The Cultural Glory of Ancient India

Reconstructing Indian History & Culture
(ISSN 0971-3824)

1. Society in Ancient India by Sures Chandra Banerji (ISBN 81-246-0000-7)
2. Political Thought in Ancient India by G.P. Singh (ISBN 81-246-0001-5)
3. Early Indian Historical Tradition and Archaeology by G.P. Singh (ISBN 81-246-0005-8)
4. Vasantotsava: The Spring Festivals of India by Leona M. Anderson (ISBN 81-246-0011-2)
5. Ecological Readings in the Veda by M. Vannucci (ISBN 81-246-0009-0)
6. Vṛndāvana in Vaiṣṇava Literature by Maura Corcoran (ISBN 81-246-0024-4)
7. Social History of the Tamils (1707-1947) by P. Subramanian (ISBN 81-246-0045-7)
8. Ancient Indian Coinage by Rekha Jain (ISBN 81-246-0051-1)
9. Buddhism and Socio-Economic Life of Eastern India by Bimal Chandra Mohapatra (ISBN 81-246-0055-4)
10. Chandragupta Maurya by P.L. Bhargava (ISBN 81-246-0056-2)
11. Mṛtyu: Concept of Death in Indian Traditions by Gian Giuseppe Fillippi (ISBN 81-246-0072-4)
12. Yama: The Glorious Lord of the Other World by Kusum P. Merh (ISBN 81-246-0066-X)
13. Sacred Complex of Ujjain by D.K. Samanta (ISBN 81-246-0078-3)
14. Vedic View of the Earth by S.R.N. Murthy (ISBN 81-246-0091-0)
15. Society in the Atharvaveda by B.S. Kharade (ISBN 81-246-0093-7)
16. Orissan History, Culture and Archaeology by S. Pradhan (ISBN 81-246-0117-8)
17. Education in Ancient India by Mitali Chatterjee (ISBN 81-246-0113-5)
18. Surā: the Liquor and the Vedic Sacrifice by M.B. Kolhatkar (ISBN 81-246-0114-3)
19. Human Ecology in the Vedas by Marta Vannucci (ISBN 81-246-0115-1)
20. Governance in Ancient India by Anup Chandra Pandey (ISBN 81-246-0135-6)

Reconstructing Indian History and Culture, no. 21

The Cultural Glory of Ancient India

— *A Literary Overview* —

by

Sures Chandra Banerji

D.K. Printworld (P) Ltd.
NEW DELHI - 110 015

Cataloging in Publication Data — DK

Banerji, Sures Chandra, 1917–
The cultural glory of ancient India.
(Reconstructing Indian history & culture; no. 21).
Includes bibliographical references (p.).

1. Vedic literature. 2. Sanskrit literature — To 1500. 3. India — History. 4. India — Civilization. I. Title. II. Series: Reconstructing Indian history & culture; no. 21.

ISBN 81-246-0137-2

First Published in India in 2000

Printed and published by:
D.K. Printworld (P) Ltd.
Regd. office : '*Sri Kunj*', F-52, Bali Nagar
New Delhi - 110 015
Phones : (011) 545-3975, 546-6019; *Fax* : (011) 546-5926
E-mail: dkprint@4mis.com

Preface

THE very first question that may arise in the mind of the reader is — what is the use of digging the past in this scientific age? The answer is that science is not the be-all and end-all of life. Every country has its own civilisation and culture; these are rooted in the past. It is particularly so in the case of India where civilisation dawned millennia before Christ. That the cultural heritage of India has not lost relevance even today is admitted by many wise people. The veteran indologist, Basham says, in his *The Wonder that was India*:

> The sages who meditated in the jungles of the Ganges Valley six hundred years or more before Christ are still forces in the world. — p. 487

Thus, we see that Indian philosophy is not 'speculative nonsense' as some detractors characterise it. Nor was ancient India 'the brooding east' as some think. The *Bhagavad Gītā* or the *Gītā*, as it is popularly called, has been highly extolled by the great German philosopher, Humboldt (1767-1853) as "the only truly philosophical peom in all the literatures known to us". Another renowned German savant, Schopenhauer (1788-1860) observed that the Upaniṣad had comforted him in his life and would comfort him while dying.

There are evidences to prove that the *Manu-smṛti* exercised influence on the Persian law at the time of Emperor Darius (sixth-fifth century BC), as also on the laws of Kandy in Ceylon (Sri Lanka) and of Burma (Myanmar). Some countries of South-east Asia, particularly Java, appear to have had Manu's influence on the legal system.

Coming to pure literature of ancient India, suffice it to say that the famous German scholar, Goethe (1749-1832) saw, in the drama *Abhijñāna-śākuntalam* of Kālidāsa (*c.* fifth century AD), the "young year's blossoms and the fruits of its decline", and what is more, "the combination of heaven and earth".

Ancient Indian works, written in Sanskrit, are not merely literary curiosities, not only of antiquarian interest. Some of them have made notable contributions to the history of human knowledge. For example, it was in the *Ṛgveda* dating back to about 2000 years before Christ, that for the first time, the plant world was declared to be endowed with life. In the domain of mathematics, India was the first country to have the concept of zero, and introduced the use of so-called Arabic numerals (1, 2, etc). In geometry, some of India's concepts may have antedated even Pythagoras (sixth century BC) of Greece. In the realm of medical science, it was India that gave the world the concept of *tridoṣa*, i.e., wind, bile and phlegm as the basic constituents of the human body. The ancient Indian methods of *yoga* have been universally accepted as very effective means of curing psychosomatic ailments. Plastic surgery was, perhaps, foreshadowed by rhinoplastic surgery of ancient India.

In realms of art and architecture, ancient India left an indelible impress on the cultural history of the world.

Thus, we see that there is enough of justification for delving into ancient Indian works. The cultural profile of ancient India is too vast to be described in a single volume. For the general reader, we have selected the most important and interesting topics. Each subject has been dealt with in a brief compass, and in a language which is generally free from jargon. There is no pretension to exhaustive treatment; it can, however, be claimed that no important aspect of a matter has been left out. Ancient Indian Śāstras are replete with technical terms. For the facility of those who want to study any Śāstra, we have added a fairly exhaustive Glossary in which the Śāstras concerned have been indicated.

Finally, a Select Bibliography of each of the subjects, dealt with in the work, has been added; this will facilitate further study and research.

My labour will be amply rewarded if this work serves as a kaleidoscope through which the reader can see the colourful scenario of ancient Indian culture changing hues from age to age.

Buddha Pūrṇimā **S. C. Banerji**
1405 B.S.

Contents

Chronological Table

Alberuni's visit to India	*c*. AD 1030
Alexander's invasion of India	*c*. 327-325 BC
Arthaśāstra of Kauṭilya	Generally assigned to fourth century BC
Aśoka	*c*. 267-232 BC
Bharata (author of *Nāṭyaśāstra*)	Perhaps earlier than fourth or fifth century AD
Buddha (Siddhārtha or Gautama)	*c*. 563-483 BC According to a tradition, *nirvāṇa* — 486 BC
Caitanya	AD 1486-1533
Cāṇakya (same as Kauṭilya, q.v.)	
Fa-hien's visit to India	AD 399
Gupta age	*c*. AD 300-647
Hiuen-tsang's stay in India	AD 630-45
Indus Valley Civilisation	*c*. 2500-1500 BC
I-tsing's stay in India	AD 671-95
Kālidāsa	Lower terminus AD 634. Generally assigned to a period around AD 400
Kāmasūtra (of Vātsyāyana)	*c*. third century AD
Kurukṣetra war (nucleus of *Mahābhārata*)	Sometime between *c*. 1000-900 BC

Mahābhārata (present form)	*c*. fourth century AD
Mahāvīra (exponent of Jainism)	*d*. 468 BC (according to others, 528 BC)
Manu-smṛti (present form)	Between *c*. second century BC — second century AD
Megasthenes' visit to India	302 BC
Pāṇini	*c*. fourth century BC
Purāṇas (Mahā)	Composition or compilation between *c*. third century AD and AD 1400
Rāmāyaṇa (present form)	*c*. second or third century AD. Highly controversial
Ṛgveda	According to Winternitz, beginning 2500 or 2000 BC According to a recent scholar, 12,500 BC. See D. Frawley, Astronomical evidences, etc., in *Glory of India*, a quarterly of Indology, Vol. V, Nos. 3-4, 1981, published by Motilal Banarsidass, Delhi
Tantras	Between *c*. fifth century AD and sixteenth century AD
Upaniṣads	*c*. 1000-600 BC
Vātsyāyana	See *Kāmasūtra*
Yājñavalkya-smṛti	*c*. AD 100-300

1

Vedic Literature

INDIAN civilisation dawned in an unknown age. The Indus Valley Civilisation is generally believed to date back to a period around 2500 BC. The recently unearthed ruins of Mehergarh in north-west India (now Pakistan) bears witness to a still earlier civilisation. We have no written record of these two ancient civilisations. Some seals, discovered in the Indus Valley, reveal what seems to be some sort of writing. But, it has not yet been deciphered.

Ṛgveda

The *Ṛgveda* is the earliest written record, known hitherto, of the Indo-Europeans. It is written in a script and language which are intelligible to us. Its study reveals the dawn of a finished civilisation, but no twilight. It is obvious that such an advanced civilisation could not be possible without a long period of development.

AGE

There is wide divergence of opinions about the age of the *Ṛgveda*. While some assign it to a stupendously ancient period. Others would bring it down to a ludicrously modern epoch. M. Winternitz, an eminent authority, steers clear of these two extremes, and suggests about 2000 BC as the time of origin of this Veda.

CONTENTS

It contains, in the popular Śākala recension, 1028 hymns including the supplementary stanzas. The *ṚV* contains ten Books, called

*Maṇḍala*s each of which comprises sections called *Anuvāka*s. Each *Anuvāka* is divided into some hymns, called *Sūkta*s. A *sūkta* consists of several stanzas called *ṛk*s. The *ṛk*s are composed in different metres. The words are accented. The three accents used are *udātta* (acute), *anudātta* (grave) and *svarita* (circumflex). *Udātta*, etc., are not stress accents, but pitch accents which are musical. The metres are determined by the number of syllables, not by short and long vowels as in classical Sanskrit. It should be noted that each *sūkta* is attributed to a sage, called *ṛṣi*. The word *ṛṣi* is derived from the root *ṛṣ* to see. According to tradition, the *ṛṣi*s did not compose the hymns, but saw them revealed by divine beings.

The hymns are mostly addressed to deities such as Agni, Indra, Varuṇa, etc. The deities are generally personifications of natural phenomena such as the sun, wind, etc., and are represented as possessed of anthropomorphic traits. There are some abstract deities too, e.g., *śraddhā* (faith), *manyu* (anger), etc.

Generally, the deities were conceived as benevolent conferring various benefits on the worshippers. Malevolent deities like Nirṛti, Kṛtyā also are conceived as doing mischief in various ways.

The Vedic text was regarded as very sacred; so much so that even a slight mistake relating to accent or syllable was believed to cause disaster to the reciter and to destroy the intended effect of a *mantra*, e.g., killing of the enemy ensured by a sacrifice for this purpose in which the above *mantra* was used. So, various methods were devised for preserving the Vedic text intact in every detail. The most popular device was called *pada-pāṭha* in which every word is separately written showing the constituents of compounds and the accents on the vowels in each word are indicated.

SECULAR MATTERS

Besides the religious hymns, there are several hymns which may be called secular. Prominent among them are as follows:

Wedding hymn, X.85
Funeral hymn, X.14-18
Gambler's lament, X.34
Didactic hymn, X.117

Riddles, I.164, VII.29
Frog hymn, VII.103

The most important among secular hymns are what are called Dialogue hymns. For example, dialogues between Yama and his sister Yamī (X.10), king Purūravas and celestial nymph Urvaśī (X.95).

Such hymns were probably the precursors of the narrative literature in later Classical Sanskrit. According to some scholars, the above dialogues foreshadowed the drama in Classical Sanskrit literature.

Certain hymns (e.g., X.107, 117), which are partly religious and partly secular, are called *dāna-stuti*s which contain eulogy of donors of gifts. These hymns have some historical value in the sense that they mention the full names of the donors and seem to be based on facts. Besides, these hymns contain some information about the genealogies of the sages and donors concerned. In them, some tribes and their habitats also are mentioned.

Secular matters, including magic, are also scattered in various contexts of this Veda. For example, hymns II.42, 43 contain prognostications. I.191 mentions *mantra* for protection against poisonous creatures. X.145 contains *mantra* for relief against the trouble created by a co-wife. Some hymns, e.g., V. 55, X.58, 60, 183 contain *mantra*s for inducing sleep, security of life, getting a child respectively.

It should be noted that there are about a dozen hymns in which philosophical ideas are set forth. Among such ideas are speculations about the universe, creation of the world, life after death, a single all-pervading soul, etc. The Creation Hymn contains the following ideas in the words of Griffith:

> Nor aught existed then, nor naught existed,
> There was no air, nor heaven beyond.
> What covered all? Wherein? In whose shelter was it?
> Was it the water, deep and fathomless?

Among the secular matters is the mention of some diseases sometimes with their cures; this is important for the history of

Āyurveda. The main diseases, mentioned, are as follows:

1. *Ajakā* — (VII.50.1) stated to be caused by a poison.
2. *Apacit* — According to Bloomfield, it is the same as *apaci*, found in medieval works, and explained by commentators as *gaṇḍamālā* (inflammation of glands of the neck).
3. *Harimāṇa* (I.50.11,12) — appears to be jaundice. Sun's rays are stated to cure it.
4. *Hṛdroga* (I.50.11) — Heart-disease the nature of which has not been stated.
5. *Śīpada* (VII. 50. 4) — Its nature has been stated neither in the text nor in the commentary.
6. *Yakṣmā* (I.122.9, X.85.31, etc.) — Probably consumption I.122.9 knows it to be an ailment of the chest.

Diseases of women are referred to in X.162.1, 2. X.162.3 mentions obstruction to pregnancy and death of the foetus. *Visuci amīvā* seems to denote infectious disease (II.33.2). *Amīvā* has been taken by Sāyaṇa to denote disease. This word reminds one of the term amoeba or ameba, used in medical science to denote a kind of protozoan. In X.39.8, it is stated that a lady, who lost her legs, got iron legs. It seems that orthopaedic appliances of a sort were known. Poison of some kinds was believed to cause certain diseases. Inflammation of the knees and heels is stated to be caused by a poison (VII.50.2).

The word *bheṣaja*, denoting medicine, occurs at several places of this Veda, e.g., I.23.19, V.53.14, VIII.9.15. The word *oṣadhi*, which denotes plant, herb, especially medicinal herb, has been used at many places, e.g., I.166.5, III.34.10, IV.33.7, V.41.8, X.145.1, etc. At some places, e.g., X.145.1 ff., it has been mentioned as possessing wonderful power like bringing others under control. As curatives of some diseases, particularly of those which are caused by poison, are mentioned sunshine (I.50.11.12), water (VII.50.4) and fire (VII.50.2).

THEOLOGY

The Ṛgvedic deities have been classified by Yāska, in his *Nirukta*, as:

1. *Dyu-sthāna* (celestial) — e.g., Sūrya, Varuṇa, etc.
2. *Antarikṣa-sthāna* (atmospheric) — e.g., Indra, Maruts, etc.
3. *Bhū-sthāna* (terrestrial) — e.g., Agni, Soma, etc.

According to Yāska, the Vedic deities are basically three, one in each of the above regions. Thus, Agni is on earth, Vāyu or Indra in the atmosphere and Sūrya in heaven. He holds that they have been proliferated in accordance with their various attributes or functions.

The renowned scholar, Bloomfield classifies the Vedic deities as:

1. Transparent — those whose basis in nature and deification in human mind are clear.
2. Translucent — the process of whose deification is not very easily comprehended.
3. Opaque — those whose basis in nature cannot be determined.

Ṛgvedic religion is clearly polytheistic. In some hymns, we notice the tendency to regard the particular deity, worshipped for the time being, as the highest divinity. This tendency was called Henotheism or Kathenotheism by Max-Müller. An example is the Hiraṇyagarbha hymn (X.121). The refrain of all the stanzas, excepting that of the last one is *kasmai devāya haviṣā vidhema* — to which (other) god shall we give sacrificial offerings? This reflects the attitude that all other gods are insignificant. According to some, this line implies a covert doubt as to the power, even existence of other gods. Thus, according to them, a monotheistic trend is noticeable in it. This tendency is reflected in some other hymns, e.g., X.14.5, X.81, 82, X.110. The monotheistic outlook gave rise to a sort of monistic belief. I.164.46 contains the following line:

ekaṁ sad viprā bahudhā vadanti
agniṁ yamaṁ mātariśvānamāhuḥ ।

The *Brāhmaṇa*s call a single existent (principle) (by various names) as Agni, Yama, Mātariśvan. This seems to foreshadow the Upaniṣadic concept of *Brahman* as the sole reality.

SOCIETY

We shall now give a brief account of the society reflected in the *Ṛgveda*. The most important matter about this society is the fourfold classification of the people of this age. The earliest reference to the four castes, brāhmaṇa, kṣatriya, vaiśya and śūdra, occurs in the *Puruṣa-sūkta* (X.90). In stanza 12 it is laid down that the above castes sprang respectively from the mouth, arms, knees and feet of the Primeval Being (*puruṣa*). This hints at the hierarchy and functions of the different castes. Brāhmaṇas, at the apex, used to study and teach, the kṣatriyas were the fighters, vaiśyas, the traders and the śūdras, in the lowest rung, were footmen.

Though Vedic Civilisation was mainly rural, yet there is mention (e.g., I.44.10) of city. Besides houses, made of clay, we find references to three-storeyed house and palace. The word *sahasra-sthūṇa*, i.e., having thousand columns (V.62.6) led the veteran scholar, Wilson to think that there were huge mansions. IV.30.20 mentions hundred cities made of stone. Also mentioned is *āyasī* or iron-made cities or forts.

Economy was mainly agricultural. We find praise of agriculture. In the Gambler's Lament, the penniless penitent gambler has been emphatically asked to take to agriculture. The existence of some sort of irrigation can be inferred from III.45.3 and VII.49.2. Cattle-rearing was a means of livelihood. There are prayers for cows, particularly milch cows, horse, goat, sheep, etc., as means of subsistence. Some of the other occupations were carpentry, medical profession, priesthood, iron-work, poetry, corn-grinding, chariot-making, making swords and axes, weaving, ship-building, rope-making, tannery, etc. (*vide* I.162.8, II.13.9, VI.9.1, VII.84.2, IX.112, X.34.13; 72.2; 112.7; 122.4, etc.).

Among the articles of foodstuff were rice, barley, pulverised grain, rice boiled in milk, cake, powdered grains mixed with curd. The word *dadhi-mantha* perhaps denotes butter churned from curd or *ghī* made with it. Dog-meat and beef seem to have been eaten, fish-eating was in vogue. People used to drink wine and *soma*-juice; the latter, extracted from the *soma* creeper, was perhaps confined to the sacerdotal class.

There is enough evidence that the government was monarchical. I.126.1 refers to a king, named Bhavya. Some *dāna-stutis*, mentioned earlier, refer to liberal gifts made by the kings to the priests.

POSITION OF WOMEN

It appears that, in the Ṛgvedic society, women had equality with men in all spheres of life, religious and secular. We find the females, Ghoṣā, Viśvavārā, Apālā, etc., who were *ṛṣis* of some hymns. The son and daughter were equally entitled to inherit patrimony and to perform the last rites of the father. We find, in VIII.31.5-6, a couple jointly performing *somābhiṣava*, and attending a sacrifice together. That the woman occupied an honoured position is indicated by several stanzas of the *Ṛgveda*. In III.53.4, 6 the wife is stated to be the house, the giver of birth to issues and the doer of salutary deeds. Though monogamy was the ideal (e.g., I.124.7, IV.3.2, X.71.4), yet the prevalence of polygamy is evident from the *mantras* (X.145), stated to be used by co-wives. The mention of *sapatnī-dhāvana-davatā* (deity driving away co-wives), as the goddess associated with the hymn, clearly points to the persecution by co-wives.

A brotherless girl was regarded as unsuitable for marriage (X.27), because the son of such a girl was treated as a son of the girl's father. From X.27.11, 12 it appears that a girl had the freedom to choose her desired man from among those who came to seek her hand. X.40.2 hints at the marrige of a widow with her husband's younger brother.

ṚV, X.85 is about the marriage of Sūryā. It throws considerable light on the customs and practices in connection with marriage in those times. Stanza 26 is a blessing to the bride to the following effect: be you an empress to your father-in-law, mother-in-law, brother-in-law and sister-in-law. Stanza 36 is an expression of the following good wishes to the husband and wife: may you live together for ever, never be separated from each other, enjoy various kinds of food, living in the own house, enjoy yourselves in company of your sons and grandsons, etc.

Dice-playing was a popular pastime. There are references to dance and acting. I.92.4 presents goddess Uṣas (dawn) as a dancing girl. Among musical instruments, mention has been made of *dundubhi* (drum), *vīṇā* (lute) and flute. Chariot-race was a popular sport. Riding swings was a common means of diversion.

Fighting appears to have been common. Nor is it surprising at a time when the Āryans attempted to subjugate the original inhabitants of the land. Of the gods, Indra appears as the master-fighter who vanquished terrible demons, and pushed into caves those who defied the Āryans. There are references to armed conflicts between kings. In VI.75 we find praise of armour, bow, arrow, adroit chariot driver, horses suitable for war, etc.

Many superstitious beliefs and practices are found in the *R̥gveda*. We have already mentioned some *mantra*s believed to produce beneficial effects. People used to believe in ghosts and evil spirits haunting forests and funeral grounds. Birds like owl were looked upon as ominous. The idea that diseases can be transferred to certain creatures occurs in I.50.12. The disease, called *harimāṇa* (jaundice?), was believed to be transferable to parrots and to turmeric. Bad dreams were dreaded, so much so that a deity, named *duḥsvapna-nāśana-devatā*, came to be recognised (I.120.12). There was belief in *vaśīkaraṇa* (bringing others under control) as we find, for instance, in X.49.5. Certain rites are prescribed for counter-acting the effect of curse. Miracles, caused by divine grace, were believed; e.g., a lame man walking, eye-sight restored to a blind person, etc. (for instance, II.15.7; IV.19.9).

R̥gvedic society was not free from vices. We have already mentioned gambling. There is reference to adultery (e.g., X.34.5). A liar has been compared with a woman hating her husband (IV.5.5). There is reference to an illegitimate child (II.29.1) being surreptiously thrown away. In Yamī's alluring her unwilling brother, Yama (X.10) for sexual enjoyment we find incest. From VII.55.3 and VII.86.5, for instance, we learn of robbers and thieves in the society. Cheating and fainting due to excessive drinking are also mentioned. People, belonging to the condemned *vrātya* class, are stated to have spoilt sacrificial rites.

Yajurveda

It is the Veda of the *yaju*s or *mantra*s used, in connection with sacrificial rites, by the priest, called *adhvaryu*.

In the introductory portion of the *Mahābhāṣya*, the Great Commentary on Pāṇini's grammar, Patañjali (*c*. second century BC) referes to 101 recensions of this Veda. The extant *YV* has two recensions, called *kṛṣṇa* (black) and *śukla* (white). The former exists in four recensions, namely.

(i) *Kāṭhaka*, (ii) *Kapiṣṭhala*, (iii) *Maitrāyaṇī* and (iv) *Taittirīya* (also called *Āpastamba-saṁhitā*).

The *Vājasaneyī-saṁhitā* is included in *Śukla YV*, the *Vājasaneyī* is named after Yājñavalkya Vājasaneya, the principal teacher of this Veda. This Saṁhitā has two recensions, *Kāṇva* and *Mādhyandina*.

While the *Kṛṣṇa YV* contains both *mantra* and *Brāhmaṇa* (a class of Vedic literature, dealt with later on), the *Śukla YV* contains only *mantra*.

This Veda contains both metrical and prose compositions. The metrical portions are mostly *ṛks* from the *Ṛgveda*. Some of the prose portions deal with magical practices, and some contain *ābhičarika kriyā* or practices designed to cause harm to others.

A characteristic feature of this Veda is riddles some of which are of the *Brahmodaya* (concerning *Brahman*) type and elitist, while others are popular. From this Veda we learn of the different occasions on which the riddles served the purpose of diversion. For instance, some riddles were used as a means of diversion among the priests in *aśvamedha* sacrifice.

A way of pleasing gods was to offer prayers in honour of them reciting many names of them and mentioning their several qualities. Of such prayers, the oldest is the *Śatarudrīya* occurring in the sixteenth chapter of the *Vājasaneyī Saṁhitā* and in the *Taittirīya Saṁhitā* (IV.5). It mentions 100 names of Rudra. This served as a model for addressing different deities mentioning their various names in later times.

This Veda has no literary merits. But, its imporatance in the history of Indian religion is undoubted. It throws considerable light on the ritualistic aspect of the Vedic literature and sacerdotalism. As Winternitz aptly says, without understanding the *YV*, one cannot understand the *Brāhmaṇas* (to be dealt with later on), and without a knowledge of these works one cannot comprehend the Upaniṣads (*History of Indian Literature*, I, 1990, p. 174).

Sāmaveda

The *Sāmaveda* is the Veda of *sāmans* (sweet songs). The priest, called *udgātā*, used to sing these songs in Vedic sacrifices.

According to a tradition, this Veda existed in a large number of recensions. There are, at present, three recensions namely. *Kauthuma*, *Rāṇāyaṇīya* and *Jaminīya*. Of these, the best known is the *Kauthuma*. This Veda, containing a total number of 1810 stanzas, is divided into two parts, called *Ārcika* and *Uttarārcika*. Some of the stanzas are repetitions. Excluding the repetitions, the number of stanzas comes to 1549. Excepting 75 stanzas all the others occur in the *R̥gveda* mostly in its eighth and ninth *Maṇḍala*s. With the aforesaid *Ārcika* are associated two song-books, called *Grāmageya-gāna* (songs to be sung in villages) and *Araṇyageya-gāna* (songs to be sung in forests). The latter contains some melodies which were considered to be dangerous and, therefore, unfit for being sung in villages. There are two other song-books, called *Ūhagāna* and *Ūhyagāna*, connected respectively with *Grāmageya* and *Araṇyageya*. These two served the purpose of giving the *sāmans* in the order in which they were used at rituals.

The *Sāmaveda*, which is the earliest work on Indian music, reveals the heptatonic system used in songs, the notes were indicated by letters; a more widely used method was to indicate the seven notes by the figures 1 to 7. At the time of singing, the priests used to stress notes by the movement of their hands and fingers. Many melodies must have been used in singing the songs. There was long-standing belief that the songs or, at least, some of them were mystic and had magical effect.

Atharvaveda

It was originally entitled *Atharvāṅgirasa*. *Atharva* denoted white magic, i.e., magic employed for the welfare of people; e.g., cure of a disease, counter-acting the effect of poison, etc., *Aṅgiras* was black magic, designed for imprecation of or mischief to the enemy. The Vedas were, in the earliest times, referred to as *trayī* (the triad), i.e., the three Vedas excluding the *Atharvaveda*. The reason for the exclusion was, perhaps, the elements of magic, particularly of hostile magic present in the *Atharvaveda*, or this Veda, having no connection with the performance of sacrifices, was not accorded the status of Veda.

This Veda is available in two recensions, called Śaunaka and Paippalāda of which the former is more widely known. The Śaunakīya recension contains 731 hymns divided into 20 chapters. Nearly one-seventh of this Veda has been taken from the *Ṛgveda*. Chapters 15 and 16 contain prose compositions of the type of *Brāhmaṇa*s (to be dealt with later).

The contents of the hymns of this Veda can be divided as:

(1) *Bhaiṣajya* — containing songs and *mantra*s for healing diseases.

(2) *Āyuṣya* — prayers for health and long life.

(3) *Pauṣṭika* — benedictions for the attainment of happiness and success.

(4) *Abhicārika* — imprecations for harm to demons and enemies and *mantra*s for exorcism.

Besides the above, this Veda contains expiatory *mantra*s for washing off sin, *mantra*s for ensuring unity in the family, magical songs relating to marriage and love, charming hymns in honour of Earth and Varuṇa. Songs and *mantra*s, relating to sacrifices, are also there. Chapter 20 contains hymns, called *kuntāpa* which are like the *dāna-stuti*s of the *Ṛgveda*.

In comparison with the other Vedas, it reflects, to the greatest extent, the life of the common people. A study of it reveals their religious and superstitious faiths, aims and aspirations, magic and charms for their material happiness and for the destruction of enemies, etc.

Āyurveda or medical science of ancient India appears to have had its roots in the *Bhaiṣajya* hymns of the Veda. Caraka, the oldest authority in Indian medicine, declares (*Caraka-saṁhitā*, I.30.19-

20) that a physician should be familiar with the medical science dealt with in this Veda. Suśruta, the highest authority on Indian surgery, makes it clear (*Suśruta-saṁhitā*, I.6) that *Āyurveda* is an offshoot of the *Atharvaveda*.

The influence of this Veda on the *Kāmasūtra* of Vātsyāyana is undoubted. Vātsyāyana acknowledges (e.g., *Kāmasūtra*, VII.1.1.) the authority of this Veda.

The *Atharvaveda* forms, as it were, a bridge between the *Karma-kāṇḍa* (ritualism) and *Jñāna-kāṇḍa* (advocating the knowledge of the ultimate truth). It contains a lot of matters relating to the state after death, immortality, continence. *Brahman*, etc., which have been elaborately discussed in the Upaniṣads. This Veda reveals the anticipations of the later concepts of pantheism, monotheism, unity underlying diversity, etc.

This Veda also foreshadows the mystic syllable and words as well as *mantras* found in the later Tāntric works.

On politics also there is influence of this Veda. XIV.146 of Kauṭilya's *Arthaśāstra*, named *Aupaniṣadika-prakaraṇa*, appears to have been written on the model of this Veda. According to Kauṭilya, at least one minister in the king's cabinet must be an Atharvavedic priest. Such a priest was versed in *Itihāsa* (history), Purāṇa, *Gāthā Nārāśaṁsī* stanzas and songs in praise of heroes). These formed the basis of the later narrative literature, the Purāṇas and Epics.

As regards pantheon, it reveals some peculiarities. In it, gods Savitā, Tvaṣṭā and Prajāpati have become fused. Some new deities have appeared; e.g. Saṁvṛtvā, Heti, Nilimpā, Vairāja, Saṁsica, etc.

Coming to the society of the *Atharvaveda*, we find that the caste-system has become more pronounced. It appears that caste was determined by birth. If necessary, a person of one caste might be a member of another. The brāhmaṇas have come to be looked upon as gods on earth, the position of the sacerdotal class has been well established. The demand of the priests for sacrificial fees is found to be growing more and more. Only the brāhmaṇas were entitled to partake of the sacrificial food. In several contexts (e.g., V.17.9, V.18.9-10) there is evidence of their concern for self-interest.

Discrimination between the Āryans and the śūdras became very prominent. There are many references to sin and expiatory rites. We meet with *vrātyas* for the first time in this Veda; they appear to have been people who defied Brāhmaṇical rites and practices.

Guests were highly esteemed, and were duly entertained (IX.6). People used to enjoy themselves in various ways of entertainment. The prevalence of music, both vocal and instrumental, and dance is noticed. Race, chariot-race and horse-race were some of the popular sports. There is mention of semi-circular race-course for horse-race. Race-competition was a noteworthy part of the *rājasūya* sacrifice by which a king was formally enthroned as a sovereign monarch. Fowling and hunting were other means of diversion.

As regards women, IX.5.27-8 testify to the vogue of widow re-marriage, V.17.8-9 bear testimony to polyandry. Despite a high ideal of conjugal life, there is evidence of the infidelity on the part of wives. As in the *R̥gveda* so also in this Veda, too, a newly married woman has been accorded the status of an empress in her husband's house. In conformity with tradition, however, the birth of a son was more desirable than that of a daughter. In VI.11.3, the birth of a daughter has been deplored. XVIII.3.1 refer to *satī-dāha* (burning of widows). *Duhitā* (daughter) used to milk cattle. Women used to weave and dress their hairs. It was a woman's duty to lighten the duties of her husband to a great extent (XIX.1). It was a part of the duty of the mistress of the house to look after domestic animals. There is a prayer, in the *Vasudhārā* hymn, to the effect that the ladies of the household may do domestic work without remissness. In this society, there appear to have been maid-servants and female slaves. They were engaged in various kinds of work, particularly husking corns.

The economy was mainly agricultural. There are references to the wide use of ploughs and cattle. Manuring was known. Among argricultural products are mentioned rice, barley, wheat, sesame, various cereals, etc. Various crafts appear to have been the occupations of both women and men. Among such women are mentioned *rajayitrī* (female dyer), *kaṇṭakikārī* (?), *vidala-kārī* (making things with split bamboo?), etc. Among craftsmen are *rathakārī* (chariot-maker), *takṣaṇa* (carpenter), *sūta* (charioteer). Weaving as a profession was in vogue. Usury appears to have been in vogue. Besides barter system, there was perhaps the use of gold coins called *niṣka*. Industry was one of the pursuits of men. Higgling prevailed at that time also, as indicated by V.15. Among the commercial commodities were clothes, bed, goat-skin, etc.

Cattle received great care; this was because, besides their usefulness in agriculture, their milk was used in sacrificial rites. Cow-slaughter, at places other than the place of sacrifice, was an offence for which death-penalty was prescribed. Pastures were carefully maintained. Spacious cow-sheds were built. Prayers for averting excessive rainfall and drought indicate that agriculture depended mainly on rain. The cultivators appear to have had an idea of irrigation.

Boats or ships seem to have been used; the word 'sambī', denoting navigator, occurs in IX.2.6 for the first time in this Veda. A kingdom, threatened with destruction, has been likened to a sinking ship.

From the use of the words *śyāmāyas* (black metal or iron) and *lohitāyas* (red metal or copper) in XI.3.1, 7, IX.5.4 and XI.3.1, 7 respectively leave no doubt about the wide use of metal in that age.

People appear to have lived mainly in wooden houses. A house contained a room for preservation of fire and also space for domestic animals. The description of houses is found in III.12, IX.3.

In an agricultural society, importance was naturally attached to villages. Residential houses, pasture, cultivable land and *araṇya* (extensive fallow land outside the village) — these together constituted a village. There were joint families in the society.

Government was generally monarchical. The king was elected by the people. There was the practice of re-installing a king who was banished. The general rate of revenue was 1/16th of the produce. The priest was a high state functionary. He used to try various means for the extension of the kingdom, destruction of enemies and the welfare of the king. This Veda testifies to the existence of several assemblies and of the practice of delivering lectures in them.

As regards food and drink, dress and decoration, there is not much difference between the *Ṛgveda* and *Atharvaveda*. In this age, conch-shells were used as amulets. The word *pravarta* (XV.2.5, 9) probably denotes a kind of ear-ornament. *Nīvi* (VIII.6.20) seems to stand for under-garment. For the preservation of the foetus, there was the practice of tying a medicinal herb at a particular part of the *nīvi*. *Upavasana* (XIV.2.41) seems to mean a veil or breast-cover. *Vavrivāsa* (VIII.6.2) perhaps stands for breast-cover. XV.2.5 appears to indicate that women of this age used some sort of head-cover (*uṣṇīṣa*). *Kumba, kurīra, tirīṭa* were perhaps different kinds of head-ornaments. Men of this age used to decorate themselves with various ornaments, called *niṣka* (necklace) *rukma*? and jewels. Some herbs also were used as ornaments. For the growth of hairs, the juice of a creeper, believed to increase hair, was sprinkled over them. The intense smell of the *śamī*-tree (*Prosopis spicigera*) with long leaves was supposed to cause baldness. For cleansing the hairs of women a device with a 100 tooth-like projections was used; it was, perhaps the earliest form of comb. From VI.68.1-3 we learn of the use of razors for cutting hairs and beards. The barber was called *vaptā* (VIII.2.17)

It is significant that the tiger appears for the first time, in the *Atharvaveda*. From this fact we can imagine that, the Ārya diaspora included the Gangetic valley, the natural habitat of this grand animal. There is evidence of the use of elephants. There is some geographical information in this Veda. For instance, it mentions the rivers Yamunā and Vārṇāvatī (probably in Vārṇāvata, modern Barnāvā in U.P.), the mountain Mujāvat (to the south of Kashmir), the regions, called Magadha (south Bihar), Bāhlīka (between the Bias and Sutlej, tributaries of the river Indus) and Aṅga (land about Bhāgalpur including Monghyr in Bihar). The Veda mentions also the Kuru king, Parīkṣit and Janamejaya as well as king Vītahavya.

Brāhmaṇas

The four Vedic saṁhitās, the contents whereof are referred to as *mantras*, along with the *Brāhmaṇas*, are together called Veda (*mantra-brāhmaṇayor-veda-nāmadheyam*).

The ritualistic aspect of the Vedas gradually became so elaborate that, for the convenience of those who performed the rites, it became necessary to write works laying down the minutiae of the rites. The result was the rise of the *Brāhmaṇa* literature. These are prose works with occasional stanzas, called *gāthā*s. Some of the *Brāhmaṇa*s are accented.

The contents of these works can be divided into three parts, viz. *Vidhi*, *Arthavāda* and *Upaniṣad*s. *Vidhi* deals with the rules to be followed in performing sacrifices. In the *Arthavāda* portion, there are discussions on the meaning of sacrifices, and *mantra*s as well as the purpose served by them. A noteworthy feature of this portion is the introduction of narratives, *Itihāsa* and Purāṇas (in the sense of *ākhyāna* and not the Purāṇic works of later times like *Agni*, *Vāyu*, etc.). For instance, the *Śatapatha Brāhmaṇa* contains the renowned stories of Purūravas and Urvaśī, the Flood Legend, etc. The Legend of Śunaḥśepa, in the *Aiṭareya Brāhmaṇa*, is interspersed with *gāthā*s which, in their language and metres, resemble Epic verses. The *gāthā*s, called *Nārāśaṁsī*s, contain eulogies of heroes. Some *ākhyāna*s lay down the origin of certain things or customs; these and stories relating to creation are called Purāṇas. The stories about gods and humans fall under the category of *Itihāsa*. That such narratives were regarded as important is proved by the fact that there was a class of litterateurs, known as *ākhyānavid* (*Aitareya*, III.25), i.e., versed in *ākhyāna*s.

The Upaniṣad portions contain explanations, polemics, theology and philosophical matter.

An important characteristic of the *Brāhmaṇa*s is *Nirukti* (etymology); in it, there are derivations and exposition of many words. Other features of these works are the determination of the true nature of objects and symbolisation.

Every Veda has its own *Brāhmaṇa*s. The *Ṛgveda* has two, viz. *Aitareya* and *Kauṣītaki*. The *Śatapatha* and *Taittirīya* belong to the *Yajurveda*, the former belonging to the *Śukla Yajurveda* and the latter to the *Kṛṣṇa*. Of the several works of this class, belonging to the *Sāmaveda*, noteworthy are the *Tāṇḍya-mahābrāhmaṇa* or *Pañcaviṁśa*, *Ṣaḍviṁśa*, *Jaiminīya* and *Chāndogya*. The only *Brāhmaṇa* of the *Atharvaveda* is the *Gopatha*.

In the *Brāhmaṇa*s of the *Ṛgveda*, *Yajurveda* and *Sāmaveda*, stress has been laid on the duties respectively of the priests, called *Hotā*, *Adhvaryu* and *Udgātā*.

The age of composition of the *Brāhmaṇas* cannot be determined. This much only can be said that these were written long after the Vedas.

The Ṛgvedic deities re-appear in the *Brāhmaṇas*, but their nature has undergone change. In this age, their omnipotence depends on sacrifices. Some deities, who were not so important in the *Ṛgveda*, have become more eminent in this period, e.g., Rudra or Śiva and Viṣṇu. The word *asura*, in the *Ṛgveda*, denoted a person or deity possessed of superhuman power. In the *Brāhmaṇas*, it has come to mean demon. These works refer to many conflicts between gods and demons. In the *Ṛgveda*, in a fight between a god and demon the former appears to be victorious. But, in these works, god and demon appear to be eager to defeat each other by the power derived from sacrifice. Thus, sacrifice assumed so much importance in these works that it became not a means to the end, but the end itself. The main pursuit of people became the performance of sacrifices. The sacrificial rites required attention to even minor details without which a rite was supposed to be imperfect and harmful to the sacrificer. For this reason, the priest was regarded as indispensable. The sacerdotal class became objects of great respect, so much so that even other *Brāhmaṇas* were looked upon as gods incarnate.

When ritualism gripped the society, some people felt the urge of knowing the truth behind all rites and rituals. This resulted in the composition of the Upaniṣads. Buddhism also arose as a protest against ritualism.

These works are dry-as-dust prose compositions dealing with ritualistic details which are jejune and insipid. The *Brāhmaṇas*, however, are important in the history of religion. Their contribution is not negligible in the study of the development of later religious and philosophical ideas. The seeds of some doctrines, which were fully developed in the Āraṇyakas and Upaniṣads, were sown in the *Brāhmaṇas*. For instance, *Brahman* who figures so prominently in the Upaniṣads, already appears in the *Śatapatha Brāhmaṇa* (XI.2.3.1) where it is held that, in the beginning, there was *Brahman* alone. It was he who created the gods, and gave, for their residence, the earth to Agni, firmament to Vāyu and the heaven to Sūrya.

In the desert of these works, the legends, historical narratives and Purāṇas, referred to earlier, serve as oases. These throw light on the development of the narrative literature of ancient India. The *Brāhmaṇas* have considerably influenced later literary works in Sanskrit. In this connection, special mention is deserved by the legends of Purūravas and Urvaśī, and of Śunaḥśepa. The Flood Legend in the *Śatapatha Brāhmaṇa*, whether indigenous or derived from a foreign source, is the oldest Indian version. The *gāthās* of these works appear to be the earliest forms of Epic poetry. As already stated, the *Gāthā Nārāśaṁsīs* contain historical elements.

We have seen above that some *Brāhmaṇas* contain *Nirukti* (etymology) which is important in the history of ancient Indian linguistics.

From certain matters, relating to sacrifices, we can get a glimpse of the moral ideas of those times. For instance, from II.5.2.20 of the *Śatapatha* we learn that it was sinful for a woman to have sexual relation with a man other than her husband; if she did so, her sin was considered to be lightened by her confession.

Āraṇyakas and Upaniṣads

The Āraṇyakas are a class of works which were written as sorts of supplements to the *Brāhmaṇas*. Āraṇyaka, a derivative of *araṇya* (forest), appears to indicate that these represent the thoughts of the sages who meditated in the jungles. The significance and mysticism of sacrifices form the main contents of these works.

The Upaniṣads of the oldest period are partly included in the Āraṇyakas, and partly supplements to them. The word *upaniṣad*, derived from root *ṣad* (to sit), preceded by the prefixes *upa* and *ni* etymologically means sittting down of a disciple near his preceptor. These works contain esoteric doctrines imparted by the preceptor to his disciple. Another name of Upaniṣad is Vedānta (*veda* + *anta*) or the end of Veda. These works originated at the end of the Vedic age. In the period of studenthood, the Upaniṣads were studied after the completion of Vedic study.

The Upaniṣads appear to have been written as a protest against the idea that the performance of sacrifices was the be-all and end-all of life. The following questions arose among the elites. Are the sacrifices, with their complicated procedure, requiring a long time and a lot of money, all-important? Are there really so many gods and goddesses? By whom is the phenomenal world kept going? Such problems are sought to be solved in the Upaniṣads.

Some of them are written in prose, some in verse and others are in mixed prose and verse. Their language is generally simple.

How many such works were composed, which of them are more authoritative than others — these questions are difficult to answer.

The following ten Upaniṣads, commented upon by Śaṅkarācārya (*c.* eighth century AD), are generally believed to be more authoritative than the others:

> *Īśā, Kena, Kaṭha, Praśna, Muṇḍa, Māṇḍūkya, Taittirīya, Aitareya, Chāndogya* and *Bṛhadāraṇyaka.*

It should be noted that, in his exposition of the *Brahmasūtra*, Śaṅkara mentions 12 Upaniṣads as authoritative. Among them, the aforesaid *Māṇḍūkya* is absent, and the additional three are the *Kauṣītaki*, *Śvetāśvatara* and *Mahānārāyaṇa*. Of these 12 Upaniṣads, the *Bṛhadāraṇyaka*, *Chāndogya*, *Taittirīya*, *Aitareya*, *Kauṣītaki* and *Kena* are older than the rest.

There are references to many more Upaniṣads. For instance, the *Muktikā Upaniṣad* refers to as many as 108 Upaniṣads.

The Upaniṣads lay greater stress on knowledge than on *karman* or rites. Their aim is to realise the highest truth that *Brahman*, the Supreme Soul (*paramātman*) is omnipresnt and omnipotent. The relation between the individual soul (residing in every creature) and the Supreme Soul has been the subject of dispute among later philosophers. The central idea of all the indisputably genuine Upaniṣads is this — the universe is *Brahman* and *Brahman* is *ātman*. *Tat-tvam-asi* (you are that). The significance of this quintessence of Upaniṣadic philosophy is — you are the universe and *Brahman*; the world exists so long as you are conscious of its existence.

The *Īśopaniṣad* aptly says (verse 11) that *vidyā* (knowledge of divinity according to Śaṅkara) and *avidyā* (sacrificial rites) are both necessary for one aspiring after liberation; one crosses death by *avidyā*, he attains immortality by *vidyā*.

Ātman could not be described as a positive entity. It has been sought to be defined by characteristics which are contradictory to one another. For instance, it has been held that *ātman* is stationary, yet faster than mind; it is near yet far, it exists inside everything and also outside. The *Bhagavad Gītā* (II.22-5), true to the spirit of the Upaniṣads, declares that weapons cannot cut *ātman*, fire cannot burn it, water cannot damp it and wind cannot make it dry. It is further stated (II.20) that *ātman* remains unaffected even when the body is killed.

The same *ātman* has different experiences in the three states of *jāgrat* (waking), *svapna* (sleep) and *suṣupti* (deep slumber). Beyond these stages is the condition called *turīya*, the fourth state in which the soul becomes one with *Brahman* (Supreme Spirit). The individual soul is covered by five *kośa*s (vestures), viz., *prāṇamaya* (made of vital air), *annamaya* (made of food), *manomaya* (made of mind), *vijñānamaya* (made of intelligence) and *ānandamaya* (made of bliss) which make the body enshrining the soul. Our ultimate goal is to realise the soul lying hidden by the above *kośa*s like a sword covered by the scabbard.

Brahman is formless. The *Kena Upaniṣad* speaks of *Brahman* as ear of the ear, mind of the mind, sentence of a sentence, breath of the breath and eye of the eye, etc. The sole Reality, *Brahman*, the imperishable one, is the cause of the creation, preservation and destruction of the world. As stated above, He is the ultimate goal for the realisation of whom are necessary *dama* (restraint), *dāna* (charity), *dayā* (kindness) and detachment. The subtle *ātman*, beyond speech and mind, is not realisable by argument, Vedic study, study of many scriptures nor by intellect. The requisites, other than those mentioned above, are truthfulness, penance, true knowledge, constant continence, etc. The successive acts for realisation are listening to what the sages say in this regard, reflection on and deep meditation of what has been said.

The Upaniṣads believe in the transmigration of soul. What makes them attractive is the attempt to inculcate doctrines by means of dialogues and narratives of various kinds. For instance, the doctrine *tat-tvam-asi* (you are that) has been analysed in the *Chāndogya Upaniṣad*. In the renowned dialogue between Yājñavalkya and Maitreyī, in the *Bṛhadāraṇyaka*, the truth about *ātman* has been expounded. The eternal quest for the knowledge of the supreme truth has been articulated in the Yama-Naciketā story of the *Kaṭha*; in it, the immortality of the soul has been sought to be established. In the legend of Prajāpati and his sons, conatined in the *Bṛhadāraṇyaka* instructions about *dama*, *dāna* and *dayā*, mentioned earlier, are given.

Some have accused the Upaniṣads of preaching pessimism. It has been argued that these treatises attach the greatest importance to knowledge. As a result, in course of time, this bred indifference to material happiness, even a feeling of aversion to all that is temporal. Pessimism is evident in the story of king Bṛhadratha in the *Maitrāyaṇī Upaniṣad* (I.2.4). But, a close study of these works reveals that Upaniṣadic philosophy is not basically pessimistic. The aim of life, according to it, is the realisation of or merging into the blissful *Brahman*. What is delusion or grief to one who has realised the oneness of all with the soul? The *Taittirīya Upaniṣad* (III.6) clearly declares — these beings are born out of joy, in joy they live, into joy they return (finally). Thus, we see that the Upaniṣads do not advocate aversion to joy. What they advocate is not gross pleasure which is *preya*, but the happiness that is *śreya* or salutary; this can be obtained by true knowledge.

The Upaniṣads are valuable in many respects. They contain a rare combination of sublime philosophical doctrines and fine poetry. The legends and parables, contained in them, have considerable importance in the history of the narrative literature of ancient India. The huge tree of Vedānta philosophy, with its ramifications in India and abroad, is rooted in the Upaniṣads. The *Bhagavad Gītā*, which has been acclaimed in India and foreign countries for advocating the threefold path of knowledge, action and devotion, and has moulded the philosophy of the lives of many people, has been stated as the essence of all the Upaniṣads.

It is noteworthy that the Islamic philosophy of Sūfism has been considerably influenced by the Upaniṣads. The renowned German philosopher, Schopenhauer paid glowing tribute to these treatises. He said that they had been the solace of his life and would be the solace of his death. According to the eminent indologist, Basham, the sages of India, who meditated in the jungles of the Gangetic valley 600 years or more before Christ, are still forces in the world.

In the Upaniṣads, we get glimpses of the society in those far-off days. It is learnt from the Yājñavalkya-Maitreyī dialogue, in the *Bṛhadāraṇyaka*, that even some women had an ardent desire to be enlightened about the highest knowledge of the *ātman*. The same Upaniṣad informs us that Gārgī embarrassed sage Yājñavalkya by volleys of philosophical questions in a learned assembly. Even common men appear to have been inquisitive about the highest truth. For instance, there is a story in the *Chāndogya Upaniṣad* (IV.1-3) that a charioteer, named Raikva was possessed of the knowledge of the Supreme truth, and that a rich man approached him for enlightenment in the matter. The story of Satyakāma Jāvāla, in the *Chāndogya* (IV.4), establishes the glory of truth.

Vedāṅgas

The study of the Vedas was a must for the upper classes of men, especially for brāhmaṇas whose main occupations were the study and teaching of the Vedas. It was believed that incorrect recitation of Vedic *mantras*, even a mistake in accentuation, was sinful, and caused harm to the reciter. Mere knowledge of the texts was not enough, the comprehension of their meaning was also indispensable for ensuring the result of the Vedic rites. Thus, accessories became necessary for the preservation of the texts intact, and also for their comprehension and details about their *ṛṣi*s, metres and application in different rites.

These reasons led to the composition of the Vedāṅgas or ancillary Vedic works. These were six, namely, *Śikṣā*, *Kalpa*, *Vyākaraṇa*, *Nirukta*, *Chanda*s and *Jyotiṣa*. These can be divided into two classes, expository and ritualistic. Those of the former class are:

(i) Śikṣā — containing rules about phonetics, the syllables, accents, analysis of words (*pada-pāṭha*), etc. The oldest works of this class are called *prātiśākhya*. Each *śākhā* (*pratiśākhā*) or recension of each Veda had its own *prātiśākhya*. For instance, to the *Ṛgveda* belongs the *prātiśākhya*, attributed to Śaunaka. Besides the *Sāma-prātiśākhya*, there are two works belonging to *Sāmaveda*. One is the *Puṣpa-sūtra* which is a sort of *Prātiśākhya* of *Uttaragāna* of the *Sāmaveda*; the other is the *Pañcavidha-sūtra* which lays down the manner in which *Sāma-gāna*s are to be sung. The *Prātiśākhya*s contain considerable grammatical matters also. The *Pāṇinīya-śikṣā* is well known. The oldest treatise on Indian music is the *Nāradīya-śikṣā*.

(ii) Vyākaraṇa — grammar. Pāṇini's (*c*. fourth century BC) *Aṣṭādhyāyī* is the oldest extant grammar. It deals not only with Vedic language and accents, but also with classical language. Pāṇini refers to earlier grammarians such as Āpiśali (Pāṇini VI.1-92), Sphoṭāyana (VI.1.123), Śākalya (VIII.3.19), etc. According to a tradition, a grammar called *Māheśa* was earlier and more elaborate than Pāṇini's grammar.

According to Patañjali (*c*. second century BC) in his *Mahābhāṣya*, holds that *vyākaraṇa* is the chief among the six Vedāṅgas. It was called *vedānāṁ veda*, the Veda of the Vedas.

(iii) Nirukta — etymology. Of the works of this class, the only one that is available is the *Nirukta* by Yāska (*c*. eighth or seventh century BC). It is a commentary on the *Nighaṇṭu* which contains five lists of words divided into three sections; called *kāṇḍa*s, namely.

(a) *Naighaṇṭuka-kāṇḍa* — a collection of Vedic words conveying special meanings;

(b) *Naigama-kāṇḍa* — comprising difficult Vedic words of doubtful import;

(c) *Daivata-kāṇḍa* — grouping of deities into three classes, namely residing in heaven (*dyusthāna*), atmosphere (*antarikṣa*) and earth (*bhū*).

(iv) Chandas —metres. The *Ṛgveda-prātiśākhya* mentions Vedic metres. The *Nidāna-sūtra* of the *Sāmaveda* contains some information about metres besides songs, etc. The *Piṅgala-chandaḥ-sūtra* is the earliest available work exclusively on metrics. In addition to Vedic metres, it deals with classical metres too.

(v) Jyotiṣa — The extant *Jyotiṣa-vedāṅga* is metrical, containing 36 stanzas in its Ṛgvedic recension and 43 stanzas in the Yajurvedic form. It discusses mainly the positions of the sun and the moon in summer and winter solstices, 27 constellations, new moon and full moon.

Jyotiṣa was indispensable for the determination of time in respect of sacrificial rituals. Elements of *Jyotiṣa* occur in the *Ṛgveda*. Of *Jyotiṣa-vedāṅga*, only two works exist—one relating to the *Ṛgveda*, attributed to Lagadha and the other relating to the *Yajurveda*, by Śeṣa. According to some scholars, these two were written about 1400 and 1200 BC.

The ritualistic Vedāṅga is called *kalpa* comprising the following four types of works written in *sūtra*s (aphorisms):

1. *Śrauta-sūtra* — dealing with the Vedic rituals. These contain details about Vedic sacrifices. Each Veda had its own *śrauta-sūtra*s, e.g., *Āśvalāyana-śrauta-sūtra* and *Sāṁkhāyana-śrauta-sūtra* belonging to the *Ṛgveda*.
2. *Śulva-sūtra* — closely connected with the *Śrauta-sūtra*s above are these *sūtra*s dealing with the measurement of sacrificial altars; *śulva* means the measuring tape. These are the earliest works on Indian geometry, and occupy a significant position in the history of mathematics.
3. *Gṛhyasūtra*—dealing with rituals right from the ceremony of impregnation (*niṣeka* or *garbhādhāna*) to funeral rite (*antyeṣṭi-kriyā*). These also are attached to particular Vedas. For instance, the *Āśvalāyana* and *Sāṁkhāyana Gṛhyasūtra*s belong to the *Ṛgveda*.
4. *Dharmasūtra*—dealing with rules and regulations relating to the four castes and four stages of life, royal duties (*rāja-dharma*) and secular law (*vyavahāra*).

Besides the above works, some works of the type of Index were written for determining the *ṛṣi*s, deities and metres of the hymns of the *Ṛgveda*. Thus, we have *Ārṣānukramaṇī*, *Devānukramaṇī* and *Chando'nukramaṇī*. The *Anuvākānukramaṇī* contains index to the *anuvāka*s into which hymns, rather the *Maṇḍala*s (books) of the *Ṛgveda* are sub-divided. Kātyāyana's *Sarvānukramaṇī*, as the title indicates, contains all the aforesaid *anukramaṇī*s. The *Bṛhaddevatā* of Śaunaka lists the names of the *ṛṣi*s to whom are ascribed the *ṛk*s of the hymns.

2

Epics

THE *Rāmāyaṇa* and the *Mahābhārata*, representing the ethos of the Indians, are the two national Epics of India.

The Rāmāyaṇa

Attributed to sage Vālmīki, it consists of the following books:

> I. Bāla-(or Ādi)kāṇḍa, II. Ayodhyā-kāṇḍa, III. Araṇya-kāṇḍa, IV. Kiṣkindhā-kāṇḍa, V. Sundara-kāṇḍa, VI. Laṅkā-(or Yuddha) kāṇḍa, and VII. Uttara-kāṇḍa.

Each of the above books comprises several cantos (*sargas*).

The main story is briefly as follows:

Daśaratha, king of Ayodhyā, has three queens, the eldest named Kauśalyā, the second Kaikeyī and the youngest Sumitrā. Four sons are born to them; Rāma was the son of Kauśalyā, Bharata and Śatrughna of Kaikeyī and Lakṣmaṇa of Sumitrā.

When they grow up, Daśaratha arranges for the coronation of Rāma, the eldest son. But, Kaikeyī asks Daśaratha for the fulfilment of the two unspecified boons which he promised to her on a previous occasion. Of the two boons, one is that Rāma would be banished; the other is that Bharata would be installed as king.

Daśaratha is extremely shocked, but, in order to honour his promise, grants her the above two boons. Accordingly, Rāma takes to forest-life. His devoted brother, Lakṣmaṇa and loving wife Sītā also accompany him.

They put up in a hut in Pañcavaṭī forest which is haunted by demons. Śūrpaṇakhā, the wicked sister of demon-king, Rāvaṇa of Laṅkā, makes overtures of love to Lakṣmaṇa. This enrages him who chops off her nose. Insulted by this act, Rāvaṇa comes to that forest. One day, seeing a golden deer moving about in the forest, Sītā is bent on getting it. At her request, Rāma keeps Lakṣmaṇa to guard Sītā, and sets out to bring the golden deer which is really demon Mārīca in disguise. The demon-deer, being struck by Rāma's arrow, cries in a plaintive tone — O Lakṣmaṇa. Agitated by this cry, Sītā, apprehending danger to Rāma, insists on Lakṣmaṇa's running for help to her dear husband.

Seeing Sītā unprotected, Rāvaṇa abducts her, and carries her away to Laṅkā. Rāma comes back only to see the hut bereft of Sītā. Having learnt of her abduction by Rāvaṇa. Rāma is determined to rescue his beloved consort.

Thereupon, Rāma allies himself with the monkey-king Sugrīva, and commissions his (Rāma's) loyal devotee, the noble monkey Hanumat to carry his signet-ring to Sītā at Laṅkā.

Having entered Laṅkā, Hanumat secretly meets Sītā. He is, however, found out by Rāvaṇa's men who set fire to his long tail as punishment. Hanumat, with his blazing tail, burns Laṅkā, and comes back to Rāma.

The simian followers of Rāma builds a bridge across the ocean. Rāma and Lakṣmaṇa, with a large ratinue, invade Laṅkā, and after many reverses, succeed in extirpating the demons, and rescue Sītā with whom Rāma returns to Ayodhyā, and is eventually anointed King.

While Rāma had been reigning, his subjects expressed their dislike of the fact that he had accepted Sītā, tainted by her association with the despicable demons. Like a true king, intent on the satisfaction of the subjects, Rāma banished Sītā into a forest where she got asylum in the hermitage of Vālmīki. There, she gave birth to two sons, Lava and Kuśa.

After many incidents, Vālmīki, accompanied by Sītā, came to Ayodhyā. Sītā, to give convincing proof of her chastity, prayed to Mother Earth to take her into herself. Earth showed a cleft into which Sītā disappeared for ever.

ORIGIN AND DATE

The Epic originated, at an unknown time, as ballads transmitted orally and sung by two classes of people, viz. Sūtas living in royal courts and Kuśīlavas who were travelling singers comparable, to a great extent, to the French troubadours.

A long period elapsed before the above ballads came to be written. It is not known when the above ballads came to be written. It is not certain when the *Rāmāyaṇa* was written for the first time. This much is certain that many interpolations crapt into the Epic, as is evidenced by the existence of more recensions than one which will be dealt with later on.

As we have stated earlier, there is neither means to determine when the *Rāmāyaṇa* ballads originated nor do we know precisely when they started to be written. After examining arguments and counter-arguments, Winternitz concludes that the extant *Rāmāyaṇa* is, perhaps, the result of evolution through the period between the fourth or third century BC and the second century AD.

GENUINE AND THE SPURIOUS

Some scholars have put forward reasons for the assumption that books I and VII and parts of books V and VI are spurious.

LITERARY VALUE OF THE RĀMĀYAṆA

In comparison with the other Epic, the *Rāmāyaṇa* is more aritstic, ornate and refined. It contains almost all the characteristics of a *mahākāvya* according to the later writers on poetics. It is called *ādi-kāvya*, the first poetical work. The story goes that a brigand, named Ratnākara, while roaming in a forest, suddenly saw a couple of birds in copulation. Of them, one was killed by a fowler. Extremely moved to pity, Ratnākara uttered the following verse:

> *mā niṣāda pratiṣṭhāṁ tvamagamaḥ śāśvatīḥ samāḥ* ।
> *yat krauñca-mithunād ekamavadhīḥ kāma-mohitam* ॥

The illiterate hoodlum was astonished at this utterance which was like a devil citing scriptures. So, he exclaimed—*kimidaṁ vyāhṛtaṁ mayā* (what is this uttered by me?). According to the legend, this was the very first verse (in classical Sanskrit literature) in which as Kālidāsa aptly remarks — *ślokatvam āpadyata yasya śokaḥ* (whose grief assumed the form of a verse). It is said that, in course of time, as a result of long and arduous penance, Ratnākara became a sage, Vālmīki by name. He is traditionally known as the author of the *Rāmāyaṇa*. As he was the first poet, his Epic came to be known as *ādi-kāvya*.

Besides occupying the place of honour in the annals of the *kāvya* literature, this Epic reveals some intrinsic qualities. Its language is limpid, style racy. Nowhere is there any attempt to show off pedantry or *tour de force* which detracts from the merit of some later poetical works, particularly of the age of literary decadence. The reader seldom or never requires the help of a commentary in comprehending what the author wants to convey. The Epic contains elements of romance, as a glance at the contents of the Sundara-kāṇḍa reveals.

Descriptions of nature in the Epic are delectable. In the Kiṣkindhā-kāṇḍa, the pen-picture of spring, rains and autumn are, indeed, graphic and testify to the fact that the poet had an eye to see and an ear to hear. A few specimens are given below in English translation:

> The sky, overcast with clouds, is visible here and invisible there. At places, being obstructed by the mountains, it assumes the beauty of a great ocean devoid of waves.
>
> — Kiṣkindhā 28/17.

> The flock of peacocks are as if performing *saṁgīta* — they are dancing at some places, loudly crying at others; at places, they are perching on tree-tops with their plumes hanging. — Kiṣkindhā 28/37

> [*Note*: In Sanskrit, *saṁgīta* donotes song, dance and instrumental music.]

Charming descriptions of aspects of nature occur in some other *kāṇḍa*s also. For example,

> The great hero, Hanumat caught sight of the rising moon

> (in Laṅkā)—it was white like milk and a lotus-stalk, bright like a conch-shell; it seemed as though a swan was swimming in a tank. — Sundara 2/55

In short, the Epic fully conforms to the ideal of poetry according to a critic who holds that poetry should be simple, sensuous and impassioned.

The delineation of some of the characters reveals the masterly hand of the poet. Rāma was not only an obedient son acting up to his father's wish, and giving up the throne without a word of protest. He was a true hero with a keen sense of honour. He did not hesitate to wage war against the powerful Rāvaṇa, the abductor of his dear wife. Overcoming heavy odds, he succeeded in rescuing Sītā and restoring her position as the queen-consort. A true king as he was, his concern was to keep his subjects pleased. They expressed resentment at his accepting Sītā whose chastity, in the custody of the powerful Rāvaṇa, was suspected by them. In order to please them, he banished Sītā though she was dearer to him than his own life. His love of her was so great that he never married again. Rāma's fraternal affection found poignant expression is his laments over the body of Lakṣmaṇa struck down by the enemy's missile.

Sītā has been depicted as an ideal woman. Sheer sense of duty and love for her husband urged her to forgo the comfort of royal harem and to resort to the arduous forest-life. This she did despite Rāma's persuasion to stay back. While in the forest, she did not flinch from her duties. She was forcibly carried away by Rāvaṇa who coaxed and cajoled her to live with him, and held out the tempting prospects of royal position in which she could enjoy all the pleasures of life. But, faithful to her husband, she spurned the overtures of the demon-king. He kept her body in captivity, but could not exercise control over her mind. No homily or threat could wean her away from her husband whose image was always before her mind's eye. When she came to know of her exile in an alien forest, she felt utterly helpless as she was in an advanced stage of pregnancy. From then, she did not accuse Rāma, but calmly accepted her wretched condition as the result of her own deeds in the previous life.

Poetical skill is revealed in the use of various figures of speech relating to both word and sense. The prosodic variety makes the Epic a pleasant read.

RECENSIONS OF THE RĀMĀYAṆA

The *Rāmāyaṇa* was a very popular Epic. Its popularity was country-wide. There was no printing press in ancient times. It was written by hand. The hand of the interpolator got ample opportunity to make changes in the text. The popularity of the Epic was responsible for the multiplicity of its manuscripts throughout the length and breadth of India. In course of time, three distinct regional recensions came into existence. These were the Kāśmīrian recension, Bengal recension and south Indian recension. These recensions differ from one another in the number, order and reading of the text.

RĀMĀYAṆA AND MAHĀBHĀRATA — WHICH IS EARLIER?

Traditionally, the *Rāmāyaṇa* preceded the *Mahābhārata*. But, for certain reasons, the fact appears to be the other way round. Some of these reasons are as follows: Pāṇini's grammar mentions the *Mahābhārata* characters Arjuna (IV.3.98) and Yudhiṣṭhira (VIII.3.95). But, it is silent about the characters of the *Rāmāyaṇa*. The *Mahābhārata* retains the old balled style, e.g., *Arjuna uvāca*, etc. But, the other Epic contains no such trace. The style of the *Rāmāyaṇa* is obviously more ornate and polished than that of the *Mahābhārata*. Again, the society, depicted in the *Mahābhārata*, is much rougher and ruder than that revealed by the *Rāmāyaṇa*. The *Mahābhārata* depicts Draupadī as having five husbands. Polyandry was a very ancient practice which is not found in the *Rāmāyaṇa*.

Those, who think the *Rāmāyaṇa* was earlier, point out that the *Mahābhārata* contains, in Vana-parva (273-90), the story of Rāma. But, it is not known whether the *Mahābhārata* got the story from the Epic *Rāmāyaṇa* or from the much older Rāma ballad. It is also argued that the *Harivaṁśa*, a part of the *Mahābhārata*, refers to the *Rāmāyaṇa*. The counter-argument is that the *Harivaṁśa* was a later supplement (*khila*) to the *Mahābhārata*.

It is noteworthy that, in the VIIth book (143-66), the

Mahābhārata contains verbatim a verse of the VIth book (81/28) of the *Rāmāyaṇa*. If this portion of the former is genuine, then it points to priority of the latter. Vālmīki is mentioned several times in the *Mahābhārata*.

Some scholars hold that the nucleus of the *Mahābhārata* may have been earlier than that of the other Epic, but, in their present forms, the Epic *Rāmāyaṇa* appears to be earlier.

INFLUENCE OF THE RĀMĀYAṆA IN INDIA AND ABROAD

In India

The influence of the *Rāmāyaṇa* on the life and literature of the Indians is deep and pervasive. The enduring impact of this Epic is expressed in the following verse:

> *yāvat sthāsyanti girayaḥ saritaśca mahītale* ।
> *tāvad rāmāyaṇī-kathā lokeṣu pracariṣyati* ॥

The *Rāmāyaṇa* story will be current among the people as long as the mountains and rivers will exist on the earth.

Children hear the story of the *Rāmāyaṇa* from their elders even before they learn the alphabets. This story is regarded as the best medium for inculcating the basic moral principles to the boys and girls. Rāma's regard for his father, Lakṣmaṇa's devotion to the elder brother, Rāma, Sītā's fidelity towards her husband, etc., have become proverbial.

That the *Rāmāyaṇa* played a great part in moulding the literature in ancient India is very nicely expressed in the following verse, attributed to Vāmana-bhaṭṭabāṇa:

> *vandyaḥ kasya na vālmīkir-yasya vāṅ-madhunaḥ kaṇān* ।
> *ādāya kavayo'dyāpi vikṣipanti sva-sūktiṣu* ॥

> To whom is notworthy of respect Vālmīki picking honey-drops of whose words the poets even today scatter into their own good speech?

Many Sanskrit works, prose, poetical and dramatic, have drawn upon the *Rāmāyaṇa* through the ages. As examples, we can mention the following poetical works: Kālidāsa's *Raghuvaṁśa*, Bhaṭṭī's *Bhaṭṭīkāvya* (*Rāvaṇa-vadha*), Kumāradāsa's *Jānakīharaṇa*, etc. Among the dramas, mention may be made of Bhāsa's *Pratimā-nāṭaka*, Bhavabhūti's *Uttara-rāma-carita*, etc., Bhoja's *Rāmāyaṇa-campū* is in mixed prose and verse.

The vernacular literatures of India also reveal the deep impact of this Epic. Besides stories, based on episodes of this work, in the different regions of India, we have adaptations of the entire *Rāmāyaṇa*. Among such adaptations, the most noteworthy are Kambana's *Rāmāyaṇa* in Tāmil, Kṛttivāsī *Rāmāyaṇa* in Bengālī, Tulasīdāsa's *Rāmacaritamānasa* in Hindī and the Nepālī *Rāmāyaṇa* of Bhānubhakta.

Many *Rāmāyaṇa* plays were written in Bengālī as also in other regional languages. In Bengal, such plays were stage for popular entertainment in what was known as *yātrā*.

Professional *kathākāras* (narrators) used to narrate the *Rāmāyaṇa* story for the entertainment and edification of the public.

Even the Buddhists and Jains took recourse to this popular Epic as a vehicle for the propagation of their respective religions among the populace. For instance, the *Daśaratha-jātaka* is an example of the Buddhist adaptation of the *Rāmāyaṇa* story. The Jainas wrote a *Rāmāyaṇa*, called *Paüma-caria*.

Naqīb Khān, Badāūnī and Hājī Sultān translated (AD 999) into Persian the *Rāmāyaṇa*; this version was the basis of a versified form produced later on by Sādullāh of Pānipath in the Mughal regime of India.

In Foreign countries

The popularity of this Epic spread far beyond the confines of India. Bhānubhakta's *Rāmāyaṇa*, written in Nepālī, is a national Epic of that country. Two *Rāmāyaṇa*-based Sanskrit dramas, composed there, are the *Mahīrāvaṇa-vadha* and *Rāmāyaṇa-nāṭaka*.

The *Jānakīharaṇa*, mentioned earlier, was composed in Ceylon.

The Cambodian version of the *Rāmāyaṇa*, called *Rāmakerti*, reveals a blend of Brāhmaṇical and Buddhistic ideas. There is epigraphical evidence of the fact that the *Rāmāyaṇa* story was popular in Indo-China and Indonesia as early as the first millennium of the Christian era. Some temples of this country, e.g., Baphoun Mountain Tample, Banteay Sri Temple depict *Rāmāyaṇa* scenes.

The popular *Rāmāyaṇa* of Thailand (Siam) is called *Rāmakir* or *Rāmakien*. A wall-painting from Phrakhee Vat, Bangkok, depicts a *Rāmāyaṇa* scene. *Rāmāyaṇa* episodes, besides being represented in sculptures and murals, are enacted on the stage, and provide themes for the popular mask-dance.

In Malaysia, themes from the Indian Epics are used in dance, drama, puppet-shows and shadow-plays. The oldest *Rāmāyaṇa* manuscript, the *Hikayat Seri Rāma* has a Tamil model.

The Epics of India profoundly influenced the literature of Java. The Javanese work, Uttara-kāṇḍa is a free old-Javanese paraphrase of the last book of the Sanskrit *Rāmāyaṇa*, with some changes in the original story. The *Serat-Rāma* is a neo-Javanese adaptation of the old-Javanese *Kakawin*.

In Champā (South Annam), the latest redaction of the *Rāma-kathā* dates back to the eighteenth century AD.

In Bali, a portion of the *Rāmakavaca* is almost identical with passages of the *Vālmīki-Rāmāyaṇa*.

Episodes of the *Rāmāyaṇa* are scenically represented on the stage in Laos. In Annam the form of *Rāmakathā* is called "The King of Demons", Rāma and Sītā have imaginary names.

Ikeda of Japan wrote a valuable treatise in Japanese about the two Great Epics of India. There is a Mongolian version of the *Rāmāyaṇa*. Siberian folklore reveals familiarity with the *Rāmāyaṇa* an abridged version of which appears in the Kalmuk language.

The Mahābhārata

Attributed to sage Vyāsa, it is an Epic consisting of 18 books, called Parvas. It has a supplement, entitled *Harivaṁśa*. Its contents are briefly as follows:

The Kauravas were cousins of Pāṇḍavas. Pāṇḍava Yudhiṣṭhira, the eldest of them, was crowned king. Duryodhana, the eldest of the Kauravas, was jealous of Yudhiṣṭhira whom he defeated in a deceitful game of dice. In accordance with the terms of a wager in the game, Yudhiṣṭhira, along with his four brothers and common wife, Draupadī, went into exile for 12 years plus one year of living incognito. Yudhiṣṭhira, having asked for the restoration of the throne after the expiry of the stipulated period, Duryodhana refused to give up the throne without a battle. In a gory battle at Kurukṣetra, the Kauravas were completely routed and lost their lives. After victory mainly with the help of Kṛṣṇa, Yudhiṣṭhira occupied the throne and, in course of time, the Pāṇḍavas attained heaven. Around this nucleous were woven various legends and anecdotes, e.g., the stories of Nala-Damayantī, Sāvitrī-Satyavān, Duṣyanta-Śakuntalā, hero-mother Vidulā, Nahuṣa, churning of the ocean, flood-legend, the story of king Śivi and so on so forth. Incidentally, attempts have been made to inculcate morality, politics, *dharmaśāstra*, philosophical precepts, heroism, Brāhmaṇical supremacy, etc. Due to the diversity of contents, it has been characterised as an 'entire literature'.

BHAGAVAD GĪTĀ

Included in the Bhīṣma-parva of the *Mahābhārata*, it comprises eighteen chapters which are named as follows:

I. *Arjuna-viṣāda-yoga* — The Yoga of Arjuna's conflict.

II. *Sāṁkhya-yoga* — *Yoga* of Knowledge.

III. *Karma-yoga* — *Yoga* of Work.

IV. *Jñāna-yoga* — *Yoga* of Divine Knowldege.

V. *Karma-saṁnyāsa-yoga* — *Yoga* of Renunciation of Action.

VI. *Dhyāna-yoga* — *Yoga* of Meditation.

VII. *Jñāna-vijñāna-yoga* — *Yoga* of Wisdom and Knowledge.

VIII. *Akṣara-brahma-yoga* — *Yoga* of the Imperishable Absolute.

IX. *Rāja-vidyā-rāja-guhya-yoga* — *Yoga* of Sovereign Knowledge and Sovereign Mystery.

X. *Vibhūti-yoga* — *Yoga* of Manifestation.

XI. *Viśvarūpa-darśana-yoga* — *Yoga* of the Vision of the Cosmic Forms.

XII. Bhakti-yoga — *Yoga* of Devotion.

XIII. Kṣetra-kṣetrajña-vibhāga-Yoga — *Yoga* of Distinction between the Field and the knower of the Field.

XIV. Guṇatraya-vibhāga-yoga — *Yoga* of the Differentiation of the Three Modes.

XV. *Puruṣottama Yoga* — *Yoga* of the Supreme Person.

XVI. *Daivāsura Saṁpad Vibhāga Yoga* — *Yoga* of Discriminating between the divine and demone as endownments.

XVII. *Śraddhātraya* — *Vibhāga Yoga* — *Yoga* of the Three Patterns of Faith.

XVIII. *Mokṣa-Saṁnyāsa Yoga* — *Yoga* of Release and renunciation.

The *Gītā*, as it is popularly called, dwells on the philosophy of life according to the different temperaments of human beings who are the followers of one or other of three paths, viz., the path of action (*karma*), the path of knowledge (*jñāna*), and the path of devotion (*bhakti*). It is in the form of a dialogue between Arjuna, brother of the aforesaid Yudhiṣṭhira, and Kṛṣṇa. Arjuna, bewildered at the sight of relatives in the opposite camp on the battlefield, is on the point of breaking down, and expresses reluctance to fight. Kṛṣṇa boosts his morale by an exhortation in which he solves the various problems spoken out by Arjuna.

The *Gītā* is regarded as a very sacred treatise which or parts of which are recited daily by some devout Indians. A laudatory verse characterises this treatise in the following words:

sarvopaniṣado gāvo dogdhā gopālanandanaḥ ।
pārtho vatsaḥ sudhīr-bhoktā dugdhaṁ gītāmṛtaṁ mahat ॥

All the Upaniṣads are cows, the son of a cowherd (i.e., Kṛṣṇa) is the milker, Pārtha; (lit. the son of Pṛthā; i.e., Arjuna) is the calf, the wise man is the enjoyer and the milk is the great nectar in the form of the *Gītā*.

This treatise has served as the gospel of life to many people. It has been interpreted by eminent scholars like Tilak, Gāndhi, Rādhākrishnan, and translated into various languages throughout the length and breadth of India.

It should be noted that the popularity of this work extended far beyond India. It has been translated into many foreign languages. According to the German philosopher Humboldt, it is, perhaps, the ony truly philosophical treatise in all the literatures known to us. Another German scholar, J.W. Hauer has described it as a work of imperishable significance.

RECENSIONS OF THE EPIC

Its popularity throughout India resulted in three recensions, viz., north Indian or Kāśmīrī, central Indian comprising the Nepālī, Devanāgarī and Maithilī versions, and the Bengal recension.

AUTHORSHIP AND EVOLUTION

Traditionally, it is attributed to sage Vyāsa. That it passed through three stages of development is borne out by internal evidence. The total number of verses in it is stated to be *śatasahasra* (hundred thousand or one lakh) in I.1.101, *caturviṁśati-sahasra* (24,000) in I.1.102 and *aṣṭau śloka-sahasrāṇi aṣṭau ślokaśatāni* (8,800) in I.2.131.

DATE

Nothing definite is known about the date of origin of the nucleus orally transmitted in the form of ballads. Nor do we know for certain when the Epic, in its written form, first appeared. Considering various evidences, Winternitz comes to the conclusion that the Epic "can have received its present form not earlier than in the fourth century BC and not later than in the fourth century AD".

The chronological relation between the *Rāmāyaṇa* and the *Mahābhārata* has already been discussed.

HARIVAṀŚA

Orthodox scholars regard it as an integral part of the Epic. But, modern scholars think that it is a much later supplement (*khila*) containing 16,373 stanzas. It is sometimes rightly referred to as the *Harivaṁśa Purāṇa*. Its connection with the Epic story is tenuous and external. It is in the three sections, called *Harivaṁśa-parva*, *Viṣṇu-parva* and *Bhaviṣya-parva*. The first section contains a full account of Kṛṣṇa in his divine form. The second section deals with Kṛṣṇa as an incarnation of Viṣṇu. The subjects, discussed in the last section, are prophecies about the future ages, creation, detailed descriptions of Viṣṇu's incarnations as Boar, Man-Lion and Dwarf, syncretisation of the worship of Viṣṇu and Śiva, good effect of the study of the Epic, account of the burning of Tripura by Śiva, epitome of the *Harivaṁśa*, good effect of listening to the recital of the *Harivaṁśa*.

INFLUENCE OF THE EPIC

This Epic has been influencing the life and literature of the Indians through ages. It is even now publicly recited for edification. Anecdotes and parables serve as media for moral instruction in the formative periods of the lives of yougsters. The righteousness of Yudhiṣṭhira, Arjuna's heroism, Draupadī's spirited reaction to the enemy's machination and devoted service of her husbands, etc., are still regarded as models for the formation of character. The *Gītā*, mentioned earlier, and the Virāṭa-parva are recited as holy texts in the obsequial rite, called *śrāddha*.

The Epic is both a great Epic and *dharmaśāstra*; its influence on *dharmaśāstra* works is marked.

The following couplet shows how the Epic provided themes for many Sanskrit works:

> *parjanya iva bhūtānāma-kṣayo bhārata-drumaḥ* ।
> *sarveśāṁ kavi-mukhyānāmupajīvyo bhaviṣyati* ।।

> The imperishable (*Mahā*)-*bhārata* tree will be, like (the god of rain) Varuṇa to creatures, the source of all the principal poets.

[*Note*: In Sanskrit, both poetical works and dramas, as well as prose compositions of certain kinds, are called *kāvya*.]

For example, the *Kirātārjunīya* of Bhāravi, *Śiśupāla-vadha* of Māgha are two noted poetical works which have derived themes from the Epic. Bhāsa's *Urubhaṅga*, Kālidāsa's *Abhijñāna-śākuntalam* are two important dramas based on it. It should be noted that the Epic legend has been drawn upon by quite a number of works in the different vernaculars of India.

Like the *Rāmāyaṇa*, the *Mahābhārata* also travelled far beyond India. It has been mentioned in a Cambodian (Kampuchean) inscription of about AD 600. There is evidence that this Epic used to be studied in ancient Champā (South Annam). The Javanese rendering of the Epic is an important treatise there. The Javanese work, *Sārasamuccaya* contains the translation of several verses from the Anuśāsana-parva of this Epic. The Javanese works, *Sang Satyavān*, *Keravāśrama*, *Navarūci* are based on the *Mahābhārata*. The translations of this Epic or of parts of it into several languages of the world testify to its world-wide popularity. In this connection, special mention is deserved by the Nala-Damayantī legend, contained in the Epic.

LITERARY VALUE OF THE EPIC

Some modern critics regard the *Mahābhārata* as a formless fermenting verbiage. It is true that the work contains exaggerations and hyperboles, etc., usual in such Epics. But, it is not devoid of literary value.

As is to be expected in bardic poetry, the *Mahābhārata* contains a lot of folk elements and a number of pithy sayings and maxims which represent the experience and wisdom of people through ages. We note below renderings of some such sayings. In this connection, the speech of Vidura, a friend of the Pāṇḍavas and an ardent devotee of Kṛṣṇa, deserves special mention. Some of his observations (Udyoga-parva, 33, Vaṅgavāsī ed.) are as follows.

> One, who is not led astray by money, is called wise. One, of whose motives and activities others do not get an inkling beforehand, is called wise.

> He is wise who listens long, but understands quickly. The characteristic of a wise man is that he gratuitously engages himself for others.
>
> He, who is not elated by honour nor resents disgrace, and is unperturbed like a Gangetic lake, is wise.
>
> He is a fool who, having neglected his own interest, acts for the interest of others, and resorts to falsehood for the sake of a friend. He is foolish who, though not invited, enters a place, and, though not asked, talks much.

Some other salutary sayings, culled from various contexts, are as follows:

> The greatest of gains is freedom from disease; of all pleasures, contentment in the best.
>
> One should strive for the truth, truth indeed is the greatest strength.
>
> Even Indra in heaven does not enjoy uninterrupted happiness.
>
> The purity of conduct is great purity, purity from a holy place comes next.
>
> Do not hurt others' feelings nor use cruel words.
>
> The wound, caused by harsh words, does not heal up.

In characterisation, the work reveals laudable skill. The ideals of Indian life have been held out through some characters. Each character has its own distinctions. Some of the female characters dispel the common impression that, in ancient India, women were looked upon as mere chattels and child-producing machines. Let us look at Darupadī. Even personalities such as Yudhiṣṭhira, Bhīma and Arjuna could not eclipse her personality as a spirited lady of uncompromising principles. Ever since her disgrace by the Kauravas in the open court, she had been nursing a strong feeling of revenge. The opportunity to feed fat her ancient grudge came after long 13 years when the selfish and insolent Kaurava king refused to hand over the throne to the Pāṇḍavas who were legitimately entitled to it. Finding the Pāṇḍavas devoid of initiative, she made a strong appeal to Kṛṣṇa to declare war. Where Duryodhana is alive even for a moment, fie upon the famed archery of Arjuna and the heroism of Bhīma. She would not rest so long as she does not see the tainted hand of Duḥśāsana, that dishonoured her, lying severed on the ground. It should not be supposed that she articulated her grievances in a fit of emotional outburst. Her speech was rational, and based on political principles. She said that *daṇḍa* (war) was the way of bringing on his knees the enemy who could not be brought to terms by *sāma* (conciliation) and *dāna* (gift). She further referred to the time-honoured wise principle that as it is a sin to kill an innocent man, so it is sinful not to kill one who deserves death.

We meet with another spirited lady, Vidulā (Udyoga-parva, 133-6). Her son, Sañjaya, vanquised by the enemy, became dispirited, and lost his will to fight again. Unlike a doting mother, Vidulā, fired by the true kṣatriya spirit, exhorts her son to take up arms. She says — up, coward, up, by accepting defeat do not enhance the delight of enemies and the grief of kinsmen. A true man goes on doing duties regardless of gain or loss, and is not stricken with the fear of life. It is better to take away the fang of a serpent than dying like a dog. The son remonstrates by saying that he is her only son, how can she, having a mother's heart, incite him to a battle in which his death is certain. But, she keeps on prodding him; the kṣatriya in her does not give in to the mother.

Some male characters also are admirable. For instance, Karṇa appears as uncompromising in his honour, loyalty and charity. When he was ridiculed as a *sūta-putra* (son of a charioteer), his spirited reply was — birth in a particular family depends on fate, but heroism is self-acquired. Karṇa was born to the Pāṇḍava-mother, Kuntī in her pre-marital life, and was abandoned by her. He was, however, picked up by a *sūta*, and reared by him. Kṛṣṇa revealed his identity, and tried to win him over from the side of Kauravas to that of the Pāṇḍavas. Kṛṣṇa held out an exalted position to be enjoyed by him as the eldest of the Pāṇḍava brothers, and as another husband of Draupadī. Moreover, Kṛṣṇa himself offered him all assistance if he defected to the Pāṇḍava camp. But,

Karṇa, owing allegiance to the Kauravas, did not flinch.

Lord Indra, disguised as a brāhmaṇa guest, approached Karṇa, and asked for his armour and ear-ring which were congenital and the protectors of his life. Knowing the risk involved in fulfilling the wish of the guest, Karṇa did not hesitate to do so remembering that honouring the guest was a sacred duty.

It should, however, be noted that the Epic depicts, in Karṇa, a human being of flesh and blood, and not as a divine being. Hence, we find some foibles too in his character. It was at his instigation that Duryodhana tried to poison Bhīma to death. Karṇa was one of those who planned the dastardly killing of the boy, Abhimanyu surrounded by great heroes. Again, Karṇa had some part in the attempted heinous undressing of Draupadī in the court.

Another noble character was Bhīṣma. For facilitating the marriage of his father with the latter's desired lady, Satyavatī, he promised never to marry. This firm resolve testifies to his devotion to father on the one hand and to the great strength of character on the other. After the death of his sonless brother, Vicitravīrya, mother Satyavatī tried, in many ways, to persuade Bhīṣma to accept Vicitravīrya's two beautiful wives as his wife according to levirate. Satyavatī argued that, by doing so, he would, at the same time, uphold religion, prepetuate the lineage and satisfy the departed ancestors. But Bhīṣma was unshaken in his resolve. He replied that he would forsake the kingdom of the three worlds rather than swerve from the truth.

Bhīṣma's appointment as the general in the Kaurava Army and his part in logistics in the battlefield bespeak his military skill.

Bhīṣma was a real appreciator of merit. Though in the opposite camp, Yudhiṣṭhira was advised to show proper honour to Kṛṣṇa who, in his opinion, was unparalleled in merit.

Bhīṣma was upright enough to utter even an unpalatable word when occasion demanded.

Hearing the pitiable appeal of Draupadī, brought to the court, Bhīṣma blamed the Kauravas. He described them as passionate and influenced by greed and delusion. He told Draupadī that the silent elderly ones such as Droṇa were like dead persons. In the Udyoga-parva, he reprimanded Duryodhana for shabby treatment towards Pāṇḍavas and disgraceful conduct towards Draupadī. He also repeatedly asked him to share the kingdom with the Pāṇḍavas.

Bhīṣma was one who could never be killed. The Pāṇḍavas felt that, without killing him, they could not defeat the Kauravas, and tried various means in vain to put an end to his life, Bhīṣma, however, embraced death voluntarily. This he did presumably for two reasons. He felt that the Pāṇḍavas were wronged; their victory would be just. Secondly, disgusted at the loss of lives in battle he lost the will to live. Thus, his voluntary death invests his life with a halo of nobility. Even today, thousands of people offer libations of water to the soul of this sonless man who was unparalleled in truthfulness and self-restraint.

3

Classical Sanskrit Literature

Poetry, Prose and Drama

CLASSICAL Sanskrit is to be distinguished from the Vedic language, and the language of the Epics. The language, standardised by Pāṇini (*c.* fifth century BC), in his monumental grammar, *Aṣṭādhyāyī*, is generally called Classical Sanskrit.

There is a vast literature — poetry, prose and drama — written in Classical Sanskrit. For the proper assessment and appreciation of this literature, we should take into account the milieu in which it originated.

We have dealt with the Vedic, Epic and Purāṇic literatures. Some Purāṇas, however, are late. Barring these late works, the other texts constituted the literary heritage of ancient India. They also supplied the themes of many works of Classical Sanskrit literature. Some ancient *śāstra*s served the purpose of shaping the ideas of the classical writers with regard to the characters delineated in their works. Of such disciplines, three deserve special mention. These are the *Nāṭyaśāstra*, *Kāmasūtra* and the *Arthaśāstra* which have been dealt with in separate chapters. These *śāstra*s influenced the different heroes and heroines of Sanskrit literary works. Ancient India was governed mainly by kings. These kings were mostly monarchs ruling over particular regions, large and small. In fact, Aśoka was the only king in ancient India who extended his sway over the largest part of the country.

The kings and potentates were patrons of learning and of learned men. This is, perhaps, the reason why most of the literary works deal with the life and the intrigues in royal courts.

The study of the Classical Sanskrit literature of ancient India reveals the following well-defined stages:

A. Creative Period (from the beginnings to *c*. fourth century AD)

B. Period of Development (from *c*. fifth century AD to the ninth century AD)

First Phase — The works of Kālidāsa

Second Phase — Post-Kālidāsa works

C. Period of decadence (from *c*. tenth century AD to the eighteenth century AD)

Even a modest account of the Classical Sanskrit literature as a whole requires a separate volume. We shall, therefore, rest content with the highlights of each of the above periods. These will be representative works of the respective periods.

A. CREATIVE PERIOD

Poetical literature

We do not know when and how this period started. The *Rāmāyaṇa* is known as the first *kāvya*. The *Mahābhārata* also, in the text itself, is called *kāvya*. To Pāṇini, who may or may not be identical with the grammarian, are ascribed some verses in anthologies. Patañjali's *Mahābhāṣya* mentions a *Vāraruca-kāvya*. Two poetical works, *Pātāla-vijaya* and *Jāmbavatī-vijaya*, are also attributed to Pāṇini of uncertain identity. The former is mentioned by Namisādhu, in his commentary on the *Kāvyālaṁkāra* of Bhāmaha, and the latter by Rāyamukuṭa in his commentary on the *Amarakośa*.

We are still in the dark about the history of Sanskrit poetical literature before Aśvaghoṣa (*c*. first century AD).

Prose literature

The origin of this species is also obscure. The aforesaid *Mahābhāṣya*, written in a lucid and eminently readable form, presupposes considerable development of literary prose. Besides, Patañjali mentions three prose works, called *Vāsavadattā* (to be distinguished from the much later work of this title by Subandhu), *Sumanottarā* and *Bhaimarathī*.

An outstanding species of prose writings of this period is the *Avadāna* literature dealing with the exploits of the Buddha, in his previous births. The works of this class date back probably to the first or second century AD. Of such works, special mention should be made of the *Avadāna-śataka*, *Divyāvadāna*, *Mahāvastu* and *Lalitavistara*, all anonymous. Somewhat later was written the *Jātaka-mālā* of Āryaśūra.

To this period belongs the world-renowned work on fable, *Pañcatantra* which is of unknown date and authorship, and, in its original form, is lost. It must have originated before AD 570 when it was rendered into Pahlavī. It exists in several versions in India (e.g., the Kāśmīrian *Tantrākhyāyika*), and abroad (e.g., Arabic, Syriac, etc.). From its extant versions it appears to have contained five topics, viz. *Mitrabheda* (dissension among friends), *Mitraprāpti* (acquisition of friends), *Sandhivigraha* (peace and strife), *Labdhanāśa* (loss of acquisition) and *Aparīkṣita-kāritva* (result of an act without deliberation).

The work attributes different human characters to beasts and birds, and is designed to inculcate worldly wisdom through stories. Written in simple prose, it is interspersed with verses.

One of the versions of the *Pañcatantra* is the *Hitopadeśa*, attributed to Nārāyaṇa who is believed to have flourished sometime between AD 900 and AD 1373. The author has left out one of the five topics of the original works.

Hertel holds that there are over 200 versions of the *Pañcatantra* in more than 50 languages, three-fourths of them being non-Indian, spreading over the vast area from Java to Iceland.

Considerable similarity between the Indian and Greek fables has been noticed by some scholars. They think that, in this respect, India is indebted to Greece.

Another noted work of the period is the *Bṛhatkathā*, referred to in such early works as the *Kāvyādarśa* (I.38) of Daṇḍin (eighth century AD) and *Harṣacarita* (introductory verse 17) of Bāṇabhaṭṭa (seventh century AD). The work is traditionally ascribed to one Gaṇāḍhya who is said to have written it in the language of the goblins (*bhūta-bhāṣāmayī*), i.e., Paiśācī Prākṛt. The original work which, as the title suggests, was a big collection of tales, is lost. We have three Sanskrit metrical versions of the work, which will be mentioned in due course. The term *kathā*, in the title, suggests that it was written in prose; *kathā* (tale) has been defined in poetics as a particular type of prose composition.

The stories of the *Bṛhatkathā* have provided themes of many later works, poetical and dramatic, e.g., Bhāsa's *Svapnavāsavadatta*, Dhanapāla's *Tilakamañjarī*, Daṇḍin's *Daśakumāracarita*, Subandhu's *Vāsavadattā*, etc. The story of king Udayana, so well-known in Sanskrit literature, is derived from the *Bṛhatkathā*.

Dramatic literature

A literary genre, called *nāṭya* (drama), originated in the Creative Period. There are quite a few theories about the origin of Sanskrit drama. A tradition, recorded in Bharata's *Nāṭyaśāstra* (probably earlier than the fourth century AD) is that god Brahmā conceived of the dramatic art as He was asked by gods, headed by Indra, to produce something for the simultaneous gratification of the eyes and ears. For this purpose, Brahmā took the element of recitation from the *Ṛgveda*, imitation of conditions from the *Yajurveda*, song from the *Sāmaveda* and *rasa* (literaray relish) from the *Atharvaveda*. Sage Bharata was asked to introduce this art on the earth.

Besides the above myth, some scientific theories about the origin of the Sanskrit drama have been suggested. We note a few of them here. According to one view, dramatic elements already existed in the so-called Dialogue Hymns of the *Ṛgveda*, e.g., between Purūravas and Urvaśī (X.95), Saramā and the Paṇis (X.108), between Yama and Yamī (X.10).

Puppet-play, in which the puppets were pulled with strings, have been a very popular entertainment in India since ancient times. According to some scholars, notably Pischel, puppet-play suggested the idea of drama. The words *sūtradhāra* (literally, one who holds the string) and *sthāpaka* (literally, one who places the puppets in particular positions) used in dramas, tend to lend countenance to this theory.

Weber, followed by Windisch, puts forward the interesting theory of the Greek origin of Sanskrit drama. According to them, the idea of drama was provided to the Indians by the dramatic performances of the Greeks, such dramas were performed in the courts of the Greek rulers who lived in India in the wake of Alexander's invasion. There was close trade relation between Ujjain and Alexandria, a seat of Greek learning. The Indians learnt the dramatic art from Greek dramas prevailing in Alexandria. Some of the arguments, put forward by the supporters of this theory, are as follows:

(i) The drop curtain in a dramatic performance is called *yavanikā*, a term formed from *yavana* meaning Greek.

(ii) The word *yavanī*, occurring in Sanskrit dramas, to indicate a female bodyguard of the king, also points to Greek influence.

(iii) There are some similarities between the dramas of the two countries. For example (a) the theme of a king's attachment to a young maiden of unknown identity, his knowledge of her identity through various obstacles and finally the union of the two, is common to Greek and Indian dramas. (b) The use of a memento for establishing one's identity, e.g., the ring in the *Śakuntalā*, the jewel (*saṁgamana-maṇi*) in the *Vikramorvaśīya*, occurs in the dramas of both the countries. (c) The blending of a political event with the plot of the drama, as we find in the Sanskrit drama, *Mṛcchakaṭika*, has been derived from the Greek drama. Windisch has pointed out many similarities between the theme of the above Sanskrit drama and the Greek drama. (d) According to Aristotle, such an incident as happens in the course of a day or a little more than that can be the plot of a drama. The supporters of the above theory think that it was due to the influence of this rule that Sanskrit dramaturgists provided that the act of a drama should describe the incidents that take place in a day. (e) Windisch has tried to show remarkable similarities between the *viṭa*, *vidūṣaka* and *śakāra* of the Sanskrit drama with the Parasite, Servus Currens and Miles glorious respectively of the Greek drama.

(iv) In the prologues of the dramas of both the countries, there is the practice of announcing the name of the dramatist, the title of the drama and the dramatist's appeal for sympathetically accepting it.

(v) The stage, discovered in the Sītāveṅgā cave in Rāmgarh hill in Madhya Pradesh, appears to have been built in imitation of the Greek stage.

None of the above arguments has been universally accepted. Some have put forward arguments against the above theories. For example, *yavana* does not necessarily mean a Greek; in fact, foreigners like Persians, Egyptians, etc., were sometimes indicated by this term. *Yavanikā* might have been so-called because it was mode of Persian tapestries; Persians were also called *yavana*s. As against the assumption of similarities in the plots of the dramas of Greece and India, it has been argued that the unities of time, space and action, essential in Greek drama, are absent in its Indian counterpart. With regard to the theatre in the above cave, the opponents hold that it is a small stage meant for a small number of spectators; it has no resemblance with the Greek theatre.

It is not known when the first Sanskrit drama was written. We know nothing more than a mention of the two dramatic works, *Amṛta-manthana* and *Tripura-dāha*, in Bharata's *Nāṭyaśāstra*. There is no evidence to prove whether these were real or imaginary titles.

A drama of this period is the *Śāriputra-prakaraṇa* or *Śāradvatī-putra-prakaraṇa* of Aśvaghoṣa (*c.* first century AD). This nine-act drama deals with the events relating to the conversion, by the Buddha, of Śāriputra and Maudgalyāyana. The work, available now, is not complete. Its importance, in the Sanskrit dramatic literature, lies in the fact that it presupposes the development of Sanskrit drama to a fair degree. The style is racy, language restrained and lucid. It is free from pedantry and literary exercise that mark some later dramas, particularly of the period of decadence.

To this period belongs Bhāsa, a proverbial figure in the domain of Sanskrit drama. As regards his date, scholars differ not by decades but by centuries. While some assign him to the fifth century BC, others would bring him down to a few centuries after Christ. This much, however, is certain that he preceded Kālidāsa who refers to him in his drama, *Mālavikāgnimitra*; this appears to be the earliest literary reference to Bhāsa. The date of Kālidāsa himself being uncertain, we cannot come to a decision on Bhāsa's date.

Till about the first decade of the present century, Bhāsa was a mere name to us. The discovery (1912-15) of a lot of 13 dramas in Trivandrum was a landmark in the history of Sanskrit drama. None of these works contains the name of the author. But, certain evidences, internal and external, were adduced by the discoverer to prove Bhāsa's authorship of all the 13 dramas. Some of the factors tending to prove the common authorship of all these plays are as follows. In the first place, a comparative study of the works reveals the similarity of language (sometimes un-Pāṇiniyan), ideas, dramatic art, style, etc. Secondly, each of these works commences with the stage-direction—*nāndyante tataḥ praviśati sūtradhāraḥ*, contrary to the usual practice. Thirdly, the prologue to each of them is called *sthāpanā* instead of the usual *prastāvanā*. Fourthly, in the initial verses of almost all of them there are hints at the principal characters of the plays. Fifthly, in many of these works, the concluding verses contain the line, sometimes with slight variations, *imāmeva mahīṁ kṛtsnāṁ rājasiṁhaḥ praśāstu naḥ*.

Now the question is—who could be the common author of these works? Bāṇabhaṭṭa, in the introductory verse 15 of his *Harṣacarita*, states that Bhāsa wrote some dramas having the following characteristics:

> Commencement with the mention of the word *sūtradhāra*, having many *bhūmikā*s or roles or characters and *patākā*s or dramatic episodes.

All these features occur in the above works.

Rājaśekhara, a renowned rhetorician and dramatist, observes

that when Bhāsa's dramas were set on fire, all excepting the *Svapnavāsavadatta* were burnt. This is a poetical way of saying that none of the Bhāsa dramas, barring the above-mentioned one, could stand the test of time. One of the Trivandrum plays is entitled *Svapnavāsavadatta*. So, it may be presumed that the others of the lot were also authored by Bhāsa.

None of the above arguments leads to a definite conclusion. Counter-arguments have also been put forward seeking to disprove Bhāsa's authorship of the plays.

The above dramas can be divided into the following four classes in accordance with the sources drawn upon by them:

1. Based on the *Rāmāyaṇa* — to this class belong the *Pratimā* and the *Abhiṣeka*.
2. Based on the *Mahābhārata* — *Madhyama-vyāyoga*, *Pañcarātra*, *Dūtavākya*, *Dūtaghaṭotkaca*, *Karṇabhāra*, *Ūrubhaṅga* and *Bālacarita*.
3. Derived from the *Bṛhatkathā* — the dramas of this class, entitled *Svapnavāsavadatta* and *Pratijñā-yaugandharāyaṇa*, deal with the story of Udayana the original source of which is the *Bṛhatkathā*.
4. Based on an unknown source—*Avimāraka* and *Cārudatta*.

Of the above works, the *Svapnavāsavadatta* is by far the most renowned. Its subject-matter is briefly as follows: A sizeable part of the territory of Udayana, king of Vatsa, has been conquered by a formidable foe. For regaining it, the minister Yaugandharāyaṇa is determined to bring about an alliance of his master with the king of Magadha. This can be possible only if Udayana marries Padmāvatī, sister of the Magadha king. But, Udayana is so deeply attached to his wife, Vāsavadattā that the above matrimonial alliance is not possible. The clever minister, firm in his objective, spreads a rumour, with the consent of the queen, that he, along with Vāsavadattā, went to a place where both of them perished in a fire. After that both of them assumed disguise, and went to the kingdom of Magadha. There, he placed Vāsavadattā, under the pseudonym Avantikā, in the custody of Padmāvatī. Having learnt that Vāsavadattā was no more, Udayana, enamoured of the beauty of

Padmāvatī, married her. In course of time, Udayana's powerful adversary was defeated, and, through strange circumstances, Udayana and Padmāvatī were united with Vāsavadattā whose identity came to light, and minister Yaugandharāyaṇa who, crowned with success, revealed his plan.

In this drama, the minister hits upon an ingenious plan which is brought to a successful denouement. The activities of Vāsavadattā incognito have been delineated deftly. Her sacrifice for the welfare of her husband and her calm deportment even at the sight of her husband's marrying another women have revealed the magnanimity of her character. Instead of breaking down, she expresses her reaction by a single utterance, *āryaputro'pi parakīyaḥ saṁvṛttaḥ* (even my husband has gone to the possession of another person!).

A specimen of Bhāsa's simple style is the following stanza, uttered by the Chamberlain to console the king, overwhelmed with grief at the news of the 'death' of his dear queen:

kaḥ kaṁ śakto rakṣituṁ mṛtyukāle rajjucchede ke ghaṭaṁ dhārayanti ।
evaṁ lokas tulyadharmo vanānāṁ kāle kāle chidyate ruhyate ca ॥

— *Svapna-vāsavadattā*, VI.10

Who can save whom at the time of death? Who can hold a pitcher when the rope is snapped? Thus, like a forest, man at one time is torn (i.e., dies) and at another grows.

B. PERIOD OF DEVELOPMENT

This period dawned in the age of the Guptas. It was in this age that the Brāhmaṇical religion was not only revived, but also became the State religion. Besides, there was the efflorescence of Indian culture in all its aspects, sculpture, architecture, painting, literature, music and dance.

Works of Kālidāsa

Kālidāsa is the brightest luminary in the literary firmament of this period. It is an irony that we know practically nothing about the greatest poet of ancient India. Tradition makes him one of the nine jewels of the court of Vikramāditya who is generally believed to be identical with the Gupta Emperor, Candragupta II (*c.* AD 380-415). The only clue about Kālidāsa's date is provided by the Aihole Inscription of AD 634 wherein there is a reference to poet Kālidāsa. Therefore, the lower terminus of his date is AD 634.

It should be noted that several poetical works of an apocryphal nature are ascribed to Kālidāsa presumably to impart a halo of authority and antiquity to them. Some such works are the *Nalodaya, Puṣpa-vāṇa-vilāsa, Śṛṅgāratilaka*, etc.

The master-poet, Kālidāsa is credited with the authorship of several poetical works and dramas. The poetical works are the *Kumārasambhava, Raghuvaṁśa* and *Meghadūta*. The dramatic works are the *Mālavikāgnimitra, Vikramorvaśīya* and *Abhijñānaśākuntalam.* Of the above, only the first eight cantos of the *Kumārasambhava*, consisting of 17 cantos, are believed to be the work of Kālidāsa. The rest is supposed to be a later interpolation mainly because there is no commentary of Mallinātha on it.

As regards the *Ṛtusaṁhāra*, its genuineness is doubted by some scholars, while, according to others, it belongs to the juvenilia of Kālidāsa.

The theme of none of the works of Kālidāsa is original. But, his originality lies in infusing life into the dry fossil of time-worn legends, as we shall see later on.

The subject-matter of the *Kumārasambhava* is a well-known Purāṇic legend. The *Raghuvaṁśa* is generally believed to be based on the *Padma Purāṇa*. The theme of the *Meghadūta* does not seem to be derived from any particular source. The idea of a man's sending, through a messenger, a message to his beloved may, however, have been suggested by Rāma's sending, through Hanumat, a message to Sītā in captivity in Laṅkā, as described in the *Rāmāyaṇa*.

The story of the *Kumārasambhava* is briefly this. The gods in heaven, extremely opposed by demon Tāraka, sought the advice of Brahmā. He told them that the demon could be slain only by Kārttikeya, a son to be born of the union of Śiva and Pārvatī, daughter of Himālaya, the lord of mountains. But, Śiva was in profound meditation. How could he be persuaded to marry Pārvatī? The gods hit upon a plan. It was to engage Cupid for causing passion in the mind of Śiva who would then be infatuated by Pārvatī's uncommon beauty. Accordingly, the god of love started hurling his flowery arrows towards Śiva sitting motionless with closed eyes. Śiva felt perturbed, and opened his eyes. Finding Cupid before him, He was incensed, and at once reduced him to ashes by the fire emerging from his eyes, disregarding the gods' appeal for mercy. This incident convinced Pārvatī that Śiva was not one to be allured by physical charm. So, she took to severe penance. Śiva, in disguise, appeared before her, and tried in vain to dissuade her from penance. Unshaken in her resolve, she succeeded in getting Śiva as her husband.

The *Raghuvaṁśa* describes some incidents which took place from the reign of Dilīpa, several generations earlier than Rāma, up to the story of Agnivarṇa, the last king of this race. Dilīpa was extremely sad as he was sonless. His *guru*, sage Vasiṣṭha advised him to serve the divine cow, Nandinī, of his hermitage. So, the king engaged himself in looking after her throughout daytime. One day, while grazing the cow in a forest, the king was confronted by a lion who was bent upon devouring the cow. The king, very faithful to his *guru*, offered himself to the lion on condition that the cow would be spared. The divine animal gave him a boon that he would get a son.

He did get a son whom he named Raghu who eventually succeeded his father, and went out for *digvijaya* (world conquest), and conquered many countries.

Raghu's son and successor, Aja attended the *svayṁvara sabhā* (assembly for self-choice of the husband) of Indumatī, daughter of king Bhoja. Bypassing all other suitors, Indumatī chose Aja as her husband. The couple's happy days were cut short by the sudden and premature demise of Indumatī. The king, overwhelmed with grief, committed suicide.

He was succeeded by Daśaratha. Eventually, his dearest son, Rāma went to exile. There Sītā was abducted by Rāvaṇa. Rāma killed the demon, rescued Sītā, and came back home. Rāma's subjects expressed resentment at their king's acceptance of a lady who lived in the house of Rāvaṇa. The righteous king, Rāma, in deference to the wishes of the people, banished Sītā, who was in an advanced stage of pregnancy, on the pretext of fulfilling her desire of revisiting the forest where she, with Rāma, spent long years in exile. When she learnt of the actual plan of Rāma from Lakṣmaṇa, she felt utterly helpless in the forest, and burst into loud wail. Hearing this, sage Vālmīki gave her asylum in his hermitage. In course of time, two sons, Lava and Kuśa were born to Sītā.

As the sons were growing up, Rāma, at the request of Vālmīki, agreed to take back Sītā on condition that she would have to undergo fire-ordeal to prove her chastity. Sītā agreed, but before she could emerge from the ordeal, her mother, the earth drew her into her bosom for ever. Rāma, having entrusted the kingdom to his sons, went out of the capital, and was whisked away in a divine chariot from heaven.

The remaining part of the work is the story of some worthless kings addicated to vices.

The *Meghadūta* is a monody. A Yakṣa (a kind of demi-god), guilty of dereliction of duty, is cursed by his master to the effect that he will have to be separated from his dear wife for one year. Accordingly, he comes to live in a hermitage on mountain Rāmagiri, far away from his home in Alakā. Disconsolate in isolation, and unable to bear the pangs of separation, he wants to send the cloud as a messenger to his beloved. At first, the Yakṣa describes the intinerary of the cloud. Then he speaks out the message intended to be conveyed to his beloved. In it, he consoles his beloved and counsels her somehow to spend the remaining four months' separation, the first eight months having already elapsed.

The *Ṛtusaṁhāra*, as the title suggests, is a description of the cycle of the six seasons (as viewed through the lover's eyes).

The *Mālavikāgnimitra*, presumably a product of the early years of Kālidāsa's literary life, is a five-act drama. The plot is briefly this. Through many vicissitudes, Mālavikā, princess of Vidarbha, appeared before king Agnimitra as a low-born girl. Already at the sight of her picture, the king was attracted by her beauty. Now, her physical presence caused deep attachment in the king's mind, so much so that he embraced her. This enraged the younger queen, Irāvatī who came there and insulted the king. The elder queen, Dhāriṇī confined Mālavikā to a place. Through the intervention of the Vidūṣaka (the pleasure-companion of the king) a reunion of the king and Mālavikā took place. At this time also, Irāvatī fumed and fretted. In course of time, with the news of the defeat of the hostile king of Vidarbha, the identity of Mālavikā was disclosed by those who came from Vidarbha. Queen Dhāriṇī was delighted at the news of the defeat of the Yavanas by her son Vasumitra. Now, she consented to the marraige of the king with Mālavikā. Irāvatī also relented. Thus, there is a happy denouement of the play.

The subject-matter of the *Vikramorvaśīya*, another drama of Kālidāsa, is the love-story of king Purūravas and the celestial nymph, Urvaśī. The king, while rescuing Urvaśī, tortured by a demon, fell in love with her. After an erotic dialogue, Urvaśī had to part company for participating in a dramatic performace in heaven.

Lord Indra permitted her to live with the king on earth on condition that she must return to heaven as soon as the king would see the face of his son by her. The couple lived happily. One day, Urvaśī, as a result of a grievous fault, was transformed into a creeper. The king was overwhelmed with grief at the separation from his beloved, and behaved like a demented person. At last, through divine favour, he got a jewel with which he embraced a creeper which, lo and behold, was turned into Urvaśī. After another spell of blissful conjugal life, through some strange circumstances, the king caught sight of the face of his son. According to the above condition, Urvaśī was to leave for heaven. Meanwhile, the divine sage, Nārada appeared with the message that, in the ongoing dour encounter between the gods and the demons in heaven, the king's help would be necessary for gods. As a reward, the king would be able to enjoy the company of Urvaśī throughout his life.

The *Abhijñānaśākuntalam* of Kālidāsa is his greatest drama, and one of the greatest in the world. The subject-matter of this work is briefly as follows: The young king, Duṣyanta, while out on a hunting excursion with his pleasure-companion, Vidūṣaka, came to the hermitage of sage Kaṇva. There he found Śakuntalā, foster-daughter of the sage and a paragon of beauty, accompanied by two female friends, named Anasūyā and Priyaṁvadā. The king and Śakuntalā fell in love with each other, and met in a bower. Before leaving the hermitage, the king gave Śakuntalā a signet-ring. Having parted company with the lover, Śakuntalā was deeply engrossed in thought about him. Meanwhile, the irascible sage, Durvāsā visited the hermitage, and announced his presence. The absent-minded Śakuntalā, did not notice him. The sage, to whom the usual hospitality was not accorded, thought that Śakuntalā, sitting there, deliberately ignored him. So, he pronounced the terrible curse that the person, about whom she had been thinking, would not remember her despite efforts to remind him. The aforesaid friends of Śakuntalā immediately tried to appease the sage, and requested him to forgive Śakuntalā who was innocent. The sage refused to go back on his words, but relented a little, and added the condition that the man concerned would recognise her only if he was shown a souvenir.

Sage Kaṇva, who was away, came back, and eventually learnt that Śakuntalā had conceived. He then arranged for her going to the capital of Duṣyanta. When she was escorted to the presence of the king, he did not recognise her. At this juncture, Śakuntalā tried to show him his signet-ring that he gave her in the hermitage. But, alas, the ring was not in her finger. It was discovered that while she was taking a bath, the ring slipped into water.

Humiliated by repudiation, Śakuntalā was on her way to the house of the king's priest. On the way, she was lifted by a divine being, and placed in the custody of sage Mārīca in his hermitage on the way to heaven.

After sometime, the aforesaid ring was found out with a fisherman who said that he had got it in a fish. As soon as it was brought to the king, he recollected the past incidents, and became full of remorse for repudiating Śakuntalā. Meanwhile, the king had to go to heaven, at the behest of Lord Indra, in order to subjugate the demons. While returning he saw, in the hermitage of Mārīca, an attractive boy whom he eventually recognised as his own son by Śakuntalā. There he was reunited with Śakuntalā, and accompanied her to the capital.

The first thing about Kālidāsa that strikes us is his ingenious innovations. As already stated, he bases his themes on well-known legends, but the magic touch of his genius transformed them almost into new creations. For instance, in the *Kumārasambhava* the description of Himālaya, the episode of Cupid's being reduced to ashes, the rigorous penance of Pārvatī, the lament of Rati, consort of Cupid, testify to his literary skill.

As regards *Raghuvaṁśa*, the description of Indumatī's *svayaṁvara*, the consequent lament of Aja, etc., are superb products of his imagination.

The subject-matter of the *Meghadūta*, and the delineation of the anguish and agnoy of the lover and the beloved pining in separation are entirely the poet's own creation.

The plot of the *Mālavikāgnimitra*, centring round a historical personage, viz. Agnimitra, testifies to the dramatic skill of Kālidāsa, and appears to have served as a model for later *nāṭikā*s (playlets) like the *Ratnāvalī* of Harṣa. The plot is entirely the product of his imagination.

In the *Vikramorvaśīya*, the demented condition of the king after the disappearance of Urvaśī, and the strange circumstances leading to their re-union have been ably depicted. The seeds of the legend occur in the Vedic literature. These not only sprouted, but also flowered in the hands of Kālidāsa.

His *Abhijñāna-śākuntalam* is universally admitted as his dramatic masterpiece. Goethe's impassioned appreciation of it as containing the young year's blossoms and the fruits of its decline and delineating the combination of earth and heaven has immortalised it in the Western world of indologists and litterateurs. The poet has introduced many innovations into the original legend. Of these, the curse of sage Durvāsā and the ring episode are the most important for the dramatic theme.

Besides innovations, the poet's portrayal of characters and power of description of nature rightly evoke the admiration of the readers. In the *Kumārasambhava*, Pārvatī's firmness of resolve to get Śiva as her husband even after hearing from Śiva in disguise, of his destitution and grotesque appearance is delineated with great skill. In the *Raghuvaṁśa*, the depiction of king Dilīpa's arduous service of his *guru*'s cow is vivid. The representation of Sītā as the ideal and chaste wife who, even when forlorn in the forest, refrains from accusing her husband and taking her miserable plight as a result of her own misdeeds in her past life invests her character with dignity and charm. On the other hand, the agony of Rāma after deserting her only to satisfy his subjects has been depicted in a poignant manner. We feel for poor Rāma who is stated to have removed her from his house, but not from his heart.

In the *Mālavikāgnimitra*, the two queens of the king show magnanimity in bringing about the union of a third woman, a co-wife, with the king. In the *Vikramorvaśīya*, the fierce-souled Urvaśī of the legend, who had not the slightest compunction in deserting the king who loved her passionately, has been represented as a soft-hearted wife. The original story, a tragedy, is transformed by the poet into a comedy. In the original Śakuntalā legend, the king is a voluptuary who fell in love with Śakuntalā, returned to the capital and forgot her. Śakuntalā of the legend is a calculating and selfish woman. Before offering herself to the king, she made it a condition that her son, to be born out of her union with the king, would be his successor. In the hands of Kālidāsa, the characters of both the hero and the heroine have been ennobled. Śakuntalā of the drama had purely romantic love for the king; there was no motive behind it. Kālidāsa's Duṣyanta was oblivious of Śakuntalā under the influence of Durvāsā's curse which is a creation of the dramatist who also devised the ring episode; how else could the curse be counteracted? Śakuntalā's two female friends are skilful innovations. But for them, Śakuntalā's life would have been permanently blighted by the curse, and the dramatic action could not proceed further.

Kālidāsa was not only a masterly describer of human characters, but also an adept in the graphic description of nature. For example, in the *Kumārasambhava*, the description of the unseasonal spring, in which Cupid tried to disturb Śiva, is superb. The influence of the season even on lower creatures is described thus:

madhu dvirephaḥ kusumaika-pātre papau priyāṁ
svāmanu-vartamānaḥ |

śṛṅgeṇa sparśa-nimilitākṣīṁ mṛgīma-kaṇḍūyata kṛṣṇasāraḥ ॥
— *Kumāra,* III.36

The drone, following his beloved, drank honey from the same flower. The spotted antelope scratched, with its horn, the female antelope whose eyes were closed at the touch (of the male antelope).

In the *Raghuvaṁśa*, the confluence of the rivers, Ganges and the Yamunā, with white and bluish water respectively, seems to be visualised by the readers. For example,

anyatra mālā sita-paṅkajānām-indīvarair-utkhacitān-tareva ।
— XIII.54.

At some place, it seems as though blue lotuses are woven into a garland of white lotuses.

kvacit khagānāṁ priyamānasānāṁ kadamba saṁsarga-vatīva paṁktiḥ ।
— XI.

At some place, it seems that a row of blue swans is mixed with white swans.

In the *Abhijñānaśākuntalam*, we get a fine picture of the hermitage in act IV at the time of Śakuntalā's departure for the capital of the king. What adds special charm is the relation between nature and human beings so finely portrayed by the author. Sage Kaṇva says:

pātum na prathamaṁ vyavasyati jalaṁ yuṣmāsvapīteṣu
yā nādatte priyamaṇḍanāpi bhavatāṁ snehena yā pallavam ।
ādye vaḥ kusuma-prasūti-samaye yasyā bhavaty-utsavaḥ
seyaṁ yāti śakuntalā patigṛhaṁ sarvaira-nujñāyatām ॥
— IV.9

That Śakuntalā, who does not drink water first when you have not drunk it, who, though fond of ornaments, does not pluck your leaves through affection, to whom it is a festival

> when you first put forth blossoms, is starting for her husband's house, let her be permitted by all.

What adds to the poignancy of the parting scene is that the entire nature seemed to have been plunged into grief as Śakuntalā had been preparing to start:

> The deer have their cud of grass dropped down, the peacocks have given up dance, the creepers with their pale leaves falling off, seem to be shedding tears. — IV.12

> Even the young deer, whom Śakuntalā reared and gave relief when it was injured, dragged her by the skirt as if it would not let her go. — IV.14

Indian connoisseurs lavishly praised Kālidāsa for his poetic achievement. He is unanimously extolled for his capacity for comparison; *Upamā Kālidāsasya* has become proverbial. A few specimens are given here. In the *Kumārasambhava* canto V, when Śiva in disguise persistently denounced Śiva of Pārvatī's dream, she decided to leave the place. Just at this juncture, Śiva assumed His real form. Overawed at the sight, she could neither go nor stay (*na yayau na tasthau*) even as a flowing river, obstructed by a rock on the way (*mārgācala-vyatikarākuliteva sindhuḥ*). *Kumāra* (V.85). In *Raghu*, (X.69), Kauśalyā, emaciated after delivering the baby Rāma, while lying down with the baby by her side, looked like a lean autumn-river with a blooming lotus on the bank. In the *Meghadūta* (Pūrva 58), the snow-clad mountain has been likened to a heap of the daily loud guffaw of Śiva. In Sanskrit poetics, laughter has been characterised as white. In the *Abhijñānaśākuntalam* the king, while reluctantly leaving the hermitage, where his beloved lived, said:

> *gacchati puraḥ śarīraṁ dhāvati paścāda-samsthitaṁ cetaḥ* ।
> *cīnāṁśukamiva ketoḥ protivātaṁ nīyamānasya* ॥
>
> — I.3

> The body moves forward, the restless mind runs backward like the silk cloth of a flag taken leeward.

In the *Svayaṁvara-sabhā* (*Raghu*, VI.67), when Indumatī bypassed the suitors one by one, they became pale like a mansion on the highway when a light at night passes leaving it behind.

Kālidāsa, with a rich experience of worldly life and a keen insight into human nature, gives us many pithy sayings of which a few specimens are given below:

atisnehaḥ pāpaśaṁkī
due to excess of affection, one apprehends untoward things.

artho hi kanyā parakīya eva
one's daughter is, indeed, the wealth of another person.

kaṣṭam khal-vanapatyatā
childlessness is, indeed, painful.

nīcair-gacchatyu-parica daśā cakra-nemi-krameṇa
the condition of a person goes down and up like the periphery of a wheel.

vikāra-hetau sati vikriyante yeṣāṁ na cetāṁsi ta eva dhīrāḥ
they, indeed, are self-possessed whose minds are not agitated despite the cause of agitation.

Yācñā moghā varama-dhiguṇe nādhame labdhakāmā
even unsuccessful solicitude before one of many virtues, is better than successful solicitude before a vile person.

satāṁ hi sandeha-padeṣu vastuṣu pramāṇamantaḥkaraṇa-pravṛttayaḥ
the propensities of the mind are guides to the good people in doubtful matters.

strīṇāma-śikṣita-paṭutvam
woman have untutored cleverness.

Post-Kālidāsa works

POETICAL LITERATURE

Among the stalwarts, succeeding Kālidāsa in this domain, are Bhāravi (before AD 634), Bhaṭṭi (before the middle of the sixth century AD), Kumāradāsa (first half of the sixth century) and Māgha (seventh century AD).

To Bhāravi is attributed the single *mahākāvya*, entitled *Kirātārjunīyam*. Based on a story of the Vana-parva of the *Mahābhārata*, it is in 18 cantos. The story is briefly given below:

While the Pāṇḍavas were in exile, Yudhiṣṭhira engaged a forest-dweller, in disguise, to gather information about the administration of Duryodhana who had been reigning. The messenger reported that Duryodhana had been ruling the kingdom cautiously and efficiently. Hearing this, Draupadī became irate, and exhorted Yudhiṣṭhira in vain to be up in arms to regain the kingdom of which he was the legitimate ruler. Bhīma supported her, but the pacifist Yudhiṣṭhira took no steps. At the instance of sage Vyāsa, Arjuna pleased Indra by hard penance. At the behest of the same god, Arjuna pleased Śiva by penance; He gave him the desired *pāśupata* weapon to be used against the powerful adversaries, the Kauravas. In the original story, the poet has made some changes. He has depicted the Himālaya in a masterly manner. He has been traditionally extolled for the dignity of meanings (*artha-gaurava*) conveyed through his composition. But, modern critics, especially of the West, denounce his poetry as laboured and full of errors of taste. For example, in XV.14 he uses only the letter *na*, which shows literary exercise. His composition, however, is not totally devoid of fine poetry conveying wise ideas. For instance,

> *sahasā vidadhīta na kriyāma-vivekaḥ paramāpadāṁ padam* ।
> *vr̥ṇute hi vimr̥śyakāriṇaṁ guṇalubdāḥ svayameva sampadaḥ* ॥
> — II.30

> Do not do anything all of a sudden; lack of discrimination is the source of great danger. Wealth, fond of virtue, voluntarily chooses one who acts with forethought.

Bhāravi shows considerable skill in characterisation. The distinct traits of the conventional characters have been ably brought to light. We are impressed by the spirited reaction of Draupadī to the humiliation caused by the enemy, Yudhiṣṭhira's unshakable firmness even in the teeth of grave provocation, Bhīma's heroic demeanour,

Duryodhana's political sagacity, etc. As stated above, Bhāravi shows commendable capacity in describing the Himālaya (canto V) and autumn (canto IV).

Some pithy sayings of Bhāravi have become proverbs, e.g., *hitaṁ manohāri ca durlabhaṁ vacaḥ* (such a speech as is, at the same time, salutary and pleasant, is rare); *āpāta-ramyā viṣayāḥ paryanta-paritāpinaḥ* (things which are, for the time being, charming cause anguish in the long run); *janmino mānahīnasya tṛṇasya ca samā gatiḥ* (the condition of one, devoid of honour, is similar to that of grass), *sulabhā ramyatā* like *durlabhaṁ hi guṇārjanam* (in the world beauty is easily available, but rare is the acquisition of virtues).

Bhaṭṭī (it is taken by some as a corrupt form of Bhartṛhari) is the author of the *Rāvaṇavadha*, popularly called *Bhaṭṭīkāvya*. It is avowedly designed as illustrations of grammatical forms and *alaṁkāra*s or figures of speech. The story goes that once when the author was teaching his pupils in the open, an elephant happened to pass between the teacher and the taught. This conventionally required the cessation of Vedic studies for one year. Grammar being a Vedic accessory (Vedāṅga), its study was also to be suspended. But the suspension of the study of such a tough subject for so long a time was likely to make the students forget the subject taught and learnt with great labour. So Bhaṭṭī devised the plan of teaching grammar through poetry, and the result was the *Bhaṭṭīkāvya*. It is divided into four distinct parts, viz., *Prakīrṇa-kāṇḍa* (cantos I-V) illustrating miscellaneous matters, *Adhikāra-kāṇḍa* (VI-IX) illustrating the *adhikāra-sūtra*s (leading aphorism of Pāṇini's grammar), *Prasanna-kāṇḍa* (X-XIII) illustrating figures of speech, and *Tiṅanta-kāṇḍa* (XIV-XII) illustrating *Tiṅanta* forms or verbs.

The banal *Rāmāyaṇa* story is the theme of the work. The poet, has sought to diversify the popular story by introducing speeches and descriptions. His description of autumn in canto II is a fine pen-picture of the season. The poet's style is at times very much laboured; it is, however, not unexpected in a work which is deliberately designed for serving a purpose. It must be said to Bhaṭṭī's credit that he is eminently successful in achieving his object which, according to Mallinātha, is an *udāharaṇa-kāvya*. The blending of poetry with grammar and rhetoric is unique. Some instances of fine poetry, flashing forth from this artificial composition, are as follows:

dattāvadhānaṁ madhulehi-gītau praśānta-ceṣṭaṁ hariṇaṁ jighāṁsuḥ ।

ākarṇayan-nutsuka-haṁsa-nādān lakṣye samādhiṁ na dadhe mṛgāvit ॥

—II.7

The hunter, willing to kill the deer, motionless on hearing the hum of bees, paid no attention to the target while listening to the cacklings of the eager swans.

Vibhīṣaṇa's speech to Rāvaṇa

rāmo'pi dārā-haraṇena tapto vayaṁ hatair-bandhubhir ātmatulyaiḥ ।
taptasya taptena yathāyaso naḥ sandhiḥ pareṇāstu vimuñca sītām ॥

—XII. 40

Rāma burns at heart due to the abduction of his consort. We have heart-burn at the demise of friends like our own-selves. As heated iron is welded with hot iron, so let there be peace between us and the enemy. Set Sītā free.

There can be no better assessment of the *Bhaṭṭikāvya* than that by the poet himself.

He says,

dīpatulyaḥ prabandho'yam śabda-lakṣaṇa-cakṣuṣām ।
hastādarśa ivāndhānāṁ bhaved vyākaraṇād ṛte ॥

—XXII.33

This composition is like a lamp to those to whom grammar is the eye; to one without knowledge of grammar, it will be like a mirror in the hands of a blind man.

Again,

vyākhyā-gamyami-daṁ kāvyamu-tsavaḥ sudhiyāmalam ।
hatā durmedhasaścāsmin vidvat-priyatayā mayā ॥

> This *kāvya*, intelligible by explanation, is a great festival to the learned. (Alas) the dullards have been killed in this by me fond as I am of the learned.

Kumāradāsa, said to have been a friend of Kālidāsa, was, according to a Ceylonese tradition, a king of Ceylon who flourished probably before poet Māgha whose work will be described later on. The poetical work, *Jānakīharaṇa*, attributed to Kumāradāsa, is not available in its complete form. Though the title indicates that the events of the story of Rāma up to the abduction of Sītā are described in it, yet from Siṁhalese commentary it seems to have dealt with the story up to the return of Rāma to Ayodhyā and his coronation. The poet has not made any great change in the original narrative. But, for diversification, he has added some minor events. What attracts the reader is the poetical descriptions of, for instance, Ayodhyā (canto I), the garden sports of Daśaratha and his queens (canto IV) and of Mithilā (canto VI). There are charming pen-pictures of the rainy season and autumn in cantos XI and XII respectively. A comparative study of Kālidāsa's two *mahākāvya*s and this work reveals the influence of the former on the latter.

A very eminent poet of this period is Māgha who is generally assigned to the earlier half of the seventh century AD. The story of his work, entitled *Śiśupālavadha* is briefly as follows:

Sage Nārada comes to Kṛṣṇa to whom he conveys Indra's directive to kill the Cedi-king Śiśupāla who is a great enemy of men and gods. Advised by Uddhava, Kṛṣṇa attends Yudhiṣṭhira's *rājasūya* sacrifice where Kṛṣṇa is warmly welcomed by Yudhiṣṭhira. Enraged at this, Śiśupāla leaves the place, and prepares for battle in which he encounters Kṛṣṇa and is eventually slain by him. Into this *Mahābhārata* episode the poet has incorporated new events, and has left the imprint of his poetic skill particularly in the erotic verses. Among the several innovations, mention may be made of the picturesque description of Nārada's appearance with Indra's message before Kṛṣṇa, the assembly for the deliberations about the battle, political analysis by Balarāma and Uddhava, etc. Cantos IV-XII are devoted to over elaboration and description of matters not related to the main theme. This has impeded the flow of the narrative, and has made it difficult for the reader to follow the continuity.

The influence of Bhāravi on Māgha, in form, language, style and literary exercise, has been discussed. It seems as though Māgha made a studied effort to surpass his predecessor. Indian critics, however, have praised Māgha in hyperbolic language. According to a long-standing tradition — *upamā kālidāsasya, bhāraver-artha-gauravaṁ, naiṣadhe padalālityaṁ, māghe santi trayo guṇāḥ.* It means — Kālidāsa has (unparalleled) similes, Bhāravi is famous for profundity of sense; the *Naiṣadhacarita* (of Śrīharṣa (to be dealt with later on) is famous for the charm of words; all the above three qualities exist in Māgha. One critic has vented his feeling about Kālidāsa and Māgha in the following proverbial words — *māghe meghe gataṁ vayaḥ*; the prime of life has been spent in the study of Māgha (i.e., *Śiśupālavadha*) and *Megha* (i.e., *Meghadūta* of Kālidāsa). By and large, the modern critics accuse Māgha of pedantry and affected style. In fairness to the poet, we must say that, at some places, he expresses a commendable sentiment in simple language. For instance,

> *pādahataṁ yadutthāya mūrdhānama-dhirohati* ।
> *svasthādevāpamāne'pi dehinastad varaṁ rajaḥ* ॥
> — II.46

> The dust-particle which, being struck by the foot, gets upon the head (of the man concerned) is superior to a man who, even in humiliation, remains calm.

Despite elaboration, his description of nature contains flashes of good poetry. For his skill in depicting nature he has deservedly earned the sobriquet *ghaṇṭā-māgha*. It owes its origin to the following description:

> On one side is the setting sun, on another the rising moon; in between stands the mountain which has been compared with an elephant who has two bells hanging on its two sides. — IV.20.

The glorious epoch of poetical works ended with Māgha. Those which followed in this period, may be broadly divided into three types, namely, didactic, satirical and pornographic.

The works of the didactic class were not designed solely to

inculcate general moral principles, but also political principles and worldly wisdom. Among the didactic poems, perhaps the most noteworthy is the *moha-mudgara* (a mace for destroying delusion) by Śaṅkarācārya *(c.* eighth century AD). In a little over dozen verses, it seeks to inculcate the hollowness of worldly pleasure, the transitoriness of life, etc. A few specimens are given below:

> *yāvad-vitto-pārjana-śaktas-tāvan-nijaḥ parivaro raktaḥ* ।
> *tadanu ca jarayā jarjara-dehe vārtāṁ ko'pi na pṛcchati gehe* ॥
>
> One's family is attached to him so long as he is able to earn money. After that, when his body becomes decrepit by old age, no one in the house speaks about him.
>
> *nalinī-data-gata-jalama-titaralaṁ tadvaj-jīvanama-tiśayacapalam* ।
>
> *kṣaṇamiha sajjana-saṁgatirekā bhavati bhavārnava-taraṇe-naukā* ॥
>
> Life is as transient as water on a lotus-petal. In this world, association with the good people (even) for a short while becomes (like) a boat for crossing the ocean of rebirths.

Besides the above, many poems of varying lenghts, seeking to inculcate detachment and true knowledge, are attributed to Śaṅkara.

A collection of verses, attributed to Cāṇakya, generally identified with Kauṭilya (*c.* fourth century BC), is variously called *Cāṇakya-nīti*, *Cāṇakya-śataka*, *Cāṇakya-nīti-darpaṇa*, *Vṛddha-cāṇakya*, *Laghu-cāṇakya*, etc. An index to its popularity is the existence of its at least 17 recensions with varying numbers of verses. The work become popular in Greater India.

A noteworthy poetical work of this period is the *Kuṭṭanīmata* attributed to Dāmodaragupta, minister of the king Jayāpīḍa (AD 779-813) of Kashmir. It created a new literary genre. It consists in instructions, given by an experienced bawd to a young courtesan, about the various tricks and deceptive show of love for alluring rich people and fleecing them. The work combines moral principles with satire. In the portion on morals, it warns the reader about the wiles of characterless women. In the satirical portion, it depicts the trickery and blandishment of such women.

Prose romance

The prose romance of this period is of great distinction. We have no earlier specimens of this class of literature. Post-Kālidāsa prose romance is represented by the works of the triumvirate, namely, Daṇḍin, Subandhu and Bāṇa; all of them appear to have flourished in the seventh century.

Before proceeding to deal with their works, it should be noted that the two broad divisions of prose *kāvya* are *kathā* and *ākhyāyikā*, the former containing imaginary events, and *ākhyāyikā* dealing with historical facts. In the history of the extant prose romance, Daṇḍin comes first. He may or may not be identical with Daṇḍin, author of the *Kāvyādarśa*, a noted work on poetics. His *Daśakumāra-carita*, as the title suggests, is a story of the adventures of ten princes. But, curiously enough, we have the activities of only eight princes. The work has two supplements, one in the beginning, called *Pūrvapīṭhikā* and at the end, called *Uttarapīṭhikā*. The former gives the accounts of the two additional princes and the latter completed the unfinished story of prince Viśruta. There are different versions of the *Pūrva-* and *Uttarapīṭhikā*s, thus confirming the suspicion that these were later additions. There is considerable diversity in the stories. The author deftly depicts the heroic exploits of the princes, their perilous adventures, love, the marriage with princesses through various obstacles, the restoration of the lost kingdom, etc. We get a variegated picture of the society. Besides members of the royal family, we come across a motley society with the wicked, magician, gambler, poison-doctor, merchant, rich people, the miserly owner of hidden treasure, courtesan, homicide, the abductor of women, etc. The story of Apahāravarman is unique in length, diversity of events and the presence of different characters.

The *Avantīsundarī-kathā*, believed by some to be the work of the above Daṇḍin, is sometimes claimed to be the missing earlier part of the *Daśakumāracarita*.

The traditional admirers of Daṇḍin credit him with *pada-*

lālitya (gracefulness of words); this is no exaggeration. Long compounds, however, occasionally prove stumbling blocks to the reader. But, the true litterateur enjoys the delectable fare provided by the work. The creation of characters, each with distinct traits, humourous situations and literary skill — for all these features Daṇḍin occupies an honourable position among the writers of prose *kāvya*. At places, he makes a conscious effort to show off literary feats. For example, in the story (seventh) of Mantragupta there is no labial letter, the amusing reason being that his lips have been badly bruised by his beloved's kisses.

The *Vāsavadattā* of Subandhu is another landmark in the history of Sanskrit prose romance. It narrates the curious story of the love of a prince and a princess. Both see each other in dream, and make attempts to meet. The prince, having met the princess, learns that her father wishes to give her in marriage to another man. Then the prince eloped her, and repaired to the Vindhya hills. One morning, the prince did not find her. After a search, he got her in a hermitage not in flesh and blood, but transformed into a stone. At the touch of the prince, she was brought back to life.

The work reveals a rich vocabulary, a wealth of thought and imagery and literary skill. But, the professed artificialities of the diction detract from its readability. The author boasts his pedantry as *pratyakṣara-śleṣamaya-vinyāsa-vaidagdhya-nidhi*. He prides himself on the frequent use of pun. The very ***double entendres***, which won the applause of ancient critics, are regarded by most modern litterateurs as literary jugglery. It must, however, be said to the credit of Subandhu that, though he draws upon the well-known traditional account of Udayana, the narrative portion of the Vāsavadattā is the poet's own creation.

Undoubtedly, the greatest of the aforesaid triad is Bāṇabhaṭṭa. Happily for us, he gives an autobiographical account in his *Harṣacarita* and in some introductory verses of the *Kādambarī*; we have got these two masterpieces from his pen, which typify the *kathā* and *ākhyāyikā* classes of composition respectively. Bāṇa enjoyed the patronage of king Harṣavardhana (reign AD 606-47).

The *Harṣacarita* deals with the main historical events from the time of Prabhākaravardhana, Harṣa's grandfather, down to the reign of Harṣa.

The *Kādambarī* of Bāṇa has been unanimously extolled by Indian critics as the greatest prose romance. It consists of two parts, *Pūrvabhāga* and *Uttarabhāga*; the former by Bāṇa himself who could not finish it, and the latter by his son, variously called Bhūṣaṇa, Pulina or Pulinda. The love-story of Candrāpīḍa and Kādambarī, in the past lives and in the present, is the staple of the work. With this runs the parallel story of the love of Puṇḍarīka and Mahāśvetā.

Bānabhaṭṭa shows his imaginative power and literary skill in the conception and execution of the theme of the *Kādambarī*. Though the *Harṣacarita* is based on a historical theme, yet he displays his greatness, in both the works, in creating situations. He has a highly commendable capacity for not only describing the beauties of nature — the mountain, lake, forest, morning, evening, etc. — but also for making the reader appreciate it. His style, with very long and involved sentences, sometimes extending over a few pages, is high flown and dignified. The richness of his fancy and vocabulary is, indeed, admirable. He has eye for colour and ear for music. Besides, natural beauty, he has also beautifully described captivating feminine charm and delineated the tenderness of the hearts of lovers and the glory of love. While going through his works, one feels like moving in an exhibition of beautiful objects all around. Rabīndranāth has characterised Bāṇa's *Kādambarī* as a picture-gallery in which the pictures are set in golden frames of discursive language.

In portraying the characters, the author shows keen insight into human nature. The rise and the gradual development of love between Candrāpīḍa and Kādambarī on the one hand, and between Puṇḍarīka and Mahāśvetā on the other, through strange circumstances, evoke our admiration. Patralekhā, another brain-child of the author, has not only a unique name but also an uncommon nature. A young princess in captivity, she has all the qualities, physical and mental by which youngmen can be attracted. She is a very close attendant of the youthful Candrāpīḍa. But, both show admirable restraint in keeping each other free from any taint the flesh is heir to.

According to orthodox Indian critics, prose is the touchstone in which a poet's ability is tested. That test has been passed by Bāṇa with great credit. The Indian critics have no reservation in their praise of this author. Some of their accolades are as follows:

kādambarī-rasajñānāmā-hāro'pi na rocate ।

even food does not taste well to those who are aware of the relish of the *Kādambarī*.

rucira-svara-varṇa-padā rasa-bhāvavatī jaganmano haratī ।
tat kiṁ taruṇī nahi nahi vāṇī bāṇasya madhura-śīlasya ॥

Is it a young damsel, with charming voice, complexion and feet, and possessed of sentiments and emotions, that captivated the mind of the world? No no, it is the speech, full of beautiful letters and words, literary flavour and feelings, of Bāṇa of sweet character. The renowned Vaiṣṇava poet, Jayadeva remarks — the five-arrowed Cupid lives in the heart (of lady Poesy).

Modern critics, especially of the West, accuse Bāṇa of use of difficult words and too long compounds. They also decry Bāṇa's technique of the Chinese box pattern of writing stories within stories by which the reader is apt to miss the main thread of the narrative. Weber characterises Bāṇa's prose as a big forest in which one has to go ahead after cutting the bushes and finds himself confronted by fericious animals in the forms of unintelligible words.

Dramatic literature

This period is distinguished for the production of some dramas of special types.

Śūdraka, presumbly a post-Kālidāsa dramatist, is credited with the authorship of the *Mṛcchakaṭika* (*mṛt* + *śakaṭikā* — a little clay-cart) which belongs to a distinct dramatic genre, called *prakaraṇa*. Written in ten acts, it makes a departure from the banalities of court-life, the usual subject-matter of the dramas. The story of the drama is briefly this.

Vasantasenā, a rich courtesan, is enamoured of Cārudatta, a wealthy and virtuous brāhmaṇa who has lost his fortune, but not his sterling character, Śakāra, brother-in-law of the reigning king, makes overtures of love to Vasantasenā who spurns his love. Naturally enraged, Śakāra, severely assaults the courtesan who falls down unconscious. He accuses Cārudatta of her murder. In a trial that ensues, Cārudatta is sentenced to death. Meanwhile, Vasantasenā, who regains consciousness, appears in the scene and Cārudatta is saved.

About this time, a revolution takes place in the state. One Āryaka, whom Cārudatta rescued from prison, succeeds in deposing the reigning king, Pālaka, and occupies the throne. Cārudatta is made by him one of his chief officers. He marries Vasantasenā.

The significance of the title is this: Cārudatta's little son was discontented with the clay-cart with which he had been playing. Out of affection, Vasantasenā stretched her arms to take him into her lap. The boy, however, refused her on the ground that his mother had not been adorned with ornaments like her. This engendered in her a feeling of disgust towards worldly riches. So, she put off the ornaments, placed them in the cart and expressed her desire that a golden cart would be made for him.

This drama has been lauded as the most Shakespearian and stage-worthy of all the Sanskrit dramas. It has also been characterised as the most human among them.

The dramatist's capacity for creating characters is striking. In Vasantasenā, though a courtesan, we find a loving woman with the usual heart-hunger for a child. She is attached to one man; to her a man's virtues are more valuable than his riches. Cārudatta, once affluent but later impoverished, did not forsake piety and other human qualities. The work, apart from testifying to the dramatic skill of the author, gives us a vivid picture of real life in which appear rogues, rakes, rascals and criminals. The court-scene, in which the sharks and other designing people abound, is true to life.

A few verses from the drama, with translation, are quoted:

A PICTURE OF POVERTY

saṁgaṁ naiva hi kaścidasya kurute saṁbhāṣate nādarāt
saṁprāpto gṛhamutsaveṣu sāvajñamā-lokyate ।
dūrādeva mahājanasya viharaty-alpacchado lajjayā
manye nirdhanatā prakāmamaparaṁ ṣaṣṭhaṁ mahāpātakam ।।
— I.37

Nobody associates with him (i.e., a poor man), talks affectionately with him. When he comes, in festivals, to the house of the rich, he is negligently looked upon. A poor man, scantily clothed, shamefully moves away from the creditor. It seems, destitution is the sixth of the grave sins.

[*Note*: The following are the five grave sins according to *Smṛti-śāstra*:

Murder of a brāhmaṇa, drinking wine of the *surā* type, theft of gold of a brāhmaṇa, adultery with preceptor's wife, and association of a person who has committed any of the above sins.]

FICKLE NATURE OF A WOMAN

samudra-vīcīva cala-svabhāvāḥ sandhyābhralekheva muhūrta-rāgāḥ ।
striyo hṛtārthāḥ puruṣaṁ nirarthaṁ niṣpīḍitā-laktavat tyajanti ।।

Women, of fickle nature like a sea-wave, of instant passion (or momentary reddish hue) like a slender evening cloud, having taken away the wealth, forsakes a destitute man like fully pressed lac.

A COURT-SCENE

cintā-sakta-nimagna-mantrī-salilaṁ dūtormi-śaṁkhā kulaṁ ।
paryanta-sthita-cāra-nakra-makaraṁ nāgāśva-hiṁsrā śrayam ।

nānā-vāśa-kaṁka-pakṣī-nicitaṁ kāyastha-sarpā-spadaṁ
nīti-kṣuṇṇa-taṭaṁ ca rāja-karaṇaṁ hiṁsraiḥ samudrāyate ||
— IX.14

The king's court is like a sea due to the presence of ferocious creatures. In it, water is the ministers, engrossed in thought. It is full of waves and conch-shells in the forms of ambassadors, on its shore are crocodiles and sharks in the forms of spies, the elephants and horses in it are like ferocious animals; it is replete with crows in the forms of shorting litigants, is the resort of serpents in the forms of *kāyasthas* (scribes), its shore is trodden by law.

We have three minor dramas, with considerable similarity of themes, all attributed to Harṣa who is generally supposed to be identical with king Harṣavardhana (AD 606-47), of Kanauj and Thāneśvar. The dramas are entitled *Priyadarśikā*, *Ratnāvalī* and *Nāgānanda*.

In the *Priyadarśikā*, we find Priyadarśikā, daughter of king Dṛḍhavarman, accidentally brought near king of Vatsa. With the pseudonym, Āraṇyikā, she is appointed a handmaid of queen Vāsavadattā. Eventually, the king becomes attached to Āraṇyikā. The king comes to learn that she is also attached to him. One day, in a dramatic performance about the marriage of the king and Vāsavadattā, the king assumes the role of the king and Āraṇyikā that of the queen. Though it is merely a dramatic performance, yet Vāsavadattā is enraged at the mutual attachment of the king and Āraṇyikā. She becomes all the more irate after learning from Vidūṣaka about the king's real attachment to the young girl. So, the queen puts her into prison. Through various circumstances, the queen comes to know that Āraṇyikā is, in reality, the daughter of her relative. Then she brings about her marriage with the king.

A similar theme is dealt with in the *Ratnāvalī*. In the latter, minister Yaugandharāyaṇa, after crossing various hurdles in strange circumstances, brings about the marriage of the Vatsa king with Ratnāvalī, daughter of the king of Ceylon.

Of the *Nāgānanda*, the subject-matter is a Buddhist story.

Jīmūtavāhana as the prince of the Vidyādharas, a class of inferior gods dwelling in the region between the earth and the sky. Of him is enamoured Malayavatī, princess of the Siddhas, a class of demi-gods supposed to live in the sky between the earth and the sun. Through various adverse circumstances, they get married. One day, having heard of the killing of serpents by Garuḍa, king of birds, Jīmūtavāhana, out of sympathy for the serpents, offered himself to Garuḍa. Jīmūtavāhana, slain by Garuḍa, was brought back to life through the mercy of goddess Gaurī. Thereafter, he and Malayavatī lived happily.

The drama, entitled *Mudrārākṣasa*, attributed to Viśākhadatta, a post-Kālidāsa playwright, is unique in the sense that it is the only work, dealing exclusively with political matters. Unlike Sanskrit dramas in general, it has no heroine; in fact, it has no female character excepting an insignificant woman. According to some Western critics, this and the *Mṛcchakaṭika* are the only two Sanskrit dramas which can be staged. The subject-matter is briefly as follows:

Rākṣasa is the faithful and able minister of the devastated Nanda dynasty. Cāṇakya, the astute statesman and the extirpator of the Nandas, is the minister of Candragupta, king of the newly-founded Maurya empire. Through various stratagems, Cāṇakya succeeds in winnings over Rākṣasa and persuading him to take over as minister of Candragupta.

The author shows commendable skill in devising complex situations through which the dramatic action proceeds up to the denouement. The portrayal of the two key characters, Cāṇakya and Rākṣasa, one serving as an excellent foil to the other, evokes our admiration. Both are of keen intellect. But, Cāṇakya is steadfast, self-confident and cautious. Rākṣasa is comparatively soft-hearted, emotional and prone to errors. The style of the work is flowing and language unaffected. Unlike many other Sanskrit dramatists, Viśākhadatta is not keen upon displaying his poetic abilities on the pretext of writing a drama. As a dramatist he is eminently successful.

Some of his observations have become proverbial, e.g.

vighnaih punaḥ punarapi pratihanyamānāḥ

> *prārabdham uttamaguṇāḥ khalu nirvahanti* ।
>
> Those, endowed with best qualities, even in the face of recurrent obstacles, carry an undertaking to conclusion.
>
> *prabhavati bimbodgrāhe maṇir na mṛdāṁ cayaḥ*
>
> A gem can contain a reflection, not a clod of earth.
>
> [*Note*: The author means to say that an intelligent student can grasp what his teacher says, but not a dull one.[
>
> *na śāleḥ stamba-karitā vaptur-guṇama-pekṣate* ।
>
> The fact that the *śāli* paddy puts forth good stalks does not depend on the sower of seeds.
>
> The idea is that *śāli*, the best kind of paddy, produces good stalks due to its own quality and does not need anybody else's help. Similarly, a qualified person himself reveals his own qualities, and does not depend on any other person.

A towering figure among the playwrights of this period is Bhavabhūti (*c.* seventh-eighth century AD), author of the *Mahāvīra-carita*, *Uttara-rāmacarita* and *Mālatīmādhava*.

The *Mahāvīra-carita*, consisting of seven acts, deals with the *Rāmāyaṇa* story. According to tradition, the portion up to verse 46 of act V is from the pen of Bhavabhūti. This part describes the events up to Rāma's exile. In the remaining portion are described the events up to the return of Rāma to Ayodhyā and his coronation. The *Uttara-rāmacarita*, in seven acts, deals with the latter part of the *Rāmāyaṇa* story, i.e., the incidents following Rāma's return and coronation. The *Mālatīmādhava* has, as its subject-matter, the love-story of a young student, Mādhava, and Mālatī, daughter of a minister. Through strange circumstances and with the intervention of the intelligent Buddhist nun, Kāmandakī, the love-affair culminates happily. With this main story runs the love episode of Madayantikā and Makaranda.

Though the first two dramas are based on the familiar *Rāmāyaṇa*, yet Bhavabhūti's innovative skill is demonstrated by the new incidents and situations. For instance, in act IV of the

Mahāvīra-carita, we find Śūrpaṇakhā's arrival in Mithilā in the guise of Mantharā, and handing over a forged letter purported to have been written by Kaikeyī stating her request for the fulfilment of two boons promised by Daśaratha. Rāma goes to Ayodhyā, and apprises Daśaratha of the above request and determines to proceed to the forest.

The originality of Bhavabhūti is striking in his *Uttara-rāmacarita*. For example, in the first act, he introduces the picture-seeing episode. We find a picture portraying the life in exile, and desire of Sītā, now in the family way, for revisiting the forest. In act III the novel features are the dialogue between the rivers, Tamasā and Muralā, Rāma's fainting at the sight of the revisited forest, and Sītā in a shadowy form (*chāyā*) comforting him, etc. It should be noted that though the original *Rāmāyaṇa* story has a tragic end, the dramatist, in compliance with the rule of dramaturgy, has re-united Rāma with Sītā. In doing so, he has resorted to superhuman events; this has made the story rather artificial.

How far the dramatist is original in the *Mālatimādhava*, it is difficult to say. Some scholars have sought to establish that Bhavabhūti was indebted to the *Bṛhatkathā* the original of which is lost and is represented by Kṣemendra's *Bṛhatkathā-mañjarī*, Budhasvāmin's *Bṛhatkathāślokasaṁgraha* and Somadeva's *Kathāsarit-sāgara*. We do not know if he had an earlier source or model. Whatever that may be, the story of the love, depicted in the work, is not confined to the hackneyed court-life. We find here the dramatised version of an incident of common life.

Bhavabhūti excels in the delineation of pathetic scenes. Though, as a king, Rāma banished Sītā, yet as husband he was consumed with grief at heart. This pathetic condition of Rāma is expressed by the dramatist in poignant words. According to him, his heart-burn was *puṭa-pāka-pratīkāśa*, like *puṭa-pāka* which is a particular method of preparing drugs (the various substances being wrapped up in leaves, covered with clay, and heated in fire). The lament of Rāma, stricken with grief at the separation of Sītā, is described as causing even granite to wail (*api grāvā roditi*) and even to crush the heart of thunder (*api dalati vajrasya hṛdayam*). Indian tradition praises Bhavabhūti's power of delineating the pathetic sentiment by saying *kāruṇayaṁ bhavabhūtireva tanute* (Bhavabhūti alone depicts pathos). It should be noted that Bhavabhūti himself holds (*Uttararāma*, canto III.47) that *karuṇā* or the pathetic is the only *rasa* which is transformed into different *rasa*s due to different causes.

Bhavabhūti richly deserves credit for the very realistic descriptions of nature. The natural objects, described by him, are not like the paintings on the walls of the parlour, but seem to be visualised by the reader. In Kālidāsa's works, we generally find the soothing gentle aspect of nature, expressed in soft language. But, Bhavabhūti does not mince words in representing the ruggedness of forests and mountains. For instance,

> *kaṇḍūla-dvīpa-gaṇḍa-piṇḍa-kaṣaṇot-kampena sampātibhi rgharma-sraṁsita-bandhanaiḥ sva-kusumaira-rcanti godāvarīm* ।
> *chāyā-paskiramāṇa-viṣkira-mukha-vyākṛṣṭa-kīṭa-tvacaḥ* ।
> *kūjat-kānta-kapota-kukkuṭakulāḥ kule kulāya-drumāḥ* ॥
> — II.9

The trees on the bank, full of nests, are worshipping (river) Godāvarī with their own flowers. Those flowers, smothered by heat and with their stems loosened, are falling on the ground as a result of the rubbing of the elephants' cheeks, the flocks of birds, scratching the ground in a shade, are dragging the worm-eaten barks of trees; on the trees, the flocks of pigeons and fowl are singing.

> *guñjat-kuñja-kuṭīra-kauśika-ghaṭā-ghūtkāravat kīcaka stambā-ḍambara-mūka-maukulikulaḥ krauñcāvato'yaṁ giriḥ* ।
> *etasmin pracalākināṁ pracalatāmu-dvejitāḥ kūjitai-rudvellanti pūraṇa-rohiṇa-taru-skandheṣu kumbhīnasāḥ* ॥
> — II.29

This is mountain Krauñcāvata where the flocks of crows are silent in the vast expanse of bamboo-clumps whistling in the air, among which the flocks of owls hoot in the groves which are their resorts; on this, the serpents, frightened by the notes of the peacocks running to and fro, climb the branches of the old sandal-trees.

Despite his poetic and dramatic skill, Bhavabhūti lacks the sense of humour; it is virtually absent in his works. While depicting austere duty and great conjugal love, he has ignored the lighter side of life.

With Bhavabhūti ends the glorious epoch of drama in the post-Kālidāsa age up to the beginning of the period of decline. More than a dozen dramas of little value were written in the intervening period.

C. PERIOD OF DECADENCE

Broadly speaking, the age started in the ninth-tenth centuries AD, and lasted till the seventeenth-eighteenth centuries. Various political and social factors were responsible for the decline of Sanskrit literature. Want of political cohesion and stablility in north India began with the fall of the Pāla empire early in the tenth century; its decline started in the ninth century. In the wake of the disruption of this empire, small states mushroomed.

In south India also, there was political disintegration. This region as well as central and west India were divided into small kingdoms. The Muslims had been invading India repeatedly from the seventh century onwards. Towards the end of the twelfth century, they succeeded in conquering Bengal, Bihar, etc., which continued to remain under their control. Towards the end of the thirteenth century, they occupied the throne of Delhi. Several Muslim dynasties beginning with Khaljīs and ending with the Moguls, ruled one after another in the span of about 500 years. During this period, some rulers oppressed the Hindus in various ways. This period saw the destructive depredations of foreigners, paticularly of Timurlane and Nādir Shāh. The rise of two powerful independent kingdoms in the Deccan was of far-reaching consequence. One was the Muslim Bahmanī kingdom and the other the Hindu kingdom of Vijayanagar.

Towards the close of the Mogul period, the formidable Mārāṭhā power arose in the south, and proved to be a menace to the Muslim rulers of Delhi.

In the Mogul regime, European merchants and missionaries started coming to India. In course of time, the British merchants grew powerful, and succeeded in vanquishing, the Muslim ruler of Bengal in AD 1757. This paved the way for the establishment of British suzerainty in India.

In such a milieu, Sanskrit literature continued to be cultivated. We shall deal with only the prominent works of the Classical Sanskrit literature of this period.

The most outstanding poetical work of this period is the *Naiṣadha-carita* of Śrīharṣa (*c*. middle of the twelfth century AD) who, according to some, hailed from Bengal. It deals with a portion of the Nala-Damayantī story of the *Mahābhārata*. The subject-matter is briefly as follows:

> Description of king Nala's manly figure and ideal royal virtues, his strong attachment to princess Damayantī on hearing of her uncommon beauty, Damyantī's irresistible desire of getting Nala as her husband, Nala's seizing a swan with golden wings in pleasure-tank, and releasing it at its request, the grateful swan's visit to the residence of Damayantī and apprising her of Nala's desire, arrangement of the Damayantī's *svayaṁvara-sabhā* (assembly for self-choice of husband), on way to it Nala's meeting with Indra and three other powerful gods, gods' request to Nala to act as their messenger for asking Damayantī to choose her husband from among them. Nala's visit to the assembly *in cognito* and futile effort to persuade Damayantī to choose a god, Damayantī adamant, then Nala's casting off disguise and the four gods' assuming the form of Nala to create confusion about the real Nala, with tips from goddess Sarasvatī Damayantī's giving the garland of choice to the real Nala, their marriage and happy conjugal life.

In this work, the poet is concerned more with manner than with the matter. Choosing a popular story, the poet makes a parade of his knowledge in various branches of learning, namely, metrics, poetics, erotics, philosophy, etc. His vast learning is, no doubt, commendable but in showing it off, he has at times lost the sense of preparation. For instance, while the story of the *Mahābhārata* is narrated in less than 200 verses, the poet has composed about three thousand stanzas. The *svayaṁvara-sabhā* in the Epic is described in just a few lines, while Śrīharṣa devotes as many as five long cantos (10-14). These examples of artificialities lead a Western critic to characterise the work as the best specimen of the worst poetic style. To many modern litterateurs, the poet is guilty of errors of taste. Like the author of the *Bhaṭṭīkāvya*, the author is conscious of the fact that it is intelligible only with the help of a commentary (22.154). In a self-complacent manner, he characterises his work as *madhu-varṣī* (showering honey). There may be honey, but before tasting it the reader has to suffer the stings of many bees in the forms of too difficult words.

Indian literary tradition, however, looks upon it as a poetic feat. The work has been deservedly praised for *pada-lālitya* (charm of words). There are occasional uses of such words. But, whatever good qualities there are in it are more than offset by a parade of pedantry. Another conventional praise of Śrīharṣa's work is — *naiṣadhaṁ vidvadauṣadham*; the *naiṣadha* is a medicine to the learned.

It must, however, be admitted that the poet reveals originality in the shaping of Nala's character. His inner conflict between love and sense of self-respect has been very deftly described by the poet. At places, dialogues have been vivified by humour. There are flashes of good poetry in the descriptions of nature, which are, however, conventional. For instance, the description of moon-rise:

> *paśyāvṛto'pyeṣa nimeṣamadre radhityakā-bhūmi tiraskariṇyā* ।
> *pravarṣati preyasi candrikābhi ścakora-cañcū-culukaṁ pratīnduḥ* ॥

> O dear, see, though covered for a moment by the screen in the form of the table-land of the mountain, the moon is quenching the thirst of the *cakora* bird by showering beams.

Description of Nala's virtue:

> *vibhajya merur na yadarthisāt kṛtaḥ na sindhuru-tsarga*

jalavyayair-maruḥ ।
amāni tattena nijāyaśoyugaṁ dviphāla-baddhās-cikurāḥ
śiraḥsthitam ॥
— I.16

Nala did not give away the (golden) Sumeru mountain to the suitors after reducing it to pieces, and (at the time of gifts) did not, while using water for consecration, reduce the ocean to a desert; he looked upon the hairs on his head, divided into two parts, as representing his above two infamies.

Poetical works with historical themes

Some scholars have complained that there is no historical writing in Sanskrit. This is a rather sweeping remark. Apart from some Sanskrit inscriptions, some Purāṇas and Jaina *Paṭṭāvalīs* (lists of teachers), which contain historical information, we have some poetical works dealing with historical themes.

The *Rāmacarita* of Sandhyākara Nandin (eleventh century) is a peculiar work. Each verse of it describes, by means of pun, the events relating to the Pāla king, Rāmapāla (reign *c.* AD 1077-1120) as also of Rāma, son of Daśaratha. The assassination of king Mahīpāla as a result of rebellion in north Bengal and the installation of his younger brother, Rāmapāla as his successor — this in brief is the subject-matter of the work. As a record of contemporary events, its value is undoubted. But, as a poetical composition, it is artificial and pedantic. The poet complacently refers to himself as *Kalikāla-vālmīki*, but his work has neither the simplicity of Vālmīki's language nor the raciness of his diction. He characterises his puns as *akleśana* (not causing difficulty) which again testifies to his self-esteem. In fact, the work is unintelligible without the help of the commentary that is available. It is difficult to gather the historical information from the portion of the text on which the commentary is lost. We quote below two verses from the work as specimens:

atha bahutarasādṛtyā yukte rāmeṇa vittapālasya ।
sūnorabhyāse sahasā saureśi-tanayaḥ praiṣi ॥
— II.36

> About Rāma — then suddenly Aṅgada (literally, son of Bālin, son of Indra) was sent, very quickly, by Rāma to Rāvaṇa (lit. to the younger brother of Kuvera, Lord of wealth).
>
> About Rāmapāla — then, that man, i.e., Bhīma whose principle was ruined and who was scared, was sent by the very powerful (or very swift) Rāmapāla to the care of his son, Vittapāla.
>
> *dātā vipakṣa-bhiduraḥ samādāna-rato vṛṣādhvarataḥ* ।
> *vilasaj-jayanta-tanayaṁ sahasra-dṛṣṭir-dadhāti padamaindram* ॥
>
> Indra is a thousand-eyed god, and is satisfied with his due share in a sacrifice. He is the destroyer of enemies, the clipper of the wings of mountains; he upholds his status as Indra along with his brilliant son, Jayanta.

The other meaning is —

> This thousand-eyed king (i.e., Rāma's son Kuśa and Madanapāla) is charitably disposed, able to destroy enemies and attached to the path of religion; he is satisfied by the performance of daily duties (or by the equitable realisation of revenue, and is possessed of a status like that of Indra by reason of resplendent victory and far-reaching policy.

To the Kāśmīrian Kalhaṇa belongs the credit of composing a work which has the greatest claim to be considered as a poetical work dealing with history. His *Rājataraṅgiṇī* (1070 Śaka = AD 1148-9). In its earlier part, it deals with legendary kings of Kāśmīr. In the latter part, it gives accounts of the kings of the historical period. It is a valuable work for the political and social history of this region as well as its topography. As is expected, the work is an amalgam of fancy and fact. After all, it is a poetical work, and not serious history. In its study, one has to be cautious in sifting the grain from the chaff.

A gem of a poem of this period is the erotico-devotional lyric, *Gīta-govinda* of Jayadeva, one of the court-poets of the Bengal king, Lakṣmaṇasena (*c.* AD 1185-1205). It deals with the vernal erotic sports of Kṛṣṇa at Vṛndāvana. The main events, described in it, are Rādhā's separation, Kṛṣṇa's sports with other cowherd women, Rādhā's anguish, yearning for union and jealousy, request to Kṛṣṇa by Rādhā's friend, Kṛṣṇa's return, remorse and appeasement of Rādhā, finally the blissful reunion. The intense human appeal of the lyric, its plain and simple language have earned the unstinted admiration not only of the Indian critics, but also of the Western connoisseurs like Lassen, Jones, Levi, Pischel and Schroeder. The wondering Rabīndranāth asks—*satya kari kaha more, he vaiṣṇava kavi, kothā hate peyechile ei prema-chavi*? Tell me the truth, O Vaiṣṇava poet, wherefrom did you get this picture of love? Though composed in the form of a poem, it contains many songs. In rural setting, theme, milieu, language and sentiment it bears the impress of true folk-fire. The lyric has all the qualities of good poetry — simple, sensuous and impassioned. It has none of the artificialities usually found in the poetical works of the age of decadence.

The existence of over 40 commentaries and a number of its imitations are an index to its wide popularity.

A few specimens of the composition are as follows:

meghair-medurama-baram vanabhuvaḥ śyāmās-tamāla drumāir-naktaṁ bhīrurayaṁ tvameva tadimaṁ rādhe gṛhaṁ prāpaya ।

ittham nanda-nideśatas-calitayoḥ pratyadhva-kuñja-drumaṁ rādhā-mādhavayor-jayanti yamunā-kule rahaḥ kelayaḥ ॥

Victorious are the secret sports on the bank of the Yamunā, of Rādhā and Mādhava (Kṛṣṇa) who proceeded towards every bower-tree on the way, at the behest of Nanda who said — the sky is overcast with clouds, the forest region are darkened by the *tamāla* trees, it is night; this one (i.e., Kṛṣṇa) is timid, so, O Rādhā, you escort him to his house.

[*Note*: The darkness under the trees is very congenial for the secret union of the lover and the beloved.]

patati patatre vicalita-patre śaṁkita-bhavadu-payānam ।

racayati śayanaṁ sacakita-nayanaṁ paśyati tava panthānam ।
dhīra-samīre yamunā-tīre vasati vane vanamālī ॥
— Canto V

As a bird (lit. the wing of a bird) falls and the leaf of a tree moves, he, apprehending your arrival, prepares the bed, and looks at your path with startled eyes (Kṛṣṇa), wearing a garland of wild flowers, stays in the forest on the bank of the Yamunā, where gentle breeze blows.

candana-carita-nīla-kalevara pītavasana-vanamālī

Vanamālī (lit. the one wearing a garland of wild flowers), clad in yellow cloth, has his dark body smeared with sandal paste.

tvamasi mama bhūṣaṇaṁ tvamasi mama jīvanaṁ ।
tvamasi mama bhava-jaladhi-ratnam ।
— Canto X.3

You are my ornament, you are my life, you are my jewel in the ocean of worldly existence.

lalita-lavaṅga-latā-pariśīlana-komala malayasamīre
madhukara-nikara-karambita-kokila-kūjita-kuñja-kuṭīre ॥
viharati haririha sarasa-vasante nṛtyati
yuvati-janena samaṁ sakhī virahī-janasya durante ॥

O friend, here Hari (i.e., Kṛṣṇa) enjoys himself and dances with young demsels in spring which is full of the juice (of flowers, etc.) and ends unhappily for those in separation, when the southern breeze is soft with the touch of the charming clove-creeper and the bower-huts resound with the songs of cuckoos mixed with swarms of bees.

mukharamadhīraṁ tyaja mañjīraṁ ripumiva keli-sulolam ।
cala sakhi kuñjaṁ satimirapuñjaṁ śīlaya nīla-nicolam ॥

O friend, put off the enemy-like anklet, which is resonant, unsteady and very fickle in sport, put on the blue cloth and go to the bower.

An example of the purely erotic poetry is the *Caurī* (or *Caura*)-*surata-pañcaśikā* or *Caura-pañcaśikā* of unknown date, generally attributed, not on definite evidence, to the Kāśmīrian Bilhaṇa. Its three recensions indicate its wide popularity. In the southern recension, it is laid down that Bilhaṇa, caught in a secret love-intrigue with a princess, was being led to the place of execution. At that time, he recited the verses contained in this poem. The king, charmed by the verses, set him free, and married the princess to him.

The language of the poem is simple and style flowing and full of erotic flavour. Vividly describing feminine beauty, and the gusto of clandestine union, it is a unique work in the history of Sanskrit poetical literature. It has inspired several works in the regional vernaculars.

In this period was produced a plethora of *dūta-kāvyas* (messenger poems) in imitation of the inimitable *Meghadūta* of Kālidāsa. But, these works lack the simplicity of Kālidāsa's lyric and the spontaneity of the expression of love. Some poets betray the tendency of showring off their literary skill. Instead of the cloud, the moon, bee or swan, has been chosen as the messenger.

The *Pavanadūta* of Dhoyī, one of the court-poets of the Bengal king, Lakṣmaṇasena, is noteworthy. The theme is as follows: Lakṣmaṇasena, out for *digvijaya* (world-conquest), goes to south India where Kuvalayavatī, daughter of a Gandharva (belonging to a class of divine beings) falls desperately in love with him. In spring, she pines in separation, and proposes to send wind as messenger to the king.' The poet's language is simple and style limpid. At places, the language and ideas betray the influence of Kālidāsa. The work deserves special mention as, contrary to the *dūta-kāvyas* in general, it deals with a historical event, and throws some light on the social condition, e.g., the prevalence of the institution of *devadāsīs* (temple-girls) in contemporary Bengal.

To this age belongs the Kāśmīrian polymath, Kṣemendra (eleventh century AD), author of a number of works on a variety of subjects. His *Deśopadeśa* and *Narmamālā* are particularly interesting. In the former, the activities of the wicked, miser, harlot, etc., have been described. The author's satirical digs and diatribes about the students from various parts of India, assembled in Kāśmīr, are highly interesting. The work contains also the ridiculous pictures of an old fellow marrying a young girl, the characterless Śaiva preceptor, a poet without poetical ability, wily merchant, hypocritical hermit, boastful grammarian, the ignorant scribe, etc. The *Narmamālā* contains extremely sarcastic remarks about the oppression of people by the high-ranking *kāyastha*s (scribes in the revenue department of the king) and their scandalous household life.

A distinct literary genre of this period is the *kośa-kāvya* or anthology of detached verses from a large number of works and on a variety of subjects. These works are valuable, because they provide a varied fare to the reader, and rescue from oblivion quite a few poets who are otherwise unknown. Some of the prominent anthologies are the *Subhāṣita-ratnakośa* of Vidyākara (c. twelfth century AD), *Subhāṣitāvalī* of Vallabhadeva (not earlier than twelfth century and not later than fifteenth century), *Subhāṣita-muktāvalī* or *Sūkti-muktāvalī* (AD 1257) of Jalhaṇa, etc.

The tradition of tale as of fable is very old in India. The lost *Bṛhatkathā* of Guṇāḍhya appears to have been a vast repository of tales. Its three extant versions all in Sanskrit verse, give us an idea of its content. Of them, the *Bṛhatkathā-mañjarī*, attributed to the aforesaid Kṣemendra, describes, like the other two versions, viz., the *Bṛhatkathā-śloka-saṁgraha* of Budhasvāmin (*c.* eighth or ninth century AD) and the *Kathāsarit-sāgara* of Somadeva (eleventh century AD), the adventure of Naravāhanadatta, son of the far-famed Udayana, his getting of Madanamañjukā as his bride and of the land of Vidyādharas (a class of supernatural beings supposed to dwell on the Himālaya) as his empire. The author sometimes unnecessarily dilates upon erotic matters, and prolongs sections on religion. The *Bṛhatkathā-śloka-saṁgraha*, referred to above and available in an incomplete form, belongs probably to the eighth or ninth century AD. The most famous of the three versions of the *Bṛhatkathā* is the *Kathāsarit-sāgara* (Ocean of the streams of tales) of Somadeva who wrote it between AD 1063 and 1082. It is the earliest and largest collection of stories in the world. It is the source of many tales in the *Thousand Nights and a Night*. Through them, it supplied ideas not only to Persian and Turkish authors, but also to the West through Boccacio, Chaucer, La Fontaine and others.

Two more prose works on tale are interesting. One is the *Vetāla-pañcaviṁśati*. In this work, 25 stories existing in four versions, are inset within the framework of the main story. The specimens of some questions are given below:

There was a king, named Trivikramasena or Vikramasena, known as Vikramāditya. A sage used to give him one fruit a day; in it was hidden a gem. For pleasing the sage, the king promised to bring a dead body hanging from a tree. When he went to fetch it, a vampire told him that he would release the corpse to the king if he could answer his questions. The vampire's questions were in the forms of riddles. For example:

> A man, while eating boiled rice, felt with his extraordinary power of smell that the rice grew in a field close to a funeral place. So, he desisted from eating.
>
> Another man could not sleep on a bed because there was a piece of hair under several layers of upholsters. Of these two, who is the more fastidious epicure?
>
> A man burns himself in the very fire which burns the dead body of his beloved. Another man spends his life, full of grief, in a hut built near the cemetery of his beloved. A third man brings back the dead beloved by a *mantra* (incantation) obtained by chance. Of these three, who is the greatest lover?

Another popular work on tale is the *Siṁhāsana-dvātriṁśikā*, also known as *Vikramacarita* (*c*. thirteenth century AD). The original work is lost. It is available in two main versions, north Indian and the south Indian. The former exists in three recensions, and the latter in two, one of which is in prose and the other in verse. The significance of the title is this. The throne of king Vikramāditya, which lay buried in the earth, is discovered, and is got by king Bhoja. As he is about to sit on it, each of the 32 magic statues, supporting the throne tells a story describing the exploits of Vikramāditya. Their object is to convince Bhoja that none can be fit for sitting on the throne before possessing the qualities like those of Vikramāditya.

A noteworthy work, containing prose tales, is the *Śuka-saptatī*, available in three versions. The original work probably dates back to about the twelfth century AD. The subject-matter is briefly given below:

> A man left home, in connection with trade, leaving behind his young wife solely in the care of his domestic pet parrot. Taking advantage of the husband's absence, the woman, at the instigation of rogues, was about to quit home. The trusted parrot restrained her by narrating 70 spicy stories, one after another, which evoked her interest. Meanwhile, the man returned, and the crisis was averted.

The stories are skilfully written so as to sustain the interest of the woman and whetting her curiosity. Rogues, rascals and rakes abound in the stories. According to some, it is an example of picaresque writing in Sanskrit. Nevertheless, it must be said that it bears the imprimatur of folk literature in its undisguised form.

Its popularity transcended the barriers of India. It was translated into Persian, in the beginning of the fourteenth century, under the title *Tutināmā*. It was followed by other Persian versions. It was translated into various foreign languages, e.g., Turkish, German, English, and so on. Through the medium of the *Tutināmā*, many Indian tales spread in west Asia and Europe. In India, some works in Sanskrit and several vernaculars were composed.

The age of decadence of Sanskrit literature produced a large number of dramas. The published and unpublished dramas of this period are more than six hundred. The works, however, are generally devoid of diversity in subject-matters. The authors appear to be eager to show off their learning; they are rather indifferent to the readers in general and the life of common people. The hackneyed heroic and erotic sentiments are delineated. The few, who have chosen common life as the subject of their plays, are of an inferior breed of authors. The playwrights of this age have a penchant for poetry. As a result, their works have generally become dramatic poems rather than true dramas. The comic element does appear in some dramas, but their authors have tried to amuse people by the introduction of vulgar witticisms and situations rather than refined humour.

One drama, however, stands alone, and deserves special mention. The *Prabodha-candrodaya* (rise of the moon in the form of true knowlege) of Kṛṣṇamiśra (*c.* eleventh century AD) breaks new ground. It is an allegorical drama in which the characters are not of flesh and blood, but abstract human propensities. It seeks to depict the conflict between two forms of the human mind, one willing to arouse true knowledge, and the other opposed to it. The subject-matter is briefly as follows:

> Mind, conceived as a king, has two wives, viz. *pravṛtti* (inclination for enjoyment) and *nivṛtti* (cessation of desire). The former gives birth to *moha* (delusion) and the latter to *viveka* (discriminative knowledge). *Moha's* attendants are *kāma* (passion) and his wife *rati* (pleasure); *krodha* (anger) and *hiṁsā* (injury); *ahaṁkāra* (egoism) and his grandson *dambha* (deceit), born of *lobha* (covetousness) and *tṛṣṇā* (hankering), *mithyādṛṣṭi* (heresy) characterised as a courtesan and Cārvāka representing materialism. On the opposite side stand, for the time being drubbed, the forces of king *viveka*, comprising *mati* (reason), *dharma* (righteousness), *karuṇā* (pity), *maitrī* (friendliness), *śānti* (peace) and her mother *śraddhā* (faith), *kṣamā* (forgiveness), *santoṣa* (contentment), *vastu-vicāra* (judgement), *bhakti* (religious devotion) and others. In course ot time, *viveka* is united with Upaniṣad; their union will breed true knowledge and learning; they will overpower *moha*. Vārāṇasī has been the scene of all favourable doctrines. Both the above forces are so acting as to occupy this holy place. At first, it was occupied by *moha*. With the main plot there is an episodical incident. *Śānti* is helpless after losing her mother, *śraddhā*. At this juncture, *śānti* is protected by *bhakti*. Here is narrated the search, by *śānti*, for *śraddhā* in Jaina, Buddhist and Brāhmaṇical doctrines. Each of these faiths has a wife whom they try to represent as *śraddhā*. But, *śraddhā* is not found in any of them. Eventually, *viveka* wins. The old king, mind is pining in separation from his son, *moha* and wife, *pravṛtti*. Meanwhile Vedānta appears, and, in order to eradicate the false view of mind, advises him to live happily with *nivṛtti*. At last, the Supreme Being appears,

> *viveka* is united with Upaniṣad, and, true to prophecy, out of this union is born true knowledge.

Many incidents have been introduced for helping the movement of the main theme. Diversification has been effected by the comic and erotic elements. The author's learning and the capacity for delineating the different moods of the human mind are undoubted. His skill in sarcastic observations about faithlessness, hypocrisy and pedantry is laudable. Psychological analysis and description of inner conflict of human mind testify to Kṛṣṇamiśra's keen perception, experience and power of discrimination. He deserves credit for composing verses, charged with emotion. His prose provides pleasant read.

Several other allegorical dramas were produced in this age.

An epoch-making event in this age is the advent of Caitanya (AD 1486-1533). Hailing from Navadvīpa in West Bengal, he renounced worldly life quite early in age and became a socio-religious reformer. He preached a new kind of Vaiṣṇavism which transcended the narrow barriers of caste. The introduction of humanism into the religion made a tremendous impact on the society. His proverbial message was *caṇḍālo'pi dviji-śreṣṭhaḥ hari-bhakti-parāyaṇaḥ*; even an (untouchable) Caṇḍāla, if solely devoted to Hari (Viṣṇu), is the greatest of *dvijas* (i.e., the twice-born). It was not a mere precept. He actually practised what he preached. He included, among his closest followers, Muslim (Yavana) Haridāsa, and converted even hoodlums to his faith. Caitanya's influence spread far and wide beyond Bengal, and claimed innumerable adherents in different parts of India, particularly in Vṛndāvana, the famous bastion of the Vaiṣṇavas.

Caitanya's exemplary life and activities inspired some scholars to produce literary works. In the dramatic literature, the *Caitanya-candrodaya* (AD 1572) of Paramānandadasa-sena Kavikarṇapūra, deserves mention. It is essentially a dramaitc representation of Caitanya's life at Navadvīpa and Purī. It lacks commendable dramatic skill, and is not a faithful record of contemporary events.

To this age belong several farcical plays, e.g., the *Bhagavadajjukīya* of uncertain authorship and date, *Laṭakamelaka* of Śaṁkhadhara (twelfth century AD), *Kautukasarvasva* of Gopīnātha, *Kautuka-ratnākara* of Kavitārkika (sixteenth century). Their contents are briefly given below:

BHAGVADAJJUKĪYA

A courtesan dies of snake-bite. An ascetic, in order to glorify himself before his disciple, manages to transfer his soul into the dead body. The messenger of Yama, god of death, appears and causes the soul of the courtesan to be put into the dead body of the ascetic. As a result of such transfer of souls, the ascetic begins to behave like the courtesan and *vice versa*. At the sight of this, Yama's messenger put back the souls into the original bodies.

LAṬAKAMELAKA

The subject-matter is this. Many characterless people assemble in the house of the bawd, Danturā seeking the love of her daughter, Madanamañjarī. Among them are a professor, named Sabhāsali and his valet, named Kulavyādhi. Unable to bear the misconduct of his wife, Kalahapriyā, the professor hankers after the company of the courtesan. Then, there throng the quarrelling Digambara Jain, Jaṭāsura, the Kāpālika, Ajñānarāśi, the cowardly village headman, Saṁgrāmavisara and his flatterer, named Viśvāsaghātaka, the brāhmaṇa, Mithyāśukla, the deceitful preceptor, Phuṁkaṭamiśra, the Buddhist debauch, named Vyasanākara, attached to a washerwoman and others. What ensues is rivalry among the lovers. At last, the Digambara, Jaṭāsura marries the old Danturā. The names of the different persons indicate their respective characters, and evoke laughter.

KAUTUKA-SARVASVA

It dramatises the story of the evil conduct of Kalivatsala, king of the city of Dharmanāśa. He is addicted to *Canabis indica* and attached to others' women. He tortures a brāhmaṇa, named Satyācāra. He has fallen out with others while coveting a courtesan. At last, he banishes all good men of the kingdom. The king's minister is named Śiṣṭāntaka, priest, Dharmānala, companion Anṛtasarvasva, and court-scholar, Pīḍāviśārada. His councillor is named Kukarmapañcānana and Abhayaśekhara, General Samarajambuka. The work is amusing. In depicting these characters the author has not transgressed the limits of decency. But, it lacks dramatic skill and literary excellence.

KAUTUKA-RATNĀKARA

The subject-matter is this: The queen of the back-boneless king, Duritārṇava, of the city Puṇyavarjita, has been abducted in the night preceding Spring festival. The king's minister is named Kumatipuñja, priest Ācārakālakūṭa, astrologer Aśubhacintaka, harem-supervisor Pracaṇḍaśepha, General Samarakātara and spiritual preceptor Ajitendriya. Advised by these people, the king placed the courtesan, Anuñjaraṅginī, in the place of the queen. At last, it comes to light that a brāhmaṇa, named Kapaṭaveśadhārī has abducted the queen. The play may have entertained the patron of the dramatist, but, according to modern readers, it betrays bad taste.

Another type of drama of this age is called *Chāyānāṭaka*. Based on Epic or Purāṇic legends, these were generally composed for the entertainment of the people on certain special occasions. It is not clear what *chāyā* actually means. A technical meaning of the word in Sanskrit is adaptation or imitation. According to some, these are shadow-plays in which the characters, represented by dolls, used to be shown on the screen through reflections.

An example of such a drama is the *Dūtāṅgada* of Subhaṭa (*c.* thirteenth century AD), known to have been staged on the occasion of Spring festival.

4

Vyākaraṇa (Grammar)

THE term *vyākaraṇa* means that branch of knowledge with the help of which words are derived (*vyākriyante vyutpādyante śabdāḥ anena iti vyākaraṇam*). As is well-known, the *Ṛgveda* (*c*. 2000-1500 BC) is the earliest written record of the Indo-Europeans. This Veda, along with the *Yajurveda* and the *Sāmaveda* were collectively called *Trayī*. Later on, the *Atharvaveda*, along with the *Trayī*, came to be regarded as very sacred. It was not sufficient merely to know the texts or committing them to memory. It was incumbent to learn their meaning as well as the etymologies of the words. The ritual application of a Vedic *mantra* in an incorrect way was considered sinful resulting in great harm to the person applying it.

For the correct recital and use of the Vedic texts six types of ancillary works (Vedāṅgas) were produced. These are *Śikṣā* (phonetics, etc.) *Kalpa* (consisting of *Śrauta*, *Gṛhya*- and *Dharma-sūtra*s dealing respectively with Vedic rituals, domestic rites and religious and civil laws), *vyākaraṇa* (grammar) *nirukta* (etymology), *chanda*s (metrics) and *jyotiṣa* (astronomy). We are concerned here with *vyākaraṇa*.

Kātyāyana, a high post-Pāṇiniyan authority, says *lakṣya-lakṣaṇe vyākaraṇam*: grammar consists of *lakṣya*s or words and *lakṣaṇa*s or rules about their formation. Patañjali (*c*. second century BC), author of the Great Commentary (*Mahābhāṣya*) on Pāṇini's grammar, regards *vyākaraṇa* as the principal Vedāṅga (*pradhānaṁ ṣaṭsv-aṅgeṣu vyākaraṇam*). According to the *Śikṣā-śāstra*, mentioned above, while *śikṣā* is the nose of the Veda. *Vyākaraṇa* is its face (*śikṣā ghrāṇam tu vedasya mukhaṁ vyākaraṇaṁ smṛtam*). The *Chāndogya Upaniṣad* (VII.1.2) characterises *vyākaraṇa* as *vedānāṁ veda* (the Veda of the Vedas).[1]

India is a land of diversities. This is true of the grammatical literature too. We shall see, in due course, that several grammatical systems arose in this country; while some have irretrievably passed into oblivion, others still exist.

Of the existing grammars, the *Aṣṭādhyāyī* of Pāṇini (*c.* fourth century BC) is the oldest and of the highest authority. A traditional verse of apocryphal nature names a pre-Pāṇini grammarian as Maheśa, and states that, in comparison with his huge ocean-like grammar, that of Pāṇini is a mere *goṣpade* (water just enough for containing a hoof of a cow). Pāṇini refers to the following predecessors each of whom was the founder of a distinct grammatical school:

> Āpiśali (VI.1.92), Kāśyapa (I.2.25), Gārgya (VII.3.99), Cakravarman (VI.1.130). Gālava (VI.3.61), Śākalya (I.1.16), Śākaṭāyana (VII.3.18), Senaka (V.4.112), Sphoṭāyana (VI.1.123), Bharadvāja (VII.2.63).

In some cases, more rules than one refer to a particular grammar; we have cited one rule only.

Besides the above, several other pre-Pāṇinian grammarians are known from various sources. The curious reader may look up G. Hāldār's *Vyākaraṇ Darśaner Itihās* (in Bengālī)

We shall give below succinct accounts of the existing Sanskrit grammatical systems. The titles of the grammars are set forth in the English alphabetical order.

Aṣṭādhyāyī

It is by Pāṇini. He is referred to, in later literature as *Śālāturīya*, i.e., hailing from Śālātura, a village, probably near Attock in

1. About the utility of grammar, Patañjali, in the introductory portion of his *Mahābhāṣya*, remarks — *rakṣohāgama-laghva-sandehāḥ prayojanam*. It means that grammar serves fivefold purpose; namely *rakṣā* (preservation of Vedic texts intact), *ūha* (conjecture or supplying what is not stated), *āgama* (scriptural injunction to study grammar), *laghu* (simplification), *asandeha* (removal of doubt about the proper import).

Pakistan, which was known to the Chinese traveller, Hiuen-tsang (stay in India AD 630-43). He writes that he saw Pāṇini's statue there. There are different opinions about his time. He is, however, generally assigned to the fourth century BC.

It is so-called as it contains eight chapters (*adhyāyas*). Each chapter is divided into four sections (*pādas*). The total number of rules is 3,981.

It is called *Trimuni-vyākaraṇa*, because Pāṇini wrote the principal *sūtras*, Kātyāyana the *vārttikas* or supplementary rules, and Patañjali wrote the *Mahābhāṣya* which, being indispensable for comprehending the rules, is regarded as a part and parcel of the grammar.

A noteworthy feature of this grammar is that it deals also with Vedic grammar and Vedic accents. Another characteristic that distinguishes it from the other grammatical systems is that its rules are not divided into the usual *prakaraṇas* or topics like *Kāraka-prakaraṇa*, *Samāsa-prakaraṇa*, etc. Moreover, it devises 14 *pratyāhāras*, called *Māheśvara* or *Śiva-sūtras*. For example, *Ac* indicates all vowels, *HAL* stands for all consonants.

It has many commentaries, sub-commentaries and commentaries on sub-commentaries. Besides the aforesaid *Mahābhāṣya*, very renowned are the *Siddhānta-kaumudī* of Bhaṭṭojī Dīkṣita (sometime between the last quarter of the sixteenth century and the first half of the seventeenth), *Kāśikā* of the joint authors, Vāmana-Jayāditya and the *Bhāṣāvṛtti* of Puruṣottamadeva (*c.* twelfth century AD). The aforesaid Vāmana flourished before AD 800 according to some, and Jayāditya died in *c.* AD 660 according to I-tsing, the Chinese traveller who visited India in AD 675 and stayed for ten years.

Mugdhabodha

Son of Keśava and pupil of Dhaneśa or Dhaneśvara, Vopadeva was the author of this grammar, written after AD 1250 under King Mahādeva of Devagiri. As the title indicates, it was written for the knowledge of the simple-minded boys (*mugdhas*). It is modelled partly on the *Aṣṭādhyāyī* and the *Kātantra* (q.v.). The Vedic portion of the *Aṣṭādhyāyī* has been omitted. It is interesting to note that, in the illustrations, the author, wherever possible, uses the names of deities, e.g., Hari, Hara, etc.

It has several commentaries, e.g., by Durgādāsa, Rāma Tarkavāgīśa, Gaṅgādhara Tarkavāgīśa.

Kātantra

Also called *Kaumāra*, *Kalāpa*, *Kātantra* (meaning a short work) is a well-known grammar which was particularly popular in that part of Bengal which is comprised in the present Bangladesh. It was written by Śarvavarman who appears to have been a protégé of the Sātavāhanas of south India (first century AD?). It, perhaps, existed in two recensions, one current in Kāśmīr and the other in Bengal. It omits the Vedic portion. A supplement for teaching Vedic grammar, called *Kātantra-chandaḥ-prakriyā*, was written by Candrakānta Tarkālaṁkāra, a Bengal scholar (1836-1909).

It has several commentaries and sub-comentaries which testify to its popularity. Of the commentaries, the *Vṛtti* or *Kātantra-vṛtti* of Durgasiṁha (eighth century AD according to some, tenth century according to others), is the most well-known.

Saṁkṣiptasāra

Attributed to Kramadīśvara (tenth or twelfth century AD), it is said to have been revised or recast by Mahārājādhirāja Jumaranandin who is credited with the commentary, called *Rasavatī*, on it.

The work appears to be eclectic, utilising different grammars, particularly that of Pāṇini. The above Jumara is said to have added the rules on *kṛdanta*, *uṇādi* and *taddhita* suffixes. It comprises eight sections (*pāda*s) of which the first seven are called *sandhi, tiṅanta, kṛdanta, taddhita, kāraka, subanta* and *samāsa*. the last section deals with Prākṛt, and seems to be a later interpolation. Most of the illustrations in the work have been taken from the *Bhaṭṭīkāvya* (c. first half of seventh century AD). Itself perhaps modelled on Bhartṛhari's *Mahābhāṣya-dīpikā*, it probably served as the model of the works, *Prakriyā-kaumudī*, a recast, by Rāmacandra (fourteenth or fifteenth century), of the *Aṣṭādhyāyī* and *Siddhānta-kaumudī* (see under *Aṣṭādhyāyī*). The *Saṁkṣiptasāra* has been popular in West Bengal.

Cāndra Vyākaraṇa

It appears to have been written to abridge and simplify the *Aṣṭādhyāyī*. It comprises 3100 rules while the latter contains 3981 rules. While the *Aṣṭādhyāyī* is in 8 chapters, it contains 6. The *Cāndra* does not give rules for Vedic grammar and accents. The grammar exists in different recensions.

The author, Candragomin (also called Candragopin, Candrayogin and Vajracandragomin) is known, from the Tibetan Tāranātha's history and other sources, to have been a Bengālī Buddhist. Several other works, some of which are Tāntric, are also attributed to him. Of these, the *Lokānandanāṭaka*, existing only in Tibetan translation, and the *Śiṣyalekha-dharma-kāvya* are well-known. The latter is a metrical epistle admonishing his disciple, prince Ratnakīrti who was under delusion, caused by power and pelf.

Candra's date is controversial. He is generally believed to have flourished in the seventh century AD or even earlier.

Sārasvata

In 700 rules, it deals with all the topics of grammar, omitting rules regarding the Vedas and the accents. According to an old tradition, the main rules were revealed, by Goddess Sarasvatī, to an ascetic, Anubhūtisvarūpācārya who is credited with the authorship of the supplementary rules. The work was probably by one Narendrācārya (according to Kṣemendra) who wrote it in the thirteenth century at the instance of the Muslim ruler of the day. It is, however, attributed to Amṛtabhāratī by some, to Viṭṭhalācārya by others. Brevity and lucidity are the two reasons for its popularity, attested by a host of commentaries on it.

Supadma

Based on the *Aṣṭādhyāyī*, it remodels the greater part of its rules, and arranges them in a methodical form, adding a short explanation under each rule. It was verry popular in East Bengal (now in Bāngladesh). The author, Padmanābhadatta (1350-1400) belonged to Mithilā according to some, to Bengal according to others. Son of Dāmodaradatta, and grandson of Śrīdatta, he is to be distinguished from his namesake, son of Gaṇeśvara and grandson of Śrīpati. The grammar has more commentaries than one.

Śabdānuśāsana

Its full title is *Siddha-hema-candrābhidha-svopajña-śabdānuśāsana*, and it is to be distinguished from a *Śabdānuśāsana* by one Śākaṭāyana. It is meant for the Śvetāmbara Jainas. Also called *Haimavyākaraṇa*, it consists of eight books, and mainly follows the arrangement and terminology of the *Kātantra*. It does not deal with Vedic grammar and accents. The eighth book deals with Prākṛt grammar. The author himself wrote two glosses, called *Laghuvṛtti* and *Bṛhadvṛtti*, and a commentary, known as *Bṛhan-nyāsa*. The author, originally named Cāṅgudeva, was son of Cāciga and Pahinī. Born at Dhanduka or Dhandukā (in Ahmedābād), he became a Jaina monk (1088-1172)

Sectarian Grammars

We know of at least three such works:

1. *Harināmāmṛta* of Jīva Gosvāmin, one of the six Gosvāmins, renowned in the history of Bengal Vaiṣṇavism. His reputation was established in the sixteenth and seventeenth centuries.

   The grammar is designed for the propagation of Vaiṣṇavism. In most of the rules, there is the mention of Viṣṇu or other Vaiṣṇava deities. For example, the first *sūtra* reads *nārāyaṇād udbhūto*, etc. The vowels are called *sarveśvara*s, and consonants *viṣṇujana*s.

2. *Saṁkṣepa* (or *Laghu*) *harināmāmṛta*: Attributed to Rūpa Gosvāmin, it is planned like the above. In fact, Jīva's work appears to be a larger version of it. Rūpa, a direct associate of Caitanya (1486-1533), was also one of the six Gosvāmins of Vṛndāvana. In this work, technical terms and illustrations

are related to Rādhā-Kṛṣṇa or Kṛṣṇa's sports.

3. *Prabodha-prakāśa*: Attributed to Balarāma Pañcānana of unknown identity and date, it aims at the propagation of Śaivism. For example, it designates vowels as Śiva.

Pāli and Prākṛt Grammars

PĀLI

The extant Pāli grammars can be divided into three groups, namely, Kaccāyana (Kātyāyana) school, Mogglläna (Maudgalyāyana) school and the *Saddanīti*.

The grammar of Kaccāyana, the *Kaccāyana-gandha* is the earliest available Pāli grammar. For historical reasons, the author cannot be identified with Kātyāyana (*c*. third century BC), author of the supplementary rules (*vārttika*s) of the *Aṣṭādhyāyī*. The major portion of Kaccāyana's work appears to have been composed on the basis of the Sanskrit *Kātantra*. There is evidence that the author utilised also the *Kāśikā* (seventh century AD) commentary on the *Aṣṭādhyāyī*. This Pāli grammar is also closely related to the *Tolkāppiyam*, the earliest Tamil grammar. Of the many commentaries on Kaccāyana's work, most well-known is the *Nyāsa* or *Mukhamattadīpanī* of Vimalabuddhi.

Two grammars, called *Mahānirutti-gandha* and *Culla-nirutti-gandha*, are also attributed to Kaccāyana.

Some other grammars of this school are:

Rūpasiddhi or *Padarūpa-siddhi* of Buddhappiya Dīpaṅkara,
Bālāvatāra of Dhammakitti or Vācissara,
Sambandha-cinta of Saṁgharakkhita,
Saddatha-bheda-cintā of Thera Saddhammasiri,
Sadda-bindu perhaps of Kyacva,
Bālappabodhana,
Abhinava-cullanirutti of Siri Saddhammālaṁkāra

Moggallāna is known to have authored the *Moggallāna-vyākaraṇa* (or, *Sadda-lakkhaṇa*) and the *Moggallāna-pañcikā* which is a commentary on the former. Other notewothy works of this school are:

Pada-sādhana of Piyadassi,
Payoga-siddhi of Vanaratana Medhaṁkara,
Moggallāna-pañcikā-padīpa.

The *Sadda-nīti* is a renowned work by Aggavaṁsa or Aggapaṇḍita. Of its 27 chapters, the first 18 are called *Mahā-saddanīti* and the rest *Culla-saddanīti.*

PRĀKṚT

Of the extant grammars, the *Prākṛta-prakāśa*, attributed to Vararūci, is the earliest. Other noteworthy works are the following: *Prākṛta-lakṣaṇa* of Caṇḍa, *Prākṛta-vyākaraṇa* of Trivikramadeva, *Prākṛta-sarvasva* of Mārkaṇḍeya Kavīndra, *Prākṛta-kalpataru* of Rāma Tarkavāgīśa, *Prākṛta-rūpāvatāra* of Siṁharāja and *Sadbhāṣā-candrikā* of Lakṣmīdhara.

5

Purāṇas

What are the Purāṇas?

'PURĀṆA' means 'old'. In some ancient works, the word denotes a particular kind of Purāṇa. In the *Atharvaveda* and some other Vedic and post-Vedic works as well as in some Buddhist treatises, Purāṇa means *itihāsa* or history. We have a distinct class of works, called Purāṇas.

Contents of the Purāṇas

The *Viṣṇu Purāṇa* (III.6.24) states that the following matters are discussed in these treatises: *sarga* (creation), *pratisarga* (new creation after dissolution), *vaṁśa* (genealogies of gods and sages), *manavantaras* (Manu periods of time), *vaṁśānucarita* (genealogies of kings).

[*Note*: Fourteen celebrated personages were called Manus; e.g., Svāyambhuva, Vaivasvata, etc. Each of them is supposed to have presided over a period of time. Such periods were called *Manavantaras*.]

According to the *Bhāgavata Purāṇa* (XII.7, 9-10), the contents of Purāṇas are as follows:

Sarga (creation), *visarga* (the world of the moving and non-moving, produced as a result of the creatures' desires in the previous existence), *vṛtti* (means of livelihood), *rakṣā* (the desire of God, residing in the beings for counter acting anti-Vedic tendencies), *antara-manavantara* (see *manvantara* above), *vaṁśa* (explained earlier), *vaṁśānucarita* (explained earlier), *saṁstha* (four kinds of *laya* or dissolution), *hetu* (the creatures who, acting through nescience, are the cause of creation, etc., of the universe), *apāśraya* (*Brahman*).

It should be noted that the Purāṇas actually deal with many other matters. The contents of the Purāṇas, as we have them now, may be analysed as (i) *gāthā* (ballad) and *ākhyāyikā* (legendary account), (ii) *vaṁśa* (genealogies of sages and kings), (iii) Mythology, (iv) Cosmogony, (v) Dharmaśāstra or Smṛti, (vi) Popular religious beliefs and practices, (vii) Miscellaneous matters.

The extant Purāṇas reveal a lot of other matters, e.g., philosophy, poetics, prosody, Dharmasūtra, botany, chemistry, medical science, music, and achitecture, sculpture, etc. In short, the Purāṇas are epitomes of ancient Indian culture. The *Agni Purāṇa* is encyclopaedic.

Number of Purāṇas

The number of major Purāṇas is traditionally 18. They are:

(i) *Agni*, (ii) *Brahma*, (iii) *Bhāgavata*, (iv) *Bhaviṣya* or *Bhaviṣyat*, (v) *Brahmavaivarta*, (vi) *Brahmāṇḍa*, (vii) *Garuḍa* (viii) *Kūrma*, (ix) *Liṅga*, (x) *Mārkaṇḍeya*, (xi) *Matsya*, (xii) *Nārada*, (xiii) *Padma*, (xiv) *Skanda*, (xv) *Vāmana*, (xvi) *Varāha*, (xvii) *Vāyu*, (xviii) *Viṣṇu*.

The minor (Upa)-Purāṇas are also 18 in number, according to some authorities. There is, however, no uniformity in their titles in the different lists. According to Raghunandana (sixteenth century), an eminent Smṛti-writer of Bengal, these are as follows:

Āścārya, Bhāskara (or Sūrya), Devī, Kapila, Kālikā, Kalki, Maheśvara, Marīci, Narasiṁha, Nandikeśvara, Nārada, Parāśara, Sāmba, Sanatkumāra, Śivadharma, Uśanas, Vāyu, Varuṇa.

Classification of Purāṇas

We have seen that the Purāṇic works have been divided into two broad classes, namely, Mahāpurāṇa and Upapurāṇa. In accordance with the predominance of the deities concerned, the Mahāpurāṇas have been divided into three classes, namely (i) *Sāttvika*—glorifying

Viṣṇu, (2) *Rājasika* — glorifying Brahmā (3) *Tāmasika* — glorifying Śiva. These are also called respectively Vaiṣṇava, Brāhma and Śaiva.

Authorship

According to tradition (e.g., *Matsya* 50/73), all the Purāṇas are attributed to the single sage Vyāsa. As a matter of fact, however, these are not the works of single authors, written at particular times. Modern research reveals that even some single Purāṇas are compilations of earlier and later compositions. For example, parts of the *Vāyu Purāṇa* appear to have been compiled between AD 200 and 1400.

Date

What we have stated above renders it difficult to ascertain the dates of the individual Purāṇas. We do not know when this class of literature originated. The *Āpastamba-dharmasūtra* (I.6.19.3) quotes verses from Purāṇas, and mentions (II.9.24.56) the *Bhaviṣyat Purāṇa*. This work dates back to a few centuries before Christ, and seems to be the earliest work to refer to Purāṇa as a class of works, though the term Purāṇa, in the sense of *itihāsa* (history), is of much earlier origin. About the age of the Purāṇas, we can say, perhaps with some degree of accuracy, that the earlier works originated before the seventh century AD. The *terminus ad quem* of the time of the later Purāṇas may, perhaps, be drawn at about AD 1400.

Importance of the Purāṇas

The Purāṇas contain many exaggerations, hyperboles and superhuman elements. Nevertheless, they are highly useful in many respects.

In the first place, they have been serving as a very good medium of mass education. The public recital of edifying Purānic legends has been an age-old practice.

The value of the Purāṇas in the political history of India is undeniable. Some information about a few royal dynasties, available in these works, is not found anywhere else. Of such dynasties, described in the Purāṇas, the following deserve special mention: Śiśunāga, Nanda, Maurya, Śuṅga and Kāṇva.

1. Śiśunāga (*Matsya* — 272, 6-13; *Vāyu* — 99, 314-22; *Brahmāṇḍa* — III.14, 127-35; *Viṣṇu* — IV.24, 3; *Bhāgavata*— XII.1, 5-8).

2. Nanda (*Matsya* — 272, 18-22; *Vāyu* — 99, 326-30; *Brahmāṇḍa*—III.74, 139-43; *Viṣṇu*—IV.24, 4-7, *Bhāgavata* —XII.1, 8-12).

3. Maurya (*Matsya*—272, 23-6; *Vāyu*—99, 331-6; *Brahmāṇḍa* —III.74, 144-9; *Viṣṇu*—IV.24, 7-8; *Bhāgavata*—XII.1, 3-16).

4. Śuṅga (*Matsya* — 272, 27-32; *Vāyu* — 99, 337-43; *Brahmāṇḍa*—II.74, 150-6; *Viṣṇu*—IV.24, 9-11; *Bhāgavata* —XII.1, 16-19).

5. Kāṇva (*Matsya*—272, 32-7; *Vāyu*—99, 343-7; *Brahmāṇḍa* —III.74, 156-60; *Viṣṇu*—IV. 24, 12; *Bhāgavata*—XII.1, 19-21).

Some Mahāpurāṇas, notably *Mārkaṇḍeya* (ch. 57 or 54 in some versions, verses 34, 59), *Vāyu* (ch. 45, verses 109-36), *Brahmāṇḍa* (ch. 114, verse 34-56), *Vāmana* (ch. 13, verses 36-58), throw light on the different kinds of people living in India. They can be divided, according to the regions, inhabited by them, into the following classes:

A. Belonging to Parvata (Himalayan region)

   For example, Hūṇa, Khaśa, Kirāta, etc.

B. Belonging to Udīcya-deśa (north India)

   For exmaple, Bharadvāja, Cīna (Tibeto-Chinese people), Gāndhāra, etc.

C. Belonging to Prācya-deśa (east India)

   For example, Bhārgava, Mālava, Malla, Muṇḍā, Pauṇḍra, etc.

D. Belonging to Madhyadeśa

For example, Ābhīra, Pulinda, etc.

E. Belonging to Vindhyaprastha (Region of the Vindhya hills)

For example, Bhoja, Kāruṣa, Mālava, etc.

F. Belonging to Dākṣiṇātya

(Deccan to the south of Vindhya Range)

For example, Āndhra, Cola, Kāruṣa, Kerala, etc.

G. Belonging to Aparānta

(Koṅkaṇ, Mālābar. According to Ptolemy, it extended toward the south from the river Narmadā).

For example, Āvantya, Kārasakara, Pāraskara, Pārasīka, etc.

The Purāṇas, belonging to the different sects, e.g., Vaiṣṇava, Śākta, etc., are useful for the history of religion in India.

These works are important also for certain branches of the history of literature. For instance, chapters 253-8 of the *Agni Purāṇa* contain useful materials in connection with the history of ancient Indian law. Chapters 336-46 of this Purāṇa appear to follow a tradition of poetics older than that of the Kāśmīrian school of Ānandavardhana who had a great impact on the later writers on poetics.

The Purāṇas contain copious information about the river-systems, mountains and topography of India. Besides, they are a mine of information about architecture, sculpture, music, dance, politics and statecraft, military matters, botany, chemistry, veterinary science, etc. Most of the above information is, however, in the nature of compilation.

The influene of Purāṇas on the life and literature of the Indians is immense. They gave women and śūdras some right to religious observances, which was denied in the traditional Dharmaśāstras. For instance, a network of *vratas*, designed in these works, satisfied, to some extent, the religious cravings of them. They allowed them, and still lower classes of people such as *mlecchas*, etc., to perform *Durgāpūjā*.

So far as Sanskrit literature is concerned, it drew freely upon these works for the themes of poetical works and dramas. Some of the prominent poetical works, based upon Purāṇic legends, are Kālidāsa's *Kumārasambhava*, Jayadeva's *Gīta-Govinda*, Līlāśuka's *Kṛṣṇakarṇāmṛta*, Kṣemendra's *Daśāvatāracarita*, etc. Some of the dramas, based on Purāṇic stories, are Bhāsa's *Bālacarita*, Rāmacandra's *Yādavābhyudaya*, Kṣemīśvara's *Caṇḍakauśika*, etc.

There is deep imprint of the Purāṇas on the various vernacular literatures of India.

The *Bhāgavata Purāṇa* is the Bible of the Vaiṣṇavas. The *Durgā-saptaśatī*, popularly called *Caṇḍī*, included in the *Mārkaṇḍeya Purāṇa*, is regarded as a holy work, so much so that it is recited in religious rites; some devout people consider it their pious duty to recite the *Caṇḍī* everyday.

6

Tantra

What is Tantra?

TANTRA is the name of a distinct literary genre. As regards the meaning of the term 'Tantra', opinions differ. Derived from the root *tan* (to spread), it is generally explained as that kind of literature by which knowledge is disseminated (*tanyate vistāryate jñānam anena*).

Classification of Tantras

These can be classified in various ways in accordance with their places of origin, the sects to which they belong, etc. The common classification is twofold, viz., *Āgama* and *Nigama*. In the former, Pārvatī is represented as questioner and Śiva as the teacher. In the latter, the process is reversed.

Antiquity of Tantra

The time of origin of Tantra is not known definitely. According to an ancient writer on Dharmaśāstra, named Hārīta, Tantra, like Veda, is Śruti or revealed literature (cf. *śrutiśca dvividhā proktā vaidikī tāntrikī tathā*, quoted by commentator, Kullūka on *Manu-smṛti*, II.1). It is true that Tāntric elements are found in the Vedas, particularly in the *Atharvaveda*. It contains a good deal of black magic, called *abhicāra*, which is designed to cause harm to others; such practices are a part and parcel of Tantras.

We cannot say precisely when Tantras, as a class of works,

began to be composed. The earliest Nepalese manuscripts of tantras appear to have been copied between the seventh and ninth centuries AD. On paleographic evidence, H.P. Sastri thinks manuscripts of some Tantras to have been written (or copied?) in the Gupta Age (*Nepal Catalogue,* I, pp. 10, 85, 117); this age, however, covers the period from *c.* AD 320-510.

The oldest Buddhist *Dhāraṇīs* (protective spells) of Tāntric type are supposed to date back to the fourth century AD.

Original Home of Tantra

Nothing definite is known about this matter. Some eminent scholars, including Winternitz, think that Bengal was the cradle of Tantra. The following anonymous couplet, of unknown origin, confirms the above impression:

> *gauḍe pracāritā vidyā maithilaiḥ prabalīkṛtā* ।
> *kvacit kvacin mahārāṣṭre gurjare vilayaṁ gatā* ॥

> This branch of learning, having been preached in Gauḍa (Bengal), was developed by the people of Mithilā (Bihar), existed at some places of Maharashtra, and met with its doom in Gurjara (Gujarat).

Some of the arguments of the protagonists of this theory are as follows:

(i) The largest number of manuscripts of the works of the Tantra class have been found in Bengal (West Bengal and Bangladesh taken together).

(ii) The worship of Kālī, the most prominent Tāntric deity, in her various forms as Rakṣā-kālī, Bhadra-kālī, Dakṣiṇa-kālī, etc., is most widespread in this province.

(iii) It is known that, in Kāmākhyā (Assam), a stronghold of Tantra, Tāntrism was preached by the Bengālī Śākta devotee, Kṛṣṇarāma Nyāyavāgīśa. The then Ahom king, Rudrasiṁha, became his disciple.

(iv) It was the Bengālī Tāntrikas who carried Tantra to the far-off Hiṁlāj in Baluchistan. The Bengālī Brahmānanda (sixteenth century AD) and his disciple Jñānānanda preached Tāntric philosophy and *sādhanā* there.

(v) Tāntric *sādhanā* in Nepal appears to have been influenced by Tāntric devotees of Bengal (*vide* Kṣitimohan Sen's *Vāṅgālīr Sādhanā*, pp. 47-8).

(vi) It is believed that, through the spread of Buddhism from Bengal, Tāntrism was introduced in Tibet and China. Several Bengālī scholars, including the most renowned Atīśa Dīpaṁkara (*c.* AD 980-1053), settled in Tibet and wrote copiously on Tantra.

(vii) Many of the *Śākta Pīṭhas* (holy resorts of Śakti) are in Bengal. For example, Kālīghāṭ in Calcutta is of wide renown.

Some scholars are inclined to think that Tantra originated in, or was strongly influenced by China. The main arguments, put forward by them, are as follows:

(i) *Cīnācāra* is a mode of Tāntric *sādhanā*. There is a distinct work, called *Mahācīnācāra(sāra)-tantra*.

(ii) The nasal sound in the mystic syllables *hrīṁ*, *krīṁ*, etc., so important in Tāntric rites, is reminiscent of the Chinese language which abounds in such sounds.

(iii) The flower *javā*, (*Hibiscus rosa-sinensis*) regarded as highly suitable in Śakti-worship, is called China rose.

(iv) The diagrams, called *maṇḍala* and *yantra*, indispensable in Tāntric rituals, remind one of the pictoral writing of the Chinese alphabet.

(v) Like the central idea of Śiva-Śakti in Tantra, there is the pivotal concept of *yang* (male principle) and *yin* (female principle), according to the Taoist doctrine of China. For reaching the highest place of mundane existence, respiratory exercise and disciplined sexual intercourse are among the practices, recommended in Taoism as well as in Tāntrism.

H.P. Sastri (in *Nepal Catalogue*, p. lxxix), on the basis of the following verse in the *Kubjikā-mata-tantra*, believes in the foreign provenance of Tantra:

gaccha tvaṁ bhārate varṣe adhikārāya sarvataḥ ।
pīṭhe pīṭhe kṣetre'smin kuru sṛṣṭimanekadhā ॥

According to him, the conception of Śakti, the worship of which plays a very important role in Tantra, was borrowed from Western Asia from where it was brought by the Magi priests of the Scythians.

Woodroffe (Avalon) thinks (*Mahā-nirvāṇa Tantra*, third edn. by him, p. 560) that there was influx of Tantra into India from ancient Chaldea, the region around which, as he believes, was the Śākadvīpa of the Indian tradition.

According to a Tāntric tradition, Tāntric principles and practices were introduced into India by the Buddhist philosopher, Asaṅga who flourished in the fourth or fifth century AD. P.V. Kane does not attach importance to this tradition as it is based mainly on *History of Buddhism* by Tāranātha (b. 1573 or 1575) who flourished over one thousand years after Asaṅga.

There are also other theories about the foreign origin of Tantra. The curious reader may look up the present writer's *A Brief History of Tantra Literature,* p. 67 ff.

Contents of Tantras

The contents of a complete Tāntric work are broadly divided as:

1. *Jñāna* or *Vidyā*,
2. *Yoga* or *Upāya*
3. *Kriyā* (instructions for making idols and constructing and consecrating temples), and
4. *Caryā* (rules about rites, festivals and social duties).

The contents of Tantra literature fall into two broad categories; one philosophical and spiritual and the other popular and practical.

The latter includes magic, *mantra* (incantations, charms and spells), *mudrā* (different postures of hands and fingers), *maṇḍala* and *yantra* (mystic diagrams used in Tāntric rituals), *nyāsa* (a part of Tāntric ritual, in which deities are conceived to be placed or felt in different limbs of the body of the worshipper). The chief magical practices, called *ṣaṭ-karma*, are *māraṇa* (killing), *stambhana* (causing paralysis), *uccāṭana* (expulsion), *vaśīkaraṇa* (bringing a hostile person under control), and *vidveṣaṇe* (causing and hatred *śānti* (propitiation or pacification). *Maraṇa*, etc., designed to cause harm to others, are known as *abhicāra* (black magic).

The principal aim of Tāntric *sādhanā* is liberation from the bondage of rebirths, and the acquisition of *siddhi*s (mystic or supernatural powers) which are as follows:

aṇimā — assuming a very small form,
laghimā — making the body very light,
mahimā — increasing one's size at will,
prāpti — power of obtaining anything,
prākāmya — irresistible will,
īśitva — overlordship,
vaśitva — bringing others under control,
kāmāvasāyitā — suppression of passion.

It should be noted that Tantra believes in the salvation not only of the disembodied soul after death, but also in *jīvanmukti* (liberation of the embodied soul while one is alive).

Importance of the Human Body

Tantra sets much store by the body which is looked upon as a microcosm or the replica of the universe.

KOŚA

The body is supposed to contain five sheaths (*kośa*s) which are as follows:

annamaya — made of food,
prāṇamaya — consisting of vital breath,
manomaya — made of mind,
vijñānamaya — consisting of special consciousness, and
ānandamaya — consisting of joy.

NĀḌĪ

The body is believed to contain a number of *nāḍī*s or arteries and veins. The most prominent of them are *iḍā*, *piṅgalā* and *suṣumnā* (See *Prāṇatoṣiṇī*, I.4; Rāghavabhaṭṭa's commentary on *Śāradātilaka*, XXV.38). *Iḍā* is on the left of the spinal cord, and *piṅgalā* is on the right. The central *nāḍī*, called *suṣumnā*, is the longest; it extends from the *mūlādhāra* (see *infra*) right up to *brahmarandhra* (see *infra*).

CAKRA

Human body is believed to contain six *cakra*s (circles or nerve-plexuses). These are as follows:

1. *Mūlādhāra*: In the lowest part of the spinal cord, shaped like a triangle with its apex downward. It resembles a red lotus with four petals.
2. *Svādhiṣṭhāna*: Above the *mūlādhāra*, but below the navel. It is like a lotus with six petals.
3. *Maṇipūra*: In the navel, and like a lotus with ten petals.
4. *Anāhata*: In the region of the heart and like a deep red lotus with 12 petals.
5. *Viśuddha*: In the region of the neck. Grey in colour and like a lotus of 16 petals.
6. *Ājñā*: In-between the eyebrows. White and like a lotus with two petals.

KUṆḌALINĪ

It is the symbol of vital energy, conceived as a serpent coiling round the *mūlādhāra*, mentioned above.

TĀNTRIC PHILOSOPHY AND SĀDHANĀ

Śiva or *Brahman* and Śakti (also called *prakṛti*) are the male and female principles underlying creation. Śakti resides in the *mūlādhāra* in the form of *kuṇḍalinī*. The highest aim of a Tāntric devotee is the rousing of *kuṇḍalinī* and raising it through *suṣumnā nāḍī*, mentioned earlier, so that it can penetrate the aforesaid six *cakra*s and unite with Śiva, supposed to reside in the *sahasrāra*-

padma (thousand-petalled lotus) which is believed to exist in the *brahmarandhra* (an aperture in the crown of the head, through which the soul or vital breath is supposed to quit the body at death).

The means of Tāntrika *sādhanā* are the following: *madya* (wine), *māṁsa* (meat), *matsya* (fish), *mudrā* (posture of finger or hand) and *maithuna* (sexual intercourse). These five are collectively called *pañca-makāra* or *pañca-tattva.*

ŚAVA-SĀDHANĀ

Some Tantras, notably *Kaulāvalī-nirṇaya* (XIV.75-260), *Tārābhakti-sudhārṇava* (IX. p. 345 ff) and *Kulacūḍāmaṇi* (VI.19-28), etc., deal with it. Among the Tantras of Bengal, the *Tantrasāra* of Kr̥ṣṇānanda (sixteenth century) describes it.

It means rituals to be performed by a devotee seated on a corpse. According to the aforesaid *Kaulāvalī*, this *sādhanā* should be performed at a funeral place or a lonely spot after the first watch of the night. The dead body should be of a young handsome warrior, killed (not by the devotee concerned) in a battle.

WAYS TO LIBERATION

According to the *Pārānanda-sūtra* (published by Gaekwad Oriental Series, pp. 1-3, 13), the following are the three paths for the attainment of the goal:

(i) *Dakṣiṇa* — prescribed in the Vedas, Smr̥tis and Purāṇas.

(ii) *Vāma* — prescribed in the Āgamas. It is so-called either because woman (*vāmā*) plays a significant role in it or because it is a crooked way practised secretly.

It is of two kinds, namely *madhyama* in which all the five *makāras*, stated above, are resorted to, and *uttama* in which only *madya*, *maithuna* and *mudrā* are used.

(iii) *Uttara* — shown by the Vedic injunction and the *guru* who is *jīvanmukta* (liberated while alive).

The *Kulārṇava* (II.7-8) mentions six paths, namely *vaiṣṇava*, *śaiva*, *dakṣina*, *vāma*, *siddhānta* and *kaula*; each succeeding is regarded as higher than the preceding one. Of these, *kaula* is prescribed for an aspirant of *divyabhāva* (divine propensities), *siddhānta* for one with *vīrabhāva* (heroic mindest); the remaining four for a devotee with *paśubhāva* (animality).

JĪVANMUKTI

Tantra recognises liberation of one while alive. For instance, the *Pārānanda* (p. 9, *sūtras* 3-8) holds that a person, liberated in this life, visualises the diety worshipped and is not affected by *karman*, pious or sinful.

Bhakti in Tantra

It is well-known that the Vaiṣṇava works, particularly the *Bhāgavata* (*c.* fifth or sixth century AD) lays (VII. 5.23-4) stress on the following ninefold *bhakti* (devotion) towards Viṣṇu:

> *śravaṇa* (hearing), *kīrtana* (reciting names), *smaraṇa* (remembrance), *pāda-sevana* (shampooing the feet), *arcana* (worship), *vandana* (salutation), *dāsya* (service), *sakhya* (friendship) and *ātma-nivedana* (self-surrender).

Some Tantras also recognise *bhakti*, but omits Viṣṇu, mentioned in the *Bhāgavata* in this connection. For instance, the *Rudrayāmala Tantra* (XXVII.103-4) mentions nine modes of *bhakti* with *manana* for *śravaṇa*, *dhyāna* for *sakhya*. Of the means to the goal, *bhakti* is accorded the highest position in the *Pārānanda-sūtra* (pp. 6-7, *sūtra*s 35, 38, 59). It goes so far as to declare *bhakti* as the sole means for those who desire enjoyment, heaven and salvation (*bhoga-svargāpavarga-kāṁkṣiṇāṁ bhaktireva ekaḥ panthāḥ*).

Guru, Śiṣya, Dīkṣā

Tantra accords a very exalted position to *guru*. One can take to *sādhanā* only when initiated by the *guru* who will decide the suitability of a *mantra* for a particular disciple. A female *guru* is highly suitable. One's mother is one's best *guru*. To be a *guru* one must be versed in *śāstra*s, calm in mind, free from avarice, truthful and of spotless character.

A disciple must be respectful and look upon the *guru*, *devatā* and *mantra* as one. He must keep secret the *mantra* and *pūjā*, taught by the *guru*.

Dīkṣā or initiation is regarded as so important that *tāntrika sādhanā* is not possible without it. It is broadly of two kinds, namely:

(i) *Bahirdīkṣā* — consisting of *pūjā*, *homa* and other external rites.

(ii) *Antardīkṣā*—it helps in awakening of *kuṇḍalinī*, described earlier.

Dīkṣā has been divided into some other kinds in different works.

Kālī in Tantra

In the Tāntric pantheon, Kālī has a very prominent place. She is the most popular deity in Bengal (West Bengal and Bangladesh taken together). Kālī is worshipped by a large number of people both publicly and in private houses. In many houses, images of Kālī are established permanently and worshipped daily. Brahmānanda (sixteenth century AD) Pūrṇānanda (b. AD 1501) Sarvānanda (b. *c.* AD 1400), Rāmprasād (*c.* AD 1720-89), Kamalākānta (AD 1772-1821), Rāmakṛṣṇa Paramahaṁsa (AD 1836-86) and Vivekānanda (AD 1863-1902) were some of the renowned Bengālī devotees of Kālī.

Of the several *śākta pīṭhas* of Bengal, Kālīghāṭ in Calcutta is very old, and has been attracting people for centuries. The Bengālī poet, Mukundarāma (sixteenth century AD) appears to be the earliest writer to refer to this Kālī image in his *Caṇḍī-maṅgala*. The earliest reference to Kālī-worship in Bangal in the *Dīvālī* night occurs in the *Śyāmā-saparyā-vidhi* (AD 1777) of Kāśīnātha.

The designations of various kinds of Kālī image, mentioned in Tantras of Bengal, are:

Ādya-kālī, Bhadra-kālī, Dakṣiṇa-kālī, Guhya-kālī, Rakṣā-kālī (or Mahā-kālī) and Siddha-kālī.

Why is Kālī so-called? Not because she is represented as dark in complexion. According to the *Mahānirvāṇa Tantra* (VI.32

Varṅgavāsī, edn., Calcutta) she is so-called as she devours time (*kāla-saṁgrasanāt*); that is she is beyond time, present, past and future. According to the same work (XII.2-13), as all other colours completely merge into black, so also all creatures fully merge in the goddess.

Tantra *vis-a-vis* Dharmaśāstra

In comparison with traditional Dharmaśāstra or Smṛti, Tantra is rational and liberal in outlook. Smṛti strongly advocates the caste-system with all its rigidities; the śūdras have been relegated to a despicable position, almost to that of sub-human species. They have no right to religious practices, their only occupation being the service of the members of the three upper castes. But, they have been given the right to Tāntric initiation like one of any other caste. A śūdra, who has undergone *pūrṇābhiṣeka* (full *abhiṣeka* or consecration), can worship *śālagrāma* (a holy stone worshipped as the symbol of Nārāyaṇa) which can be saluted even by a brāhmaṇa. Such a śūdra is entitled to recite *praṇava* (i.e., *oṁkāra*) which is a taboo for śūdras in general. An *avadhūta* (a Tāntric devotee of a very high order) of any caste is worthy of being saluted even by a brāhmaṇa.

In Dharmaśāstra, women are generally discriminated against in comparison with men. For example, while men enjoy unfettered right in rites and rituals, Manu ordains (V.155) that women have no independent right to perform sacrifices, observe vows, even fast; they attain heaven simply by serving their husbands.

Tantra, however, accords an exalted position to women. A female *guru* has been declared as preferable to a male. One's mother is the best person to impart Tāntric initiation (*dīkṣā*) to her son. For Tāntric *sādhanā*, a man must have a woman, preferably his wife, as his partner; such a woman is called *śakti*.

The worship of virgin girls of a certain age and possessed of certain qualities is a must in certain important Tāntric rituals as also in *Durgāpūjā*. Girls of any caste, even a casteless cāṇḍāla girl, with requisite qualities, can be worshipped even by a brāhmaṇa who can take her *prasāda* or remnants of food.

Tantra Beyond India

The rational and liberal outlook of Tantra made it popular not only in India, but also in some foreign countries. Tibet, for example, was imbued with Tāntric influence. Several Tāntric scholars from Bengal went to Tibet, settled there and wrote many treatise on Tantra; these works are lost; their Tibetan versions exist in the works, *Tanjur* and *Kanjur* of that land. Of such Bengālī scholars, the most renowned was Dīpaṁkara Śrījñāna Atīśa who flourished towards the close of the tenth century AD.

Nepal is another country where Tantra produced a great impact.

Among the countries of south-east Asia, Cambodia appears to have been deeply influenced by Tantra. There is epigraphical evidence testifying to the introduction of at least the following four Tantras into Cambodia:

Śiraścheda, *Vināśikha*, *Sammoha* and *Nayottara*

Importance of Tantra

While Dharmaśāstra was confined to the elites, Tantra influenced people down to the grassroot level. Hordes of people welcomed Tāntric *dīkṣā*, and took to some Tāntric rituals. Tantra laid more stress on *antaryāga* (mental worship) and *cittaśuddhi* (purification of mind) than on the external formalities of religious practices. Instead of self-mortification, taught in the conventional Brāhmaṇical Śāstra, Tanta preached the principle of *mukti* (liberation) through *bhukti* (enjoyment), and did not advocate the repression of natural human propensities. It did away with the narrow caste-restrictions in the observance of Tāntric rituals.

All this gave a humane face to Tāntrism.

It is noteworthy that Tantra developed a system of medical treatment of diseases of children, men and women. The following are some of the noteworthy Tantras dealing with the healing of maladies. The drugs prescribed are mostly herbal, and, in some cases, chemical. The body being considered essential for Tāntric *sādhanā*, various drugs were prescribed for the preservation of youth and virility. There are medicines for rejuvenation and destroying the effects of various kinds of poison. The Tāntric Rasa school played an important role in the society.

Tantra gave rise to the Sahajiyā cult in which love of humanity and easier ways of worship were the essence.

The popularity of Tantra compelled the orthodox Brāhmaṇical Śāstra to incorporate Tāntric practices. For instance, the Tāntric concepts of *maṇḍala*, *mudrā*, *yantra*, the mystic *bīja-mantras* like *hrīṁ*, *krīm*, *kumārī-pūjā*, etc., crept into the traditional works of the brāhmaṇas. The great social reformer of Bengal, Raghunandana (sixteenth century), who was a staunch brāhmaṇa, for the first time recognised Tāntric initiation in the above province.

Buddhism was deeply influenced by Tantra. Many Tāntric works were written by Buddhists. The *Guhya-samāja*, *Hevajra*, *Sādhanamālā*, *Prajñopāya-viniścaya-siddhi* are some of the noted works on Buddhist Tantra.

There is hardly any religion or religious sect, major or minor, which has not been influenced by Tantra in some way or other. The Śaiva Tantras of Kashmir have earned the acclaim of the specialists. The Śaiva Siddhānta of south India bears the indelible impress of Tantra.

The Pañcarātra works of the Vaiṣṇavas reveal a close relation with *Śākta Tantra*. The *Bhāgavata Purāṇa*, the *Bible* of the Vaiṣṇavas, acknowledges (e.g., XI.3.47, 5.28, 31, etc.) authority of Tantra in matters concerning worship, initiation, etc. Śrīdharasvāmin, in his commentary on a passage of the above Purāṇa, refers to Tāntric authority on both *bhukti* and *mukti*. The highly authoritative Vaiṣṇava treatises of Bengal, by Rūpa and Jīva Gosvāmins, are replete with references to and quotations from Tantras. (For details, see S.K. De, *Vaiṣṇava Faith and Movement*, 1961, pp. 418-19).

Tantra inspired quite a lot of works in different vernaculars of India. For instance, the Nātha *sāhitya* of Bengal is renowned.

Not only literatue, art and architecture also were considerably influenced by Tantra. There are many images of various Tāntric deities, particularly of Kālī in her different forms. Many temple sculptures, particularly of Orissa and south India, show an abundance of Tāntric motifs. The Haṁseśvarī temple (completed in AD 1814) at Bānsberiā in the Hoogly district of West Bengal shows the influence of Tantra on architecture. The interior of the temple is like the six Tāntric *cakras*, mentioned above, through which *kuṇḍalinī*, represented by goddess Haṁseśvarī, goes upward. The Tāntric nerves (*nāḍī*) are indicated within the temple by ladders. The above goddess is seated on a lotus which rests on a stem emerging from the navel of Śiva lying on a *Trikoṇa-yantra*. The goddess has a human skull in her lower left hand, and *abhaya mudrā* in her upper right hand, while, in her other hands, there are a sword and a conch-shell.

There are paintings galore of Kālī and other Tāntric deities as also of *maṇḍalas*, *mudrās*, *yantras*, *kuṇḍalinī*, etc.

Degeneration of Tantra

In course of time, among some people, particularly of the lower echelons of the society, Tāntric practices degenerated into immoral behaviour. Under the cover of religion, they became excessively self-indulgent. Excessive drinking and promiscuous sexual unions marked their so-called rituals. As too much importance was attached to the *guru*, he often turned to be an extortionist. *Gurus* being hereditary even the worthless and avaricious son of a *guru* exploited his disciples only to fleece them and fill his own pocket.

The following line betrays the attitude of a Tāntric devotee turned an epicure

> *vāme rāmā ramaṇakuśalā dakṣiṇe pāna-pātram-*

> on the left, a woman expert in sexual intercourse, on the right a decanter. This reminds one of Omar Khaiyām with *surā* (wine) and *śākī*, his beloved woman.

7

Darśana-śāstra (Philosophy)

Introductory remarks

THE germs of Indian philosophy are found in the *Ṛgveda*. For example, in the Hymn of Creation (X.129), there is speculation about the beginning of creation. The Vedic seer appears to be groping for the correct answer to the question — what was there in the beginning? The groping is indicated by his contradictory statements, e.g., there was neither the non-existent nor the existent; there was neither death nor immortality. Again, in stanza 7, it is stated thus — he who in the highest heaven is its surveyor, he only knows or else he knows not.

In the funeral hymn (X.11.1-6) it is stated that, after death, one gets a life as deserved as a result of his deeds in the mundane existence. This testifies to the belief in the existence of soul and its transmigration; an ethical idea is also there. In X.14, the wish is expressed that the soul of the deceased may be united with that of his forbears.

Indra was regarded as the mightiest god in the Ṛgvedic pantheon. But, in this very Veda, doubt arose in the mind of some people about the power, even the very existence of Indra. In II.12, the sage appears to be anxious to impress upon the sceptics by emphatically asserting *sa janāsa indraḥ* (he, O men, is Indra) which is the refrain of the stanzas of this hymn. Stanza 5 urges these people to have faith in Indra (*śrad asmai dhatta*). The scepticism of the unbelievers is clear from the lines *yaṁ smā pṛcchanti kuha seti ghoram, utemāhur-naiṣo astītyenam* ।

The terrible one about whom they say — where is he, he is not.

In VIII.100.3f, the priests are urged to offer an eulogistic song in honour of Indra if He really exists (*yadi satyam asti*).

In the polytheistic milieu of the *Ṛgveda*, a philosophic doubt about the plurality of gods is articulated in X.121 where the refrain of each stanza is *kasmai devāya haviṣā vidhema* (barring Prajāpati) to which deity shall we offer sacrifice? A monotheistic tendency is implied in it.

Stanza 46 of the hymn I.164 declares:

ekaṁ sad viprā bahudhā vadanti,
agniṁ yamaṁ mātariśvānamāhuḥ ।

The brāhmaṇas variously designate the only existent one as Agni, Yama and Mātariśvan. Here, the sole reality appears to foreshadow the Upaniṣadic *Brahman*, the one and only one.

According to some, the *Puruṣa-sūkta* (X.90) of the *Ṛgveda* contains elements of what was later known as Sāṁkhya philosophy. To quote Radhakrishnan,

> The whole world according to it (i.e., *Puruṣa-sūkta*) is due to the self-diremption of the Absolute into subject and object, *puruṣa* and *prakṛti*
>
> — *Indian Philosophy*, I, p. 105

The Ṛgvedic *puruṣa* re-appears in Sāṁkhya in a modified form.

Elements of philosophy occur also in the *Yujurveda* (*Vājasaneyī Saṁhitā*, section XXXI). It is stated that the world originated through the sacrificing of the *puruṣa*, the Highest Being with whom the world is identified.

The *Atharvaveda* (X.2, XI.8) appears to contain the idea that man, as *Brahman*, has become what he is, and acquired all his power.

The Āraṇyakas (forest texts) and Upaniṣads (esoteric texts), originally forming parts of the works, called *Brāhmaṇas* which followed the Vedic Saṁhitās, contain clearer philosophical ideas. *Brahman*, as the Supreme Being, identified with the individual and universal soul, emerges in a more prominent perspective.

The independent Upaniṣadic texts, of which the ten, called *Īśa*, *Kena*, *Kaṭha*, *Praśna*, *Muṇḍaka*, *Māṇḍūkya*, *Taittirīya*, *Aitareya*, *Chāndogya* and *Bṛhadāraṇyaka*, commented upon by Śaṅkarācārya, dating back approximately to a period between 1000 and 300 BC, are regarded as authentic and most authoritative. These texts contain ideas which were later developed in orthodox philosophy.

There are six systems of orthodox philosophy, viz., Sāṁkhya, Yoga, Nyāya, Vaiśeṣika, Mīmāṁsā (also called Pūrva Mīmāṁsā) and Vedānta (also called Uttara Mīmāṁsā). We shall briefly describe the literature of each of the above systems.

Works on Orthodox Systems of Philosophy

SĀṀKHYA

Ideas of Sāṁkhya are scattered in the Upaniṣads. For instance, in the *Kaṭha Upaniṣad* (I.3.10-11) there is reference to the *avyakta* (i.e., *prakṛti*) and *puruṣa*; this dual principle is the pivot round which Sāṁkhya philosophy revolves. The *Praśna Upaniṣad* (IV.8) declares that all objects are resolved into the imperishable in the order of the five gross elements (*pañca-mahābhūtas*) with their respective subtle elements (*tanmātras*). The last two, as we shall see later on, are the final evolutes according to Sāṁkhya. The *Bṛhadāraṇyaka Upaniṣad* (II.4.14; III.4.2, IV.3.15) seems to foreshadow the Sāṁkhyaite idea that true knowledge is the means to liberation. It may be noted that, in the *Śvetāśvatara Upaniṣad* (VI.13), the term 'Sāṁkhya' means true knowledge which Sāṁkhya philosophy advocates. The same Upaniṣad mentions (I.4) three *guṇas* which came to be called *sattva*, *rajas* and *tamas*.

We do not know when Sāṁkhya, as a distinct philosophical system, originated. Tradition ascribes a *Sāṁkhyasūtra*, believed to have been the earliest work on systematic Sāṁkhya, to sage Kapila of unknown date and identity. It is also said that, as this work was too short and terse, the sage wrote also a work entitled *Sāṁkhya-pravacana-sūtra*.

The earliest available work on this system is the *Sāṁkhya-kārikā*, attributed to Īśvara-kṛṣṇa whose precise date is unknown; he, however, came to be regarded as the greatest exponent of Sāṁkhya since the fifth century AD. The above work, in its present form, contains 71 memorial verses in *āryā* metre. It is also called *Sāṁkhya-saptatī*; in Chinese, it is entitled *Suvarṇa-saptatī*. Both the alternative titles suggest that it contained 70 verses.

The other noteworthy works are *Sāṁkhyakārikā-bhāṣya* of Gauḍapāda (fifth-sixth century AD, according to some, seventh-eighth century according to others) who commented on 69 verses omitting the last two; *Tattvakaumudī* of Vācaspati (ninth century AD) — a commentary on the *Sāṁkhyakārikā*; *Sāṁkhyapravacana-bhāṣya* and *Sāṁkhyasāra* of Vijñānabhikṣu (*c.* sixteenth century AD).

YOGA

Some ideas of this system appear in the Veda. For instance, *Ṛgveda* V.81.1 speaks of the concentration of mind which is a fundamental theme of Yoga philosophy. The term *yoga* occurs in some Upaniṣads (e.g., *Kaṭha*, II.3.11.18.3; *Taittirīya* II.4, etc.). Some of the Yogāṅgas, mentioned in the *Yogasūtra*, are found in certain Upaniṣads. For example, the *Śvetāśvatara* mentions *āsana* and *prāṇāyāma*. The word *dhyāna-yoga* occurs in it (I.3). It is clear from the *Āpastamba-dharmasūtra* (I.8.23.3-6), which perhaps dates back to a period between the seventh century BC and the fourth, that *yoga*, as a means of mental discipline, developed to a great extent. The Buddha (*c.* 563-483 BC) is known to have practised *yoga*.

The first systematic work on Yoga philosophy is the *Yogasūtra*, attributed to Patañjali; hence, it is also called *Pātañjala-sūtra*. The author is identified, by some scholars, with Patañjali, author of the *Mahābhāṣya* (*c.* second century BC) commentary on Pāṇini's grammar. The celebrated commentary on it is the *Yogabhāṣya*, also known as *Vyāsabhāṣya*, by Vyāsa. Two popular works are Bhoja's *Vṛtti* and *Yogamaṇi-prabhā*. Well-known manuals of the Yoga philosophy are the *Yoga-vārttika* and *Yogasāra-saṁgraha* of Vijñānabhikṣu (*c.* sixteenth century AD).

Yoga and Sāṁkhya are regarded not as two distinct systems of philosophy, but two aspects of the same system. In other words, one is considered to be complementary to the other. While Sāṁkhya represents the theory, Yoga prescribes the practice. The former ordains *viveka-jñāna* as the means to the goal, the latter teaches the methods of attaining that. According to the *Bhagavad Gītā* (V.4), it is naive to regard these two as separate from each other.

NYĀYA

Nyāya or logic is the *sine qua non* for ascertaining the truth. Therefore, a methodology of argumentation developed in early times to get at the truth. Some of the Upaniṣads, which date back to a period long before Christ, mention assemblies for debates and disputations on matters philosophical and theological. In this connection, mention may be made of the *Chāndogya*, V.3.1, *Bṛhadāraṇyaka*, VI.2.1 and *Praśna*, I.6. The *Chāndogya*, VII.1.2 mentions *Vākovākya* which means *Tarkaśāstra* or the science of logic, it is also called *Ānvīkṣikī*. Debating assemblies are mentioned also in Buddhist literature, e.g., Parivāra of *Vinayapiṭaka*. The Jaina *Āgamas* testify to the prevalence of logical methods in remote antiquity.

We know of the adoption of logical methods in ancient Greece for ascertaining the truth. For instance, we may refer to Socrates (d., 399 BC) and Plato (d., 347 BC). The Greek intellectuals adopted the mode of disputation, called Dialectic consisting of questions and answers. Methods of argumentation and disputation can be known from Plato's *Dialogue*, Aristotle's (d., 322 BC) *Topics* and *Sophisticate Refutations*.

Though logical discussions and debates were current in ancient times, yet no systematic work on the methodology of argumentation appears to have originated before the *Nyāyasūtra*, attributed to Gotama (also called Gautama and Akṣapāda) of *c.* sixth century BC. Its celebrated commentator was Pakṣilasvāmin Vātsyāyana (*c.* fourth century AD) who is to be distinguished from Mallanāga Vātsyāyana (*c.* third or fourth century AD), the celebrated author of the *Kāmasūtra*.

The writers on Nyāya are broadly divided into two schools, viz., Prācīna (old) and Navya (new).

Among the works of the old school, besides the above *Nyāyasūtra*, the following are prominent:

> *Nyāyavārttika* of Uddyotakara (c. seventh century, first half),
>
> *Nyāyavārttika-tātparya-ṭīkā* of Vācaspati Miśra (c. fifteenth century, middle)
>
> (*Nyāya*)*Kusumāñjali* and *Nyāyavārttika-tātparya-pariśuddhi* of Udayana (c. eleventh century, last quarter),
>
> *Nyāyamañjarī* of Jayanta.

The school of Navya-Nyāya which appears to have originated in Mithilā, gave rise to the renowned Gauḍīya or Bengal school of Navya-Nyāya. It should be noted that the fundamental difference between Prācīna Nyāya and Navya-Nyāya is that while the former is concerned with *padārtha*s (substances), the latter discusses *pramāṇa*s (means of valid knowledge).

With the *Tattvacintāmaṇi* of Gaṅgeśa (thirteenth-fourteenth century AD) of Mithilā, we get the definitive period of Navya-Nyāya in that land. The formative period may be said to have started with Udayana though he is usually regarded as belonging to the school of Prācīna Nyāya. Some of the writers of the pre-Gaṅgeśa and post-Gaṅgeśa periods have also left evidence of their scholarship in this field.

The exposition, of the highly scholastic *Tattvacintāmaṇi*, led to the foundation of Navya-Nyāya in Navadvīpa (now in West Bengal). The greatest exponent of this school was Raghunātha Śiromaṇi (sometime between fifteenth and sixteenth centuries). His *Tattvacintāmaṇidīdhiti* stands as a monument to his enormous erudition and intellect of a very high order. This work led several writers to produce learned lucubrations.

The entire system of Navya-Nyāya is an elaboration of the follwoing 16 philosophical topics (*vide Nyāyasūtra* and *Bhāṣya* 1.1.1, 1.2.20):

1. *Pramāṇa*s — valid means of knowledge.
2. *Prameya* — object of true knowledge.

3. *Saṁśaya* — doubt.
4. *Prayojana* — necessity.
5. *Dṛṣṭānta* — example.
6. *Siddhānta* — doctrine accepted as true.
7. *Avayava* — a member of syllogism.
8. *Tarka* — hypothetical argument.
9. *Nirṇaya* — certain knowledge of a thing.
10. *Vāda* — discussion aimed at ascertaining the truth.
11. *Jalpa* — wrangling intended only for defeating the opponent, not for ascertaining the truth.
12. *Vitaṇḍā* — debate solely for refuting the view of the opponent without establishing one's own view.
13. *Hetvābhāsa* — fallacy of inference.
14. *Chala* — quibble in which one tries to contradict a statement by taking it in a sense other than the intended one. For example, one utters the word *nava* to mean new, but another takes it in the sense of nine.
15. *Jāti* — evasive and shifty answer to an argument.
16. *Nigrahasthāna* — ground of defeat in a debate.

VAIŚEṢIKA

It is so-called as it discusses, *inter alia*, *Viśeṣa* as a category of knowledge. The earliest work on this system is the *Vaiśeṣikasūtra*, attributed to Kaṇāda, also called Kaṇabhakṣa, Kaṇabhuk, Kaśyapa, Ulūka or Aulūkya. According to some scholars, he was a contemporary of the Buddha. The *Padārtha-dharma-saṁgraha* of Praśastapāda (about the end of the fourth century AD, according to Radhakrishnan) generally regarded as a commentary on the *Vaiśeṣikasūtra*, is like an independent exposition of this system of philosophy.

Nyāya and Vaiśeṣika are allied in some respects, viz. (i) ultimate goal is the liberation of the individual self, (ii) ignorance is the root of all suffering, (iii) atomic theory of the universe. Besides, both recognise the same nature and qualities of the self.

The fundamental difference between the two systems is this. While Nyāya recognises 16 *padārthas*, mentioned earlier, Vaiśeṣika admits the following seven only: *dravya* (substance), *guṇa* (quality), *karma* (action), *sāmānya* (generality), *viśeṣa* (particularity), *samavāya* (relation of inherence) and *abhāva* (non-existence).

There are some works which combine Nyāya and Vaiśeṣika. Of them, prominent are the following:

Saptapadārthī of Śivāditya (twelfth century), *Tarkakaumudī* of Laugākṣī Bhāskara (*c.* fourteenth and fifteenth century), *Nyāyalīlāvatī* of Vallabhācārya (AD 1376-1430), *Kārikāvalī* or *Bhāṣāpariccheda* with its commentary *Siddhāntamuktāvalī* both by Viśvanātha (seventeenth century according to some, the latter by Kṛṣṇadāsa Sārvabhauma, according to others). (*vide* D.C. Bhattacharya in his *Vāṅgālīr Sārasvata Avadāna*, Pt. I, *Vaṅge Navya-Nyāyacarcā*, p. 117).

MĪMĀṀSĀ

The term generally means settlement of a dispute. This system originated out of the need for resolving the problems of interpretation of Vedic injunctions relating to rituals. It is also called Pūrva Mīmaṁsā as distinguished from Uttara Mīmāṁsā or Vedānta. This philosophical system developed on the lines, viz. (i) methodology of interpretation, and (ii) philosophical justification of the faith on which ritualism was based.

The founder of this school was Jaimini (*c.* fourth century BC) to whom is attributed the *Mīmāṁsāsūtra*. Śabarasvāmin (*c.* sometime between AD 100 and 300) appears to have been the earliest commentator of this work. There are many other commentaries on this work. Also available are some other works like epitomes or of an introductory nature of which the notable ones are the *Mīmāṁsā-nyāya-prakāśa*, also called *Āpadevī* (*c.* seventeenth century, early part) and the *Mānameyodaya* (*c.* AD 1600). Of the *Mānameyodaya*, the *māna* (i.e., *pramāṇa*) section is believed to have been written by Nārāyaṇa Bhaṭṭa and the *meya* (i.e., *prameya*) section by Nārāyaṇa

Paṇḍita.

In course of time, two schools of Mīmāṁsā developed; one founded by Kumārila Bhaṭṭa (*c.* AD 600-60) and popularly known as Bhāṭṭa school, and the other by Prabhākara (also known as *guru* of *c.* sixth-seventh century AD), popularly called Prābhākara school. The *Ślokavārttika* and *Tantravārttika* are the works of the former and the *Bṛhatī* of the latter; all these are commentaries on the *Mīmāṁsā-sūtra*. The main difference between the two schools lies in the fact that while Kumārila rocognises six means of valid knowledge, Prabhākara admits five, as we shall see later in our discussion on epistemology.

VEDĀNTA

It is so-called in the following senses:

(i) It is the last product of the Vedic period.

(ii) Of the Vedic literary works, it is studied last of all.

(iii) It contains the culmination of the Vedic thought.

The earliest stage of Vedānta philosophy is represented by the Upaniṣads. The term *upaniṣad* is derived from the root *sad* (to sit), preceded by the prefixes *upa* and *ni*, and literally means sitting (of the disciple) near (the preceptor). Thus, the Upaniṣads came to represent a particular type of esoteric teachings. The central theme of the Upaniṣads is — the universe is *Brahman* and *Brahman* is *ātman*. There were many Upaniṣads containing diverse strands of thought, different problems and their solutions.

As in the case of other systems of philosophy, so also in the present case, the need was felt for systematising the Upaniṣadic thoughts. As a result, the *Brahma-sūtra* (also called *Vedānta-sūtra*, *Śārīraka-sūtra*, *Śārīraka Mīmāṁsā*, *Uttara-mīmāṁsā*) came into existence. It is attributed to Bādarāyaṇa who is assigned to a period between 500 and 200 BC by some scholars. According to others, the *terminus ad quem* is AD 200.

Like the other *sūtra* works, it also necessitated exposition. As a philosophy of life, not dealing with the nitty-gritty of rituals or niceties of the interpretation of Vedic texts, this system become very popular. Naturally, the *Brahma-sūtra* was commented upon by a number of scholars of whom very eminent were Śaṅkarācārya (eighth-ninth century AD), Rāmānuja (b., AD 1017), Nimbārka (*c.* eleventh century AD), Madhva (b., AD 1197 or AD 1199) and Vallabhācārya (AD 1376-1430). Each of them had his independent opinion, and thus became the founder of a distinct school. The schools, founded by them, were respectively known as *Advaita-vāda* (non-dualism), *Viśiṣṭādvaita-vāda* (qualified monism), *Dvaitādvaita-vāda* (dualistic non-dualism), *Dvaita-vāda* (dualism), and *Śuddhādvaita-vāda* (pure monism). The main point of difference among the above schools lies in the conception of the relation between *jīva* (individual soul) and *Brahman* (universal soul).

In course of time, at least five other schools arose (*vide* Rama Chaudhuri, *Ten Schools of Vedānta*, Calcutta, Pt. I, 1973, Pt. II, 1975, Pt. III, 1981).

Among other works on Vedānta the *Pañcadaśī* is a classic of later *Advaita-vedānta*. It is written in 15 chapters of which the first six are said to have been written by Vidyāraṇya and the rest by Bhāratītīrtha. According to another scholar, the first ten chapters were by Vidyāraṇya and the rest by Bhāratītīrtha.

Of the epitomes or manuals of Vedānta, noteworthy are the following:

Vedānta-dīpa of Rāmānuja who summarises in it his *Śrībhāṣya* commentary on the *Vedānta-sūtra*;

Vedānta-kāmadhenu (also called *Siddhānta-ratna*, and *Vedānta-siddhānta-sāra-daśaślokī*) of Nimbārka;

Vedānta-paribhāṣā of Dharmarāja;

Vedanta-sāra

(i) By Rāmānuja;

(ii) By Sadānanda

Contents of Orthodox Philosophical Systems

We shall give a resume, under important heads, of the contents of the six philosophical systems described earlier.

Epistemology

SĀṀKHYA

It admits, as sources of valid knowledge, perception (*pratyakṣa*), inference (*anumāna)* and verbal testimony (*śabda* or *āptavacana*, i.e., Vedic authority).

YOGA

It agrees with Sāṁkhya in this respect.

NYĀYA

Besides the above, this system recognises comparison (*upamāna*).

VAIŚEṢIKA

The four sources of valid knowledge are perception (*pratyakṣa*), inference (*laiṅgika*), recollection (*smṛti*) and intuitive knowledge (*ārṣa-jñāna*). According to this system, besides ordinary perception by which one perceives gross substances, there is Yogic perception which leads to *ātma-pratyakṣa* or cognition of the soul (*Vaiśeṣika-sūtra*, IX.1.11-15). In the Vaiśeṣika view, *upamāna* (q.v.), *aitihya* (tradition) and *śabda* (q.v.) are included in inference (*Padārtha-dharma-saṁgraha*, p. 212 ff).

MĪMĀṀSA

Besides the four sources, mentioned under Nyāya, it admits two more, viz., *arthāpatti* (postulation) and *anupalabdhi* (non-perception).

Example of arthāpatti

Ostensibly, a man is fasting. But, paradoxically he is getting fat. The contradiction can be explained by postulating that he eats at night beyond the eyes of others.

Example of anupalabdhi

A jar is not on a table. How can one know of its absence? Non-existence, being a negative fact, cannot be perceived. It cannot be inferred; inference is possible if we already have the knowledge of a universal relation between non-preception and non-existence. Thus, for a direct knowledge of the non-existence of jar there, we have to admit *anupalabdhi*.

VEDĀNTA

According to Śaṅkarācārya, the sources of valid knowledge are perception, inference and testimony. Post-Śaṅkara scholars add comparison, implication and negation.

Conception of God

SĀṀKHYA

The Sāṁkhya literature is twofold, viz., classical and non-classical. According to the former, the existence of God need not be presumed. What caused the world to come into existence is not God, but *prakṛti* or nature consisting of the three qualities of *sattva*, *rajas* and *tamas*. It is because of this atheistic attitude that Sāṁkhya has been characterised as *nirīśvara* (godless).

According to later writers, the most eminent of whom is Vijñānabhikṣu, there may not be a Creator-God. It must, however, be admitted that an eternally perfect spirit, or God is the passive onlooker at the world. His very presence (*sannidhi-mātra*) activates *prakṛti* as a magnet moves a piece of iron. Vijñānabhikṣu adds that such a god is supported by both reason and the Vedas.

YOGA

Patañjali prescribes (I.23) *īśvara-praṇidhāna* (contemplation of and devotion to God) as one of the requisites for the attainment of *samādhi*, the final aim of Yoga. According to later commentators and interpreters, God in Yoga philosophy is the perfect eternal spirit, omniscient, omnipotent and omnipresent. He is the Supreme Ruler of this world, and is distinct from all other selves.

NYĀYA

It is theistic. God's grace is regarded as indispensable for true knowledge and attainment of liberation. God, the eternal infinite self, is the creator, preserver and destroyer of the world.

One of the pro-God arguments in this philosophy is this. Every effect has a twofold cause, material and efficient. The phenomenal world is an effect being produced out of the combination of atoms which, therefore, are the material cause. There must be an intelligent organiser to build the world with the atoms. This organiser is the efficient cause, called God.

VAIŚEṢIKA

According to this system, the creation and destruction by God proceed respectively from the creative will and destructive will of the Supreme Lord. God directs Brahmā to create.

MĪMĀṀSĀ

The position of God in this system is rather confusing. Some followers of this philosophy believe in the atomic theory of creation of the world. But, they do not recognise a Creator-God. According to them, the inexorable law of *karman* is believed to regulate the atoms so as to form the world of the type deserved by the souls. This system, however, cannot be called atheistic. According to Max-Müller, the fact that all the schools of Mīmāṁsā recognise the authority of the Vedas. So, it is not proper to say that this system rejects god outright. Some point out that, in Mīmāṁsā, deities are not believed to have existence anywhere except in the Vedic *mantras* describing them (*vide Introduction* to *Ślokavārttika*, Eng. tr. by Jha).

VEDĀNTA

This system recognises God as immanent and transcendent. According to Śaṅkara, from the empirical standpoint God is omnisceint and ominipotent creator, possessed of qualities. In reality, He is consciousness, infinite and devoid of any quality and distinction. To think of God as possessed of qualities is to limit one who is really limitless. *Māyā* (illusion) may be a predicate of God from the lower point of view. Those, who are possessed of true knowledge, know the world to be unreal, a mere show; as such, it has no real creator.

Ethics

SĀṀKHYA

According to this system, creatures are subject to three kinds of suffering, viz., *ādhyātmika* (physical and mental disorder), *ādhibhautika* (caused by beings like men, animal, etc.) and *ādhidaivika* (produced by supernatural causes). Suffering is believed to be due to *aviveka* or non-discrimination. For escape from pain one has to acquire *viveka-khyāti* or discriminative knowledge. The veil of illusion that conceals our real self is removed by such knowledge as *nāsmi* (I am not), *na me* (nothing is mine); one must feel that the ego is non-existent.

Every individual is possessed of three *guṇas* or qualities, called *sattva*, *rajas* and *tamas* in some degree. The preponderance of the three *guṇas* makes one spiritually advanced, restless and dull respectively. One, desirous of perfection, must gradually increase the quality of *sattva*, and reduce the other two. Sāṁkhya recommends the method of Yoga as the means to the end. It emphasises the necessity of ethical virtues in realising deeper consciousness.

Sāṁkhya reveals originality and rational thinking. It declares (*Sāṁkhya-kārikā*, 2) that the remedy of pain is neither in scriptures nor in the science of medicine. Contrary to tradition, it does not set much store by Vedic rites, because they involve animal sacrifice which militates against the sublime moral principle of *ahiṁsā*. Unlike conventional *dharmaśāstra*, it gives the śūdras the right to higher studies, and recognises, as teachers, not only brāhmaṇas but also those who have freed themselves. Contrary to the traditional acceptance of the existence of God, Sāṁkhya holds an agnostic view.

YOGA

According to this system, the means to the goal is Yoga which, according to Patañjali, is *citta-vṛtti-nirodha*. Plainly speaking, it means the suppression of the mental functions. For this purpose, the following accessories (*yogāṅgas*) have been recommended.

Yama, *niyama*, *āsana* (posture), *prāṇāyāma* (breathing exercise), *pratyāhāra* (withdrawal of senses from their objects), *dhyāna* (meditation), *dhāraṇā* (fixing the mind on the object, e.g., navel, nose-tip), and *samādhi* (absorption of mind in the object of contemplation).

Of these, we are concerned here with *yama* and *niyama* which are ethical. *Yama* consists in abstention from injury to life, falsehood, theft, incontinence and avarice. In connection with *yama*, *ahiṁsā* has been accorded a very exalted position. It means not only abstinence from physical harm, but also the abjuration of the mental attitude of enmity (*vaira-tyāga*). *Ahiṁsā* of *Yoga-śāstra* is universal, and cannot be compromised under any circumstances, whether for religious purpose or maintenance of family custom.

Niyama means the cultivation of the qualities of *śauca* (purification of body and mind), *santoṣa* (contentment), *tapas* (e.g., enduring heat and cold, and practice of austerities), *svādhyāya* (Vedic study), and *īśvara-praṇidhāna* (meditation on and surrender to God).

The practice of *yama* and *niyama* leads to *vairāgya* which consists in the absence of passion or desire for things temporal or for worldly pleasures (*Yogasūtra,* I.15).

The suppression of mental modifications, stated above, depends on *vairāgya* (detachment) and *viveka* (discriminative knowledge).

NYĀYA

According to this system, as interpreted by Vātsyāyana (*Nyāya-bhāṣya*, IV.1.19-21), everything in life does not depend on God; there is scope for human effort (*puruṣakāra*). Man should aim at freedom from pain and not enjoyment of pleasure, because pleasure is mixed with pain. Śrīdhara, however, regards (*Nyāyakandalī*, p. 260) bliss as something positive; mere negation of pain is not pleasure. Pain is caused by attachment (*rāga*), aversion (*dveṣa*) and delusion (*moha*). All of these are the result of false knowledge (*avidyā*) which should be overcome. One should strive for true knowledge which arises from virtuous acts; it also enables one to distinguish between the soul on the one hand, the body and the senses on the other. Meditation and augmentation of righteousness are requisites for the acquisition of true knowledge. Also prescribed are study of the scriptures, philosophic thought and Yogic practices (*Vātsyāyana-bhāṣya*, IV.2.46). Suppression of all desires and abjuration of all worldly pleasures and forest-life have been advised by some authorities. Devotion (*bhakti*) to God is stated to result in peace and happiness. Like other Brāhmaṇical systems, Nyāya also believes in the doctrine of *karman*; the kind of deeds, done in this life, determines the kind of future existence.

VAIŚEṢIKA

Dharma, according to Vaiśeṣika (I.1.2), is that which leads to prosperity (*abhyudaya*) and spiritual well-being or final beatitude (*niḥśreyasa*). Of these two, the former is attainable by ritualistic practices, and the latter by the knowledge of reality (*tattva-jñāna*).

According to this system, the following duties are obligatory for all irrespective of caste and conditions of life:

> *Śraddhā* (faith), *ahiṁsā* (non-violence), *bhūta-hitatva* (quality of being benevolent to creatures), *satyavacana* (truthful utterance), *asteya* (non-theft), *brahmacarya* (continence), *anupadhā-bhāva-śuddhi* (purity of mind, devoid of deceit), *krodha-varjana* (discarding anger), *abhiṣecana* (bath), *śuci-dravya-sevana* (use of pure substances), *viśiṣṭa-devatā-bhakti* (devotion to a particular deity), *upavāsa* (fasting), *apramāda* (lack of inadvertence).

The usual duties of the different castes and stages of life have been set forth in the *Vaiśeṣika-sūtra*, VI.2.3 and *Padārtha-dharma-saṁgraha* (p. 273). Duties are stated to produce virtue only when done without any desire for visible results such as acquisition of wealth, etc., and with the purest motive. Self-control is emphasised (e.g., *Vaiśeṣika-sūtra*, VI.2.8). Yoga is recognised as the means to self-restraint (*Vaiśeṣika-sūtra*, V.2.16-18).

It is believed by Vaiśeṣika that past lives can be recollected by proper discipline (*Upaskāra*, V.2.18, VI.2.16). According to this system, suitable practices enable one to be elevated to a superior order of existence, and the lack of proper observances reduces one to a subhuman state.

MĪMĀṀSĀ

According to it, a good life is based on *dharma*. *Dharma* has been defined as — *codanālakṣaṇo'rtha* (*Mīmāṁsā-sūtra*, I.1.2) or a beneficial act prompted by an exhortative Vedic text. Thus, black magic, though mentioned in the Veda, is not *dharma* as it is meant for causing harm to others.

This system aims at happiness which is not mundane, but attainable in the other world. So, it recommends a code of conduct for right living on earth so that it may result in happiness in the life beyond. Mīmāṁsā holds that the result of good deeds, done in this life, is stored as *apūrva* which produces fruit in the other world.

The deeds of a person in the earthly life are of three kinds, viz. *nitya* (obligatory), *naimittika* (done on certain occasions) and *kāmya* (done with an object in view). An example of *nitya-karma* is daily prayer. The performance of *nitya-karma* does not produce any good result, but non-performance causes sin. By avoiding *kāmya-karma*, one can be free from selfish motives which are impediments to salvation. By refraining from prohibited acts, one can avoid fall into hell.

It should be noted that *dharma* in Mīmāṁsā is confined to rituals alone (*yāgādireva dharmaḥ — Arthasaṁgraha*); human activities in general have not been teken into consideration.

Buddhism, which is basically an ethical religion, had a powerful impact on society. The inclusion of the Buddha as an incarnation in the Brāhmaṇical religion is a strong evidence of the Buddha's influence. Kumārila, a great exponent of Mīmāṁsā and follower of Vedic authority, could not ignore Buddhist ethics. So, he lauded the Buddhists' stress on *ahiṁsā* (non-injury), but deplored their denunciation of Vedic authority. In a bantering manner, he compared Buddhist ethical precepts with milk, which though nourishing, is spoilt by being thrown over a dog's leather (*Tantravārttika*, I.3.6).

It is interesting to note that, besides allowing the three upper classes to perform sacrifices, he allows also some other people of low classes to perform certain specified sacrifices. For instances, chariot-makers (*rathakāra*s) are eligible for *agnyādhāna* (*Ibid.*, VI.1.44-50). He recognises the right of *niṣāda*s to the performance of *Raudra yajña* (*Ibid.*, VI.1.51-2).

VEDĀNTA

According to this system, both *avidyā* (ritual) and *vidyā* (true knowledge) are necessary for attaining the highest goal. The *Īśā Upaniṣad* (stanza 11) states that by rituals one can cross death, and the knowledge of the Supreme Being leads to salvation. Thus, a judicious combination of both *karman* and *jñāna* is necessary for attaining the *summum bonum*.

For the realisation of *ātman* or *Brahman*, the following three in succession are necessary:

> *śravaṇa* (listening to scriptures from knowledgeable persons),
> *manana* (comprehending what has been heard), and
> *nididhyāsana* (profound and repeated meditation).

The realisation of the truth, by a person, should be followed by his leading worldly life with indifference. Such a person is free from the constraints imposed by convention.

With the acquisition of true knowledge, the aspirant must have good conduct and devotion to God. Vedānta also stresses the importance of control of mind for such a person.

Bondage and Liberation

According to all the six systems, liberation is the highest goal. There is, however, difference of views about the meaning of liberation and the means of its attainment.

SĀṀKHYA

As mentioned earlier, what one should strive for is freedom from three kinds of suffering, which are facts of worldly existence. It is held that the cause of suffering is ignorance or lack of knowledge discriminating between the self and the non-self. For getting rid of ignorance and, for that matter, of suffering one must acquire *viveka-jñāna* or discriminative knowledge. Liberation consists in the recognition of the self as the reality beyond space and time, above mind and body and as free, eternal and immortal.

Sāṁkhya recognises two kinds of liberation, viz., *sadeha* (with body, i.e., while one is alive) and *videha* (in disembodied state, i.e., after death).

YOGA

As stated earlier, Yoga and Sāṁkhya represent two aspects of the same philosophy. While the former is practical, the latter is largely theoretical. Discriminative knowledge is the means to the end in both. According to Yoga, liberation lies in *kaivalya*, i.e., knowledge of the self as distinct from the physical world including the body, mind and ego. The contribution of *yoga* is that it suggests practical methods for the acquisition of the above knowledge; these are the eight accessories of Yoga (*yogāṅgas*) enumerated earlier. Sāṁkhya, of course, prescribes *śravaṇa*, *manana* and *nididhyāsana*, already explained, which are also practical.

NYĀYA-VAIŚEṢIKA

Liberation means the freedom of the soul from all kinds of sufferings. It is possible when its bonds with the body and the senses are completely severed. In the disembodied state after death, the soul ceases to experience pleasure or pain and even consciousness. This is not for a limited time, but for eternity. In such a state, the soul is calm (*śānta*), free from decay (*ajara*), immortal (*amṛta*) and free from fear (*abhaya*). Eternal freedom from suffering means the cessation of pain-causing rebirths; this is liberation. The stepping stones to liberation are *śravaṇa*, *manana* and *nididhyāsana*, explained earlier. As a result of these, the true knowledge of the self dawns; the self is understood to have no connection with the body and mind. Thus, one becomes fit for liberation.

MĪMĀṀSĀ

In the early phase of Mīmāṁsā, the highest goal was considered to be the access to heaven after death, where the soul enjoys perfect bliss, free from a shred of pain. In course of time, the exponents of the system realised that the highest goal was the liberation from the bondage of flesh. On realising the hollowness of worldly pleasures, man abstains from action with desire. While doing disinterested action with the knowledge of the self, man dies never to be re-born. Thus, the soul is liberated.

VEDĀNTA

According to Śaṅkara, liberation of the soul is possible both in the embodied and disembodied states. In the former case, the soul never again identifies itself with the body. The phenomenal world still appears before a *jīvanmukta* person, but he is indifferent and disinterested. So, he is not affected by the misery of worldly existence.

For an aspirant, besides *śravaṇa*, *manana* and *nididhyāsana*, it is necessary to prepare the mind in the following ways:

(1) *Nityānitya-vastu-viveka* — discrimination between what is eternal and what is non-eternal.

(2) *Ihā-mutrārtha-bhoga-virāga* — detachment to enjoyment in this life and in the next.

(3) *Śama-damādi-sādhana-sampat* — the wealth of means consisting in repose, self-restraint, etc.

(4) *Mumukṣutva* — the state of one desiring liberation.

Creation and Evolution

SĀṀKHYA

It recognises the two principles, underlying creation. One is *puruṣa* or the conscious principle, a passive onlooker at *prakṛti*, the other principle which is unconscious matter. The order of evolution of *prakṛti* in relation to *puruṣa* is as follows.

puruṣa-prakṛti
|
mahat (*buddhi*)
|
ahaṁkāra (ego)

manas (mind)	*jñānendriya* (five-sense-	*karmendriya* (speech, hand,	*pañcatanmātra* (five subtle elements,

organs, viz., *cakṣu*, *karṇa*, *jihvā*, *nāsikā*, *tvak*)	foot, *anus* and genital organ)	*śabda*, *sparśa* *rūpa*, *rasa*, *gandha*)
		|
		pañcamahābhūtas (Five gross elements, viz., ether, air, fire, water, earth).

NYĀYA-VAIŚEṢIKA

These systems believe in the atomic theory of creation. The eternal constituents of the universe are the four kinds of atoms of the gross elements, called earth, water, fire ether and air. The atoms are activated by the creative will of the Supreme Being. The actual fashioning of the world is entrusted to *Brahman*.

VEDĀNTA

Under this we shall consider the views of only Śaṅkara and Rāmānuja, the two outstanding figures.

According to Śaṅkara, creation is a magic show arranged by God through his magical power, *māyā* (illusion) which is a part of Himself. It is only the ignorant who, through false knowledge, (*avidyā*) look upon the world as real. Those, who have true knowledge, discern God behind the illusory appearance (*vivarta*) of the world.

According to Rāmānuja, God is both the material and efficient causes of the world. Through the will of the Omnipotent God, the undifferentiated subtle matter is transformed into the three kinds of subtle elements, viz., fire, water and earth. Such elements reveal three kinds of qualities (*guṇa*) called *sattva*, *rajas* and *tamas*. In course of time, these elements get mixed up, and lead to all gross objects perceived in the material world.

Other Systems of Theistic Philosophy

All that we can do is to give a broad outline of each of these systems.

ŚAIVA PHILOSOPHY OF KĀŚMĪR

Śaivism of this land passed through two successive forms. In the earlier from, it belonged to the Pāśupata sect, and advocated dualism. It was supplemented by the *Trika* system which believed in *Advaita-tattva* or idealistic monism. The *Trika* system can be broadly divided into three classes, namely, *Āgama-śāstra, Spanda-śāstra* and *Pratyabhijñā-śāstra*.

Āgama-Śāstra

It comprises mainly the following Tantras:

> *Mālinī-vijaya* (or, *-vijayottara*), *Svacchanda*, *Vijñāna-bhairava*, *Ucchuṣma-bhairava*, *Ānanda-bhairava*, *Mṛgendra*, *Mātaṅga*, *Netra*, *Niḥśvāsa*, *Svāyaṁbhuva*, *Rudrayāmala*.

In the early phase, the above works were interpreted from the dualistic, even pluralistic standpoint. These were followed by the *Śiva-sūtra* (*c*. AD 850) of unknown authorship. It rejected the dualistic view; pure Advaitism was advocated by it, and elaborated by commentaries on it.

Spanda-Śāstra

It is based mainly on the *Spanda-sūtra*s, generally known as *Spanda-kārikā*s. *Spanda* means vibration, activity. Śiva is regarded as the sole substratum of the universe. His activity is believed to be the cause of all distinctions.

Pratyabhijñā-Śāstra

It is so-called as it considers *pratyabhijñā* or recognition of the reality as essential for liberation. Somānanda (end of ninth century AD), author of the *Śiva-dṛṣṭi*, was the founder of this Śāstra. The writer, preceding him, dealt only with principles. It was Somānanda who appears to have introduced the method of argumentation and philosophical reasoning for rebutting the views of opponents and establishing his own. He is called the originator of reasoning (*tarkasya kartā*). The most important work of this Śāstra is the *Īśvara-pratyabhijñā*, also called *Pratyabhijñā-sūtra* or *Pratyabhijñā-kārikā* by Utpala, pupil of the aforesaid Somānanda.

The salient ideas of the Śaiva philosophy of Kāśmīr are set forth below:

Ātman, called *caitanya* or *cit*, is Paramaśiva. He, in his Śakti aspect, manifests the universe; this manifestation is variously called *unmeṣa*, *udaya*, *ābhāsana*, *sṛṣṭi*, *prakṛti* and *puruṣa*, the ultimate realities in Sāṁkhya philosophy, are regarded as derivatives in this philosophy. According to this system, the apearances are real and not illusory as the advocates of Vedāntic *vivarttavāda* think.

The bonds, with which the individual soul is tied, are *avidyā* (false knowledge or ignorance), *karman* (action, rites, etc.) and *māyā* (illusion). Such a soul identifies itself with the body, oblivious of its identity with Śiva. The continuous recognition (*pratyabhijñā*) of a person's identity with Śiva, through true knowledge and deep Yogic meditation, is liberation from bondage. Though the individual soul is the same as the universal soul, yet the knowledge of this fact on the part of the former is essential for liberation. This is brought home to us by an analogy. A love-lorn woman is extremely anxious to meet her lover. But, the mere presence of the man is not enough. She must recognise him as her lover; otherwise her yearning connot be set at rest.

According to Abhinavagupta, the liberated souls are of three classes, namely.

(i) Those merged in the Supreme Being (*para-mukta*),

(ii) Those united with Him in his manifested phase (*apara-mukta*).

(iii) Those yet remaining in the body (*jīvan-mukta*).

As regards the means of attaining the goal, the *spanda* system holds a different view. According to it, the dawning of the vision of God in the mind, in course of meditation, purges the mind of its impurities and makes it fit for the devotee's realisation of his identity with God.

According to the *Rudrayāmala*, a work of high authority in Kāśmīr Śaivism, the following seven stages of *bhakti* (devotion) lead to *jīvan-mukti* (liberation while alive):

manana (reflection), *dhyāna* (meditation), *kīrtana* (narration), *smaraṇa* (remembrance), *pāda-sevana* (shampooing feet), *arcana* (worship) and *nivedana* (surrender).

Śaiva philosophy of Kāśmīr includes also the *krama* system. Some scholars believe that, having originated in the seventh or eighth century AD, it lasted till the eighteenth. It has a rich literature, broadly divided into two classes, namely, revealed, comprising some anonymous works and *krama*, *āgama*s, and non-revealed, comprising the non-Āgamic works.

The *krama* system, as the name indicates, believes in spiritual progression. It equally stresses each step towards self-realisation.

South Indian Śaiva Philosophy

The time of its origin is not known. Apart from a number of Śaiva *Āgama*s, an important work on this system is the *Śataratna-saṁgraha* by Umāpati Śivācārya (thirteenth-fourteenth century AD). The essence of its contents is as follows: Paśupati (Śiva), with His inherent powers *dṛk* (Supreme consciousness) and *kriyā* (action) is the efficient cause of the universe. The devotees, favoured by him, attain salvation of different stages according to their individual deserts. Induced by Prakṛti, Lord Śiva performs his five functions, viz., *sṛṣṭi* (creation), *sthiti* (stability), *laya* (dissolution), *anugraha* (favour) and *tirodhāna* (disappearance). She plans the universe manifested in forms, with matter as the material cause.

The central concepts of *Śaiva-siddhanta* are *pati*, *paśu* and *pāśa*. *Pati* or Lord is Śiva. To him belong the *paśu*s (lit. animals) which are the countless fettered souls. The fetters (*pāśa*) are *avidyā* (nescience), *karman* (action) and *māyā* (illusion).

Liberation is eternal rest from worldly sufferings brought about by desire. It does not mean the merging of the soul in God. It will remain for ever with Śiva like his servant. Liberation cannot be attained by mere philosophical reflection. The aspirant has to realise the truth of the following great Vedic *mahāvākya*s (sentences with great import):

prajñānam ānandaṁ brahma (*Brahman* is perfect knowledge and bliss).

ahaṁ brahmāsmi (I am *Brahman*).
tat-tvam-asi (That thou art).
ayamātmā brahma (This self is *Brahman*).
jīvan-mukti (liberation while alive or liberation of the embodied soul) is recognised.

It is noteworthy that, according to this philosophy, only true knowledge is not enough for liberation. Some ethical virtues are also necessary. It is declared by Siddhiyar (XII.2) that love of God is not possible without love of mankind. It is important to note that this system does not insist on the strait-jacket of the caste-system. Later Śaiva stalwarts like Paṭṭanāthu, Piḷḷai, Kapilar and the Telugu poet, Vemana are sceptical about the restrictions imposed by this system. Tirumular holds that there is only one caste as there is one God. The reformer Bāsava (middle of twelfth century AD), himself a brāhmaṇa, led a movement denouncing the supremacy of brāhmaṇas.

Nakulīśa Pāśupata System

The philosophy of this system is briefly as follows:

It recognises the follwoing five principal categories:

(1) *Kāraṇa* (cause) — Lord (*pati*) who, creates, preserves and destroys the entire creation.

(2) *Kārya* (effect) — it comprises knowledge (*vidyā*), organs (*kalā*) and individual souls (*paśu*). Dependent on the above cause are, besides the aforesaid knowledge, etc., the five subtle elements (*tanmātra*), five gross elements, the five sense-organs and the five motor organs, the three internal organs of intelligence, egotism and mind.

(3) *Yoga* — the mental process through which the soul attains God.

(4) *Vidhi* — rules regarding the practices required for righteousness.

(5) *Duḥkhānta* — cessation of suffering. It means the final

liberation or destruction of misery and attainment of sublimation of spirit with full powers of knowledge and action. Even in this condition, the individual soul (*jīvātman*) does not lose its individuality; it can assume many forms, and do anything instantaneously.

Vaiṣṇava Philosophy of Bengal

Caitanya (AD 1486-1533) was the greatest exponent of Bengal Vaiṣṇavism. He added new dimensions to this religion by infusing into it great emotionalism, and rising above the narrow barriers of casteism. To him, even a cāṇḍāla, devoted to Hari (Viṣṇu), was the greatest of the brāhmaṇas.

This basic work of this philosophy is the *Bhāgavata Purāṇa* (*c*. fifth or sixth century AD). Among the later philosophical works of this system, prominent are the following:

Bṛhad-bhāgavatāmṛta of Sanātana,

Saṁkṣepa-bhāgavatāmṛta of Rūpa Gosvāmin, and

Ṣaṭ-sandarbha of Jīva Gosvāmin;

all these authors were contemporaries of Caitanya.

According to Jīva Gosvāmin, *śabda* (scriptural testimony) is the only source of valid knowledge. All other sources, namely, perception, etc., suffer from the following defects:

Bhrama — mistaking one thing for another.

Pramāda — mistake due to inadvertence.

Vipralipsā — mistake caused by a desire to deceive.

Karaṇāpāṭava — mistake due to the defects of the senses.

Besides the Vedas, *itihāsa* and Purāṇa also have been included in *Śabda-pramāṇa*.

This system believes in non-dualism. The Supreme Being is *Brahman*, also called *paramātman* and *bhagavat*. The powers of God are of three kinds, viz. *parā* or *svarūpa-śakti*, *taṭastha* or *jīva-śakti* and *bahiraṅga* or *māyā-śakti*. The difference of *śakti* from the *śaktimat* (possessor of *śakti*) is not known. Nor are they known to be identical. This peculiar relation is called *acintya-bhedābheda* (incomprehensible difference and non-difference).

In this philosophy, *bhakti* (devotion) is recognised as superior to other means of reaching the ultimate goal. *Bhakti* is of three kinds, namely.

Āropasiddhā — generated by work done for God, in the absence of natural *bhakti*.

Saṅgasiddhā — caused by association with good people.

Svarūpasiddhā — spontaneous.

The last kind of *bhakti* is *akaitavā*; it is inspired by no other reason than pleasing God. It has two stages, viz., *vaidhī* (induced by scriptural injunction) and *rāgānugā* (following natural impulse). It imitates *rāgātmikā* (in which there is *rāga* alone) *bhakti* which the divine attendants of god, as His own *śakti*, show towards *Him*.

Liberation of the *jīvātman* after death may be of five kinds:

(i) *Sālokya* — access to the divine region.

(ii) *Sārṣṭya* — acquisition of power like that of God.

(iii) *Sārūpya* — attainment of a divine form.

(iv) *Sāmīpya* — nearness to God.

(v) *Sāyujya* — union with God.

Heterodox Philosophical Systems

In ancient India, the authority of the Vedas which had firm hold on the Brāhmaṇical society, was not universally recognised. Prominent among the anti-Vedic people were the Buddhists, Jains and the Cārvākas (also called Lokāyatas). We shall focus on the highlights of their philosophical views.

BUDDHIST PHILOSOPHY

Gautama, who attained Buddhahood or enlightenment (*c.* 486 BC), protested against the conventional Brāhmaṇical religion. He denounced ritualism, animal sacrifice, etc. He preached ethical practices, and discouraged metaphysical discussions and debates on matters beyond comprehension and proof. In his opinion, the following enquiries are about imponderable matters and are, therefore, futile:

(i) Is the world eternal?

(ii) Is it non-eternal?

(iii) Is it finite?

(iv) Is it infinite?

(v) Is the soul identical with the body?

(vi) Is it different from the body?

(vii) Does a person, knowing the truth, return after death?

(viii) Is there no rebirth for him?

(ix) Does he live, re-live and not re-live after death?

(x) Does he neither live nor not live again after death?

The highest goal is the attainment of *nirvāṇa*, i.e., the extinction of passions and, therefore, also of misery; it is a state of perfect and perpetual calm, repose.

The aspirant must know the four noble truths (*ariyasaccāni*, Skt. *āryasatyāni*), viz., *duḥkha* (life is full of sufferings), *samudaya* (source of suffering), *nirodha* (suppression of suffering) and *mārga* (means of suppression of suffering).

The following eightfold ethical code (*aṭṭhaṅgika magga*, Skt. *aṣṭāṅgika-mārga*) has to be observed as preparatory for *nirvāṇa*:

(i) *Sammā diṭṭhi*, Skt. *samyak dṛṣṭi* — right view about the self and the world.

(ii) *Sammā samkappa*, Skt. *samyak saṁkalpa* — right resolution.

(iii) *Sammā vacā*, Skt. *samyak vākya* — right speech.

(iv) *Sammā kammanta*, Skt. *samyak karmānta* — right conduct.

(v) *Sammā ājīva*, Skt. *samyak ājīva* — right livelihood.

(vi) *Sammā vāyāma*, Skt. *samyak vyāyāma* — right effort.

(vii) *Sammā sati*, Skt. *samyak smṛti* — right mindfulness.

(viii) *Sammā samādhi*, Skt. *samyak samādhi* — right concentration.

The four means to the attainment of the pleasure of living in the Brahma-world consist in the cultivation of the mental attitudes, called *maitrī* (friendliness), *karuṇā* (compassion, pity), *muditā* (genuine delight at others' happiness) and *upekṣā* (equanimity, indifference to pleasure and pain).

Buddhism stresses the importances of disciplining the conduct (*śīla*), mind (*citta*) and intellect (*prajñā*).

This philosophy recognises the doctrine of *karman* according to which actions done in one existence determine the kind of the existence in another. But, the connecting link of one existence with another is not the soul which is denied, but the five *khandhas* (Skt. *skandha*) which are *rūpa* (form), *vedanā* (feeling of pleasure, pain and indifference), *saṁjñā* (perception including understanding and naming), *saṁskāra* (impression caused by past experience) and *vijñāna* (consciousness).

SCHOOLS OF BUDDHIST PHILOSOPHY

There were four schools, called Vaibhāṣika, Mādhyamika, Yogācāra and Sautrāntika. Their doctrines are briefly stated below:

Vaibhāṣika is so-called as it is based on the *abhidharma-mahāvibhāṣā*. In this school, the existence of both mind and external things is recognised. The knowledge of phenomenal world is acquired by perception, not inference.

Mādhyamika is so-called as it follows the middle course by avoiding the two extremes of absolute realism and absolute non-realism. According to it, *śūnyavāda* does not mean absolute emptiness, but the emptiness of the phenomenal world. The sole reality, behind the phenomenal world, can be comprehended by only *nirvāṇa*.

Yogācāra takes its name from the fact that it emphasises the practice of *yoga* (see account of Yoga philosophy) and *ācāra* (conduct). It advocates the doctrine of Vijñanavāda according to which mind, properly controlled, can remove the delusion about the reality of the external world and attachment to it.

Sautrāntika: The significance of the name of Sautrāntika is that it is based on the *Suttapiṭaka* comprising several texts, called *Suttanta*. It declares that knowledge of the external world can be acquired through inference. The knowledge about the objects arises from their forms and impressions about them.

It should be noted that the Buddhists were divided into two sects, viz., Hīnayāna (lesser vehicle) and Mahāyāna (great vehicle). The former and the older one adhered to the Buddhist teaching that every devotee must achieve his own salvation — *ātmadīpo bhava* (light your own lamp). This was the difficult path of self-help, and could be resorted to by the devotees of the upper class. The mass of ordinary converts did not find it suitable. So, the Mahāyāna sect came into being. According to it, the ideal of *bodhisattva* was the acquisition of perfect wisdom whereby suffering of all beings could be removed. The term *bodhisattva* (Pāli: *bodhisatta*) denotes a person in a state of existence prior to the attainment of Buddhahood.

Two important philosophical doctrines of the Buddhists were:

1. *Pratītyasamutpāda* (Pāli: *Paṭiccasamuppāda*): It is the theory of dependent origination or Conditional Existence of Things. According to it, the origin of everything depends on a cause. Likewise, nothing perishes without leaving an effect.
2. Doctrine of impermanence and universal change, momentariness: According to it, everything disappears with the disappearance of its cause; everything is impermanent. This theory led to the belief that everything lasts only for a moment.

JAINA PHILOSOPHY

According to it, knowledge is immediate (*aparokṣa*) and mediate (*parokṣa*). The former, gathered through the senses and mind, is ordinary or empirical (*vyavahārika*). The latter, gained by the soul, purged of the obstacles created by *karmans*, is absolute (*pāramārthika*).

Jaina philosophers believe in two broad kinds of substances, viz., extended (*astikāya*, i.e., existing like a body) and non-extended.

Extended Substances
(*Astikāya-dravyas*)

- Animate (*jīva* or soul)
  - Emancipated (*mukta*)
  - Fettered (*baddha*)
    - Moving (*trasa*)
      - With five senses e.g., man mind,
      - With four senses e.g., bees
      - With three senses e.g., ants
      - With two senses e.g., worms
    - Non-moving (*sthāvara*)
- Inanimate (*ajīva*)
  - *dharma*
  - *adharma*
  - *ākāśa*
  - *pudgala* → Material substances capable of being combined to form larger and larger entities and of disintegrating into smaller and smaller particles, the minutest being *aṇu* (molecule): our body, speech, breath also are the products of matter
    - *aṇus* (molecules) of earth, water, etc.
    - *saṁghātas* (Compounds)

(*anastikāya*). To the latter class belongs only time (*kāla*). The divisions and sub-divisions of extended substances are as follows:

Bondage and Liberation

According to Jaina philosophy, the soul has endless potentiality, and is intrinsically perfect. Its limitations are, however, due to its identifying itself with the material body. As an effect of past deeds (*karman*), the soul is associated with the matter constituting the body of a particular kind. Anger, pride, infatuation and greed, called *kaṣāyas* (sticky substances), cause the bondage of the soul. The above passions, being in the soul, cause matter-particles stick to it. The influx of these particles, called *karma-pudgala* or *karman*, into the soul is called *āsrava*.

Bondage may be of two kinds, viz., *bhāva-bandha* (ideal or internal) and *dravya-bandha* (material). In the former, there is bondage to bad dispositions. As an effect of it, in the latter there is actual association of the soul with matter.

Liberation means ridding the soul of matter and the above passions engendered by ignorance. Ignorance can be dispelled only by right knowledge (*samyag-jñāna*). Such knowledge is possible only by the careful study of the teachings of the *tīrthaṁkaras* who attained liberation and, as such, became fit for leading others along the path of liberation. It should be noted that *samyag-jñāna* must be preceded by faith (*samyag-darśana*) in the above teachings.

Samyag-jñāna, to be fruitful, must be accompanied by *samyag-carita* (right conduct). Right conduct means all-round control — control of passions, senses, thought, speech, action. Right knowledge, coupled with right conduct, gradually roots out the past *karmans*, and thereby causes the annihilation of matter which holds the soul in bondage. The triad of right faith (*samyag-darśana* — see *Tattvārthādhigama-sūtra*, I.2-3), right knowledge (*samyag-jñāna* — see *Dravya-saṁgraha*, verse 42) and right conduct (*samyak carita* — *Ibid.*, verse 45) is called *Triratna* the three gems or essentials for liberation (*Tattvārthādhigama-sūtra* — first *sūtra*).

With the bondage to matter eliminated, the soul attains the fourfold perfection (*ananta-catuṣṭaya*), viz., infinite knowledge, infinite faith, infinite power and infinite bliss.

The Jainas do not believe in God; instead of God, they worship the liberated souls. The five kinds of pure souls (*pañca-parameṣṭi*) are:

> *arhats*, *siddhas*, *ācāryas*, *upādhyāyas* and *sādhus*. (See *Dravya-saṁgraha*, 49).

They worship them as guides and neither for their mercy nor for pardon. They believe that the results of past misdeeds cannot be overcome by anybody's help but by self-exertion in cultivating good thoughts, good speech and good action. This religion teaches self-help and courage. So, the liberated soul is called *jina* (victor) and *vīra* (hero).

CĀRVĀKA PHILOSOPHY

It is so-called as it is believed by some to have been propounded by a sage, Cārvāka. This philosophy is also known as materialistic philosophy, as it recognises matter as the sole reality. Some think that the appellation Cārvāka applied to the materialists as they used to utter words pleasant to hear (*cāru vāk* — pleasant speech). This school is also called *Lokāyatika* or *Lokāyata-mata* (view of the common people). Materialistic teachings are associated with the name of Bṛhaspati in the *Mahābhārata* and some other works. The philosophical views of this school were, until recently, pieced together from the mention or refutation of them in different works. In recent times, the only available work of this school, called *Tattvopaplava-siṁha*, has come to light. Attributed to Jayarāśi, it advocates full-fledged scepticism. Different sections of the work are devoted to the various definitions of the means of knowledge in general and perception in particular. The systems, criticised in it, are: Nyāya, Mīmāṁsā, the epistemological school of Buddhism (Diṅnāga and Dharmakīrti), Sāṁkhya (Vārṣagaṇya and Vindhyasvāmin).

In this philosophy perception has been recognised as the only means of valid knowledge. There are arguments to establish that testimony and inference, recognised in the orthodox systems, are not free from flaws.

According to this view, God, soul, heaven and life before the earthly existence or after death cannot be perceived, and hence cannot be believed. The material world is declared to be composed of four elements instead of the traditional five, viz., the gross elements of earth, water, fire, wind and ether; ether is rejected as it is not perceived. This system identifies soul with the body possessed of consciousness (*caitanyaviśiṣṭo deha evātmā*).

The materialists do not believe in liberation in the sense of complete cessation of suffering. According to them, such a condition can only mean death (*maraṇam evāpavargaḥ — Bṛhaspati-sūtra*).

Hedonistic as they are, they declare that pleasure is the highest goal of life. Of the four traditional ends of life (*puruṣārthas*), viz., *dharma*, *artha*, *kāma* and *mokṣa*, they reject the first and the last ones.

8

Arthaśāstra

(Politics and Statecraft)

LITERALLY, it means the *śāstra* dealing with *artha* or wealth which was regarded as one of the four ends of life. In reality, however, this *śāstra* deals with politics, statecraft, trade, commerce, economics, etc. The work, entitled *Arthaśāstra* (fourth century BC), attributed to Kauṭilya, is the earliest extant work on *Arthaśāstra*, Kauṭilya, however, mentions quite a few authorities who probably flourished earlier. Some of them were Viśālākṣa, Piśuna, Vātavyādhi, Parāśara, etc. The other principal works, dealing particularly with *Rājadharma* (royal duties), are the *Manu-smṛti* (chapter VII), *Mānasollāsa* (AD 1129) of Someśvara, and the *Śukranīti(sāra)* which was written, according to P.V. Kane, in the thirteenth or fourteenth century AD. As regards the *Manu-smṛti*, P.V. Kane thinks that the present version is the result of evolution between about the second century BC and second century AD.

The *Kauṭilīya Arthaśāstra*, being the earliest, most authoritative and exhaustive work, we shall briefly indicate its contents, occasionally adverting to the *Manu-smṛti*.

At the outset, it may be noted that, according to Kauṭilya, of the three ends of the life (*trivarga*), *artha* is of prime importance, because *dharma* and *kāma* are dependent on *artha* (*artha eva pradhāna iti kauṭilyaḥ — arthamūlauhi dharmakāmāviti*, I.7). The contents of this work, *adhikarṇa* (section)-wise, are as follows:

I. Upbringing and education of a prince; appointment of ministers and ministerial officers, spies, emissaries, counsels, measures for a king's personal safety.

II. Duties of a vast army of superintendents.

III. Law of discussed.

IV. Repression of evil-doers by police action and heavy penalties; deceitful doctors and tradesmen, artificial increase of prices, adulteration, use of false weights are some of the practices condemned.

V. Means of getting rid of an undesirable minister, extortion of taxes for filling the treasury, remuneration of the royal entourage.

VI. Description of the seven elements of politics, interstate relations.

VII. The six *guṇa*s or political expedients.

VIII. Evils arising from a king's addiction to vices; misfortunes which fire, water, etc., may bring on a land.

IX. War.

X. War.

XI. Dissension among, and destruction of the cohesion of hostile aristocracies of warriors.

XII. Means by which a weak king may aggrandise himself.

XIII. Capture of fortified cities.

XIV. The secret part consisting of recipes to enable one to murder, to cause blindness or madness and so on.

XV. Plan of the work, 32 methodological principles used in the discussion.

The *Arthaśāstra* has often been regarded as comparable to the work of Machiavelli. Some scholars think that it is not a work of Kauṭilya, but rather of a school which followed his views.

We shall discuss a few interesting topics in some detail.

Ministers

First of all, we take up the appointment of ministers who are next, in importance, to the king. To denote minister the terms *saciva* (*Manu-smṛti* VII.54), *amātya* (*Arthaśāstra* I.8) and *mantrin* (*Ibid.*) have been used. *Saciva* appears to denote minister in general. *Amātya* and *mantrin*, both denoting minister, have not only terminological difference, but also functional. After mentioning some qualifications, Kauṭilya ordains that men, endowned with these virtues, should be appointed as *amātyas*, but not as *mantrins* —*amātyāḥ sarva evaite kāryāḥ syur na tu mantriṇaḥ* (I.8). Kauṭilya, appears to mean that a person, possessed of some (not all) qualities of a minister, mentioned by him, should be an *amātya*. One, endowed with all the prescribed qualities, should be made *mantrin*. From the trend of his discussion, it appears that *amātya* was *karma-saciva* or executive minister while *mantrin* was *dhī-saciva* whose sole duty was to give counsel to the king. The curious reader may refer to the *Arthaśāstra* (I.9) for the 25 qualities that are required in a first-class minister.

What Kauṭilya means by *mantrin*, Manu means by *saciva* (VII. 54). Manu's *amātya* (VII.60) has been taken by Kullūka as *karma-saciva*.

Mere possession of the prescribed qualities does not make one fit for ministership. He must have to pass four tests called *Upadhās*, briefly described below. These tests were based on stratagem.

A spy will tell the minister that the ruling king is not pious. So, it has been decided by all to depose him, and instal another person on the throne. If the minister does not agree to the proposal, he will be regarded as loyal. This method of test is called *dharmopadhā*.

Besides instigating a minister in the above manner, a spy will offer him an attractive amount of money, and ask him to give his consent to the decision of murdering the king. If the minister rejects the proposal, he will be regarded as honest. This is called *arthopadhā*.

A female wandering mendicant, honoured by the queens in the harem, will entice a minister saying that the queen longs for union with him, and has made a plan. If he (the minister) spurns the proposal, he will be considered as pure. This is called *kāmopadhā*.

A spy will tell a minister, who has been humiliated by the king, that the king has taken recourse to an evil way. So, it has been decided by others to kill the king all of a sudden, and to instal another person on the throne. If the minister rejects the proposal, he will be regarded as loyal. This is called *bhayopadhā*.

Morality and Politics

A study of the *Arthāśāstra* reveals that what we generally understand by morality and ethics has hardly any place in politics. A few instances are given here:

In XII.1, the author provides that, being attacked by a stronger king, a weak king should seek self-defence by trying to make peace or diplomatic war. If his effort be abortive, he is advised to resort to *kūṭa-yuddha* or deceitful war at an undeclared place and time (X.3). At such a juncture, the spies of the weak king may try to occupy the enemy's fort or camp by resorting to poisoning and incendiarism. All sorts of disturbance and disruption should be created at the rear of the powerful king's army. The weak king may even try to get the enemy's territory devasted by the forces of the forest-chiefs. Attempt may be made to get the enemy ousted by some powerful person among the king's kin or by a prince who may have been confined by that king as a measure of punishment.

In connection with ministers, we have seen that all the methods of testing their integrity and loyalty were based on deceit.

It was nothing wrong for a king to create dissension among the people of his rival's kingdom, particularly to provoke sedition among the people, who were somehow or other, humiliated by that king.

State-control of the detestable profession of prostitution seems to have been resorted to for enriching the exchequer with the income derived from this source.

From IV.4 and 5 it is learnt that for detecting anti-social elements, various kinds of stratagem were recommended by the author of the *Arthaśāstra*.

Perhaps the climax of ruthlessness, advised for the security of a king is found in I.17. In this connection, Kauṭilya refers, apparently with approval, to the views of some authorities. Of them, Bharadvāja holds that princes, like crabs, devour their fathers. So, it is safe for a king to put to death such a son as does not love his father. Another authority, Vātavyādhi, says that it should be so arranged that such a son becomes excessively addicted to sensual pleasures. In V.1, Kauṭilya's advice is this. If a powerful member of the royal council (*sabhā*) proves to be a menace to the kingdom, then the king may instigate the brother of that man to kill him. For this service, the king will promise to induct him into the post of the murdered person. After the operation, the king will convict him of fratricide, and put him to death. In V.2, the king has been advised to fill his depleted treasury with the wealth forcibly taken away from temples.

Adhikaraṇa XIV, called Aupaniṣada (secret ways of destroying enemies) is a catalogue of nefarious tactics recommended for the destruction of enemies. For instance, the secret administration of poison is recommended for liquidating the enemy.

It is interesting to note that the ancient Greeks, particularly the Spartans, strongly felt that principles of morality were to be shunned in the interest of the State. In this respect, the opinion of Lysander (395 BC), a great military and political leader, is well-known (Plato, *Lysander*, p. 7). Those, who believed that the descendants of Heracles (AD 575-641), an inspiring military leader, should not take recourse to deceitful means in battle, were ridiculed by the opponents; their argument was that when the lion's skin fails to protect us, the jackal's skin ought to be sewn over it.

System of Espionage

In ancient India, a king was characterised as *cāra-cakṣu* (one whose eyes are the spies). In all the ages and countries, the spies were an indispensable part of the administrative machinery. The system of espionage, envisaged in the *Arthaśāstra*, evokes our admiration for its organisation. We shall briefly discuss the system.

In this work (V.1.11, 12), the spies have been divided into two broad classes, viz., *saṁstha* (those who remain at one place and gather information) and *saṁcāra* (those who go from one place to another in the kingdom to gather information). Those of the first class are of five kinds, namely.

(1) *Kāpaṭika* — a hypocritical student.

(2) *Udāsthita* — a wise man fallen from mendicancy, (or, according to some, initiated to this way of life).

(3) *Gṛhapatika* or *gṛhapati-vyañjana* — an impoverished cultivator who is wise and honest.

(4) *Vaidehaka-vyañjana* — an impoverished merchant who is wise and honest.

(5) *Tāpasa-vyañjana* — one who, with a shaven head or matted locks, takes to this occupation.

To the second class i.e., *saṁcāra*, belonged to the following four kinds of roving spies, namely:

(1) *Satrī* — being related to the king, he has to be maintenaned. Such a person will be versed in magic, erotics, music, the art of bringing others under control, the duties in the four stages of life, etc.

(2) *Tīkṣṇa* — One who, like a gladiator, becomes engaged in fighting animals like elephant, tiger, etc., utterly disregarding his own body.

(3) *Rasada* — one who is ruthless, and does not hesitate even to administer poison (*rasa*) to others.

(4) *Parivrājikā* — A poor old brāhmaṇa widow, in quest of means of livelihood, who enjoys respect in the royal seraglio, and frequents the houses of dignitaries. Buddhist nuns and śūdra widows also belong to this class.

The principal duty of the above spies was to collect secret information about the high functionaries of the kingdom. The spies of the *tīkṣṇa* class were to join, incognito, as various employees under them, like shampooer, carrier of water-pots and sandal, etc. Then they would gather external information about them, and communicate it to the spies of the *saṁstha* class through *satrīs*.

The internal information about the dignitaries will be gathered by the *rasada* class of spies after working as thier cooks, shampooers or pretending to be dumb, deaf, etc., or in the guise of dancers, singers, etc. After gathering information from them the above female spies will communicate it to the spies of the *saṁstha* class. The followers of these spies will communicate the information to the king by cipher.

The system was so well-organised that the spies did not know one another. The king would take a piece of information as true only when it was confirmed by three spies.

Besides the above, there was another class of spy known as *ubhaya-vetana*. A king's spy would, concealing his identity, take up a job under the enemy-king and supply secret information to his former master. The king, before appointing such a spy, was to keep his wife and sons as hostages; this was a security-measure against the possible betrayal by the *ubhaya-vetana* man.

Prostitution

This profession was under state control. There was a high official, designated as *gaṇikādhyakṣa* (superintendent of courtesans).

A beautiful young courtesan, versed in various arts like music, was to be appointed for service in the royal palace on 1,000 *paṇa*s (a year?). Among her duties were carrying umbrella, water-pot, etc., for the king. When such a courtesan lost her beauty and youth, she was appointed as the trainer of her successor. If the royal courtesan wanted to be free from service, she had to pay a ransom of 24,000 *paṇa*s.

Some rules in respect of courtesans are as follows: Such a woman, depositing her ornaments with someone other than her mother, was to pay a fine of 4¼ *paṇa*s. A fine of 50¼ *paṇa*s was payable by a courtesan for selling her clothes, etc. A fine of 24 *paṇa*s was imposed for abusing a person. Double this amount was payable for assaulting a person.

Heavy penalty was prescribed for a man who raped a virgin girl against her wish. Less punishment was prescribed for sexual union with such a girl even with her consent.

A fine of 1,000 *paṇa*s was payable by a man for confining a reluctant courtesan to his house or concealing her elsehwere as well as for disfiguring her with teeth, nails, etc.

A courtesan, not complying with the royal order for yielding her body to a particular person was to be punished with 1000 lashes or 5,000 *paṇas*. Liable to punishment was also a courtesan who, even after receiving her fees, from a man, did not satisfy him. For stealing a courtesan's ornaments, other things or her fees, a man would have to pay eight times the value of the things concerned.

A public woman was to pay, as tax to the king, two days' income every month, i.e., 2/30 or 1/15 of her monthly income.

Out of the revenue, realised from cities and villages, the king was to spend an amount for the maintenance of the person training the courtesans and the wives of actors in the following subjects: vocal and instrumental music, dance, drama, writing, painting, divining other's feelings, production of perfumes, making garlands, shampooing, harlotry, etc.

System of Taxation

In the *Arthaśāstra* (II.22), there is provision for different kinds of tax, these are:

(1) *Bāhya-śulka* — levied on commodities produced in the countryside.

(2) *Ābhyantara-śulka* — levied on things grown in forts, cities, etc.

(3) *Ātithya-śulka* — levied on foreign goods.

Each of the above classes is sub-divided into two kinds, namely:

(i) *Niṣkrāmya-śulka* — payable for exported goods.

(ii) *Praveśya-śulka* — payable for imported goods.

The general rule is that, in the case of imported goods, ¼ of the price is payable as tax. The tax is 1/6 in respect of the following:

> Flowers, fruits, vegetables, paddy-seeds, dried fish and meat.

1/10 or 1/15 will be the rate of tax for the following:

> silk, cloth, metal, sandal, aloewood, seed used in the fermentation of spirituous liquor, wine, ivory, deer-skin,

woollen goods, asafoetida, red arsenic, yellow orpimont, etc.

The rate will be 1/20 or 1/25 for cloth, animals, linen, perfumes, herbs, timber, bamboo, bark, leather, earthen vessel, paddy, oily substances, salt, molasses, cooked food, etc.

For articles, brought into the city, the keeper of the main gate will realise 1/5 of the tax determined for them; this is called *dvārādeya śulka*.

Besides the above taxes, there was *vartanī*. For things, brought into the city from outside, the *antapāla* (principal officer-in-charge of the boundary of the kingdom), will realise 1¼ *paṇa* for security of the road. It will be one *paṇa* for one-hoofed animals, ½ for cattle, ¼ for small animals and one *māṣa* for porters.

The following were tax-free:

articles required for marrige, those taken by the newly wed girls from her father's house to that of the husband, things presented for a charitable purpose, milk, curd, etc., meant for sacrifice, medicines required for delivery of a woman, things necessary for obligatory rites, for such rites as *upanayana*, tonsure, rite of initiation, etc.

There is provision for *parihāra* or total exemption from tax (II.1) to the cultivators in distress.

9

Smṛti or Dharmaśāstra
(Religious and Civil Law)

Origin

THE origin of Dharmaśāstra, also called Smṛti, harks back to hoary antiquity, and it has a very long history of development. The Vedic literature can be broadly divided into two classes, viz., revealed and non-revealed. The three Vedic Saṁhitās, viz., *Ṛgveda*, *Yajurveda* and *Sāmaveda* are believed by the orthodox Indians, to have been revealed by divine beings and seen by certain specially gifted persons, called *ṛṣis* (from root *ṛṣ* to see) and in a later period, the *Atharvaveda* was also included as the fourth Saṁhitā. These are also believed to have been orally transmitted through centuries; hence they are referred to as Śruti (from root *śru* to hear). At long last, they were reduced to writing.

The ancient Indians were very particular about the preservation of the Vedic texts intact. Even a wrong accent in pronouncing them was thought to mar the effect of a Vedic *mantra*. In course of time, the cult of sacrifice developed to an enormous extent. Apart from elaborate ritualism, the society expanded to a great extent. For guidance in the performance of sacrifices in all minute details, the preservation of the authenticity of the Vedic texts as also for the regulation of the people in their secular life, works of various sorts came to be composed; these were called Vedāṅgas or accessories of the Vedas. These accessories admit of two broad divisions, viz., exegetical and ritualistic. To the former class belong *śikṣā* (mainly phonetics), *vyākaraṇa* (grammar), *nirukta* (etymology), *chandas* (metrics) and *jyotiṣa* (astronomy). To the latter class of Vedāṅgas belongs *kalpa*. All of these were written in the mnemonic *sūtra* or aphoristic style. *Kalpa-sūtras* comprised *Śrauta-*, *Gṛhya-*, *Dharma-* and *Śulva-sūtras*. Of these, *Śrauta-sūtras* deal with the minutiae of the Vedic sacrificial rites, *Gṛhya-sūtras* with the rules meant for *gṛhasthas* (householders), Dharmasūtras with the secular life of people in general and *Śulva-sūtras* with the measurement of the sacrificial altars. *Śulva* means a measuring string.

The above Dharmasūtras were the precursors of Dharmaśāstras which may be characterised as the enlarged versions of the former. The burgeoning society, with greater complexities of life, demanded the formulation of more elaborate rules and regulations about religious and civil law, than what was prescribed in the *sūtra* works.

The Dharmasūtras were a few in number. The major works were those attributed to Āpastamba, Baudhāyana, Gautama, Vasiṣṭha, Viṣṇu and Vaikhānasa. The existence of a few other works of this kind can be inferred from quotations in the later works, particularly in the later Smṛti digests and commentaries on the Dharmaśāstra texts. The contents of Dharmaśāstra may be broadly divided into four classes, viz. *ācāra* (rules of conduct), *prāyaścitta* (rules of expiation), *vyavahāra* (legal matters) and *rājadharma* (royal duties or politics and statecraft). The age of Dharmasūtras cannot be determined with certainty. There is, however, little doubt about their origin centuries before Christ.

Dharmaśāstras — Forms and Number

The Dharmaśāstra, written in metrical form, deal with the same topics as Dharmasūtras, albeit in a more elaborate manner. Traditionally, the writers of Dharmaśāstra are 20 in number (*vide Yājñavalkya-saṁhitā*, I.4-5). They are Manu, Atri, Viṣṇu, Hārīta, Yājñavalkya, Uśanas, Aṅgiras, Yama, Āpastamba, Saṁvarta, Kātyāyana, Bṛhaspati, Parāśara, Vyāsa, Śaṁkha, Likhita, Dakṣa, Gautama, Śātātapa and Vasiṣṭha. This list is not exhaustive. For example, Nārada is absent; may be that when the *Yājñavalkya-smṛti* was composed (*c.* first-second century AD), the other Dharmaśāstra writers were not born or did not become so eminent as to merit mention by Yājñavalkya.

Commentaries

India is a vast country with diverse social and cultural conditions, customs and practices. Sanskrit learning was popular; in fact, the acquisition of this learning was widespread; in fact, the acquisition of this learning was considered as a must, particularly for brāhmaṇas. The texts of the Dharmaśāstras required commentaries. *Vyākhyā buddhibalāpekṣā* (explanation or interpretation depends on intellectual capacity) — this was the attitude of scholars. This is the reason why scholars interpreted texts according to their own ideas and to suit their respective regional practices. A noteworthy feature of the commentaries is that they incorporated the authority of the Purāṇas and Tantras which deeply influenced the populace chiefly by considerable latitude in religious practices to women and śūdras who were denied the right to perform Vedic rites.

Of the commentators of Manu, Medhātitihi (*c.* ninth century AD) is the earliest and Kullūkabhaṭṭa (perhaps earlier than fifteenth century AD) the most popular. Another noteworthy commentator is Govindarāja (*c.* latter half of eleventh century AD). Among the commentators of Yājñavalkya, the most famous, authoritative and ancient is Vijñāneśvara (eleventh-twelfth century). Other notable interpreters of the work of Yājñavalkya are Aparāditya or Aparārka (first half of twelfth century), Viśvarūpa (*c.* ninth century AD) and Śūlapāṇi (*c.* sometime between eleventh and the fifteenth centuries). There are commentaries on the Dharmaśāstras of some other authors too.

Mitākṣarā and Dāyabhāga

Vijñāneśvara's *Mitākṣarā* commentary had been the sole authority in matters relating to inheritance and succession throughout India excepting Bengal, until recent times when Hindu Law was reformed. In Bengal, the sole authority in such matters was Jīmūtavāhana (*c.* after thirteenth century), a scholar of Bengal and author of the *Dāyabhāga*. Though not a commentator of the entire *Yājñavalkya-smṛti*, he interpreted independently the text of this Smṛti relating to inheritance and succession. The fundamental difference between

Vijñāneśvara and Jīmūtavāhana is this. With regard to a person's ancestral property, he shares the right of inheritance, by his very birth, equally with his father. This is called *janma-svatva-vāda*, according to Vijñāneśvara. Jīmūtavāhana holds that one acquires right of inheriting the ancestral property only after the death of the parents. This is known as *uparama-svatva-vāda*.

Contents of Dharmaśāstras and Schools of Smṛti

As we have seen, there was a number of Dharmaśāstras dealing with all kinds of matter relating to religious and civil law. There was also a bewildering bulk of commentaries. These proved quite unwieldy to the people in general as also to the priests conducting various rites and rituals. Therefore, the need was felt for short-cuts on each of the various topics like *vivāha*, *śrāddha*, *prāyaścitta*, *vyavahāra*, etc. The result was the composition of digests (*nibandhas*) on different topics. The digest-makers can be broadly divided into the following schools:

1. *Gauḍīya or Bengal school* — the greatest exponent was Raghunandana (sixteenth century AD). Jīmūtavāhana as stated earlier, was the sole authority in matters relating to inheritance and succession.
2. *Maithila or Bihar school* — perhaps the greatest representative of this school was Caṇḍeśvara Ṭhakkura (fourteenth century AD) and the most popular was Vidyāpati (fourteenth-fifteenth century AD) who is better known for his succulent Vaiṣṇava *Padāvalīs*.
3. *Vārāṇasī school* — perhaps the most well-known was Lakṣmīdhara (twelfth century AD).
4. *Dākṣiṇātya or south Indian school* — the most prolific writer was Hemādri (thirteenth century AD).
5. *Kāmarūpīya or Assam school* — Nīlāmbarācārya appears to have been the most well-known digest maker.
6. *Orissa school* — Pratāparudradeva (fifteenth-sixteenth century AD) was renowned both as the king of Orissa and a Smṛti scholar.

Commentaries on some of the prominent Smṛti digests also were written.

Manu-smṛti

As is well-known, the society was divided into four castes, viz., brāhmaṇa, kṣatriya, vaiśya and śūdra. The life of a man of any of the three upper castes was divided into four stages, viz. *brahmacarya* (studenthood), *gārhasthya* (householdership), *vānaprastha* (forest-life) and *saṁnyāsa* (complete renunciation of all worldly attachments).

WHAT IS DHARMA?

According to Manu (II.1), *dharma* is a practice which is always observed by those who are learned (i.e., versed in the Vedas), pious, free from hate and attachment, and which is heartily approved by them. Besides the *dharmas*, specified for the four castes and four stages of life, mentioned above, Manu ordains (X.63) the following as the *dharma* common to all irrespective of caste: *ahiṁsā* (non-injury), *satya* (truthfulness), *asteya* (non-theft), *śauca* (purification by water), *indriya-nigraha* (restraint of the senses), *prajanaṁ sveṣu dāreṣu* (procreation in own wives), *anasūyatā* (absense of jealousy). Instead of the last two, Yājñavalkya states (I.122) *dāna* (charity), *dama* (control of mind, according to the *mitākṣarā* (commentary), *dayā* (kindness) and *kṣānti* (absence of mental agitation even in harm done by others).

We shall give a brief account of the salient matters which are of interest and relevance even today. In doing so, we shall confine our observations only to the Smṛti works of Manu and Yājñavalkya, which are the most authoritative and widely known.

STUDENT-LIFE

The period of studenthood was of strict discipline, hard work and study. After a certain age, a boy had to live in the preceptor's house, serving him and studying under him. The teachers were of two kinds, viz., *ācārya* and *upādhyāya*. The former is one who, after performing the *upanayana* (initiation to Vedic study) of a boy, teaches him the Veda along with the sacrificial lore and Upaniṣad (*Manu*, II.40). The latter is one who, for the sake of livelihood, teaches a pupil only a part of the Veda or only the Vedāṅgas. In point of honour, an *ācārya* is equal to ten *upādhyāyas*; the father is equal to a hundred *ācāryas*, and the mother exceeds a thousand fathers (*Manu*, II.145). Again, Manu holds (II.146) that between the progenitor and the teacher of the Veda, the latter is superior to the former, because *brahma-janma* (i.e., initiation to the Veda which is the intellectual birth) of a brāhmaṇa is eternal which endures even in the other world. Kullūka's commentary on II.147 observes that the birth, given to a man by his parents out of passion (*kāma*), is common to animals also.

HOUSEHOLDER'S LIFE AND POSITION OF WOMEN

As regards householder's life, Manu says (III.60) that there is abiding welfare in a family in which the husband is satisfied with the wife and the wife with the husband. If the wife cannot please her husband, then the couple becomes childless (III.61). It is further held (III.56) that gods are pleased where women are honoured. That family perishes in which women are sorrowful (III.57). *Manu* (III.45 ff.) ordains that one should meet his wife in her menstrual period (i.e., sixteen days from the start) leaving out four days from the start of the menstrual flow; even in the remaining days one should avoid union on such occasions as new moon. In III.48, Manu says that union in the even number of nights produces a male child, and in the odd number of nights leads to the birth of a female one.

It is rather curious that, despite rules urging honour to women, *Manu* (IX. 3) declares that a woman does not deserve self-dependence; she is protected by the father in her virginity, by the husband in her youth and by sons in her old age.

It is also ordained (V.155) that a woman is neither entitled, independently of her husband, to perform sacrifice, observe a vow (*vrata*) nor to fast. By her service to her husband, she is glorified in heaven.

Some rules of Manu, however, reveal a humane attitude to women. Though the general rule is that a girl should be given in marraige before her menstruation starts, yet Manu firmly ordains that she should never be married to a man devoid of qualifications and learning, etc., even if she has to live at her father's house till death (IX.89). A girl who has menstruated before marriage, should wait for three years; if, in this period, her guardians do not arrange for her marriage, then she will be at liberty to find out a suitable husband (IX.90).

Ordinarily, the marriage-tie is unbreakable. Manu clearly says (IX.46) that the wife cannot be released from the husband even by sale or desertion. Manu allows (II.80 ff.) a man to supersede his wife under certain circumstances, i.e., if she drinks wine, is unchaste, etc., and to marry another women. Even in such a circumstance, the marriage-tie remains unbroken. P.V. Kane makes it clear that even when an extremely guilty wife is *tyajyā* (worthy of being forsaken) as in *Manu* (IX.83), "divorce, in its ordinary sense (i.e., divorce *a vinculo matrimonii*) has been unknown to Dharmaśāstras and to Hindu society . . . except on the ground of custom among the lower castes". So abandonment meant only separation in bed and board.

As regards widow-remarriage, *Manu* (IX.175) seems to allow a widow to re-marry. The next verse provides that if a woman, whose marriage is not consummated, resorts to another man, then her marriage with the latter may be solemnised. Incidentally, it may be noted that Nārada, probably later than Manu, clearly allows (*Strī-puṁsa-prakaraṇa*, 97) a woman to re-marry (*patiranyo vidhīyate*) under the following circumstances: when the husband is untraceable, dead, has become a mendicant, is impotent or apostate. The same verse occurs in the *Parāśara-smṛti* also. The *Parāśara-mādhava* commentary remarks that remarriage is meant for another age (i.e., not for *kali* age). The commentator, Medhātithi on *Manu* (V.157) remarks that *pati* (in the aforesaid verse of Nārada and Parāśara) means not husband, but one who maintains the widow (*pālanāt patimanyamā-śrayeta*). It can, perhaps, be concluded that, by the time the commentaries were written, the practice of remarriage of a widow ceased to be lawful. Medhātithi, mentioned above, is supposed to have flourished in the ninth century AD, and Mādhava in the fourteenth.

As regards the position of women *vis-a-vis* secular law, the main rules will be stated in our discussion on the *Yājñavalkya-smṛti*.

RĀJADHARMA

Chapter VII. of the *Manu-smṛti*, dealing with *rājadharma* (royal duties), is both interesting and instructive. Much of it agrees with what Kauṭilya provides in his *Arthaśāstra*. We shall touch upon a few important matters. According to *Manu* (VII. 3ff.), the king was created by God with elements taken from different deities. So, he should not be regarded as a human being.

Manu prescribed (VII.43) the following subjects to be learnt by the king: *trayī vidyā* (the three Vedas, called *Ṛk*, *Yajus* and *Sāman*), *daṇḍanīti* (*arthaśāstra* or economics, according to Kullūka), *ānvīkṣikī* (logic), *ātma-vidyā* (*brahma-vidyā*, knowledge about *Brahman*) and *vārtā* (according to Kullūka, agriculture, cattle-rearing, trade, etc.)

Manu insists on the constant control of the senses; it is with this that a king can control his subjects (VII.44).

He asks the king carefully to avoid vices (VII.45 ff.), which are divided into two groups, viz., arising out of passion (*kāmja*) and arising from anger (*krodhaja*). The first group comprises hunting, dice-playing, day-sleep, slander, women, drinking, dance, music (vocal and instrumental) and loitering. The second group includes falsely finding fault of others, *sāhasa* (according to Kullūka, persecution like imprisonment of an innocent person; violence according to others), *droha* (according to Kullūka, killing on a pretext; malice, according to others), jealousy, discovering fault in others who have merit, abuse, assault, etc., *arthadūṣaṇa* (theft of money or non-repayment of debt).

In VII.40 ff. Manu stresses the importance of modesty (*vinaya*) on the part of a king, and cites instances of how many kings were ruined due to the lack of it, and how several kings prospered by this virtue.

DAṆḌA

VII.14ff. deals with the importance of *daṇḍa* (royal sceptre symbolising the royal power to punish the wrong-doers and protect those who act rightly). Manu advises judicious application of *daṇḍa* avoiding the two extremes of too much severity and too much leniency. Manu draws a picture of chaos and confusion in the absence of *daṇḍa*.

MINISTERS

Manu advises (VII.54) the king to appoint seven or eight *saciva*s (*amātya*s, according to commentator, Kullūka) who must be born in a high family which served the king for generations, versed in scriptures, heroic, makrsmen; before appointment they must be tested. The king is to take an action after consulting them severally and jointly. As regards their number, stated above, it is not rigid. There should be as many of them as may be necessary.

AMBASSADOR

As peace and war depend on the ambassador (VII.65), Manu mentions (VII.63, 64) the qualities required in him. These are versed in all scriptures, able to understand hints, the motives indicated by others' physical movements and activities, pure in money matters and unaddicted to sexual enjoyment, skilful, born in a high family, loyal, possessed of good memory, and of the knowledge of countries and times, having a good physique, free from fear, eloquent.

FORTS

Manu's directions about forts and military matters have been discussed in a separate chapter.

POLITICAL EXPEDIENTS

Manu provides for two kinds of political expedients; one is called *upāya* and the other *guṇa*. *Upāya*s (VII.107 ff.) are four, viz., *sāma* (conciliation), *dāna* (gift), *bheda* (dissension) and *daṇḍa* (war). Manu's advice is that a king should never take recourse to war so long as the other three *upāya*s serve the purpose (VII.198, 200). The *guṇa*s are six (VII.160), viz., *sandhi* (peace, treaty), *vigraha* (conflict), *yāna* (expedition), *āsana* (sitting on the fence, i.e., to wait and see), *dvaidhībhāva* (splitting the army into two parts, one in the rear and the other in the van; according to others, duplicity, i.e., outwardly behaving as a friend of the enemy, but actually preparing for a strike) and *saṁśraya* (alliance with a stronger king).

Rājamaṇḍala

The concept of the political circle (*rājamaṇḍala*), according to *Manu* (VII.155 ff.), can be made clear in the following way:

	arimitramitra	
	mitramitra	
	arimitra	*udāsīna*
	mitra	
	(Friend or ally)	
madhyama	*ari*	
	(Enemy)	
	vijigīṣu	
	(The central power)	
	pārṣṇigrāha	
	ākranda	
	pārṣṇigrāhāsāra	
	ākrandāsāra	

The principle is that the immediately next power is hostile. *Madhyama* is a king who can help both the *vijigīṣu* and the *ari* whether they are allied to each other or not, and can resist any of them individually when they are not in alliance. *Udāsīna* is a king whose realm is beyond the sphere of the territories of the *vijigīṣu*, his *ari* and the *madhyama* and who can help these three kings whether they are allied or not, and can resist any of them when they are not allied.

Manu lays down the following rules for rural administration (VII.114 ff). A sort of police outpost should be set up for units of two, three, five or one hundred villages. A village will be administered by a headman. One man will be in charge of each of the units of ten, twenty, hundred and thousand villages; each succeeding being superior to the preceding one. Food, drink, fuel, etc., which are to be given to the king daily by villagers, will be used as the maintenance of the village headman. The head of ten villages will get, for his maintenance, as much land as can be tilled by two ploughs, each drawn by six cows. The head of 20 villages will get five times of the above. The head of a hundred villages will get an entire village, and that of a thousand villages will enjoy a city. A minister will be in the over-all charge of rural affairs.

Regarding taxation (VII.127 ff.), Manu's directive is that, before levying taxes on traders, the king should consider the following factors: purchase price, sale price, the distance covered, expenses for food, security expenses, and the profit. The king should neither impose too heavy taxes nor should he be over-lenient. The rates are briefly as follows: 1/50th of animals and gold, 1/8th, 1/6th or 1/12th part of corns. A brāhmaṇa is completely exempted from tax or revenue. So far as craftsmen artisans, śūdras and all those who earn livelihood by physical labour are concerned, they should be made to work gratis for the king once every month.

DELIBERATION WITH MINISTERS

Manu emphasis (VII.146ff.) the importance of the secrecy of counsel (*mantra*) given by ministers to the king. He should hold deliberations at one of the following places: top of a hill, lonely place, lonely forest.

The following should be removed from the place of deliberation: idiot, dumb, deaf, blind, (talking) birds, too old, woman, a *mleccha* (see Glossary), diseased, one with one limb less than usual (e.g., one-eyed person, one with 19 fingers) women have been stated to be the most prone to the leakage of counsel. The suitable time is midday or midnight.

ESPIONAGE

The system of espionage has been briefly touched upon by Manu. In VII.154 he refers to the five kinds of spies (*pañca-varga*) which are explained by Kullūka as *kāpaṭika*, *udāsthita*, *gṛhapati-vyañjana*, *vaidehaka-vyañjana* and *tapasa-vyañjana*. These have been described in a chapter in *Arthaśāstra*. It is one of the daily duties of the king to hear the reports of the spies.

Yājñavalkya-Smṛti

It deals with all the usual topics of Dharmaśāstra. Its chapter on secular law (*vyavahāra*) had been of a very high authority in Hindu Law. As stated earlier, its *Mitākṣarā* commentary played a very important role in the interpretation of the rules laid down in the *Yājñavalkya-smṛti*. The highlights of his discussion on law are briefly stated below:

JUDICIAL PROCEDURE — GENERAL PRINCIPLES

Yājñavalkya-smṛti (hereafter *Y*) states (II.5) that a cause of action or a subject of litigation arises when a person, wronged by another person, seeks redress from the king. Thus, according to him, a king cannot *suo motu* start a lawsuit.

A judicial proceeding consists of four parts, viz. lodging of a complaint, evidence, reply (of the defendant), and judgement (*Y*, II. 8). In a suit, in which the defendant admits the charge against him, the question of evidence and judgement does not arise.

If there is conflict between two Smṛti texts, equity based on usage prevails (*Y*, II.21). But, if of two Smṛti texts, one relates to *arthaśāstra* or politics and the other is in accord with Smṛti-śāstra, then the latter will prevail (*ibid.*) For example, a text of Dharmaśāstra provides that a property, though not acquired by a valid mode of acquisition, will be regarded as belonging to one who has been in hereditary possession of it, i.e., what has been possessed by three preceding generations including one's father). But, a Smṛti text of the *arthaśāstra* type ordains that such a person should be punished like a thief. In this case, the earlier text will be of stronger authority.

TITLES OF DISPUTE

There are 18 titles of dispute or subjects of litigation (*vyavahāra-padas*) according to *Manu* (VIII.4-7) which are given below:

1. *Ṛṇādāna* — giving of debt, non-repayment of debt, etc.
2. *Nikṣepa* — deposit.
3. *Asvāmi-vikraya* — sale by one not the owner.
4. *Sambhūya-samutthāna* — partnership business.
5. *Dattasyā-napākarma* — non-delivery of gift.

6. *Vetanasyā-dāna* — non-payment of wages.
7. *Saṁvid-vyatikrama* — breach of contract.
8. *Kraya-vikrayā-nuśaya* — repentance after purchase and sale.
9. *Svāmī-pāla-vivāda* — dispute between owner and herdsman.
10. *Sīmāvivāda* — boundary dispute.
11. *Daṇḍa-vācika-pāruṣya* — abuse and defamation; assault.
12. *Steya* — theft.
13. *Sāhasa* — crime of violence.
14. *Strī-saṁgrahaṇa* — adultery.
15. *Strī-puṁ-dharma* — duties of wife and husband.
16. (*Dāya*) *vibhāga* — partition of heritage.
17. *Dyūta* — gambling.
18. *Āhvaya* — Animal-betting.

SUBSTANTIVE LAW — EVIDENCE

Evidences are threefold, viz., document, possession and witness. In the absence of all of them, ordeal (*divya*, divine) should be resorted to (*Y*, II.22).

ADVERSE POSSESSION

If one's property (other than wealth) is enjoyed by another without protest by the owner, for 20 years, then the latter will be its owner. In case of wealth, ten-year uninterrupted possession by another person will cause his ownership over it. The law of adverse possession, however, will not apply to the properties of an idiot, minor, a king, woman, a brāhmaṇa versed in the Veda. A mortgaged property, boundary, sealed deposit and open deposit, will not come within the purview of the above law (*Y*, II.24, 25).

MODES OF ACQUISITION AND POSSESSION

A valid mode of acquisition (i.e., by purchase, gift, etc.) is stronger than possession, provided the possession is not hereditary, (i.e., by three preceding generations including one's father). But even a valid mode of acquisition will be of no avail where there is not even slight possession (*Y*, II.27).

AUTHORITIES FOR ADMINISTRATION OF JUSTICE

In a lawsuit, among those mentioned below, each preceding is of higher authority than the succeeding one:

Persons appointed by the king, *pūga*, *śreṇī* and *kula* (*Y*, II.30). (For *pūga*, *śreṇī* and *kula*, see Glossary).

It should be added that even against the highest body above complaint will lie with the king.

LAWS OF DEBT

Interest on money lent may be of the following kinds:

(i) *Kālikā* — payable monthly.

(ii) *Kāritā* — fixed according to the wish of the parties.

(iii) *Kāyikā* — in the form of physical labour and realisable per day.

(iv) *Cakra-vr̥ddhi* — compound interest.

(v) *Śikhā* — realised daily.

(vi) *Bhoga* — in the form of enjoyment (e.g., rent of a house, crops, etc.).

If a creditor, out of greed for more interest, does not accept repayment by the debtor, then the latter will give the money to a mediator; since then, no further interest will accrue (*Y*, II.44).

A woman is not liable for the debt of the husband or son; father is not responsible for the liabilities of the son; the husband is not liable for the debt of the wife. In every case, however, if a debt is incurred for the sake of the family, the head of the family will be liable for repayment (*Y*, II.46). The son is not responsible for the debt incurred by the father for the following purposes: drinking, gratifying passion, gambling, balance of fine or tax, purposeless gift (*Y*, II.47).

The husbands of the following classes are responsible for the debts of their wives, because their occupations depend on the women: cowherd, distiller of wine, actor, washerman, hunter (*Y*, II.48).

A mortgaged property is forfeited if it is not released even when the interest becomes equal to the principal. A mortgage for a specified period will be forfeited after the expiry of the time-limit. A usufructuary mortgage is never forfeited. (*Y*, II.58).

WITNESS

Generally, witnesses for a litigant should not be less than three (*Y*, II.69). But a single witness will do if he is approved by both the parties to the suit (*Y*, II.72). As a rule, men with certain qualifications like piety, learning, etc., are eligible as witnesses, yet everyone, irrespective of the requisite qualifications, is eligible as witness in suits relating to theft, abuse, assault and crime of violence.

In the event of difference of opinion among the witnesses, that of the majority will be accepted. If two groups of equal number of witnesses differ, then the evidence furnished by the group consisting of meritorious persons will be acceptable. If there is difference among the meritorious, the version of those who are the most meritorious will be valid (*Y*, II.78).

It is interesting to note that, though perjury is a penal offence (*Y*, II.81), yet Yājñavalkya himself ordains (*Y*, II. 83) that a witness will tell a lie if his true statement is likely to lead to the death-penalty of a member of any of the four castes.

PARTITION OF INHERITANCE

When the father makes partition, he may either divide the property equally among the sons or give the eldest one more than what other sons severally get (*Y*, II.114). If the division is done equally, then the wife also should get a share equal to that of a son, provided she has got no *strīdhana* (woman's exclusive property) from the husband or father-in-law. But, if a greater share is given to the eldest son, then the wife will get a share equal to that of a son out of what remains after giving the excess to the eldest son (*Y*, II.115).

After the death of the parents, the sons may partition the inheritance as well as debt (if incurred by father) equally among themselves. The property of the mother, however, will go to her daughters after deduction of debt, if any (*Y*, II.117). One, who himself earns something without using the paternal property, and whatever is earned by means of learning are not to be shared with others (*Y*, II.118, 119).

Sons of different fathers will inherit the shares of their respective fathers. In other words, they will inherit per stirps, not per capita (*Y*, II.120). It may be made clear in the following way:

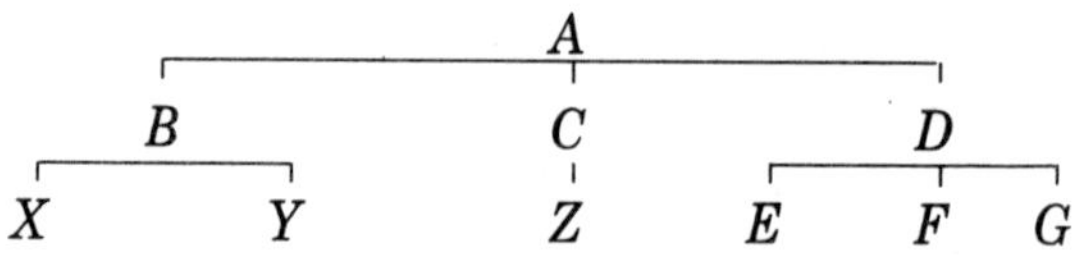

> *A* has three sons, *B*, *C* and *D*. *B* has two sons, *X* and *Y*. *C* has one son, *Z*. *D* has three sons, *E*, *F*, *G*. Each of *B*, *C*, *D* will get 1/3. Each of *X* and *Y* will get 1/6. *Z* will get 1/3. *E*, *F*, *G* will get 1/9 each. Thus 1/6 +1/6 + 1/3 + 1/9 + 1/9 + 1/9 = 1.

To a land and other things, belonging to the grandfather the right of the father is equal to that of his son (*Y*, II.121). In the event of partition after the death of the father, the mother will get a share equal to that of a son. The unmarried brother will be married by those who are already married. The unmarried sisters will be married after giving a *turīyaka* from the share of a brother (*Y*, II.124). The word *turīyaka*, according to the *Mitākṣarā*, means a fourth part. Thus, the property will be divided equally into as many parts as there are brothers and sisters. Then one-fourth of one part will be set apart for the sister. The remaining property will be equally divided among the brothers.

KINDS OF SONS

The following kinds of sons are recognised by *Yājñavalkya-smṛti* (*Y*, II.128-32):

1. *Aurasa* — born of one by his wife of the same caste.
2. *Putrikāputra* — of two kinds — (a) A daughter, appointed by a sonless man, to be like his son; and (b) the son of the daughter of a sonless man who appoints him as his own son.
3. *Kṣetraja* — begotten by one on the wife of another.
4. *Gūḍhaja* — secretly born in the house (the begette being one other than the father).
5. *Kānīna* — son of girls before her marriage.
6. *Paunarbhava* — son of a woman, called *punarbhū* (see Glossary).
7. *Dattaka* — adopted.
8. *Kṛta* — purchased.
9. *Kṛtrima* — a parentless boy treated like a son after alluring him with money, land, etc.
10. *Dattātmā* — a boy, bereft of parents or cast away by them, offers himself as a son.
11. *Sahoḍhaja* — born to a woman who was pregnant before marriage.
12. *Apaviddha* — one, who, cast away by parents, is taken by a person as his son.

In all the cases, the son is to be understood as belonging to the caste of his father. In offering oblations to the deceased ancestors and inheriting properties, each succeeding in the list will be eligible only in the absence of the preceding one.

ORDER OF SUCCESSION RELATING TO A SONLESS MAN'S PROPERTY

Among all the castes, the following is the order of succession in respect of the property of a sonless man who is dead (*Y*, II.135-6):

> Wife, daughter, parents, brother, brother's son, one with the same *gotra*, *bandhu* (see Glossary), disciple, fellow student.

PERSONS DEBARRED FROM INHERITANCE

The following persons are not entitled to any share of the property, but only to maintenance (*Y*, II.140):

> impotent, apostate, son of an apostate, lame, insane, mentally retarded, blind, afflicted with an incurable malady, etc.

The *Mitākṣarā* commentary adds that if the defects of the above persons arise before partition, then they will be excluded. But, if the defects arise after partition, they will continue to enjoy their rights. Their *aurasa* and *kṣetraja* sons, if free from defects, are, however, entitled to inheritance. But, the son of an apostate will have no share.

STRĪDHANA

The subject of *strīdhana* (see Glossary) has been dealt with in *Y*, II.143 ff. The *strīdhana* of a woman, dying childless, goes to her *bāndhavas*. In the cases of those childless women, who were married in any one of the four forms of marriage, viz., *brāhma*, *daiva*, *ārṣa* and *prājāpatya*, their property will be inhertited by their husbands. If such a woman dies leaving daughters, then they will inherit the property. In the cases of women, married according to any one of the other forms of marriage (viz., *gāndharva*, *āsura*, *rākṣasa*, *paiśāca*) the property will go to her father. The *Mitākṣarā*, quoting authority, declares that the order of succession among the daughters, mentioned above, is as follows:

> unmarried, married but poor and married and established.

SOLATIUM IN SUPERSESSION

To the superseded wife the husband shall give equal amount (*samam*), provided no *strīdhana* was given to her. If, however, she had got *strīdhana*, she would be given half (*Y*, II.148). The word 'equal' means equal to what has been spent on the subsequent marriage. According to others, it means equal to what has been given to the other wife.

Śūdras

WHO WERE THE ŚŪDRAS?

The earliest reference to the stratification of the society is contained in stanza (*ṛk*) 12 of the *Puruṣa-sūkta* of the *Ṛgveda* (X.90). Though the term *varṇa* does not occur there, yet the four castes, brāhmaṇa, kṣatriya, vaiśya, and śūdra are stated to have sprung from the mouth, arms, knees and feet respectively of the Great Primeval Being. Thus, the śūdras appear to have belonged to the lowest rung of the social ladder.

There are different opinions about the identification of the śūdras. Some think that they were pre-Āryan aborigines of India, referred to in the *Ṛgveda* as *dāsa* or *dasyu* (e.g., *ṚV*, I.51.8, II.11.2, 4; III.29.9, V.70.3, VII.5.6, IX.88.4, etc.). Others are of opinion that the reference, in the aforesaid Ṛgvedic stanza, to śūdra as born out of the feet seems to suggest that śūdras were within the Āryan fold, serving the three higher castes. The *dāsa*s (perhaps referring to the non-Āryan tribals) are stated, in this very Veda (II.12.4), to have been pushed into caves by the Āryan deity.

In course of time, the word *dāsa* came to mean servant in general, and also, in some cases, slaves.

CLASSIFICATION OF ŚŪDRAS

From Pāṇini's rule II.4.10 and Patañjali's commnet thereon, we come to learn that śūdras were divided into two classes, viz., *aniravasita* and *niravasita*. The former included those the utensils, used by whom in eating, could be purified and used. The utensils, used by the other class, had to be thrown away. Again, śūdras were classed as *sat* and *asat*. Those of the former class followed good avocations or trades, served the people of the higher castes, and abstained from meat, intoxicating drinks, and did not sell wine. Those of the other classes acted in a contrary manner. A third division of śūdras was as *bhojyānna* (i.e., the food cooked by whom could be eaten by brāhmaṇas) and *abhojyānna* (those whose cooked food was a taboo for brāhmaṇas).

DUTIES OF THE ŚŪDRAS, THEIR PRIVILEGES AND CONSTRAINTS

The authorities are almost unanimous in holding that their principal duty is to serve the members of the three higher castes (*Manu*, I.91, VIII.413, 414). The servitude on the part of śūdras was so much insisted upon that Manu (II.32) prescribes that they should be given names indicating service.

All the religious rites for śūdras were to be without Vedic *mantras*. It should be noted that the śūdras had no *saṁskāras* (sacraments) excepting *vivāha*. They have one stage of life, that is *gārhasthya*. All other stages are denied to them. It should be noted that, according to *Y*, II.241, as read by commentator Viśvarūpa, a person was punishable for inviting a śūdra ascetic to a feast in rites for gods and the manes. This implies that śūdras also could adopt the fourth stage of life (see Kane, *HDH*, II, p. 945).

According to *Manu* (II.223), one should emulate a śūdra who performs a good deed. One should respectfully acquire knowledge even from an *avara* (II.238); *avara* means śūdra according to Kullūka, any one of a low caste (*hīnajātīya*) according to Medhātithi.

Manu (IV.80-1) shows a very contemptuous attitude towards śūdras. His strict rule is that no one should give any advice, religious or secular, to a śūdra nor give him the residue of what has been offered in a sacrifice. A śūdra should wear the old or thrown-away clothes, umbrellas, sandals, mattresses, etc., of his master whose remnants of food should be given to him (*Manu,* X.125). A śūdra can perform *vratas* but without *homa* and *mantras*. He is forbidden to utter *oṁkāra*. *Manu* (IV.211) forbids a brāhmaṇa to take food from a śūdra unless the latter is his cowherd, own servant or barber or tills the former's field or is a hereditary friend of the family (*Manu*, IV.253).

Manu (IV.61) prohibits the residence of a brāhmaṇa in the kingdom of a śūdra. Even if a śūdra has capacity, he should not accumulate wealth, because, by so doing, he may be proud and cause trouble to brāhmaṇas.

A śūdra, reviling a person of a higher caste, shall have his tongue cut off (*Manu*, VIII.270). But, for a similar offence of a brāhmaṇa towards a śūdra, he would have to pay a small fine (*Manu*, VIII.268). *Manu* ordains (VIII.20) that a king may appoint a brāhmaṇa as a judge even if he does not perform all his duties, but never a śūdra even of good conduct and self-restraint.

In times of distress, a śūdra was allowed to take to agriculture or some crafts. But, as *Y*, I.120 and the *Mitākṣarā* thereon clearly state, whatever calling a distressed śūdra may adopt, it must be conducive to the benefit of the members of the higher castes.

Śūdras were so much detested that, according to *Manu*, XI.66 and *Y*, III.236, the killing of a person of this class was regarded as an *upapātika* (minor sin). The rite for expiating this sin was the same as that for killing such lower animals and birds as cat, frog, crow, etc., (*Manu* XI.131).

Śūdras were debarred from the study of the Vedas and even from listening to their recitation. From *Manu* II.16, it appears that a śūdra was not eligible even for the study of the *Manu-smṛti* and for hearing its study.

For adultery with a brāhmaṇa woman, a śūdra would be given death-penalty (*Manu*, VIII.366). For a similar offence of a brāhmaṇa, with an unguarded śūdra woman, he would be fined (*Manu*, VIII. 385).

Slavery

The word *dāsa*, in post-Vedic works, denotes both servant and slave in different contexts. For example, Bhartṛhari's (mid-seventh century AD), *Śṛṅgāra-śataka* (I.1) uses the expression *gṛha-karma-dāsaḥ*. We are concerned here with slaves only. From *Manu* VIII. 299 it is clear that *dāsa*, in some contexts, means slave; *dāsa* and *preṣya* (servant) are separately mentioned.

Manu (VIII.415) names the following seven kinds of *dāsa*s or slaves: (i) captured in a battle, (ii) one who voluntarily becomes so for food, (iii) born in the house (to a female slave), (iv) purchased, and (v) given by parents or relatives, (vi) inherited, and (vii) voluntarily becoming so for paying fine or debt. According to *Manu* (VIII.416) a slave cannot own any property; whatever he earns belongs to his master. *Yājñavalkya-smṛti*, II.182 ordains that one enslaved by force, one sold by a thief, one who saves the life of the master from a danger, by giving up food (in the case of one who volunteered as a slave for food) must be set free. A slave who pays the ransom (i.e., the money paid by the master for paying fine or debt) shall also be manumitted. According to *Manu* (VIII.299, 300), in the matter of physical punishment for doing something wrong, the slave is to be treated like one's wife, son, servant, brother. If necessary, they can be beaten with a rope or a thin piece of bamboo. But, they can be struck only on the back, but never on the head.

10

Kāma-śāstra (Erotics)

Of the four ends of life (*puruṣārtha*), recognised in ancient India, namely *dharma*, *artha*, *kāma* and *mokṣa*. *Kāma* belongs to *trivarga*, the other two being *dharma* and *artha*. *Kāma* means desire in general. When we say *Kāma-śāstra*, *kāma* means sexual desire, and the *śāstra* relating to it means erotic literature. The very existence of this *śāstra* proves that the wise people of ancient India were not averse to enjoyment. What they insisted upon was not brutal indulgence in sex gratification, but restrained enjoyment of women. The works on erotics look upon it as one of the many arts.

Among the extant works on erotics, the *Kāmasūtra* of Vātsyāyana, also called Mallanāga, is the most well-known and authoritative. His date is uncertain. Different scholars assign him to different periods ranging from the third to sixth century AD. According to Keith, he cannot have been earlier than the fifth century AD (*vide A History of Skt. Lit.*, p. 469). S.K. De assigns him approximately to the third century (*vide Ancient Indian Erotics and Erotic Literature*, p. 91). That there was a long tradition of erotics as a discipline, is evident from the above work. Vātsyāyana names the following predecessors in this *śāstra*:

> Śvetaketu, Bābhravya, Dattaka, Cārāyaṇa, Ghoṭaka-mukha, Gonardīya, Goṇikāputra, Suvarṇanābha, and Kucu(i)māra.

From the story of Uddālaka-Śvetaketu, in the *Bṛhadāraṇya-kopaniṣad*, it seems that, even in that remote age (pre-Christ), the problems of sex-life, especially in connection with genetics, attracted the attention of the sages. The following statement of Vātsyāyana also testifies to the existence of an exhaustive *Kāmaśāstra* before him:

> *saṁkṣipya sarvamarthamalpena granthena kāmasūtra-midaṁ praṇītam* ।

Most probably, the above Kucumāra was the author of the *Kucimāra-tantra* which deals with erotics in eight chapters (*paṭala*s).

Vātsyāyana's *Kāmasūtra* is a fairly exhaustive work, divided into seven sections, called *adhikaraṇa*s. The titles of the *adhikaraṇa*s, as given below, indicate their contents.

I. *Sādhāraṇa* (generalities).

II. *Sāṁprayogika* (sexual intercourse).

III. *Kanyā-saṁprayuktaka* (courtship and marriage).

IV. *Bhāryādhikārika* (wife).

V. *Pāradārika* (another person's wife).

VI. *Vaiśika* (prostitutes).

VII. *Aupaniṣadika* (secrect love or extraneous stimulation).

The work incidentally mentions 64 arts to be learnt particularly by women. These include music, dance, decoration, painting, sewing, gardening, making garlands, dyeing of teeth, nails, hair, clay-modelling, etc. To these arts, called *śilpakalā*s are added 64 *kāmakalā*s or various ways of erotic acts. The life of a *nāgaraka* (man about town) has been described in detail. The prostitutes have been divided into various classes. Sections five and six clearly show that the author did not conform to conventional morality. He has sought to guide people in their efforts to fulfil their carnal desire in the different ways that were in vogue in the society.

The author sounds a sceintific note when he says that erotic satisfaction is as necessary as food for the preservation and well-being of the body (I.2.46). The learned commentator adds that mental health, too, requires it; because, repression is likely to result in mental derangement. This is a well-known view of the modern psychiatrists. Some of the recipes, given in the last section of the

Kāmasūtra, for whetting sexual vigour, are reported by doctors to be of practical value.

It seems that the quality and reputation of Vātsyāyana's work eclipsed earlier works on the subject. The works which follow the *Kāmasūtra* are either professedly its epitomes, imitations or of the nature of manuals intended for the rogue. It should be noted that most of the later works omit the topic of prostitutes. Among these works, mention may be made of the following:

Anaṅga-raṅga of Kalyāṇamalla (sixteenth century).

Kandarpa-cūḍāmaṇi (AD 1577) of King Vīrabhadra of Vaghelā dynasty.

Nāgara-sarvasva of Padmaśrī (sometime between the tenth century and the fourteenth).

Pañcasāyaka of Maithila Jyotirīśvara Kaviśekhara (fourteenth century, first half).

Rati-mañjarī of Jayadeva whose identity is uncertain.

Rati-ratna-pradīpikā of Mahārāja Devarāja (seventeenth century).

Rati-rahasya of Kukkoka (sometime before thirteenth century).

The above are published works which deal almost exclusively with sexual union (*sāṁprayogika*) or give some recipes for artificial stimulation (*aupaniṣadika*). The *Rati-rahasya*, mentioned above, expatiates on the last-mentioned subject. The aforesaid *Kandarpa-cūḍāmaṇi*, however, is an exception. It deals with the entire subject.

Two other published works, namely *Ratiramaṇa*, attributed to Siddha Nāgārjuna and *Kucimāra-tantra* could not be examined by us.

There are several unpublished works which are insignificant.

11

Alaṁkāra-śāstra (Poetics)

General Remarks

POETICS is called *Alaṁkāra-śāstra*. In its wider sense, *alaṁkāra* means ornament, embellishment, that which beautifies. One of the meanings of *alam* is *bhūṣaṇa*. In its narrower sense, *alaṁkāras* means the figures of speech, called *śabdālaṁkāras* like *anuprāsa*, *yamaka*, etc., and *arthālaṁkāras* like *upamā*, *rūpaka*, etc.

The word *upamā* occurs in the *Ṛgveda* (I.31.15, V.34.9). At certain places of this Veda, we find the use of figures of words, like *anuprāsa* and *yamaka* as well as the figures of sense like *upamā*, *rūpaka*, *atiśayokti*, etc. The *Śatapatha Brāhmaṇa* uses some figures of speech in, for example, I.2.5.16. The *Kaṭhopaniṣad* contains instances of *rūpaka*. Pāṇini (*c*. fourth century BC) has used the words *upamāna* (II.1.55) and *upamita* (II.1.56). There are instances galore of the use of several figures of speech in the *Rāmāyaṇa* (present form completed *c*. second or third century AD) and the *Mahābhārata* (completion of the extant form in about fourth century AD).

The litterateurs unconsciously use figures of speech in order to embellish their compositions. So, the use of figures of speech, in the above cases, does not necessarily prove that there was an *Alaṁkāra-śāstra*. In fact, we have no means to determine the time of origin of this discipline. Rājaśekhara, in the latter part of the ninth century AD, records a tradition which regarded this *śāstra* as the seventh Vedāṅga. But, there is evidence of the later origin of this *śāstra*. For instance, the *Chāndogya Upaniṣad* (Böhtlingk's ed., VII.1.2, 4) does not mention it among the subjects to be learnt. The *Āpastamba Dharmasūtra* mentions the conventional six Vedāṅgas. *Alaṁkāra-śāstra* is conspicuous by its absence in Yājñavalkya's (*c.* first century AD) list (I.3) of 14 *śāstra*s and the list in the *Viṣṇu Purāṇa* (earlier than sixth century) which adds four more branches of learning.

The *Lalitavistara*, a fairly early *Avadāna* treatise, mentions (Lefmann's ed., I, p. 156) a *Kāvya-karaṇa-grantha*. The *Śukranīti* (*c.* thirteenth or fourteenth century, according to P.V. Kane) appears to be the earliest work to refer to *Alaṁkāra-śāstra* among 32 *śāstra*s.

There are reasons to believe that this *śāstra* originated much earlier than the seventh century AD. The poeticians Bhāmaha (*c.* seventh-eighth century) and Daṇḍin (*c.* eighth century) refer to earlier writers or their views. Both Bhāmaha and Daṇḍin presuppose a fairly long period of development of this *śāstra*. Otherwise, it would not, perhaps, have been possible to write such systematic and well-thoughtout treatises. Thus, it is not, perhaps, unjustifiable to suppose that this *śāstra*, as a distinct discipline, was considerably developed about the sixth century AD. Had it been so, the *śāstra* must have originated much earlier.

In the fourth and fifth centuries, in the Gupta regime, there was an efflorescence of Sanskrit literature. Kālidāsa is generally believed to have belonged to this period. Might be that the *Alaṁkāra-śāstra* also flourished in this milieu of cultural resurgence.

For the present, we shall give a resume of the developement of *Alaṁkāra-śāstra*.

A study of this *śāstra* reveals four principal schools. The question that naturally arises is — what is it that led to so many schools of opinion about the *Alaṁkāra-śāstra*?

With the gradual development of this *śāstra*, the connoisseurs started thinking about what constituted the essential element or the soul of *kāvya*. It was *alaṁkāra* according to some, *rīti* in the opinion of others, while yet others considered *rasa* to be the soul of *kāvya* and it was *dhvani* according to some writers.

Alaṁkāra School

The time of its origin is unknown. The strongest exponent of this school was Bhāmaha. He, for the first time, declared — *kāvyaṁ grāhyama-laṁkārāt*; i.e., a poetical composition is acceptable (or delightful to the connoisseur) by reason of embellishment.

Of all the extant treatises on poetics, the earliest one is the *Kāvyālaṁkāra* of Bhāmaha. It was commented upon by Udbhaṭa, an eminent theoretician of this school. Bhāmaha's date has not yet been determined with certainty. Considering all the evidences and the opinions of different scholars, S.K. De concludes that he probably flourished between the last quarter of the seventh century, and the middle of the eighth.

Bhāmaha recognises separate figures of word (*śabdālaṁkāra*) and sense (*arthālaṁkāra*) which, together, constitute *kāvya*. He is of the opinion that the indispensable element of all *alaṁkāra*s whatsoever is *vakrokti* which means the speciality or charm of expression. This idea so strongly appealed to later writers that they recognised it as a distinct figure of speech. The above idea of Udbhaṭa found a great exponent in Kuntaka (*c.* eighth-ninth century) the title of whose treatise, *Vakrokti-jīvita* speaks for itself. He recognised *vakrokti* as the very life (*jīvita*) of *kāvya*. In explaining this, he holds that *vakrokti* contains a kind of *atiśaya* (surpassing element) which is an unavoidable factor of the *vicitra mārga* (wonderful style) which consists in *vakrokti-vaicitrya*. Daṇḍin also subscribes to this view when he maintains that all *alaṁkāra*s are based on *atiśayokti* (hyperbole). An expositor, commenting on this view of Daṇḍin, says — *alaṁkārāntarāṇāmapi eṣa* (i.e., *atiśayokti*) *upakārī bhavati, atiśaya-jananatvaṁ vinā bhūṣaṇatayā na syāt*; i.e., *atiśayokti* is good for other *alaṁkāra*s too; embellishment is not possible without the quality of producing *atiśaya*. The *dhvani*-exponent, Ānandavardhana, too, admits that *atiśayokti* is included in all *alaṁkāras*, *atiśayokti* is *sarvālaṁkāra-sāmānya-rūpa*, according to Abhinavagupta, and, according to Mammaṭa, with respect to *alaṁkāras*, it exists like the life-breath (*prāṇatvenāvatiṣṭhate*). In the opinion of Bhāmaha, the *atiśaya*, that inheres in the *vakratā* of *alaṁkāras*, means *lokātikrānta-gocaratā*; that is to say that *alaṁkāra*s create superhuman charm.

Though not recognising the separate existence of *rasa*, Bhāmaha has fancied its presence in *rasavat alaṁkāra*, and, perhaps, also in the *alaṁkāras*, *preyas* and *urjasvī*. He has not explicitly mentioned *dhvani* or *vyaṅgyārtha*. But, it appears from the characteristics of the *alaṁkāras paryāyokta, vyāja-stuti, aprastuta-praśaṁsā* and *samāsokti*, that these are based on *vyaṅgyārtha*. Thus, it is clear that the ideas, however embryonic, of *dhvani* and *rasa* existed in hoary antiquity.

Another stalwart of this school was Udbhaṭa (*c.* end of eighth century to earlier part of the ninth). Besides expositions, called *Bhāmaha-vivaraṇa* and *Kāvyālaṁkāra-vivṛtti*, of Bhāmaha's work, he wrote the *Kāvyālaṁkāra-saṁgraha* which appears to have followed Bhāmaha in the order of the *alaṁkāras* and in the definitions of most of them. Udbhaṭa's work reveals some independent thinking. For example, while Bhāmaha mentions *saṁsṛṣṭi*, the combination of two or more independent *alaṁkāras*, Udbhaṭa makes a distinction between *saṁsṛṣṭi* and *saṁkara*. The latter is far more advanced than the former in the concept of *rasa*, and its place in *kāvya* and *alaṁkāra*. Udbhaṭa mentions the terms *bhāva* and *anubhāva* which are absent in Bhāmaha's work.

Although Bhāmaha is regarded as the founder of the *alaṁkāra* school, yet the doctrine of *alaṁkāra*, as the essential element of *kāvya*, finds the fullest explication in Udbhaṭa's work. He, indeed, is the pioneer in dealing with the subtle divisions and sub-divisions of the *alaṁkāras*, and in showing their distinctions from one another. His commentator, Pratihārendurāja has not, in all cases, presented the views of Udbhaṭa strictly as they are. Flourishing more than a century later, Pratihārendurāja was naturally influenced, to a great extent, by the schools of *rīti*, *dhvani* and *rasa*.

Another outstanding figure in the *alaṁkāra* school was Rudraṭa (*c.* ninth century). In his *Kāvyālaṁkāra*, he betrays considerable influence of the *rasa* doctrine. Nevertheless, he emphasises *alaṁkāra*. Despite the mention of four *rītis*, he does not set much store by *rīti* and *guṇa*. *Dhvani* has neither been mentioned by him nor does he indicate his familiarity with its place in *kāvya*. It should, however, be noted that he has hinted, in connection with figures like *paryāyokta*, *bhāva*, etc., at suggested meaning (*vyaṅgyārtha*) in addition to the denoted sense (*vācyārtha*), Rudraṭa has defined several additional *alaṁkāras*, and has mentioned sub-divisions of many principal *alaṁkāras*. He has very clearly shown the difference between *śabdālaṁkāra* and *arthālaṁkāra*. It was he who, for the first time, divided the *alṁkāras* into different categories. According to him, the *śabdālaṁkāras* can be divided as *vakrokti*, *ślesa*, *citra*, *anuprāsa* and *yamaka*. The *arthālaṁkāras* have been categorised as *vāstava*, *aupamya*, *atiśaya* and *śleṣa*.

Rīti School

The idea of *rīti*, in a poetical composition, perhaps originated even before Bhāmaha. But, it came to be better understood in Daṇḍin's work, and was declared by Vāmana as the soul of *kāvya*. Daṇḍin appears to stand midway between the *alaṁkāra* school and the *rīti* school; his predilection, however, for the latter is more pronounced. Like the adherents of the former, Daṇḍin (*c.* first half of ninth century) also feels that both the word and sense, constituting *kāvya*, should be embellished. But, he shows originality in thinking that only the *śabdālaṁkāras* and *arthālaṁkāras* do not embellish a *kāvya*; another requisite is *guṇa*. The *guṇa*-based style, emphasised by Daṇḍin, is *rīti* extolled by Vāmana. Daṇḍin does not use the word *rīti*, but its synonyms, *mārga* and *vartman*. His emphasis on *guṇa*, to which the *alaṁkāra* theorists were indifferent, marks his speciality in comparison with them. He holds that the *mārga* imparts grace to a composition; this idea shows him as a supporter of the *rīti* school. Of the two *mārgas*, *gauḍa* and *vaidarbha*, the latter is lauded by Daṇḍin as having, as its life-breath (*prāṇa*), a combination of the following qualities: *śleṣa*, *prasāda*, *samatā*, *mādhurya*, *sukumāratā*, *arthavyakti*, *udāratva*, *ojas*, *kānti* and *samādhi*. He declares — *eṣāṁ viparyayaḥ prāyo dṛśyate gauḍa-vartmani*; thus, the *gauḍa-mārga* seems to be devoid of these *guṇas*. Older commentators, however, think that the word *prāyas* signifies that these *guṇas* are generally (but not entirely) absent in the *gauḍa-mārga*.

Unlike the supporters of the *alaṁkāra* school, Daṇḍin thinks that *guṇa* also comes within the purview of *alaṁkāra*; in his opinion, any property that beautifies a *kāvya* (*kāvya-śobhākara*) is *alaṁkāra*.

All the poeticians, preceding Vāmana (eighth-ninth century), were concerned with the body of the *kāvya* which is constituted by a series of words conveying the desired sense (*iṣṭārtha-vyavachinnā padāvalī*). Vāmana appears to have been the first to concern himself with the soul of poetry. In his *Kāvyālaṁkāra-sūtra-vṛtti*, he clearly declares — *rītirātmā kāvyasya*. He has defined *rīti* as *viśiṣṭapada-racanā* (composition of special words or special composition of words). He mentions three *rīti*s, viz. *vaidarbhī, gauḍī* and *pāñcālī*. In his opinion, the first one possesses all the ten *guṇa*s, mentioned above, the second one copiously contains the *guṇa*s, *ojas* and *kānti*; *mādhurya* and *saukumārya* are the elements of *pāñcālī*. The *guṇa*s are the essential elements of the *rīti*s concerned. For the first time, in Vāmana's work, we find the twofold division of *guṇa*s, viz., *śabdaguṇa* and *arthaguṇa*.

It is not proper to render *rīti* as style. According to Western critics, the style is the man, i.e., the persona of the writer is reflected in the way he writes. But, *rīti* is not exactly like this. A composition, possessed of certain characteristics, is said to have a particular *rīti*. In short, while style is subjective, *rīti* is purely objective.

Like the protagonists of the *alaṁkāra* school, Vāmana too admits *alaṁkāra* as the essence of *kāvya*. But, he does not use the term *alaṁkāra* in the earlier and narrower sense of figure of speech, but in the broader sense of charm (*saundaryam alamkāraḥ*).

The *rīti*-theory failed to achieve wide popularity. Ānandavardhana subjected it to trenchant criticism. Mammaṭa has sought to refute the main thesis of Vāmana. The inherent weakness of the *rīti* doctrine lies in the fact that it busied itself with only the form or external element of *kāvya*. It could not get into its core. The advocates of the *rasa* and *dhvani* theories penetrated into the vitals of *kāvya*. This is why the *rīti* theorists proved to be no match to the other two schools, mentioned above.

Rasa School

Viśvanātha (*c*. fourteenth century, first half), in his *Sāhityadarpaṇa* (I.31), for the first time, defined *kāvya* as a *rasātmaka-vākya*, i.e., a sentence of which the soul is *rasa*. He explains *rasa* as follows:

vibhāvenā-nubhāvena vyaktaḥ sañcāriṇā tathā ।
rasatāmeti ratyādiḥ sthāyī bhāvaḥ sacetasām ॥
— (III. 1)

The permanent feeling, (love), etc., of the connoisseurs, being manifested by *vibhāva* (excitant), *anubhāva* (ensuant) as well as by *sañcārī bhāva* (accessory feeling), is transformed into *rasa*. For instance, in the *Rāmāyaṇa* story, the love of Rāma has Sītā as the *ālambana-vibhāva* (substratum) and moon-rise, etc., as *uddīpana-vibhāva*. The *anubhāva* may be *stambha* or stupefaction. The *sañcārī bhāva* may be *āvega* or agitation. Love in Rāma's mind, being manifested by the aforesiad *vibhāva*, etc., is transformed into *śṛṅgāra rasa* (erotic sentiment).

In the words of Viśvanātha, the above *rasa* is *vedyāntara-sparśa-śūnya* (devoid of the trace of any other knowledge), *brahmāsvāda-sahodara* (like the bliss of the attainment of *Brahman*), and *lokottaracamatkāra-prāṇa* (possessed of superhuman charm as its life-breath). When one experiences the bliss of the attainment of *Brahman*, he has knowledge of nothing else nor can he express it to any other person. So also a connoisseur, experiencing the *rasa* of *kāvya*, becomes oblivious of any other knowledge and cannot communicate to another person his literary relish. A man is delighted by the birth of a son or at the acquisition of wealth; such joy is human. But, the joy, produced by *kāvya-rasa*, is not mundance.

It is important to note that the idea of *rasa* originated in connection with dramaturgy. Bharata was the first writer to moot the concept of *rasa* in his *Nāṭyaśāstra*. His celebrated *Rasa-sūtra* is as follows:

vibhāvā-nubhāva-vyabhicāri-saṁyogād rasa-niṣpattiḥ ।

The combination of *vibhāva*, *anubhāva* and *vyabhicārī* (or *sañcārī*) *bhāva* with (the *sthāyī bhāva*) leads to *rasa-niṣpatti*. The word *niṣpatti* has been variously construed as *utpatti* (according to Lollaṭa), *anumiti* (Śaṁkuka), *bhukti* (Bhaṭṭanāyaka) and *abhivyakti* (Abhinavagupta); the terms mean respectively production, inference, enjoyment and manifestation.

The story of the incorporation of *nāṭya-rasa* as *kāvya-rasa* is interesting. While the former was discussed by some writers following in the footsteps of Bharata, the latter received a casual treatment in early times. Bhāmaha does not show much familiarity with the concept of *rasa* in *kāvya*. Only in defining *rasavat alaṁkāra*, he mentions the term *rasa*: *rasavat darśita-spaṣṭa-śṛṅgārādi-rasam* (*Kāvyālaṁkāra*, III.6). He does not mention the terms *vibhāva, anubhāva*, etc. He holds that a *mahākāvya* should contain all *rasas* (*ibid.*, I.21); he mentions also *Kāvya-rasa* (V.3). It seems, in these cases, he mentions *rasa* in the general sense of enjoyability, and not in its technical import.

In his *Kāvyādarśa*, Daṇḍin appears to have been influenced by the advocates of *rasa* to a greater extent than Bhāmaha. Like the latter, the former also admits the presence of *rasa* in *alaṁkāras* like *rasavat*. Moreover, he has attached the importance of *rasa* also as a constituent of *mādhurya guṇa* (*mādhuryaṁ rasavad vāci vastunyapi rasasthitiḥ* — *Kāvyādarśa*, I.51). It should be noted that, according to him, the *rasa* of speech arises from *Śrutyanuprāsa*, and the *rasa* of subject-matter (*vastu*) means the absence of vulgarity (*grāmyatā*). From this it appears that, unlike the *rasavādins*, he has not accepted the technical sense of *rasa*. This does not indicate his ignorance of their standpoint; he has clearly stated (I.18) that, in a *mahākāvya*, the delineation of *rasa* and *bhāva* is indispensable. Besides, in connection with the *alaṁkāras*, *rasavat, preyas* and *urjasvī*, he clearly hints at his familiarity with eight kinds of *rasa*. In fact, as elements of the *alaṁkāras* discussed, he has given examples, mentioning the *rasas* — *śṛṅgāra*, *raudra*, *vīra* and *karuṇa*.

In his *Kāvyālaṁkāra-sūtra-vṛtti*, he has admitted that the *artha-guṇa*, called *kānti*, is a constant factor in *kāvya*. In his opinion, *dīpta-rasatvaṁ kāntiḥ* (III.2.15); that is, in *kānti-guṇa*, *rasa* will clearly be present.

From the foregoing discussion, it appears that, according to Bhāmaha, Daṇḍin and Vāmana, *rasa* is not an indispensable element of *kāvya*. In their opinion, *rasa* exists only as an element of *alaṁkāra* or *guṇa*, but not as an independent entity. As a matter of fact, the writers down to Vāmana make no attempt to get at the soul of *kāvya*; they were engaged in dealing with such external elements as *alaṁkāra*, *rīti*, etc. Despite the importance, attached by Daṇḍin to *guṇa*, he regards *guṇa* as the life-breath of *rīti*, but not of *kāvya*. These early writers were concerned more about the body and embellishment of *kāvya* than about its soul. Like Bhāmaha, too, he has recognised *rasa* as an element of some *alaṁkāras*.

In the history of poetics, Rudraṭa was the first writer to discuss *rasa* in a somewhat detailed manner. To the eight *rasas* of Bharata, he has added two more, viz., *preyas* and *śānta*. Rudraṭa, though belonging to the Alaṁkāra school, has lauded those poets whose *kāvyas* are scientillating with *rasa*. He has, however, elaborately laid down his views about *alaṁkāras*; but shows no concern about the relation of the *rasa* theory with his theory of *alaṁkāra*. These are the reasons why some scholars are inclined to regard the portion of his work, devoted to a discussion of *rasa*, as a later interpretation.

Dhvanikāra, in his *Dhvanyāloka*, for the first time, clearly spells out the predominance of *rasa* in *kāvya*. The importance, he attached to *rasa-dhvani*, paved the way for *rasa* to be well-established in the history of poetics.

Dhvani School

Dhvani means suggested sense. Such a sense is not supposed to be conveyed by the verbal functions of *abhidhā* (denotation), *lakṣaṇā* (indication) and *tātparya* (import, recognised by some writers). For the comprehension of the suggested sense (*vyaṅgyārtha*), another function of the word and sense, called *vyañjanā* (suggestion) has been postulated by some writers. *Dhvani* has been admitted as the soul of *kāvya*, for the first time, in the *Dhvanyāloka*. The very first line of the initial verse of this work reads:

kāvyasyātmā dhvanirīti budhairyaḥ samāmnāta-pūrvaḥ ।

The word *pūrva* clearly indicates that there was an earlier tradition of *dhvani* as the soul of *kāvya*. But, the origin of this concept is shrouded in obscurity. The term *dhvani* was first used by the grammarians in connection with *sphoṭa*, Ānandavardhana clearly states that the *dhvani* theory, established by him, is based on grammar.

Dhvani, which is regarded in this school as the soul of *kāvya*, is threefold, namely *vastu-dhvani* (suggestion of a matter or idea), *alaṁkāra-dhvani* (suggestion of a poetic figure) and *rasa-dhvani* (suggestion of a mood or feeling). The greatest importance has been attached to the last one. This shows the influence of the Rasa school on that of *dhvani*. As a matter of fact, although the importance of *rasa* was recognised in drama (*dṛśya-kāvya*) earlier, yet, it was not established in the domain of poetical literature (*śravya-kāvya*) before Dhvanikāra. From this point of view, some scholars characterised the theory of *dhvani* as merely an extension of *rasa*. This view is not tenable; because the Dhvanikāra does not mention *rasa* as the principal element or the sole aim of *kāvya*; it is only one of the kinds of *dhvani* as the soul of *kāvya*.

The *dhvani* theorist had to encounter heavy odds in order to establish his theory. Many renowned writers were not inclined to admit even *vyañjanā*, the basis of *dhvani*, not to speak of *dhvani*. Of the opponents, the most prominent was Mahimabhaṭṭa, author of the *Vyaktiviveka*. His main anti-*vyañjanā* arguments are noted below:

(1) Some say that cause is inferred from effect. Similarly, when we find a suggested sense, we can realise that it has been comprehended from the denoted sense (*vācyārtha*). So, for the suggested sense, it is not necessary to assume the function of *vyañjanā*; *abhidhā* is enough for the purpose. The word is the cause, and the suggested sense is the effect.

(2) According to *dīrgha-vyāpāra-vādin*s, an arrow, discharged by a strong man, is capable of piercing the enemy's armour, skin and heart. Similarly, a word, used by a good poet, is able, by the single function of *abhidhā*, to convey its relation with other words as well as the suggested sense. So, the assumption of *vyañjanā* is not necessary.

yat-paraḥ śabdaḥ sa śabdārthaḥ ।

(3) In a sentence like *rāmo'smi sarvaṁ sahe*, *rāmeṇa priya-jīvitena tu kṛtaṁ premṇaḥ priye nocitam*, *rāmo'sau bhuvaneṣu vikramaguṇaiḥ prāptaḥ prasiddhiṁ parām*, the single word *rāma*, through *lakṣaṇā*, conveys the following meanings:

he who bears all kinds of suffering, is ruthless and son of Daśaratha.

So it is not necessary to admit *vyañjanā* as distinct from *lakṣaṇā*.

(4) The Naiyāyikas and the rhetoricians like Mahimabhaṭṭa deny *vyañjanā*, and think that the suggested sense is comprehended through inference.

The opponents of *dhvani* theory can be divided into three classes, namely:

(i) Those who hold that there is nothing like suggested sense in *kāvya*.

(ii) Those who think that *dhvani* is not comprehended from words; *dhvani* is only *sahṛdaya-hṛdaya-saṁvedya*, i.e., comprehensible only to a connoisseur.

(iii) Those who say that *dhvani* can be comprehended through the well-known functions, called *abhidhā*, *lakṣaṇā* and *tātparya* or through inference. So, it is unnecessary to postulate *vyañjanā* as a distinct *vṛtti*.

The exponents of the *dhvani* theory, however, succeeded, even in the teeth of trenchant criticism, in establishing the predominance of it in *kāvya*. The later writers admitted that poetry, containing *dhvani*, was regarded as the best. That poetry, in which the suggested sense is subordinate to the denoted sense, was regarded as a comparatively inferior *kāvya*. That poetry, which is devoid of *dhvani*, has been termed as *citra* by Dhvanikāra followed by Mammaṭa who characterises *citra* as the worst kind of poetry. Viśvanātha has not recognised this type a *kāvya*. Jagannātha, in his *Rasagaṅgādhara*, has divided *kāvya*, on the basis of *dhvani*, as *uttamottama, uttama, madhyama* and *adhama*. The last variety is devoid of *dhvani*. He has called it *citra*.

Agni Purāṇa

— Its place in the history of Alaṁkāra Literature.

It is a Mahāpurāṇa of an encyclopaedic nature. Its contents do not strictly conform to the conventional topics of Purāṇas, viz., *sarga* (creation), *pratisarga* (re-creation after dissolution), *vaṁśa* (genealogies of gods and sages), *manvantaras* (Manu periods of time) and *vaṁśānucarita* (genealogies of kings). It deals with a variety of other subjects including poetics (ch. 336-46). Parts of this Purāṇa appear to have been composed or compiled in different periods. The aforesaid portion, dealing with *Alaṁkāra-śāstra*, probably originated about AD 900. Many topics, discussed in early works on poetics and in the *Nāṭyaśāstra* of Bharata, even some verses or part-verses from them have been incorporated in this Purāṇa. Besides mentioning Bharata (339.6), it cites verbatim Daṇḍin's definitions of *kāvya* and *alaṁkāra*. Parts of Bhāmaha's work and of the *Dhvanyāloka* have been reproduced in it. Some similarity is noticed in the characteristics of *vakrokti* given in this Purāṇa and by Rudraṭa. In this Purāṇa, *dhvani* is included in the *alaṁkāra*, *ākṣepa*. In this, the Purāṇa agrees with the writers preceeding Dhvanikāra.

A noteworthy feature of the Purāṇa is the discussion on certain matters of dramaturgy, besides the important topics of *Alaṁkāra-śāstra*. It follows Bharata in connection with *nāṭya*, *nṛtya*, *abhinaya* and *rasa*. Though it is mainly a compilation of the views of earlier writers, it is not entirely devoid of independent thinking which reveals a distinct departure from the earlier ideas. May be that the Purāṇa was familiar with a school of poetics the works of which sank into oblivion with the passage of time. It is also not unlikely that the Purāṇa-maker, urged by his own genius, laid down some novel ideas. The innovations are briefly set forth below:

The *dhvani*-theory is absent in it. We have already mentioned the position, accorded in the Purāṇa to *dhvani*. The term *dhvani* is mentioned also in the opening verse. But, the Purāṇa, like *Vākyapadīya*, has used the term in the sense of the *sphoṭa* of a word.

In 336/33, the Purāṇa states — *vāg-vaidagdhya-pradhāne'pi rasa evātra jīvitam*. Thus, *rasa* has been clearly declared as the soul of poetry. Viśvanātha, who makes a similar statement, cites the authority of this Purāṇa in support of his own view. It is true that, in pursuance of Bharata's opinion, the Purāṇa has described *rasa* and *bhāva*. But, it does not testify to the rise of a systematic doctrine of *rasa* on the basis of this concept. According to the Purāṇa, the process of the rise of *rasa* is as follows:

ānanda
|
ahaṁkāra
|
abhimāna
|
rati

The erotic and other *rasas* are the transformations of *rati*. Like the *Nāṭyaśāstra*, the Purāṇa admits four basic *rasas*; the other five (including *śānta-rasa*) are believed to rise from them. The predominance of *śṛṅgāra-rasa* has been stressed.

The Purāṇa cannot be affiliated to the *rasa* school; because, though *rīti*, *guṇa* and *alaṁkāra* are recognised as requisite elements of *kāvya*, yet these have not been regarded as helpful to *rasa*.

Vāmana and Daṇḍin regard *guṇa* as the basic element of *rīti*. The Purāṇa does not directly connect *guṇa* with *rīti*, and does not appreciably make any difference between *guṇa* and *alaṁkāra*. *Guṇa* has been characterised as *yaḥ kāvye mahatīṁ chāyām anugṛhṇātyasau guṇaḥ*. *Alaṁkāra* has been defined, in the words of Daṇḍin (*Kāvyādarśa*, II.1), as *kāvya-śobhākarān dharmānalaṁkārān pracakṣate*.

In the names and classification of the *guṇas*, the Purāṇa has some originality. The usual practice is to classify them as *śabda-guṇas* and *artha-guṇas*. In the Purāṇa, at first *guṇas* have been divided as *vaiśeṣika* and *sāmānya*. Those of the first kind are related to some part or characteristic of a poetical composition. Those of the second kind are applicable to a composition in a general way. *Sāmānya guṇas* are threefold, viz., those of *śabda*, of *artha* and of both *śabda* and *artha*. This threefold division appears to have been made, for the first time, in this Purāṇa. Each of the ten *guṇas*, mentioned by Vāmana, pertains to *śabda* as well as *artha*. According to the Purāṇa, *śabda-guṇas* are seven, and *artha-guṇas* six.

Mutatis mutandis, the *śabdālaṁkāras* of the Purāṇa are similar to those of the *Kāvyādarśa*. In case of *arthālaṁkāras*, the Purāṇa does not accept the earlier classification and definitions.

In the present state of our knowledge, it is difficult to assert whether the *Agni Purāṇa* is the innovator of the above departures from the conventional ideas or it merely followed some work or view, now lost.

Causes of Kāvya

What is it that prompts a person to compose *kāvya*? This question arose in the minds of some early as well as later rhetoricians. Different writers tried to ascertain the reasons underlying the poetical compositions. All of them are unanimous in stating *pratibhā* as the first and the foremost cause of *kāvya*. There is, however, difference in their conceptions of *pratibhā*.

According to Bhāmaha and Daṇḍin, the main requisite for a poetical composition is *pratibhā*. It is *naisargikī* (natural) or *sahajā* (inborn). *Pratibhā* is generally regarded as such intellect as has ever-new flashes (*prajñā nava-navo-nmeṣa-śālinī*; this occurs in a quotation by Hemacandra). According to Daṇḍin, it is *pūrva-vāsanā-guṇānubandhi* (following or resulting from latent impressions of the previous existence). In the words of Vāmana, it is *janmāntaragata-saṁskāra-viśeṣaḥ* or a particular impression coming from the previous life. Abhinavagupta, in his *Dhvanyāloka-locana*, defines it as *apūrva-vastu-nirmāṇa-kṣamā prajñā*, i.e., intellect capable of creating original or wonderful subject-matter. Bharata characterises it as the inner feeling of a poet. Instead of *pratibhā*, Mammaṭa uses the term *śakti*, and describes it as *kavitva-bīja-rūpaḥ saṁskāra-viśeṣaḥ yaṁ vinā kāvyaṁ na prasaret, prasṛtaṁ vā upahasanīyaṁ syāt*; it is a kind of *saṁskāra* which is of the nature of the germ or source of poetical ability, without which poetry does not flow or even if it flows, it would be liable to ridicule.

Besides *pratibhā*, Daṇḍin states two more reasons underlying poetry; one is *bahu-nirmalaṁ śrutam*, i.e., clear knowledge of many branches of learning, and *amanda abhiyoga* (vigorous practice).

Rudraṭa holds that, besides being *sahajā*, *pratibhā* may also be *utpādyā* (derived from the cultivation of learning). According to Mammaṭa, besides *śakti*, mentioned above, the other causes of *kāvya* are *loka-śāstrādy-avekṣaṇa* (knowledge of the world and proficiency in various branches of learning) and *kāvyajña-śikṣābhyāsa* (practice according to the training by those who can produce and critically examine poetry).

It should be noted that Daṇḍin mentions three causes of poetry, but mentions them as *kāraṇam* in singular number. It, therefore, seems that he considers the three together, and not severally, as the cause of poetry. Mammaṭa's text concerned reads *trayaḥ samuditā na tu vyastas-tasya kāvyasyodbhave . . . hetur na hetavaḥ.* Jagannātha, however, in his *Rasagaṅgādhara*, has stated *pratibhā* as the sole cause of *kāvya*.

Purpose or Necessity of Kāvya

Human nature is varied; each person is different from the other not only in outward appearance, but also in mindset. Of the poets, some are gifted with poesy. They write poetry spontaneously. Others are laboured poets. Their poetry does not flow from their hearts, but from their heads.

The rhetoricians had been thinking about the necessity or purpose of *kāvya* since ancient times. According to early rhetoricians, the main purpose, served by poetry, is the fame of the poet and the pleasure of the reader. About this, Bhāmaha, Daṇḍin, Vāmana, Rudraṭa, Bhoja, etc., are unanimous. They have, however, a lot of difference about the various materials of peotry. In course of time, the three ends of life, viz. *dharma, artha* and *kāma* have been recognised as the results obtained through poetry. After that, *mokṣa* was added in the list of the results. Gradually, the predominance of *rasa* being recognised, pleasure or delectation came to be regarded as the principal necessity of *kāvya*. In this connection, the following opinion of Abhinavagupta is noteworthy:

dharmārtha-kāma-mokṣeṣu vaicakṣaṇyaṁ kalāsu ca ।
karoti kīrtiṁ prītiṁ ca sādhu-kāvya-niṣevaṇam ॥
prītireva pradhānam . . . prādhānyena ānanda eva uktaḥ
(Remark on Bhāmaha's *Kāvyālaṁkāra*, I/2 — See *Locana*).

Mammaṭa, in his *Kāvyaprakāśa*, writes:

kāvyaṁ yaśase'rthakṛte vyavahāravide śivetarakṣataye ।
sadyaḥpara-nirvṛtaye kāntā-sammitatayo-padeśayuje ॥

The purposes of *kāvya* are: achievement of fame, acquisition of money, knowledge about the conduct of kings, etc., destruction of evil, instant experience of the highest bliss, obtainment of advice like that of one's wife. In explaining *śivetarakṣataye*, it is stated, as an example, that poet Mayūra got rid of leprosy by composing a hymn in eulogy of the sun. In explaining *sadyaḥ-para-nirvṛti*, Mammaṭa observes that, a soon as a poetical composition is written or read, the poet or the reader gets such pleasure that, for the time being, there remains in his mind, no awareness of any other thing. The teaching, derived from *kāvya*, is not harsh like that of the scriptures which give directions like one's master (*prabhu-sammita*). Nor is the teaching, derived from the Purāṇas which act like one's friend (*suhṛt-sammita*). The lesson, derived from *kāvya*, is tender and pleasant like the pleasant advice given by one's wife. The delight, caused by *kāvya*, has been characterised by Mammaṭa as *sakala-prayojana-mauli-bhūta*, i.e., the greatest of all the necessities. In later times, Jagannātha described poetic delight as *alaukika* (supramundane). In his *Sāhityadarpaṇa*, Viśvanātha has stated that even a person of mean intellect can easily acquire, from *kāvya*, the results of the four ends of life. Why should a person set store by *kāvya* when scripture are available? To this question, his answer is this. If a disease be curable by a bitter medicine as well as by sugar, then the patient will naturally prefer the latter.

Kāvya-Lakṣaṇa

The word *kāvya-lakṣaṇa* seems to mean definition of *kāvya*. In reality, however, in dramaturgy and poetics, the word *lakṣaṇa* has been used in a special sense.

Lakṣaṇa has been discussed, for the first time, in connection with poetics, dealt with in the *Nāṭyaśāstra*. From this discussion, it is learnt that the *lakṣaṇa*s relate partly to the form of *kāvya*, and partly constitute elements of it. The above work names and defines 36 *lakṣaṇa*s. The author lays greater stress on *lakṣaṇa* than on *alaṁkāra*. According to Bharata, like *guṇa* and *alaṁkāra*, *lakṣaṇa* also helps *rasa*.

In the works of later rhetoricians, *lakṣaṇa*s have no importance; most of them have been inextricably mixed up with *alaṁkāra*s and *guṇa*s. In his *Kāvyādarśa* (II.366), Daṇḍin has made a brief mention of *lakṣaṇa* in connection with *alaṁkāra* in the wider sense. He has placed *lakṣaṇa* on equal footing with *sandhyaṅga* and *vṛttyaṅga*; the last two, however, belong to the province of dramas. Similar is the treatment of *lakṣaṇa* by Dhanañjaya in his *Daśarūpaka*.

A more detailed discussion on this topic is found in Viśvanātha's *Sāhityadarpaṇa*. Including it in his discussion on dramaturgy, he has designated some *lakṣaṇas* as *nāṭyālaṁkāras*. He has further stated that, though some of them are included in *guṇa*, *alaṁkāra*, *bhāva* and *sandhi*, they deserve special treatment as they should be carefully used in dramas. Like Bharata, Viśvanātha also mentions 36 *lakṣaṇas*, but they differ in their names. Some of Bharata's *lakṣaṇas* are included in Viśvanātha's *nāṭyālaṁkāras*. Viśvanātha has mentioned 33 *nāṭyālaṁkāras*. As a matter of fact, he does not make any distinction between *lakṣaṇa* and *nāṭyālaṁkāra*. He says —

> *eṣāṁ ca lakṣaṇānāṁ nāṭyālaṁkaraṇam eka-rūpatve'pi*
> *bhedena vyapadeśaḥ gaḍḍalikā-pravāheṇa* ।

In later works on poetics, *lakṣaṇa* has practically lost its separate entity; it figures only in the works on dramaturgy. Among later rhetoricians, only Jayadeva, in his *Candrāloka*, has discussed *lakṣaṇas* in detail. It should be noted that he has defined and illustrated only ten *lakṣaṇas*.

In course of time, it lost importance even as characteristics of dramas.

Kavi-Śikṣā

The education of poets is an indispensable prerequisite of *kāvya*. Poetry, to a great extent, owes its origin to the genius (*pratibhā*) of a poet. This genius has been characterised, by some rhetoricians, as *sahajā* (inborn) and *utpādyā* (to be produced by learning, knowledge of the world, etc.). In the beginning of poetics, there was no provision for the system of the training of poets. All that is found in those times is some advice to poets asking them to avoid certain faults, and attain some excellences. Besides, there is the description of embellishments which should augment the beauty of expressions.

In course of time, the education of poets received greater attention, so much so that it became a separate subject of study. Some writers devoted themselves exclusively to *kavi-śikṣā*.

In this connection, Kṣemendra and Rājaśekhara deserve special mention. Kṣemendra's *Aucitya-vicāra-carcā* contains instructions about the do's and don'ts for poets. He emphasises *aucitya* or propriety, particularly in delineating a *rasa* of which it is stated to be the essence (*rasa-jīvitabhūta*). The *aucitya* may relate to the various elements of a poem, such as *pada* (word), *vākya* (sentence), *prabandhārtha* (the sense of the composition as a whole), *guṇa* (literary excellence), *alaṁkāra* (poetic figure), *rasa* (sentiment in a poem), grammatical factors like verb, gender, etc. *Aucitya* may relate also to time (*kāla*) and place (*deśa*).

Kṣemendra's other work, *Kavi-kaṇṭhābharaṇa* states two impulses required for the attainment of poetic ability, these are divine help (*divya prayatna*) and personal effort (*pauruṣa*).

From the standpoint of plagiarism, Kṣemendra divides poets into the following classes:

(i) *Chāyopajīvin* — one who imitates the general idea of another poet.

(ii) *Padaka* — and *pādo-pajīvin* — one who borrows a word or a verse-line.

(iii) *Sakalopajīvin* — one who imitates the entire poem of another poet.

(iv) *Bhuvanopajīvya* — one who borrows from sources universally regarded as legitimate, e.g., Vyāsa.

Then the author gives, in detail, rules for regulating the life, character and education of the poet. After this, he discusses *camatkāra* or poetic charm without which poetry is not possible.

The above discussion is followed by the treatment of the *guṇa*s (excellences) and *doṣa*s (blemishes) of *śabda* (verbal expression) and *artha* (sense).

The work is concluded with a list of the arts and sciences in which a poet should be proficient.

Rājaśekhara's *Kāvyamīmāṁsā* deals mainly with the usual topics of poetics, incidentally referring to *kavi-śikṣā*. He refers to the view of some authorities who think that *kāvya-śakti* (poetic capacity) is the only source of poetry, and it causes *pratibhā* (genius) and *vyutpatti* (knowledge). He sets forth also another opinion according to which *samādhi* (concentration) and *abhyāsa* (practice) too are required.

According to him, *pratibhā* may be either creative (*kārayitrī*) or discriminative (*bhāvayitrī*). The former may be natural (*sahajā*), adventitious (*āhāryā*) or derived from instructions (*aupadeśikā*). In accordance with these three, poets can be classed as *sārasvata*, *ābhyāsika* and *anupadeśika*.

Rājaśekhara mentions ten grades of apprenticeship through which a poet, aspiring to be a *kavirāja*, has to pass; it indicates a status higher than that of a *mahākavi*. He also describes the literary test to be passed by a poet in order to qualify himself for such honour and recognition.

We find, in this work, the author's idea about the purity of the body, mind and speech necessary for a poet. There are rules of conduct of the poet about his lifestyle, house, etc.

The author devotes considerable space to plagiarism. In short, his opinion is that practically no poet is above it. But, he is the best who knows how to conceal the fact of plagiarism (*yo jānāti nigūhitum*). An entire chapter (XIII) enumerates 32 methods by which a poet may deftly utilise the plagiarised matter to his advantage.

Arisiṁha, Amaracandra and Deveśvara were some other writers who dealt with *kavi-śikṣā*.

12

Nāṭya-śāstra (Dramaturgy)

In the chapter on Classical Sanskrit Literature, we have discussed some theories about the origin of drama. Whatever the origin, it is certain that Sanskrit drama arose a few centuries before Christ. Pāṇini (*c*. fourth century BC or earlier) mentions (IV.3.110) *naṭasūtra* which means aphorism for *naṭa*s or actors. The *Arthaśāstra* of Kauṭilya (*c*. fourth century BC) mentions *kuśīlava* which appears to have denoted dramatis personae. Patañjali (*c*. second century BC), in his *Mahābhāṣya* (III.1.26.34) commentary on Pāṇini's grammar, has mentioned two dramas, *Kaṁsavadha* and *Balibadha*.

When dramaturgy, as a distinct discipline, came into existence we do not know. The earliest extant work on dramaturgy is the *Nāṭyaśāstra*, attributed to Bharata. The date of the work is controversial. Generally, it is believed to have originated around the third century AD.

The author of this work mentions the names of several predecessors some of whom were, perhaps, historical personages. The text, as we have today, comprises 36 chapters which deal with the topics, indicated below:

I. Origin of drama, II. Description of the auditorium, III. Worship of the stage-deity, IV. Characteristics of *tāṇḍava* (see Glossary), V. Preliminaries of a dramatic performance, VI. *Rasa*s (see Glossary), VII. *Bhāva*s (see Glossary), VIII. Accessories, IX. Acting by hand, X. Acting by different parts of the body, XI. *Cārī* (see Glossary), XII. *Maṇḍala* (see Glossary), XIII. Rules about movements of actors, actresses, Stage-directions; XIV. Stage-directions; XV. Matters relating to words, pronunciation, etc., XVI. Metres, XVII. Vocal acting, XVIII. Languages, XIX. Intonation, XX. Ten types of drama, XXI. *Sandhyaṅgas* (see Glossary), XXII. Dramatic styles, XXIII. Acting effected by dress and decoration, XXIV. Generalities of acting, XXV. Courtesans and other women, types of men, XXVI. Various matters relating to acting, XXVII. Accomplishment of dramatic performance, obstacle, etc., XXVIII. Instrumental music, XXIX. Stringed instruments, XXX Wind-instruments, XXXI. *Tāla* (see Glossary), XXXII. *Dhruva*, XXXIII. Percussion instruments, XXXIV. Nature of actors and actresses, XXXV. Roles, and XXXVI. Concluding remarks throwing light on curiosities about dramatic performance.

The most outstanding contribution of the author of the *Nāṭyaśāstra* is the formulation, for the first time, of the theory of *rasa*. He discusses it in connection with drama. But, later writers introduced this concept in the domain of poetical compositions in general. For a discussion on it, see our observations on *rasa* school in the chapter on *Alaṁkāra-śāstra*.

Of the other noteworthy works, some deal exclusively with dramaturgy, while others discuss it as one of the subjects, the other topics relating to poetics. We shall briefly deal with the prominent works.

Daśarūpaka

It is by Dhanañjaya of the tenth century AD and is divided into four parts in which he discusses the following subjects:

1. Subject-matter and plot of the drama.
2. The hero, heroine and other characters; the language of the drama.
3. The prologue and its varieties and different kinds of drama.
4. Emotions and sentiments.

The work takes its name from the ten *rūpakas* (major types of drama) dealt with in the *Nāṭyaśāstra*. It has a commentary, called *Avaloka*, attributed to Dhanika.

Abhinaya-Darpaṇa

Attributed to Nandikeśvara, it deals mainly with the gestures and postures used in drama and dance. It appears to have been compiled later than Bharata's *Nāṭyaśāstra*.

Nāṭaka-Lakṣaṇa-Ratna-Koṣa

Ascribed to Sāgaranandin of uncertain date, perhaps not earlier than the tenth century and not later than the thirteenth. It deals with:

1. *Rūpaka* and its ten varieties.

2-5. *Avasthās* (see Glossary), dialects to be used and *Artha-prakr̥tis* (see Glossary).

6-10. *Upakṣepakas*, *sandhis*, *patākāsthānas* and *vr̥ttis* (see Glossary).

11. Qualities of the hero.

12-13. Thirty-six *nāṭya-lakṣaṇas*, *guṇas* and *nāṭyālaṁkāras*.

14-16. *Rasas* and *bhāvas* (see Glossary).

17. Types of heroine and their qualities.

18. Minor types of drama.

The treatise is important mainly for two reasons. First, it brings together different views on the topics discussed. Secondly, it refers to a large number of dramas and works on dramaturgy.

Nāṭyadarpaṇa

It is attributed jointly to Rāmacandra and Guṇacandra, both pupils of the renowned Jaina scholar, Hemacandra, believed to have flourished *c.* AD 1100 and 1175. It deals, in four chapters, with dramaturgy. It should be noted that the work mentions 12 kinds of *rūpaka* (major drama) instead of the traditional ten, and a number of *uparūpakas* (minor dramas).

Nāṭaka-Paribhāṣā

By Śiṅgabhūpāla, variously called Siṁhabhūpāla, Śiṅga-dharaṇīśa, Śiṅgarāja, Śiṅgamahīpati, identified by some with king Śiṅgama Nāyaḍu of Veṅkaṭagiri and assigned to a period about AD 1330. He is better known as the author of the *Saṁgīta-sudhākara* commentary on the *Saṁgīta-ratnākara* of Śārṅgadeva.

This work deals, in 268 verses, with the technical terms of dramaturgy; it has the qualities of brevity and lucidity. It contains a treatment of the languages used in drama, modes of address, names of the dramatic elements along with the ten types of drama.

Rasārṇava-Sudhākara

By Śiṅgabhūpāla (*c.* fourteenth century), author of the *Nāṭaka-paribhāṣā*, dealt with above, discusses almost all the topics of dramaturgy and *rasa*. Written in three chapters, called *vilāsa*s, its subject-matter is as indicated below:

I. *Nāṭya-lakṣaṇa* and *rasa-lakṣaṇa*; merits and classification of heroes, incidental discussion on the *rīti*s, *gauḍi*, *vaidarbhī* and *pāñcālī*, four dramatic *vṛtti*s or styles, *pravṛtti*s and *sāttvika bhāva*s.

II. Treatment, in extenso, of 33 *vyabhicārī-bhāva*s and eight *sthāyi bhāva*s; aspects of *rati*; *śṛṅgāra* and other *rasa*s; opposition and commingling (*saṁkara*) of *rasa*s, *rasābhāsa*.

III. *Rūpaka* — its different kinds and subject-matter; five *arthaprakṛti*s, *patākā-sthānaka*, five *avasthā*s; five *sandhi*s and their accessories (*aṅga*); *bhūṣaṇa*s; *nāṭaka* as the main *rūpaka*; other kinds of *rūpaka*; use of languages; naming of characters.

Though drawing directly on Bharata's *Nāṭyaśāstra* and the *Daśarūpaka*, the author appears to be indebted to his other predecessors like Bhoja's *Śṛṅgāra-prakāśa* and Śāradātanaya's *Bhāva-prakāśana* and some other works on dramaturgy and *rasa*.

Ekāvalī

Attributed to Vidyānātha (according to some, *alias* Agastya Paṇḍita) who can probably be assigned to a period between the end of the thirteenth century and beginning of the fourteenth.

The *Ekāvalī*, in the form of *kārikā* and *vṛtti*, consists of nine chapters (*prakaraṇas*) in the third of which are illustrated the requirements of a *Nāṭaka* by a model drama. The treatment is based chiefly on the works of Bharata and Dhanañjaya. The rest of the work is devoted to poetics.

Sāhityadarpaṇa

A very popular work mainly on poetics, by Viśvanātha (*c*. fourteenth century, first half). Chapter VI of this work deals exclusively with dramaturgy. Besides the traditional ten *rūpaka*s, it describes 18 *uparūpaka*s or minor dramas.

Nāṭaka-Candrikā

By Rūpa Gosvāmin, a contemporary of Caitanya (1486-1533). The author states that he consulted the *Bharata-śāstra* and the *Rasārṇava-sudhākara*, but not the *Sāhityadarpaṇa* which is opposed to Bharata's views. The work contains eight sections dealing with topics mentioned below.

I. General characteristics of a drama.

II. The hero.

III. Divisions of *rūpaka*.

IV. Elements of action and their classification.

V. *Arthopakṣepaka*s and their divisions.

VI. Divisions of acts and scenes.

VII. Distribution of dialects.

VIII. Styles of dramatic compositions and their application. The illustrations are taken mostly from Vaiṣṇava works.

Main Topics of Dramaturgy

As we have seen, the *Nāṭyaśāstra* speaks of ten dramas, called *rūpaka*s. According to later writers, there are also 18 *uparūpaka*s or minor dramas. We shall briefly deal with the principal topics of dramaturgy on the basis of the *Sāhityadarpaṇa* which is the most popular in academic circles.

Rūpaka, Abhinaya

Rūpāropāt to rūpakam;

> a drama is called *rūpaka*, because forms (of certain persons or characters) are attributed (to actors and actresses).

Abhinaya means the imitation of a situation or condition (*avasthānukāraḥ*). It is of four kinds, namely

(i) *Āṅgika* — by means of the bodily movements.

(ii) *Vācika* — by means of speech.

(iii) *Sāttvika* — physical manifestation in the actor, of the feelings and emotions of the characters, e.g., perspiration.

(iv) *Āhārya* — by means of dress and decoration, etc.

Types of Rūpakas (Major Dramas)

The following ten are called *rūpakas*: (i) *nāṭaka*, (ii) *prakaraṇa*, (iii) *bhāṇa*, (iv) *vyāyoga*, (v) *samavakāra*, (vi) *ḍima*, (vii) *ihāmṛga*, (viii) *aṅka*, (ix) *vīthi*, (x) *prahasana*.

Nāṭaka is the basic form; the others have their individual characteristics. We note the broad characteristics of *nāṭaka*, *prakaraṇa*, *bhāṇa* and *prahasana* which are more common. The main criteria for distinguishing the various types are the *vastu* (plot), *netā* (hero) and *rasa* (sentiment).

NĀṬAKA

Vastu — a well-known event.

Netā — a man of excellent qualities, e.g., a king of renowned lineage or a divine being or semi-divine character (e.g., Rāma).

Rasa — principal sentiment erotic or heroic, other sentiments are subsidiary.

An act of the *nāṭaka* should represent such an event as can happen in the course of a day. The following practices are prohibited for representation:

> Calling from afar, killing, fight, revolution, marriage, eating, curse, answering calls of nature, death, sexual union, such shameful mark on the body as biting with teeth, scratching with nails, lying down, kiss, siege of cities, bath, application of cosmetics, etc.

Preliminaries

Pūrvaraṅga — what is done by actors before commencing a drama. Of the Preliminaries, indispensable is the *Nāndī* which contains benediction (towards the audience) and eulogy of gods, the twice-born people (i.e., brāhmaṇa, kṣatriya, vaiśya) or kings, etc.

[*Note*: Viśvanātha does not endorse the practice of regarding the initial verse of a drama as *Nāndī*. He would call it *Raṅgadvāra* included among the preliminaries. According to him, *raṅgadvāramārabhya kaviḥ kuryāt* (the poet or dramatist begins with *Raṅgadvāra*). The preliminaries appear to have been of two kinds, viz., *antaryavanikā* (behind the curtain) and *bahiryavanikā* (outside the curtain). The *Nāndī* formed a part of the former, and the dramatist had nothing to do with it. The direction *nāndyante tataḥ praviśati sūtradhāraḥ* which is followed by the opening verse of a Bhāsa drama, supports the contention of Viśvanātha.]

The number of acts in a *nāṭaka* may be from five to ten.

PRAKARAṆA

Vastu — a worldly subject conceived by a dramatist. It should represent the activities of wicked people, gamblers, etc.

Netā — a brāhmaṇa, minister or merchant. The heroine must be a housewife or a courtesan or both.

Rasa — principal sentiment is the heroic. Example, *Mṛcchakaṭika* of Śūdraka.

BHĀṆA

One-act monologue play. The only character is an expert and learned *Viṭa* (see Glossary). Example: *Caturbhāṇī*.

PRAHASANA

Farce. One-act play in which the subject-matter is imaginary. The principal sentiment is the comic (*hāsya*). It deals chiefly with the tricks and quarrels of low characters of every sort. Example: *Laṭaka-melaka*.

Plot of Nāṭaka — Analysis

The subject-matter has two broad divisions, viz., the main (*ādhikārika*) and the eventual (*prāsaṅgika*); the former running up to the denouement, as the love of the king and Śakuntalā in the *Abhijñānaśākuntalam*. The latter is of two kinds, viz., episode (*patākā*) covering a comparatively longer portion and only an incident (*prakarī*).

The fully developed action passes through five *avasthās* (stages of development), viz., *ārambha* (commencement), *yatna* (effort), *prāptyāśā* (hope of getting the desired object), *niyatāpti* (certainty of success) and *phalāgama* (attainment of the object).

The five *arthaprakṛtis* or elements of the plot are *bīja* (germ or seed), *bindu* (lit. drop, link when the main subject-matter is interrupted), *patākā* (episode), *prakarī* (an incident), and *kārya* (denouement).

Based on the above parallel sets, there is another division into *sandhis* (junctures). These are: *mukha* (opening), *pratimukha* (progression), *garbha* (development), *vimarśa* or *avamarśa* (pause) and *nirvahaṇa* (conclusion).

We illustrate, after the renowned commentator, Rāghavabhaṭṭa, the *sandhis* with reference to the *Abhijñāna-śākuntalam*; thus, *avasthās* and *arthaprakṛtis* also will be clear. After the prologue, the hero, i.e., the king begins the drama. Here we get the *mukha-sandhi*. The *pratimukha* begins where the king tells the *vidūṣaka* that he is deprived of the result of having eyes (act II). The *garbha* extends throughout act IV up to *iti yathoktaṁ karoti* (act V). The *avamarśa* spreads all over the remaining part of act V. The *nirvahaṇa* occurs in the act where divergent incidents converge for the single object of the reunion of the king with Śakuntalā and his son.

Viśvanātha names the following 18 *uparūpaka*s or minor types of drama:

> *nāṭikā, troṭaka, goṣṭhī, saṭṭaka, nāṭyarāsaka, prasthāna, ullopya, kāvya, preṅkhana, rāsaka, saṁlāpaka, śrīgadita, śilpaka, vilāsikā, durmallikā, prakaraṇī, hallīśa, bhāṇikā.*

13

Chandaḥ-śāstra (Metrics)

THE *Ṛgveda*, the earliest available Indian treatise, is metrical. It comprises *ṛk*s or stanzas in different metres; e.g., *Gāyatrī*, *Triṣṭubh*, etc. It does not seems to be a mere accident that all stanzas, in a particular metre, have uniform characteristics. We can, perhaps, say that the different metres presuppose a common code or discipline. We do not, however, meet with any work on metrics before the Vedāṅgas. Some *Brāhmaṇa*s contain scattered references to metre. It is in the *Sāṁkhāyana-śrauta-sūtra* (VII. 27) and *Ṛgveda Prātiśākhya* (last three *paṭala*s or sections) that we get a separate treatment of the subject. In this connection, the *Nidāna-sūtra*, belonging to the *Sāmaveda*, should also be mentioned. The portion of Kātyāyana's *Anukramaṇī* (index) on metres appears to follow the *Ṛgveda Prātiśākhya*.

Though *chanda*s has been mentioned as a Vedāṅga, yet there is no work exclusively on this subject. The *Chandaḥ-sūtra* of Piṅgala, claimed to be a Vedāṅga, in reality, deals mainly with post-Vedic metres and partly with Vedic metres. Piṅgala, also called Piṅgalanāga or Piṅgalācārya, is sometimes identified with Patañjali (second century BC), author of the *Mahābhāṣya*, commentary on Pāṇini's grammar. The text of Piṅgala's work appears to be earlier than chapters XIV and XV of the *Nāṭya-śāstra* of Bharata (probably earlier than fifth century AD) dealing with metres. The *Chandaḥ-sūtra* is earlier also than the *Agni Purāṇa* (c. ninth century AD) of which chapters 328-34 deal with prosody. As a matter of fact, the Purāṇic chapters concerned are derived from Piṅgala's work. The text on Prākṛt metres, attributed to Piṅgala, is of a much later date. There are several commentaries on Piṅgala's *Chandaḥ-sūtra*. Notable among them are those by Halāyudha (printed), Yādavaprakāśa (printed), Śrīharṣaśarman, Vāṇīnātha, Lakṣmīnātha and Dāmodara. The difference between Vedic and classical metres is that while the former is determined by the number of syllables, the latter is determined by both the number and quality of the sounds. Thus, the Vedic *gāyatrī* metre, for instance, consists of three octosyllabic verses (feet). The classical metre, *indravajrā*, for instance, contains 12 syllables of specified quantities.

For classical metres, Piṅgala uses the letters *LA* and *GA* to indicate the short and long vowels respectively. He also adopts an algebraic code of mnemonics to indicate groups (*gaṇa*) of short and long vowels, each group containing three syllables. The groups are as follows: ∪ and the sign '–' indicate short and long vowels respectively for example.

> MA – – –, NA – ∪∪∪, Bha – ∪∪,YA ∪ – – , JA ∪ – ∪, RA – ∪ –, SA ∪∪ –, TA – – ∪.,

A short vowel, preceding a conjunct consonant, is taken as long. A short vowel, at the end of a foot (*pāda*) can be taken as long, if necessary for metre.

In some cases, in the determination of a metre, *yati* (pause or caesura) is also a factor.

The metres may be of two kinds, namely, *vṛtta* (determined by syllables), and *jāti* (regulated by the number of syllabic instants i.e., (*mātrā*; a *mātrā* is the measure of time required for pronouncing a short vowel). *Vṛtta*s may be of three kinds, namely, *samavṛtta* (in which all the feet are of similar metrical scheme), *ardha-samavṛtta* (in which the alternate feet are similar) and *viṣamavṛtta* (in which all the feet are dissimilar).

Examples are given below:

(i) *Upendravajrā* metre — *jatau jagau gaḥ; mŭkŭndă mūrdhnā pră ṇipătyă yācē* ।

(ii) *M̄andākrāntâmbŭdhi-răsă-năgāir mō bhănāu tāu gă-yūgmam* ।

It consists of the groups *ma, bha, na, ta, ta, ga, ga,* with pause on the fourth letter, then the sixth letter and thereafter on the seventh letter.

(iii) *kāścīt kāntā vīrăhă gŭrŭṇā svādhīkārā pramāttāḥ* ।

Works on Metre

Besides the *Chandaḥsūtra* of Piṅgala, mentioned earlier, there are many works, published and unpublised. A very popular work, especially among the beginners of the study of *kāvya*, is the *śrutabodha*, a metrical work attributed, on no definite evidence, to Kālidāsa.

The line *chandovicityāṁ sakalas-tatprapañco nidarśitaḥ*, occurring in the *Kāvyādarśa* (I.12 in the BORI edn.) of Daṇḍin (*c.* eighth century AD) is worth considering here. The word *chandoviciti* has been taken by some to have been a work of Daṇḍin. Others think that it was, perhaps, a chapter of the *Kāvyādarśa*. Yet others think that it refers to metrics in general. The question has been discussed by the present writer in his *Chandoviciti*—a note, in *IHQ*, XXIX, 1953. The *Chāndomañjarī* of Gaṅgādāsa is very popular. He introduces himself as son of Gopāladāsa Vaidya of Bengal, and describes, in six chapters, varieties of metres illustrating them by verses in eulogy of Kṛṣṇa. An index to its popularity is the existence of several commentaries on it. Gaṅgādāsa's work must be distinguised from works of the same title, one by Gopāladāsa and the other on Vedic metres. Gaṅgādāsa is generally believed to have flourished in the fifteenth-sixteenth century AD.

A noteworthy work is the *Vṛttaratanākara* of Kedārabhaṭṭa, son of Pibveka (Pathvaka), who is believed to have lived earlier than the fifteenth century AD. Judging by the fact that it has been extensively quoted by commentators, most notably by Mallinātha (*c.* fifteenth century AD) and that it has over a dozen commentaries, it must be taken as the most popular work.

Most of the later works, of which we have a lot, are like manuals for students or paraphrases of eralier works.

14

Saṁgīta-śāstra
(Vocal Music, Instrumental Music and Dance)

THE word *saṁgīta*, in Sanskrit, denotes vocal music, instrumental music and dance. At several places, *saṁgīta*, has been called *Gāndharva-vidyā* or *Pañcama-veda*.

Saṁgīta appears to have been co-eval with civilisation in India. Among the ruins of the Indus Valley Civilisation (*c.* 3000-2500 BC) are found the flute, *mr̥daṅga* (tabor), *vīṇā* (lute), *karatāla* (cymbal) and figures of dancing men and women. The Vedic age (*c.* 2000-1500 BC) reflects considerable development in these arts. The stanzas (*r̥ks*), constituting the *R̥gveda*, are composed in musical accents, called *udātta* (acute), *anudātta* (grave) and *svarita* (circumflex). The eighth book (*Maṇḍala*) of this Veda, with songs predominating, is called *Pragātha*, derived from root *gai* (to sing). The main elements of the *Sāmaveda* are the *mantras* of the *R̥gveda*, meant for being sung at the time of sacrificial rites.

There are references, in the Vedic literature, to the musical instruments, called *kṣoṇi*, *vāṇa* (same as *vīṇā* above), *dundubhi*, a sort of drum, etc.

The later Vedic literature, comprising *Brāhmaṇa*s, Āraṇyakas, Upaniṣads and Sūtras, contains copious references to music with which the people's familiarity is undoubted. Of the exegetical Vedāṅgas (accessories to the Vedas), the *Nāradīya Śikṣā* bears eloquent testimony to a high degree of development of music. It mentions seven notes (*svara*s), three *grāma*s (gamut), 21 *mūrchanā*s (rise and fall of sounds) and 59 *tāna*s (protracted tones).

Many scholars think that the songs, sung by travelling singers and the minstrels in royal courts formed the nucleus of the *Rāmāyaṇa* and the *Mahābhārata* in the hoary past. These Epics testify to the wide vogue of music and dance.

The Purāṇas contain a good deal of information about *saṁgīta*. For instance, the *Mārkaṇḍeya* (*c.* third-fourth century AD), clearly refers to seven notes, *grāma*, *rāga* (musical mode), *mūrchanā*, *tāna*, *tāla* (beating time) and *laya* (time). Mention has been made of the instruments *veṇu* (flute), *vīṇā*, *paṇava*, *mṛdaṅga*, *paṭaha* (kettle-drum), *dundubhi* and *śaṁkha* (conch). Dance also is mentioned. Chapter 23 deserves special mention as it is full of information on music. The following matters, relating to music, occur in the *Vāyu Purāṇa*, (evolved between AD 200 and 1400), chapters 86 and 87; seven notes; three *grāma*s, 21 *mūrchanā*s, 59 *tāna*s, relation between *grāma*s and *mūrchanā*s, *gītālaṁkāra*, *varṇa*, *sthāna*, *tāla*, etc. Certain *rāga*s are mentioned in the *Kālikā Purāṇa* (*c.* tenth or eleventh century AD).

Some Tāntric works contain information on music. Special mention should be made of the *Vīṇātantra*, included in the *Yāmala-tantra*.

Of the early works on Dharmaśāstra, the *Yājñavalkya-smṛti* (*c.* first or second century AD), Prāyaścittādhyāya, 115, mentions the playing of the *vīṇā*, *śruti*, *jāti* (seven primary notes of the gamut) as means to salvation.

Classical Sanskrit works, prose, poetical and dramatic, are replete with references to music and dance. Among the very noteworthy works are the *Pañcatantra* (before the middle of the sixth century AD), *Meghadūta* and *Abhijñāna-śākuntalam* of Kālidāsa (*c.* fourth century AD) and the *Mṛcchakaṭikam* of Śūdraka (*c.* sixth century AD).

Ancient Indians looked upon music and dance not only as a means of entertainment and diversion, but also as a medium of worship and meditation. The idea that God is pleased by songs is expressed in the following line of the *Bhagavad Gītā* (X.22), a part of the *Mahābhārata* which is believed by Winternitz, to have assumed its extant form about the fourth century AD — *vedāṇām sāmavedo'smi* (of the Vedas, I am the *Sāmaveda*). Dance also was believed to please God. This belief led to the rise of the system of *devadāsī*s (temple-girls).

In course of time, as *saṁgīta*, in all its three branches, developed to a considerable degree, the need for systematisation was felt. The time of origin of *Saṁgīta-śāstra* is not known. The earliest extant work is the *Nāṭyaśāstra*, attributed to sage Bharata. The author names several predecessors. The title of the work is apt to lead one to think that it is a treatise on *nāṭya* (drama) only. As a matter of fact, however, it deals with vocal and instrumental music and dance. The work is so named perhaps because song and dance developed as an essential accompaniment of drama. Elements of drama occur in the *R̥gvedic* Dialogue hymns, viz. Dialogues between Yama and Yamī (X.10), between Purūravas and Urvaśī (X.95), etc. A tradition, contained in the *Nāṭya-śāstra*, is as follows. According to a request of the gods to produce something that would simultaneously please the eyes and ears. Brahmā created *Nāṭyaveda*, the fifth Veda, for which, He took the element of song from the *Sāmaveda* and to which Śiva and Pārvatī contributed the fierce *tāṇḍava* and the graceful *lāsya* dances respectively. It was Bharata who introduced the art on earth, and composed the *Nāṭya-śāstra*. Some scholars would attribute the latter part (Chapters 28-33) to one, Kohala. The work, of which different parts appear to have been written in different periods, is assigned by scholars to periods ranging between the second century BC and the fourth century AD. The most authoritative commentary on the work is entitled *Abhinavabhāratī*, by the celebrated Kāśmīrian Abhinavagupta (tenth-eleventh century AD).

Of the works on *saṁgīta*, published hitherto, the following are important:

Br̥haddeśī of Mātaṅga (*c*. between fifth century and seventh century AD).

Dattila of Dattilācārya.

Hr̥daya-kautuka and *Hr̥dayaprakāśa* of Hr̥dayanārāyaṇa-deva (seventeenth century AD).

Rāganirūpaṇa or *Catvāriṁśacchata-rāga-nirūpaṇa*, attributed to Nārada.

Rāgataraṅgiṇī of Locanapaṇḍita (seventeenth century AD).

Rāgavibodha of Somanātha (seventeenth century AD).

Saṁgīta-dāmodara of Śubhaṁkara (*c.* fifteenth century AD).

Saṁgīta-darpaṇa of Dāmodara (seventeenth century AD).

Saṁgīta-makaranda of Nārada.

Saṁgīta-pārijāta of Ahobala (seventeenth century AD).

Saṁgīta-ratnākara of Śārṅgadeva (thirteenth century AD).

Saṁgīta-samaya-sāra of Pārśvadeva (*c.* thirteenth century AD).

Saṁgīta-sāra-saṁgraha of Narahari (eighteenth century AD).

Saṁgīta-sudhā of Govindadīkṣita (seventeenth century AD).

Svaramela-kalānidhi of Rāmāmātya (sixteenth century AD).

Besides the above works, the *Abhilāṣitārthacintāmaṇi* (also called *Mānasollāsa*, AD 1129) of Someśvara deals (Vol. III, GOS 1961 edn.), with music and musical instruments in 2500 verses.

Of the above works, the most well-known, authoritative, exhaustive and systematic is the *Saṁgīta-ratnākara* of Śārṅgadeva. Its importance lies in the fact that it deals with vocal and instrumental music as well as dance. Kallinātha and Siṁhabhūpāla are well-known commentators on this work.

Vocal Music

GĪTA, GĀNDHARVA, GĀNA

A group of *svaras* (notes), causing delight to the mind, is called *gīta*. It is of two kinds namely:

(1) *Gāndharva* — It is traditional (believed to be) used by *gandharvas* (a class of demi-gods regarded as musicians of gods), and is regulated by *mūrchanā*, etc.

It should be noted that a person, versed in both *mārga* (q.v.) and *deśī* types of songs, is called *gāndharva*.

(2) *Gāna* — That which is composed by an expert composer in conformity with the characteristics described in connection with *deśī-rāga*, etc., and that gives delight to the people. It is of two kinds:

(i) *Nibaddha* — Composed in words and structured on a certain pattern; it is also called *prabandha*.

(ii) *Anibaddha* — Not composed in words and free from structural limitations; it is also called *ālapti* or *ālāpa*.

MĀRGA, DEŚĪ

These two are applicable to each of the three constituents of *saṁgīta*. These are, however, mainly associated with *rāgas* (q.v.). *Mārga-rāga* is strictly controlled by the rules and regulations of *grāma* (q.v.) — *mūrchanā* (q.v.) system. But, *deśī-rāga* is mostly free from such regulations, and delights the mind of the people of different tastes in different regions.

RĀGA

Derived from root *rañj* (to please), it means a group of notes which gives delight to the people. According to Śārṅgadeva, *rāgas* are of 20 kinds. According to most of the later authors, however, there are the following six *rāgas*: *śrī*, *vasantaka*, *bhairava*, *pañcama*, *megha* and *naṭṭanārāyaṇa*. Each of them is supposed to have some consorts which are called *bhāṣā* by Śārṅgadeva and *rāgiṇī* by later authorities. It is interesting to note that some *rāgiṇīs* have regional names; e.g., *gurjarī* (from Gujarat), *vaṅgālī* (from Vaṅgāla), *saindhavī* (from Sindhu or Sind), *bhūpālī* (from Bhopal), *karṇāṭī* (from Karṇāṭaka), *gāndhārī* (from Gāndhāra), *mālavī* (from Mālava), *saurāṭī* (from Saurāṣṭra).

Anthropomorphic features are attributed to the *rāgas* and *rāgiṇīs*. For example, *śrī-rāga* is conceived as follows:

> *aṣṭādāśābdaḥ smara-cāru-mūrtiḥ, dhīro lasat pallava*
> *karṇapūraḥ* ।

ṣaḍjādi-sevyo'ruṇa-vastra-dhārī śrī-rāga eṣa kṣitipāla mūrtiḥ ||

This *śrī-rāga*, 18 year old, having his body beautiful like that of Cupid, wearing a reddish brown cloth, adorned with dazzling leafy ornaments, is calm, served by *ṣaḍja,* etc., and appears like a king.

Vasantī, a *rāgiṇī* of *śrī-rāga*, has been described thus:

śikhaṇḍi-varhoccaya-baddhu-cūḍā karṇāvataṁsīkṛta-śobhanāmrā |
indīvara-śyāma-tanuḥ sucitrā vasantikā syādali-mañjula śrīḥ ||

The exquisitely beautiful Vasantikā, decked with bees, having a body dark-blue like a blue lotus, with top-knot tied with many peacock-plumes, has beautiful ear-ornaments in the forms of mango-blossoms.

Rāgas are classified from different points of view. These are divided as *mārga* (classical) and *deśī* (regional). Again, in accordance with the number of basal *svaras*, they are divided into three types, namely *auḍava* (based on five *svaras*), *ṣāḍava* (based on six *svaras*) and *sampūrṇa* (based on all the seven notes).

Śārṅgadeva lays down (IV.374-9) the merits and defects of songs. The merits are as follows:

Vyakta — clearly articulated *svara*, *rāga*, etc.

Pūrṇa — with complete *gamaka.*

Prasanna — clear and easily intelligible meaning.

Sukumāra — with *svaras* arising from the throat.

Alaṁkṛta — embellished in the *sthānas*, *mandra*, *madhya* and *tāra*.

Sama — even in *varṇa*, *laya* and *sthāna*.

Surakta — harmonious in lute, flute and voice.

Ślakṣṇa — uniform smoothness in low and high tones, *druta* and *madhya*, etc.

Vikṛṣṭa — loud pronunciation.

Madhura — possessed of special grace and delightfulness.

The defects of songs are stated below:

Lokaduṣṭa — disgusting to people.

Śāstraduṣṭa — defective according to rules.

Śrutivirodhī — lacking in *śruti*.

Kālavirodhī — sung at a prohibited time.

Punarukta — repetitive.

Kalā-bāhya — inartistic.

Gatakrama — disorderly.

Apārthaka — meaningless.

Grāmya — vulgar.

Saṁdigdha — of doubtful import.

The author mentions (III.13-18) many qualities of the best singer. Among them are charming voice, sound knowledge of the art, tirelessness even after singing many songs, regular practice, etc.

Singers have been divided into three classes (III.22-4), namely, *ekala* (soloist), *yamala* (duetist) and *vṛnda-gāyana* (singing in a chorus). They have again been divided into five classes, namely, *śikṣākāra* (learning different types of songs with ease), *anukāra* (imitating the style of others), *rasika* (according to some, one who, after hearing a sweet song, becomes horripilated and sheds tears of joy), *rañjaka* (one who can cause delight to the mind of the listeners) and *bhāvaka* (one who can turn an insipid song into a succulent one, inspire emotion and sings according to the desire of the audience).

Śārṅgadeva enumerates 25 kinds of condemned singers (III.25-7). Some of them are:

Saṁdaṣṭa — one who sings with clenched teeth.

Bhīta — scared.

Kampita — trembling.

Kākī — having a raucous voice.

Vitāla — devoid of the sense of *tāla*.

Tumbakī — one whose throat is inflated like a bottle-gourd while singing.

Vinimīlaka — one who sings with closed eyes.

Sānunāsika — one singing with a nasal tone.

Instrumental Music

Musical instruments are divided into the following four classes (*Saṁgīta-ratnākara*, Vādyādhyāya, 4-5):

Ānaddha or *Avanaddha* — percussion instruments the ends of which are covered with leather; e.g., drum.

Tata — stringed instruments; e.g., lute.

Suṣira — wind instruments having holes; e.g., flute.

Ghana — metallic instruments; e.g., cymbal, bell.

Śārṅgadeva has enumerated (*ibid.*, 12-14) 23 varieties of *avanaddha* instruments. As regards stringed instruments, he divides lutes (*vīṇā*) into two main classes (*ibid.*, 7-8) viz., *śruti-vīṇā*, and *svara-vīṇā*. The former is divided into two types, namely *dhruvā* or *acalā* and *calā* (*ibid.*, I.3.17). *Svara-vīṇā* is divided into ten types (*ibid.*, 9-10). *Suṣira* instruments are also of ten varieties (*ibid.*, 11-12). Seven types of metallic instruments are mentioned (*ibid.*, 15-16).

The notes, produced by particular strokes on instruments, are called *dhātu* (VI.125). *Vādya* has been stated (VI.23) to make up the deficiencies of songs and dance.

In Chapter VI (Vādyādhyāya) of the *Saṁgīta-ratnākara*, Śārṅgadeva discusses, in details, the measurement, dimensions and the materials of the different instruments. He deals also with the modes of playing the instruments. Incidentally, he dwells on the merits and defects of the instrumentalists.

Dance

Usually, dance is called *nṛtya*. But, Śārṅgadeva draws (VII. 26-28) a distinction between *nṛtya* and *nṛtta*. *Nṛtya* is that which, by means of acting (*abhinaya*), delineates certain *bhāva*s (emotions). *Nṛtta* means physical gestures and postures without acting. So, dance should be properly called *nṛtta*. The *Daśarūpaka* of Dhanañjaya (tenth century AD) defines *nṛtya* as *bhāvāśraya* (based on *bhāva* or emotion) and *nṛtta* as based on *tāla* and *laya*. The former is pantomime or tableau.

Śārṅgadeva describes the various postures and gestures of dancers from head to foot. Thus, he describes 19 positions of the head, 70 of the hand 13 of the foot, 17 of the arm, 8 kinds of *rasa-dṛṣṭi* (glance indicating a sentiment), 28 kinds of *bhāva-dṛṣṭi* (glance indicating an emotion), 9 positions of the eye, 10 of the lips.

Towards the end of the work, Śārṅgadeva lays down the qualifications of *ācārya*, *naṭa*, *nartaka*, *vaitālika*, *cāraṇa*, *sabhāsada* and *sabhāpati*. Then he describes the *sabhā* of the audience-hall and its paraphernalia. Finally, he analyses the nine *rasa*s.

Ācārya should be well-versed in dance, vocal and instrumental music. Moreover, he should be eloquent, good-looking, well-dressed, appreciative, skilled in eulogy. He must also be able to realise jokes in the assembly and to play instruments.

Naṭa (actor) is one who knows, the distinction between the different kinds of drama and is versed in the art of acting.

Nartaka (dancer) is one who has mastered the classical dance.

Vaitālika (panegyrist of the king and proclaimer of the hour of the day) should be a linguist capable of pleasing the audience and of criticising others.

Cāraṇa (wandering actor or singer) is capable of playing *kiṅkiṇī*, surrounded by dancers awkwardly dressed, versed in the *rāga*s and clever.

A *sabhāsada* or member of the audience is of moderate opinion, careful, eloquent, just, experienced in dance, modest, devoid of pride, appreciator of *rāga*s and *bhāva*s, skilled in dance and music, clever, devoid of jealousy and a connoisseur.

A man, possessing the following qualifications, deserves to be *sabhāpati* (president of the assembly):

> Versed in erotic matters, charitable, respectable, rich, capable of praising even slight virtues, interested in amusement, eloquent, devoid of jealousy, skilled in jokes, learned, grave, skilled in all arts, versed in all sciences, desirous of fame, sweet-tongued, capable of reading other's minds, meritorious, endowed with good memory, specialist in music and dance, experienced in giving rewards, possessed of all materials, wise, calm, having members of family under control, capable of appreciating beauty and enjoying *rasa*, truthful, aristocratic, possessed of a delighted face, grateful, kind, pious, friendly to the learned, etc. As regards the audience-hall, it will be decorated with flowers. With various kinds of canopies and jewelled posts, it will have a beautiful throne on which the *sabhāpati* will be seated. He will have ladies of the harem on his left, principal men on the right with the treasurer behind them. Near them will stay people versed in Vedic and classical lore. There will also remain poets skilled in all kinds of diction. Among the learned will be seated respectable astrologers and physicians. On the south will sit the ministers. Also seated there will be the commander-in-chief and other persons. Sportive men and women will be on all sides of the ladies of the harem and *sabhāpati* will be in front of the king. Young and charming women will stay behind the king; they will wave *chowrie*s, and attract the minds of the audience by the jingling of their bangles. In front of the king, to his left will sit those who compose songs, reciters, bards, learned men, those who are skilled in sweet speech and eulogy. Then on all sides will sit the royal retinue. In the hall, there will also be present skilful people with canes in hands. On all sides there will remain armed bodyguards of the king. In the assembly hall, thus arranged, the leader will enjoy music.

15

Vāstuvidyā (Architecture)

THERE are references to architecture in the *Ṛgveda* (*c*. 1500 BC), the earliest Indo-European text. For instance, the words *harmya*, *pastya*, denoting mansion, occur in *ṚV*, VII.55.6 and X.96.11 respectively. The expression *sahasra-sthūṇa* (*ṚV*, V.62.6) led Wilson to think that huge buildings, supported by one thousand *sthūṇa*s (pillars or columns), existed in the Vedic age. Besides earthen houses, there are references also to three-storyed house and palace as well as to their pillars. In *ṚV* (IV.30.20) it is stated that Indra, siding with Divodāsa, destroyed a hundred stone cities. In some verses of this Veda, mention is made of *āyasī* (made of iron?) cities or forts. At several places, references are found to village and city. As regards sculpture, we cannot say definitely whether or not images of deities existed in that age. Nor is there any indication of other sculptural designs or motifs. The anthropomorphic characteristics of various deities tend to make us think that some sort of image might exist.

The ruins of Indus Valley Civilisation, which is generally believed to have preceded the Vedic by about a millennium, contain many indications of the development of architecture to a great extent and of the sculptural technology of a sort.

Information about architecture, especially house-building, is found, *inter alia*, in *ṚV*, I.67.5, I.166.8, II.15.3, III.8, III.54.20; IV.30.20, V.32.5, VII.55.6, VII.76.2, IX.71.4, etc. The *Atharvaveda* contains the *mantra*s recited at the time of building houses. The *Śatapatha Brāhmaṇa* (ch. III) refers to three kinds of stone structures; namely, *vāstu* (wherein the remains of the bodies of great men were preserved), *gṛha* (residential house) and *prajñāna* (memorial column or stone boulder). References to house-building, etc., are available also in the *Sāṁkhāyana Gṛhyasūtra* (III.2), *Āśvalāyana Gṛhayasūtra* (II.7-9); *Gobhila-gṛhyasūtra* (IV.7.15-19), and *Hiraṇyakeśi-gṛhyasūtra* (I.8.27). In post-Vedic times, particularly in the technical works on architecture the term *vāstu-vidyā* included also the construction, of images of deities.

The great Epics contain many references to cities with palatial buildings and images of divine and human beings. Rāma, unable to bear the pangs of separation from his banished beloved, is stated to have made her golden image. These two Epics contain many references to cities, mansions, forts, palaces, etc. There is mention also of persons expert in architecture; they appear to have enjoyed great prestige in the society. *Rāmāyaṇa* (*Rām*) (I.13.8, V.15, 43) throws some light on architecture. It may be noted that the description of Ayodhyā, contained in the *Rāmāyaṇa*, is much similar to the description of a city, occurring in such works on architecture as the *Mānasāra*. The *Mahābhārata* (*Mbh.*) refers to cities, ramparts, temples, etc. From I.184.19, it appears that palaces, etc., in that age also were white-washed, the word *Sudhāvadāta* indicates it, *sudhā* denotes lime. The following are some of the passages of the *Mahābhārata*, which throw light on architecture: I.128.41, II.1.18, XII.62; XIV.10, V.143.30. The time of origin of these Epics is not known. They evolved through centuries before assuming the present forms. According to Winternitz, if the *Mahābhārata* had its present form about the fourth century AD, the *Rāmāyaṇa* did so a century or two earlier.

The word *vāstu*, in the *Arthaśāstra* of Kauṭilya (III.8) (*c*. fourth century BC), includes *gṛha* (house), *kṣetra* (town?), *ārāma* (garden), *setubandha* (demarcation of boundary) and *taḍāga* (tank). Many things relating to house-building, etc., have been dealt with in the *Arthaśāstra* (II.1-4, III.8).

Some Purāṇas contain information about *vāstu-vidyā*. For instance, the *Matsya Purāṇa* names 18 persons versed in this *śāstra*. While some of these names may be imaginary, others are believed to be historical personages (*vide* T.P. Bhattacharya, *A Study on Vāstuvidyā*, ch. X). In chapter 254 of *Matsya Purāṇa*, there is a brief discussion on this lore. Some discussion on it occurs also in the *Mārkaṇḍeya Purāṇa* (ch. 49), *Vāyu Purāṇa* (chap. 8), *Angi Purāṇa* (ch. 104), etc. Of the above Purāṇas, the *Matsya Purāṇa* dates back to a period between the third century AD and the fourth, the *Mārkaṇḍeya Purāṇa* between the third century AD and the fifth; the *Agni Purāṇa* to the ninth century AD; the dates are, however, conjectural. Besides the Purāṇas, mentioned above, the following Purāṇas also deal with this subject: *Skanda Purāṇa* (*c.* AD between 700 and 1050), *Garuḍa Purāṇa* (*c.* AD 800-1000), *Nārada Purāṇa* (*c.* ninth century AD), *Bhaviṣya Purāṇa* (upper limit *c.* AD 500), *Brahmavaivartta* (present form between *c.* tenth-sixteenth century AD). These Purāṇas deal with such matters, relating to house-building, as *stambha* or column, measurement of brick-built houses, building plan, classification of buildings, etc.

Some other important works incidentally refer to architecture. For example, the *Kāmasūtra* of Vātsyāyana (*c.* third century AD) mentions 64 arts including *vāstu-vidyā*. The first section (*adhikaraṇa*) of this work contains a graphic description of the beautiful house of the *nāgaraka* (man about town) and of the city. The *Bṛhat-saṁhitā* of Varāhamihira (*c.* AD 475-550) contains five chapters about architecture and sculpture. Among the architectural subjetcs are suitable site for a residential house, method of testing the soil, plan of the house, storey, measurements of doors, etc.; these are deftly discussed. There is classification of brick-built houses and the ways of building them have been mentioned.

Some Purāṇas deal with the subject which comprises the construction of temples, forts, quarters for ministers, generals, ordinary houses (*sāmānya-gṛha*). The following Purāṇas deserve special mention in this connection: *Agni*, *Garuḍa*, *Matsya*, *Vāyu* and *Viṣṇudharmottara*. Some interesting information, contained in the Purāṇas, is set forth below:

> The city (*nagara* or *pura*) will extend over an area of one *yojana* = 4 *krośas* or 8/9 miles. *Kheṭa* (small town or hamlet) covers half a *yojana*. *Grāma* (village) spreads over ¼th. *yojana* (*Vāyu* 9. 116, 117).

The *Vāyu Purāṇa* mentions various kinds of roads; e.g., *rathyā* (for movement of chariots?), *rāja-mārga* (highway), *pratoli* (main road), *ghaṇṭāpatha* (perhaps so-called because cattle, with small bells tinkling round their necks, used to pass along it), *gṛharathyā* (perhaps the path leading to a house), *vṛttimārga* (used by people pursuing different professions?) (*Vāyu* 11.33-4, 30.220, 41.50-4, etc.).

The space between two houses should be three *padas* (strides). Among the various kinds of rooms and houses is mentioned the *prāgvaṁśa* (*Vāyu*, 8.121). It means a sacrificial chamber or a room in which the family and the friends of the sacrificer used to assemble.

According to *Vāyu* (40.8, 41-54, 59.126-7), a city should contain, among other things, gardens and *dharmaśālā*s (charitable institutions?). Details about the sites and layouts of cities are discussed in some Purāṇas, e.g., *Matsya* (254.14-16). Areas appear to have been earmarked for different classes of people, e.g., ministers, *śilpin*s (artists), and *kāruśilpin*s (craftsmen), physicians, etc., and even for prostitutes.

The *Matsya Purāṇa* (253, last verse, 254.1 ff.) describes different types of buildings, e.g., *sarvatobhadra* (palace or temple has four entrances, four doors and *alinda*s or terraces before house-doors on all sides), *nandyāvarta* (devoid of door in the west), *svastika* (without door in the east), etc.

It is interesting to note that the dimensions of the houses were specified for different castes; the higher the caste, the greater is the dimension.

For the construction of a house, the timber of the following trees was prohibited (*Matsya*, 257.4-7):

> milk-exuding trees, trees on which birds live, those battered by wind, burnt by fire, struck by lightning, broken and dry, grown in *caitya*s (see Glossary), temples, funeral ground, etc.

According to *Vāyu* (257.7-8), also to be avoided are thorny trees, *kadamba* (*Anthocephalus chinensin*), *nīm* (*Azadirachta indica*), *bibhītaka* (*Terminalia balerica*), *śleṣmātaka* (*Dillenia indica*) and mango-tree (*Mangifera indica*).

In some Tāntric works of the *āgama* class, there is considerable information about architecture and sculpture. As many as 60 chapters of the *Kālikāgama* are devoted to these subjects. Three kinds of construction, called *nāgara*, *drāviḍa* and *vesara* have been described. Among other *āgamas*, dealing with the same subjects, most noteworthy are the *karaṇāgama*, *suprabhedāgama* and *vaikhānasāgama*.

The prose, poetical and dramatic works of the Classical Sanskrit literature are replete with references to various architectural patterns. For instance, the *Rājataraṅgiṇī* of Kalhaṇa (twelfth century AD) mentions *vānaśālā* which means a huge mansion well-protected with ramparts, moats, etc. Besides, there is mention of *vihāra* (Buddhist monastery) and *caitya* which generally denotes Buddhist or Jain prayer-halls, most of which contained memorial columns. In his *Harṣacarita*, Bāṇabhaṭṭa (early seventh century AD) vividly describes the royal palace. Besides the harem, there are at least three compounds in the palace. There are references to multi-storeyed huge buildings, floors studded with shining stones, walls with precious stones, columns, etc. The assembly hall and *prāgvaṁśa* (small room by the side of the sacrificial hall) are also mentioned.

Some works on astronomy and mathematics, too, discuss *vāstu-vidyā*. For instance, the *Garga-saṁhitā* mentions the measurement of the compound and the rooms as well as the mode of placing doors, etc. In constructing a house, the gnomon was considered to be very useful. This matter has been discussed, in extenso, in works like the *Sūryasiddhānta* (*c.* AD 400), *Siddhāntaśiromaṇi* (AD 1150), etc.

Various matters, relating to the subject concerned have been discussed in the Vaiṣṇava work *Hayaśīrṣa-pañcarātra* (between the seventh century and the ninth). A voluminous work on architecture is the *Aparājitapṛcchā*. It is believed that a work on the construction of columns was composed, on the authority of Jaya and Aparājita, at the instance of Mahārāṇā Kumbha (1433-68) of Chittor (Rājasthān).

There are works dealing exclusively with architecture and sculpture. Very important among them are the following:

(For dates of works, we have taken T.P. Bhattachrya's *Study on Vāstuvidyā* as authoritative.)

1. *Viśvakarma-prakāśa* of Vāsudeva — perhaps earlier than the *Matsya Purāṇa* (q.v.).
2. *Mayamata* — tenth century AD or earlier.
3. *Samarāṅgaṇa-sūtradhāra* of Bhoja — eleventh century AD.
4. *Mānasāra* — the extant version probably dates back to a period between the eleventh century and the fifteenth.
5. *Śilparatna* — attributed to Śrīkumāra (sixteenth century AD).
6. *Vāstu-ratnāvalī*.
7. *Aṁśumadbheda* — attributed to Kāśyapa.
8. *Vāstusūtra-upaniṣad* — attributed to Pippalāda, it is the earliest known work on image-making. In six chapters, it deals with stones, compositional diagram, carving disposition of parts of the image, the basic emotions connected with images, total composition of the image panel. The metaphysical question of the origin of form and its importance for the attainment of *mokṣa* is the central idea.

The following is a brief account of the matters dealt with in the extant works on *Vāstu-śāstra*. The fact that some ancient works are lost is known from references to or citations from them in later works. The main topics discussed in the available works are:

> *Vāstu-devatā* and related worship, testing and selection of sites for residential house, construction of house, especially of its doors. In connection with house-building, the system of drainage and other sanitary arrangements also have recieved the attention of the authors. There is discussion about the trees to be grown around the house and also those which should be avoided. Brick, stone, wood, etc., are mentioned as the principal materials of a house. Some of the other subjects are — auspicious moments for starting

construction, different kinds of houses, measurements of the house, etc., temple-building, different schools of architecture, art of the lay-out of *janapada* (village) and *nagara* (city), decorative elements, etc.

It is not possible here to dwell at length on all the above subjects. We shall describe only a few interesting topics. A method of testing the soil of the selected site of a house is this: First of all, a square hole, one cubit deep, is to be dug. After filling it with water, one has to wait for one day and one night. If the water fully dries, during this time, then the site is to be regarded as bad. But, if some water still remains, the place may be considered suitable. In building a house, one had to be careful about the health and convenience of the neighbours. The *Arthaśāstra* clearly states that a person making doors and windows in a manner inconvenient to others, will be liable to punishment. The owner of the house, from which water falls into another's house, will be punished. It was obligatory to leave the specified space between two adjacent houses; this space was one cubit and eight fingers or three steps wide (*vide* R.G. Basak's Bengali translation, first edition, p. 212).

It appears to have been customary to make various attractive artistic designs and images in different parts of the house, particularly at the doors. The motifs related to myths or nature.

Doors appear to have attracted the attention of most of the authors. They have laid down do's and dont's about their location, material, size, etc. It is noteworthy that they are very particular about ventilation. An important rule is that the doors should be located in one or other the four principal directions just in the middle of the wall.

Different works differ on the size of the bricks. The largest brick was 18" × 18" × 6" and the smallest one 8" × 4" × 2".

According to the *Mānasāra*, among the high-rise mansions, the highest one was twelve-storeyed; it was suitable for a paramout monarch.

As stated earlier, architecture was divided into two main schools, viz. Northern (*Nāgara*) and Southern (*Drāviḍa*). In the *Śilpa-śāstra* of southern India, a third school, named *Vesara* is mentioned. It is not definitely known in which part of India *Vesara* prevailed. According to some, this was the appellation given to Orissan architecture only. Others hold that *Vesara* had two sub-classes, named *Āndhra* and *Kāliṅga*. In some works, the architectural patterns, called *Lāṭa*, *Vairāṭa*, *Bhūmija*, etc., are also mentioned. It should be noted that originally temple-architecture of different types gave rise to the above classifications. In the *Śilparatana* and some other works, as many as 20 types of temple-architecture, named *nalina*, *pralīna*, etc. are mentioned. The south Indian work of the *Āgama* class, entitled *Atri-saṁhitā*, mentions four types of temples, called *Brahmāchanda*, *Viṣṇucchanda*, *Indracchanda* and *Rudracchanda*. In some later works, mention is made of temple architecture, called *Brahmākānta*, *Viṣṇukānta*, etc.

Some scholars hold that Buddhist topes (*stūpa*s) were the precursors of temples. It is difficult to determine the extent to which Indian architecture, especially temple-architecture was influenced by the Buddhists. It should be noted that later temples might have been originally influenced by the Buddhist topes; but the former, in course of time, developed independent characteristics to a great extent. Temple with *śikhara*s (tapering summits) were of independent development.

It is difficult to say when, how and to what extent south Indian architecture was influenced by that of the Āryans. It should be noted that, in course of time, the architecture of both these parts of India coalesced. According to some scholars, Aryan architecture of north India was, to some extent, influenced by that of the non-Āryans like Asuras and Nāgas (see Bhattacharya, *A Study on Vāstuvidyā*, pp. 298-301).

Most of the temples in India appear to have been constructed from the sixth century onward. Although no earlier models exist, yet some scholars, on certain evidences and other reasons, conclude that temple architecture originated in India as early as the second or first century BC (*ibid*., p. 291).

Scholars are not unanimous as to whether or not, in the domain of architecture, India was indebted to Rome. Similarity of the work of the Roman architect, Vitruvius (first century BC), with Indian

Śilpaśāstra, particularly the *Mānasāra*, has been found. But which work was the borrower, if at all, cannot be ascertained (*ibid.*, pp. 198-201). The extant *Mānasāra* appears to have been composed centuries later than Vitruvius. It may be supposed that this work may have been a later recast or an earlier version of the *Mānasāra* or that the present form records a time-honoured tradition which originated in the period following Vitruvius:

> *Vāstu-vidyā* did not remain within the confines of India. Like several other Indian *śāstras*, this *śāstra* also had considerable impact on the architecture of Tibet, Sikkim, Nepal, Ceylon (Śrī Laṅkā), etc., and on the south-eastern countries, Siam (Thailand), Combodia (Kampuchea), Campā (South Annam), Sumātrā, Bāli, Borneo, Jāvā, etc. Indian influence on the architecture of Khoṭan and Tunhuang in Central Asia is not negligible. One wonders how the distant lands of China and Japan bacame indebted to Indian architecture. The ruins of the Maya civilisation of America remind one of Indian *Vāstu-vidyā*. The similarity of the name Maya with the title of the Sanskrit work, *Mayamata*, is not, perhaps, accidental.

16

Aśva-śāstra (Horselore)

THE horse has been a very useful animal ever since the Vedic age. Besides being a swift means of transport, horses constituted a wing of the army. They were used in hunting excursions too. *Aśvamedha* sacrifice was a very important rite for kings. It was a long-standing practice to send letters through horses. It was, therefore, natural for scholars to write treatises on horse. Kauṭilya's *Arthaśāstra* contains details about the duties of a high royal functionary, called *Aśvādhyakṣa*.

Several works, dealing exclusively with horselore, are available. These can be broadly divided into two classes, viz: (1) those which discuss the different species of horses, their good and bad signs, etc. and (ii) those dealing with various maladies of horses and their treatment.

A single work, belonging to the first class above, has as yet been published. It is entitled *Aśva-śāstra*, and attributed to Nakula. It is edited by S. Gopalan, Sarasvati Mahal Library, Tanjore, 1952. The editor informs us that, in this Library, there are many manuscripts on horselore.

The above Nakula is identified, in verses 4 and 5, with the Pāṇḍava brother of this name. The date of its composition is unknown. That it is only a compilation, and not an original work is indicated in verse 5 (*dṛṣṭvā samastaṁ . . . śāstraṁ . . . brūte tattvārtham . . . . śāstraṁ kṛtvā samāsataḥ*). May be that the compiler, desiring to impart a halo of sanctity and antiquity to the work, associated it with Pāṇḍava Nakula who is mentioned, in the

Mahābhārata, as a physician of horses. It may be noted that the manuscript, on which the above edition is based, contains 21 pictures of different kinds of horses.

The topics, dealt with in the work, are briefly as follows:

Vāji-praśaṁsādhyāya — the horse has been characterised as fearless, obedient, swift, fit to be used in all seasons, and capable of enduring hunger and thirst. Its usefulness in war has been expressed by the statement *aśvair-hastagatā pr̥thivī*; by means of horses the world is conquered.

Raivata-stotra — no harm can be done to the horses of one who recites this hymn in the morning.

Praśnādhyāya — it is stated that, in times of yore, horses had wings which were clipped by Śālihotra at the request of Indra.

Pradeśādhyāya, *Aṅga-lakṣaṇaprakaraṇādhyāya*, *Aśva-lakṣaṇopodghātādhyāya* — the following are some of the good signs of a horse: red complexion, soft lips devoid of hairs, soft sides of the face, hard neck. Longevity of a horse is 32 years.

Āvartādhyāya — *āvarta* means hairy circular mark; such *āvarta*s of various shapes, are classified as *dhruva* (fixed), *nindya* (blameable), *śubha* (auspicious) and *aśubha* (inauspicious).

Miśrita-lakṣaṇādhyāya — signs of the best horse — all-white, white at certain parts of the body, viz., hoof, face, well-formed body, graceful gait. Horses of some mixed colours are the best, e.g., red or black with white ears, hoofs, face and legs. Some mixed colours indicate the worst kind; e.g., black hoofs, and white legs.

Puṇḍra-lakṣaṇādhyāya — a white mark above the nose, but below the ear is called *puṇḍra*. *Puṇḍra*s of the following shapes forebode the prosperity and victory of the owner of the horse:

lotus-petal, pitcher, plough, flag, good (useful in driving elephants), *bel* tree, conch, umbrella, *svastika*, etc.

Marks of the dark colour and of the shapes of chain, etc., are inauspicious.

Puṣpa-lakṣaṇa — some marks, seen on the body of a horse, disappear after sometime. Such a mark is called *puṣpa*. *Puṣpa*s in some parts of the body are auspicious, while, in others, these are ominous.

Heṣita-śubhalakṣaṇa — some modes of neigh are auspicious, while others inauspicious.

Gandha-lakṣaṇa — the smell of a horse's body, like that of lotus, sandal, etc., is good while the smell like that of a camel, ass, etc., is ominous.

Chāyā-lakṣaṇa — different kinds of shadow covering the body of the horse, e.g., that of the water, the rising sun, etc. Such shadows are visible when the horse drinks water, eats grass or is asleep.

Gati-lakṣaṇa — discussion on different kinds of gait of the horse; e.g., auspicious is the gait like that of a peacock, bull, etc. The horse which strikes the ground or jumps while moving is inauspicious.

Sattva-lakṣaṇa — threefold division of the nature of horses into *sāttvika*, *rājasa* and *tāmasa* each of which is sub-divided into several kinds.

The other chapters, in order, deal with *Mahādoṣa*, *Tālu-raṅga* (colour of palate), *Kula-lakṣaṇa* (signs of pedigree), *Vayo-jñāna* (knowledge of age), *Varṇa-lakṣaṇa*, *Rājavāha* (fitness for a king's ride), *Āyu-lakṣaṇa*, *Utpāta* (various signs and actions of a horse foreboding natural calamities), *Vāhana-śikṣā* (training of the horses), *Dhārā* (different kinds of gait), *Ārohavidhāna* (rules for the rider).

The manuscript, *Sārasindhu* (also called *Śālihotra Vaiśampāyanīya*), in the Sarasvati Mahal Library, Tanjore, by Malladeva Paṇḍita, contains certain matters relating to horses. It deals, *inter alia*, with horses having deformities, their psychology, the appurtenances for their maintenance as well as for the riders.

A treatise about the treatment of equestrian diseases, entitled *Aśva-cikitsita* in 18 chapters, is also attributed to Nakula (ed. by U. Gupta, *Bib. Indica*, Calcutta, 1887). The topics discussed are: teeth of horses, size of their limbs, speed, mode of riding them, their different species, colour of their different limbs, their good and bad signs, their maintenance in different seasons, administration of snuff, their diseases and treatment, maintenance of stable, etc.

Another work on the same subject is the *Aśva-vaidyaka* (*Bibliotheca Indica* ed., Calcutta, 1887) by Jayadatta Sūri, son of

Vijayadatta. According to the editor, some internal evidences indicate that it was written after the thriteenth century or even the fifteenth. Some of the topics, dealt with in its 68 chapters, are signs of long or short life of a horse, different species of horses, called *pārasīka*, *turaṣka*, *saindhava*, etc., growth of worms in horses as a serious malady, remedy for the barrenness of a mare. Among other ailmets, of a horse are ulcer, pain, dropsy, piles, insanity, etc. There is mention of several drugs in connection with treatment of horses.

From the verse VII.1, it appears to be an epitome of various treatises.

17

Gaja-śāstra (Elephantlore)

ELEPHANTS constituted one of the wings of the army which, as always, was indispensable for defence. Again, they added to grandeur of royal processions and expeditions. This animal served as an excellent conveyance in hunting excursions; it was comparatively safer when there was the risk of attack by tigers, etc., and convenient for targeting an animal from a good distance. Its usefulness as a beast of burden and in charging the enemy in battle is well-known. These were the reasons why the pachyderms received the careful attention of their owners. It was, therefore, quite natural for scholars to write treatises dealing with the capture, training, maintenance and medical treatment of the elephants. We shall briefly describe the highlights of elephantlore.

A lot of information can be gathered about this leviathan from different works, notably the *Arthaśāstra* (II. 31, 32) of Kauṭilya who designates a particular high official as *Hastyadhyakṣa* (superintendent of elephants). In the *Rāmāyaṇa* (I.6.24), there is mention of the various species of this animal. The *Śukranīti* (IV.7.79) and Varāhamihira's *Bṛhat-saṁhitā* contain various matters relating to elephants. The poetical work, *Yaśastilaka-campū* (Kāvyamālā ed., Vol. I. p. 482) contains certain matters connected with elephantlore.

Besides the above works, which incidentally mention facts about this animal, there were several treatises, devoted exclusively to this Śāstra. Some of these works are still unpublished. Among the manuscripts, special mention is deserved by MS. no. 12295 preserved in Sarasvati Mahal Library, Tanjore. As far as we know, the following two works are available in print:

Nīlakaṇṭha's *Mātaṅga-līlā* and Pālakāpya's *Hastyāyurveda*.

The first work, edited by Ganapati Sastri, was published in Trivandrum in 1910. Its German translation, by Zimmer, was published in Berlin in 1929, and England rendering, by F. Edgerton, was published in New Haven, Yale University Press, 1931. The other treatise was published in Ānandāśrama Series, Poona, 1894. We know nothing about Nīlakaṇṭha mentioned (perhaps erroneously, as Nārāyaṇa by A.B. Keith in *History of Sanskrit Literature*, p. 465). As the *Mātaṅga-līlā* is very well-known in Kerala, Sastri thinks that probably the author belonged to that region.

The *Mātaṅga-līlā*, comprising 263 verses, is divided into 12 *paṭalas* (section) the contents of which are briefly as follows:

I. Different synonyms, with their derivative meaning, of the word *hastin*.

II. Good signs of an elephant, e.g., high tusk and backbone, 20 nails, etc.

III. Bad signs, e.g., having a limb more or less than usual, very much emaciated, curved tail.

IV. Marks indicating the longevity of an animal, e.g., smooth tusk, long ears and tail indicate long life.

V. Marks indicating age and different conditions of life, e.g., coppery complexion, fondness for breast-feed, undeveloped limbs indicate the first year of age. V. 3 states that an elephant lives for 120 years.

VI. Length of the body is determined from the eye to the tail, height from the nail to the neck.

VII. General principle of determining the price of an elephant.

VIII. Different kinds of nature of elephants and their external signs.

IX. Discussion on the flow of ichor on the elephant's body due to excitement or excessive joy. In such a condition, the animal trumpets loudly, and tries to run away from the place where it is tied. In such a condition, a tablet prepared with the barks of certain trees, mixed with honey and milk shoud be administered to it.

X. Methods of capturing wild elephants. These are fivefold, viz., laying a trap, enticing a male elephant by a female one, chase, striking or beating, making it fall into a deep pit. The last method is as follows:

a pit, four cubits deep, two cubits wide and five cubits long, has to be dug and covered with tempting fodder. When a very young elephant comes there to eat, if falls into the pit. Then it is to be captured.

XI. Maintenance of elephants, a few matters are noted below: Daily bath in cold water is good. Lotus-stalk, banana plant, grass, sugarcane, bamboo-leaves, uncooked and cooked rice are among the favourites of an elephant. Application of *ghee* is good for its eyes and teeth. A good quantity of salt is an antidote for its worms and loss of appetite, etc. The treatment of certain elephant-diseases like fever is like that of humans.

XII. Qualifications of drivers and supervisors.

The *Hastyāyurveda* is attributed to sage Pālakāpya who is stated (I.1.155) to have been so culled because of his rearing (*pālana*) a herd of elephants and his belonging to (the place called?) Kāpya. The work is in mixed prose and verse. Many of the verses seem to be quotations. The entire treatise appears to be a compilation, this impression is confirmed by the word Saṁhitā (Collection) in its full title *Hastyāyurveda-saṁhitā*, contained in the final colophon.

The above work comprises four parts called *sthāna*s, the contents of which are briefly indicated below. Each of the parts is divided into some chapters:

I. *Mahāroga-sthāna*: It deals with the symptoms and treatment of serious diseases of elephants. In its chapter, called *roga-vibhakti*, the diseases are divided into two main categories, namely, *ādhyātmika* (those caused by internal causes) and *āgantuka* (infectious). Of the diseases, 76 are caused by *vāta* (wind), 27 by *pitta* (bile) and 32 by *śleṣma* (phlegm).

II. *Kṣudra-roga-sthāna*: Dealing with minor ailments and their remedies.

III. *Śalya-sthāna*: Discusses surgery. The following ten kinds of surgical instruments are mentioned:

(i) *vṛddhi-patra*, (ii) *kuśa-patra* (like a blade of *kuśa* grass), (iii) *maṇḍalāgra* (with a circular tip?), (iv) *vrīhi-mukha* (whose tip is like a rice grain), (v) *kuṭhārākṛti* (looking like an axe), (vi) *vatsa-danta* (like the tooth of a calf?), (vii) *utpala-patra* (like the leaf or petal of a lotus?), (viii) *śalākā* (a probe or a kind of pointed surgical instrument), (ix) *sūcī* (needle), and (x) *rampaka* (?).

IV. *Uttara-sthāna*: Deals with the following topics:

Various eatables and drinks, flow of ichor, construction of elephant-stalls, description of different kinds of elephants, lustration of elephants.

In chapter XXX, called *Pāṁśudāna*, elephants have been divided into four classes, namely.

Āraṇya (wild), *damyamāna* (under training), *dānta* (trained), and *purāṇa* (old?).

18

Kṛṣi-śāstra (Agriculture)

Agriculture has been the main source of livelihood of the Indians ever since pre-historirc times. The earliest extant literary work, the *Ṛgveda* contains enough of evidence that economy was largely agricultural. In the well-known Gambler's Lament (*Ṛgveda*, X.34), the wretched gambler, who has become a pauper due to his addiction to gambling, has been strongly advised to take to agriculture (*kṛṣim it kṛṣasva, ibid.*, stanza 13). There are references, in this Veda, to seeds and sowing (e.g., I.17.2.21; X.9.2.3, etc.). There is mention of the bull and plough, required for the cultivation of fields (e.g., IV.5.12.1-8; X.10.5.7, etc.). IX.4.1.7; III.3.4.3, 7, etc., appear to refer to some kind of irrigation. The *Ṛgveda* (V.6.12.9, 10) and *Yajurveda* (109.2) contain references to harvesting and storing corns. The *Atharvaveda* contains references to various matters relating to agriculture; the word *kṛṣi* has been frequently used (e.g., III.17, 24; VI.50, 142, etc.). There are prayers (VII.18, 39, etc.) for the luxuriant grwoth of crops. III.24.1-7 contain a beautiful account of the requirements of cultivators. Crop-damaging pests and the means of saving the crops are also mentioned. Some sort of irrigation appears to be referred to in III.13. *Ṛgveda* (IX.4.1.7; III.4.3.7) should also be mentioned in this connection. The *Atharvaveda* mentions several classes of people connected with agriculture; e.g., *gopa* (one who looks after cattle), *kṛṣībala* and *kīnāśa* both denoting cultivator, *dhānyakṛt* (producer of *dhānya* which may denote rice or any corn or grain), etc. Among the corns are mentioned *vrīhi* (rice), *yava* (barley), *mudga* (a kind of kidney-bean), *māṣa* (a bean), *tila* (sesame), *godhūma* (wheat). *Taṇḍula* also is mentioned; it may denote rice or the kernel of any corn. The word *śariśāka* means *śāli dhānya*, according to some; *śāli* is regarded as paddy of a very good quality. Śugarcanes are also mentioned.

This Veda mentions various parts of the plough, made of strong *khadira* wood (*Acacia catechu*), *sītā*, meaning furrow, is of frequent occurrence. We find incantations and magic rites for averting the various impediments to agriculture; e.g., locusts, mischievous birds, wild beasts, plunderers, excessive rain, thunderstroke, drought, etc.

It is interesting to note that the *Atharvaveda* stresses the use of animal manure (III.14.3, 8; XIX.31.3). Natural manure is mentioned; other manures such as cowdung are also mentioned.

Various kinds of information about agriculture are available in a number of works e.g., Pāṇini's grammar, Epics, Purāṇas (e.g., *Brahmāṇḍa*, II.7.162, *Vāyu*, 79.71, etc.), *Arthaśāstra* (particularly *sītādhyakṣa* II.24), *Bṛhat-saṁhitā* of Varāhamihira, Parāśara, *Jyotistattva* of Raghunandana, *Vīramitrodaya* of Mitramiśra. It is interesting to note that in the *Arthaśāstra* (II.1), there is mention of irrigation canals, catchments and dams. According to the *Manu-smṛti* (VII.43) and *Arthaśāstra* (II.1), *vārtā* has been prescribed as one of the subjects of study for princes. *Vārtā* has been explained by commentator Kullūka, on the above text of Manu, as *Kṛṣivāṇijya-paśupālanādi*, i.e., agriculture, trade, cattle-rearing, etc.

The *Kṛṣi-parāśara*, is a published work dealing exclusively with agriculture. Also called *Kṛṣi-saṁgraha, Kṛṣi-karma-vivecana* and *Kṛṣi-paddhati*, it appears to be a work by a late compiler who fathered it upon the ancient sage, Parāśara in order to impart a halo of antiquity and sanctity to it. It deals with all the agricultural operations right from sowing up to harvesting and storing in granaries. A brief resume of the contents is given below:

Though entitled *Kṛṣi-parāśara*, it deals with paddy only. Seeds are to be collected in the month of *Māgha* or *Phālguna*. After drying them in the sun and removing husk and all particles of grass, these must be kept away from fire, smoke, rain-water and fish. For sowing, the month of *Vaiśākha* is the best and *Śrāvaṇa* worst (verses 159-77). After sowing, the land must be levelled by a *madikā* (a ladder-shaped appliance used in crushing the hard soil and clods of earth. For sowing of seeds for transplantation, the month of *Jyeṣṭha* or *Āṣāḍha* is the best time. Seedlings should be transplanted in *Śrāvaṇa* at proper intervals from one another; it should never be done in low lands (V.190). For weeding out and levelling the field, after the sprouting of seeds the months of *Āṣāḍha* and *Śrāvaṇa* are the best. In *Bhādra*, arrangement should be made for the excess water to flow out; only as much water as is necessary for dipping the roots of the plants should be allowed to remain in the field (V.195).

After harvest, the grains should be separated from the stalks by the process called *mardana*; it is nowadays done by getting the paddy plants trampled again and again by cows.

Personal supervision is stressed for ensuring the good growth of the plants and substantial yield. Bulls are stated to be essential elements in agriculture, and great care of them has been emphasised. Cowdung as manure has been highly spoken of.

Some of the main agricultural implements, mentioned in the work, are *hala* (plough), *madikā* (described earlier), *īṣā* (pole of a plough), *yuga* (yoke), *pāśika* (rope), *paccanī* (stick). *Phāla* (ploughshare) is also mentioned.

It seems to be a superstitious belief that black bulls are the best, black-and-red ones tolerable, and white ones the worst.

The only other published work on agriculture, known hitherto, is the *Kāśyapīya-kṛṣi-sūkti*, which despite our best effort, could not be procured.

19

Gaṇita-śāstra (Mathematics)

SOME salient features of ancient Indian mathematics are as follows: The most outstanding contribution of ancient India, in the realm of mathematics, is the concept of Zero (0) and the numbers 1 to 9. The eminent scholar, Sarton observes, "Our numerals and the use of Zero were invented by the Hindus and transmitted to us by the Arabs (hence the name Arabic numerals)." (*The Appreciation of Ancient and Medieval Science During the Renaissance*: *1450-1600*, Philadelphia University and Pennsylvania Press, 1955, p. 151). Some scholars, however, are inclined to trace the origin of the above to old Babylon and China (*vide* O. Neugebauer, *The Exact Sciences in Antiquity*, Copenhagen, 1951, p. 20; J. Needham, *Science and Civilisation in China*, III, Cambridge, 1959, pp. 11-12).

As in astronomy, so also in mathematics we have to trace its origin to the Vedic times. The *Śulvasūtra*, a Vedāṅga (accessory of Veda) originated for the correct measurement of the sacrificial altars; it was believed that no sacrifice could be entirely fruitful unless the altar was constructed with absolute accuracy; *Śulva* means a measuring string. Thus, the *Śulvasūtras* are the earliest available works on Indian geometry. What is known as the Pythagorean theorem in geometry is generally attributed to the Greek Pythagoras (*c.* 540 BC). This geometrical concept occurs in the *Baudhāyana Śulvasūtra*; Baudhāyana is supposed to have been anterior to Pythagoras. The application of this theorem is found in such ancient Indian texts as *Budhāyana Śrauta-sūtra* (X.19, XIX.1, XXVI). For some reasons, the idea of this theorem seems to occur in the much earlier *Taittirīya* and other Vedic Saṁhitās.

The Bakhshāli Manuscript (AD 400), discovered (AD 1881) near Peshāwar, and lodged in Bodleian Library, Oxford, appears to be the earliest work to express operation of fractions in terms of symbols. Later on, Mahāvīra (d. 468 BC, according to others, 528 BC) and Brahmagupta (b. AD 598) formulated rules for the operation of fractions and methods of reducing fractions to common denominations. The above Bakhshāli manuscript and some other later works contain the method of analysis of arithmetic progression series. Piṅgala's *Chandaḥ-sūtra* (*c.* 200 BC) appears to be the earliest work to mention the geometric progression series. Bhāskara (b. *c.* AD 1114) appears to have been the first mathematician to conceive and prove that $x/0$ is infinity. Āryabhaṭa I (b. AD 476) is credited with a remarkably accurate value of *ñ*, viz. 3.1416.

Some of the prominent works on mathematics in ancient India, are, besides the *Śulva-sūtras* (e.g., of Baudhāyana and Āpastamba) and the Bakhshāli manuscript, noted above, are:

> *Āryabhaṭīya* (*Gaṇitapāda* section) of Āryabhaṭa I, *Līlāvatī* and *Bījagaṇita* of Bhāskara, *Brahma-siddhānta* of Brahmagupta, *Gaṇita-sāra-saṁgraha* of Mahāvīrācārya (ninth century AD).

20

Āyurveda (Medical Science)

Origin of Āyurveda and Āyurvedic Works

THE indigenous medical science of India is called Āyurveda. The foundation of this science is found in the Vedas, particularly the *Ṛgveda* and *Atharvaveda*. For instance, the *Ṛgveda* (e.g. I.34.6) mentions *Tridhātu* or the triad of humours of the body, called *vāyu* (wind), *pitta* (bile) and *kapha* (phlegm). It also mentions some diseases, for example.

> *Harimāṇa* (jaundice?) (I.50, 11, 12); *hṛdroga* (heart disese) (I.50.11); *yakṣmā* (consumption) (I.122.9, X.163.1), etc.

The *Atharvaveda* (I.17.1;VI. 90.2) reveals knowledge of anatomy. The human body is stated to contain 100 *dhamanī*s (major blood-carrying tubes), 1,000 *hira*s (minor veins, etc.), 72,000 *hita*s (very minute capillaries) and 10,800 *pesa*s (muscle fibres). Perhaps dissection was in vogue. This Veda mentions some maladies; e.g., *apacit* (scrofula) (VI.25.83); *apasmāra* (epilepsy) (IV.20.37); *jalodara* (dropsy) (I.10); *vidratha* (abscess) (VI.127), etc.

It is noteworthy that this Veda contains, *inter alia*, *Bhaiṣajya-sūkta*s (hymns concerning the healing of diseases) and *Āyuṣya-sūkta*s (hymns concerned with health and long life). The *Kauśika-sūtra*, attached to this Veda, throws some light on the methods of healing diseases.

Both these Vedas speak of many magical rites, spells, prayers and amulets designed to cure diseases. Occasionally, healing herbs are also mentioned. Sometimes we find also a scientific attitude regarding etiology.

The efficacy of herbs is mentioned in both the above Vedas; e.g., *R̥gveda*, (X.97.11, 18-20); *Atharvaveda*, (XII.1.2.) Some of the herbs and herbal products, used as medicine in the Atharvavedic India, are *Apāmārga* (*Achyranthes aspera*), *Aśvagandhā* (*Withania somnifera*), *Āmalakī* (*Phyllanthus emblica*), *Kumuda* (*Nymphoea esculenta*).

Besides curing diseases by drugs (*bheṣaja*), the *Atharvaveda* (and, to a lesser degree, the *R̥gveda*) reveals considerable knowledge of osteology and surgery. For example, the *Atharvaveda* (I.11) recommends, in a case of complications in the delivery of a baby, operation in the *mehana* (birth channel), *yoni* (womb) and *gavīnaka* (connecting canal). There are references to incision for boil, surgical remedy of swelling caused by arrows stuck to the body, etc. (*AV*, VII.78.1), treatment of fractured limbs (*ibid.*, III.12.1, 2, 7), use of a sort of catheter for relief in blocked urination (*ibid.*, I.3), removal of an injured eyeball (*R̥V*, I.116.16). We do not know whether the references to the replacement of an amputated leg by an iron-made one indicates orthopoedic knowledge or is merely a figment of imagination (*ibid.*, I.116.15).

From the *R̥gveda* and the *Atharvaveda*, we learn that diseases are caused by congenital (*kṣetrīya*) factors, infection (*R̥V*, X.97.1; *AV*, III.7.1-6; V.30.3; VI.83.1; VII.76.4), change of seasons especially in the case of *takman* (a kind of fever) (*AV*, V.22.13; XIX. 39.10, etc.) as well as *kr̥mis* (minute insects within the body) (*AV*, II.31.2-5, V.2.3).

It is noteworthy that dietetics plays an important part in the Vedic medical science. For example, in the *R̥gveda* (I.187.9), *Taittirīya Saṁhitā* of *Yajurveda* (VI.2.5.3), milk is stated to cause strength, nutrition, intelligence, bright complexion, and also to help the growth of the human foetus. The *Atharvaveda* (IV. 35.5; VII.140.2) states that rice of a good quality, eaten as a cereal, improves virility, and helps the growth of the teeth of infants.

As *Āyurveda* was regarded as very important for life, it was given the status of the Veda, and was referred to as *Pañcamaveda*.

Its close relation with the *Atharvaveda* led people to characterise it as an *upāṅga* (accessory) of this Veda.

Some later Vedic works also reveal considerable knowledge of the medical science. For example, the *Kauśika-sūtra* (XXVI.17) recommends milk, compounded with turmeric, as a cure for jaundice. The *Aitareya Brāhmaṇa* (I.1) prescribes fresh butter for the good health of children and women in the family way, but clarified butter for the grown-ups. Clarified butter, mixed with certain drugs, is stated, in the *Kauśika-sūtra* (XXV.12.21), as a preventive against miscarriage.

It should not be supposed that medical science developed only in the brāhmaṇa community. The Buddhists also made considerable contribution to this science. It is, however, probable that they also drew upon the common source, namely the *Atharvaveda*. As an instance of the development of this science amongst the Buddhists, we can cite the *Cīvaravastu* (Pt. 2, Vol. 3 of the Gilgit manuscripts). It mentions some wonderful cures effected by Jīvaka, personal physician of king Bimbisāra (*c.* middle of the sixth century BC). There is mention of surgical operations removing a portion of the skull for reaching the brain, eye surgery, curetting the cervical region, removal of vaginal tumour, etc. There is mention also of the treatment of dropsy, internal tumour, vericos vein, optical disease, etc. The *Vinaya Piṭaka* (*Mahāvagga*, VI.1-14; *Majjhima-nikāya*, 101, 105) and some other works show the knowledge of surgical instruments, use of hot bath, etc. If the testimony of the above work as also of some other Buddhist canonical texts is to be believed, then it must be admitted that there was appreciable development of this science two or three centuries prior to the Christian era. (See R.C. Majumdar in *A Concise History of Science in India*, 1971, p. 221).

The follow-up of the Vedic medical tradition proceeded in two streams, one represented by the Dhanvantari school, and the other by the Ātreya school.

Another tradition, known as Tāntric, also developed. According to some scholars, this method of medical treatment was in vogue in India before the advent of the Āryans. It developed on two lines; one was *Rasa-sādhaka* and the other *Viṣa-sādhaka*. Those, belonging to the former school, claimed to cure diseases by various drugs prepared with mercury. The followers of the latter claimed to use various poisons in preparing drugs as palliatives or cures of diseases. Besides the renowned *Rasārṇava-tantra*, various other works were written in the *rasa* school. In later times, quite a few Tantras were written on medical treatment by means of chemical and herbal drugs. Some such works are: *Kumāra-tantra*, *Bīja-cintāmaṇi-tantra*, *Arkaprakāśa*, *Matsya-tantra*, *Prayoga-cintāmaṇi*, *Ḍāmara-tantra*, etc.

Āyurveda has been divided into the following eight principal branches, hence it is called *Aṣṭāṅga*:

> 1. *Kāya-cikitsā*, 2. *Śalya-cikitsā*, 3. *Śālākya-cikitsā*, 4. *Bhūta-vidyā*, 5. *Kaumāra-bhṛtya*, 6. *Agada-cikitsā*, 7. *Rasāyana-cikitsā*, and 8. *Vājīkaraṇa-cikitsā*.

The above branches deal with the diseases of humours and their treatment. To these is added a ninth, called *Paśu-cikitsā*. *En passant*, it may be added that there is a separate treatise on the treatment of diseases affecting trees.

Under *Kāya-cikitsā*, diseases are divided into two classes, physical and mental. Physical ailments are of three kinds, namely.

(i) *Svābhāvika* — natural, arising out of imbalance or disorder of the three humours, called *vāyu* (wind), *pitta* (bile) and *kapha* (phlegm).

(ii) *Saṁkrāmaka* — infectious; e.g., small-pox, skin disease, etc.

(iii) *Āgantuka* — adventitious or accidental; e.g., injury caused by fire or fall, etc.

Śalya-cikitsā deals with surgery. Over 100 instruments and 14 kinds of bandages are mentioned. Considerable knowledge of osteology is evident from this part. Some scholars hold that the Indians excelled in surgery long before Hippocrates (fifth century BC), the father figure in Greek medical science. Plastic surgery was known; nose or ear, with a portion chopped off, could be repaired.

Śālākya-cikitsā — deals with the surgical treatment of diseases affecting eyes, ears, nose, tongue, mouth and throat.

Bhūta-vidyā — deals with the treatment of diseases such as insanity, epilepsy, etc., in which people are believed to be possessed by demons.

Kaumāra-bhṛtya — deals with paediatrics.

Agada-tantra — toxicology.

Rasāyana — dealing with tonics and methods of arresting physical and mental decay.

Vājīkaraṇa-tantra — deals with virilifics.

Of the existing works on *Āyurveda*, the *Caraka-saṁhitā* is the oldest and most authoritative. The text, in its present form, appears to be the result of revision by one Dṛḍhabala who admits to having added the last two chapters and to having written 17 out of 28 or 30 chapters of book VI. The work does not claim to be original; it appears to have been a revision of a number of Tantras on special topics written by Agniveśa. The contents of the work are as follows:

Part I — *Sūtra-sthāna*: It deals with remedies, diet, duties of a physician.

Part II — *Nidāna-sthāna*: It deals with eight chief diseases.

Part III — *Vimāna-sthāna*: It deals with general pathology and medical studies. It also contains regulations for the conduct of the newly fledged student.

Part IV — *Śārīra-sthāna*: Anatomy and embryology.

Part V — *Indriya-sthāna*: Diagnosis and prognosis.

Part VI — *Cikitsā-sthāna*: Special therapy.

Parts VII, VIII — *Kalpa-sthāna* and *Siddhi-sthāna*.

General therapy.

The work is in prose mixed with verses. Caraka is assigned by some scholars to the second or first century BC. It was rendered into Persian at a fairly early date, and into Arabic *c*. AD 800.

Next in importance to the *Caraka-saṁhitā* is the *Suśruta-saṁhitā*, a famous treatise on *Āyurveda*, traditionally attributed to Suśruta. According to some, it is not the personal work of a certain

Suśruta, but the anonymously edited manual of a school which chose Suśruta as patron. Also called *Āyurveda-prakāśa*, it is divided into five sections called *sthānas*. The sections and their corresponding contents are as follows:

I. *Sūtra-sthāna* (46 chapters) — it deals with general questions, and gives the name of Suśruta's teacher.

II. *Nidāna-sthāna* (16 chapters) — it deals with pathology.

III. *Śārīra-sthāna* (10 chapters) — anatomy and embryology.

IV. *Cikitsā-sthāna* (40 chapters) — therapeutics.

V. *Kalpa-sthāna* (8 chapters) — toxicology.

The *Uttara-tantra*, which appears to be a later addition, is a supplement to the work. A Nāgārjuna is credited with having worked over the text. It is the earliest work to deal with dissection of bodies and surgery. Some eminent authorities think that the Saṁhitā originated in the last centuries before the Christian era, and appeared in the early centuries AD in an already systematic form. The Saṁhitā, in its present form, appears to have been fixed by the seventh century AD.

In the history of *Āyurveda*, the Bower Manuscript, also called *Nāvanītaka*, discovered in Central Asia, occupies an important place. It is written in a kind of barbarous Sanskrit copiously mixed with Prākṛt. It has been dated between AD 350 and 375.

Some other noteworthy Āyurvedic works are:

Aṣṭāṅga-hṛdaya of Vāgbhaṭa I or elder Vāgabhaṭa,

Aṣṭāṅga-hṛdaya-saṁgraha of Vāgbhaṭa II or younger Vāgbhaṭa (between seventh and eighth century AD).

Rug-viniścaya or *Nidāna* of Mādhavakara (eighth-ninth century AD).

Siddha-yoga of Vṛnda (eighth or ninth century AD).

Cakra-saṁgraha or *Cikitsā-sāra-saṁgraha* of Cakrapāṇidatta (*c.* AD 1050).

Cikitsā-saṁgraha of Vaṅgasena (eleventh or twelfth century AD).

Śārṅgadhara-saṁhitā of Śārṅgadhara (thirteenth century AD).

Bhāva-prakāśa of Bhāvamiśra (sixteenth century AD).

Some medical dictionaries also were compiled. As examples, mention may be made of the *Dhanvantari-nighaṇṭu*, Sureśvara's *Śābda-pradīpa* (1075), Narahari's *Rāja-nighaṇṭu* (1235-50), etc.

Influence of Āyurveda

Āyurveda was not confined only to the Hindus and Buddhists. The Muslim *Ūnānī* system of medicine was considerably enriched by the Āyurvedic system. As pointed out by R.C. Majumdar (*Concise History of Science in India*, 1991, p. 54), important medical works, written by Indian practitioners of the *Ūnānī* system from the thirteenth or fourteenth century onward, testify to the impact of *Āyurveda*. For instance, Hakim Diya Muhammad's *Majmual-Diyaiyya* (AD 1320) refers to a Persian translation of an Āyurvedic treatise. There was a Persian translation of Vāgbhaṭa's work by 'Ali Muhammad (fifteenth-sixteenth century AD). In the Mogul regime, many Hakims and Āyurvedic physicians were engaged in translating and adapting Āyurvedic works.

It is noteworthy that *Āyurveda* travelled far beyond India. It is learnt that Hārun-al-Rashid (AD 763-809), Caliph of Baghdād, got the works of Caraka and Suśruta and some other Āyurvedic works rendered into Arabic. The Indian physician, Maṅkha is known to have adorned his court. It was at the instance of the Caliph that the toxicological portions of *Āyurveda* were rendered into Persian. The treatises of Caraka and Suśruta have been quoted as authoritative by the Arabian physician, al-Razi (d. AD 932).

The Muslim traveller, Al-Biruni (stay in India AD 1017-30) informs us that the aforesaid Hārun sent many students to India for learning the Indian system of medicine. It is also stated that he invited many Indian physicians to his country, and appointed them at the hospitals of Baghdād and other places. The Persian medical work, *Firdaus ul hikmat* contains detailed information on Indian medicine.

The Tibetans adopted Indian medicine. The *Yoga-śataka* of Nāgārjuna or Vararuci was translated into Tibetan. The treatise, entitled *Amṛtahṛdaya* is stated to have been translated into this language; in the eighth century AD; the original is lost. The Tibetan *Tanjur* preserves the translation of the *Aṣṭāṅga-hṛdaya* of Vāgbhaṭa with two commentaries. It also contains the translation of Śālihotra's *Aśvāyurveda* (on horse-diseases).

The medical work, *Yogaśataka* had been in use in Ceylon up to the end of the nineteenth century.

Some works of Java on medicine contain several words of Indian origin. We have already mentioned the Indian medical works contained in the Bower Manuscript, discovered in Kashgar (Central Asia) in AD 1890.

Some scholars have pointed out remarkable similarities between *Āyurveda* and the Greek medical science. For instance, in the Greek *Hippocratic Collection (HC)*, the treatment of the pneumatic system is very similar to the Indian concept of *vāyu* or *prāṇa*. Plato's (d. 347 BC) *Timaeus* appears to be familiar with the Āyurvedic doctrine of *tridoṣa*. In the above *HC*, there are references to Indian drugs. It has, however, not yet been established whether there was parallel development in the two countries or the one borrowed from the other. The curious reader may consult A.B. Keith's *History of Sanskrit Literature*, Pt. III, Ch. XXVI for a succinct account of the similarities as also for references to important works dealing with the matter in detail.

The Roman Celsus (*c.* first century AD), Galen (AD 131-201) and some other medical men reveal familiarity with the Indian medical science. The Latin translation, by Farachi (*c.* thirteenth century AD), of al-Rhazi's *Kitāb al-haur*, which incorporated Indian medical knowledge, was regarded as an authoritative work in Europe. In his book, *Eating for Health*, the Russian author, Y. Nikolayev acknowledges his indebtedness to *Āyurveda*.

The ethno-botanical use of plants and their ecological importance were recognised in ancient India. So, we have some treatises on plant diseases and their cures. This subject has been dealt with in our observations on botany.

Veterinary Science

Side by side with the growth of the medical science for humans, veterinary science also was considerably developed. This is borne out by such works as the *Pālakāpya-saṁhitā* dealing with elephant-diseases, *Śālihotra-saṁhitā* on horse-diseases and *Gotama-saṁhitā* concerning bovine diseases.

21

Jyotiṣa (Astronomy)

Origin and Works

THE origin of astronomy can be traced in the Vedic Saṁhitās which, however, do not reveal systematic knowledge of it. *Nakṣatras* are mentioned in the *Ṛgveda*. This Veda knows (I.105.9) the seven colours of sun-rays. The moon is known to have no light of its own; it shines by sunlight (*ṚV*, IX.71.9). The year of 360 days and 12 months is referred to in *ṚV*(I.164.48). The solar eclipse is indirectly mentioned in *ṚV* (V.40.59). The conception of lunar mansions is clear from *ṚV* (X.85.2). An occasional year with a thirteenth (intercalary) month is referred to in *ṚV* (I.25.8). But, the entire series, comprising 27 or 28 *nakṣatras*, headed by Kṛttikās occur, for the first time, in the *Yajurveda*. Details about seasons, months and month-names are also found in this Veda. Importance is attached to the winter solstice through *mahāvrata* rites. The *Sāmaveda*, its *Brāhmaṇas* and *Sūtras* contain considerable material of calendrical astronomy, in connection with some rituals designed round the daily course of the sun.

The *Atharvaveda* also reveals some information of astronomical interest. It mentions Rāhu for the first time, eclipse, intercalary or the thirteenth month and enumerates 28 *nakṣatras* including Abhijit.

The works of the class of *Brāhmaṇas*, which elaborate the rituals, reveal clearer astronomical ideas that germinated in the Vedic texts. The *Aitareya Brāhmaṇa* (III. 44.4) knowns that the sun never rises nor sets. It, however, naively believes that, after the end of night, the sun makes day below and night on the reverse side. After reaching the end of day, it makes night below and day on the other side. The same *Brāhmaṇa* (XVIII.18) reveals the knowledge of solstices. In this connection, the *Kauṣītaki Brāhmaṇa* (XIX.3) also deserves mention. The materials, contained in the Vedic Saṁhitās and *Brāhmaṇas*, appeared afresh in the Sūtra works. This is particularly the case with the Vedic calendars. Calendrical elements are no doubt mentioned in the Vedic texts. But, various ways of year-reckoning and calendar-making clearly emerge in the Sūtras. For this purpose, the *Lāṭyāyana Śrauta-sūtra* and the *Nidāna-sūtra* of the *Sāmaveda* deserve special mention.

Astronomical knowledge appears to have been systematised in the treatises known as *siddhānta*s of unknown authorship and dates. It is not known how many such works were composed; their exact contents are also unknown. Five such works are described by Varāhamihira (*d.* 587) in his *Pañcasiddhāntikā*. These works are named (i) *Paitāmaha-siddhānta*, (ii) *Romaka*-s, (iii) *Pauliśa*-s, (iv) *Vasiṣṭha*-s and (v) *Sūrya*-s.

The other renowned authors of astronomical works are Āryabhaṭa, Brahmagupta, Bhoja and Bhāskarācārya. There appear to have been two persons of the name of Āryabhaṭa. Of them, Āryabhaṭa I (b. AD 476) is credited with the authorship of the *Āryabhaṭīya*, divided into the following broad sections: *daśa-gītikā-sūtra*, *gaṇita-pāda*, *kāla-kriyā* and *gola*. It was he who, for the first time, dealt with mathematics in relation to astronomy. He declared that the earth is spherical, and rotates on its axis. He used letters of the alphabet to indicate numerals.

Āryabhaṭa II, known to the traveller Al-Biruni (AD 973-1048), wrote the *Ārya-siddhānta* (*c.* 950 AD). The astronomical work, *Mahāsiddhānta*, is attributed to an Āryabhaṭa.

Brahmagupta (b. AD 598) was the author of the *Brāhma-siddhānta* (AD 628), also called *Sphoṭa-siddhānta* and the *Khaṇḍakhādyaka*. The former is a famous mathematical-astronomical work. The latter, to be distinguished from the Vedāntic work *Khaṇḍana-khaṇḍa-khādya* of Śrīharṣa, was written *c.* AD 656. It consists of the following chapters:

(i) *Tithyādhikāra*, (ii) *Grahādhikāra*, (iii) *Tri-praśnādhikāra*, (iv) *Candra-grahaṇādhikāra*, (v) *Sūrya-grahaṇādhikāra*, (vi) *Udayāstādhikāra*, (vii) *Śṛṅgonnatyadhikāra*, (viii) *Graha-yutyādhikāra*.

To Bhoja is attributed the *Rāja-mṛgāṅka* (AD 1042).

Two persons of the name Bhāskara figure in the history of Indian astronomy. Bhāskara I (b. *c.* AD 600) appears to have composed the *Mahā* (or, *Bṛhat*)-*bhāskarīya*, a treatise on astronomy in eight chapters, and its abridgement, called *Laghu-bhāskarīya*, Bhāskara II (b. *c.* AD 1114) was a noted mathematician and astronomer. Of the several works, attributed to him, the most well-known is the *Siddhānta-śiromaṇi* (AD 1150) in four parts, named *Līlāvatī*, *Bījagaṇita*, *Graha-gaṇita* and *Gola*. The first two contain the mathematical portion, and the last two deal with astronomy proper. The last one contains a section on astronomical problems, a part on astronomical instruments and a description of the seasons.

India's Relationship with Foreign Countries *vis-a-vis* Astronomy

Astronomy is one of the subjects which prove that culture knows no geographical bounds. The titles of two of the *siddhāntas* mentioned earlier, are clear indications of foreign influence. The term *romaka* does not necessarily indicate knowledge derived from the city of Rome itself. The knowledge probably was gathered from Alexandria which was included in the Roman Empire; the widespread fame of the Empire was, perhaps, responsible for labelling it as *romaka*.

The *Pauliśa* is reminiscent of the Greek Paulus Alexandrinus. Among other things, which indicate its Greek derivation, mention may be made of the fact that this treatise gives the difference in longitude between Yavanapura (city of the Greeks) and Ujjain. Without going into the intricacies of astronomical matters, in which India may have borrowed from Greece, we can point out the following Greek terms which infiltrated into Indian astronomical and astrological texts:

The names of the Zodiacal signs, used in the *Bṛhajjātaka* of Varāhamihira — *Kriya* (*Meṣa*), *Tāvuri* (*Vṛṣa*), *Jituma*

> (*Mithuna*), *Leya* (*Siṁha*), *Kulīra* (*Karkaṭa*), *Pāthona* (*Kanyā*), *Jūka* (*Tulā*), *Kaurpya* (*Vṛścika*), *Taukṣika* (*Dhanus*), *Ākokera* (*Makara*), *Hṛdroga* (*Kumbha*) and *Ittha* (*Mīna*).

Other examples of borrowed Greek terms are as follows:

> *liptā* (minutes), *horā* (hour, horoscope), *dreṣkāṇa* or *dṛkkāna* (deccan), *āpoklima* (inclination), *kendra* (anomaly), *jyāmitra* (chord), etc.

The respectful eulogy of the Greeks in the domain of astronomy, articulated by some eminent astronomers of ancient India, bears ample testimony to the fact that the latter were heavily indebted to the former. Garga and Varāhamihira speak of their admirable knowledge, and go so far as to declare that, though they are *mlecchas* (degraded people beyond the four castes and four stages or life), they deserve honour like *ṛṣis* (sages).

It has been stated, on good grounds, that there was Babylonian influence on the planetary theory of Āryabhaṭa I. There is evidence proving the impact of Babylonian astronomy on the computation of lunar motions, as dealt with in the *Vasiṣṭha-siddhānta*.

In the history of astronomy, India is not only a taker but also a giver.

Sino-Indian contacts in matters, religious and cultural, date back to a period about the beginning of the Christian era. These contacts got a fillip from the time of Yuch-Chi Dharmarakṣa (third-fourth century AD) and the Kāśmīrian Kumārajīva (fourth-fifth century AD). In the following centuries many Buddhist scholars from India went to China mainly to propagate Buddhism, and also to disseminate secular learning such as astronomy. It is interesting to note that the catalogue of the Sui dynasty (AD 610) mentions a number of Brāhmaṇical works on astronomy. In the seventh century AD, we learn of an Astronomical Board at Chang-Nan. There, Indian *siddhāntas*, attributed to Gautama, Kāśyapa and Kumāra are said to have been taught. From about the eighth century AD, the *navagraha* (nine planets), Rāhu-Ketu theory of eclipse and some other matters of Indian astronomy started appearing in the Chinese astronomical literature.

The Arabs came into contact with Indian astronomy as early as in the reign of Caliph al-Mansur, when an Indian astronomer visited his court. He brought with him planetary tables, texts for the calculation of eclipses and other matters of astronomical importance. Ābu-Māshar, an astrologer of Balkh, mentions an Indian astronomer from whom he learnt about Indian great cycle of *kalpa*. At the behest of al-Mansur, Brahmagupta's *Brahmasphoṭa-siddhānta* and *Khaṇḍa-khādyaka* were rendered, with the co-operation of Indian scholars, into Arabic by Muhammad ibn Ibrāhim al-Fazāri (d. 796 or 806) and also by Ya'qūb ibn Tāriq (d. 796); the translations were named *Sindhind* and *Arkand*.

From al-Biruni we come to learn that the *Zik-i-Shatro-ayār*, (the Pahlavī astronomical tables) was based on Indian astronomical methods. Some of the notable works, influenced by Indian astronomy, are the *Astronomical Tables* by al-Khwārizmi (*c*. 840), *Az-Zijal-Mukhtari* of al-Hasan bin Misbāḥ (*c*.870), *Az-Zij al-Kabur* of an Nairizi (*c*. AD 900), *Mukhtasar az Zij* of ibn as-Saffār (*c*. AD 1100). In the transmission of the knowledge of Indian astronomy to Arabia, al-Biruni played a great role. In his *Ta'rikh al-Hind*, *al-Quanun al-Ma'sūdi*, he discusses Indian astronomy, astronomical methods, and compares and contrasts it with other systems.

Elements of Indian astronomy spread in Latin Europe through the Latin translations of Islamic works. The most outstanding example is Adelard of Bath's (*c*. AD 1142) translation of al-Khwārizmi's astronomical tables in the version of the Spanish astronomer, Maslama al-Majrīṭi. The stream of Indian astronomy, fed by the elements of Babylonian and Greek astronomy, flowed, through the channel of Arabic language, to the remote West as far as England.

22

Udbhid-vidyā (Botany)

Origin and Works

THE plant-kingdom is one of the richest creations in the world. Man was born in the cradle of nature. Even when he was a cave-dweller, he fed on the fruits and roots of trees and plants, besides the meat of the animals they hunted. They were clad in barks after the period of nudity was over. The plant-world has played a vital role in the cultural and practical life of the people. The forests provided solitude to the Indian sages, who meditated on the meaning and ultimate goal of life; the results of their meditations are enshrined in the Upaniṣads and Āraṇyakas, the repositories of the highest truth, which is a source of inspiration even today. The attitude of admiration of the wise ancient sages towards forests is expressed in the well-known Forest Hymn of the *Ṛgveda* (X.146).

Glimpses of the culture of *āśrama*s (hermitages) can be had from many works, prose, poetical and dramatic, of Classical Sanskrit literature, particularly the immortal drama, *Abhijñāna-śākuntalam* of Kālidāsa (*c*. fourth century AD). The *Rāmāyaṇa* (present form *c*. second or third century AD) and the *Mahābhārata* (final form *c*. fourth century AD) depict forests in connection with the exile of Rāma and Pāṇḍavas respectively.

The modern science of Ethnobotany is investigating the various uses served by the plant-world in human life. The most important service that trees render to us is the supply of oxygen without which we cannot survive. The leaves and barks of some trees and a number of herbs are used for preparing drugs which cure diseases. Moreover, trees protect riparian lands from erosion.

The ancient Indians learnt many lessons from trees. We are advised to learn tolerance and kindness from trees which, themselves suffering the scorching rays of the sun, give cool shades to those who seek relief under them. The tree does not withdraw its shade even from one who axes it. The famous social and religious reformer, Caitanya, looked upon trees as models of tolerance, and asked his followers to be even more tolerant than them.

Naturally, therefore, the ancient Indian thinkers paid due attention to them, observed the different classes of trees, and prescribed means of their growth and of their protection from diseases as also from the negligent and mindless people causing harm to them.

That the trees and plants have life and sensation was known even to the Vedic people. *R̥gveda* (X.97.21) appears to hint at this fact. This Veda is generally assigned to a date around 1500 BC. The *Manu-smr̥ti*, which is supposed to have evolved in the period between 200 BC and AD 200, is very explicit on this matter. It declares (I.49), in no uncertain terms, that *antaḥ-saṁjñā bhavantyete sukha-duḥkha-samanvitāḥ* (these, endowed with consciousness within, have the sensation of pleasure and pain).

We do not know whether or not any work, exclusively dealing with botany, was written in ancient India. There is, however, a *Vr̥kṣāyurveda* which, as the title indicates, is on the diseases of plants and their remedies. It is attributed to Surapāla. A work of the same title is attributed to Parāśara (*Journal of Asiatic Society*, Calcutta, Vol. III, No. 2, 1961, pp. 85-6). While the date of the former is unknown, the latter is assigned to pre-Christian age by some, to *c.* twelfth century AD by others. The English translation of a *Vr̥kṣāyurveda*, by N.N. Sarkar and R. Sarkar is reported to have been publised in Delhi. It should be noted that the *Br̥hat-saṁhitā* contains a chapter, called *Vr̥kṣāyurveda*; this is the name also of chapter 282 of the *Agni Purāṇa* (Calcutta, 1389 BS). Information about various branches of botany is available in works on *Āyurveda*, *Kr̥ṣi-śāstra*, Dharmaśāstra, *Arthaśāstra*, Purāṇa, *Jyotiṣa*, etc. The following are some of the principal works throwing light on this science.

Ṛgveda (*c*. 2000-1500 BC) — X.97.15, 21; 117, 145, etc.

Atharvaveda (later than the *Ṛgveda*) II.8.3, 8.7; X.7.38; XI.6.10, etc.

Upaniṣads (*c*. 1000-600 BC)

Bṛhadāraṇyaka, III.9, IV.6.1

Chāndogya I.1.2, VI.12.1, 2

Aṣṭādhyāyī of Pāṇini (*c*. fourth century BC)

Mahābhāṣya of Patañjali (*c*. second century BC)

Mahābhārata (present form completed *c*. fourth century AD), Śānti, ch. 184.

Kauṭilya's *Arthaśāstra* (*c*. 300 BC). Particularly *adhikaraṇa* II. ch. 24 (*sītādhyakṣa*)

Manu-smṛti — *c*. 200 BC to AD 200. I.46-49,

Bṛhat-saṁhitā of Varāhamihira (*c*. AD 475-550).

Purāṇas (the dates given below, are conjectural, and mostly in accordance with the *Purāṇic Records* by R.C. Hazra)

Agni (ninth century AD), ch. 13, 70/194, 246, 248, 281; 282.

Padma (between tenth and eleventh century AD), ch. 26.

Matsya (third-fourth century AD), ch. 59, 154, 227; 91-5, 255-6.

Varāha (between AD 800 and 1500), *gokarṇa-māhātmya*.

Viṣṇu (earlier than sixth century AD) 4.25, 7/37-9.

Bhāgavata (lower terminus AD 500-650) — Skanda 3-10.19, 20

Caraka-saṁhitā (*c*. first or second century AD)

Sūtra-sthāna I.36, 37, chs. 4 and 27

Śārīra-sthāna III.22-6.

Kalpa-sthāna V.3

Suśruta-saṁhitā (post-Caraka)

Sūtra-sthāna I.23, XXXV.34-42, ch. XXXVIII

Śārīra-sthāna II.39, III.18, IV.20-3.

Kāmasūtra of Vātsyāyana (*c*. third century AD)

Amarakośa (*c*. fourth century AD)

Vanauṣadhi-varga, 135.

Bhūmi-varga 8

Kāmandaki-nītisāra (*c*. fourth-fifth century AD), XIV, 27-42.

Kṛṣi-parāśara (not earlier than fifth century AD).

Śārṅgadhara-paddhati (thirteenth century). ch. named Upavana-vinoda.

Śukranīti (*c*. thirteenth or fourteenth century AD, according to P.V. Kane), IV.2.56., 57, IV.4.91-108, 113-14, 123-4.

Besides the above works, some botanical information is available also in the following works:

Hemacandra's (1088-1172) *Nighaṇṭuśeṣa*,

Buddhaghoṣa's *Sumaṅgala-vilāsinī* (commentary),

Dhanvantari-nighaṇṭu, etc.

For other works, B.N. Seal's *Positive Sciecnes*, etc., may be consulted.

The botanical information, gleaned from the above works, can be divided broadly under the following heads in accordance with the modern science of botany:

Morphology, Plant physiology, Taxonomy, Ecology, Miscellaneous.

Morphology

This branch of botany is divided into external morphology and internal morphology or histology. Both these divisions were known to Indian scientists. External morphology appears to be found, for the first time, in the *Atharvaveda*. Trees of different descriptions are mentioned in viii.7 of this Veda; e.g., trees with spreading branches (*viśākhā*), those with leaves having long clusters (*mañjarī*) those having only one sheath (*ekaśuṅgāḥ*), those which are bushy (*stambinī*), those which expand (*prastṛnatīḥ*), those which creep (*pratanvatīh*), those having many stalks (*aṁśumatīḥ*) and those which are knotty or have joints (*kāṇḍinīḥ*) (*AV*, VIII.7). The different parts of a plant are mentioned in the *Vājasaneyī-saṁhitā* (22.28), and the *Taittirīya-saṁhitā* (VII.3.20.1) state the different parts making up a plant. These are *mūla* (root), *tūla* (panicle), *kāṇḍa* (stem), *valśa* (twig), *puṣpa* (flower) and *phala* (fruit).

The other parts are *skandha* (corona), *śākhā* (branch), and *parṇa* (leaf). Pāṇini mentions different parts of a tree in different *sūtras*. Patañjali mentions these together (I.2.19). These are *mūla*, *skandha*, *phala* and *palāśa* (leaf). According to Pāṇini (IV.1.64), plants are named after the characteristics of their leaves, flowers, fruits and roots; e.g., *śaṁkhapuṣpī* (having flowers white like conch-shells), *bahumūlī* (having many roots), etc. From Pāṇini (IV.3.43), we learn that plants and creepers were called after names of their flowering seasons, e.g., *vāsantī kundalatā*, as illustrated in the *Kāśikā* commentary.

The *Viṣṇu Purāṇa* (VII.37-9) mentions the various parts of trees, namely, sprouts, roots, trunks, leaves and flowers. Parasitic plants, growing on trees, were not unknown in ancient India. Mushroom is mentioned in Suśruta's *sūtrasthāna* (Chp. 46). From the mention of *eka-patra*, *dvi-patra*, *tri-patra* and *sapta-parṇa*, it is clear that, in those times, leaves, both single and joint, were known. In accordance with their shape, the leaves were variously designated as *aśva-parṇaka* (*Shorea robusta*), *mūṣika-parṇī* (*Salvinia*), etc.

The different stages in the growth and bloom of flowers are differently named. Before blossoming they were called *koraka*, *kalikā*; when blooming they were styled *kuṭmala*, *mukula*. When in full bloom, they were described as *sphuṭa*, *vikaca*, etc.

The use of words like *bīja-kośa* (seed-vessel), *śasya* (endosperm) and *bīja-patra* (cotyledon) demonstrates that different parts of seeds were not unknown in those far-off ages.

Gross histology was very well-known. The people knew of the existence of the wood and pith inside the trees. In the *Bṛhadāraṇyaka Upaniṣad* (Ch. III — *Brāhmaṇa* ix), the bone, flesh marrow and nerve of the human body have been stated to be like the wood, *śakara*,[1] pith and fibrous tissue of the tree. Guṇaratna, in his commentary on the six philosophical systems, observes that, like the wounds on human body, those on trees also can be healed up by the application of medicaments.

Plant Physiology

In his commentary on the *Ṣaḍ-darśana-samuccaya*, Guṇaratna holds that, as human body is nourished by milk and other articles of food, so also fertile land and water contribute to the nourishment of trees. Want of proper nutrition impairs both human body and the body of trees. It is with their roots, corresponding to human mouths, that trees absorb the sap; this is why they are called *pādapa* (that which drinks with foot). The intake of food by trees and plants, the distribution of food over their different parts; assimilation of food and the vital role played in the matter by wind — these have been beautifully described in the *Mahābhārata* (Śāntiparva — Ch. 184). These are fully in accord with the modern science of Botany.[2]

Works such as the *Arthaśāstra*, *Bṛhat-saṁhitā* and *Agni Purāṇa* contain rules for planting trees. The people used to believe in the benign and malign influences of stars on the planting of trees.[3] Different seasons are supposed to be good for planting different kinds of saplings. According to the *Bṛhat-saṁhitā*, winter is the best season for planting trees whose branches have not grown. Dewy season and the rainy season have been prescribed for planting respectively those trees which have grown their branches and those whose branches have become nature. Besides growing trees from seeds, the ancient Indians knew the process of growing trees from the cut branches as well as by grafting the branch of one tree to that of another. Trees grown by planting the branches cut from other trees are called *kāṇḍa-ropa* in the *Bṛhat-saṁhitā*. Two methods of grafting appear to have been adopted. The branch of one tree used to be grafted to the root or trunk of another tree. While planting trees, sufficient space was kept between them so that the root of one could not be mixed with another resulting in damage to them.[4] Watering has been prescribed for the growth of plants. The proper time for watering is morning and evening in summer and afternoon in winter. In the rainy season, water should be sprinkled only when the earth is dry.

The ancient botanists knew various methods of keeping the ground fertile and sappy; they knew quite well that trees and plants draw sustenance from the earth. There are elaborate rules regarding this matter in the *Bṛhat-saṁhitā*, *Agni Purāṇa* and *Upavana-vinoda*. The *Atharvaveda*[5] was perhaps the earliest treatise to contain such rules. An admixture of the prescribed quantities of sesame, goat's dung, barley-powder, beef and water was regarded as a very effective manure. Cow-dung was considered to be a good fertiliser even in remote ages.

The *Bṛhat-saṁhitā* contains detailed procedure of preserving seeds. Seeds, mixed with *ghī*, are to be thrown into milk. The next day, they are to be separately kept. After repeating this process for ten consecutive days, the seeds have to be smeared with cow-dung. Then these have to be heated in pots full of the flesh of boars or deer. Such seeds will lead to the growth of flowering trees. A different method is prescribed for preparing the seeds with a view to growing trees rich in foliage. For the development of trees, particularly mango-trees, the washing of fish is to be sprinkled according to the *Agni Purāṇa* (ch. 194).

Diseases of plants and their treatment have been dealt with in the *Bṛhat-saṁhitā* (chapter called *vṛksāyurveda*), *Agni Purāṇa* (ch. 281) and *Upavana-vinoda*. Guṇaratna, in his commentary, has also dealt with the subject. Excessive increase or decrease of heat and violent wind are some of the causes of the maladies of trees. Yellowish colour of the leaves, under-development of the buds, dryness of the branches exuding juice — these are some of the symptoms of their diseases. A decoction of *kulattha* (*Dolichos biflorus*), *māṣa* (*Phaseolus radiatus* var *Roxburghil*), *mudga* (*P. mungo*), *tila* (*Seasamum indicum*) and *yava* (barley) is to be applied to roots of trees in order to cure them of barrenness. As preventives of diseases, the following articles are prescribed for application to the roots of trees: mud mixed with *ghī*, milk mixed with fish and flesh.

The sleep,[6] waking up and reaction to touch, etc., have been mentioned in Dharmottara's commentary on the *Nyāyabindu* and

Udayana's *Kiraṇāvalī*. Guṇaratna, in his commentary, has noticed the reaction to touch on the part of creepers and shrubs such as *Mimosa pudica*. He has further observed that, as the lotus blooms at sunrise and the lily at moonrise, so also some flowers bloom at particular times.

In some treatises,[7] just as human beings trees also have been described as having infancy, childhood, youth, old age and death. Guṇaratna mentions 10,000 years as the longest period of life of trees. Their death is attributed to disease and lack of food.

As stated above, the ancient Indian was aware of the consciousness of trees. In the *Bhāgavata Purāṇa* (III.10.19, 20), trees have been declared to be threefold: *ut-srotasaḥ* (taking sap upwards), *avyakta-caitanya* (with subdued consciousness) and *antaḥsparśa* (with inward sensation of touch).[8] According to Udayana, trees and plants have very slight consciousness. The Śāntiparvan of the *Mahābhārata* speaks of their reaction to cold, heat, thunder, good and bad smell.

The ancient Indians had some idea, though not scientifically accurate, of the process of procreation among trees as a result of the union of the male and the female species. The division, made by them, of trees into male and female is not based on scientific basis. According to Caraka, *kuṭaja* has male and female species. Those which have white flowers and bear large fruits are male. Those which have red or yellow flowers and bear small fruits are female.

The idea of rotation of crops is found in the *Taittirīya-saṁhitā* (V.1.7.37) which is a very early text.

Taxonomy

In ancient India, trees were designated by terms which referred either to their external features or to their efficacy. For instance, a tree with curved flowers was called *vakrapuṣpa* (*Sesbania grandiflora*), and as it contained property that could cure boils, it was called *vraṇāri* (lit. enemy of boils or sores).

The following classification of trees is found in ancient Indian works:

(a) Botanical classification,

(b) Classification according to properties,

(c) Classification based on food-value.

BOTANICAL CLASSIFICATION[9]

In the *Ṛgveda*,[10] the earliest work of the Indo-Āryans, trees have been classified as *phalinī* (bearing fruits), *aphala* (not bearing fruits), *apuṣpa* (devoid of flowers) and *puṣpiṇī* (having flowers). In the same Veda, the plant-kingdom has been divided into *vṛkṣa* (tree), *gulma* (shrub), *bheṣaja* (medicine), and *latā* (creeper).

In the Dharmasūtras, a twofold division of trees is discernible. The broad divisions are *oṣadhi* and *vanaspati*. Govindasvāmin, commentator on the *Baudhāyana-dharmasūtra*, has sub-divided *oṣadhi* into *vallyauṣadhi* and *tṛṇauṣadhi*; to the former class belong *kulattha*, etc., and to the latter *vrīhi* (paddy).

Pāṇini also appears to classify forests as:

(1) *Oṣadhi-vana* — those producing herbs, e.g. *Dūrvā-vana*, *Mūrvā-vana*, etc.

(2) *Vanaspati-vana* — those producing timbertrees, e.g., *Devadāru-vana*. (VIII.4.6). It should be noted that Pāṇini uses the word *vana* in a twofold sense, namely natural and cultivated. Natural forests are like *puragāvaṇa*, *miśrakāvaṇa*, etc. (VIII.4.4.) and cultivated groves are *āmravaṇa*, *ikṣuvaṇa* etc. From Pāṇini (IV.1.49) and Kātyāyana's *Vārtika* thereon we learn that an ordinary forest was called *āraṇya*, while an extensive forest was known as *vaṇānī*.

The following classification of trees and plants is found in the *Manu-smṛti* (1.46-48):

(1) *Oṣadhi* — a plant of this class withers after the ripening of fruits.

(2) *Vanaspati* — Any tree or that which bear only fruits, but not flowers. According to a lexicon, *vanaspatirvṛkṣamātre vinā puṣpa-phale drume*. Scientifically speaking, the absence of flower is only apparent, not real.

(3) *Vṛkṣa* — That which bears flowers and fruits.

(4) *Gulma* — Shrub.

(5) *Tṛṇa* — Grass and grass-like plant.

(6) *Pratāna* — Plants with tendrils.

(7) *Vallī* — Creepers entwining a support.

According to the *Sūtra-sthāna* (I.36-7) of *Caraka-saṁhitā*, trees and plants are of four classes:

(1) *Vanaspati* — Those bearing only fruits, but not flowers.

(2) *Vānaspatya* — Trees bearing flowers followed by fruits.

(3) *Oṣadhi* — Those producing herbs.

(4) *Vīrudh* — Same as *latā* and *gulma* above.[11]

Suśruta's classification is like that of Caraka.

In the *BhāgavataPurāṇa* (III.10.19), the classification is as follows:

(1) *Vanaspati* — See above.

(2) *Oṣadhi* — See above.

(3) *Latā* — Corresponding to *vallī* of Manu above.

(4) *Tvaksāra* — Those whose bark is very tough; e.g., bamboo.

(5) *Druma* — Those which bear both flowers and fruits.

In the *Upavana-vinoda* (verse 43), trees and plants have been divided into four kinds: *vanaspati*, *druma*, *latā* and *gulma*. In the same context, these are stated to grow from seed, stem and bulb. The mango-tree, the jackfruit tree, etc., grow from seeds, the *sindhuvāra*, *tagare*, etc., grow from stems. *Rasona*, *kuṅkuma*, etc., grow from bulbs. *Dāḍīma, mallikā* grow form seeds and stems. The lotus and some other plants grow from seeds and bulbs.

In Vaiśeṣika philosophy, Praśastapāda gives the following classification:

Tṛṇa, *oṣadhi*, *latā*, *avatāna*,[12] *vṛkṣa* and *vanaspati*.

The following classification is found in the *Vanauṣadhi-varga* and *Vaiśya-varga* of the *Nāmaliṅgānuśāsana*:

(i) *Kāṣṭhadāru* — Those which bear fruits and have trunks.

(ii) *Kṣupa* — Those having short roots (*śilpha*) and branches.

(iii) *Latā*

(iv) *Oṣadhi*

(v) *Tṛṇa* — Bamboo belongs to this class.

(vi) *Tṛṇa-druma* — Trees such as coconut, date and areca-nut trees.

CLASSIFICATION ACCORDING TO PROPERTIES[13]

Caraka, in *sūtrasthāna* (iv) broadly divides trees and plants into purgative and astringent. According to him, 600 species belong to the first class and 500 to the second. The latter class has been sub-divided into ten groups (*varga*),[14] Suśruta has divided (*sūtra-sthāna* XXXVIII) the entire plant-kingdom into 37 classes (*gaṇa*).

CLASSIFICATION BASED ON FOOD-VALUE

Caraka's classification is as follows (*sūtra-sthāna* XXVIII)

(i) *Dhānya-varga* (*Graminaceae*) — Those corns which have husk. These have been sub-divided into 11 varieties; e.g., *śāli*, *vrīhi*, *yava*, *godhūma*, etc.

(ii) *Śamīdhānya-varga* (*Leguminoseae*)—twelve kinds of corns, viz., *mudga*, *māṣa*, etc.

(iii) *Śāka-varga* —eighteen varieties of vegetables belong to this class.

(iv) *Phala-varga* — Those bearing fruits.

(v) *Harid-varga* (green class) — *ārdraka* (*Zingiber officinale*), *mūlaka* (*Raphanus sativus*), *Palāṇḍu* and *Laśuna* (*Allium cepa* and *Allium sativum*), etc., belong to this class.

(vi) *Āhārayogī-varga* — Oils of sesame, mustard, etc., belong to this class.

In his *sūtrasthāna*, Suśruta's classification is as given below:

(i) *śālidhānya*, (ii) *ṣaṣṭika*, (iii) *vrīhidhānya*, (iv) *kudhānya-varga*, (v) *vaidala*, (vi) *tila*, (vii) *yava*, (viii) *śimba*, (ix) *phala-varga*, (x) *śāka-varga*, (xi) *puṣpa-varga*, (xii) *udbhid-varga*, (xiii) *kāṇḍa-varga*, (xiv) *taila-varga* and (xv) *ikṣu-varga*.

The *Nāmaliṅgānuśāsana* mentions a number of corns and condiments as articles of food and commerce.

The following classification occurs in the *Bhāvaprakāśa*:

(i) *Harītakyādi-varga*,

(ii) *Karpūrādi-varga*,

(iii) *Guḍucyādi-varga*,

(iv) *Puṣpa-varga*,

(v) *Vaṭādi-varga*,

(vi) *Āmrādiphala-varga*,

(vii) *Dhānya-varga*,

(viii) *Śāka-varga*,

(ix) *Taila-varga*,

(x) *Ikṣu-varga*.

Ecology

The growth and development of trees depend, to a great extent, on climate and the nature of the soil. According to nature, soils have been divided by Caraka (*kalpa-sthāna* I), into the following classes and the names of the trees and plants growing on them have been mentioned by him:

I. *Jāṅgala* (Arid) — The trees growing on such lands are called Xerophytes in modern science; e.g., *khadira* (*Acacia catechu*), *sāla* (*Shorea robusta*), *vadarī* (*Zizyphus jujuba*).

II. *Anūpa* (marshy) — Trees growing on such a soil are called Hydrophytes and Hygrophytes; e.g., *hintāla* (*Phoenix paludosa*).

III. Common soil — Trees of the Mesophytes class grow on such soil; e.g., *vanaspati*, *vānaspatya*, etc.[15]

The classification of soil is similar in the *Upavana-vinoda* and *Suśruta-saṁhitā* (*sūtra-sthāna*, 35). Some ecological information is found in the *Bṛhat-saṁhitā* (ch. 54) and *Nāmaliṅgānuśāsana* (*svarga-varga*).

The ancient Indians used to believe that, in the order of creation, trees and plants preceded the creatures.[16] Botany was regarded as a science to be learnt. This science was utilised in various ways in practical life. By means of botanical knowledge the future growth and availability of crops could be forecast.[17] From certain signs in the trees and plants, excessive rainfall or drought could be predicted. In agricultural operations, the knowledge of Botany served useful purposes, as is borne by such works as the *Bṛhat-saṁhitā* and *Kṛṣi-parāśara*.

From the foregoing pages it is abundantly clear that botanical speculations started in India in hoary antiquity. In fact, India cultivated this science, in howsoever rudimentary a form, at a time when most of the ancient lands, including Greece and Rome, did not have much idea of it. The *Ṛgveda* attests the high antiquity of this science in India.

There was remarkable progress in the medical science of India through botanical knowledge. The treatment of diseases with medicinal herbs is borne out by the *Ṛgveda*[18] and the *Atharvaveda*. With the progress of medical science from the *Atharvaveda*[19] down to the age of Caraka and Suśruta, the knowledge of the plant kingdom grew to an appreciable degree. From the *Atharvaveda* we learn that trees and plants were used not only for the preservation and improvement of health but also for the acquisition of sons and warding off the influence of evil spirits.

The science of Botany and trees played a vital role in the life of the people in various other ways too.[20] Trees were utilised for making dress, furniture and vehicles. In some religious festivals, the use of certain trees and plants was indispensable. Trees also provided the people with materials for trade and commerce. These were also some reasons why the science of botany had to be cultivated.

In modern times, the American Botanist, Luther Barbank,

made astounding contributions to this science by bringing into existence some botanical products out of a combination of several things.[21] India can justly feel proud of the fact that the creation of botanical marvels was not absolutely unknown in this country even in the remove past. The *Bṛhat-saṁhitā* (ch. 54) and *Upavana-vinoda* contain evidences of this fact. For instance, in the latter work, we find a process of producing fragrant flowers in a tree that bears odourless flowers. To the root of such a tree is to be applied earth mixed with fragrant flowers. Then a decoction, made with the bark of the trees called *dhava* (*Grislea tomentosa* or *Anogeissus latifolia*) and *khadira* (*Acacia catechu*), is to be sprinkled and the tree should be smeared with *ghī* and fumigated with the smoke of incense. We are informed that red cotton may be grown in the very tree in which white cotton grows.

In ancient India, the art of grafting plants was well-known. The matter has been dealt with by P.K. Gode.[22]

Arthaśāstra and Ethnobotany

The *Arthaśāstra* of Kauṭilya (*c*. fourth century BC) contains copious information about ethnobotany. We give here some ideas about the various uses of plants according to this work. For details, the reader may consult the book *Ethnobiological Information in Kauṭilīya Arthaśāstra*, P. Sensharma, Calcutta, 1998. Besides the contribution of the plant kingdom to materials for food and fodder, to the welfare of humans and animals, to pharmacognosy, pharmacology and pharmacopoea to agriculture, this work dwells also on the use of plants for military purposes. For example, there are references to the use of branches of trees, canes, bamboos, etc., for hitting the enemy as well as for self-defence. Maces, clubs, bows and arrows, etc., and other weapons, both for offence and defence, were made of plant materials. Plants are stated to have been used in setting fire to the forts and camps of the enemy. Certain types of shields, e.g., *peṭī tālamūla*, *kavāṭa*, etc., appear to have been made of materials derived from plants. Some plants were used in biological warfare. For instance, a kind of poisonous smoke, caused by burning, *inter alia*, the roots of *kāli* (*Tragia involucrata*), *śatāvarī* (*Asparagus racemossus*), etc., might be used against the enemy. Some plants were used in destroying the animals of the enemy.

Notes

1. The portion just below the bark.
2. See G.P. Majumdar, *Vanaspati*, pp. 31-3.
3. C.f. *Bṛhat-saṁhitā*, chap. 54.
4. Vide *Agni Purāṇa*, 281/8-9.
5. II.8.3.
6. The contraction of leaves at night has been described as their sleep.
7. E.g. Guṇaraṭna's commentary.
8. For the consciousness of trees and plants, see G.P. Majumdar, *Vanaspati*, pp. 53-8.
9. Only a few of the works are mentioned here. For a detailed account, see G.P. Majumdar, *Vanaspati*, pp. 79-89.
10. X.97.15.
11. *Vide* Cakrapāṇi's commentary.
12. Same as *Gulma*.
13. For the names of trees healing diseases, occurring in ancient Indian works, see K. Biswas and E. Ghosh, *Bhāratīya Vanauṣadhi* (in Bengali), Calcutta.
14. See G.P. Majumdar, *Vanaspati*, pp. 90-8.
15. For meaning, see above.
16. Cf. *Chāndogya Upaniṣad*, I.1.2, and *Rāmāyaṇa* (Uttara-kāṇḍa, canto 72).
17. Cf. *Bṛhat-saṁhitā*, ch. 29.
18. VII.18; X.145, etc.
19. I/2, 3, 23, 24; II/7, 25; IV/17, 18, 20, 37; V/4, 14, 15; VI/85; XIX/39, etc.
20. For details, see G.P. Majumdar, *Some Aspects of Indian Civilisation*, etc.
21. For example, he produced a fruit called Primus-berry out of a combination of Black-berry and Rasp-berry. Some such marvels are associated also with the names of Lysenko and Michurin. For details about this topic, see Harwood: New *Creations in Plant Life*, 1905.
22. *Indian Culture*, Vol. XIII. No. 1, 1946.

23

Popular Beliefs and Practices

THE approach of the writers in ancient India was mainly elitist. But, occasionally we have glimpses of the ideas and practices of the common people right from the Vedic age. We shall briefly deal with the subject. For this purpose, we shall utilise not only Sanskrit literature, but also Pāli, Prākṛt and Apabhraṁśa literatures.

Evil Spirits in General

In the *Ṛgveda* (henceforth *ṚV*), (X.97.146) we find peculiar ideas of the people about forests. These were believed to be haunted by dangerous spirits. In some contexts (*ṚV*, X.14.9), we find the belief that ghosts move about in cemeteries. The evil spirits, called *kimīdins* were believed to cause diseases and spoil cows' milk (e.g., *Atharvaveda*, henceforth *AV*, I.7, III.9, XVI.1).

The *Rāmāyaṇa* (e.g., II.10.29-30, II.58.34, II.60.1) lays down the following characteristics of people possessed by ghosts: long sigh, tremor in body, impairment of memory, unconsciousness. Belief in ghosts appears to have been widespread in the age of *Arthaśāstra* also (*vide* IV.3.40-1, V.2.41, XIII.2.21-35). The *Harṣacarita* (Ch. II) refers to the practice of driving away ghosts by white sesame. It also mentions (Ch. V) the recitation of an incantation, called *mahāmāyūrī* for the same purpose. Bhavabhūti's *Mālatīmādhava* (IV V) refers to the practice of offering fresh meat for appeasing ghosts in the cemetery. It also mentions the custom of offering the flesh of a virgin girl to goddess Cāmuṇḍā for this purpose.

The *Khettūpamā* (pp. 1-9) of the *Petavatthu* commentary mentions a tree-spirit who stole away a maiden, called *sulasā*. The *dhāraṇīs*, belonging to the Buddhist Mahāyānist literature, are protective spells designed to ensure well-being after destroying evil forces. From the *Losaka Jātaka* as well as *Asilakṣaṇa-jātaka*, we learn that an evil spirit, called *kālaparṇī*, was believed to cause mischief, and people were supposed to be possessed by it. In the latter, we find the following procedure of exorcism. At first, a circle is drawn. Then, a bed is spread over a corpse. The person, supposed to be possessed by the aforesaid *kālakarṇī*, is made to lie down on it. Finally, the person is bathed with 108 pitcherfuls of Gaṅga-water.

Personified Evil Forces with Grotesque Features

People's imagination did not rest by merely conceiving ethereal evil spirits. It went on creating mental images of certain malevolent forces with grotesque forms. In the Vedic age, some such forces are conceived as red, having horns in hands and heads; the front portions of their feet are turned backward, and heels forward. One has one thousand eyes. Those, belonging to the class of Mūradeva, are throatless. The terms Mūradevī or Sahamūlā (R̥V, III.30.17) seem to suggest that they were in the forms of roots of trees. In the *R̥gveda* (e.g., I.35.10, VII.104.15, X.14.9, etc.) we meet with demons with three heads, six eyes, three feet, red complexion, etc.

It was a belief that some malevolent forces wandered in the forms of dogs, owls, hawks, etc. A class of demons, called *kimīdin* (e.g., R̥V, VII.104.2. X.87.24), was supposed to move about shouting *kim idam, kim idam* (what is this? what is this?) Another class of demons, called *kṣviṁkā* (e.g., R̥V, X.87.7) was thought to be shouting. *Kr̥tyā* (e.g., R̥V, X.85.28, 29) and *Nirr̥ti* (e.g., R̥V, I.38, X.10.11, etc.) were believed to be demi-goddesses causing injury or mischief.

Bad Dreams

Bad dreams have been dreaded throughout the ages since Vedic times. In the *R̥gveda*, (X.164.12) a distinct deity, called *duḥsvapna-nāśana* (Destroyer of bad dreams) has been conceived. The entire hymn is a prayer for getting rid of the evil effects of bad dreams. In

R̥V (V.82.4) there is a prayer to God Savitr̥ (Sun) for the above purpose. Protection has been sought from Varuṇa (*R̥V*, II.28.10). For matters, relating to bad dream, the following texts may be referred to *R̥V* (VIII.47.14-18; X, 36.4, X.37.4). The *Sāmaveda* (ch. II, Aindra Kāṇḍa, hymn 7) also reflects the faith that sun-god can destroy the effects of bad dreams. There are charms against bad dreams in the *Atharvaveda* too (e.g., XVI.5, IV.5, IV.17.5). The practices for averting bad dreams are given in the *Kauśikasūtra*, Kāṇḍa 48, 9-13.

According to the *Aitareya Āraṇyaka* (III.2.4), the sight of the following in dreams is inauspicious:

> Dark man with black teeth, such a man killing the dreamer, a boar killing him, an ape jumping on him, wind carrying him swiftly, having swallowed gold he vomits it, drinking honey, chewing lotus-stalks, carrying one (red) lotus, driving a herd of assess or boars, wearing a garland of *nalada* flowers, flowers, driving a black cow with a black calf towards the south.

The *Rāmāyaṇa* (e.g., II.4.17, III.73.33, V.27.6, VI.33.28) mentions both good and bad dreams.

The following creatures and things, seen in dreams, were believed to portend evil:

According to the *Matsya Purāṇa* (242.15-20), the bad effects of dreams can be averted by the following practices:

According to the *Bhujabala-nibandha* (p. 304) the sight of all dark objects, in dreams, excepting cow, image of god, elephant, horse and brāhmaṇas, is ominous.

> Monkey, beating by a dark woman, going southward on an ass-cart, wearing a garland of red flowers, flaming meteor, falling of cow-dung from above a hill into a pit, drying of an ocean, fall of the moon on the earth, all-engulfing darkness, cracking of the ground, withering of a tree, emission of smoke from the peak of a hill.

The ominous dream of demoness Trijaṭā (*Rāmāyaṇa*,

Sundara-kāṇḍa, Canto 27; *Mahābhārata*, Vana-parva, ch. 280, verse 64-5) is well-known. Among the evil omens about Rāvaṇa, seen by himself, were: he had red garments, his fall on earth from his aerial car, riding an ass-drawn cart, etc.

declaring the dream to another, sleeping after seeing it, bath with water mixed with the viscous sediment of oily substances, *homa* with sesame, honouring brāhmaṇas, eulogy of Vāsudeva, worshipping Him and hearing the story of the liberation of Gajendra.

Some Buddhist Jātakas, e.g., *Mahāsvapna* (77), *Lauhakumbhī* (314), *Astaśabda* (418) refer to the performance of a sacrifice designed to transform bad dreams into good ones. In the *Lauhakumbhī*, we find that, in such a sacrifice, the meat of four of each of the following classes of creatures had to be offered: elephant, horse, bull, human being, sparrow.

The *Bhavisyatta-kahā* (Dalal and Gune) refers (I.14) to belief in the good and bad effects of dreams.

It is interesting to note that, in many ancient countries, dreams were supposed to indicate future events. For example, the Chaldean astrologers and interpreters of dreams were highly respected in Babylonian and Assyrian courts. Plato, in his *Timaeus* (ch. 46, 47), regards dreams as prophetic visions. The Muslims have the science of *tabir* or interpretation of dreams (*vide JRAS*, Old Series, Vol. 16, pp. 118-17).

As there were bad dreams, so were good dreams too. Consideration of space forbids accounts of them.

Magic and Miracle

Some ancient works testify to the people's belief in magical practices and miracles. Some such beliefs are found, even in modern times, among some tribes and other backward people.

The *R̥V* contains charms and magical practices designed to cure diseases, curb *rākṣasas*, revive a dying person, counteract the effects of omens and portents, bring back an animal that strayed away from the herd, etc. *Ṛ̥V* (I.50.12) reflects the curious belief that some human diseases can be transferred to other creatures and objects. The disease, called *harimāṇa* (jaundice), was believed to be transferable to male and female parrots and to turmeric. It was believed that, through divine favour, a blind man could see and a lame man could walk (*Ṛ̥V* (II.15.7, IV.19.9). Youthful vigour is said to have been restored, through divine favour, to the old and infirm Cyavana (*Ṛ̥V*, I.117.13, 118.6, etc.).

We learn of wine flowing out of a horse's hoof (*Ṛ̥V*, I.110.8). In some hymns (e.g., *Ṛ̥V*, X.159.4), we read of the magical power of sacrifice in destroying enemies. Demons appear to have recited some *mantras* for inducing sleep among the inmates of a house (*Ṛ̥V*, VII.55). An evil force was to be invoked for causing miscarriage to a woman (*Ṛ̥V*, X.122).

The *AV* contains many magical practices, particularly those for causing mischief to the enemies. A portion of this Veda is called *Ābhicārika* which contains curses and exorcisms against evil spirits, demons, wizards and enemies. The *AV* refers to the use of various kinds of amulets for driving away evil spirits, bringing others under control, acquisition of material prosperity, cure of diseases, averting evil, etc. Some important amulets are called *vīrudh*, *śatampuṣpa*, *trivṛ̥t*, *tilaka*, *jaṅgiḍa*, *śatavāra* (*AV*, IV.20, V.28, VIII.5, etc.). A characteristic of the age of the *AV* is symbolical magic. Processes of some symbolical magic are laid down in the *Kauśika-sūtra*. For instance, a blade of grass, cut into two pieces, is to be thrown towards the enemy. The splitting of the grass indicates the division of the enemy-army and consequent dispersal (*Kauśika-sūtra*, I.6.10). The burning of an iguana, after killing it, indicates the killing of the enemy (*ibid.*, 40.7.39, 54). Before starting for trade, a merchant was to place a ball of cowdung on the body of the priest and ask him — how is the day? If the priest answered that it was auspicious and conducive to fortune, then the journey was undertaken (*Kauśika-sūtra*, I.15). The recitation of *AV* (V.13) was believed to destroy snake-venom. In this connection, the use of such words of unknown meaning as *taimāta*, *apodaka*, *āligī*, *viligī*, *urugulā*, *asiknī*, etc., tends to indicate non-Āryan influence (*vide AV*, V.6, etc.).

Tantra is a mine of magic and miracle. In this Śāstra, we find the use of magic for both benevolent and malevolent purposes. Among the good purposes, served by Tāntric magic, are victory in dispute, prevention and cure of diseases, getting rid of idleness, making a dead man alive. The main result of malevolent magic was *abhicāra* (causing mischief to enemies) which comprises *mārana* (killing), *utsādana* (ruination), *stambhana* (causing paralysis), *vaśīkaraṇa* (bringing others under control), *vidveṣaṇa* (causing enmity), *uccāṭana* (expulsion), *mahāhāni-karaṇa* (causing serious damage). Some procedures are as follows:

> After cooking rice, a portion of it should be offered as *bhūtabali* (offering to birds and beasts) in a lonely place. Then that rice is to be buried in a pit in the enemy's house at midnight; this ensures the death of the enemy within a week. In order to bring a person under control, any one of the following things, consecrated with a *mantra*, recited 108 times, should be given to the person concerned; by using it he will come under domination:
>
> Betel-leaf, a fruit, clove, a piece of cloth, etc.

On a specified day, a human bone, measuring four fingers, should be collected. Towards the close of night, that person's name is to be written on a bone which should be thrown into his residential house. By this his expulsion is ensured. Details about *abhicāra* are available in, *inter alia*, the following works on Tantra:

> *Śāradātilaka* (XXIII.123-25), *Śaktisaṁgama*, (Kālī, VIII.102-5).

In the *Arthaśāstra* (IV.5.1-7) we find a class of people, called Mānava who committed robbery by using magical methods.

In the *Kādambarī* (Kale's ed. 1928), it is stated (p. 338) that a kind of collyrium, called *siddhāñjana*, when applied to the eyes, could enable the person concerned to visualise hidden treasure. There is mention of an incantation, called *antardhāna* (disappearance), which was believed to make one invisible to others (*ibid.*, p. 339).

The *Gaüḍavaho* (ed. N.G. Suru, 1965) testifies (1071) to the prevalence of *abhicāra*.

The *Kathā-sarit-sāgara* of Somadeva is a mine of information on popular beliefs and practices. In this connection, one may look up Penzer's edition of Tawney's *Ocean of Story*. Demon Maya was believed to have a vessel, a stick and shoes all of wonderful magical power (II, p. 22). The vessel became filled with whatever was wanted to be eaten. Whatever was written with the stick came to be true. It was possible, with the shoes on, to fly in the sky.

In the *Kevaḍḍha Sutta* (*Dīghanikāya* I, pp. 211-23) we find magical practices by which miraches can be performed. There are means by which gods are clearly manifested to one with great concentration. The *Valāhassa Jātaka* (vol. II) refers to some shipwrecked mariners who escaped from a city of goblins with the help of a flying horse. The *Dhammapada* commentary (III, pp. 134ff.) mentions flying through air on the back of a wooden Garuḍa bird. According to the *Campeyya Jātaka* (IV, pp. 451-68), Bodhisatta, born as a serpent-king, had magical power by which he could perform miracles. The *Kathāvatthu* (ch. 21) deals, among other things, with *iddhi* (means supernormal potency). The *Sumaṅgalavilāsinī* states that the Buddha performed double miracles at the gate of Sāvatthi. While fire was raging on the upper part of his body, water flowed down the lower part. In the *Dhammapada* commentary (III. pp. 113 ff.), the Buddha is stated to have created a girl of exquisite beauty by his miraculous power.

The *Karpūramañjarī*, a Prākr̥t drama by Rājaśekhara, reflects belief in magic; a magician is also mentioned. There are references to the carrying of a person by magical power (I), making flowers bloom out of season (II) and a magic car moving through the air or walls (IV).

The *Karakaṇḍa-cariu* refers to a bamboo-clump (II.7) which grew from the eyes on a human skull, a horse flying through the sky (VIII.9), conjurers who could control demons by spells (II.12).

Miscellaneous Superstitious Beliefs and Practices

Superstitions of various kinds have been playing a prominent role in the life of the people from time immemorial. Omens and portents have been dealt with separately. We shall deal here with superstitions of a miscellaneous nature.

As in many other ancient countries, in Vedic India too we find traces of totemism. In the *R̥V*, some tribes are called *matsya* (fish) and *aja* (goat). They trace their origin from fish and goat respectively. Some sects of priests are named Gotama, Vatsa, Śunaka and Kauśika; they claim their origin from the cow, calf, dog and owl respectively.

Fetishism has been prevalent in some form or other ever since Vedic times. For instance, tree-worship is mentioned in *Śāṁkhāyana* (I.15-16) and *Kauṣitaki-gr̥hya-sūtras* (I.9.12). The worship of a *palāśa* tree (*Butea frondosa*) was a must in the festival of *Medhājanana* (generating intellect or retentive memory). Tree-worship is also mentioned in the *Rāmāyaṇa* (II.55.25-6). Also mentioned (II.25) is the worship of the hill, lake, season, sky, wind, etc. It was believed that forests had presiding deities (I.31.14).

Madhuvidyā can turn poison into nectar. (I.191.13) contains the idea that the recitation of the names of 99 rivers, can counteract poison. The same purpose is said to be served by 21 female peacocks and *sapta-svasāraḥ* (seven sisters, i.e., seven rivers (*R̥V*, I.191.14). A priest is believed to heal diseases by reciting *mantras* (*R̥V*, X.161, 163). In *AV*, IV.90.1-2, the priest assures the patient that he is going to take away the malady. The disease, called *jalodara*, commonly known as *udarī* (accumulation of water in the belly) was supposed to be caused as a result of the transgression of the laws of God Varuṇa. A peculiar practice for curing the above disease was as follows. Certain specified herbs were taken near water. The severed heads of a sheep and a dog were thrown into water. Human hairs were tied to a bamboo top along with a worn out shoe *AV* (II.29) was believed to remove thirst.

The recital of *AV*, VI.56 was considered to result in the shutting of the mouth of a serpent for good so that it could never bite any body.

AV, II.36, VI.60, etc., appear to provide remedies for a girl who fails to get a husband owing to some defects or any other reason.

Some Vedic Sūtra works refer to serpent-worship. For instance, in *Śravaṇā* festival, it was customary to worship serpents with comb, collyrium, fruits, cosmetics, etc. (*Pāraskara-gr̥hya-sūtra*

II.14.17, *Śāṁkhāyana*, IV.15.8, *Āpastamba*, VII.18.11). According to *Baudhāyana* (III.10.4), powdered rice, ghī, wheat, etc., boiled in sugarcane-juice, should be offered in such a worship. The *Arthaśāstra* testifies (IV.3) to the prevalence of the worship of not only serpents, but also of fire, river, rats, etc., in order to get rid of the ravages caused by them. In this work, there are provisions for milching a cow and burning a torso, made of the powder of rice and some other grains, in a funeral ground.

In the *Mahābhārata* (Anuśāsana 127/3) we find that bath in the water, in which a cow's horn was washed, was regarded as holy. The cow was looked upon as a deity and drinking cow's urine was believed to cause internal purification (Sabhā, 18/2).

According to some Purāṇas, e.g., *Kālikā*, a part of the festivities, on the *daśamī* day of *Durgāpūjā*, was *śabarotsava* (borrowed from the tribe, Śabara?). It consisted in the participants' smearing their bodies with mud and covering them with leaves and creepers and then abusing one another in filthy language. Chapter 142 of the *Agni Purāṇa* contains various practices designed for skill in snake-charming, safe delivery of babies, acquisition of a son, etc.

In some works of Classical Sanskrit, we find the custom of the father's kissing the head of the son proceeding for a journey. The *Kādambarī* (Kale's ed., 1928, p.120) records the practice of burning the powder of a snake-slough and of the horn of a ram, mixed with the *ghī* of goat's milk, for getting good results. Those who come to see a newly born baby should touch water and fire, before doing so; this was believed to protect the baby from the evil eye (*ibid.*, p. 121). For the same purpose, a tiger's nail, covered with gold, was also kept hanging from the neck of the child.

Omens and Portents

As far as we know, belief in omens and portents existed in the past, and still exist among the people of all countries of the world. However scientifically developed a country may be, such beliefs cannot be eradicated from a section of its people. As for India, omens and portents have been a part of life ever since the Vedic times. We cannot say anything about the matter in the pre-Vedic period as we have no record. We find several Sanskrit words denoting omens and portents; e.g., *nimitta*, *adbhuta*, *utpāta*, *śakuna* (or *apaśakuna*), *lakṣaṇa* (*aśubha-lakṣaṇa*, *durlakṣaṇa*, *alakṣaṇa*, *apalakṣaṇa*, etc.), *nirghāta*, etc. *Nimitta* has been used to mean both good and evil omens. For example, in the *Abhjñānaśakuntalam* (I.15), the king says that his arm is throbbing; this indicates something great to be acquired. Again, in the same work, Śakuntalā expresses (V after verse *abhyaktamiva*, etc.) fear at the throbbing of her right eye, which, in the case of a women, indicates danger. *Adbhuta* has been explained as an event that did not occur before *Prakṛteranyathā utpātaḥ*. *Utpāta* means something abnormal, *śakuna* appears to denote good omen. Monier-Williams mentions *apaśakuna* to mean an evil omen. *Lakṣaṇa* is used to denote a bodily sign indicative of good or bad luck. *Upasarga* is that which causes suffering. *Nirghāta* means the same as *utpāta* above.

The great importance, attached to omens and portents in ancient India, is proved by the fact that separate treatises and parts of some works are devoted to them, and prescribe ways and means for overcoming their influence. The *Adbhuta-sāgara* of the Bengal king Ballālasena (*c*. AD 1158-70) deals with these topics exhaustively. These have been dealt with in some important Smṛti works also; e.g., *Caturvarga-cintāmaṇi* (on Vrata) of Hemādri (thirteenth century), *Madana-ratna* (on Śānti) of Madana Siṁhadeva (*c*. fifteenth century — first half). Several Purāṇas, particularly the *Matsya* (ch. 228), *Viṣṇu* (ch. 2), *Vāyu* (ch. 19), *Brahmavaivarta* (Gaṇeśakhaṇḍa, 34), *Agni* (ch. 229), *Padma* (4), *Viṣṇudharmottara* (2), *Bhaviṣva* (1), etc.

Even the *Arthaśāstra* of Kauṭilya contains information on the above matters.

Some Tāntric works, notably the *Ārya-mañjuśrī-mūlakalpa* (ch. 20), *Pīṭhamālā-mahātantra* (ch. 21) throw considerable light on the beliefs relating to omens and portents.

Varāhamihira's (*c*. AD 475-550) *Bṛhat-saṁhitā* (ch. 85-95), *Bṛhad-yogayātrā* (ch. 16), which though dealing with astronomy, devote considerable space to these popular subjects. Even the renowned *Āyurveda* treatise, *Caraka-saṁhitā* (Indriya-sthāna, ch. 12) provides that the physician should observe some physical signs of the patient. Among other works, the *Bhujabala* (*c*. AD 1040-50) of

Bhoja deals with omens. Curiously enough, even the great Vedāntist, Śaṅkarācārya (c. eigth-ninth century), in his commentary on the *Vedānta-sūtra* (III.24), mentions some omens.

There are scattered references to omens and portents in many works of Classical Sanskrit literature. Belief in these things was so ingrained and widespread that it was considered necessary to write works devoted exclusively to them. Of such works, the most notable is the *Vasantarāja-śakuna* (between c. AD 700-1100). Attributed to one Vasantarāja, it is divided into 20 sections of which section 5 deals with auspicious and inauspicious things and sights, section 6 with inauspicious and auspicious appearance, dress, gestures, speed, throbbing of limbs of men and women. Prognostications from the cries, sight, glance, movement, etc., of some birds, e.g., female cuckoo, swan, crane, cakravāka, parrot, peacock, vulture, owl, pigeon, cock, etc. Among the animals are dog, jackal, etc. The work was so popular that it was commented upon by Bhānucandra-gaṇi who enjoyed the patronage of Akbar the Great (sixteenth century). The *Vasantarājaśakuna* was translated into Hindi.

The poet-saint Tulasīdāsa (AD 1532-1623) is credited with the authorship of two works, on these subjects (*vide* G.A. Grierson, *Indian Antiquary*, Vol. XXII, pp. 204 ff.).

The *Nimitta*, attributed to *Bhadrabāhu*, contains 26 chapters and nearly 1460 verses.

We shall set forth some omens and portents mentioned in some prominent works right from the Vedic age. For this purpose, the omens and portents can be classified as follows:

(a) Relating to natural phenomena.

(b) Relating to human body.

(c) Relating to birds, beasts, insects and other creatures.

(d) Relating to dreams.

(e) Relating to images of deities.

(f) Relating to genetic aberrations.

(g) Miscellaneous.

OMENS AND PORTENTS RELATING TO NATURAL PHENOMENA

The *AV* (XIX.19) mentions the following phenomena as portending evil:

> falling star, rise of a comet.

The *Kauśika-sūtra* (ch. 13, Kaṇḍikā 93) mentions, *inter alia*, the following *utpāta*s:

> Shower of blood and other terrible things from the sky, spurting up of water in a waterless place, a comet darkening the Great Bear, fall of a meteor at daytime.

Some *utpāta*s, according to the *Mahābhārata* (e.g., Sabhā 80.28-31; Virāṭa 39.4-5; Udyoga 84.5-9; Bhīṣma 2.20-3; Śalya 23.22-3, etc.) are:

> lightning or thunder in the cloudless sky, fierce-looking cloud, unkindled fire, the moon without its spot, shower of flesh from the sky, fall of a mountain-peak, etc.

Some of the *utpāta*s, mentioned in the *Rāmāyaṇa*, (e.g., Ayodhyā 4.17, Araṇya 23.1-3, Yuddha 28.4-6, etc.) are:

> violently runbling grey cloud showering rain with blood, the sun looking like a firebrand, surrounded by a dark circle with red fringe, appearance of a torso near the sun, shaking of mountain-tops, fall of a ball of fire from the sun, flight of planets, etc.

Some omens are stated to portend evil not always but at specified times. For example, the unnatural phenomenon of heavenly bodies being visible by day is not ominous in the months of *Āśvina* and *Kārttika*.

OMENS RELATING TO HUMAN BODY

From the *AV* (6.140) we learn that the appearance of teeth in the upper jaw of a child before those in the lower one portends danger to the lives of the parents.

The throbbing of different limbs was looked upon as indicating good or bad effects. The knowledge of prognostications from the movement or some characteristics of limbs appears to have been cultivated as *Aṅga-vidyā* by which some mean palmistry while others mean the interpretation of the throbbing of different limbs. Some marks on the palm and the body were regarded as ominous. For example, the *Kāśikā* commentary (*c.* seventh century), on Pāṇini III.2.53, mentions *Patighnī pāṇirekhā* or a particular line in the palm of a woman indicates that she will lose her husband. In the same context, it states *jāyāghnas-tilakalakaḥ*, i.e., a black *tila* (mole, spot) on the body of a man indicates that he will lose his wife.

The *Rāmāyaṇa* (III. 69-21, VI. 65-50, etc.) mentions the following as inauspicious for men: throbbing of the left eye and left arm, lack-lustre face, hoarse vioce, agitation of mind. The following are auspicious for women (V.27.50-2, V.29.2-5): throbbing of the left eye, horripilated left arm and left thigh slipping off cloth.

The *Matsya Purāṇa* (241.1-14) deals with the effects of the throbbing of the various parts of the body; e.g.

Part of body	Result
Top of head	Acquisition of earth which may mean kingdom or land.
Space between eyebrows and nose	Union with persons who are dear.
Back	Defeat
Chest	Victory

The *Garuḍa Purāṇa* (ch. 63) deals with the auspicious and inauspicious physical signs.

The *Gāthā-saptaśatī* (II.37) of Hāla refers to the throbbing of the left eye of a woman as auspicious.

It is interesting to note that, in Shakespeare's drama, *Othello* (sixteenth century), Desdemona speaks about the itching of her eyes as a bad omen.

OMENS RELATING TO BIRDS, BEASTS, ETC.

The owl was regarded in the *Ṛ̥V* (II.42.1, 3) as ominous. The cry of the *kapiñjala* (heath-cock, *Franuslinus francolinus*) was believed to be auspicious. The pigeon was looked upon as the messenger of Yama (*Ṛ̥V*, X.165.4) and of the malevolent goddess Nirṛ̥ti (X.165.1). According to the *Kauśika-sūtra* (46.4.6; 51.7) serious misfortune is indicated by the falling of birds like the crow, pigeon, etc., on the body of a person with flesh in the beak or by their dropping something from their beaks on him.

According to the *Rāmāyaṇa*, the following are ominous in the battlefield: sight of a jackal (III.23.10), fall of a torso near a person (IV.34.32). According to the same Epic, the following are inauspicious signs:

> horripilation on the body of camels, asses and snake, etc., tears rolling down their eyes, the presence of a snake in the kitchen, loud scream of birds facing the sun.

The following are some other inauspicious omens according to this Epic:

> cry of a jackal vomiting fire, fall of a vulture on a chariot, horse stumbling on an even ground, unusual cries of birds; e.g., a crane crying like an owl, etc.

According to the *Mahābhārata* (Bhīṣma III.65.74), the following are good: peacock, swan or crane following a person, chirping of auspicious birds like the peacocks and curlews to the right.

The *Bṛ̥hatsaṁhitā* (ch. 92, 93) deals in detail with the prognostications to be drawn from elephants and horses.

OMENS RELATING TO DREAMS.

See Discussion on Bad dreams, *supra*.

OMENS RELATING TO IMAGES OF DEITIES

Belief in omens in connection with images of deities was widespread and very old. Our chief sources of information are:

Ātharvaṇa-pariśiṣṭa (LXXII), *Kauśikasūtra* (Kaṇḍikā 105), *Mahābhārata* (Bhīṣma 112.11), *Matsya Purāṇa* (163.243), *Viṣṇudharmottara*, *Padma Purāṇa* (V.42.137-8), *Bṛ̥hat-saṁhitā*,

Adbhuta-sāgara, *Caturvarga-cintāmaṇi* (*Vrata*), *Madana-ratna* (*śānti*).

The inauspicious signs, relating to images, are mainly the following:

> Their fall, tremor, dance, laughter, weeping, closing and opening the eyes, scream, emission of snake, blazing, singing, perspiring, oozing blood, moving.

Some of the evil effects indicated by the above are:

> drought, danger particularly from weapons, famine, epidemic, destruction of the king and his ministers.

OMENS RELATING TO GENETIC ABERRATIONS

The omens of this class have been mentioned as relating to both humans and animals. The main sources of information are the

> *Kauśikasūtra* (Kaṇḍikās 110, 111) *Mahābhārata* (Bhīṣma 3.2-7), *Matsya Purāṇa* (235.1-3), *Viṣṇudharmottara* (II.140.1-3), *Bṛhatsaṁhitā* (45.51-4), *Adbhuta-sāgara* (pp. 559-69).

Among the aberrations, relating to women, are the following:

> giving birth to monstrosities, twins, triplets, quadruplets, etc., delivery long before or after the due time, giving birth to eagles or peacocks.

The birth of a female baby after the successive births of three males was believed to result in disastrous consequences.

Extremely ominous were the following in case of animals:

> Birth of a cow-calf to a mare, of a jackal to a bitch, birth of twins to mares, camels, she-buffaloes and female elephants.

MISCELLANEOUS OMENS

According to the *Kauśika-sūtra* (Kaṇḍikā 93), the following are some ominous incidents: wrangling of family members, two ploughitares getting entangled, village fire burning a house, a bamboo splitting open with a sound, a jar splitting in a reservoir of water.

It is stated, in the *Śatapatha Brāhmaṇa* (XIII.8.1), that if the land, on which a mound is raised, to commemorate the death of a person, is sloping to the north, it indicates the prosperity of his childern. Slope to the south forebodes their imminent death.

Some of the omens, portending serious calamities to the householder, according to some Gṛhyasūtras (e.g. *Gobhila*, III.3.29-34, *Āpastamba*, VIII.23.8-10) are:

> falling of a bird's dung on the body, falling of water on the body from the cloudless sky, being caught in a tornado, sight of a single jackal or a she-wolf.

According to the *Rāmāyaṇa* (VI.58.39, VI.78.17), the dropping of a stick from the hand of a charioteer is inauspicious.

According to the *Mahābhārata*, the following are ominous:

> trees bearing fruits or flowers out of season, sudden fall of a flag, lack of lustre in fire. The spreading of the flame of smokeless fire to the right side was regarded as auspicious (Bhīṣma III.74).

According to the *Kṛṣiparāśara*, the breaking of the plough, at the time of ploughing the field, forebodes the death of the master of the land.

Upaśruti (oracular voice or word) has been dealt with in the *Vasantarāja-śakuna*, mentioned earlier. The author states that, before undertaking any matter, one should carefully listen to and ponder over voices heard at nightfall or about the morning twilight when people scarcely speak anything. What a child says, without being prompted, is infallible.

24

Yuddha (War)

FIGHTING has been a fact of life ever since the origin of mankind. The primitive people, for their very existence, had to fight with not only hostile people, but also for keeping at bay or killing ferocious animals which were menacing to their lives. In the hunting stage, when people used animal flesh as their food, animals had to be killed. The ruins of the Indus Valley Civilisation (*c.* 3000 or 2500 BC) reveal stone weapons. Coming to the Vedic age (*c.* 2000-1500 BC), we read about fight between the Āryans and the non-Āryans as also between gods and demons. The Epics, *Rāmāyaṇa* (present form *c.* second or third century AD) and *Mahābhārata* (present form *c.* fourth century AD) testify to organised wars. The Purāṇas and the Classical Sanskrit literature contain copious information about war and war-materials.

There is no separate treatise dealing with various matters relating to war. There are a few works, entitled *Dhanurveda* or *Dhanurvidyā* which are not comprehensive. To Uśanas, Vyāsa, Sadāśiva are attributed works bearing the title *Dhanurveda*. The *Dhanurveda prakaraṇa* of the *Agni Purāṇa*, attributed to Vikramāditya, is only a paraphrase of the *Dhanurveda* of Sadāśiva. It refers to the school of Vīreśvara. A *Dhanurveda* is quoted in Kṣīrasvāmin's (*c.* eighth century according to some, eleveenth according to others) commentary on the *Amarakośa*, as well as in the *Abhidhāna-cintāmaṇi* of Hemacandra (eleventh-twelfth century AD). A *Dhanurveda-cintāmaṇi* is attributed to Narasiṁhabhaṭṭa. A *Dhanurveda-saṁhitā*, attributed to Vasiṣṭha, has been printed, (1) with Hindī trs., Barantha, 1897, (2) with Bengālī trs., Calcutta,

1922. The *Viṣṇu Purāṇa* (Wilson's trs. VIII.67) mentions *Dhanurveda* as a distinct branch of knowledge. Among the works, incidentally throwing light on aspects of war, prominent are the following: the Kauṭilīya *Arthaśāstra* (*c*. fourth century BC), *Mahābhārata*, *Manu-smṛti* (present form evolved from *c*. second century BC. to *c*. second century AD). Some Purāṇas, to which references will be made in due course, throw considerable light on matters relating to war. Among other works, mention may be made of the *Abhilaṣitārtha-cintāmaṇi* (also called *Mānasollāsa*), composed in Śaka 1051 (AD 1129) by the Cālukya King Someśvara; *Kāmandaka-nītisāra* (*c*. eighth century AD), *Yukti-kalpataru* attributed to Bhoja of Dhārā (eleventh century AD), *Śukranītisāra* (*c*. thirteenth or fourteenth century AD, according to P.V. Kane, nineteenth century according to others).

Besides purely literary sources, certain inscriptions refer to war and military matters. Some archaeological remains include weapons.

It is noteworthy that some foreign sources, e.g., Greek, Chinese and Muslim throw light on warfare in ancient and medieval India.

We shall attempt to give an outline of the subject, based mainly on the *Mahābhārata*, *Rāmāyaṇa*, *Manu-smṛti*, *Arthaśāstra* and the Purāṇas.

While there is enough of evidence about war on land, we get very little information about aerial and naval warfare in ancient India. In the *Rāmāyaṇa*, we find Rāvaṇa carrying away Sītā through the air, Rāvaṇa's son fighting from behind clouds, Rāma and Sītā returning to Ayodhyā in an aerial car, etc. Some Purāṇas refer to aerial fight. For example, the *Mārkaṇḍeya* (ch. 90) describes the aeiral encounter of goddess Caṇḍī with demon Śumbha. The word *vimāna*, denoting aerial car, occurs, besides some Purāṇas, in several ancient texts, e.g., *Raghuvaṁśa* 7/51, 12/104, 13/1; *Kumārasambhava*, 2/45, 7/40, *Vikramorvaśīya* 4/43; *Kirātārjunīya* 7/11, etc. But, the above works deal with legendary themes. So, these cannot be taken as positive proofs of the existence of aerial vehicles in those times. But, the testimony of the *Samarāṅgana-sūtradhāra* (ch. 33, *GOS*, ed.) of king Bhoja (eleventh century AD), a well-known historical personage, cannot, perhaps, be similarly brushed aside as imaginary; this chapter deals with the mode of construction of various flying machines. Three movements of flying machines are mentioned as ascending, surveying vast areas in the space and then descending. It is also stated (31.45-74) that these cars fly so fast that only a faint drone is audible to those who are on the ground. These are spoken of as having different shapes — like elephants, horses, monkeys, some kinds of birds and chariots. An aerial car, made of light wood, is durable having mercury inside and fire at the bottom. It has two wings propelled by wind. It can carry several persons.

As regards naval warfare, the textual evidence is meagre. In view of the vulnerablity of India, especially of south India, from the sea, it is quite probable that some sort of fleet for guarding the coastal region was maintained. But, the *Arthaśāstra*, while laying down the duties of the superintendent of boats or ships (*Nāvadhyakṣa*, II.28) is silent about navy or naval war. Book X of this work, called Sāṁgrāmika, devoted to war, also does not mention navy. The following line in II.28 deserves notice:

amitra-viṣayātigāḥ paṇya-pattana-cāritropaghātikaśca (*Arth*, II.28).

(*nirghātayet*, which is the last word in the immediately preceding line, is obviously understood here). *Amitra-visyātigāḥ* has been interpreted by some as sea-going men of war belonging to the enemy. As a matter of fact, the above expression means any boat or ship (not necessarily men of war), laden with merchandise, heading for a belligerent country, should be destroyed. The context is about the realisation of toll and the destruction of those vessels which try to evade it or fail to abide by the rules of the emporium. Destruction, however, does not imply battle. The idea seems to be that the vessel, containing merchandise, should not be allowed to fall into the hands of the enemy, and add to his resources.

Of the ancient texts, the *Manu-smṛti* clearly refers to naval war (*yudhyed-anūpe nau-dvipaistathā*, VII.192; at a place abounding in water, one should fight with boats and elephants). Another clear reference to such a battle is available in the *Raghuvaṁśa* in which Kālidāsa states that king Raghu, in course of *digvijaya*, conquered Bengal which had a fleet (*nausādhānodyatān*, IV.36).

In later times, naval war is referred to in some inscriptions and literary works. For example, the Allahabad Stone Pillar Inscription, eulogising Samudragupta (*c.* 330-80) refers to his conquest of some islands (*vide Corpus Ins. Ind.*, III, p. 14); this implies the utilisation of navy. The same inscription (p. 217) contains a reference to a fleet of war-ships belonging to Jīvitagupta II. From the *Yuktikalpataru*, mentioned earlier, we come to know of a kind of ship used for naval battle.

Weapons

The main weapons, used in ancient India, will be mentioned here. It should be noted that both the words *astra* and *śastra* have been used to denote arms in general, though their derivative meanings are different. *Astra*, derived from the root *as* (to throw) primarily denotes a missile hurled at the enemy. *Śastra*, derived from root *śas* (to destroy) may mean those which are hurled or held in the hand. We shall see that both these kinds of weapons were in use.

In the Vedic age, the following were the chief weapons:

> *Śara* (arrow), *aṅkuśa* (hook or goad), *paraśu* (axe), *kr̥pāṇa* (sword), *vajra* (stated to be made of *ayas* which may denote any metal, particularly iron), *śataghnī*.

The above terms are used, for example, in the *R̥gveda* (V.57.2; VIII.17.10; X.28.8; X.22.10; X.48.3); *Taittirīya Saṁhitā* (or Black *Yajurveda*). *R̥ṣi*, mentioned as a weapon in *R̥gveda* (V.52.6, V.57.2), is of unknown description. Of these, *vajra* appears to denote any weapon destructive like the thunderbolt. Opinions differ about the exact meaning of *śataghnī*. The apparent meaning is that which kills one hundred persons (at one throw ?). May be that *śata* here was used to indicate a large number, and not precisely one hundred. According to some, it is a huge boulder with barbed wires on all sides, meant for being thrown from a high place. The name of this thing occurs at several other places, e.g., *Rāmāyaṇa* (Yuddha 3/13; Sundara 2/11) *Mahābhārata* (Vana 169/16; 284/3, Ādi 207/34); Droṇa 156/70; Karṇa 11/8; Śalya 45/110, etc.) From the Vana-parva of *Mahābhārata* (284/31), it seems to have been fitted with wheels with a round stone within.

The *Atharvaveda* (14/6/6) appears to refer to a poisoned arrow.

Of the various weapons, mentioned in the *Rāmāyaṇa* (e.g., I.5.11, I.27.8, II.16.2, II.31.30, II.52.11, III.12.20, 21; V.4.17, 21, 22; V.41.12, VI.7.3, VI.9.4, etc.) prominent are the following :

> *Aśani* (perhaps the same as *vajra*, *supra*), *asi* (sword), *ṛṣti* (double-edged sword), *kārmuka* (bow), *kṣepaṇī* (a sort of missile hurled at the enemy?), *khaḍga* (sword), *gadā* (mace, club), *cakra* (wheel), *tomara* (iron club or javelin), *triśūla* (trident), *dhanus* (bow), *paṭṭiśa* (a kind of sharp-edged spear), *paraśvadha* (hatchet, battle-axe), *parigha* (iron club in general; stick or club studded or tipped with iron), *pāśa* (noose), *prāsa* (dart, barbed missile), *mudgara* (hammer, mallet, club, mace), *musala* (mace, club), *vajra* (see *supra*), *śakti* (spear, dart, lance), *śataghnī* (see *supra*).

In the above list, some words appear to mean the same thing. It seems such words denote different types of the same thing; the same weapons of different shapes may have been differently named.

The arrow appears to have been the commonest weapon. There is mention of a variety of arrows; e.g., *agnidīpta-mukha* (with fire at the tip), *ardhacandra* (crescent-shaped), *āśīviṣānana* (with snake-shaped tip), *karṇī* (ear-shaped), *kāka-mukha* (with crow-like tip), *kṣura* (like a razor), *pañcāsya* (five-tipped), *vyāghra-mukha* (with the tip like a tiger's face), and many other kinds. From certain contexts, e.g., VI.64.25, it appears that, in some cases, the names of the heroes, using the arrows, were inscribed on them. The word *yantrāyudha* (e.g., I.5.10) seems to mean a missile hurled from machines. We learn of *yantras* (machines) placed in the hill-fort of Kiṣkindhā (IV.14.5). Huge machines for hurling missiles are stated to have been placed over the fort-gate of Laṅkā, (VI.3.12). Over the city-gate of Laṅkā, there was the *śataghnī* too (VI.3.13).

The Epic mentions (VI.102.43-4) a powerful blazing weapon capable of drying up a sea or at least a part of it. It seems to be legendary.

The *Mahābhārata*, in which the great war is the main theme, naturally refers to a number of weapons and other war materials.

The principal sources of information, in this regard, are the following books (*parvans*) of the Epic :

Ādi 19/12-17; 32/12-14; 139/6; 227/25.

Vana 20/33, 34; 21/2, 25; 42/4, 5; 169/15, 16.

Virāṭa 32/10; ch. 42.

Udyoga 19/3, 4; 154/3-12.

Bhīṣma 16/9; 18/17; 46/13, 14; 58/3; 62/27; 76/4-6.

Droṇa, ch. 146 and 177.

The main weapons were as follows:

Aṅkuśa (goad made of iron); *aśmaguḍaka* (rounded piece of stone), *asi* (sword), variously called *viśasana*, *khaḍga*, *tīkṣṇadhāra*, *durāsada*, *śrīgarbha*, *vijaya*, *dharmapāla*, and *nistriṁśa* (*vide* Virāṭa 42/6 and Nīlakaṇṭha's comment thereon, Śānti, ch. 166).

Twenty-one modes of wielding the sword have been mentioned (Droṇa 190/37-40; Karṇa 25/31, 32). Some swords are stated to have been overlaid with ornamental work in gold.

Sheaths for swords appear to have been made of the leather of cows, tigers and of five-toed animals as also of gold. Perhaps the hides of rhinoceros and alligator (*godhā*) also were used for this purpose (Virāṭa, ch. 42, 43).

The other weapons were:

Bhalla — long, with curved tip (Ādi 139/6 and Nīlakaṇṭha's commentary).

Bhindipāla — cubit-long arrow or a mace to be hurled by the hand.

Bhusuṇḍi — a device, made of leather and rope, by which stones can be hurled (Ādi 227/25 with Nīlakaṇṭha's commentary)

Cakra — sharp-edged wheel.

Cakrāśma — a wooden mechanism which, while turning round, can throw even big slabs of stone (Ādi 227/25, Nīlakaṇṭha's commentary)

Dhanus — bow.

Gadā — see *supra*. (Udyoga 51/8).

Hala — plough.

Kacagraha-vikṣepa — a weapon which drags the enemy by his hairs, and brings him down to the ground (Udyoga, 154/5, Nīlakaṇṭha's commentary).

Kampana — ? (Bhīṣma 76/6).

Kaṇapa — a mechanical device of iron from inside which bullets, being hurled, spread on all sides (Ādi 227/25, Nīlakaṇṭha's commentary).

Karṇī — (Karṇa 81/12). The term occurs in *Manu* (VII.90) where Kullūka explains it as an arrow with ear-like blades.

Kṣura — a weapon with sharp edge, pointed tip and straight (Ādi, 139/6, Nīlakaṇṭha's commentary).

Kṣurapra — arrow sharp like a razor (Karṇa 25/36).

Kuliśa — same as *vajra* (*supra*).

Mudgara — see *supra*.

Musala — see *supra*.

Nakhara — a weapon sharp as nail.

Nālika — a kind of arrow.

Nārāca — a sharp-edged, straight iron arrow (Ādi 139/6 Nīlakaṇṭha's commentary).

Paraśvadha — see *supra*.

Parigha — see *supra* (Ādi 19/17 — Nīlakaṇṭha's commentary)

Pāśa — see *supra* (Udyoga 154/4, Nīlakaṇṭha's commentary)

Prāsa — see *supra* (Ādi 19/12, Nīlakaṇṭha's commentary), Vana 42/4).

Rathacakra — a chariot-wheel used as a missile.

Ṛṣṭi — see *supra* (Vana 20/34, Udyoga 154/2, Nīlakaṇṭha's commentary).

Śakti — see *supra* (Ādi 19/13, Nīlakaṇṭha's commentary).

Śara — arrow. It appears to have been of various kinds, e.g., made of iron, bamboo. There is reference to bird-feather (probably of vulture), attached to the base of the arrow, and to the arrow-base, overlaid with gold.

Śūla — perhaps same as *triśūla* (*supra*).

Tomara — see *supra* (Ādi 19/12, Nīlakaṇṭha's commentary).

Tulāguḍa — ? (Vana 42/5, Nīlakaṇṭha's commentary). It is described as a weapon, mounted on wheels, causing violent gusty wind and cracking sound (*vāyu-sphoṭa* and *nirghāta*).

Vipāṭha — a kind of broad-tipped arrow (Ādi 139/6, Nīlakaṇṭha's commentary).

Yamadaṁṣṭrā — ? Literally meaning the tooth of God of Death.

Yaṣṭi — stick.

In addition to the above, there are references to some other weapons. In Vana 154/45-8, we find *aśani*. It seems to have been carried on an eight-wheeled conveyance to a certain place from which it was hurled towards the target which was burnt. The Udyoga (181/1-14, 184/10-14) mentions the following three classes of weapons:

(i) *Prasvāpana* — inducing sleep among the soldiers of the enemy.

(ii) *Prabodha* — waking up the sleeping soldiers of the enemy.

(iii) *Brahmāstra* — causing conflagration in the enemy camp.

A strange weapon was the *tvāṣṭra* (Droṇa 18/11-15). It is stated to have caused the image of the person, using it, to be reflected on the face of the enemy.

Droṇa (151/12-15) refers to an eight-wheeled mechanical vehicle used against the enemy. Vana (23/2-9) mentions ground-to-air, air-to-ground and ground-to-ground missiles following the track of sound. The *Saubhapura* (Ādi 57/12-14, 63/11-14) appears to have been a flying mechanical contrivance.

The *Manu-smṛti* (VII.90) mentions *āyudha* (weapon), and adds the following adjectives: *kūṭa, karṇī, digdha* and *agni-jvalita-tejana*. The terms are explained by the commentator, Kullūka, as follows: *Kūṭa* means a secret sharp weapon covered with wood and the like. *Karṇī* stands for an arrow having an ear-shaped blade. *Digdha* means a poisoned arrow. The last term indicates an arrow with a blazing blade. Manu does not mention any other weapon.

Some Purāṇas contain information about weapons. In accordance with the mode of discharging weapons, the *Agni* (249/2) mentions four kinds, namely

(i) *Yantramukta* — discharged from a machine.

(ii) *Pāṇimukta* — thrown by hand.

(iii) *Mukta-sandhārita* — thrown and held; e.g., a noose which, while held in the hand, is hurled at the target.

(iv) *Amukta* — not discharged or thrown; e.g., a sword.

In places of the (iii) and (iv) above, the *Matsya* (215/40) reads *muktadhārita* and *vimukta*. The last one, perhaps, denotes arrow and other weapons thrown at the target. One wonders why *amukta* (sword, etc.) is not mentioned.

Some Purāṇas mention a few weapons, but do not describe them. It should be noted that, from different contexts, we learn of 42 kinds of weapons. The principal weapons mentioned are *āgneyāstra* (*Vāyu* 88/124,135), *aṅkuśa* (see *supra*), *aśani* (*Matsya* 162/31, *supra*), *asi* (same as *khaḍga* q.v.), *bhindipāla* (*Agni* 252/15, *Matsya* 162/32 — see *supra*), *bhusuṇḍi* (see *supra*), *cakra* (*Agni* 136, 236/29; *Matsya* 129/35. 217/32), *gadā* (*Agni* 252/12, *Matsya* 162/31 — see *supra*), *khaḍga* (*Matsya* 162/31, 217/30; *Agni* 245/17-27, 252/1-4), *kṛpāṇa* (*Agni* 252/17 — see *supra*), *kuliśa* (same as *aśani* q.v.), *kunta*, *kuṭhāra* (*Matsya* 217/31, same as *paraśu* q.v.), *paraśu* (*Agni* 252/13 — see below), *paraśvadha* (*Matsya* 217/32 — see *supra*), *pāśa* (*Agni* 251, 252/6, 7 — see *supra*), *paṭṭiśa* (*Agni* 252/16, *Matsya* 217/31 — see *supra*), *prāsa* (*Matsya* 162/31, 217/32 — see *supra*), *śakti* (*Matsya* 135/76, 150/79, 151/22, 153/208, 160/22, 163/12, etc., 217/32 — see *supra*), *śataghnī* (*Matsya* 129/35, 162/32, 177/11, 217/8 — see *supra*), *śatapatra*, *śūla* (*Agni* 252/9, *Matsya* 129/35, 217/32), *tomara* (*Matsya* 217/29, *Agni*, 252/10 — see *supra*), *triśūla* (*Matsya* 217/31 — see *supra*), *vajra* (*Agni* 236/29, 252/16; *Matsya* 162.31 — see *supra*).

Āgneyāstra, mentioned above, obviously denotes *fire-arms*, but it is not known how it was. We have seen that Manu refers to a kind of arrow with blazing blades. According to some, it is a mythical weapon, so-called because it was believed to be presided over by *agni* (fire).

The *Mastya Purāṇa* mentions (153/138) a weapon called *ayoguḍa*. According to different scholars, it may mean (i) iron-ball hurled from a sling; (ii) iron-bullet, and (iii) iron.

As regards *bāṇa* or arrow, we learn of the following types of arrow-heads:

Vatsa-danta — shaped like a calf's tooth.

Karṇika — ear-shaped.

Śatapatra — one hundred (does it mean many?) blades bundled together.

Ardhacandraka — crescent.

Gardhapatra — ?

Cakra, described as a disc-shaped weapon, is stated to have eight spokes, sometimes with sharp-toothed edges. Its functions in war are

> *Chedana* — piercing, *bhedana* — splitting, *pāta* (causing one to fall down ?), *śayana* (causing one to lie down ?).

We get a fairly detailed description of the *khaḍga* or sword. That which is *khaṭi-khaṭṭara-jāta* (*Agni* 245/21) is beautiful; the Sanskrit expression is obscure. One, made at the place, named Śūrpāraka (= Supārā to the north of Mumbai), is very strong. That, made in the region, called *arsika* (?), cuts the body. The one, made in Bengal, is sharp and capable of cutting. Swords are stated also to be made in Aṅga (part of Bihar about Bhāgalpur, including Monghyr). A sword, 150 *aṅgulas* (fingers) long, is the best. One, of half this length, is medium and a smaller one is the worst and should not be used. A sword, with its tip like a lotus-petal, and one with a round tip, are commendable. One, coloured like a crow or owl, is awkward and dangerous. Thirty-two modes of holding swords have been mentioned.

Four functions of the *kṛpāṇa*, mentioned above, are *haraṇa* (causing loss of life?), *chedana* (cutting), *ghāta* (hitting), *baloddharaṇa* (?) and *āyata* (causing a wide injury?). Seven modes of wielding it have been mentioned.

Kṣepaṇa(-ya), mentioned in *Agni* (252/16) and *Matsya* (217/29), appears to have been a sling or an instrument with which missiles could be hurled.

Mudgara (*Matsya* 162,32, 217/31; *Agni* 252/14), variously rendered as hammer, mallet, club, mace, etc.) appears to have been a sharp weapon made of iron. Its functions in a battle are stated as follows:

> *Tāḍana* (beating), *chedana* (cutting), *cūrṇana* (pulverising), *plāvana* (? the ordinary meaning of flooding or inundating does not suit the context) and *ghātana* (killing).

A weapon, called *nālika*, has been mentioned at some places. The following meanings of it have been suggested : (a) a kind of metallic arrow, (b) a sort of barbed missile, (c) a kind of gun, (d) arrow discharged with the help of a hollow tube (*nalikā*).

The above-mentioned *paraśu* is generally identified with *kuṭhāra* (axe). According to *Kauṭilīya Arthaśāstra* (Book II, ch. 18) *kuṭhāra* and *paraśu* are of different kinds. The functions of the axe in battle are stated as follows :

> *karāla* (causing gaping injury ?), *ayoghāta* (hitting with iron ?), *daṁśa* (?), *upapluta* (causing the enemy's body to be smeared with blood ?), *kṣiptahasta* (hurled by the hand), *sthita* (striking while held in hand ?), *śūnya* (thrown into

the air so that it can fall on the enemy ?).

As regards *pāśa*, it is described as ten cubits long and circular; the strings are made of *kārpāsa* cotton, *muñja* grass or *bhagna-snāyu* (broken guts or bow-string). It may also be made of strong thongs. Thirty strings should be rolled into one. It is held in the left hand, and hurled at the enemy with the right. The modes of holding the noose in battle are stated to be eleven. The modes of throwing it are stated to be five.

Śakti, mentioned above, is described thus. Resounding with golden or gold-plated bells, it is sharp and fierce. While falling down, it appears like a big fire-brand with sparks falling from the sky. It is shining and elevated at the top.

Śarapañjara is interesting. Literally, it means a cage of *śara*s or arrows. It probably means a number of arrows discharged from all sides so as to form a sort of cage with the target inside it.

It should be noted that there is mention also of *bāhu-yuddha* or duel fought with the hands only. The term *niyuddha* was used to denote close personal fight in which no weapons were used. It was a sort of wrestling bout, also called *dvandva-yuddha* and *bāhukaṇṭaka-yuddha*. Such fights were of various kinds, e.g., *kṛta* (torturing any part of the enemy's body), *susaṅkaṭa* (tightening the grip), *sannipāta* (rubbing one's body with that of the enemy, etc.), *avadhūta* (throwing away the enemy to some distance), *pramātha* (pressing the enemy very hard after felling him on the ground), etc. See *Mahābhārata*, Virāṭa, ch. 13, Nīlakaṇṭha's commentary. The *Agni Purāṇa* (252/19-23) mentions various modes of *niyuddha*. The term *vimāna* in *Agni* (252/21) has led some scholars (e.g., P. Sen Sarma, *Military Wisdom in the Purāṇas*, p. 121) to think that *niyuddha*, in Purāṇas, means aerial fight. As a matter of fact, it was a kind of *niyuddha*.

Military Array (*Vyūha*)

There are specific descriptions of the modes in which soldiers are to be arranged in a battlefield. The *Arthaśāstra* provides for four basic kinds of array; these are called *daṇḍa* (see under *Manu-smṛti*), *bhoga* (like a serpent), *maṇḍala* (circular) and *asaṁhata* (loose).

Each of these has been subdivided into several kinds (*Arthaśāstra*, X.6.3.43).

Bhoga is of unequal depth in its wings, flanks and the van. *Maṇḍala* has its wings, flanks and the van close to one another without intervening space. In the *asaṁhata* type, these are apart from one another.

The following *vyūhas* are mentioned in the *Mahābhārata*; all the *vyūhas* have not been described.

Ardhacandra — (Bhīṣma 56/11-18) with a very famous hero on the right, many heroes on the left, a group of elephant-soldiers in the middle.

Krauñca or *krauñcāruṇa* — (Bhīṣma 50/40-58, Droṇa 6/15). Soldiers arrayed in the form of a curlew. A famous fighter will be in the forefront. Another hero, with a band of soldiers, will remain on the imaginary head of the bird. Thus, one hero, accompanied by a group of soldiers, will remain ready on each of the imaginary limbs, e.g., eyes, neck, wing, back, tail, etc.

Garuḍa (*Suparṇa*) — (Bhīṣma 75/15-26, Droṇa 19/4). Arrayed in the form of the mythical bird *garuḍa*, the mount of Viṣṇu. Two heroes, with two bands of soldiers, will be ready on the imaginary head. A larger number of soldiers will be stationed in the imaginary tail and back. The two wings will be widespread and long.

Cakra — (Droṇa 33/13). The name indicates its form.

Vajra — (Bhīṣma 19/7).

Makara — (Bhīṣma 69/4-6, 75/4-12). It has a hero with soldiers in the van, and, in the rear, are charioteers, infantry and elephant-soldiers in succession.

Maṇḍalārdha — (Droṇa 19/4).

Śakaṭa or *Cakraśakaṭa* — (Droṇa 6/15, 73/27, 85/21). The rear is lotus-shaped.

Śṛṅgāṭaka — (Bhīṣma 87/17). Shaped like a *Śṛṅgāṭaka*; this word may denote a particular aquatic plant or crossing of four roads. According to Nīlakaṇṭha, it looks like a crossing of four roads.

Śyena — (Bhīṣma 69/7-12). Of the form of a hawk.

Sarvatobhadra — (Bhīṣma 99/1-8.) Round with soldiers and ordinary fighters within and guarded on all sides by renowned heroes.

Sāgara — (Bhīṣma 87/5). Extensive like a sea.

Sūcīmukha — (Bhīṣma 19/5, 77/59; Śānti 100/40). This form of array is necessary when the rival soldiers are larger in number. Besides the above arrays, the heroes are stated to have resorted to different kinds of *maṇḍalas*. *Maṇḍala* means the change of the course of chariots, etc., having ascertained the weakness of the enemy.

The *Manu-smṛti* (VII.187, 188) mentions the following *vyūhas*; their descriptions, according to commentator, Kullūka, are given below:

Daṇḍa — like a stick with the commander in the van, the king in the middle; the General at the rear, elephants at the flanks, heroes near them, then the infantry. It is necessary when danger is apprehended on all sides.

Śakaṭa —
like a cart. The van is like a needle and the rear wide. It should be formed when there is danger at the rear.

Varāha —
like a boar. Slender in van and rear, but wide in the middle.

Garuḍa —
like *varāha*, but wider in the middle. *Varāha* and *garuḍa* are necessary when danger is apprehended from the sides.

Makara —
like a shark. The opposite of *varāha*. It should be formed when there is danger both at the van and the rear.

Sūcī —
like a needle. It resembles a row of ants, with soldiers closely following one another.

Padma —

like a lotus with the king at the centre, surrounded by soldiers who are evenly distributed.

Vajra —

in it troops are arranged in three ways.

The *Agni Purāṇa* (ch. 242) mentions and describes a number of *vyūha*s which are classified into four groups the names of which are identical with those of the four basic types of Kauṭilya, mentioned above.

Defensive Weapons

The *Mahābhārata* mentions *varman* (Virāṭa 31/15, Karṇa 81/27), *tanu-trāṇa* or *kavaca* (Virāṭa 31/10-14, Udyoga 152/21) and *godhāṅguli-trāṇa* (Virāṭa 5/1, Ādi 134/23). As regards *varman*, it appears to have been made mostly of iron. In connection with *kavaca*, it has been stated that a variety of it was overlaid with ornamental work of gold. Various pictures were painted over a particular type of *kavaca*. *Aṅguli-trāṇa* (finger-protector) was meant for the protection of the fingers of an archer. It appears to have been made of alligator's leather.

The following are mentioned in the Purāṇas

Carman (*Agni* 252/4; *Matsya* 217.32) — Shield usually made of the hide of rhinoceros. The modes of wielding it are stated to be thirty-two.

Kavaca (*Matsya* 217/30) — Armour which appears to have been of various types.

Kheṭa(ka): Perhaps shield in general.

Sannāha: Same as *kavaca* (q.v.). *Sannāha* occurs also in the *Manu-smṛti* VII.92.

Śirastrāṇa: Helmet made of metals or non-metallic material.

Varman: (*Matsya* 217/32, *Agni* 251/9-12, *Mārkaṇḍeya* ch. 123) Same as *kavaca* (q.v.). The way of using it appears to have been different.

Ethics in War

The wise people of ancient India did not believe in the principle that nothing is unfair in war. They would not have supported Hiroshima and Nagasaki types of holocaust, caused by war.

MANU-SMṚTI

Manu, for example, provides the humane rule that a secret weapon (e.g., a sharp weapon hidden in a wooden cover), arrows with ear-shaped or flaming blades, poisoned arrows, etc. (VII. 90), should not be used against the enemy. The following persons should not be killed:

> enemy on the ground (while the rival fighter is on a chariot), an eunuch, one with folded hands (indicating surrender), one with dishevelled hairs), a sitting person, one who says — I am yours, (i.e., declares surrender), one in sleep, a person devoid of armour, an onlooker who is not fighting, one fighting with another person, naked person, one who is not armed, one whose weapons are broken, an ailing person, one who is grievously injured, one who is alarmed, one who is running away (VII.91-3).

MAHĀBHĀRATA

Besides the practices forbidden by Manu for a warrior, the following main moral principles are laid down in the Epic (e.g., Śānti 95/7-17, Vana 18/13, 14, Karṇa 69/25, 26, Śalya 60/6-24, etc.).

> Everyday, after the cessation of battle, the parties will treat each other in a friendly way. One who is engaged in verbal duel, must be fought verbally. Fight must be between equal rivals; for example, one on a chariot should fight with the enemy who is also in a chariot. An enemy should be addressed before hitting him. One, engaged in some other work, should not be struck. A charioteer, the mounts like horse or elephant and a performer of war-music should not be hit. One, who fights in conformity with moral principles, should be fought in a similar manner, but an immoral

> fighter should be encountered immorally. The Epic categorically prohibits the killing of women, minors and the old in battle. Hitting the enemy below his navel is forbidden; this accords well with the principle of later times that condemns striking below the belt.

It should be noted that the Epic itself contains instances of flagrant violation of some of the above principles. Attack at night is mentioned in Droṇa, ch. 152, Karṇa ch. 160. The killing of Bhīṣma, Droṇa and Karṇa through deceitful means is a glaring example of flouting the ethical principles inculcated in the Epic. Bhīma is stated to have shattered the knees of his formidable adversary, Duryodhana.

PURĀṆAS

The Purāṇas do not appear to bother about the ethical norms of war prescribed by earlier authorities. There are instances of many warriors attacking a single fighter in the opposite camp (e.g., *Matsya*, ch. 135; *Mārkaṇḍeya*, ch. 123, *Padma*, *Pātāla* ch. 33, etc.). We find also instances of hitting the charioteer and the mounts like elephants and horses of the enmy (e.g., *Matsya* ch. 150, *Vāmana* ch. 10, etc.).

ARTHAŚĀSTRA

One, going through the *Arthaśāstra*, is apt to form the impression that the author always prefers expendiency to morality in political matters. In fairness to the author, it should be stated that, according to him, so long as a fair fight (*dharmiṣṭha yuddha* 10/3) is possible, a king should not deviate from the moral principles in war (13/4) which are almost the same as those laid down by Manu. But, when the object of a king cannot be achieved by this means, he is advised to resort to deceitful and violent means. *Dharmiṣṭha yuddha* (righteous war) is called *prakāśa-yuddha* (7/6). On failure of it, a king is advised to resort to *kūṭa-yuddha* or deceitful war (*ibid*). In an extreme case, *tūṣṇīṁ-yuddha* (*ibid*) is recommended. The tactics in it are administering poison and sowing seeds of dissension in the enemy's side through spies.

Fort

Durga (fort) was regarded as one of the essential things of a kingdom. It was rightly so, because the security of the king was indispensable for him to function properly. The fort protected the king not only against foreign enemies but also from those in his own kingdom. A rebellious prince and the disaffected royal functionaries might attack the monarch. The word *durga*, meaning a place difficult of access, is very old. For instance, the Upaniṣad declares *durgaṁ pathastat*, i.e., the path (of human qualities) is difficult to traverse. The fort, which was the resort of the king, was generally in the capital of the kingdom concerned; there were also forts outside the capital. According to the *Yājñavalkya-smṛti* (I.321), the fort is necessary for not only the security of the person of a king, but also for the safety of his people and the treasury (*jana-kośātma-guptaye*).

That the king in ancient India used to live at a fortified place is borne out by the *Ṛgveda*. For instance, in *ṚV*, II.20.8, Indra is stated to have destroyed the *dasyus*' cities of *ayas* (copper); this tends to point to the fact that walled cities existed even in that hoary age. Megasthenes (*c*. 302 BC) testified that the city of Pāṭaliputra was surrounded by a wall of wooden palisades.

The *Manu-smṛti* (VII.70) names the following kinds of *durgas*; we describe them after the commentator, Kullūlka:

1. *Dhanva-durga* — surrounded by deserts and devoid of water up to five *yojanas* (1 *yojana* = eight or nine miles). One wonders how the king and the people, living in it, could procure water. May be that the *durga* contained tanks, etc., but the surrounding areas up to the above distance was without water, thus rendering it difficult for the enemy to reach the fort.

2. *Mahī-durga* — encircled by a rampart of stone or brick, higher than 12 cubits, the height being twice the width and fit for the movement of the army, over it, for battle and provided with covered windows.

3. *Ab-durga* — surrounded by a very deep moat.

4. *Vārkṣa-durga* — having outside, in all directions up to one *yojana* (see supra), huge trees, thorny shrubs and creepers, etc.
5. *Nṛ-durga* — guarded, on all sides, by many foot-soldiers equipped with elephants, horses and chariots.
6. *Giri-durga* — mountain-top accessible with difficulty only through a narrow pass; within it there are rivers, falls, etc., and many corn fields and trees.

In the next verse, Manu recommends the last one as the best. As regards the utility of *durgas*, Manu holds (VII.74) that one archer on a rampart can fight with a hundred rival soldiers or a hundred archers on a rampart can battle with ten thousand adversaries.

The *Mahābhārata* (Śānti 86/4, 5) also mentions the same kinds of a *durgas* with *mṛd-durga* for *mahī-durga*. Some think that *mṛd* is a misreading, because it means the same as *mahī*. It may, however, be noted that *mahī*, according to Kullūka, here means stone or brick. *Mṛd* is *mṛthikā* or clay. We find houses, walls, etc., made of clay. It should be noted that, according to Śānti (56/35), *nṛ-durga* is the most difficult to conquer.

The *Arthaśāstra* (II. 3) names four main types of forts, these are *audaka*, *pārvata*, *dhānvana* and *vana*. Each of these has been divided into two kinds. *Audaka* may be of two kinds — (i) that which is surrounded by river and the like; and (ii) that which is surrounded by deep tanks, etc. *Pārvata* may be (i) made of rocky stone, and (ii) that which is a natural cave. *Dhānvana* may be (i) devoid of water and grass, and (ii) arid or sandy. *Vana-durga* may be difficult of access (i) due to loam and slush all around, and (ii) due to densely grown trees. Kauṭilya ordains that forts should be built in all directions in the periphery of the kingdom for resisting the enemy. He also advises the laying out of the capital in one of them.

Some Purāṇas mention various types of forts. The number of types is six in each of them. But, besides the following three types, common to them, the others are differently named:

Fort surrounded by water or moat (called *audaka*, or *ambu* or *jala*).

Fort in the midst of trees all around (called *vārkṣa* or *vṛkṣa*).

Fort on a mountain (*giri*, *parvata* or *śaila*).

The other types, mentioned in the *Bṛhaddharma* (ch. 33), are *bhūmi*, *vana* and *parikhāta*. The *Agni* (239/29) names *airiṇa*, *dhānvana* and *kālasaha* (?). The *Matsya* (217/6-7) names *dhanu*, *mahī* and *nara*. *Dhanu-durga* appears to be a mistake for *dhanur-durga* or desert fort (see Monier Williams, *Skt.-Eng. Dictionary*). The *Viṣṇudharmottara* (Khaṇḍa II, chap. 26, verses 6-7) mentions *dhanva*, *mahī* and *nara*, *airiṇa* is derived obviously from *iriṇa*. *Iriṇa*, according to Monier Williams, may mean, in Classical Sanskrit, a desert, an inhospitable region, a bare plain, barren soil and salt soil. Which meaning is intended here is not clear. If it is taken in the sense of desert, then the next word *dhanvana*, also meaning desert, becomes redundant. If taken to convey any other of the above meanings, then a fort in such a place as becomes unfit for human habitation.

The *Vāyu Purāṇa* (ch. 8, verse 108), however, states that *durgas* are of four kinds; of them, three are natural (*sva-samutthāni trīṇi*), and one is artificial (*kṛtrima*). The last one contains high rise mansions, has a surrounding wall and a moat of deep water; its gate should be connected with a bridge.

Glossary

The following abbreviations have been used:

A — *Arthaśāstra* | *Al* — *Alaṁkāra-śāstra*

As — *Aśva-śāstra* | *Ay* — *Āyurveda*

C — *Chandaḥ-śāstra* | *D* — *Darśana-śāstra*.

G — *Gaja-śāstra* | *J* — *Jyotiṣa-śāstra*

K — *Kāma-śāstra* | *Kr̥* — *Kr̥ṣi-śāstra*

N — *Nāṭya-śāstra* | *S* — *Saṁgīta-śāstra*

Sm — *Smr̥ti*

T — *Tantra* | *U* — *Udbhid-vidyā*

Vy — *Vyākaraṇa*

Ābhāsa (*D*): (1) Unreal or fallacious appearance.

(2) The processes of manifestation of the universe, according to the *Trika* system of Kāśmīr, is called *ābhāsana* or *ābhāsa*. The above manifestation is the expression of the ideas or the experience of Parama Śiva. The *ābhāsa* of the *Trika* system is much the same as the *vivartta* (q.v.) of the Vedānta with some marked difference. According to those, who recognise *vivartta*, the appearances are mere names and forms (*nāma-rūpa*) which are not essentially real, being for ever non-existent in the Supreme Reality which, according to the Vedānta, is *Brahman*. The *ābhāsavādin*s, however, hold that the appearances are real inasmuch as they are aspects of the Ultimate Reality which, according to the *Trika*, is Parama Śiva. *Ābhāsa* is the name of that

process by which the source, revealing manifestations, itself remains unaffected and undivided.

Abdurga (*Sm*): A fort surrounded by deep water.

Ābalīyasa (*A*): Guiding principles for a king weaker than the king hostile to him.

Abhāva (*D*, *Vy*): Non-existence. It stands for all negative facts, and is of four kinds, viz., *prāgabhāva*, *dhvaṁsābhāva*, *ātyantābhāva* and *anyonyābhāva*. The first means the non-existence of a thing before (*prāk*) its production, e.g., the non-existence of a pot in clay before it is made by the potter. The second means the non-existence of an object after its destruction (*dhvaṁsa*) e.g., the non-existence of a pot after it is broken up. The third is the absolute absence of a thing at all times, e.g., the non-existence of colour in air. The fourth is the mutual non-existence of two different things, e.g., the jar is not the cloth and *vice versa*. The first three together are called *saṁsargābhāva*.

Abhicāra (Sm, *T*): Magic spells or rites for malevolent purposes, viz., killing an enemy (*māraṇa*), causing paralysis (*stambhana*), expulsion (*uccāṭana*), bringing one under control (*vaśīkaraṇa*), creating bad blood (*vidveṣaṇa*), pacification (*śānti*). Instead of *śānti*, *mohana* (causing delusion) is also found.

Abhidhā (*Al*): Denotation. The function by which a word denotes its primary or conventional sense.

Abhidhāna (*Vy*): Designation, denotation. It is usually done by means of *tiṅ*, *kṛt*, *taddhita* and *samāsa*.

Abhihitānvayavāda (*D*): This view of a school of Mīmāṁsakas is thus explained by Mammaṭa, the author of *Kāvyaprakāśa*: when the meanings of the words are connected in accordance with expectancy, compatibility and proximity, another sense arises called purport, which has a distinct form and which, though not constituting the sense of the words, is yet the sense of the sentence. See *Kāvyaprakāśa*, ii, 1. *Vṛtti* as explained by S.K. De in *Sanskrit Poetics* II, p. 149 (1960).

Ābhīkṣṇya (*Vy*): Repetition of an action.

Abhiśasta (*Sm*): Used in the following senses:

(i) Murderer of a brāhmaṇa.

(ii) Murderer of a woman who is Ātreyī (q.v.).

(iii) One guilty of a mortal sin.

(iv) Murderer of a person of the brāhmaṇa or kṣatriya caste, who has studied the Veda or has been initiated for some sacrifice.

(v) One who has destroyed the foetus of a brāhmaṇa.

Abhiṣeka (*T*): A kind of Tāntric *dīkṣā* (initiation). The *guru* performs different forms of *abhiṣeka* for his disciple in the different stages of the spiritual life of the latter. *Abhiṣeka* is of eight kinds.

Abhividhi (*Vy*): Limit inclusive. It is of two kinds, viz., *kālika* (relating to time) and *daiśika* (relating to place). *Kārtikyāḥ caitraṁ yāvat śītam* is an example of the former; it means that winter lasts from *Kārttika* up to *Caitra* (inclusive). *Kāśītaḥ pāṭaliputraṁ yāvat vṛṣṭo devaḥ* is an example of the latter; it means that it rained from Kāśī up to the region, called Pāṭaliputra (inclusive).

Abhivyaktivāda (*Al*): Doctrine of Abhinavagupta. According to this view, *rasa* is revealed by *vyañjanā* (q.v.).

Abhyāsa (*D*, *Vy*): Reduplication, repetition. In grammar it stands for the earlier part of a reduplicated root. For example, in *bhub bhub*, the first *bhub* is called *abhyāsa*.

Abhyasta (*Vy*): That which undergoest *abhyāsa* (q.v.) is called *abhyasta*.

Ābhyudayika (*Sm*): Same as *Vṛddhi-śrāddha* (q.v.).

Ācārya (*Sm*): (i) One who, having performed the *upanayana* of his pupil, teaches him the Veda together with the Kalpasūtra and the Upaniṣads.

(ii) One from whom the pupil learns his duties.

Ādeśa (*Vy*): Substitute as contradistinguished from *sthānin*, the origin.

Ādhāna (*Sm*): Pledging or mortgaging.

Ādhi (*Sm*): Pledging or mortgage of a chattel or immovable property to the creditor himself with or without possession.

Adhikāra-sūtra (*Vy*): Leading or governing rule. The aphorism that serves to make the following rule or rules complete. It is of four kinds, viz. *Goyūtha*, *Siṁhadṛṣṭi*, *Maṇḍūkapluti* and *Gaṅgā-srotaḥ-pravāha*. For example, the rule *kārake* (I.4.23) leads the rules about *kāraka* that follows.

Adhikaraṇa (*D, Vy*): Substratum. A complete argument treating of one subject. According to the followers of Mīmāṁsā and Vedānta, a complete *adhikaraṇa* consists of five members, viz., *viṣaya*, *saṁśaya*, *pūrvapakṣa*, *uttara* and *siddhānta*. Locative case in grammar.

Adhimāsa (*J*): That lunar month in which the sun does not pass to a Zodiac. Or, that solar month in which there is *kṣaya* of two New Moons. Intercalary month. See *malamāsa*.

Adhi-māsa (*Sm*): Same as *malamāsa* (q.v.).

Adhivastra: Part of a garment; outer cover or veil.

Adhivedana (*Sm*): Marrying another woman when there is already the lawfully wedded wife.

Ādhivedanika (*Sm*): A kind of *strīdhana*, presented to a woman by her husband on his marrying another woman.

Ādhmāna (*Ay*): Flatulence.

Adhyagni (*Sm*): A kind of *strīdhana*, given to a girl at the time of her marriage, before the nuptial fire.

Adhyāhāra (*D, Vy*): Supplying words not stated. For example, in *rathastham̐ vāmanam̐ dr̥ṣṭvā punarjanma na vidyate*, the words *sthitasya janasya* have to be supplied between *dr̥ṣṭvā* and *punarjanma* for grammatical accuracy.

Adhyavāhanika (*Sm*): A kind of *strīdhana*, obtained by a woman while taken from her father's house to that of the husband.

Adhyāsa (*D*): False attribution, wrong supposition, e.g., nacre mistaken for silver.

Ādhibindu (*J*): In the *rāśi-cakra* the end of Revatī *nakṣatra* and the beginning of Aśvinī *nakṣatra*.

Aditi (*A*): A woman who collects alms by showing images of deities.

Advaita (*D*): Absence of duality, non-dualism. According to this doctrine, advocated by Śaṅkarācārya and his followers, *Brahman* is the only One Reality, and the world is not real but an appearance which *Brahman* conjures up with His inscrutable power, called *māyā*.

[See L.S. Betty, *Vādiraja's Refutation of Śam̐kara's Non-dualism*, Delhi, 1978.]

Āgama (*Sm*, *Vy*): Valid mode of acquisition of a property, e.g., inheritance, purchase, gift, etc.

Augment, added to the primitive or basic word, during the process of formation of a complete word.

Agnihotra (*Sm*): Oblation to *Agni*, the sacred fire.

[See P.E. Dumont, *Agnihotra*; P.D. Navathe, *Agnihotra of the Kaṭha Śākhā*, Poona, 1980.]

Agniṣṭoma (*Sm*): Name of a ceremony or sacrifice forming one of the chief modifications of the *Jyotiṣṭoma* offered by one desirous of obtaining heaven. The performer is a brāhmaṇa maintaining the sacred fire; the offering is the *soma*; the deities are Indra, etc., the number of requisite priests is 16; the ceremonies continue for five days.

[See W. Caland and H. Henry, *L'Agniṣṭoma*, 2 Vols.,

Paris, 1906-7.]

Agrayaṇa: A religious rite in which the first crop, harvested in the season, is offered to deities.

Agredidhiṣu (*Sm*): Younger sister married before the elder.

Āhārya (*N*): The kind of acting in which the actor represents the states or conditions of a person by means of his appearance or dress.

Āhavanīya (*Sm*): Name of one of the fires with which Vedic sacrifices are to be performed.

Āhiṇḍika (*Sm*): One born of a *niṣāda* (q.v.) by a *vaideha* (q.v.) female. A class of men who used to serve as gate-keepers and watchmen.

Ajapā (*T*): A kind of effortless meditation. The sounds *haṁ* and *saḥ*, arising automatically within the body due to inhalation and exhalation, constitute this *mantra*.

Ajātavāda (*D*): A Buddhist doctrine according to which there is nothing like origin of the universe.

Ajahalliṅga (*Vy*): The word that never gives up its gender, e.g., *bhājanam*, *pātram*, etc.

Ājñā (*T*): See *Cakra*.

Akarṣa: A kind of game played on a board.

Ākhyāta (*Vy*): Verb, verbal form.

Ākhyāyikā (*Ay*): A composition in prose with a historical theme.

Ākranda (*Sm*, *A*): The king ruling over a territory just beyond that of Pārṣṇigrāha (q.v.). The rear friend of a neighbouring king.

Ākrandāsāra (*Sm*, *A*): The king of the territory just beyond that of the Pārṣṇigrāhasāra (q.v.). A friend of the Ākranda (q.v.).

Ākṛtigaṇa, (*Vy*): A group or class of words in which some words are stated and there is scope for including other words undergoing the same operation.

Akṛtya (*A*): A person who cannot be alineated from his own king, and seduced to owe allegiance to another king.

Akṣa (*A*): (i) The number five and its multiples; (ii) A weight.

Akṣapaṭala (*A*): The records and audit office.

Akṣabhā (*J*): Shadow of gnomon at noon or on the day of vernal equinox.

Akṣajyā (*J*): Sine of latitude.

Ākṣepa (*D*): Inference or postulation (*arthāpatti*).

Akusīda (*D*): One who does not hanker after the fruit or result like the attainment of *siddhi* (?)

Āḷāpa (*S*): Name given to the practice of demonstrating or spreading out a *rāga* without any wording and *tāla*.

Ālīḍha (*T*): A particular posture of an archer who stretches his right knee forward, and retreats his left leg.

Āmukha (*N*): Same as *prastāvanā* (q.v.).

Alpa-prāṇa (*Vy*): Non-aspirate letter, also called unaspirate. The first and third consonants of each class or group (*varga*); the nasals and the semi-vowels belongs to this category.

Āmāśaya (*Ay*): Receptacle of undigested food.

Āmātisāra (*Ay*): Dysentery.

Amātya (*Sm*, *A*): In early times, a companion of a king. Later a minister generally of a lower rank or *karma-saciva*, one of the seven limbs (*aṅga*) of the State.

Āmavāta (*Ay*): Acute rheumatism.

Ambaṣṭha (*Sm*): One sprung from the union of a brāhmaṇa male and a vaiśya female.

Āmreḍita (*Vy*): The latter portion of a reduplicated word. For example, in *Upary-upari*, the latter portion is called *āmreḍita*.

Amṛta (*Sm*): (1) Food obtained without begging; (2) Remnants of what is offered in a sacrifice.

Aṁśa (*S*): The note that manifests the *rañjakatva* (the quality of causing delight) of a song; the note whose *saṁvādī* and *anuvādī* are largely perceived and, being used as *graha* (q.v.), *nyāsa* (q.v.) in singing is abundantly felt. Abundance and pervasion in *rāgas* are the characteristics of *aṁśa*.

Aṁśa (*J*): 1/360 part of a circle or 1/90 of a right angle.

Aṁśapatha (*A*): Land-route, an overbridge.

Anabhihita (*Vy*): Not specified generally by anyone of the following: Verbal affix, *kr̥t* affix, *taddhita* affix and compound. Sometimes the specification is done by *nipāta* (q.v.).

Ānaddha (*S*): See *vādya*.

Anadhyāya (*Sm*): Suspension of study caused by a number of factors, e.g., disturbance in village, conflagration, *amāvasyā*, *paurṇamāsī* of certain months, storm, rainfall, eclipse, earthquake, etc.

Anāhata (*T*): See *cakra*.

Anavasthā (*D*): Infinite regress. Absence of finality or conclusion, an endless series of statements of causes and effects; a fault of reasoning.

Andhra (*Sm*): One sprung from the union of a Vaidehaka (q.v.) male and a Kārāvara (q.v.) female.

Anekaparigrahā: A prostitute attached to many persons.

Aṅgādhikāra (*Vy*): Portion of the *Aṣṭādhyāyī* covering VI.4.1 to end of ch. VII.

Aṅganyāsa (*T*): Touching certain limbs with the hand, accompanied by proper *mantras*.

Aṅgahāra (*N*): Graceful rhythmic movement of limbs, especially of the sides or flanks, or the bending of the body in accordance with *tāla*.

Āṅgika (*N*): Acting in which there is expression of feelings by gestures.

Anna-prāśana (*Sm*): Name of the ceremony in which a child is fed with rice for the first time after birth. It is to be held in the sixth month from the child's birth, according to Yājñavalkya.

Antapāla (*A*): The chief person in charge of the frontiers of a kingdom.

Antarāla (*Sm*): A sub-caste sprung from the union of a male born in a *pratiloma* (q.v.) marriage and a female born in an *anuloma* (q.v.) marriage.

Antarvaṁśika (*A*): Principal guard of a royal harem.

Antaryāga (*T*, *D*): Mental worship.

Antra-vṛddhi (*Ay*): Hernia.

Antyāvasāyin (*Sm*): A mixed caste sprung from the union of a cāṇḍāla (q.v.) male and a niṣāda female.

Anubandha (*D*, *Ay*, *Vy*): According to Vedānta, it stands for the four, namely *viṣaya*, *prayojana*, *adhikārī* and *sambandha*. In *Ay*, it means the absence of the excess of *vāta*, *pitta*, etc. In grammar, it stands for a letter, technically called 'it' (that which is elided), belonging to *prakṛti*, *pratyaya*, *āgama* or *ādeśa*. For example, '*k*' in the suffix *kta* is an *Anubandha*. When added to, say, the root *bhū*, '*k*' is elided and the form obtained is *bhūta*.

Anubhāva (*Al*): Ensuant. It follows and strengthens a mood and comprises such outward manifestations of feeling as sidelong glance, smile, movement of the body. It is a factor of *rasa* (q.v.).

Anūcāna (*Sm*): One who has mastered the Vedas and the Vedāṅgas.

Anudātta (*Vy*): Grave accent which is produced from the lower places of articulation in the mouth.

Anuloma (*Sm*): In regular order; generally applied to marriage between a male of the higher caste and a female of the lower.

Anumāna (*D*): Inference as a means of valid knowledge.

Anumiti-vāda (*Al*): The doctrine of Śaṅkuka, according to which *rasa* (q.v.) is inferred.

Anunāsika (*Vy*): Nasal letter, i.e., a letter uttered simultaneously through both the nose and the mouth.

Anupala (*J*): A measure of time equal to 1/60 *vipala*.

Anupalabdhi (*D*): Non-perception. It is the source, according to a school of Mīmāṁsā, of our immediate cognition of the non-existence of an object. For example, the non-existence of a jar is known by non-perception of it.

Anupapatti (*D*): Logical non-consequence, absence of validity; discord.

Anu-pātaka (*Sm*): A class of sins comprising falsehood, theft, adultery, etc.

Anuśaya (*Sm*, *A*, *D*): (1) Revocation, annulment. (2) Dormant passion according to Buddhists.

Anuvādī (*S*): The note that makes the *saṁvādī* note clearer. Literally, it means the note that follows the note called *vādī* (q.v.). In the works on music, all notes other than *saṁvādī* and *vivādī* are called *anuvādī*.

Anuvākyā (*mantra*) (*D*): Formula of invitation to gods.

Anuvr̥tti (*Vy*): Continuity, repetition. When a particular aphorism or a part of it is necessary for completing the sense of a following aphorism, it is said that the former has *anuvr̥tti*. The repetition is sometimes continuous when the word or words concerned are repeated in the immediately following rules. Sometimes the *anuvr̥tti* applies not to the immediately following rules but to the remote ones.

Anvādheyaka (*Sm*): A kind of *strīdhana*, obtained by a woman, after her marriage, from her husband or parents.

Anvāhita (*Sm*): Sub-mortgage, i.e., mortgage of a property by the mortgagee.

Anvaṣṭakā (*Sm*): The ninth day in the latter half of the three (or four) months following the full moon in *Agrahāyaṇa*. *Pauṣa*, *Māgha* and *Phālguna*.

Anvaya-vyatireka (*D*): *Anvaya* means agreement in presence between two things, e.g., where there is smoke, there is fire, *Vyatireka* means agreement in absence between two things. For example, where there is no smoke there is no fire. *Anvaya-vyatireka*, therefore, holds when both the above relations are present. *Anvaya* ordinarily means logical connection of words.

Ānvīkṣikī (*Sm*, *D*): (i) *Tarka-vidyā* or Logic.

(ii) *Ātma-vidyā* or spiritual knowledge.

(iii) Sāṁkhya, Yoga and Lokāyata (*Kauṭilīya Arthaśāstra*, I.2).

(*Lokāyata* in this context has been taken in the sense of *Nyāyaśāstra*).

Anviābhidhānavāda (*D*): Doctrine of a school of Mīmāṁsakas. According to it, words have a power to denote not only things but also their purport or connection along with them. In other words, words do not express their sense generally but connectedly. They reject the view of the *Abhihitānvaya-vādins*, and deny the necessity of postulating the function of *tātparya*. See S.K. De, *Sanskrit Poetics*, II, p. 149, 1960.

Anyathā-khyāti (*D*): Error. For example, a mother of pearl is erroneously assumed to be silver.

Apādāna (*Vy*): Ablative case; the limit of separation.

Apa-Pātra (*Sm*) (1) Cāṇḍālas, etc., with whom no social intercourse is possible.

(2) Rajakas, etc., born in the reverse order of marriage.

(3) One ostracised by kinsmen for the commission of some degrading sin. Literally, one not allowed to use vessels out of which members of other castes are to take food.

Aparā-vidyā (*D*): The kind of knowledge leading to the acquisition of the desired things. The scripture that lays down rites and rituals. According to *Muṇḍaka Upaniṣad*, the *vidyā* comprises the four Vedas and the six Vedāṅgas.

Aparigrahā: A prostitute not attached to a particular individual.

Apasarpa (*A*): A secret agent, spy.

Apātrīkaraṇa (*Sm*): A class of sins rendering the sinner unworthy of receiving gifts. Acceptance of money from condemned persons, trade, service of śūdras, to utter and untruth — these are sins of this class for a brāhmaṇa.

Apavāda (*D*, *Vy*): Special rule, exception.

False statement, according to Sāṁkhya. A special injunction to bar out a false object, according to the philosophers advocating the doctrine of *māyā*.

Apavarga (*D*): Liberation. Absolute cessation of suffering, attainment of *nirvāṇa*.

(*Vy*): Attainment of the result of an action.

Apaviddha (*Sm*): One cast off by one's parents, and accepted by another person as his son.

Apoha (*D*): Excluding all things not coming under the category in point. For example, *nīlatva* (blueness) excludes all things that are not *nīla*.

Apūrva (*D*): Unperceived potencey generated by the performance of rites, in the soul of the performer. It bears fruit in future. Thus, the *apūrva* generated by a particular rite, performed in this life, leads to the acquisition of heaven in the next world.

Arahata (*D*): Skt. *Arhat*. In Buddhism, one who has attained *nirvāṇa*. According to Theravāda school, this is the ideal of personal life. In pre-Buddhistic times, *arhat* denoted anyone who attained the ideal of his religion.

Ārakṣaka: Guard; police magistrate.

Ārālika (*A*): seller of cooked meat, etc.

Ārambha (*N*): One of the *avasthās* (q. v.).

Āraṭṭa (*Sm*): Name of a region a visit to which taints a man (brāhmaṇa?) with sin, and renders him liable to expiation.

Ārabhaṭī (*N, S*): (1) A kind of dramatic manner or style, generally translated as violent. It suits the sentiments of horror and fury.

(2) A kind of dance.

Ārdhadhātuka (*Vy*): Technical term used to indicate affixes other than *sārvadhātuka* (q.v.), i.e., the conjugational signs of the eighth and tenth classes, the affixes added to form the causal base and a few denominatives, the affixes *-sya*, *-ta*, *-sa* and *-ya* added to the bases of the two future tenses, the Desiderative and the Aorist, and the Passive and the Frequentative respectively, and those forming the Past Participle (Active and Passive), the Infinitive and the verbal indeclinables, and some others. The significance of the name is that the endings of this type are added to the root without *vikararaṇa* (q.v.), i.e., before these endings only half the root or a part thereof is discernible.

Ardhasama (*C*): A *vṛtta* (q.v.) in which the first and the third feet and the second and fourth feet have the same metrical scheme.

Ardhasīrin or *ardhasītika* (*A*): A cultivator who tills another person's land on condition that he (the tiller) will take half the produce.

Ardhodaya (*J*): A particular conjunction which takes place if, in the month of *Pauṣa* or *Māgha*, there are New Moon, Sravaṇā *nakṣatra* and *vyatīpātayoga* (q.v.) on Sunday.

Ariyasacca (*D*): *Āryasatya* in Skt. Four Noble Truths, viz., *duḥkha* (suffering), *samudaya* (origin of suffering), *nirodha* (its suppression) and *mārga* (way of suppression).

Āroha (*S*): Ascent of the notes in a song, in the order *SA*, *RA*, *GA*, *MA*, *PA*, *DHA*, *NA*.

Arśa (*Ay*): Piles.

Ārṣa (*vivāha*) (*Sm*): A kind of marriage in which a girl is given away after taking from the bridegrooms's family a pair or two of cattle as a matter of form, and not as the price of the girl.

[See J. Gonda, Reflections on the *ārṣa* and *āsura* forms of marriage, *Sarup Comm. Vol.*, 1954.]

Arthāpatti (*D*): A means of valid knowledge, according to Mīmāṁsā philosophy. Circumstantial inference; deduction of a matter from that which could not otherwise be. For example, a rat has eaten up the stick. So, by *arthāpatti*, we may infer that the cake also, that was on the stick, was eaten up by it.

Artha-prakṛti (*N*): Element of the plot of a Sanskrit drama. There are five elements, viz., *bīja*, *bindu*, *patākā*, *prakarī* and *kārya*. The first is the germ whence springs the action. For example, in the *Abhijñānaśākuntalam*, the germ is cast when the hermit blesses the king that he may have a great son, and says that Kaṇva has gone away leaving Śakuntalā to perform the rites of hospitality. *Bindu* is the drop which spreads out as oil in water; the course of the drama, which has seemed to be interrupted, is again set in activity. In the same drama (Act II), we get it when the king speaks of Śakuntalā to the Vidūṣaka when the main action is interrupted by such incidents as the talk about the chase, the double call of duty to the king, etc. The other three elements are the episode, the incident and the denouement.

Arthavāda (*D*): Explanation or a remark in praise. It usually recommends a *vidhi* or precept by stating the good result of its observance and the evil resulting from its non-observance.

Arthin (*Sm*): Plaintiff, suitor.

Arvuda (*AY*): Swelling, tumour.

Āryāvartta (*Sm*): (1) That part of India which lies between the Himālayas and the Vindhya mountain, and extends up to the eastern and western seas.

(2) The region between the rivers Gaṅgā and Yamunā.

(3) That region of India where spotted antelopes roam about naturally.

Āsana (*Sm*): A political expedient by which a king assumes an attitude of indifference to the activities of a belligerent power.

(*D*) Practice of steady and comfortable postures; e.g., *padmāsana*. It is a *yogāṅga* (q.v.).

Asatkāryavāda (*D*): The doctrine according to which the effect is something new, and does not pre-exist in the cause.

Āsava (*D*): Primarily, it denotes wine. In Buddhism, it is the name of the following regarded as intoxicants: sensuality, longing for rebirth, false doctrine, ignorance.

Āsedha (*Sm*): Restraint under the king's order. It is of four kinds, namely

(1) Restraint as to place (e.g., you cannot go elsewhere from specified places).

(2) Restraint as to time (e.g., you must present yourself before court on specified dates).

(3) Restraint from proceeding on a journey (till the suit is disposed of).

(4) Restraint as to certain activities (e.g., you are not to sell a certain property or plough a certain field till the disposal of the suit).

Aśmarī (*Ay*): A disease, called stone (in the bladder).

Āsrava (*D*): According to Jains, the action of the senses, which compels the soul towards external objects.

Aṣṭakā (*Sm*): The eighth day after full moon (especially that in *hemanta* and *śiśira*) on which the progenitors or manes are worshipped. There are three kinds of *aṣṭakā-śrāddha*, namely

(1) *Pūpāṣṭakā* — in which cakes are offered;

(2) *Māṁsāṣṭakā* — in which meat is offered;

(3) *Śākāṣṭakā* — to be performed with vegetables.

Aṣṭakūṭa (*J*): The eight factors, *varṇa*, etc., which are examined and calculated in determining the suitability of a match in marriage.

Aṣṭapāśa (*T*): See *Pāśa*.

Aṣṭa-siddhi (*T*): See *Siddhi*.

Āstika: (*Sm*): One believing in the existence of god, the other world, etc.

Astikāya (*D*): In Jaina philosophy, all substances excepting *kāla* (time), are so called, as every substance of this kind exists (*asti*) like body (*kāya*) possessing extension. An ontological category. It denotes the five groups of existence, viz., *jīva* (soul), *pudgala* (non-soul), *dharma* and *adharma* (principles of rest and motion) and *ākāśa* (space).

Āsura (*Vivāha*) (*Sm*): A form of marriage in which a girl is given away, at the father's will, after the bridegroom gives as much wealth as he can afford to the relatives of the girl and to the girl herself.

[See J. Gonda, Reflection on the *ārṣa* and *āsura* forms of marriage, *Sarup Comm. Vol.*, 1954.]

Aśvakrānta (*T*): In certain Tantras, India has been divided into three regions one of which is called *aśvakrānta* or *gajakrānta*. According to the *Śaktimaṅgala-tantra*, the tract of land from the Vindhya hill to the great ocean is called *aśvakrānta*.

Aśvamedha (*Sm*): Name of a sacrifice in which a horse was to be immolated. The horse was to be placed by a king under the charge of military men and then let loose. On its return after a year, the sacrifice was to be performed. The practice, which reaches back to the Vedic times, was regarded as a symbol of sovereignty and power.

[See J. Puhvel, Vedic *aśvamedha* and Gaulish Epomeduous, *Language*, Linguistic Soc. of America, 31; R.C. Hajra, The *aśvamedha* etc., *ABORI*, 36. Also see P.E. Dumont, *L' Aśvamedha*, 1927.]

Ātatāyin (*Sm*): Designation of the following hostile persons: incendiary, poisoner, one armed with weapons, robber, one who wrests a field or carries away one's wife.

Āṭavika (*A*): Principal person protecting the forest-region.

Aticāra (*A*): Transgression, misconduct.

(*J*): Movement of a planet from one Zodiac to another before the usual time.

Atisarga (A): (1) Giving up, surrender.

(2) Granting permission, allowing.

Atisāra or *atīsāra* (*Ay*): Diarrhoea or dysentery.

Atikr̥cchra (*Sm*): A form of expiation in which the sinner has to eat merely one morsel of food for three days in the morning only, for three days in the evening only, one morsel each for three days without asking for it and has to fast for three days.

Atipātaka (*Sm*): A class of sins comprising adultery with one's mother, daughter, daughter-in-law.

Atithi (*Sm*): One not staying permanently at another's house; a brāhmaṇa guest who stays for one night only.

Ativyāpti (*D*): The fault of being too wide. For example, if we define 'cow' as a quadruped having two horns, then it will include also buffaloes, etc.

Ātodya (*S*): A kind of musical instrument; percussion instrument.

Ātreyī (*Sm*): A woman who has bathed after her monthly impurity.

Aucitya (*Al*): Propriety or appropriateness. Kṣemendra elaborates, in his *Aucitya-vicāra-carcā*, the view that whatever is improper in any way detracts from *rasa* (q.v.) and is to be avoided.

Auḍa(u)va (*S*): Designation of a *rāga*. A *rāga*, consisting of five notes, takes this name. In it, the initial note *ṣaḍja* is never given up.

Aupariṣṭaka (*K*): Sex-act into the mouth of an eunuch.

Aupaśleṣika (*Vy*): Arising from immediate contact.

Aurasa (*Sm*): A son begotten by a man on his wife.

Avakīrṇī (*Sm*): A *brahmacārin* who has had sexual intercourse with a woman.

Avabhṛtha (*Sm*): Ablution to be performed after the conclusion of a sacrifice.

Avadātikā: A kind of wine.

Avadhūta (*T*): A Tāntric *sādhaka* of a very high order.

Avama (*J*): The end of one and the beginning and end of another on the same day.

Āvantya (*Sm*): Offspring of a *vrātya* (q.v.) brāhmaṇa by a woman of the same caste.

Āvāpa (*D*): Putting in, experimental insertion.

Avaroha (*S*): The reverse order of *āroha* (q.v.), e.g. *NA*, *DHA*, *PA*, *MA*, *GA*, *RA*, *SA*, Lit. it means 'descent'.

Āvarta (*Kṛ*): A kind of cloud.

Avasthā (*N*): Stage of development of dramatic action. There are five stages, namely, *ārambha*, *yatna*, *prāptyāśā*, *niyatāpti*, and *phalāgama*. "There must be at the beginning (*ārambha*) the desire to attain some end, which leads on to the determined effort (*prayatna*) to secure the object of desire; this leads to the stage in which success is felt to be possible (*prāptyāśā*) having regard to the means available and the obstacles in the way of achievement; then arrives the certainty of success (*niyatāpti*), if only some specific difficulty can be surmounted; and finally, the object is attained (*phalāgama*). Thus, in the *Abhijñana-śākuntalam*, we have the king's first anticipation of seeing the heroine; then his eagerness to find a means to meet her again; in act IV we learn that the anger of the sage, Durvāsas, has in some measure been appeased, and the possibility of the reunion of the king and Śakuntalā now exists; in act VI the discovery of the ring brings back the king's memory and the way for a reunion is paved, to be attained in the following act."[1]

Avayava (*D*): One of the number of sentences, used to project one's conclusion into another. According to *Māṭharavṛtti* on *Sāṁkhyakākrikā*, *anumāna* (inference) has three *avayavas*, viz. *pakṣa* (*pratijñā*), *hetu* and *dṛṣṭānta*.

Avidyā (*D*): Nescience, non-knowledge, often identified with ritual practices.

[See E.A. Solomon, *Avidyā — A Problem of Truth and Reality*, Ahmedābād, 1969.]

Avīrā (*Sm*): (I) A woman having neither husband nor son.

(II) A woman who is independent, but not gone astray.

Avyaya (*Vy*): Indeclinable. A word which does not undergo any change in any gender, any case-ending and in any number.

Āvṛta (*Sm*): One sprung from a brāhmaṇa male and an *ugra* (q.v.) female.

Avyāpti (*D*): The fault of being too narrow, as opposed to *ativyāpti*. For example, if we say that a student is one who reads in a school, the definition is too narrow because it excludes those who read in a college or other educational institutions.

Avyayībhāva (*Vy*): Adverbial compound in which the sense of the first member predominates.

---

1. Keith, *Sanskrit Drama* (1924), pp. 297-8.

Ayanānta Bindu (*J*): The maximum declination of the sun (North or South).

Āyogava (*Sm*): (1) One born of the union of a śūdra male and a vaiśya female.

(2) One born of the union of a vaiśya male and a kṣatriya female.

Ayogavāha (*Vy*): The letters or phonetic elements *anusvāra*, *visarga* and so called as they are always uttered only in combination with another phonetic element or letter like'a', and never independently. The *ayogavāha* letters possess the characteristics of both vowels and consonents.

Bahula (*Vy*): Used in connection with a rule, affix or the like. It denotes four kinds of operation, namely, applicable, not applicable in certain cases, optionally applicable in some cases and quite something else in others.

Bahumūtra (*Ay*): A kind of diabetes.

Bahuvrīhi (*Vy*): Attributive compound in which the sense of a word, other than the members of the compound, is predominant.

Balikarman (Sm): Same as *bhūtabali* (q.v.).

Bāṇaliṅga (*T*): A particular form of Śiva phallus. So called as such a *liṅga* is believed to have been installed by Bāṇa, a demon-devotee of Śiva.

Bandhaka (*Sm*): Pledge or mortgage.

Bandhakī: A prostitute attached to many men.

Bandhakī-poṣaka: Keeper of a brothel.

Bāndhava (*Sm*): The following three classes of relatives —

(I) *Ātma-bandhu* — son of one's father's sister, mother's sister and of one's maternal uncle.

(II) *Pitṛ-bandhu* — son of one's father's sister, father's mother's sister and of one's father's maternal uncle.

(III)*Mātṛ-bandhu* — son of one's mother's mother's sister, mother's father's sister and of one's mother's maternal uncle.

Bandhu (*Sm*): Same as *bāndhava* (q.v.).

Bavri: A kind of garment.

Bhākta (*D, Al*): Secondary, attributed.

Bhairavī-cakra (*T*): A ritual in which man and woman together perform certain rites of which drinking and sexual intercourse are parts.

Bhakti: Devotion which is of several kinds.

(1) *Āropasiddihā*: In the absence of spontaneous devotion, it is engendered by rites, performed in honour of god.

(2) *Saṁgasiddhā*: Arising out of association with the good people.

(3) *Svarūpasiddhā*: Spontaneous, natural. When motivated by any other factor, it is called *sakaitavā*. When there is no motive other than pleasing god, it is *sakaitavā*. It is of two kinds, namely.

(a) *Vaidhī*: Evoked by Śāstric injunctions.

(b) *Rāgānugā*: It follows natural tendency, and not from Śāstric injunctions. It is an imitation of *rāgātmikā bhakti*, in which the essence is *rāga* or attachment. The kind of *bhakti* that the divine associates have for god is *rāgātmikā*. *Jñānamiśrā Bhakti* may lead to *śuddhā* or pure *bhakti*. Divine pleasure is stated to lie in *śuddhā bhakti* alone; it is regarded as the best mode of attaining the highest good.

Bhakti may also be *karmamiśrā* and *yogamiśrā*.

Bhāṇa (*N*): One-act monologue drama depicting herroic or erotic sentiment.

Bharata-vākya (*N*): The concluding verse of a drama. It was so called becasue it used to be recited by *bharatas* or actors. Some think that it takes its name from Bharata, founder of Dramaturgy. In it, we find prayer to god or benediction to spectators.

Bhāratī (*N*): A dramatic style based on sound, the verbal manner. In it, the voice is the only means of expression. As the actors are called *bharata*, this manner is named *bhāratī*. According to some, it suits all sentiments.

Bhāṣā (*Sm*): Plaint in a lawsuit.

(*S*): It denotes what was, in later times, called *rāgiṇī*, fancied as a consort of a *rāga*.

Bhāṣitapuṁska (*Vy*): A word in the feminine gender having a corresponding masculine form; e.g., *sundarī*. But, *latā* is not so, as it has no corresponding masculine form.

Bhāṭaka (*A*): Fare for boats, etc.

Bhāva (*Al*): Emotion, feeling, complete psychosis as the basis of *rasa* (q.v.). Divided into two kinds, viz. *sthāyī* (permanent or principal mood) and *sañcārī* or *vyabhicārī* (accessory feeling).

Bheda (*Sm*): A political expedient by which seeds of dissension are sown in the territory of a hostile king.

Bhrū(u)kuṁsa or *Bhrakuṁsa* (*N*): A man in the role of a woman in a drama.

Bhrūṇa (*Sm*): (i) A brāhmaṇa conversant with the Veda, who has performed *soma* sacrifice.

(ii) Foetus.

(iii) Any brāhmaṇa.

(iv) A brāhmaṇa who has studied the Veda with its six accessories.

Bhukti (*Sm*): Possession.

Bhuktivāda (*Al*): According to this view of Bhaṭṭa Nāyaka, *rasa* is enjoyed, and it is neither inferred nor produced.

Bhūrjakaṇṭaka (*Sm*): Offspring of a *vrātya* (q.v.) brāhmaṇa by a similar woman sometimes also called *āvantya*, *vāṭadhāna*, *puṣpadha*, *śaikha*.

Bhūta-bali (*Sm*): Offering to creatures, as a part of the householder's duty.

Bhūta-śuddhi (*T*): A process by which the five elements of the body are supposed to be purified.

Bhūta-yajña (*Sm*): Same as *bhūtabali* (q.v.)

Bīja (*N*): An *artha-prakṛti* (q.v.).

(*T*): Mystic syllable like *hrīm*; semen; Supreme Spirit.

Bījin (*Sm*): The owner or giver of seed, the real progenitor (as opposed to *kṣetrin*, the nominal father or merely the husband of a woman.

Bindu (*N*): One of the *artha-prakṛtis* (q.v.).

Bodhi (*D*): Perfect wisdom, enlightenment. According to Buddhist philosophy, the sole Absolute embracing this consciousness which, in its turn, includes in itself all psychic processes, is *bodhi*. It is the one and only truth attainable to him who practises *yoga*, and even to him only in stages, after he has gone through all the ten stages (*daśabhūmi*) of the career of a *bodhisattva*.

Bodhisattva (Pāli-*Bodhisatta*) (*D*): A being destined for perfect enlightenment for bringing salvation to all people. The Buddha, in his previous births, was so called.

Bradhna (*Sm*): Sun.

Brahmāñjali (*Sm*): Hands folded by a pupil as a preliminary to Vedic study with a teacher.

Brahmadeya (*A*): Land, etc., given by a king to a brāhmaṇa.

Brahmadeyā (*Sm*): A woman married in the *Brāhma* (q.v.) form of marriage.

Brahmapura (*T*): Designation of the human body.

Brahma-rākṣasa (*Sm*): The ghost of a brāhmaṇa who used to lead an unholy life.

Brahmarandhra (*T*): An aperture in the crown of the head through which the soul is supposed to exit at the time of death.

Brahmasatra (*Sm*): Sacrifice in the form of devotion or meditation; constant repetition of Vedic texts.

Brahma-vihāra (*D*): Name given by the Buddhists to *maitrī*, *karuṇā*, *muditā* and *upekṣā*, the qualities necessary for the attainment of *nirvāṇa*. These mean respectively love, pity, sympathy in joy and equanimity.

Brahmāvarta (*Sm*): The part of India between the rivers Sarasvatī and Dṛṣadvatī.

Brāhma-vivāha (*Sm*): The form of marriage in which the daughter is given away, after decking her with valuable garments and honouring her with jewels, etc., to a man conversant with the Vedas and of good conduct, whom the father of the girl himself invites.

Brahma-yajña (*Sm*): See *pañca-mahāyajña*.

Brahmodya (*Sm*): Such riddles, questions and answers as are found in the *Taittirīrya-saṁhitā* (VII.4.18) and the *Vājasaneyi-saṁhitā* (XXIII. 9-12), etc.

(2) Legends narrated in the Vedas.

(3) Talks relating to the exposition of *Brahman*.

Caitya (*V*): In ancient times, it stood for altar, holy tree, temple or palace. Later on, it came to denote temples on *citā*s (funeral places). In course of time, it was used to denote any temple.

Cakra (*T*): Mystical circle, according to Tantras. The human body is supposed to have the following *cakra*s:

(I) *mūlādhāra*, (II) *svādhiṣṭhāna*, (III) *maṇipūra*, (IV) *anāhata*, (V) *viśuddha* and (VI) *ājñā*.

These are supposed to be located respectively in the following regions: lowest extremity of spinal cord, above *mūlādhāra*, naval, near heart, near the neck, between eyebrows.

Cakrabheda (*T*): Literally, penetration of *cakras*. The ultimate aim of a Tāntric devotee is to make *kuṇḍalinī* (q.v.) penetrate the six *cakras*, and reach *sahasrāra* (q.v.).

Cakracara (*A*): A roving person who does not remain at a place for more than one day.

Cakra-vṛddhi (*Sm*): Compound interest, i.e., interest on interest.

Camatkāra (*Al*): Literary delight. The supernatural and inexplicable joy produced by a literary composition. It is the essence of *rasa*.

Campū (*Al*): A literary composition in prose and verse.

Cāṇḍāla (*Sm*): (I) Name of the caste sprung from the union of a śūdra male and a brāhmaṇa female.

(II) Offspring of an unmarried woman.

(III)One born as a result of a man's union with a *sagotrā* girl.

(IV)Son of one who, after becoming an ascetic, comes back to the householder's life.

Cāndramāsa(mukhya) (*J*): Lunar month beginning in the first lunar mansion of the bright half of the month, and ending with the conclusion of New Moon.

Cāndramāsa(gauṇa) (*J*): Lunar month beginning with the first lunar mansion of the dark half, and ending with the conclusion of the Full Moon.

Cāndrāyaṇa (*Sm*): A form of penance in which a sinner is required to eat 15 morsels of food on each day of the dark fortnight and to fast completely on the New Moon day. This is of many kinds, viz., *pipīlikā-madhya*, *yati-cāndrāyaṇa* and *śiśucāndrāyaṇa*.

Cāpa (*J*): A portion of the circumference of a circle, cut by a straight line.

Cara (*Cāra*) (*Sm*): Spy.

Cāraka (*A*): Place where an offender is kept confined.

Chāyānāṭaka (N): Some think, it means outline of a drama. Others think, it is the shadow of a drama or half drama. There is an opinion that it is an epitomical adaptation of a previous play on the subject concerned.

Cārī (S): Simultaneous graceful movement of the feet, shanks, thighs and the hip in various ways in dance. It is of two main kinds, namely *ākāśikī* (aerial) and *bhaumī* (terrestrial).

Caritrabandhaka (Sm): A mortgage. In it the creditor, relying on the honesty of the debtor, lends a big amount against the mortgage of a small property. Or, the debtor, relying on the honesty of the creditor, borrows a small sum by mortgaging a big property.

Carmakāraka(-kāra, Carmāvakartin, Carmopjīvin):

(i) Offspring of a śūdra by a kṣatriya girl.

(ii) One sprung from the union of a vaidehaka (q.v.) and a brāhmaṇa female.

(iii) Offspring of an *āyogava* (q.v.) by a brāhmaṇa female.

Cuñcu (Sm): Offspring of a brāhmaṇa by a *vaidehaka* (q.v.) woman.

Caturaṅga (A): Army consisting of four wings, namely elephants, horses, chariots and infantry.

Caturasra (J): A place within four lines.

Cāturmāsya (Sm): Name of the three sacrifices, namely *vaiśvadeva*, *varuṇapraghāsa* and *śākamedha*, performed in the beginning of the three seasons of four months each.

Chālikyagāna: A kind of chorus.

Cīnācāra (T): A mode of *kaulācāra* or *kaulamārga* (q.v.).

Citraghāta (A): Torturing to death.

Cորarajju (A): *Cnowkidārī* tax.

Corarajjuka (A): A government officer whose duty is to arrest thieves.

Cūcuka (*Sm*): Offspring of the marriage of a vaiśya with a śūdra woman.

Cūḍākarman or *cūḍākaraṇa*, *cūḍā* (*Sm*): A sacrament in which the hairs on a child's head are cut for the first time. *Cūḍā* means the tuft of hair kept on the head when the major part is shaved off.

Cūḍāmaṇi (*J*): Name of a *yoga* or conjunction when there is solar eclipse on Sunday or lunar eclipse on Monday.

Dadhimantha: Perhaps *ghī* or buttermilk.

Dāha-jvara (*Ay*): Inflammatory fever.

Daiva vivāha (*Sm*): The form of marriage in which a father gives away his daughter after decking her with ornaments, etc., to a priest who duly officiates at a sacrifice, during the course of its performance.

Daiva Yajña (*Sm*): Same as *devayajña* (q.v.).

Dakṣiṇāyana (*J*): The period of the sun's stay in the southern hemisphere.

Dāna (*G*, *Sm*): A liquid substance exuding from elephant's body, ichor. Gift; one of the four means (*upāya*) of influencing one's enemy in one's favour.

Daṇḍa (*Sm*): (I) Staff, especially that held by one at the time of *upanayana*.

(II) Punishment, sometimes personified.

(III) Fine.

(IV) Sceptre or Rod as a symbol of royal power or judicial authority.

(V) A political expedient by which a king invades an enemy's country.

(VI) The army: military power and sovereignty.

(VII) 1/30 part of a day or night.

Daṇḍa (*J*): 1/60 part of 24 hours, equivalent to 24 minutes.

In some cases, one *daṇḍa* is equal to 1/32 part of 24

hours.

Daṇḍadāsa (*Sm*): One enslaved for non-payment of fine.

Daṇḍanīti (*Sm*): (i) Judicature as science; application of the rod; administration of justice.

(ii) *Arthaśāstra*.

Daṇḍa-vyūha (*Sm*): A kind of soldiers' array looking like a stick.

Darśa (*Sm*): New Moon or a sacrifice performed at that time; the day on which the moon is seen only by the sun and by no one else.

Dāsa or *dāśa* (*Sm*): Same as *kaivarta* (q.v.).

Daśa-mahāvidyā (*T*): Ten manifestations of Goddess Bhagavatī. These are Kālī, Tārā, Ṣoḍaśī, Bhuvaneśvarī, Bhairavī, Chinnamastā, Dhūmāvatī, Vagalā, Mātaṅgī and Kamalā.

Daśavargika (*A*): Commander of a group of ten soldiers.

Dattaka (*Sm*): A boy who, being given by his parents, is adopted by a person as a son.

Dattātmā (*Sm*): A boy who, either bereft of parents or forsaken by them, offers himself to a person as his son.

Dattrima (*Sm*): Same as *dattaka* (q.v.).

Dāyāda (*Sm*): One who is entitled to inheritance.

Dāyāda-bāndhava or *-bandhu* (*Sm*): Such *bandhus* or *bāndhavas* (q.v.) as are entitled to inheritance.

Devadāsī: A girl engaged for dancing in a temple.

Devalaka (*Sm*): (1) A brāhmaṇa who performs the worship of an image for wages for three years, and who thereby becomes unfit to officiate in *śrāddha*.

(2) One who maintains himself on the treasury of a shrine.

(3) Worshipper of Śiva for wages.

Deva-yajña (*Sm*): See *Pañca-mahāyajña*.

Dhaivata (*S*): The sixth note of the Indian gamut; it is denoted by *DHA*.

Dhamanī (*Ay*): A tube or canal of the human body; a vein; a nerve.

Dhanva-durga (*Sm*): A kind of fort surrounded by deserts and devoid of water for five *yojana*s.

Dhāraṇā (*D*): Fixing the mind on the desired object; a *yogāṅga*.

Dhāraṇī (*T*): Protective spell used by Tāntric Buddhists. Formed parts of Mahāyāna Buddhist literature.

Dharmamegha (*D*): According to Vedānta, it is *nirvikalpa samādhi*, so called as it showers the ambrosia of *dharma* which is the cause of salvation. According to Yoga, it is the culmination of *samprajñāta samādhi* (see *samādhi*).

Dhyāna (*D*): Steady contemplation of the desired object without any break; a *yogāṅga* (q.v.).

Dharmastha (*A*): Judge, particularly for trying civil suits.

Dharmasthīya: Prison, a sort of lock-up.

Dhātu (*S*): Element of a *prabandha* (q.v.). There are four principal *dhātu*s, namely, *udgrāha*, *melāpaka*, *dhruva* and *ābhoga*. A fifth, namely, *antara* or *antarā* is also added.

Dhigvana (*Sm*): Offspring of a brāhmaṇa by an *āyogava* (q.v.) female.

Dhruva (*Nakṣatra* or *Tārā*) (*J*): North polar star which is always fixed on the north point of the earth.

Dhruva (*S*): A kind of song. It is chiefly of three kinds, namely, *uttama*, *madhyama* and *adhama*. According to Bharata, it is of five kinds, namely *praveśa*, *ākṣepa*, *niṣkrama*, *prāsādika* and *āntara*.

Dhvajabhaṅga (*Ay*): A kind of impotency.

Dhvani (*Al*): Suggested sense, the best kind of *kāvya*, according to some.

[See M.M. Sharma, *The Dhvani Theory in Sanskrit Poetics*, 1968.]

Didhiṣu (*Sm*): An elder sister before whom her younger sister has been married.

Dīkṣā: Initiation. Its modes vary in different Tantras. According to *Viśvasāra*, it is of four kinds, viz. *kriyāvatī*, *kalāvatī*, *varṇamayī* and *vedhamayī*.

Prāṇatoṣiṇī II.4.

According to *Kulārṇava* (XIV), it is sevenfold, viz., *kriyā*, *varṇa*, *kalā*, *sparśa*, *vāk*, *dṛk* and *mānasa*. Each of these has sub-divisions.

According to *Rudrayāmala*, it is of three kinds, viz., *āṇavī*, *śāktī* and *śāmbhavī*.

Prāṇatoṣiṇī II.4.

Other types of *dīkṣā* are *krama*, *pañcāyatana*, *ekamantra*, etc.

Ḍima (*Al*): One of the ten kinds of major drama.

Ḍimba (*A*): An affray, a riot, revolt of subjects.

Dimbāhava (*Sm*): (a) a battle where no king is present.

(b) A quarrel in which no weapon is used.

Divākīrti or *Kīrtya* (*Sm*): Cāṇḍāla or barber.

Divya (*Sm*): Divine proof, e.g., ordeal of fire, water, etc.

Draviḍa (*Sm*): Same as *karaṇa* (q.v.).

Drāviḍa (*V*): Designation of the type of architecture that was current in south India.

Drekkāna or Dreṣkāṇa (*J*): 1/3 of a *rāśi*.

Droṇa (*Kṛ*): A kind of cloud.

Droṇamukha (*A*): A sort of satellite town, set-up for the administration of 400 villages.

Dvaidha or *Dvaidhībhāva* (*Sm, A*): One of the six kinds of royal policy (*guṇa*). According to some, it means double-dealing, keeping apparently friendly relations with the enemy. According to others, it means dividing one's army and encountering the enemy in detachments.

Yet others take it to mean 'making peace with one king and carrying on war with another'.

Dvāmuṣyāyaṇa (*Sm*): A son of two fathers. Usually, an only son given in adoption on condition that he will be treated as the son of both the natural father and the adoptive father.

Dvandva (*Vy*): Copulative compound in which the meaning of both the members is equally prominent.

Dvigu (*Vy*): Numeral appositional compound, i.e., a kind of *karmadhāraya* (q.v.) in which the first member is a numeral.

Ekaliṅga (*T*): A field or place, (up to 5 *krośa*s or a little over two miles), in which there is but one *Śiva-liṅga*; designation of a *liṅga* at such a place.

Ekaparigrahā: A prostitute attached to one person.

Ekaśeṣa (*Vy*): Name of a *vṛtti* (q.v.). It is a phenomenon in which, of the words having the same form and same case-ending one remains, or of words of different forms but of the same meaning only one remains. For example,

(1) *naraḥ naraḥ* = *narau*.

(2) *vakradaṇḍaḥ kuṭiladaṇḍaḥ* (both words meaning 'curved stick') = *vakradaṇḍau* or *kuṭiladaṇḍau*.

Ekoddiṣṭa (*Sm*): A kind of *śrāddha* performed in honour of one individual.

Gajakrānta (*T*): Same as *aśvakrānta* (q.v.).

Gamaka (*S*): Such trembling of a musical note as is pleasant to the listeners.

Gaṇa (*Sm*, *C*, *Vy*): (i) An Association of merchants, etc.

(ii) A guild of horse-dealers.

(iii) An association of men living in a village, etc.

(iv) An association of warriors, etc., who pursue the samc vocation.

(v) A tribal community.

In Metrics it is a metrical unit consisting of three syllables, represented by a letter. For example, three consecutive long syllables are represented by *Ma*, three consecutive short ones by *Na*. There are eight *gaṇas* representing the various permutations and combinations of the long and short syllables. In grammar, lists of words undergoing similar grammatical operation, constitute *gaṇapāṭha*.

Gāṇanika (*A*): Government accountant.

Gaṇḍamālā (*Ay*): Inflammation of the glands of the neck.

Gāndhāra (*S*): The third of the seven notes in a song. It is indicated by *GA*.

Gāndharva (*Sm*): That form of clandestine marriage in which the parties marry by mutual consent.

[See L. Sternbach, Juridical aspects of the Gāndharva form of marriage, *Proc. of All-India Oriental Conference* (12th Session), Vol. II, Banaras, 1946.]

(*S*): One conversant with music of both *mārga* and *deśī* types.

Garbhādhāna (*Sm*): A sacrament performed to ensure the birth of a good child. Authorities differ as to the proper time for performing it.

Garbha-kendra (*J*): Centre of a circle.

Garbhasrāva (*Ay*): Abortion.

Gārhapatya (*Sm*): The householder's fire received from his father, and transmitted to his descendants; one of the three sacred fires, being that from which sacrificial fires are lighted.

Garuḍa (*Sm*): Name of a particular array (*vyūha*) of soldiers resembling the *varāha-vyūha* (q.v.) with the only difference that, in the former, the middle part is wider.

Gati (*Vy*): Another name of certain particles which are also called *upasarga* (q.v.). Other words, receiving the designation of *gati*, are those which are listed with *ūri* leading, words formed by adding the affix-*cvi* as well as affix-*ḍāc*, provided all such words precede verbs.

Gauḍī (*Sm, Al*): (1) Wine distilled from molasses.

(2) Name of a *rīti* or a particular mode of arrangement of words in a literary composition.

Gāyatrī (*T*): The basic *mantra* of an initiated *dvija* — *tat-sa vitur-vareṇyam*, etc. (*Ṛgveda* III.62.10).

Gha (*Vy*): Technical term for the *taddhita* affixes *tarap* and *tamap*.

Ghana (*S*): See *vādya*.

Ghāta (*J*): Multiplication.

Ghaṭarī (*S*): A kind of lute.

Ghaṭikā (*J*): Same as *daṇḍa* (q.v.).

Ghi (Vy): Technical term for noun-bases or *prātipadika*s (q.v.) ending in short *i* or short *u*, excepting the bases *sakhī*, *pati* and those included in *nadī* (q.v.).

Ghoṣavat (*Vy*): A consonant having *ghoṣa* (depth in tone), called sonant; third and fourth letters of a *varga*.

Ghu (*Vy*): Technical term for the roots *dā* and *dhā*; root *dāp* is excluded.

Giri-durga (*Sm*): A kind of royal fort situated on a hill very difficult to climb, accessible through a narrow path, with a supply of water from rivers and falls and with many productive lands and trees.

Glaha (*Sm*): Wager mutually agreed upon by gamblers.

Godāna (*Sm*): The ceremony of tonsure, performed in the sixteenth year of age for a brāhmaṇa, in the twenty-second year for a kṣatriya and in the twenty-fourth year for a vaiśya.

Golaka (*Sm*): Illegitimate son of a widow.

Gopa (*A*): Head of five or ten villages.

Gopura (*V*, *A*): City-gate. In course of time, it came to denote the entrance to a temple. It means a particular kind of entrance according to south Indian works on architecture.

Gosava (*Sm*): Name of a one-day *soma* sacrifice.

Goṣṭhī: Something like a club where people used to relax by light talks and jokes.

Gotra (*Sm*): "All persons who trace descent in an unbroken male line from a common male ancestor." (Kane) According to some authorities, *gotra* means the earliest traceable brāhmaṇa ancestor from whom descent is claimed through generations. *Gotra*s are eight according to some, while others recognise a few more.

Graha (*S*): Same as *aṁśa* (q.v.) according to Bharata, while later writers take it to denote the secondary note in a *rāga*. Generally, the note from which a *rāga* is commenced is called the *grahasvara* of that *rāga*.

Grahaṇa (*J*): The phenomenon called eclipse, when the sun or moon, even though remaining in the clear sky, becomes invisible.

Grahaṇi or *Grahaṇī* (*Ay*): Diarrhoea, dysentery, especially when the disease is old.

Grahayuti (*J*): Denotes the equality of two *graha*s in *rāśi*, *aṁśa* and *kalā*.

Grāma (*S*): A gamut, scale in music.

Grāmakūṭa (*A*): Village headman.

Gṛhabali (*Sm*): Domestic oblation; offering of remnants of food to all creatures.

Gṛhapatikavyañjana: A cultivator, unable to earn a living by his own occupation, acting as a spy with Government help.

Gūḍhaja (*Sm*): A son born to a woman during the absence of her husband, the real father being unknown.

Gūḍhapuruṣa (*A*): Spy.

Gulma (*Sm, A, Ay*): (i) A troop or guard of soldiers.

(ii) A police-station, outpost.

(iii) Chronic enlargement of the spleen.

Guṇa (*Vy, Sm, A, Al*): (1) A technical term denoting *AR, AL, E* and *O* in place of *Ṛ, Ḷ, I* (and Ī), *U* and (*Ū*) respectively.

(2) A political expedient; these are six, viz.; *sandhi, vigraha, yāna, āsana, dvaidhībhāva* and *saṁśraya*.

(3) Literary excellence as essential for *rasa* (q.v.).

Guru-talpa (*Sm*): (i) Mother. (ii) Wife of a Vedic teacher. (iii) Mother, or step-mother belonging to the same caste as that of the father.

Gurvaṅganā (*Sm*): Same as *guru-talpa* (q.v.).

Haituka (*Sm*): A rationalist, sceptic, heretic.

Haiyaṅgavīna: *ghī* made of the milk obtained on the previous day.

Haṁsa (*T, D*): (1) One of the four classes of *saṁnyāsin*s (in the fourth stage of life).

(2) A Tāntric devotee of a high order.

(3) *Ajapā-mantra* which arises spontaneously and involuntarily in the mind. So named as the *S*-sound arises in exhalation (*recaka prāṇāyāma*) and *H*-sound in inhalation (*pūraka prāṇāyāma*).

Hastinī (*K*): A class of women.

Haṭhayoga (*T*): A kind of *yoga* in which the mind is forced to withdraw from external objects. *HA* and *ṬHA* stand for sun and moon respectively.

Havya (*Sm*): A sacrificial gift or food.

Hayamedha (*Sm*): Same as *aśvamedha* (q.v.).

Hetvābhāsa (*D*): The semblance of *hetu* (logical reason, reason for inference, middle term); a fallacious reason. This fallacy is of five kinds according to Nyāya philosophy.

These are:

(i) *Savyabhicāra* (irregular middle).

(ii) *Viruddha* (contradictory middle).

(iii) *Satpratipakṣa* (counter-balanced middle).

(iv) *Asiddha* or *sādhyasama* (unproved middle).

(v) *Bādhita* (sublated middle).

Hikkā (*Ay*): Hiccup.

Horā (*J*): Considered to be a Greek word borrowed by Sanskrit. Attempts have been made to give it an Indian tinge by deriving it from the word *ahorātra* with the initial *a* and final *tra* dropped. It is half of a *rāśi* or 15°. At some places, it is taken to denote 2½ *daṇḍa*s or one hour.

Iḍā (*T*): According to Tantras, it is the principal nerve in the human nervous system, being on the left side of the body.

Īhāmṛga (*N*): A kind of drama.

Indradhvaja: A popular festival.

Iṣṭa (*Sm*): (i) Whatever is offered in the *gṛhya* fire and the *śrauta* fire, and gifts made inside the *vedī* in the *śrauta* sacrifices.

(ii) Honouring a guest and performance of *vaiśvadeva*.

(iii) Oblation to fire, penance, truthfulness, Vedic study, hospitality, performance of *vaiśvadeva*.

Iṣṭāpūrta (*Sm*): *Iṣṭa* and *pūrta*. Of these, *iṣṭa* has been defined above. *Pūrta* has been defined as (i) Dedication of deep wells, oblong large wells and tanks, temples, distribution of food and maintaining public gardens. (ii) To the above are added, by some, gifts made at the time of eclipse or on the sun's passage into a Zodiacal sign or on the twelfth day of a month. (iii) Nursing of those who are ill.

Īśvara-praṇidhāna (*D*): A kind of devotion to God; surrendering all actions to god without any desire for fruit. It consists in the repetition of *praṇava* (*oṁkāra*) which stands for god, and contemplation of its meaning.

It (*Vy*): Elision.

Īti: The following six factors causing severe damage to crops: excessive rain, drought, locusts, rats, birds, a king who is very close.

Jalpa (*D*): A mode of argumentation in which a man carries on while knowing himself to be wrong or unable to defend himself properly against his opponents except by trickery and other unfair means of arguments. In it the main object is the overthrow of the opponent rightly or wrongly.

Jambhakavidyā: The Śāstra containing rites designed to destroy enemies, secure long life, love, wealth, son, etc.

Jāmi (*Sm*): (i) Sister, (ii) a lady of the family, (iii) a lady with her husband alive.

Janapada: Union of villagers.

Jāṅgala (*Sm*, *A*): (i) A tract or land, with scanty water and grass, where there are sufficient sunshine, air, paddy, etc. (ii) A place with water, trees and hills.

Jāṅgalavit (*A*): A toxicologist who treats animals like the horse.

Jāṅgulika: Snake-doctor; dealer in antidotes of poison.

Jātakarman (*Sm*): A sacrament performed after the birth of a son to ensure his welfare.

Jāti (*C*, *D*, *Vy*): (1) a kind of *padya* (q.v.) in which the metre is determined by the number of *mātrās*.

(2) Genus, generality.

(3) Evasive and shifty answer to an argument.

(4) In grammar, it has been used in a threefold sense:

(a) Whatever is distinguishable from another (species) on account of its possessing certain form or figure (common to the individuals of that class), e.g., *taṭī* (a bank, a place near the river).

(b) A word, which, not being used in all genders, is used to denote a single individual and, therefore, is singular in number. It will apply to other individuals of the class without their being specially mentioned, e.g., *vṛṣalī* (a low caste woman); it implies her sons, brothers, etc.

(c) A word formed with a patronymic affix and expressive of a person belonging to a particular branch of Vedic school and studying a particular portion of the Vedas.

Jātibhraṁśakara (*Sm*): A class of sins, believed to cause loss of caste to the sinner.

Jhalla (*Sm*): Same as *karaṇa* (q.v.)

Jighāṁsada: A kind of thief.

Jīvanmukti: See *mokṣa*.

Jñāti (*Sm*): Agnatic relation.

Jvara (*Ay*): Fever.

Jyotiṣṭoma (*Sm*): Name of a *soma* sacrifice.

Kairātaka: A kind of wine.

Kaivalya (*D*): Detachment of the soul from matter; identification with the Supreme Being, final emancipation.

Kaivarta (*Sm*): One born to a *niṣāda* (q.v.) by an *āyogava* (q.v.) woman.

Kākaṇi (*A*): (i) A cowrie-shell (used in gambling). (ii) Name of a copper coin (1/64 of a *paṇa*).

Kāku (*Al*): Intonation, changed voice.

Kalabha (*G*): It denotes a young elephant. According to some, it denotes an elephant in the fifth or thirteeth year from its birth.

Kalāpaka (*Al*): A kind of *kāvya* consisting of four stanzas related to one another.

Kālarātri (*J*): Name of the sixth, fourth, second, seventh, fifth, third, first and eighth *yāmārdha* of Sunday, Monday, Tuesday, Wednesday, Thursday, Friday and Saturday respectively. One *yāmārdha* = 1/8th of the duration of a night. It is regarded as inauspicious.

Kālavelā (*J*): Designation of the fifth, second, sixth, third, eighth, fourth and eighth *yāmārdha* respectively of Sunday, Monday, Tuesday, Wednesday, Thursday, Friday and Saturday. One *yāmārdha* = 1/8 part of a day. It is considered to be inauspicious.

Kālikā (*Sm*): (i) Interest accruing and payable every month.

(ii) In literature, a kind of wine.

Kañcuka (*D*): Sheath or cloak enveloping the *puruṣa* or the limited individual. The following are the five *kañcuka*s:

(i) *Kala* — limitation with regard to duration of presence and simultaneity of experience.

(ii) *Niyati* — restriction in regard to presence as in space.

(iii) *Rāga* — limitation in regard to some objects or selection.

(iv) *Vidyā* — limitation as to the sphere of cognition.

(v) *Kalā* — limitation as to the authorship or power to accomplish, leading to limited activity.

Kañcukī (*N*): Designation of a character in a Sanskrit drama. He is an old brāhmaṇa, endowed with various good qualities, moving about in the harem and expert in all kinds of work.

Kānīna (*Sm*): Son of an unmarried woman.

Kapāla (*A*): A treaty in which excessive demands are made.

Kāpālika (*T*): An extremist Śaiva resorting to the cult of Śakti, and drinking wine from human skulls.

Kāpaṭika (*Sm*): A student acting as a spy.

Kapiśāyana: A kind of intoxicating drink.

Kāraka (*Vy*): Case, that which has some connection with a verb. Six *kārakas* are distinguished in grammar. These are *kartā* (nominative), *kārma* (objective), *karaṇa* (instrumental), *saṁpradāna* (dative), *apādāna* (ablative), *adhikaraṇa* (locative).

Karaṇa (*Vy*): Instrumental case, that which is the most helpful in the accomplishment of an action.

(*Sm*): (1) One born of the union of a vaiśya and a śūdra female.

(2) One born of a *vrātya* (q.v.) kṣatriya by a kṣatriya woman.

(*J*): Half of the duration of a *tithi*.

(*N*): Simultaneous and graceful movement of hands and feet in dance.

Kāraṇa (*T*): Wine used in Tāntric rituals. The word means cause. Such wine is supposed to be the cause of knowledge of *dharma*, *artha*, *kāma* and *mokṣa*.

Kāraskara (*Sm*): A region a visit to which renders a man (brāhmaṇa?) liable to expiation.

Kārāvara (*Sm*): A sub-caste that springs from the union of *niṣāda* (q.v.) and a *vaideha* (q.v.) woman.

Kāritā (*Sm*): The interest stipulated by the debtor himself.

Karkarikā: A kind of lute.

Karma (*Vy*): Accusative or objective case; that which is the most desired object of the agent.

Karmadhāraya (*Vy*): Appositional compound. It is a variety of *tatpuruṣa* in which the members are in the same case relation; in other words, it is a compound of an adjective with a noun.

Karmānta (*Sm*, *A*): Workshop, factory.

Karmapravacanīya (*Vy*): The particles *prati*, *anu*, etc., receive this designation when governing a substantive and modifying a verb. These are to be distinguised from *upasarga* and *gati*. For example, *japam anu prāvarṣat*; here *anu* is a *karmapravacanīya*.

Karṇa (*J*): The side opposite to the right angle in a right-angled triangle.

Kārṣāpaṇa: A coin or weight of different values (if of gold = 16 *paṇa*s or 1280 *cowries*, if of copper = 80 *rattikā*s or about 176 grains; but according to some = only 1 *paṇa* of *cowries* or 80 *cowries*).

Kartā (*Vy*): Nominative case; that is independent in the performance of an action.

Kāruṣa (*Sm*): A sub-caste sprung from the union of a *vrātya* (q.v.) vaiśya and a vaiśya female.

Kārtāntika (*A*): One who earns a living by showing the picture of Yama; astrologer.

Kaṭakāra (*Sm*): One born as a result of the clandestine union of a vaiśya and a śūdra female.

Kārya (*N*): An *Artha-prakṛti* (q.v.).

Kathā (*Al*): A literary composition in prose dealing with an imaginary theme.

Kavya (*Sm*): Oblation of food offered to deceased ancestors.

Kāyastha (*Sm*): (i) A scribe in the revenue department of a king. (ii) Name of a caste which, according to some, is śūdra.

Kāyikā (*Sm*): (i) Interest of a *paṇa* or quarter *paṇa* to be paid everyday without the principal being liable to be reduced whatever interest may have been recovered.

(ii) Interest received from the body, e.g., milk received from a cow pledged or the work put in by a slave or by a bull pledged.

Keśānta (*Sm*): Ceremony of tonsure.

Khanaka (*Sm*): One born of an *āyogava* (q.v.) by a kṣatriya woman.

Khandha (*D*) Skt. *Skandha*: The constituents of the individual. These are *rūpa* (form), *vedanā* (feeling), *saññā* (Skt. *saṁjñā*—notion), *saṁkhāra* (Skt. *saṁskāra*—mental disposition) and *viññāna* (Skt. *vijñāna* — clear consciousness or discrimination).

Khyāti (*D*): Knowledge, faculty of discriminating objects by appropriate designation.

Khaṇḍitā (*Al*): A woman angry at the sight of nail- or tooth-marks of another woman on the body of her husband.

Khārvaṭika (*A*): One in charge of a small township, set-up by the king, for the administration of a unit of 200 villages.

Kitava: Gambler in dice.

Kleśa (*D*): Suffering of five kinds, viz., *avidyā* (false knowledge), *asmitā* (ego), *rāga* (attachment), *dveṣa* (hatred), *abhiniveśa* (instinctive clinging to worldly life and bodily enjoyments and the fear of being cut off from them by death.

Klīva (*Ay*): Impotent.

Kośa (*T*, *Sm*, *A*, *D*): According to Tantra, the human body consists of five *kośa*s or sheaths, namely:

(i) *annamaya-kośa*, (ii) *prāṇamaya-kośa*, (iii) *manomaya-kośa* (iv) *vijñānamaya-kośa* and (v) *ānandamaya-kośa*. In works, dealing with politics and *rāja-dharma*, it means treasury, exchequer; one of the seven constituents (*aṅga*) of the State.

Krānti-vṛtta (*J*): The circular route along which Ravi is supposed to move constantly.

Kṛcchra (*Sm*): (i) Bodily mortification, penance, (ii) A particular kind of penance. For an incapable person, one cow is substituted for penance.

Krīta or *Krītaka* (*Sm*): One who is purchased from one's parents in order to be treated as a son.

Kriyā (*Sm*): Proof in a law-suit.

Kr̥mi-roga (*Ay*): Worms.

Kr̥t (*Vy*): Primary affixes, added to verbs.

Kr̥ti (*J*): Square, e.g., $a \times a = a^2$.

Kr̥trima (*Sm*): A parentless boy adopted by a person as his son after alluring him with money, land, etc.

Kr̥tya (*A, Vy*): (1) Seducible, liable to be disaffected.

(2) Designation of the following *kr̥t* suffixes; *tavya, anīyar, nyat, yat, kyap*.

Kṣātra (*Sm*): A form of marriage, which is the same as *rākṣasa* (q.v.). A *pratiloma* caste sprung from a śūdra father and kṣatriya mother.

Kṣattā (*Sm*): A *pratiloma* caste sprung from a śūdra father and kṣatriya mother.

Kṣaya-māsa (*J*): A lunar month in which there are two *ravi-saṁkrāntis*. It happens once in 19 years or 131-7 years.

Kṣetraja (*Sm*): A kind of son, begotten by a person, by means of *niyoga* (q.v.), on the wife of a sonless person.

Kṣetrin (*Sm*): The husband of a woman on whom a son is begotten by another person, called *bījin*, according to *niyoga* (q.v.).

Kṣitija-vr̥tta (*J*): Same as *kuja* (q.v.).

Kuja (J): Horizon where the earth and the sky seem to meet. Planet Mars.

Kukkuṭaka (*Sm*): (1) A particular *pratiloma* (q.v.) caste.

(2) One born of a śūdra by a *niṣāda* (q.v.) woman.

(3) One born of a vaiśya by a *niṣāda* woman.

Kula (*Sm*): (i) As much land as can be tilled with two ploughs.

(ii) A multitude.

(iii) Family.

Kula (*Sm*): (i) A group of relatives (cognates and agnates) of the litigant.

(ii) According to *Aparārka* commentary, cultivators.

Kulaka (*Al*): A kind of *kāvya* consisting of five stanzas related to one another.

Kula-kuṇḍalinī (*T*): Same as *kuṇḍalinī* (q.v.).

Kullukā (*T*): Designation of a *mantra*, recited before *japa* after the worship of Mahāvidyā (q.v.).

Kumba: Perhaps a kind of head-dress.

Kumbhadāsī: A woman in keeping.

Kumbhakāra (*Sm*): (1) One born out of the clandestine union of a brāhmaṇa with a vaiśya female.

(2) A particular section of śūdras.

Kumbhaka (*D, T*): A kind of *prāṇāyāma* in which the breath is held up.

Kuṇḍa (*Sm*): One born out of a male with a woman whose husband is alive.

Kuṇḍalinī (*T*): Name of the dormant spiritual energy in the human body. It is fancied to encircle, like a serpent, the *mūlādhāra* (q.v.).

Besides the individual *kuṇḍalinī*, the Tantras conceive also of Mahākuṇḍalinī at the root of the universe.

[See R.C. Prasad, *Lifting the Veil* (*Kuṇḍalinī-yoga*), Delhi, 1971; G. Krishna, *Kuṇḍalinī*: *The Evolutionary Energy*.]

Kupya (*Sm, A*): A base metal; any metal but gold, silver, brass, etc.; bamboo, creeper, bark, rope, etc.

Kurīra: Perhapas a dress or ornament for the head.

Kuśīlava (*Sm*): A professional dancer.

Kuṣṭha-Roga (*Ay*): Leprosy; elephantiasis. There are 18 kinds of it — 7 *mahākuṣṭhas* and 11 *kṣudrakuṣṭhas*.

Kusuma (*Ay*): Ophthalmia.

Kūta-sākṣin (*Sm*): A perjurer.

Kūṭa-śāsana (*A*) : A forged royal edict.

Kūṭatāna (*S*): Those complete and incomplete *mūrchanā*s (q.v.) in which the notes are uttered in irregular order.

Kūṭa-yuddha (*A*): Deceitful war at an undeclared place and year.

Kuṭṭanī: Procuress.

Kvātha (*Ay*): Decoction.

Lagna (*J*): Rise of a zodiac.

Lakṣaṇā (*Al*): A function of words. By it a word expresses a sense other than its primary sense with which the former is connected. For example, in the sentence *gaṅgāyāṁ ghoṣaḥ vasati* the word *gaṅgāyām* means not in the Ganges but on the bank which is connnected with the Ganges.

Lamba (*J*): Perpendicular.

Laya (*S*): Uniformity of interval of time in music. It is of three kinds, namely, *druta* (fast), *madhya* (medium) and *vilambita* (delayed).

Lāsya (*S*): Tender and voluptuous dance; it is stated to increase passion.

Lingastha (*Sm*): A religious student.

Lepabhāgin(*bhuj*) (*Sm*): Paternal ancestors in the fourth, fifth and sixth degrees, who are entitled to *lepa*, i.e., particles or remnants wiped from the hand after offering oblation to the three ancestors.

Madhukoṣaka: Perhaps a drinking vessel.

Madhuparka (*Sm*): A mixture of certain delicious substances offered to deities in religious rites or to distinguished guests. Opinions of some authorities, who differ on the ingredients, are as follows:

(i) Mixture of curd and honey.

(ii) Mixture of water (or, milk) and honey.

(iii) Meat.

Nowadays used in the worship of deities only, it consists of a mixture of curd, *ghī*, water, honey and sugar.

Madhuvidyā: The science which turns poison into nectar.

Mādhvī (*Sm*): A spirituous liquor distilled from the flowers of the *madhuka* plant (*Madhuka longifolia*).

Madhyama (*S*): The fourth of the seven notes of the Indian gamut; it is indicated by *MA*.

Mādhyamika: Name of a school of Buddhist philosophy. The significance of the name is that, in this school, the two extremes, viz., everything is real or everything is unreal, are avoided, and the middle path is adopted. According to it, *śūnyavāda* does not mean absolute emptiness or void; only the phenomenal world is regarded as void. But, all realities are not denied. *Śūnya* indicates the indescribable nature of the phenomenal world. It is a sort of relativity. The idea is that the reality behind the world, that we see, can be realised only by *nirvāṇa*. What is denied is the incomprehensibility of the reality through the senses, not the reality itself.

Madhyamā (*D*): A special type of sound in between *paśyantī* (q.v.) and *vaikharī* (q.v.). It is within the body, and connected with intellect. Regarded as a state of equilibrium of *parā* (q.v.) and *paśyantī*. According to Bhāskara Rāya, a Tāntric scholar, *Brahman* as sound, being manifested as *paśyantī*, is specially articulated with the help of wind in the region of the heart as *nāda*. This state is called *madhyamā*, the third stage of sound. It is supposed to reveal words. See commentary on the Tāntric work, *Prapañcasāra*, II.43: *Cidvallī* on *Kāmakalāvilāsa*, XXVI; Saubhāga-bhāskara on *Lalitāsahasra-nāma*, 99.

Magadha (*Sm*): (1) A caste sprung from the union of a vaiśya male and a kṣatriya female.

(2) Offspring of a vaiśya by a brāhmaṇa female.

(3) Offspring of a śūdra by a kṣatriya female.

Mahābhūta: Same as *pañca-bhūta* (q.v.).

Mahākāvya (*Al*): A poetical composition of certain characteristics of which the chief are: number of cantos more than eight, hero a divine being or a kṣatriya of good lineage and noble character, principal *rasa* (q.v.) erotic and accessory *rasa*s heroic or quietistic, theme historical event or an event relating to a good person. There should be descriptions of nature, sacrifice, marriage, expedition, birth of son, etc.

Mahālayā (*Sm*): The latter half of *Bhādrapada*, when the sun is in the zodiac Kanyā, is so called.

Mahāmāyūrī: Prayer for exorcism.

Mahānāṭaka (*N*): A kind of drama, in ten acts, containing all kinds of *patākā-sthāna*s (q.v.).

Mahāpātaka or *-pāpa* (*Sm*): A class of sins comprising the following: murder of a brāhmaṇa, drinking of wine called *surā*, theft of gold belonging to a brāhmaṇa, incestuous connection with one's mother and association with one who has committed one or other of the above sins.

Mahāprāṇa (*Vy*): Aspirate. Consonants requiring hard breathing for pronunciation. The second and fourth consonants of each class or group (*varga*) and the sibilants belong to this category.

Liṅga (*D*): In logic, the predicate of a proposition.

Lokāyata or *Lokāyatika* (*D*): Cārvāka, materialist. According to them, the body, with consciousness, is the soul. Hedonism is the highest goal of their lives. They do not recognise God as also the existence of the other world.

Madhubhūmika (*D*): A *yogin* who, by practising *yoga*, has attained *Ṛtambharā prajñā* (q.v.).

Mahāsāntapana (*Sm*): An expiatory rite about the nature of which the divergent views are as follows:

(1) Lasting for seven days. One has to drink cow's urine, dung, milk, curd, *ghī* and water in which *kuśa* grass has been soaked, one each on the successive days, and to fast on the last day.

(2) Of 20 days' duration. Each of the above substances is to be taken for three successive days, and fast undergone for the last three days.

(3) Spreading over 15 days. Cow's urine, dung, milk, curd, and *ghī* — each of these is to be taken for three days consecutively.

Mahāvidyā (*T*): See *daśa-mahāvidya*.

Mahat (*D*): According to Sāṁkhya and Yoga, the first evolute of *prakṛti* (q.v.); *buddhi*.

Mahāvrata (*Sm*): Name of a *sāman* or *stotra*. Appointed to be sung on the last day but one of the *gavāmayana*, a sacrifice performed through a year.

Mahāvyāhṛti (*Sm*): Name of the mystical formula *bhūr bhuvaḥ svaḥ*.

Mahāyajña (*Sm*): Same as *Pañca-mahāyajña* (q.v.).

Māheśvara-sūtra (*Vy*): See *Śiva-sūtra*.

Mahī-durga (*Sm*): A kind of fortress which is surrounded by a wall made of stone or brick, twice the width in height, which will not be less than 12 cubits, provided at the top with sufficient space for the movement of troops and fitted with covered windows.

Māhiṣa (*Sm*): One who acquiesces in the conduct of his wife gone astray.

Māhiṣya (*Sm*): A caste sprung from the marriage of a kṣatriya male with a vaiśya female.

Maitra (*Sm*): Same as *kāruṣa* (q.v.).

Maitreyaka (*Sm*): Offspring of a Vaidehaka (q.v.) by an Āyogava (q.v.) female.

Makara (*Sm*): A military array which is the reverse of *varāha-vyūha* (q.v.).

Mala (*D*): Impurity which is an obstacle in the way of the individual self's realisation of identity with the Supreme Soul. It is threefold, viz., *āṇava* (by this the soul is subjected to limitation); *māyīya* (caused by *māyā*) (q.v.) and *kārma* (arising from actions).

Malamāsa (*J*, *Sm*): Intercalary month; an intercalated thirteenth month in which no religious ceremony should be performed. See *adhimāsa*.

Malāvaha (*Sm*): A class of sins comprising killing of birds, aquatic creatures, worms and insects, eating things similar to intoxicating drinks.

Malla (*Sm*): Same as *jhalla* (q.v.).

Maṇḍa (*Ay*): Thick scum forming on the surface of any liquid; the scum of boiled rice, gruel.

Maṇḍala (*Sm*, *T*): (i) The circle of a king's near and distant neighbours with whom he must maintain political and diplomatic relations.

(ii) a kind of mystical diagram used in invoking a divinity; e.g., *sarvatobhadra*.

Maṇḍūka-pluti (*Vy*): 'Frog-leap'. A kind of *adhikāra* (q.v.) in which a *sūtra* or a part of it is to be understood in a remote *sūtra* without being applicable in the intervening *sūtra*s.

Mānuṣa (*Sm*): A form of marriage similar to *āsura* (q.v.).

Manuṣya-yajña (*Sm*): Same as *nṛ-yajña* (q.v.).

Mārga (*S*, *Al*): (i) Classical music. Derived from the root *mṛg* (to seek), it literally means that music which Brahmā obtained after seeking. The word *mārga* is also interpreted as way, path, i.e., the path shown by the sages. The term is used to indicate that music which is performed in strict conformity with the rules laid down in authoritative works.

(ii) Same as *rīti* (q.v.).

Mārgava (*Sm*): Same as *kaivarta* (q.v.).

Māruta-vrata (*Sm*): Kullūka, on *Manu* (IX.306), explains it thus. As the wind, called *prāṇa*, enters into all creatures, and moves about in their bodies, so also the king should penetrate, through spies, all the places in his own territory as well as in that of another, in order to gather the intended information; this is *māruta-vrata*.

Maryādā (*Vy*): Limit exclusive. It is of two kinds according as it relates to time and place. For example, in *āmukteḥ saṁsāraḥ*, 'ā' is in the sense of *maryādā* so that it excludes the time when *mukti* is obtained. Again, in *prayāgāt prabhṛti ā kāśyā vṛṣṭo devaḥ* 'ā' excludes the region known as Kāśī.

Māsadagdhā (*J*): Certain inauspicious lunar mansions in the solar month, e.g., *śuklā ṣaṣṭhī* in *Vaiśākha*, *kṛṣṇā caturthī* in *Jyeṣṭha*, etc.

Manana (*D*): Comprehending the instructions of the preceptor about *Brahman* through reasoning until all doubts are set at rest, and firm conviction arises. The second of the three requisites for realisation of *Brahman*.

Mātrā (*C*): Mora, syllabic instant. A short vowel is said to be of one *mātrā* while a long one has two.

Mātṛ-bandhu (*Sm*): See *Bāndhava*.

Mātsya-nyāya (*A*): The rule of might; anarchy; oppression of the weak by stronger persons. The analogy is drawn from the finny world in which a big fish devours smaller ones.

Mātu (*S*): *Vāk* or words constituting a *kāvya*. It differs from *dhātu* (q.v.) in that the latter is a matter worthy of being sung.

Maula (Sm): One holding office from a previous generation; hereditary.

Māyā (*D*): In Vedānta philosophy, it means illusion by which one considers the unreal universe as really existent and as distinct from the Supreme Spirit. It is regarded as a power of God. *Māyā* is considered by some to be synonymous with *ajñāna* or *avidyā* which is the cause of false knowledge. In Sāṁkhya philosophy it means the *pradhāna* or *prakṛti*. *Māyā* is believed to have two forces (*śakti*) by which it causes the distrection of mind (*vikṣepa*) and veiling the reality (*āvaraṇī*).

[See A.K. Ray Chaudhury, *Doctrine of Māyā*; T. Goudriaan, *Māyā: Divine and Human*, Delhi, 1978; L.T.O. Neil, *Māyā in Śaṅkara*, Delhi, 1980.]

Meda (*Sm*): Offspring of a Vaidehaka (q.v.) by a Niṣāda (q.v.) female.

Mleccha (*Sm*): (1) Persians and the like.

(ii) Those who live in Ceylon and such other places as are devoid of the caste-system and the four stages of life.

Mleccha-deśa (*Sm*): According to *Manu* (II.23) the land beyond the region which is the natural habitat of Kṛṣṇasāra (spotted antelope?).

Mokṣa (*D*): Also called *mukti*, *niḥśreyasa*, etc.

It is of different kinds according to different philosophers. For instance, Abhinavagupta recognises three classes of emancipated souls, viz., *pramukta* — those merged in the Supreme Being; *aparamukta* — those united with Him in his manifested phase and *jīvanmukta* or those yet residing in the body.

Other kinds of liberation are : *sālokya* (getting access into the region of God), *sāyujya* (entrance into or absorption in the divine self), *sāmīpya* (acquiring the proximity of God), *sārṣṭya* (attainment of the power or status like that of God).

Excepting *jīvanmukti*, in all other kinds of *mokṣa* the soul is believed to attain liberation in the disembodied state, i.e., after the death of the individual concerned.

Mṛgī (*K*): A class of women.

Mṛta (*Sm*): Food obtained by begging.

Mudrā (*T,S*): Derived from the root *mud*, it literally means 'that which causes delight'. Generally, it denotes various positions of the fingers and hand, made by one at the time of worship, e.g., *matsya-mudrā*, *śaṅkha-mudrā*, etc. This word also denotes certain postures of the body at the time of practising *yoga*, e.g., *aśvinī-mudrā*. Several *mudrā*s are used also in dance.

Muhūrta (*J*): Measure of time = ten *daṇḍa*s or 1/16 part of a day or night. According to some, it is 1/15.

Mukhebhagā (*K*): A woman satisfying the carnal desire of a man by her mouth.

Muktaka (*Al*): (1) A single independent verse.

(2) A kind of composition devoid of prose.

Mūlādhāra (*T*): Name given, in the Tantras, to a mystical circle supposed to exist above the organ of generation.

Mūlakarman (*A*): A magical rite performed with the help of herb-roots.

Mūrchanā (*S*): The rising of sounds, an intonation, duly regulated rise and fall of sounds, conducting the air and the harmony through the keys in a pleasing manner, changing the key or passing from one key to another.

Mūrdhavasikta (*Sm*): (i) A caste sprung from the marriage of a brāhmaṇa with a kṣatriya woman.

(ii) Offspring of the clandestine union of a brāhmaṇa with a kṣatriya woman.

Nāda (*T*): Sound. First vibration of *parā śakti* expressing itself in creation. Manifestation of the Supreme Being's consciousness revealed in sound.

Nadī (*Vy*): A technical term which generally denotes words in feminine gender, ending in long *I* and long *U*. There are exceptions.

Nāgara (*V*): Designation of the type of architecture current in north India.

Nagnikā (*Sm*): (i) A ten-year old girl.

(ii) A girl whose first menstruation is imminent.

(iii) A girl in whom sexual desire has not yet grown.

(iv) A girl whose menstrual flow has not yet started, and whose breasts are not yet fully developed.

(v) A girl who looks beautifiul even without dress.

Naigama (*Sm*): The *pāśupatas*, etc., who accept Vedic authority.

Naiṣṭhika (*Sm*): A life-long *brahmacārin*.

Nālikā (*A*): Water-clock.

Nāmakarman or *Nāmadheya* (*Sm*): The sacrament in which a child is named for the first time.

Nāman (*Vy*): Noun, substantive. One of the four categories of words, according to the *nirukta* and some other ancient works.

Nāṇaka (*Sm*): A coin or anything stamped with an impression.

Nāndī (*N*): Name of one of the preliminaries of a drama. By it the gods, the twice-born or kings, etc., are eulogised along with benediction to actors or spectators.

Nāndīmukha (*Sm*): Designation of the *pitṛs* (ancestors) in whose honour *vṛddhi-śrāddha* (q.v.) is performed.

Nāndī-śrāddha (*Sm*): Same as *vṛddhi-śrāddha* (q.v).

Nāṣṭika (*Sm*): Owner of a lost thing.

Nāstika (*Sm*): (i) Atheist or unbeliever.

(ii) One denying the consequence of works.

(iii) One who speaks ill of the Vedas, *Brāhmaṇas*, *Dharmas*, etc.,

(iv) One denying the existence of future life in the other world.

Naṭa (*Sm*): Same as *karaṇa* (q.v.).

Nāṭikā (*N*): A four-act drama with following characteristics: imaginary plot, hero, a well-known noble king, heroine an unmarried girl of a royal family with newly grown attachment to king, her union with the king after many obstacles.

Nāṭya (*N*): Imitation of a condition. Drama.

Navāṁśa (*J*): 1/9 of a *rāśi*.

Nāyaka (*A*): Principal military officer over ten generals.

(*N*): Hero of a poetical composition or drama.

Nibaddha (*S*): Song composed in words; as opposed to *anibaddha* which means a *rāga* without words.

Nibandha (*Sm*): (1) "A periodic payment or allowance in cash or kind permanently granted by a king, a corporation or a village or a caste to a person, family or a temple."

(2) "Delivery or payment of so many leaves (of betel or the like) on each bundle of leaves or so many rupees on each load of merchandise or so many betelnuts on each load of betelnuts."

(3) "The wealth to be obtained under the order or direction of king or other authority that dealers in commodities should pay every year or month a certain amount to a certain brāhmaṇa."

Nicchivi (*Sm*): Same as *karaṇa* (q.v.).

Nidhi (*Sm*): Treasure-trove, i.e., gold, etc., lying underground for a long time.

Nididhyāsana (*D*): Constant meditation, with a concentrated mind, on what the preceptor has said about *Brahman*. The third of the three requisites for the realisation of *Brahman*.

Nigrahasthāna (*D*): Points of defeat in a debate. These are as follows:

(1) *Pratijñāhāni*—surrendering the proposition to be established.

(2) *Pratijñāntara* — shifting the argument by bringing in new considerations.

(3) *Pratijñāvirodha* — self-contradiction.

(4) *Pratijñā-saṁnyāsa* — disclaiming the proposition.

(5) *Hetvantara* — shifting the reason.

(6) *Arthāntara* — shifting the subject.

(7) *Nirarthaka* — senseless talk.

(8) *Avijñātārtha* — use of unintelligble jargon.

(9) *Apārthaka* — incoherent talk.

(10) *Aprāptakāla* — overlooking the order of argumentation.

(11) *Nyūna* — leaving out essential steps of the argument.

(12) *Adhika* — elaboration of the obvious.

(13) *Punarukta* — repetition.

(14) *Ananubhāṣaṇa* — to keep silent.

(15) *Ajñāna* — not understanding the proposition.

(16) *Apratibha* — lacking in resourceful reply.

(17) *Vikṣepa* — evasion of discussion by pretending to be ill.

(18) *Matānujñā* — admission of defeat by pointing out that it exists also in the opponent's view.

(19) *Paryanuyogyopekṣaṇa* — overlooking the censurable.

(20) *Niranuyogyānuyoga* — censuring the non-censurablerable.

(21) *Apasiddhānta* — deviation from an accepted tenet.

(22) *Hetvābhāsa* — semblance of a reason, fallacy.

Niḥśreyasa (*D*): Liberation. Freedom from the bonds of birth and death and the complete cessation of all sufferings. Also see *mokṣa*.

Nikṣepa (*Sm,A*): (i) A deposit entrusted to a man after counting the articles in his presence.

(ii) Deposit of one's articles with another through confidence.

(iii) Delivery of one's articles to another for handing over to a third.

(iv) A container, a storing place.

Nimitta-kāraṇa (*D*): Efficient cause. For example, in the making of a table, the carpenter is the *nimittakāraṇa*.

Nipāta (*Vy*): Certain particles such as *ca*, etc., when not denoting a substance, are known by this name.

Nipātana (*Vy*): The fact of a word, given in an authoritative work, especially in that of Pāṇini, regardless of its derivation, is called *nipātana*. For example, in the rule *Acaturavicatura*, etc. (Pāṇini V.4.77), the words are vaild by *nipātana*.

Nirdhāraṇa (*Vy*): Selection of one from a group by means of genus, quality, action or name.

Nirākṛti (*Sm*): (1) One who does not perform the five *mhāyajñas* (q.v.).

(2) One who has not studied his own Veda or does not perform *vratas*.

Nirodha (*D*): Suppression (of *duḥkha* in Sāṁkhya and Buddhist philosophy); (of mental modifications according to Yoga).

Nirṛti (*Sm*): Name of a malevolent goddess.

Nirvāṇa (*D*): According to the Buddhists, the highest bliss. It means purification of the mind, its restoration to its primitive simplicity or radiant transparency. Sometimes four kinds of *nirvāṇa* are distinguished, viz.

(i) Synonym of *dharmakāya* — the undefiled essence present in all things.

(ii) *Upādhiśeṣa nirvāṇa* — that *nirvāṇa* in which some residue is left.

(iii) *Anupādhiśeṣa nirvāṇa* — that which has no residue

(iv) Absolute enlightenment having, for its object, the benefiting of others; it is the highest kind of *nirvāṇa*.

Niṣāda (*Sm*, *S*): (i) Offspring of the marriage of a brāhmaṇa with a śūdra woman, such an offspring being called *pāraśava* by some. According to some authorities, Niṣāda is the offspring of a brāhmaṇa from a vaiśya woman.

(ii) The seventh note of the Indian gamut; it is indicated by *Nl*.

Niṣeka (*Sm*): The ceremony of impregnation.

Niṣka: (i) A kind of coin.

(ii) Gold or silver necklace.

Niṣkramaṇa or *Niṣkrama* (*Sm*): The sacrament by which a child is taken out of the house for the first time after birth.

Niṣkraya (*Sm*): Price, hire, ransom.

Nisṛṣṭārtha (*A*): One authorised to negotiate in a matter, plenipotentiary, envoy, *charge d'affaires*.

Nisṛṣṭi (*A*): A kind of royal edict authorising somebody to do some work.

Niṣṭhā (*Vy*): Designation of the *kṛt* suffixes *-kta* and *-katavatu*.

Nīvī (*A*): (1) The remainder after deducting expenses from the income.

(2) Capital amount.

Nivītin (*Sm*): One wearing the sacred thread round the neck like a garland.

Niyama (*D*, *Vy*, *Al*): (i) Restriction relating to one when another alternative is available. The Vedic sentence *vrīhīn-*

avahanti (threshes paddy) is an instance of *niyamavidhi*. When unhusking can be effected either by using the mortar and pestle or by some other method (such as by using nails), this rule restricts one to threshing only.

(ii) In Yoga philosophy, it is a *yogāṅga* (q.v.). It means the practice of the following: *śauca*, *santoṣa*, *tapas* (austerity), *svādhyāya* (study of scriptures, particularly Vedic study) and *Īśvarapraṇidhāna* (q.v.).

(iii) In Rhetoric, a poetical commonplace or convention: e.g., the description of the cuckoo in spring, peacocks in the rains.

Niyatāpti (*N*): One of the *avasthās* (q.v.).

Niyoga (*Sm*): Appointment of a wife or widow to procreate a son from intercourse with an appointed male, usually her brother-in-law younger than her husband.

Nṛ-durga (*Sm*): A kind of royal fort guarded, on all sides, by infantry, with elephants, horses and chariots.

Nṛtta (*N*): Dance based on *tāla* (q.v.) and *laya* (q.v.).

Nṛtya (*N*): It represents, by gestures, an emotion which is expressed by words. Pantomime.

Nṛ-yajña (*Sm*): See *Pañca-mahāyajña*.

Nyāsa (*Sm*, *T*, *S*): (i) An open deposit for safe custody.

(ii) Handing over, to some member in the house, an article in the absence of the head of the house, for delivery to the latter.

(iii) In Tantras, it is the name of the process by which a *sādhaka* imagines different parts of his body as identical with the body of the deity meditated upon or worshipped by him. *Nyāsa* is of many kinds, e.g., *aṅga-nyāsa*, *kara-nyāsa*, *mātṛkā-nyāsa*, etc.

(iv) In music, it is the note in which a song or *rāga*, being completed, is concluded.

Oṣadhi (*U*): It denotes a tree that dies out after its fruits ripen.

Pācana (*Ay*): (i) A medicine prepared by cooking the ingredients.

(ii) A dissolvent, digestive medicine.

Pada (*Vy*): A basic form (*prātipadika*) with *sup* affixes attached and a root with *tiṅ* affixes attached pare designated as *pada*.

Pāda (*C*): A foot of a verse.

Pādakr̥cchra (*Sm*): A form of penance in which the sinner takes food on one day only once by day, only once at night, then once only (by day or at night) but without asking for it, and observes total fast for one day.

Padika (*A*): A military officer-in-charge of ten parts of an Army, particularly of ten chariots and elephants.

Padma-vyūha (*Sm*): A kind of military array in which the king remains at the centre, and spreads the army on all sides.

Padminī (*K*): A class of women.

Padya (*C*): According to the *Chandomañjarī*, it is a composition having four feet. It is of two kinds, viz., *vr̥tta* and *jāti*, the former being determined by syllables and the latter by syllabic instants.

Paiśāca (*Sm*): The basest and most sinful form of marriage in which a man has sexual intercourse with a girl stealthily while she is asleep.

Paiṣṭī; (*Sm*): Spirituous liquor distilled from rice or other grains.

Pāka-yajña (*Sm*): A sacrifice in which cooked offerings are given. According to some, the following are the *pāka-yajña*s *vaiśvadeva*, *bali*, *śrāddha*, entertainment of guests.

Pakṣa (*D*, *Sm*): (i) A point under discussion; the subject of a syllogism or conclusion (minor term); alternative view. A way of presenting a matter.

(ii) Plaint in a lawsuit.

Pakṣābhāsa (*D*): Fallacy of the minor term.

Pakṣiṇī (*Sm*): The period of one night with one day immediately preceding it and one day immediately following. It generally denotes a period of impurity (*aśauca*) consequent upon the birth and death of certain relatives.

Pala (*J*): A measure of time = 1/60th part of a *daṇḍa* (q.v.).

Palabhā (*J*): Same as *akṣabhā* (q.v.).

Paṁkti-pāvana (or *-pāvaka*) (*Sm*): One who sanctifies society.

Paṁkti-dūṣaṇa (or *-dūṣaka*): (*Sm*): One who defiles society, and, as such, should not be associated with.

Paṇa (*Sm*): (i) A weight of copper used as a coin (20 *māṣas*).

(ii) A bet or wager.

Pañcabhūta (*D*): Five gross elements, viz., *kṣiti* (earth), *ap* (water), *tejas* (fire), *marut* (wind) and *vyoma* (ether).

Pañca-gavya (*Sm*): The five products of cow, viz., milk, curd, *ghī*, cow's urine, cowdung.

Pañcāgni (*Sm*): The five sacred fires, viz., *āhavanīya*, *gārhapatya*, *dakṣiṇa*, *sabhya* and *āvasathya*.

Pañcakāruki: The following five classes of people: potter, blacksmith, carpenter, barber, washerman.

Pañcakleśa: See *Kleśa*.

Pañcakṛṣṭi: Cultivation of five crops by rotation in the same field or in different fields.

Pāñcālī (*Al*): Name of a style of literary composition possessing, according to Vāmana, the qualities of *mādhurya* and *saukumārya*.

Pañcalikā: Perhaps doll.

Pañcama (*S*): The fifth note of the Indian gamut; it is indicated by *PA*.

Pañca-mahāyajña or *Yajña* (*Sm*): The five religious acts to be performed by a householder, viz., *brahma-yajña* (study and teaching of the Vedas), *pitṛ-yajña* (offering libation to the manes), *daiva-yajña* (*homa*), *bhūta-yajña* (offering of food, etc., to birds, beasts, etc.), *nṛ-yajña* (rites of hospitality).

Pañcāmṛta (*Sm*): The five kinds of divine food, viz., milk, coagulated or sour milk, butter, honey and sugar.

Pañcamuṇḍī (*T*): An *āsana* (seat) for Tāntric *sādhana*, made with the severed heads of two cāṇḍālas, one jackal, one monkey and one snake.

Pañcanakha (*Sm*): Five-toed animal.

Pañcāṅga (*J*): A book, containing details about days of the week, lunar mansions, stars, *karaṇa* (q.v.) and Yoga (q.v.) is called by this name. It is called *pañjikā* (almanac) is Bengālī; in it, there is mention of also days of the solar month. The solar month is observed in Bengal, Orissa, Assam and Punjab.

Pañcarātra (*T*): A form of ritualistic Vaiṣṇavism. Mystic knowledge said to have been imparted by Viṣṇu to Brahmā who learnt it in five nights.

Pañca-sūnā (*Sm*): The five things in a house, by which animal life may be accidentally destroyed, viz., the fire-place, slab for grinding condiments, broom; pestle and mortar, water-pot.

Pañca-tattva (*T*): Also called *kula-dravya* or *kula-tattva*. In common parlance, it is called *pañca-makāra*. The five *tattva*s or *makāra*s are :

(i) *madya* (wine).

(ii) *māṃsa* (meat),

(iii) *matsya* (fish),

(iv) *mudrā* (position of fingers).

(v) *maithuna* (copulation).

Mudrā in this context sometimes means particular kinds of grains.

Pañca-varga (*Sm*): Five classes of people, appointed as spies, viz., a pilgrim or a rogue, an ascetic who has violated his vows, an agriculturist in distress, a decayed merchant and a fictitious devotee.

Pañca-yajña (*Sm*): Also called *pañcamakha*, *pañca-satra*, these are *brahma-yajña* (q.v.), *pitṛ-yajña* (q.v.), *daiva-yajña* (q.v.), *bhūta-yajña* or *bhūtabali* (q.v.) and *nṛ-yajña* (q.v.).

Pañca-varga (*Vy*): See *varga*.

Pāṇḍu (*Ay*): Jaundice.

Pāṇḍusopāka (*Sm*): Offspring of a cāṇḍāla (q.v.) by a Vaidehaka (q.v.) woman.

Parāka (*Sm*): An expiatory rite consisting in fast for 12 days and control of the senses.

Paramahaṁsa (*T*): A Tāntric devotee of a very high order, who was attained success in *Haṁsa-mantra* (q.v.).

Parāmarśa (D): Deduction, ascertaining that the *pakṣa* or subject possesses the *hetu* which is concomitant with the *sādhya*.

Pārśava (*Sm*): Offspring of a brāhmaṇa by a śūdra woman; sometimes called *niṣāda*.

Parihāra (*A*): (1) Total exemption of revenue.

(2) A kind of royal edict laying down exemption of tax at the behest of the king.

Parimitārtha (*A*): A kind of ambassador. He lacks one-fourth of the qualifications of a minister, and is given charge of limited affairs.

Parā (*Dy*): According to Rāghavabhaṭṭa on *Śāradātilaka* (I.1), it is the unmanifested sound. Also see *Setubandha* on *Nityaṣoḍaśikārṇava* (VI.10-11).

Pāramitā: Perfection, transcendental virtue. A state of spiritual fullness or success gained by *bodhisatta* for attaining Buddhahood. Generally, six or ten, viz., *dama*, *śīla*, *kṣānti*, *vīrya*, *dhyāna*, *prajñā*. To these are sometimes added *satya*, *adhiṣṭhāna*, *maitra*, *upekṣā*.

Pariṇāha (*Sm*): A space of 100 *dhanus* (1 *dhanu* = 4 cubits) between a village and a field.

Pāriṇāhya (*Sm*): Household furniture and utensils.

Pariṇāma (*D*): Transformation, assuming new characteristics. For example, curd is the *pariṇāma* of milk.

Parisaṁkhyā (*D*, *Vy*): Restriction relating to a part when the whole may be applicable. For example, when all five-toed animals may appear to be edible, the injunction permitting the eating of five species of five-toed animals only (*pañca pañcanakhā bhakṣyāḥ*) is a *parisaṁkhyā*.

Pariṣat (*Sm*): An assembly of learned men for the removal of doubts about *dharma*.

Parisrut: A kind of wine.

Parivedana (*Sm*): The act of one's marrying before one's elder brother.

Parivettā (*Sm*): The younger brother who has married before the elder.

Parivindaka (*Sm*): Same as *parivettā* (q.v.).

Parivinna (*Sm*): Same as *parivitti* (q.v.).

Parivitta or *Parivitti* (*Sm*): The unmarried elder brother whose younger brother has married.

Parivrājikā (*A*): A female spy disguised.

Parṇakūrca (*Sm*): Name of an expiatory rite.

Pārṣṇi-grāha (*Sm*, *A*): A king, considered to be hostile, just behind the territory of another king; the rear enemy.

Pārṣṇi-grāhasāra (*Sm*, *A*): The king ruling over the territory just behind that of the *ākranda* (q.v.), ally of the rear enemy of a king.

Pārśvaka: Cheat.

Pārvaṇa (*Sm*): (i) Name of *homa* performed on Full and New Moon days.

(ii) Name of a kind of *śrāddha*.

Paryudāsa (*D, Vy*): A kind of restriction. In it, stress is laid on what should be done rather than on what should not be done. For example, *abrāhmaṇān ānaya*. Here, the stress is on who should be brought and not on who should not be brought. So, the negative particle in *abrāhmaṇān* is in the sense of *paryudāsa*.

Pāṣaṇḍa (*Sm*): Heresy, heretic.

Paśyantī (*D*): A constituent of sound, considered to be the second stage of its development. It arises from the region of the navel, and has little vibration. It is supposed to reveal letters. See commentary on the Tāntric work, *Prapañcasāra*, (II.43).

Patākā-sthāna (*N*): An equivocal speech or situation in a drama, which foreshadows an event whether near at hand or distant.

Paunarbhava (*Sm*): Son or daughter of a *punarbhū* (q.v.).

Paurṇamāsa (*Sm*): A sacrifice performed on the Full Moon day.

Peraṇī (*S*): A dancer who dances in a way pleasing to the spectators. (For details, see *Saṅgīta-ratnākara*, Nartanādhyāya, verse 1303 ff.).

Peyūṣa (*Sm*): Beesting.

Phalāgama (*N*): One of the *avasthās* (q.v.).

Phāṇṭa: A sort of hot drink.

Phiṭ-sūtra (*Vy*): A *rātipadika* (q.v.) is called *phiṭ*. A *sūtra* (aphorism), dealing with the accentuation of *phiṭ*, is called *phiṭ-sūtra*.

Piṅgalā (*T*): A principal nerve in the nervous system of the human body, being on the right side.

Pīṭhamarda (*N*): The associate of the hero in the episode of a drama. He is a little less qualified than the hero, and helps him in sentiments other than the erotic.

Pitṛ-bandhu (*Sm*): See *bāndhava*.

Pitṛ-yajña (*Sm*): See *pañca-mahāyajña*.

Pitta-jvara (*Ay*): Bilious fever.

Pitta-śūla (*Ay*): Colic pain.

Plavaka: Acrobat.

Pluta (*Vy*): Designation of a vowel having three *mātrās* (*mora*). The vowels of words, used to express calling from afar, used in singing and weeping receive this name.

Prabandha (*S*): A kind of *nibaddha* (q.v.) song.

Prācīnāvītin (*Sm*): One whose sacred thread hangs over the right shoulder, and under the left arm.

Pradara (*Ay*): The disease called *Flour albus*.

Pradeṣṭā: Superintendent of the residence of cowherds.

Pradoṣa (*Sm*): Period of six *ghaṭikās* after sunset.

Prāḍvivāka (*Sm*): A judge in a lawsuit.

Pragṛhya (*Vy*): Certain words receive this designation, and the final vowels of such words do not enter into *sandhi* with the following vowel. The most commonly known words of this class are those in the dual number ending in *ī*, *ū* or *e*.

Prājāpatya (*Sm*): (i) That form of marriage in which the father gives the daughter after addressing the couple with the words 'may both of you perform your religious duties together', and honouring the bridegroom with *madhuparka* (q.v.), etc.

(ii) A mode of expiation on the description of which authorities differ. According to Manu, it consists of four periods of three days each following one another in which there are respectively eating once only by day, once only by night, once only without asking for food and complete fast.

Prakaraṇa (*N*): A major type of drama having the following main characteristics: Plot — temporal and imaginary; Hero

— brāhmaṇa, minister or merchant; Principal sentiment — erotic. Heroine — housewife, courtesan or both. Example: *Mṛcchakaṭika* of Śūdraka.

Prakarī (*N*): An *artha-prakṛti* (q.v.).

Prakṛti (*D, Vy, Ay, Sm*): Stem, root, primary material or form of rite. According to Sāṁkhya, the equilibrium of the qualities of *sattva*, *rajas* and *tamas*. According to Mīmāṁsā, *prakṛti* is that for which all the accessories are ordained. For example, the chief sacrificial rites such as *darśa* and *pūrṇamāsa* are called *prakṛti*. Among the followers of Vedānta, the school of Śaṅkara divides *prakṛti* into *māyā* and *avidyā*. The followers of Vallabha take *prakṛti* to mean matter which is a part of God. According to the followers of Madhvācārya, *prakṛti* is two-fold, viz., *cit-prakṛti* and *jaḍa-prakṛti*, the former is Lakṣmī or the will of God and the latter is the entire immovable world such as earth, stone, etc.

In Grammar this word means the base-form of a word or root before the addition of suffixes.

In *Āyurveda*, it means the condition of body.

In *Rājadharma*, the following seven limbs of a state are called *prakṛti*; king, minister, ally, treasury, territory, fortress and forces.

Prameha (*Ay*): A general name for a urinary disease (such as gleet, diabetes).

Pramṛta (*Sm*): Agriculture as a means of livelihood for a brāhmaṇa. So-called as agriculture, causing the death of many creatures in the land, engenders many kinds of pain.

Prameya (*D*): Object of valid knowldege. That which is known by *pramāṇa* like preception.

Praṇava (*Sm*): The mystical and sacred syllable *Om*.

Praṇaya (*A*): Special revenue and the like wanted by a king from the subjects in dire economic distress.

Prāṇāyāma (*Sm*, *T*, *D*): Name of the three breath exercises, viz., *pūraka*, *kumbhaka* and *recaka*, to be performed during daily prayers. By it, the vital breath is supposed to be controlled. The Tāntric worshipper believes that this practice secures for him rousing the energy, freedom from disease, aversion to objects of sense and bliss.

Praṇidhi (*Sm*): Spy.

Praṇīta: A son begotten on a woman by a person other than her husband.

Prāṅ-nyāya (*Sm*): The kind of reply in a lawsuit, in which the defendant proves that the point at issue has already been decided in his favour in a previous lawsuit.

Prapatti (*D*): Absolute self-surrender.

Prāptyāśā (*N*): One of the *avasthā*s (q.v.).

Prārabdha karma: That action done previously, which has started bearing fruit. This fruit is threefold, namely.

(1) Voluntary adoption of the life of a mendicant wandering for alms.

(2) Food and drink, etc., offered by disciples and the like, when a person is in the state of *samādhi*. It is called by others desire.

(3) Sudden or accidental fall of a stone or piercing by thorns when a person is in *samādhi* or *vyutthāna*. It is not caused by any one's desire.

Prasajya-pratiṣedha (*D*, *Vy*): A kind of restriction. In it, stress is laid on what should not be done rather than on what should be done. For example, in the grammatical rule *na nirdhāraṇe* (II.2.10), the emphasis is on the prohibition.

Prasaṅga (*Sm*): Name of the principle by which an act done in connection with one thing is helpful in another also. For example, expiation for a grave sin is capable of washing off a light sin also committed by the same person.

Prasannā: A kind of wine.

Praśāstā (*A*): The head of prisons.

Prastāra (*S*): Spreading out. Name given to the method of arranging, in a different way, the normal order of the seven musical notes; e.g., normal order *SA RA GA* may be arranged as *RA SA GA, SA GARA, GA SARA, RA GA SA* and *GA RA SA*.

Prastāvanā (*N*): Prologue in which the chief actress and the *vidūṣaka*, etc., converse with the stage-manager relating to their own work or the plot of the drama.

Prātibhāsika; Apparent, existing only in appearance. The silver exists in a mother of pearl only in imagination; it has no real existence.

Prātibhāvya (*Sm*): Suretyship.

Pratibhū (*Sm*): Surety. *Pratibhū*s are generally of three kinds viz.

(i) *Darśana-pratibhū* — one who stands guarantee for producing a man.

(ii) *Pratyaya-pratibhū* — one who creates confidence in the mind of the creditor, etc., about the debtor and the like.

(iii) *Dāna-pratibhū* — one who gives assurance like this — if so and so fails to repay the money, I shall make the payment.

Pratidhi: A part of female garment.

Pratiloma (*Sm*): The reverse order, usually applied to marriage between a male of the lower caste and a female of the higher caste.

Prātipadika (*Vy*): That which has some meaning, but which is neither a root nor a suffix, is so called. Words ending in *kṛt* suffixes, *taddhita* suffixes and *samāsa*s are also called *prātipadika*s.

Pratiprasava (*D, Vy*): Counter-exception. Exception to exception.

Pratītyasamutpāda (*D*): A Buddhist doctrine which means that the existence of everything is conditional, dependent on a cause; nothing happens fortuitously or by chance.

Pratoli (*A*): Road.

Pratyabhijñā (*D*): Recognition. Knowledge produced by *saṁskāra*s through sense-organs. The *Pratyabhijñā Śāstra*, founded by Somānanda, is a class of literature belonging to the Śaiva philosophy of Kāśmīr.

[See R.K. Kaw, *Doctrine of Recognition*, Hoshiarpur, 1967.]

Pratyāhāra (*D*, *Vy*): Restraining the sense from the objects. In grammar, the comprehension of several letters or affixes into one syllable, effected by combining the first letter of a *sūtra* with the final indicatory letter, or in the case of several *sūtra*s with the final letter of the last member. For example, *AN* is the *pratyāhāra* of the *sūtra AIUN*.

Pratyarthin (*Sm*): A defendant in a lawsuit.

Pratyavaskandana (*Sm*): The defendant's reply of special plea or demurrer.

Pravara (*Sm*): Also called *ārṣa* or *ārṣeya*, it denotes one or more illustrious *ṛṣis* who are the ancestors of a person and are associated with his *gotra* (q.v.).

Praveśaka (*N*): It is a device used for indicating some matter in a drama. It is inserted in between two acts. In it low characters speaking *Prākṛt* take part. *Entr'acte*.

Pṛṣṭhīya kendra (*J*): The polar centres of a spherical body.

Pudgala (*D*): Atom. According to Buddhists, something endowed with *sparśa*, *gandha* and *varṇa*. It is of two kinds, namely, *aṇu* and *skanda*.

Pūga (*Sm*, *A*): (1) According to *Mitākṣarā*, corporation of men belonging to different castes and occupations but living at the same place.

(2) According to *Dīpakalikā* of Śūlapāṇi, association of grocers and the like.

(3) Association of brāhmaṇas, etc., according to the

Bālakrīḍā of Viśvarūpa.

Pukkasa (*Sm*): (1) Offspring of a niṣāda (q.v.) by a śūdra female.

(2) Offspring of a śūdra by a kṣatriya female.

(3) Offspring of a vaiśya by a kṣatriya female.

Pulkasa (*Sm*): Same as *pukkasa* (q.v.).

Puṁsavana (*Sm*): A sacrament performed before the throbbing of the foetus in the womb, for obtaining a male child.

Puṁścalī: Demi monde corrupting young men.

Punarbhū (*Sm*): It generally means a re-married widow. *Punabhū*s are of 7 kinds:

(i) A girl who had once been promised to be given away in marriage.

(ii) A girl round whose wrist the auspicious band was tied by the husband.

(iii) A girl already intended to be given in marriage.

(iv) A girl who had been given away with water by the father.

(v) A girl whose hand was held by the bridegroom.

(vi) A girl who went round the fire.

(vii) A girl who bore a child after marriage.

The above girls are called *punarbhū* when married to another person. Regarding the different classes of *punarbhū*s, authorities differ.

Puraścaraṇa (*T*): A form of *sādhanā*. In it, the *sādhaka*, after partaking of *haviṣyānna* or *pañca-gavya*, recites, with a concentrated mind, a particular *mantra* many a times and feeds *Brāhmaṇa*s.

Pūrta or *pūrtaka* (*Sm*): Act of pious liberality, such as feeding brāhmaṇas, digging wells, etc.

Puruṣa (*D*): *Jīva*, consciousness. According to Sāṁkhya, there is a plurality of selves of which one is connected with each body. Along with *prakṛti*, *puruṣa* of Sāṁkhya is the uncaused cause of the universe. But, according to the Trika system of Kashmir, *prakṛti* and *puruṣa* are produced by *māyā*.

Puruṣārtha (*D*): End or purpose of human life. There are four ends, namely, *dharma*, *artha*, *kāma*, *mokṣa*.

Pūrva-nyāya (*Sm*): Same as *prāṅ-nyāya* (q.v.).

Puṣkara (*Kṛ*): A kind of cloud.

Puṣpadha (*Sm*): Same as Bhūrjakaṇṭaka (q.v.).

Pusta (*N*): Stage-properties, appurtenances required in a dramatic performance. These are of three kinds — *sandhima* (q.v.), *vyājima* (q.v.) and *ceṣṭima* (q.v.).

Puṭapāka (*Ay*): A particular method of preparing drugs, in which the various ingredients are wrapped up in leaves, and being covered with clay are roasted in the fire.

Putrikā or *Putrikā-putra* (*Sm*): (1) One's daughter's son appointed to be one's own son. (2) One's daughter appointed as one's son.

Rāga (*S*): That which pleases (*rañjayati*) the minds of listners is called *rāga*. According to Mataṅga, a number of notes, causing delight is called *rāga*. Generally, six *rāga*s are spoken of. As a matter of fact, however, many more *rāga*s are described in various works on music. There are differences of opinion about the names of six *rāga*s. Several *rāgiṇī*s of each *rāga* are imagined. Authorities differ on the names and number of *rāgiṇī*s.

Rāhu (*J*): Ascending node of the moon; eclipse, rather the moment of an occultation.

Rajaka (*Sm*): (1) Offspring of a *pulkasa* (q.v.) or *vaideha* (q.v.) by a brāhmaṇa woman.

(2) Offspring of a *pulkasa* (q.v.) by a vaiśya girl.

Rājasūya (*Sm*): Sacrifice performed at the coronation of a king, by himself and tributary princes; this confirms his title.

[See Heesterman, *Ancient Indian Royal Consecration*, The Hague, 1957; A. Weber, *Uber die* Konigs, des/Rajasu . . . Berlin, 1893.]

Rājayakṣmā or *Rājajakṣmā* (*Ay*): Consumption, phthisis.

Rājayoga (*D*): A method of *yoga* (q.v.) which aims at the complete control of the mind with all its functions or modifications suppressed.

Rākṣasa (*Sm*): A form of marriage in which a maiden in forcibly abducted.

Raṅgadvāra (*N*): The opening verse of a drama. Sometimes wrongly called *Nāndī*.

Rañjaka (*Sm*): Offspring of the clandestine union between a śūdra and a kṣatriya female.

Rasa (*Al*, *Ay*): An inexplicable inward experience of a connoisseur on witnessing a dramatic performance or reading a poetical composition. Supernatural literary delight. According to Bharata, its *niṣpatti* follows from a combination of *vibhāvas*, *anubhāvas* and *vyabhicārī-bhāvas* with the *sthāyī-bhāva*. The word *niṣpatti* has been interpreted by different scholars as *utpatti* (production), *anumiti* (inference), *bhukti* (enjoyment) and *abhivyakti* (revelation or manifestation). The following 8 *rasas* are generally recognised: *śṛṅgāra* (erotic), *vīra* (heroic), *raudra* (furious), *bībhatsa* (disgustful), *hāsya* (comic), *adbhuta* (marvellous), *karuṇa* (pathetic) and *bhayānaka* (terrible). *Śānta* (quietistic) is accepted by some as the ninth *rasa*.

In the literature of the Vaiṣṇavas of Bengal, *bhakti*, which was regarded as a *bhāva* in the earlier works on poetics, came to be regarded as a *rasa*. They divide *bhakti-rasa* into 5 main *rasas* and 7 subsidiary *rasas*.

In *Āyurveda*, it may mean any mineral or metallic salt, mercury.

[See T.P Chakravarti, Impact of the concept of *sphoṭa* on the idea of *rasa*, *Summaries of Papers*, *AIOC*, 1969.]

Rasada (*A*): A kind of spy who administers poison.

Rāśi (*J*): Zodiac.

Rathakāra (*Sm*): (1) Offspring of the marriage of a vaiśya and śūdra female.

(2) Offspring of a *māhiṣya* (q.v.) by a *karaṇa* (q.v.) woman.

(3) Offspring of the clandestine union of a kṣatriya and a brāhmaṇa woman.

Rathakrānta (*T*): Name of one of the three zones or regions into which India is divided in certain Tantras. It extends from the Vindhya hill to Mahācīna including Nepal.

Recaka (*T, D*): Exhalation, a kind of *prāṇāyāma* (q.v.).

Riktā (*Sm*): Name of the following *tithis* (lunar mansions): 4th, 9th and 14th day of lunar fortnight.

Riktha (*Sm*): Same as *r̥ktha* (q.v.).

Rikthin (*Sm*): An heir.

Rīti (*Al*): Also called *mārga*. It is defined as *viśiṣṭa padaracanā*, i.e., a particular mode of composition or arrangement of words. There are several *rītis*, e.g., *vaidarbhī*, *gauḍī*, *pāñcālī*, etc. Of these, *vaidarbhī* is generally regarded as the best.

R̥ktha (*Sm*): Any property, wealth, especially that left by one at death; inheritance.

R̥ṇa-traya (*Sm*): Threefold debt or obligation, namely:

(i) *Deva-r̥ṇa* — divine debt repayable by sacrifice.

(ii) *R̥ṣi-r̥ṇa* — debt to sages repayable by Vedic study, teaching.

(iii) *Pitr̥-r̥ṇa* — paternal debt repayable by begetting a legitimate son.

R̥ṣabha (*S*): The second of the seven notes in a song. It is so called as it is supposed to have been obtained from the bellow of a bull (*r̥ṣabha*). It is indicated by *RA*.

Ṛṣi-yajña: See *Pañca-mahāyajña*.

Ṛta (*Sm*): (i) True, truth.

(ii) Gleaning of corns as a means of a brāhmaṇa's livelihood.

Ṛtambharā prajñā (*D*): A peculiar power of knowing, which is full of truth (*ṛta*). It is different from the usual ways of knowing like perception, inference and verbal testimony. It can be acquired by *śravaṇa*, *manana* and *nididhyāsana*. See *Yogasūtra*, (I.48).

Ṛtvik (*Sm*): Priest, usually of four kinds, viz., *hotā*, *adhvaryu*, *brahmā* and *udgātā*.

Rukma: An ornament of the neck.

Rūpaka (*N*): Drama of a major type. Generally regarded as of ten types.

Śabara (*Sm*): An aboriginal tribe living in jungles.

Sabhika: Keeper of a gambling house.

Sada (Sm): Agricultural produce.

Ṣāḍava (*S*): A *rāga*, consisting of six notes, receives this designation. In *ṣāḍava*, the initial note *ṣaḍja* is never given up.

Ṣaḍguṇa or *Ṣāḍguṇya* (*Sm*, *A*): The six measures of royal policy, viz., *sandhi*, *vigraha*, *yāna*, *āsana*, *dvaidhībhāva* and *saṁśraya*.

Sādhya (*D*, *Sm*): The predicate of a proposition, the major term in a syllogism. For example, in *parvato vahnimān dhūmāt*, *vahṇi* is *sādhya*.

In Smṛti, *sādhya* is that which, in disputes of various kinds, is to be established by evidence.

Ṣaḍja (*S*): The first of the seven notes in a song. It is so called because it has originated from six notes. Some think that the name means 'that which has given birth to the other six notes'. It is indicated by *SA*.

Sāhasa (*Sm*): (i) "Punishment, fine regarded as of three kinds, the highest being called *uttama*, half of that *madhyama* and half of that *adhama*" (M. Wms.). (ii) Violence, rape, felony.

[See L. Rocher, in *V. Raghava Fel. Vol.*, Delhi, 1975.]

Sahasrāra (*T*): Thousand-petalled, multi-coloured lotus supposed to exist in *brahma-randhra* (q.v.).

Sahoḍha or *Sahoḍhaja* (*Sm*): A kind of son brought with a woman pregnant at her marriage.

Sahṛdaya (*Al*): Connoisseur. One having the capacity for appreciating a drama or a poetical composition.

Śaikha (*Sm*): Same as *āvantya* (q.v.).

Sairindhra: A class of men who used to arrange the dress of rich people.

Śakaṭa (*Sm*): The form of military array in which the van is very narrow and the rear wide, such an arrangement being resorted to in the event of danger from behind.

Śakti (*T*): 1. Power of the Supreme Being, imagined as a Female Principle thorugh which the universe is manifested. The immanent aspect of Śiva; it is not an independent entity, but His creative energy. Śakti has an infinite variety of modes of which the principal ones are:

(i) *Cit* (intelligence). By this Parama Śiva shines by Himself like the sun even when there is no object to reveal or shine on.

(ii) *Ānanda* (bliss). With the help of this Śakti, the Supreme Lord realises absolute bliss.

(iii) *Icchā* (will). The volition which makes Parama Śiva feel supremely able and of irresistible will, so that he can do or create something.

(iv) *Jñāna* (knowledge). By this Parama Śiva brings

all objects into conscious relations with Himself, and with one another.

(v) *Kriyā* (action). It is His power of assuming all kinds of form.

2. Female partner of a Tāntric devotee. Of three kinds — *svakīyā* (own wife), *parakīyā* (wife of another) and *sādhāraṇī* (public woman or prostitute).

3. According to Tantra, one of the six limbs of a *mantra*.

Sakulya (*Sm*): The three paternal ancestors above the paternal great-grandfather, and the three male descendants beyond the great-grandon.

Śakunavidyā: The science of omens and portents.

Sāma or *Sāman* (*Sm*): Policy of conciliation, negotiation being one of the four *upāyas* or means of successs against the enemy.

Samādhi (*D*): Absorption of mind in the object of contemplation. It is of two broad kinds, viz., *savikalpa* or *saṁprajñāta* (in it there is a clear and distinct consciousness about the object of contemplation) and *nirvikalpa* or *asaṁprajñāta* (it stops all mental modifications, and does not rest on any object). These are also called *sabīja* and *nirbīja* respectively.

Samādhi-mokṣa (*A*): Release of one's son and the like, kept as a pledge with the enemy.

Samāhartā (*A*): Collector of income from the fort, state, etc.

Samāhvaya (*Sm*): Setting animals to fight for sport, betting with living creatures.

Sāmājika (*Al*): Same as *sahṛdaya* (q.v.).

Samānādhikaraṇa (*Vy*): Having the same case-ending or case-relation. See *vyadhikaraṇa*.

Samānodaka (*Sm*): "Having only libation of water to ancestors in common", distantly related (the relationship, according to some, extending to the 14th degree, the first 7 being both *sapiṇḍa*s and *samānodaka*s, while the remaining 7 are *samānodaka*s).

Samāsa (*Vy*): Compound. The reducing of two or more words syntactically connected with one another, into one word.

Samāvartana (*Sm*): Return home of a student after completion of Vedic studies in the preceptor's house. Also the *saṁskāra* performed on this occasion.

Samavāya (*Vy, D, Sm*): (i) Inherence. For example, the relation of fragrance to flower is one of inherence.

(ii) One of the categories in Vaiśeṣika philosophy.

(iii) Concourse, assemblage.

Sama-vr̥tta (*C*): A kind of *vr̥tta* (q.v.) in which all the feet have the same metrical scheme.

Samaya (*Sm*): Agreement, contract.

Samayādhyuṣita (*Sm*): The time when the sun has not yet appeared, and the stars are invisible.

Śambhalī: Same as *Kuṭṭanī* (q.v.).

Sambhūyasamutthāna (*Sm*): Partnership business.

Sambuddhi (*Vy*): Designation of a word in vocative singular.

Saṁcara (*A*): A class of roving spies, who go from place to place for gathering information.

Saṁgrahaṇa (*Sm, A*): Rape. A very small township, set-up for the administration of ten villages.

Saṁhitā (*Vy*): Euphonic combination, *sandhi*.

Śaṁkhinī (*K*): A class of women.

(*Ravi*) *Saṁkrānti* (*J*): The passing of the sun from one Zodiac to another.

Saṁnidhātr̥ (*A*): Director of Stores.

Saṁnipāta-jvara (*Ay*): A combined derangement of the three humours of the body, causing fever which is of a dangerous kind.

Saṁpradāna (*Vy*): Dative case; the person whom one wishes to connect with the object of a gift, i.e., one to whom something is given.

Saṁprapada (*Sm*): Moving about.

Saṁprasāraṇa (*Vy*): It means the transformation of *Y*, *V*, *R*, and *L* into *I*, *U*, *R* and *L* respectively.

Saṁpratipatti (*Sm*): The kind of reply in a lawsuit, in which the defendant admits the charge brought against him.

Saṁsāra (*D*): Re-birth.

Saṁśraya (*Sm*): One of the *guṇas* or measures of policy, according to which a king, pressed hard by the enemy, takes the help of a more powerful king.

Saṁsr̥ṣṭa or *Saṁsr̥ṣṭin* (*Sm*, *Al*): One re-united with coparceners after partition of the property. Simultaneous presence of figures of speech, independent of one another.

Saṁstha (*A*): A class of spies staying at one place, and collecting information for the king.

Samudaya (*Sm*, *A*): Source of revenue, revenue.

Saṁvādī (*S*): A note that helps develop a *rāga* manifested by the *vādi-svara* (q.v.).

Saṁvarta (*Kr̥*): A kind of cloud.

Saṁvit (*Sm*): Contract.

(*D*): Knowledge, consciousness.

Saṁyama (*D*): *Dhāraṇā* (q.v.), *dhyāna* (q.v.) and *samādhi* (q.v.) with respect to a single object, are together called *saṁyama*.

Sanābhi (*Sm*): Kinsman on the paternal side.

Sañcārī-bhāva (*Al*): Same as *vyabhicārī-bhāva* (q.v.).

Sandhi (*Vy*, *N*, *Sm*): (1) Euphonic combination.

(2) Juncture in the action of a drama. There are five junctures, based on the parallel sets called *avasthā*s (q.v.) and *artha-prakṛti*s (q.v.). The junctures are *mukha, pratimukha, garbha, vimarśa* and *upasaṁhṛti* meaning respectively opening, progression, development, pause and conclusion. "Thus in the *Abhijñana-śakuntala* the opening extends from Act I to the point in Act II where the General departs; the progression begins with the king's confession to the Vidūṣaka of his deep love, and extends to the close of Act III. The development occupies Acts IV and V up to the point where Gautamī uncovers the face of Śakuntalā; at this moment the curse darkens the mind of the king who, instead of rejoicing in reunion with his wife, pauses in reflection, and this pause in the action extends to the close of Act VI, while the conclusion is achieved in the last Act". (See A.B. Keith, *Sanskrit Drama*, 1924, p. 29).

(3) Treaty, peace; one of the six *guṇa*s or measures of policy.

Sandhinī (*Sm*): (1) A cow in heat.

(2) A cow that gives milk in its pregnancy.

(3) A cow that is milched with the calf of another cow.

(4) A cow that is milched every alternate *velā* (time for milching?)

Sandhyā (*Sm*): 400 years at the beginning of *satya-yuga*.

Sandhima (*N*): A kind of *pusta* (q.v.), made up from bamboo, covered with skin or cloth.

Sandhyakṣara (*Vy*): Diphthong(oe). A vowel, produced by a combination of two vowels, looked upon as a single vowel for a single effort being required for its pronunciation. The vowel *e, ai, o, au* are called diphthongs.

Sandhyaṁśa (*Sm*): 400 years towards the end of *satya-yuga*.

Saṅgīta (*S*): Vocal music, instrumental music and dance are together designated by this term.

Saṅketa (*Al*): Convention. Theorists differ as to the locus of convention in the case of words. Some think that convention lies in *jāti* (genus), *guṇa* (quality), ***kriyā*** (action) and *saṁjñā* (name). Others think that it lies in the genus alone.

Sannidhātā (*A*): A top-ranking official in charge of the protection of treasury, etc.

Sāntapana (*Sm*): A form of penance. It is of five kinds, viz., the first for two days, the second for seven days, the third for 12, the fourth for 15 days and the fifth for 21 days.

Sapiṇḍa (*Sm*): It generally means one's (i) ancestors up to the sixth degree from one's father, and descendants down to the sixth degree from oneself, (ii) ancestors up to the fourth degree from mother and descendants down to the fourth degree from father.

Sapiṇḍīkaraṇa (*Sm*): Name of a *śrāddha*, performed after one year from one's death. It is supposed to unite the deceased with the body (*piṇḍa*) of his ancestors.

Sārvadhātuka (*Vy*): Name of the terminations of all tenses and moods, except those of the Perfect and the Benedictive, and of the affixes having the indicatory 'S'; i.e., the various conjugational signs of the nine classes of roots (excepting the eighth) and terminations of the Present Participle (*parasmaipada* and *ātmanepada*). These are so-called because the endings are added to the entire root. The *Vikaraṇa* (q.v.) is regarded as part and parcel of the root, so the endings before which the *vikaraṇa* is preserved is known by this designation.

Sarvanāman (*Vy*): Pronoun like the words *sarva*, *viśva*, etc.

Sarvanāmasthāna (*Vy*): The case of masculine and feminine words, the suffixes *su*, *au*, *jas*, *am* and *au* are so-called. In the case of neuter words, *jas* and *śas* receive this designation.

Śaśaka (*K*): A class of men according to writers on erotics. Such a man is soft-spoken, of good character, soft-bodied, possessed of good hair, a repository of all virtues and truthful.

Śāsana (*Sm, A*): An edict, royal command.

Śataghnī: Cannon or, according to some, a huge piece of stone covered with barbed wire. It is supposed to have been wielded for killing a hundred people at a time.

Ṣaṭkarma (*T*): Six acts included under *abhicāra* (q.v.).

Satkāryavāda (*D*): The doctrine according to which the effect pre-exists in the cause, and is made manifest by operation which that cause undergoes.

Sātvata (*Sm*): Same as *kāruṣa* (q.v.).

Satrin (*A*): A class of spies, known to be versed in various scriptures.

Satyānṛta (*Sm*): Trade and commerce.

Saudāyika (*Sm*): (i) Wealth received by a woman, whether as a maiden or as a married lady, in her father's or husband's house from her parents or relatives of the father and mother.

(ii) All property donated by the husband to a woman excepting immovable property.

Śaudra (*Sm*): "The son of a man of either of the three classes by a śūdra woman (the last of the twelve kinds of sons acknowledged in ancient Hindu Law". Monier-Williams.

Saumyakṛcchra (*Sm*): A kind of expiation about the nature of which there are different views. According to Yājñavalkya, it is a penance lasting for six days, on the first five of which one subsists, in succession, on oilcake, foamy scum of boiled rice, buttermilk, water and *saktu* (pulverised grain), and on the last day total fast is observed.

Śauṇḍika: Distiller or seller of wine.

Sauramāsa (*J*): The period from the sun's entrance into one Zodiac to its passing into another.

Sautrāntika (*D*): A school of Buddhist philosophy, so called as it is based on the *Suttapiṭaka*, known as *Suttanta*. It differs from the Vaibhāṣikas in its *Bāhyānumānavāda*, is the doctrine according to which, knowledge of the external objects arises from inference. Their forms lead to their knowledge.

Savana-māsa (*J*): A month counted with 30 days.

Savarṇa (*Vy, Sm*): Letters having the same place of articulation and requiring similar effort to pronounce are called *savarṇa*s of one another. A vowel cannot be a *savarṇa* of a consonant.

In Smṛti literature, it means one of the same caste.

Sāvitrī (*Sm*): (1) *Ṛgveda* (III.62.10).

(2) "Initiation as a member of the three twice-born classes, by reciting the above verse and investing with the sacred thread." Monier-Williams.

Sāvitrī-Patita (*Sm*) : Same as *vrātya* (q.v.).

Śeṣa (*Vy*): Pāṇini uses this in the sense of 'the remainder after what has been said'.

[See K.C. Varadachari, The evolution of the concept of *śeṣa, B.C. Law Volume*, II, Poona, 1946.]

Setu (*A*): That which marks the boundary of a house, etc.

Setubandha (*A*): (1) Dam for artificially accumulating the water of the river, etc., for the production of crops.

(2) Fixing the boundary of a house, etc., by posts and the like.

Siddhi (*T*): Superhuman faculty or power which is achieved by a *sādhaka* when he reaches the highest stage of *sādhana*. Besides faculties or powers of little importance, the following eight are called *aṣṭa-siddhi*:

aṇimā, laghimā, mahimā, prāpti, prākāmya, īśitva, vaśitva, and *kāmāvasāyitā*. The highest *siddhi* is liberation.

Śila (*Sm*): Gathering stalks or ears of corn.

Sīmantonnayana (*Sm*): The parting or dividing of the hair; name of one of the sacraments observed by a woman in the fourth, sixth or eight month of her pregnancy.

[See S.S. Dange, Symoblism in the rite of *sīmantonnayana*, *J of Asiatic Soc.*, Bombay, New Series, Vols. 52-3.]

Śiśnadeva: A non-Āryan worshipping phallus or indulging in sexual pleasure.

Śiśu-cāndrāyaṇa (*Sm*): A form of Cāndrāyaṇa (q.v.). In it, a brāhmaṇa eats, for a month, four mouthfuls in the morning and four after sunset.

Sītātyaya (*A*): Name of fine imposed on cultivators for reducing or misappropriating corns.

Śiva-sūrta (*Vy*): Also called *Māheśvara-sūtra*. The 14 *sūtras*, *a i u n*, *r̥ ḷ k*, etc., which are believed to have been taught by Śiva to Pāṇini by the sounds of the drum at the end of his dance.

Skandha (*D*): Aggregate. According to the Buddhists, there are five *skandhas*, viz., *rūpa* (form), *vedanā* (feeling of pleasure and pain), *saṁjñā* (perception), *saṁskāra* (tendencies created by impressions of past experiences) and *vijñāna* (consciousness). According to them, there is no soul beyond these five *skandhas*.

Snātaka (*Sm*): One who has perfomed ablutions marking the end of studenthood.

Sopāka (*Sm*): Son of a cāṇḍāla (q.v.) by a *pulkasa* (q.v.) woman.

Śotha (*Ay*): Swelling, dropsy.

Spanda (*D*): A term used in the Śaiva philosophy of Kāśmīr. Vibration or activity. The activity of Śiva, the only substratum of the universe, is supposed to be the cause of all distinctions.

Sphoṭa (*D*): The idea which bursts out or flashes on the mind when a sound is uttered; the impression produced on the mind on hearing a sound, the eternal sound. *Sphoṭa* is considered to be of eight kinds, namely, *varṇa-sphoṭa*, *pada-sphoṭa*, *vākya-sphoṭa*, *akhaṇḍapada-sphoṭa akhaṇḍavākya-sphoṭa*. *Varṇajāti-sphoṭa*, *Padajāti-sphoṭa*, and *vākyajāti-sphoṭa*. Of these, *vākya-sphoṭa* alone is real and the others are unreal. This is the view of grammarians.

[See *Sphoṭanirṇaya* of K. Bhatta, ed. S.D. Joshi with Intro., Eng. trs. notes. Also see H.G. Coward, *Sphoṭa Theory of Language,* Delhi, 1980; G.N. Shastri, *A Study in the Dialectics of Sphoṭa*.]

Śravaṇa (*D*): Listening to the preceptor's instructions about *Brahman*. The first of the three requisites for the realisation of *Brahman*.

Śreṇī (*Sm*, *A*): (i) A guild or association of traders dealing in the same articles. (ii) A band (of harmful persons). (iii) Banded troops.

Śṛṅgāṭaka (*A*): A 'forked rod', a kind of trap for the enemy.

Śruti (*S*): Sound having no resonance. According to some, Bharata recognised 22 *śruti*s. *Śruti* is a unit of measurement of the gradual rise of the notes of the Indian gamut.

Sthāna (*Sm*, *A*): (i) Props of a kingdom, namely, Army, treasury, capital city and territory. (ii) A condition of stability. (iii) Position, high position.

Sthānapāla (*Sm*): Appears to be the same as *sthānika* (q.v.).

Sthānika (*A*): (i) A revenue officer-in-charge of a quarter of the realm.

(ii) A city officer-in-charge of a ward.

(iii) A person able to see objects buried underground.

Sthānīya (*A*): A sort of town, set-up for the administration of 800 villages.

Sthāyī-bhāva (*Al*): Permanent or dominant feelings residing in the human mind. These are generally eight, namely, *rati*, *hāsa, krodha, utsāha, bhaya, jugupsā*, *vismaya* and *śoka*. A factor of *rasa* (q.v.). According to those, who recognise *śānta* as the ninth *rasa*, *śama* or *nirveda* is the *sthāyī-bhāva* of this *rasa*.

Strīdhana (*Sm*): A woman's exclusive property. Certain special kind of property given to a woman by relatives on certain occasions or in different stages of her life, over which she has absolute right. Authorities differ on the various kinds of *strīdhana*. According to Manu, it is of the following varieties: (i) *adhyagni* — given before the nuptial fire; (ii) *adhyāvahanika* — given in the bridal procession; (iii) *dattaṁ ca prītikarmaṇi* — given as a token of love; (iv) *bhrātr̥-mātr̥-pitr̥-prāptam* — received by the girl from her parents and brothers.

Strī-saṁgrahaṇa (*Sm*): Adultery, incest, rape, etc.

Sūcaka (*Sm*): Offspring of the union of a vaiśya and a śūdra female.

Sūcī (*Sm*): A kind of military array in which the van and the rear are compact like a row of ants.

Suda (*A*): One who cooks meat, etc.

Śuddha-vadha (*A*): Killing without torture.

Sudhanvācārya (*Sm*): Same as *kāruṣa* (q.v.).

Śuklakuṣṭha (*Ay*): Another name of *śvitra* (q.v.).

Śukriya (*Sm*): Name of the *pravarga* section of the *Vājasaneyī-saṁhitā*, (39-40).

Śukta (*Sm*): (i) A sweet substance turned sour through staleness. (2) Harsh word.

Śulka (*Sm*): (i) Bride's price, i.e., money paid by the bridegroom's side to the bride's guardians. (ii) Toll, tax, especially money levied at ferries, passes and roads.

Sūnā: See *pañca-sūnā*.

Suṇḍā: Bar.

Sūnika (*Sm*): One born of an *āyogava* by a kṣatriya woman.

Śūnyapāla (*A*): One who guards the vacant capital during the absence of the king, engaged in war.

Śūnyavāda (*D*): This doctrine of the Mādhyamika school of Buddhism advocates negatively the non-existence of substances, and positively the ever-changing flux of *saṁsāra*.

Surā (*Sm*): Spirituous liquor distilled from rice, molasses and the flowers of the *madhuka* plant. Primarily it denotes the first kind.

Sūrmi (*Sm*): A hollow metal column made red hot for burning a condemened criminal (especially, adulterer) to death.

Suṣira (*S*): See *vādya*.

Suṣumnā (*T*): The most important nerve in the human nervous system, being in the middle of the body. It is also called *brahma-vartma*.

Suṣupti (*D*): Great insensibility, spiritual ignorance.

Sūta (*Sm*): One sprung from the union of a kṣatriya and a brāhmaṇa female.

Sūtaka (*Sm*): Child-birth; impurity of parents consequent upon the birth of their child or miscarriage.

Sūtikā-roga (*Ay*): Diseases like fever, dysentery, etc., of a woman delivered of a child.

Sūtradhāra (*N*): Experienced in music, both vocal and instrumental, and dance, and skilful in organising a dramatic performance, he largely corresponds to the modern stage-manager. He figures in the prologue of a drama, as conversing with the chief actress, *vidūṣaka*, etc.

Svāṅga (*Vy*): See Pāṇini (IV.1.54). Literally meaning *sva-aṅga* (own limb), its grammatical meaning is stated in the following couplet:

adravaṁ mūrtimat svāṅgaṁ prāṇiṣṭham avikārajam ।
atatsthaṁ tatra dṛṣṭaṁ ca tena cet tat tathā yutam ॥

A word of the following descriptions is a grammatical *svāṅga*:

1. Not something liquid, as *sveda*.

2. Having a form that which can be perceived by senses.

3. Found to belong to an animate being, e.g., *stana*.

4. Not caused by any deformity, e.g., boil.

5. Though not remaining in an animate being, yet it is generally found in it; it must be in such a position as is found in an animate being, e.g., an image of a female, having *stanas*.

Śvapāka or *Śvapaca* (*Sm*): (i) Offspring of an *ugra* male from a *kṣatṛ* female.

(ii) Offspring of a *kṣatṛ* male from an *ugra* female.
(iii) Offspring of a cāṇḍāla male from a vaiśya female.
(iv) Offspring of a cāṇḍāla male and a brāhmaṇa female.

Svara (*S*): It is that which is produced immediately after *śruti*, has resonance and is charming and delightful. There are seven *svaras* in the Indian gamut; these are *ṣaḍja*, *ṛṣabha*, *gāndhāra*, *madhyama*, *pañcama*, *dhaivata* and *niṣāda*.

Svarita (*Vy*): Circumflex accent. Designation of the accent that is produced by the combination of *udātta* (q.v.) and *anudātta* (q.v.) tones.

Svayaṁdatta (*Sm*): A kind of son who, bereft of parents or forsaken by them, voluntarily offers himself to a person.

Śvetakuṣṭha (*Ay*): Another name of *śvitra* (q.v.).

Śvitra (*Ay*): Leucoderma.

Syādvāda (*D*): A Jaina doctrine which is also known as *saptabhaṅgī*. It is so called as it holds all knowledge to be only probable. According to it, there are seven different ways of speaking of a thing or its attributes, in accordance with the point of view. There is a point of view from which substance or attribute (i) is (*syād asti*), (ii) is not (*syād nāsti*), (iii) is and is not (*syād asti nāsti*), (iv) is unpredicable (*syād avaktavya*), (v) is and is unpredicable (*syād asti avaktavya*), (vi) is not and is unpredicable (*syād nāsti avaktavya*), and (vii) is, is not and is unpredicable (*syād asti nāsti avaktavya*).

Tādarthya (*Vy*): 1. The nature of being meant for another.
2. Meant for another.

It takes place when a thing is transformed into another, e.g., *kuṇḍalāya hiraṇyam* — gold meant for being transformed into a *kuṇḍala*.

Taddhita (*Vy*): Secondary affixes added to substantives so as to form secondary nominal bases.

Tadguṇa-saṁvijñāna (*Vy*): A kind of *buhuvrīhi* compound. For example, *lambakaraṇam ānaya*; bring the person or animal having long ears. In it, the person or animal as well as his characteristic comes along.

Tāla (S): Beating times in music.

Tanmātra (*D*): Five subtle elements, viz., *gandha* (smell), *rasa* (taste), *rūpa* (form), *sparśa* (touch), and *śabda* (sound) underlying *pañca-bhūta*s (q.v.).

Tantratā (*Sm*): The principle by which a sinner becomes free from several similar sins by performing only once the penance prescribed for the perpetrator of such a sin.

Tāpasavyañjana (*A*): A hypocritical ascetic acting as a spy.

Tāpatraya (*D*): Threefold suffering, viz., *ādhyātmika* (caused by mind), *ādhidaivika* (caused by fate) and *ādhibhautika* (caused by beings, e.g., animal).

Taptakṛcchra (*Sm*): (i) A form of expiation in which the sinner has to subsist on hot water, hot milk, hot *ghī* for three days each and to fast for the last three days when he should inhale hot vapour or atmosphere.

(ii) A form of penance of four days' duration when the sinner has to take hot milk, hot *ghī* and hot water in the first three days and to fast on the fourth day.

(iii) A penance of two days' duration.

(iv) A penance of 21 days' duration.

Tara(*śulka*) (*A*): Tax for ferrying across rivers, etc.

Tārpya : A kind of garment.

Tata (*S*): See *vādya*.

Taṭastha (*D*): Indifferent, neutral. In argument, one who is other than the person who questions and one who answers.

Tātparya (*Al*): See *Abhihitānvayavāda*.

Tatpuruṣa (*Vy*): Determinative compound in which the sense of the latter member predominates.

Ṭi (*Vy*): Part of word, consisting of the last vowel and the consonants following it.

Tīkṣṇa (*A*): A class of spies who are very brave, and do not care for their bodies.

Timira (*Ay*): An optical disease.

Tirīṭa: Perhaps a kind of head-dress.

Tretāgni or *Tretā* (*Sm*): The sacred fires, viz., *gārhapatya*, *dakṣiṇa* and *āhavanīya*.

Trika (*D*): A system of Śaiva philosophy of Kāśmīr. It taught *advaita-tattva* or idealistic monism. The literature of the *trika* system can be broadly divided into three classes, viz. *āgamaśāstra*, *spandaśāstra* and *pratyabhijñāśāstra*. The followers of this system recognise a threefold division into *para* (works dealing with the doctrinal aspect), *apara* (those dealing with the practical and ritual part) and *parāpara* (those which combine the nature of both *para* and *apara*).

Triphalā (*Ay*): Three myrobalans together are so called. These are *āmalaka*, *harītakī* and *vibhītaka*.

Tryahasparśa (*J*): It takes place if, from one sunrise to another, two lunar mansions end and a third begins.

Tuṅgī (J): A planet is called *tuṅgi* (placed in height) if it resides in a particular Zodiac; e.g., Mars in *makara* (Capricornus), Venus in *mīna* (Pisces).

Tulā-puruṣa (*Sm*): (i) Gift of gold, etc., equal to the weight of the

donor's body.
(ii) A ten-day penance.

Tunnavāya: Tailor.

Tuṣṇīm-yuddha (*A*): War by administering poison against the enemy or carried on by dissension caused through spies, diplomatic war.

Ubhayavetana (*A*): A spy, paid by one king, also serving another king in order to supply information about the latter to the former.

Udāsīna (*Sm*): A king who is able to help the *vijigīṣu* (q.v.) and *madhyama* when they are united or to harass them when separated from each other.

Udāṣthita (*A*): A kind of spy, disguised as an indifferent ascetic.

Udātta (*Vy*): Acute accent. It is produced from the higher places of articulation in the mouth.

Udaya (*Sm*): Increase, gain, interest, etc.

Udbandhaka (Sm): (1) One born of the union of a *sūnika* (q.v.) and a kṣatriya female.
(2) One born of the union of a *khanaka* (q.v.) and a kṣatriya woman.

Uddhāra (*Sm*): (i) The best part of things obtained by conquest.
(ii) That which is set aside, e.g., for the eldest brother in the partition of patrimony among brothers.

Udvartana: Rubbing perfumed substances on the body.

Ugra (*Sm*): (1) Child of a kṣatriya male by a śūdra female.

(2) One born of the union of a brāhmaṇa male and a śūdra female

(3) One born of the union of a vaiśya male and śūdra female.

Ūha (*D*, Vy): (1) Imagining. For example, in the sentence *agnaye juṣṭaṁ nirvapāmi* the word *sūryāya* is to be imagined for *agnaye* as occasion arises.

(2) Change, modification.

(3) Logical consequence or connection.

Uṇādi (*Vy*): Affixes, headed by the affix *uṇ*, similar to *kṛt* affixes of Pāṇini. the *Uṇādi-sūtras* give derivation mostly of such words as cannot be derived by the rules of Pāṇini. There are, however, *Uṇādi-sūtras* of Kātantra and some other systems of grammar also.

Uñcha (*Sm*): Gathering of abandoned corns, one by one.

Unmāda (*A*): Mania, insanity.

Upadaṁśa (*Ay*): Venereal disease.

Upādāna-kāraṇa (*D*): Material or inherent cause.

Upadeśa (*Vy*): Original enunciation, first or original precept or teaching.

Upadhā (*Vy, A*): (i) Name of the penultimate letter in a word. (ii) A secret test of loyalty and integrity. There are four such tests, viz., *dharmopadhā*, *arthopadhā*, *kāmopadhā*, and *bhayopadhā*.

Upādhi (*D*): (1) A general property other than the generic attribute (*jāti*).
(2) A limiting adjunct.
(3) A vicious condition.

Upādhyāya (*Sm*): One who teaches, for livelihood, a pupil, a portion of the Veda or the Vedāṅgas.

Upajāpa (*A*): Seduction, instigation for creating dissension.

Upākarman (*Sm*): Commencement of Vedic study.

Upakurvāṇa (*Sm*): A pupil who, on completion of Vedic studies and becoming a *gṛhastha*, honours his religious teacher by a gift.

Upamāna (*D, Vy*): Comparison, analogy as a means of valid knowledge. In grammar, it stands for an object with which something is compared. For example, when one's face is compared to the moon, the latter is called *upamāna*.

Upāṁśu-vadha (or *-Daṇḍa*) (*A*): Secret killing.

Upanayana (*Sm*): Initiation of a pupil by a preceptor to Vedic studies.

[See J. Gonda, *Indologica Taurinensia*, Vol. VII, Turin (Italy), 1981.]

Upanidhi (*Sm, A*): A sealed deposit, i.e., an article deposited with a person in a sealed receptacle without disclosing the contents.

Upanikṣepa (*Sm*): An open deposit, i.e., an article kept by one with another for safe custody showing the latter the nature of what is deposited.

Upaniṣat-prayoga (*A*): Secretly arranging to cause mischief to the enemy.

Upapada (*Vy*): Such words as are indicated by the seventh case-ending in Pāṇini's rules from III.1.90 to the end of III.4. Certain indeclinables also receive this designation.

Upapātaka (*Sm*): A class of sins, lighter than *mahāpātaka*s (q.v.), and comprising such sins as incest, giving up of Vedic study, allowing the time for initiation to Vedic study to pass, following the profession of dancing, singing, acting, cow-killing, fornication, etc.

Upapatti (*D*): Logical consequence.

Uparūpaka (*N*): Minor drama. These are 18, according to Viśvanātha.

Upasaṁvyāna: A lower garment.

Upasarga (*Vy*): The particles *pra*, etc., when prefixed to verbs, receive this designation.

Upasarjana (*Vy*): (i) Name of a word indicated by the first case-ending in a grammatical rule relating to *samāsa*.

(ii) Name of a word that is always used in the same case-ending in expounding a *samāsa*, and does not become the first member of a compound.

Upavasana: A kind of garment.

Upāya (*Sm*): Expedient of royal policy. The four expedients are *sāma*, *dāna*, *bheda* and *daṇḍa*. These terms mean respectively conciliation, gift, dissension and war.

Urustambha (*Ay*): Paralysis of the thigh.

Uṣmavarṇa (*Vy*): Letters *Ś*, *Ṣ*, *S* and *H*.

Uṣṇaka: A labourer who works promptly.

Utpāta (*Sm*): (i) An abnormal natural phenomenon foreboding a calamity.

(ii) Portent.

Utpattivāda (*Al*): This is the view of Bhaṭṭa Lollaṭa. According to it, *rasa* is produced (*utpanna*) in the minds of persons having the capacity for appreciation.

Utsarga (*Vy*, *D*): A general rule as opposed to a special rule or exception. For example, the general rule is that no creature should be killed. But, an exception is that an animal may be killed in a sacrifice.

Uttara (*Sm*): (1) Defendant's reply in a law-suit. *Uttara*s are broadly of four kinds, viz., *saṁpratipatti* (admission), *mithyā* (denial), *pratyavaskandana* (special plea) and *pūrva*-(or, *prāṅ*-)*nyāya* (plea of a former trial, *res judicata*).

(2) Obsequial rites performed after *spiṇḍīkaraṇa* (q.v.)

(3) an indirect witness who learns from another witness who has seen or heard of a transaction, when the latter is going to a distant country or is on the point of death.

Uttarābhāsa (*Sm*): Vitiated reply in a law-suit.

Uttarāyaṇa (*J*): The period of the sun's stay in the northern hemisphere.

Vāda (*D*): A mode of argumentation. It consists in a number of declarations put forward by various speakers purporting to be reasons in support of several theories, leading ultimately to the acceptance of one of these theories as the demonstrated truth. The sole object of *vāda* is to ascertain truth.

Vādī (*S*): The note that manifests the form of a *rāga*. The principal note in relation to which other notes are determined.

Vādya (*S*): Musical instrument. The instruments are divided into the following classes:

(i) *Tata* — stringed instruments, e.g., *vīṇā* (lute).

(ii) *Śuṣira* — possessed of holes and played with the help of wind, e.g., *vaṁśī* (flute).

(iii) *Ānaddha* (or *vitata*) — covered with skin, e.g., *ḍhakkā* (drum).

(iv) *Ghana* — metallic instruments played by striking, e.g., *ghaṇṭā* (bell), *karatāla* (cymbal).

Vaibhāṣika: A school of Buddhist philosophy, so-called as it is based on the *Abhidhamma-mahāvibhāṣā*. According to it, the Buddha is a common mortal. By Buddhahood he attained *nirvāṇa*, and by death *Mahāparinirvāṇa*. His divine characteristic lay in the fact that he acquired highest knowledge about the truth without the assistance of others. In this view, both mind and external objects have real existence, knowledge about the phenomenal world is directly acquired, and not through inference.

Vaiḍālavratika (*Sm*): Acting like a cat, hypocritical, a religious impostor.

Vaidarbhī (*Al*): Name of a *rīti* or particular mode or arrangement of words in a literary composition. It is regarded as the *rīti par excellence*. It consists of the ten *guṇas*, viz., *śleṣa, prasāda, samatā, mādhurya, sukumāratā, arthavyakti, udāratva, ojas, kānti* and *samādhi*.

Vaidehaka (*Sm*): (1) A caste sprung from the union of a vaiśya and a brahmaṇa female. (2) Offspring of a śūdra by a kṣatriya woman. (3) Offspring of a śūdra by a vaiśya female.

Vaidehakavyañjana (*A*): A merchant, having lost his livelihood serving as a spy.

Vaidhṛti or *Vaidhṛta* (*J*): A particular conjunction of the sun and the moon, harmful to people.

Vaikharī (D): An ingredient of sound. It is that kind of sound which is carried by the wind within the body and is articulated in the throat. The gross sound. It is supposed to reveal sentences. Vide commentary on *Śāradā-tilaka* (I.1). *Setubandha* on *Nityaṣoḍaśikārṇava*.

Vaiṇa (*Sm*): Same as *veṇa* (q.v.).

Vaiśvānarī (*Sm*): A sacrifice performed in the beginning of every year.

Vajra (*Sm*): A kind of military array in which the Army is arranged in three ways.

Vākovākya (*Sm*): Vedic texts in the form of catechism.

Vākapāruṣya (*Sm*): Abuse, harsh speech.

Vāmācāra (*vāmamārga*) (*T*): A Tāntric way of *sādhanā*. According to some, it is a rite in which a woman, placed on the left of the devotee, plays on important part. Or, it is a crooked way practised secretly. *Vāma* is of two kinds, viz., *madhyama* in which all the five *makāra*s are resorted to, and *uttama* in which *madya*, *maithuna* and *mudrā* are used.

Vanaspati (*U*): A tree which bears fruits without any flower. Sometimes it means any tree.

Vāra (*J*): Day of the week, e.g., *somavāra* (Monday).

Varāha (*Sm*): A form of military array in which the army is so arranged that it is tapering at the van and rear, but wide in the middle.

Vāravelā (*J*): Designation of the fourth, seventh, second, fifth, seventh, third, sixth (and first) *yāmārdha* of Sunday, Monday, Tuesday, Wednesday, Thursday, Friday and Saturday respectively. One *yāmārdha* = 1/8th part of a day. It is considered to be inauspicious.

Vārdhuṣi or *Vārdhuṣika* (*Sm*): Usurer.

Varga (*Vy*): A group of five consonants. There are five *vargas* beginning with *K*, *C*, *Ṭ*, *TA*, *PA* respectively.

Vāri-durga (*Sm*): Same as *ab-durga* (q.v.).

Vārkṣa (*Sm*): A kind of fortress which is surrounded, up to one *yojana*, by huge trees, thorny shrubs, creepers and rivers.

Varṇa (*S*): The act of singing.

Varṣavara (*N*): An eunuch generally engaged as a keeper of the royal harem.

Vārtā (*Sm*): Agriculture, cattle-rearing and trade, etc., as a profession usually adopted by vaiśyas.

Varttanī: A sort of octroi on foreign goods.

Vāruṇī: A kind of wine.

Vāta (*Ay*): Wind, as one of the three humours of the body.

Vāṭadhāna (*Sm*): Same as *āvantya* (q.v.).

Veṇa (*Sm*): (1) Offspring of a Vaidehaka (q.v.) by an Ambaṣṭha (q.v.) woman.

(2) Offspring of the union of different castes in the reverse order (*pratiloma* q.v.) subsisting by cutting bamboo or cane, etc.

Vesara (*V*): A type of architecture. According to some, the architecture of Orissa is so called. Some think that it had two forms, viz. *āndhra* and *kāliṅga*.

Veṣṭima (*N*): A kind of *pusta* (q.v.). Clothes.

Vibhāva (*Al*): Excitant. A factor of *rasa* (q.v.). It is of two kinds, viz., *ālambana* and *uddīpana*. For example, Sītā is the *ālambana-vibhāva* of Rāma's love while moonrise, spring, etc., are the *uddīpana-vibhāvas*.

Vidradhi (*Ay*): Abscess.

Vidūṣaka (*N*): A character in a drama. The hero's confidant and devoted friend. He is a brāhmaṇa, ludicrous in dress, speech and behaviour. He is generally represented as a dwarf, bald-headed, with projecting teeth and red eyes. He evokes laughter by his silly chatter in Prākṛt and his revenous greed for food.

Vighasa (*Sm*): It is what is left after the brāhmaṇas and guests have partaken of.

Vigraha (*Sm*, *Vy*): War. In grammar, it means a sentence that expresses the meaning of a *vṛtti* (q.v.).

Vijigīṣu (*Sm*): 'One desiring to conquer'. The central power in the *maṇḍala* (q.v.).

Vikāra (*D*, *Vy*): (i) The transformation of *prakṛti*. It means the assumption of a different form after giving up the original form. For example, curd, sprout, earring are the *vikāras* respectively of milk, seed and gold.

(ii) A rite in which not all subsidiaries are directly prescribed.

(iii) Modification of word-base or an affix, caused generally by the addition of suffixes.

Vikaraṇa (*Vy*): Lit. meaning 'modification', it generally denotes the conjugational characteristic inserted between the root and the suffix or ending, or between the last vowel and the following consonant of the root. For example, *śap* coming between the root *bhū* and the termination *tip* (present, third person singular), is called a *vikaraṇa*.

Vikṛti: Same as *vikāra* (q.v.).

Vimaṇḍala (*J*): The circular course in which a planet moves.

Vinaśana (*Sm*): The place where the river Sarasvatī disappeared; regarded as a holy place.

Vinna (*Sm*): Married.

Viniyoga (*D*): Application.

Vipala (*J*): A measure of time = 1/60th *pala* (q.v.).

Vīpsā (*Vy*): *Vi* + *īpsā*, Special desire.

Vīra (*T*): A Tāntric *sādhaka* of the second grade, who has advanced faculties, and follows *vīrācāra* (q.v.).

(*Al*): Name of a *rasa*, heroic.

Vīrācāra (*T*): A way of Tāntric *sādhanā*.

Viṣakanyā (*A*): A poisoned woman with whom an enemy is induced to cohabit, and die as a result.

Viṣama-vṛtta (*C*): A *vṛtta* in which the feet are of different metrical schemes.

Viṣkambhaka (*N*): A device in a drama, placed in the beginning of an act, which serves as a connecting link between what has happened and what is going to happen.

Viṣkira: A kind of bird that eats things after scratching the earth.

Viṣṇukrānta (*T*): Name of one of the three regions into which India has been divided in certain Tantras. The tract of land from the Vindhya hill to Chittagong (in Bangladesh) is called Viṣṇukrānta.

Viṣṭapa (*Sm*): 1. A world, region.

2. Heaven.

3. *Brahman* who is free from pain.

Viṣṭi (*A*): Labourers who work for things instead of wages; sappers and miners.

Visūcikā (*Ay*): Cholera.

Viṭa (*N*): Paramour, passionate rogue. Associate of a king or a characterless young man. Accomplice of a prostitute.

Vitaṇḍā (*D*): A kind of debate in which the rival party does not establish his position, but merely tries to refute that of the opponent.

Vitata (*S*): Same as *ānaddha* (q.v.).

Vivādī (S): The note that causes loss of charm to a *rāga*. If, between two notes, there exists one *śruti*, then those two notes are *vivādī* of each other.

Vivarta (*D*): False knowledge of a substance when the real thing remains unchanged. For example, the mistake of a rope for a serpent.

Vivīta (*Sm*): An enclosed spot of ground (esp. pasture ground), paddock, levy on pasture.

Vrātya (*Sm*): (i) One born to a member of the regenerate class by a wife of his own caste, on whom or on whose ancestors the sacrament of *upanayana* has not been performed.

(ii) Anyone born of the mixture of *varṇa*s or castes.

[See L.B. Keny, The *Vrātyas*, etc.; *Proc. of Indian History Congress* (9th Session), 1946, *Summary of Papers* 8th and 9th *Indian History Congress*; *Proc. of Indian History Congress*, 10th Session, 1947; H.P. Sastri, *Absorption of the Vrātyas*, London, 1926; R.K. Chaudhury; *Vrātyas in Ancient India*.]

Vr̥ddhi (*Vy*, *Sm*): (i) A technical term denoting *Ā*, *AI*, *AU*, *ĀR* and *ĀL* in place of *A*, *I* (long and short), *U* (long and short), *R̥* and *L̥* respectively. (2) Interest. (3) A kind of *śrāddha* performed before some ceremonies, e.g., marriage.

Vr̥kṣa-durga (*Sm*): Same as *vārkṣa* (q.v.).

Vr̥tta (*C*): A kind of *padya* in which the metre is determined by the number of syllables.

Vr̥tti (*N*, *Vy*): Dramatic style. *Vr̥tti*s are four according to the *Nāṭya-śāstra*, viz., *kaiśikī* (the graceful), *sāttvatī* (the grand), *ārabhaṭī* (the violent), *bhāratī* (the verbal). *Kaiśikī* is appropriate to the erotic sentiment. *Sāttvatī* is suitable for heroism, wonder, fury and, in a less degree, for the pathetic and erotic. *Ārabhaṭī* accords with fury, horror and terror. The verbal manner is based on sound as the other three are on sense. It is suited, according to *Nāṭya-śāstra*, to heroism, wonder and fury.

In grammar, it means that in which a word, besides expressing its own meaning, also declares the meaning of another. Grammatical *vr̥tti*s are five, viz., *kr̥t*, *taddhita, samāsa, ekaśeṣa* and roots taking the affixes like *san, yaṅ*, etc.

Vyabhicāri-bhāva (*Al*): Transient mood, subordinate or accessory feeling such as *śaṅkā* (apprehension). A factor of *rasa* (q.v.). Also called *saṁcārī-bhāva*.

Vyadhikaraṇa (*Vy*): Possessed of different case-relations or case-affixes. For example, *vīṇā pānau yasyāḥ*. The words *vīṇā* and *pāṇi* have different case-endings.

Vyāhṛti (*Sm*): The mystical utterance of the names of the seven worlds, viz. *bhūḥ, bhuvaḥ, svaḥ, mahaḥ, janaḥ, tapas* and *satya*.

Vyājima (*N*): A kind of *pusta* (q.v.). It denotes what is done by a *yantra* (mechanical contrivance).

Vyañjanā (*Al*): A function by which a word expresses a suggested sense which is other than its primary sense.

Vyāpaka (*D*): A thing which prevades another (*vyāpaka*). In *parvato vahnimān dhūmāt, vahni* is *vyāpaka*.

Vyāpti (*D*): (1) Invariable concomitance between two things (*vyāpya* and *vyāpaka*). (2) A general proposition. For example, the relation of smoke to fire is one of *vyāpti*.

Vyāpya (*D*): A thing that is pervaded by something else (*vyāpaka*). For example, in *parvato vahnimān dhūmāt*, smoke is *vyāpya* while fire is *vyāpaka*.

Vyatipāta (*Sm, J*): The day of New Moon when it falls on Sunday, and when the moon is in the *nakṣatras Śravaṇā, Aśvinī, Dhaniṣṭhā, Aśleṣā* or *Ārdrā*. It is harmful to people.

Vyatireka (*D*): See *anvaya-vyatireka*.

Vyavahāra (*Sm, A*): (i) Legal procedure, consisting of four stages, viz., *bhāṣā* (plaint), *uttara* (reply), *kriyā* (proof of evidence) and *nirṇaya* (judgement). (ii) Administration of justice. (iii) Contract. (iv) Competency to manage one's own affairs, majority.

Vyavahāra-pada (*Sm*): Subject-matter of litigation or dispute.

Vyāvartaka (*D*): Distinguishing quality or characteristic.

Vyūha (*Sm*): Logistics; particular arrangement of soldiers in a battle. Manu mentions the following *vyūhas*: *daṇḍa, śakaṭa, varāha, makara, sūcī, garuḍa, padma.*

Yakṣmā (*Ay*): Consumption, phthisis.

Yama (*D*): A *yogāṅga* (q.v.). It generally consists in *ahiṁsā, satyavacana, brahmacarya, asteya* (non-theft) and *aparigraha* (non-acceptance of gifts).

Yamapaṭika: A class of men who used to go around showing torments of hell on a canvas.

Yamapaṭṭaka: A piece of canvas on which infernal torments were depicted.

Yama-vrata (*Sm*): Punishing the subjects, like Yama, without respect for persons and without partiality, as one of the duties of the king.

Yāmya (*J*): South.

Yāmyottara-rekhā (*J*): Meridian line.

Yāna (*Sm*): One of the six *guṇas* to be resorted to by kings; marching against the enemy.

Yantra (*T*): A mystical diagram painted with minerals on something or on the ground at the time of worship. The worshipper imagines that the deity, which is being worshipped by him, for the time being resides in the diagram in accordance with his prayer. The diagrams differ in form according as the forms of desired deity differ.

Yati (*C, S*): (i) Pause in a metre.

(ii) Pause in a song.

Yati-cāndrāyaṇa (*Sm*): A penance where the sinner eats eight mouthfuls of food only once at noon for a month, and exercises control over himself.

Yatna (*N*): One of the *avasthās* (q.v.).

Yautuka or *Yautaka* (*Sm*): A kind of *strīdhana*. Authorities differ on the nature of this:

(i) Wealth received, as a gift, from anybody by a woman while seated together with her husband at the time of marriage.

(ii) Separate property of a woman, her *strīdhana*.

(iii) Wealth obtained from the family of the woman's father, which is separate in its characteristics.

Yava-Madhyama (= *Madhya*) (*Sm*): A kind of *Cāndrāyaṇa* (q.v.). The word literally means — large in the middle like a grain of *yava* corn.

Yoga (*Sm*, *D*): In Smṛti literature it means —

(i) Acquisition of what has not been acquired; (ii) A trick; (iii) Connection, relation; (iv) Power, zeal. In philosophy it means the restraint of the functions of the mind; concentration of the mind.

Yogācāra: A school of Buddhist philosophy. It denies the existence of the external world, and recognises the existence only of mind. In this school, great stress is laid on *yoga* (q.v.) and *ācāra* (conduct); hence the name. The doctrine of the school is called Vijñānavāda (q.v.). The advocates of the school hold that, properly controlled, mind can dispel delusion about the external world, and can remove attachment to it.

Yoga-kṣema (*Sm*, *A*): (i) Sacrificial acts performed with *śrauta* or *smārta* fire and charitable gifts such as construction of tanks, parks, etc. (ii) Royal minister and *purohita* who bring about the welfare of people. (iii) Umbrella, cowrie, weapons, shoes and the like. (iv) Comfortable life or easy and happy way of maintenance or annuity descending from the father (to the son) at a royal place. (v) *yoga* means ship and *kṣema* fort. (vi) The wealth gained by a learned brāhmaṇa resorting to a rich man for his maintenance. (vii) Acquisition of what has not been acquired and the preservation of what is acquired. Also see *Gītā* (IX.22).

Yoga-vibhāga (*Vy*): A device by which a portion of a grammatical rule is cut off, and treated as an independent rule. This has been adopted in the school of Pāṇini. For example, Pāṇini's rule *Saha supā* (II.1.4), has been split up into two, viz., *saha* and *supā*.

Yogāṅga (*D*): Accessories of *yoga*. These are *yama*, *niyama*, *prāṇāyāma*, *pratyāhāra*, *dhyāna*, *dhāraṇā*, *āsana* and *samādhi*. These terms have been separately defined.

Yuganaddha (*T*): Male Principle united with Female Principle, a motif often represented in Buddhist Tāntric art.

Yugmaka (*Al*): A kind of *kāvya* consisting of two interrelated stanzas.

Bibliography

VEDIC LITERATURE AND SAṀHITĀS

Ṛgveda

TEXT

Ṛgveda-saṁhitā with Sāyaṇa's comm., Vols. I-IV, Vol. V (Index of words and lines), Poona, 1993-41.

TRANSLATION

Eng. tr. by Wilson, 6 Vols., Poona, 1925-28.

German tr. by A.L. Ludwig, 6 Vols., Prag, 1876-88.

French tr. by Langlois

Spanish tr. by F. Tola, Buenos Aires, 1968.

Bengali tr. by R.C. Dutta, Calcutta, 1963.

STUDIES

Bregenhoi, C., *Ṛgveda as the Key to Folklore*, Copenhagen, 1987.

Chakraborty, C., *Common Life in ṚV and AV*, Calcutta.

Chandra, A.N., *Ṛgvedic Culture and the Indus Valley Civilisation*, Calcutta, 1980.

Chawla, J., *The Ṛgvedic Deities and their Iconic Forms*.

Frawley, D., Astronomical evidences, etc. *Glory of India*, Journal pub. by Motilal Banarsidass, Delhi, Vol. V, Nos. 3-4, 1981.

Griswold, H.D., *Religion of ṚV*, London, 1923.

Hariyappa, H.L., *ṚV. Legends Through the Ages*, Poona, 1953.

Mankad, D.R., *Date of ṚV*.

Sastri, P.S., *Ṛgvedic Aesthetics*, 1988.

Upadhyay, B.S., *Women in ṚV*.

Yajurveda

TEXT

Kāṭhaka-saṁhitā, ed. by Satavalekar, Aundh, 1943.

Taittirīya-saṁhitā, ed. by Dhupkar, Pardi, 1957.

Kāṇva-saṃhitā, ed. by Satavalekar, Aundh, 1940.

Mādhyandina Śukla YV., ed. by Satavalekar, Pardi, 1957.

Maitrāyaṇī-saṁhitā, ed. by L.V. Schroeder, Leipzig, 1881-6.

Mūla-yajurveda-saṁhitā, ed. by Daivarata, Varanasi, 1973.

TRANSLATION

Eng. tr. (in verse) by R.T.H. Griffith (The Texts of the White *YV*), Banaras, 1957.

Bengali tr. by D.D. Lahiri, 1919.

Hindī tr. by D. Sarasvati, 1906.

Tamil tr. by M.R. Jambunathan, Bombay, 1938.

MISCELLANEOUS

Svami, V. and Svami, N., *Complete Alphabetical Index of all Words in YV.*

Sastri, P., *Word-index to Tait. Saṁ.*, 1930.

Visvabandhu, *A Grammatical Word-Index to the Tai. Saṁ.*; 1963.

Desai, G.C., *Thinking with the YV.*

Pandey, U.K., *Political Concepts and Institutions in Śukla YV.*

Dey, S., *Indian Life in Śukla YV.*, 1985.

Sāmaveda

TEXT

Ed. with comms. of Mādhava and Bharatasvāmin, by Raja, Adyar.

Saṁhitā of the Rāṇāyanīyā, ed. and tr.by J. Stevenson, London, 1842 (Rep. Banaras, 1961).

Saṁhitā of the Kauthumas, by T. Benfey, Leipzig, 1948.

Jaiminīya Saṁhitā, ed. by Raghuvira, Lahore, 1938 (with Sāyaṇa's comm.).

TRANSLATION

Besides the above :

Eng. metrical tr. by Griffith (new ed., 1916, 1926 — in two parts).

Bengali tr. by D.D. Lahiri (with text), 1899.

Hindī tr. by J. Sharma (with text) 1890-91.

Tamil tr. by M.R. Jambunathan, Bombay, 1935.

MISCELLANEOUS

For bibliography of studies, see M. Winternitz, *Hist. of Ind. Lit.*, I.

Faddegon, B., *Studies on the Sāmaveda*, Amsterdam, 1951.

Svami, V. and Svami, N., *Complete Alphabetical Index of all Words in Sāmaveda*.

Raghavan, V., S.V. and Music, *Journal of Music Academy*, Vol 33, Madras, 1962.

Tarlekar, G.H., *The Sāman Chants*, 1985.

Ganapati, S.V., Sāmaveda (whole text, Eng. tr., some comments with a new light, exhaustive and critical intro.), Delhi, 1992.

Atharvaveda

TEXT

Śaunaka recension, with Sāyaṇa's comm., annotations, etc., pub. from V.V.R.I., Hoshiarpur, 1960-4.

Paippalāda-saṁhitā, ed., with notes, by D.M. Bhattacharya, 2 Vols., Calcutta, 1964.

TRANSLATION

Eng. tr. by R.T.H. Griffith, Banaras, 1895-6 (New edn., 1916).

French tr. by V. Henry, Paris, 1894-1916.

Bengali tr. (with text) by D.D. Lahiri, 1919.

Hindī tr. (with text) by K. Trivedi, 1912-21.

Tamil tr. by M.R. Jambunathan, Bombay, 1940.

Spanish tr. by F. Tola, Buenos Aires, 1968.

German tr. (selection) by A. Ludwig in his *Ṛgveda*, Vol. III, Prague, 1898.

Persian tr. (983 AH) By Mullā Ibrāhimi, Fayzi and Badāuni with Ākbar's patronage.

STUDIES

Bali, S., *Historical and Critical Studies in the* AV, Delhi, 1981.

Chakraborty, C., *Common Life in ṚV and AV*, Calcutta.

Karambelkar, *AV and Avesta, AV and Āyurveda, Atharvavedic Civilisation.*

Lal, K., *Historical and Critical Studies in AV*.

Modak, B.K., *A Study of Ancillary Literature of AV with Special ref. to Pariśiṣṭas*.

Shende, N.J., *The Religion and Philosophy of the AV*, Poona, 1952.

Svami, V. and Svami, N., *Complete Alphabetical Index of all Words in the AV*.

Brāhmaṇas

TEXT AND TRANSLATION

Aitareya

Ed. Pillai, with *Sukhapradā* comm., in 3 vols., TSS, Vol. III, pub. in 1955.

Eng. tr. by A.B. Keith, along with *Kauṣītaki*, HOS, 1920.

Kauṣītaki

Eng. tr. by A.B. Keith, HOS, 1920.

Śatapatha

Kāṇva recension, (ed.), Caland, Lahore, 1926.

Mādhyandina recension, pub. in 5 vols., Kalyan, 1940-1 (with comms. of Sāyaṇa and Harisvāmin).

Also ed. by A. Weber, with comms. of Sāyaṇa, Harisvāmin and Dvivedaganga, Banaras, 1964 (23rd edn.).

Eng. tr. by Eggeling, SBE, Vols. XLI, XLIII, XLIV, XXVI.

Taittirīya

Ed., with comm. of Bhāskara, R.S. Shastri and Srinivasacharya.

STUDIES

Banerjee, A.C., *Studies in the Brāhmaṇas*, Delhi, 1963.

Basu, J.R., *India of the Age of Brāhmaṇas*, Calcutta, 1969.

Pandey, U.C., *The Cosmogonic Legends of the Brāhmanas,* Gorakhpur, 1992.

Tilak, S.K., *Cultural Gleanings from the Brāhmaṇa Literature*, New Delhi, 1990.

Upaniṣads

TEXT AND TRANSLATION

Twelve Principal Upaniṣads, with comm. of Śaṅkara, gloss of Ānandagiri, Eng. tr. and notes, ed. by Roer, Madras, 1931-2.

Principal Upaniṣads, Text in Roman script and Eng. tr. by S. Radhakrishnan.

STUDIES

Bahadurmal, *The Religion of the Buddha and its Relation to Upaniṣadic Thought*, Hoshiarpur, 1958.

Deussen, P., *The Philosophy of the Upaniṣads.*

Jacob, G.A., *Concordance of the Principal Upaniṣads and the Bhagavadgītā*, Delhi, 1963.

Modak, M.S., *Spinoza and the Upaniṣads*, Nagpur, 1970.

Mukhopadhyay, P.C., *Journey of the Upaniṣads to the West*, Calcutta, 1987.

Radhakrishnan, S., *The Philosophy of the Upaniṣads.*

Sharma, S., *Life in the Upaniṣads*, 1985.

Sadhale, S.S., *Upaniṣad-vākya-mahākośa*, 1940-1 (Rep. 1989).

Subrahmanian, N.S., *Encyclopaedia of the Upaniṣads.*

VEDĀṄGAS

Śikṣā

NĀRADĪYA ŚIKṢĀ

Ed., with *Vivaraṇa* and *Vivaraṇa-prakāśa*, Mysore, 1949; with Eng. tr. and notes, by S.C. Banerji, Calcutta.

Pāṇinīya Śikṣā

Ed. M. Ghosh, with two comms., tr. and notes, Calcutta, 1938.

On Śikṣā, see F. Kielhorn, *Indian Antiquary*, 5, 1876; W.S. Allen, *Phonetics in Ancient India*, London, 1953.

Kalpa

TEXTS AND TRANSLATIONS

Āśvalāyana Śrautasūtra

Ed., with Nārāyaṇa's *Vṛtti*, by G. Sastri, 1917. Eng. tr. (Pt. I) by H.G. Ranade, Poona, 1981.

Gobhila-gṛhyasūtra

Ed., with German tr., by F. Knauer, Dorpat, 1884, 1886. Eng. tr. by H. Oldenberg, *SBE*, vol. 30.

Gautama-dharmasūtra

Āpastamba-śulvasūtra, with comms. of Kapardisvamin, Karavinda and Sundararaja, Mysore, 1931. German tr. by A. Burk, *ZDMG*, vols. 55, 56, 1901-02.

STUDIES

Apte, V.M., *Social and Religious Life in the Gṛhyasūtras*, Bombay, 1953 (2nd edn.).

Banerji, S.C., *Dharmasūtras, —A Study in their Origin and Development*, Calcutta, 1962.

Datta, B.B., *The Science of the Śulba —A Study in Early Hindu Geometry*, Calcutta, 1932.

Gonda, J., *The Ritual Sūtras*, 1977.

Kashikar C.G., *A Survey of the Śrautasūtras*, Bombay, 1966.

Ram Gopal, *India of Vedic Kalpasūtras*, Delhi, 1959.

Sharma, R.N., *Culture and Civilisation as Revealed in Śrautasūtra*.

Vyākaraṇa

See bibliography on *Vyākaraṇa* works.

Nirukta

Ed. L. Sarup, in 6 vols., 1920-29 (with Eng. tr. and ed. of Madhva's comm.).

Chandaḥ

See bibliography on *Chandaḥ-śāstra*.

Jyotiṣa

See R. Shama Sastri, Light on the Vedāṅga-jyautiṣa, *Kuppuswami Sastri Comm. Vol.*, Madras, 1937.

EPICS

Rāmāyaṇa

Critical edn. reported to be under preparation by Raghuier and Chandorkar. Another critical edn. reported to have been undertaken by Oriental Institute under M.S. University, Baroda.

North-western recension ed. by D.A.V. College, Lahore.

Southern recension ed. by R.N. Aiyar, Madras, 1933.

Bengal recension, with Lokanatha's comm. and Bengali trs. Calcutta Skt.

Ser., 1933 onward.

Tr. into English by M.N. Dutt, Calcutta, 1892-94.

For discussion on various problems relating to the Epic see M. Winternitz, *History of Indian Literature*, Vol. I.

See N.A. Gore, *Bibliography of the Rāmāyaṇa*.

The following are some of the important works relating to the *Rāmāyaṇa*:

Bhatt, G.H., *Pāda-index of Vālmīki-Rāmāyaṇa*, GOS, 1961, 1966.

Bulcke, C., *Rāmakathā* (in Hindi), Prayag, Allahabad, 1950.

Datta, R., *Rabīndranātha on the Rāmāyaṇa and the Mahābhārata*, Asiatic Society, Calcutta.

Dharma, P.C., *The Rāmāyaṇa Polity*.

Vyas, S.N., *India in the Rāmāyaṇa Age*, Delhi, 1967.

Mahābhārata

Crit. edn. pub. by BORI, Poona, 1927-54.

Eng tr. by P. Lal.

For discussion on various matters relating to the Epic, see M. Winternitz, *History of Indian Literature*, Vol. I.

Banerji, S.C., *Smṛti Material in the Mahābhārata*, Vol. I, Calcutta, 1972.

———., *Indian Society in the Mahābhārata*, Varanasi, 1976.

Jayal, S., *Status of Women in the Epics*, 1966.

Lal, P., *An Annotated Mahābhārata Bibliography*, Calcutta.

Sorensen, S., *Index to Names in the Mahābhārata*, Delhi, 1963.

CLASSICAL SANSKRIT LITERATURE

GENERAL

De and Dasgupta, *History of Skt. Lit.*, Calcutta, 1947.

Keith, A.B., *History of Skt. Lit.*, Oxford, 1924.

———., *Sanskrit Drama*, Oxford, 1924.

POETICAL LITERATURE

Aśvaghoṣa, *Śāriputra-prakaraṇa*, See H. Lüders,

———, *Das Śāriputra-prakaraṇa*, ein Drama des Aśvaghoṣa in *Sitzungsberichte d Berliner Akad*, 1911.

Bhāsa, for works, Bhāsa-problem, etc., see A.D. Pusalker, *Bhāsa, a Study*, Lahore, 1937.

Kālidāsa

Complete works of Kālidāsa (Texts with Eng. tr.,) ed. by R. Dvivedi, Vol. I Poetry, Vol. II Drama. Each of the poetical and dramatic works has been edited and translated by different scholars.

See S.A Sabnis, *Kālidāsa, His Style and His Times*, Bombay.

For various works and papers relating to Kālidāsa and his treatises, see S.P. Narang, *Kālidāsa Bibliography*, New Delhi, 1976.

Bhāravi

Kirātārjunīya, ed. by Godabole and Parab, with Mallinātha's comm., 1907.

See S. Pittor, K. of Bhāravi, a critical study, Calcutta, 1983.

Bhaṭṭi

Bhaṭṭikāvya, Eng. tr., with notes, by G.G. Leonardi, Leiden, 1972.

S.P. Narang, *Bhaṭṭikāvya, a Study*, 1969.

Kumāradāsa

Jānakī-haraṇa, ed. by V. Raghavan, Delhi, 1977.

See A critical study of text, crit. edn. (XVI-XX), with Eng. tr. by C.R. Swaminathan, *Critical Study of Jānakīharaṇa* by S. Suri, Delhi, 1984.

Māgha

Śiśupāla-vadha, NSP. ed., with commentary of Mallinatha, 1927 (9th edn.)

GRAMMAR

TEXTS

Aṣṭādhyāyī

Many editions; most noteworthy are:

NSP ed. with *Sid. Kaumudī*, *Tattvabodhinī* comm., Bombay, 1933.

With *Bhāṣāvṛtti* comm. and Sṛṣṭidhara's sub comm., *Bib. Indica,* Calcutta, 1912.

With *Mahābhāṣya, Pradīpa* and *Uddyota* and Eng. version of opening portion, J.R. Ballantyne, Vol. I (Navāhnika); Mirzapore, 1856.

Ed. Kielhorn, BSS, 1906ff.

With comm. *Prabhā* by editor D. Vidyāratna, with rules in Pāṇini's order (in Bengal characters).

Bālamanoramā

Ed. with *Sid. Kau.*, by C.S. Sastri, Madras, 1927 (3rd edn.)

Dhātupradīpa

Ed. by B.C. Maitra, Rajashahi (Bangladesh), 1919.

Durghaṭa-vṛtti

Ed. in Roman script, and tr. into French by L. Renou, Paris, 1940-5. Also ed. by R.S. Banerjee, Calcutta.

T. Ganapati Sastri, Delhi, TSS 6.

Gadā (Kāśikā) — by V. Payagunda.

Ed. Anandasrama 72.

———, (Bhairava Miśra) Pt. Benares, 1886.

*Gaṇamālā (*of Kātantra School*)*

Ptd. Calcutta 1907.

Gaṇapāṭha

R. Birwe, *Der Gaṇapāṭha*, Wiesbaden, 1961.

Gaṇaratna-Mahodadhi

Ed. by J. Eggeling, London, 1879, 1881. Also pub. in Allahabad, 1894.

Gaṇaratnāvalī

Ptd. Baroda, 1874.

Harināmāmṛta Vyākaraṇa

Ed. by Puridas, 1947 — with *Bālatoṣaṇī* comm., G. Das (2nd edn. B. Misra), Mursidabad, 1337 BS.

Kalā

Comm. on Nāgeśa's *Vaiyākaraṇa-Siddhānta (laghu) mañjūṣā* Ptd. Chowkhamba Skt. Ser. 191-2.

Kāśikā (of Vāmana Jayāditya*)*

Ed. by B. Sastri, Banaras, 1928 (3rd edn.); D.D. Sastri and K.P. Shukla with *Nyāsa* and *Padamañjarī*, Banaras, 1967 (Portion only).

Ed. tr. by L. Renou and Y. Ojihara, Paris, 1960.

Ch. 14, *pādas* 1, 2 of *Kāśikā*, tr. into German by B. Liebich, Breslau, 1892.

Kāśikā-Vivaraṇa-Pañjikā (or *Nyāsa*)

Ed. with notes, S. Chakravarti, Rajshahi (Bangladesh), 1913, 1919-24, 1925.

Kātantra

Ed. with Durgasiṁha's comm., by J. Eggeling, *Bib. Indica*, 1874-8.

German tr. by Liebich, 1919.

Kātantra-Chandaḥ-Prakariyā

Pub. in Calcutta, 1896, 1907, 1921.

Kavikalpadruma (*Vopadeva*)

Several editions. Ed. with *Dhātudīpikā*, Calcutta, 1831, 1904; with *Paribhāsā-ṭīkā*, Calcutta, 1848; with Sinhalese comm., with index and list of roots, etc., Colombo, 1911.

Kavikalpadruma (*Hemacandra*)

Ptd. Jaina Yaśo Grantha 12, Benares, 1909.

Kriyāratna-Samuccaya

Ptd. *Jaina-yaśovijaya-granthāvalī*, Benares, 1908.

Laghuśabdendu-Śekhara

Pub. Andhra Univer. Series, No. 26, 1941; Kashi Skt. Series, 1954.

Madhya-Siddhānta-Kaumudī

Ed. by Govindasiṁha, Venk. Press, Bombay, 1900.

Mahābhāṣya

Ed. D.E. Soc., Poona, Vol. VII.

Several other editions. Most important among them are :

with *Pradīpa* and *Uddyota* and Eng. rendering of the opening portion by J.R. Ballantyne, Vol. I (*Navāhnika*), Mirzapore, 1856.

Ed. Kielhorn, BSS, 1906 ff. Vol. I, 3rd ed., by K.V. Abhyankar, 1962.

With comm. of Kaiyaṭa, Nāgeśa and R. Jha, by G. Sarma Chaturvedi, *Āhnikas*, 1-9.

Paśpaśāhnika, ed. and tr. by K.C. Chatterji, Calcutta; *Samarthāhnika*, with Eng. tr. and notes, by S.D. Joshi, Poona, 1968.

Karmadhārayāhnika, ed. tr. by S.D. Joshi and J.A.F Roodbergen, Poona, 1971.

Tatpuruṣāhnika, ed. Do, Poona, 1971, Āhnikas I-III, ed. Abhyankar and Shukla, with Eng. tr. and notes, Poona, 1975.

Avyayībhāva and *Bahuvrīhi Āhnikas* also ed. by Joshi and Roodbergen. *Word-index to the Mahābhāṣya*, BORI, Poona, 1927.

Mahābhāṣya-Pradīpa

M.S. Narasimhacarya, *Mbh.-pradīpa-vyākyānāṇi*, Adhy. II, *pāda* 4, Pondicherry.

Ed. Böhtlingk, St. Petersburg, 1847; G. Vidyāratna, with comm. based on comm. of Dargādāsa, Rāma Tarkavāgīśa and Gaṅgādhara Tarkavāgīśa and notes, Calcutta, 1891.

Manoramā-Kucamardinī

Same as *Prauḍha-manoramā-kucamardinī* (q.v.).

Nirukta (Yāska)

Ed. L. Sarup in 6 vols. 1920-29 (with Eng. tr. and Madhva's comm.)

With Devarāja Yajvan's comm. BSS, 2 vols., 1918 and 1942.

With *Nirukta-vṛtti* and notes by M. Jha Bakshi, NSP, 1930.

With comm. of Durgācārya and gloss by S. Sarma (with Eng. tr. and edn. of Madhva's comm).

Padamañjarī

Ed. by D.D. Sastri and Shukla with *Nyāsa* of *Jinendrabuddhi*,Varanasi, Pts. I, II, 1963 (up to 2nd section of chapter III);

Ramacandra and Sarma, chaps. 1-4, Hyderabad, 1981.

Pāṇiniprabhā

Ptd. by author at Dacca, 1318 B.S.

(*Sūtras* in Pāṇini's order and comm.)

Prabodhacandrikā

Ptd. in Telugu script, Madras, 1858, Do, 1871; in Benares, 1889; Vizagapattam, 1895.

Prabodha-Prakāśa

Ptd. Calcutta, 1911.

Pradīpa

M.S. Nṛsimhācārya, *Mahābhāṣya-pradīpa-vyākhyānāni*, I-II, Pondicherry, 1973-74.

——, Vols. VII, VIII, Pondicherry, 1980-81.

Prakriyākaumudī

Ptd. Bombay Skt. Series 78, 82 in two pts., with comm. *Prasāda*.

In two parts with comm. *Prakāśa* by Kṛṣṇa, Varanasi, 1972.

Prakriyā-Saṁgraha

Ed. Oppert, Madras, 1898.

Also pub. at Kolhapur, 1902.

Prauḍhamanoramā

Ed. by S. Shastri, Banaras, 1934; with comm. of Hari Dīkṣita and *Laghuśabdaratna* of Nāgeśa, by S. Shastri, Vol. I, Banaras, 1964; ed. by V.L. Joshi with *Śabdaratna,* several comms. and Skt. intro., pp. 3-110, Poona, 1960. There are other ed. and tr.

Prauḍhamanoramā-Kucamardinī (or *-Khaṇḍana*)

Ptd. Partly with *P-manoramā.*

Rasavatī-Vṛtti

Pub. with *Saṁkṣiptasāra*, Calcutta, 1888, 1901, 1904, 1911.

Śabdakaustubha

Ed. with the *Aṣṭādhyāyī*, Banaras, 1874 (comm. on *pāda* I only of the *Aṣṭādhyāyī*), CSS., 1898, V.P. Dvivedi and G.S. Mokate, CSS, Vol. II only, Banaras, 1917.

Śabdānuśāsana

See *Kielhorn's Report*, for 1880-81, p. 46.

Saṁkṣiptasāra

Ed., with comm. and Bengali tr., by G. Vidyanidhi, Calcutta, 1911; with comm. of Jīvānanda, Calcutta, 1901.

Sārasvata-Vyākaraṇa

Ed. with Anubhūtisvarūpācārya's exposition, three *Vṛttis* and *Subodhinī* comm. and a Hindī comm., CSS, 1955; with comms. of Candrakīrti and Vāsudeva, notes, Index, etc., by N.K. Sarma.

Sarasvatīkaṇṭhābharaṇa

Ed. by K.S. Sastri, TSS, 1935-38.

Siddhahemacandra

See Kielhorn, *WZKM,* ii; Pathak in *Indian Antiquary,* Oct., 1914, p. 200.

Siddhāntakaumudī

Ed. and tr. into Eng. by S. Vasu, Allahabad. 8 vols. 1891-8, Ed. with *Tattvabodhinī* and *Subodhinī* by Pansikar, NSP, 1933 (7th edn.). *Vaidikīprakriyā* ed. with HindI comm. by U. Sarma, Benares, 1962.

Śṛṅgāraprakāśa

Of Bhoja, ed. V. Raghavan (see Intro. for an account of Bhoja).

Supadma-Vyākaraṇa

Ed., with Viṣṇumiśra's comm. and notes, by T. Bhattacharya, Calcutta, 1900.

Tattvabodhinī

Ed., with *Aṣṭādhyāyī* and *Sid. Kau.*, by Pansikar, NSP, 1933 (7th edn.)

Tripādī

(Abridged version of Buiskool's *Pūrvatrāsiddham*), London, 1939.

Uddyota

Ed. by J.R. Ballantyne, vol. I (*Navāhnika*), with Eng. tr. of the opening portion, Mirzapore, 1856, Ed. by B. Sastri, *Bib. Indica,* Calcutta.

Uṇādisūtras

Ed. by T. Aufrecht, Bonn, 1859.

Vākyapadīya

Ed., with Puṇyarāja's comm., Banaras. Skt. Ser. 1887-1907; with Helārāja's comm. (3rd *Kāṇḍa*), TSS, 1935; with *Bhāvapradīpa* comm. and notes, by Shukla CSS, 1871; Ch. II ed., by K.A.S. Iyer, Delhi, 1977.

Ch. I, II, with Eng. tr. by K.R. Pillai, Delhi, 1971; K.V. Abhyankar and Limaye, Poona, 1965. Eng. tr. by S.K. Iyer. Ed. by S. Verma, *Vākyapadīyam* (*Brahmakāṇḍa*) with Eng. and Hindi, Delhi, 1970; with intro. and Appendices, by Abhyankar and Limaye; *Kāṇḍa* II Eng. tr. with notes by K.A.S. Iyer, Patna, 1977; *Brahmakāṇḍa*, tr. into Eng. by K. Subrahmanyam, 1992; see Bhat and Kar, *Word-index to the Vākyapadīya of Bhartṛhari*, Delhi, 1992. *Vākyapadīya-prameya-saṁgraha*, München, 1981.

Vārtikas

Ptd. in eds. of *Aṣṭādhyāyī*. Alphabetical list of *Vārtikas* given at the end of *Sid. Kaumudī*, NSP ed., 1932.

STUDIES

Abhyankar and Shukla, *A Dictionary of Skt. Grammar*, Baroda, 1986.

Agrawala, V.S., *Gotras in Pāṇini*.

———, *India as known to Pāṇini*.

Allen, W.S., *Sandhi*, Poona.

Balasubramaniyam, M.D., *Systems of Kṛt Accentuation in Pāṇini and the Phonology in Pāṇini, B.C. Law Vol.*

Banerji, S.C., *Contribution of Bihar to Skt. Lit.*, Patna, 1973.

Bare, J.S., *Phonetics and Phonology in Pāṇini*, Univ., of Michigan, Phonetics Laboratory, 1975.

Belvalkar, S.K., *Systems of Skt. Grammar*, Poona, 1980 (2nd edn.).

Biardeau, M., *Theorie de...... brahmanisme classique*, The Hague, 1964.

Bhattacharya, B., *Yāska's Nirukta and the Science of Etymology*, Calcutta, 1958.

Birwe, R., *Studies in ch.* III-V *of the Aṣṭādhyāyī*.

———, *Der Gaṇapāṭha*, Wiesbaden, 1964.

Böhtlingk, O., *Pāṇini's Grammatik*.

Bühler, G. , *Uber das Laben das Jaina Monches Hemacandra*, Wien, 1889.

———, *Report*, 1875-76.

Buiskool, *Pūrvatrāsiddham*, Amsterdam, 1934.

(Abridged recast, *The Tripādī*, Leiden, 1939).

Cardona, C., *Pāṇini — A Survey of Research*, 1980.

———, *Pāṇini, His Work and Translation*, Delhi.

Coward, H.G., *Encyclopaedia of Indian Philosophies. The Philosophy of Grammarians*.

Chakrabarti, P.C., *Philosophy of Skt. Grammar*, Calcutta, 1930.

Chatterji, K.C., *Technical Terms and Technique of Skt. Grammar,* Pt. 1, Calcutta, 1948.

Chaubey, B.R., *Ṛṣi-mantra nirvacanabhāṣya of Yāska*, Hoshiarpur.

De, S.K., *Sanskrit Poetics,* Calcutta, 1960.

———, *Early History of Vaiṣṇava Faith and Movement in Bengal,* Calcutta, 1961.

———, *Padyāvalī* (Intro.).

Deshpande, M.M., *Critical Studies in Indian Grammarians,* Vol. I, Michigan, USA, 1975.

———, *Evolution of Synthetic Theories in Skt. Grammar,* 1980.

Devaraja, Y., *Comm. on the Nirukta,* Calcutta, 1952.

Devraja, G.V., *Anubandhas of Pāṇini.*

Diksit, R., *Patañjalicarita* (in Grantha script), Chidambaram, 1888.

Dvivedi, H.P., *Studies in Pāṇini,* Delhi, 1978.

Dyen, I., *The Skt. Indeclinables of the Hindu Grammarians and Lexiccographers,* Baltimore, 1939.

Encyclopaedia of Religion and Ethics, VI (About Hemacandra).

Faddegon, *Studies in Pāṇini's Grammar.*

Filliozat, J., *Le Mahābhāṣya de Patañjali.*

———, *Le Pradīpa de Kaiyaṭa et Uddyota of Nāgeśa*, 3 vols. Tr. into French up to nine *Āhnikas*, Pondicherry, 1975-80.

Ganguli, *The Philosophy of Languages.*

Ghosh, B.K., *Linguistic intro. to Skt.*

———, *Pūrvācāryas in Pāṇini.*

Gode, P.K., *Studies in Indian Literary History.*

Goldstücker, *Pāṇini and His Place in Skt. Lit.*

Gonda, J., *Remarks on the Skt. Passive*, Leiden, 1951.

———, *La place del particula negative na dans la phras Indian*, London, 1952.

———, *The Aspectual Function of the Ṛgvedic Present and Aorist*, 1962.

———, Character of IE moods with special regard to Greek and Skt., Gottingen, 1956. Remarque surla on verve dans la . . . on langua sanscrite, Utrecht, 1952.

Haldar, G.P., *Vyākaraṇ Darśaner Itihās* (in Bengali), Vol. I, Calcutta, 1330 BS.

Henrich, H.H., (ed.), *Studies in Sanskrit Syntax,* 1886.

Indische Studien XIII, pp. 293-302 (About *Mahābhāṣya*).

Iyer, K.A.S., *Bhartṛhari, a Study of the Vākyapadīya in the Light of Ancient Comms.,* Poona, 1969.

Iyer, K.A.S., *Some Lost Works on Vyākaraṇa, Raghavan Fel. Vol.,* Delhi, 1975.

Jha, R.K., *A Glimpse of the History of Sanskrit Grammar,* Varanasi, 1990.

Joshi, S.D., *Pāṇini Rules* I.4.49-I.4.51. *Summaries of Papers,* AIOC, 1974.

———, *Some Theoretical Problems on Pāṇini' Grammar,* Poona, 1982.

Junnarkar, P.B., *Intro. to Pāṇini.*

Joshi and Roodbergen, *Patañjali's Vyākaraṇa Mahābhāṣya.*

Katre, S.M., *Dictionary of Pāṇini,* 3 vols., Poona, 1968-9.

Kielhorn, F., *Kātyāyana and Patañjali — their Relation to Each other and to Pāṇini,* Banaras, 1963 (2nd edn.).

Kielhorn's Report for 1880-1 MSS 35, 36, (about Jinaprabhasūri).

Kiparsky, P., *Pāṇini as a Variationist.*

Laddu, S.D., *Evolution of the Skt. Language* (Pāṇini to Patañjali), *Primary formations,* Poona, 1974.

Leidecker, K.F., Sanskrit Essentials of Grammar and Language, Madras, 1976.

Liebich, *Pāṇini,* 1891.

Limaye, V.P., *Critical Studies in Mahābhāṣya,* Hoshiarpur, 1974.

Mahavir, *Pāṇini as Grammarian,* Delhi, 1978.

———, Some Anomalies reg. the *Aṣṭādhyāyī. Sum. of Papers,* AIOC, 1974.

Majumdar, P.K., *Philosophy of Language in the Light of Pāṇini and Mīmaṁsā Schools of Indian Philosophy,* Calcutta, 1977.

Mehendale, M.A., *Nirukta Notes,* Series I, Poona, 1965.

———, *Nirukta Notes,* Series, II, Poona.

Mimamsak, Y., *Sanskrit Vyākaraṇ kā Itihās.*

Mishra, H., *A Critical Study of Some Aspects of Skt. Grammar.*

Misra, S.S., *A Comparative Grammar of Sanskrit, Greek and Hittite.*

Palsule, G.B., *Sanskrit Dhātupāṭha,* Calcutta, 1968.

Pathak and Chitra, *Word-Index to Pāṇini,* followed by *Aṣṭādhyāyī-sūtrapāṭha* and *Vārtikas, Dhātupāṭha, Gaṇapāṭha,* etc., Poona, 1935.

Pawate, *The Structure of the Aṣṭādhyāyī,* 1950.

Peterson's Report for 1890-2 Index (About Jinaprabhasūri).

Prasad, M., *Language of the Nirukta*, Delhi, 1963.

Puri, B.N., *India in the Time of Patañjali,* Bombay, 1957.

Raghavan, V., *Inaugural Address to Seminar on Contribution of Bihar to Different Indological Studies,* 1970, Deptt. of Sanskrit, Vikram University, Ujjain.

Raghuvir, *Critical Study of the Kāśikā.*

Rao, V.S., *The Philosophy of Sentence and its Parts,* Delhi, 1970.

Rau, W., *Handschriftioche Uber lieferung des Vākyapadīya and Seminar Kommentare,* München, 1971.

Renou, L., *Etudes Vediques of Pāṇinianeeness,* Paris, 1957.

———, *Le Grammaire de Pāṇini,* Vols. I-III, 1965.

———, *Traduite du Sanskrit,* Paris, Vol. I, 1948; II, 1951; III. 1954.

———, *Terminologie grammatical du Skt.*, Paris, 1959.

Rocher, R., *La theorie des voix Du Verhe dans Lecola Pānineene* (Le 14 Āhnika), Bruxelles, 1960.

Sarangi, A.C., *Development of Skt. from Pāṇini to Patañjali.*

Sarma, M.K., *Pāṇini, Kātyāyana and Patañjali,* 1971.

Scherfe, H., *Pāṇini's Metalanguage,* Philadelphia.

Schefts, B., *Grammatical Method in Pāṇini.*

Sen, S., *Pāṇinica,* Calcutta, 1970.

Sharma, M.A., *A Comp. Study of Kāśikāvṛtti and Siddhāntakaumudī.*

Shastri, *Pāṇini-vyākaraṇa-śāstre Vaiśeṣika-tattva-mīmāṁsā,* Calcutta, 1959.

Shastri, G.N., *Philosophy of Word and Meaning,* Delhi, 1976.

Shastri, C., *Pāṇini Re-interpreted*, Delhi, 1990.

Shastri and Varma, *The Etymologies of Yāska*, Hoshiarpur, 1953.

Shastry, P.V.N., *Vai. Sid. Kau.* (analytical discussion in contents in English), Delhi, 1974.

Shukla, S., *Pāṇini Vyākaraṇ evaṁ Agnipurāṇ men nirūpit Vyākaraṇa* (in Hindi).

Singh, J.D., *Pāṇini, His Description of Skt.*, New Delhi, 1991.

Skold, H., *The Nirukta* etc., Lund, 1926.

Thieme, P., *Pāṇini and the Veda.*

Tripathi, R.P., *Some Works of Secondary Derivatives — an Historical Comparative and Critical Study in Skt.*

Tripathi, T.R., *A Critical Study of the Padamañjarī*, New Delhi, 1981.

Tripathi, R., *Skt. Vyākaraṇ Darśan,* Delhi, 1972 (in Hindī).

Wezler, A., *Paribhāṣā*, IV, V, XV, Hamburg Y.D.H., Gelden, 1969.

Whitney, W.D., *Roots, Verb-forms and Primary Derivatives of the Skt. language.*

———, *Sanskrit Grammar.*

Wilson, H.H., *Grammar of the Skt. Language.*

Zachariae, Th., *Ind. Woerterbucher,* Strassburg, 1897.

JOURNALS, COMMEMORATION VOLUMES, ETC.

ABORI (Diamond Jubilee Vol.) 1978 (about Patañjali).

ABORI, Vol. 62, 1981 (S. Bhate's paper on Pāṇini and Yāska).

Asutosh Mookherji Silver Jubilee Vol. Pt. 1, p. 202 (about *Tantrapradīpa*).

BEFEO, III, 1903, pp. 38-53 (Regarding date of Candragomin).

BSOAS, XL5, (H. Falk, Three Groups of particles in *Nirukta*).

D.R. Bhandarkar Vol., Calcutta, 1940 (B.K. Ghosh — Pūrvācāryas in Pāṇini).

Indian Antiquary, Vol. X, p. 79, Vol. XVI, p. 27 (about *Aindra Vyākaraṇa*).

IA, Oct., 1914 (about *Amogha-vṛtti*).

IA, X, p. 75 (About *Pañcavastu*).

IA, Oct., 1914 (Path on all Jaina *Śākaṭāyana*).

IA, Vol. V, (re: metrical *vārtika*s),

IA, XXV, p. 103 (On *Dharmadāsa*),

IA, I, II, XV, XVI (about *Patañjali*),

IA, Vol. 43, 1914, pp. 205-12 (For *Amoghavarṣa*).

Indian Historical Quarterly, VII, pp. 418-19 (K.C. Chatterji).

IHQ, XIV, pp. 256 ff. (Re. Candragomin),

IHQ, XIX, 1943, pp. 201 ff. (about Puruṣottamadeva).

JASB, 1911, Sup., p. 85 (Csoma da koros about Candrakīrti).

JOR, Madras, XII, p. 7 (about Goyīcandra).

JRASB, VI (Preface about Aindra Vyākaraṇa).

La Vallee Poussin Memo. Vol., Calcutta, 1940 (Renou on identification of Two Patañjalis).

Studies in Indian Literary History, by P.K. Gode, Vol. II, pp. 65-74. (on date of Bhaṭṭoji); p. 75 (List of Bhaṭṭoji's works).

Poona Orientialist, XX, 1955 (about Aindra Vyākaraṇa)

Pro. of 5th Oriental Conf., Vol. I, 1912 (G. Deva, critical study of Bhartṛhari, with sp. reference to *Vākyapadīya* and its comm.).

RASB, VI, Preface, p. lxvi (about Goyīcandra)

R.K. Mookerji Vol., Bhāratakaumudī, Allahabad, 1945, 1947. (A.B. Keith, Pāṇini's vocabulary).

Siddhabhāratī, S. Varma, Vol. II, Hoshiarpur, 1950. S.B. Chaturvedi, Pāṇini's vocabulary and his date.

Studie Indologica, Festschrift Für H. Kirfel (R. Birwe-Interpretation in Pāṇini's *Aṣṭādhyāyī*, Bonn, 1955).

Woolner Com. Vol. Lahore, 1940. S.B. Chaturvedi, Pāṇini's Vocabulary, its bearing on his date.

Summaries of Papers, AIOC, 1924. (Karandikar on date of Haradatta).

WZKSO, V, P. 125 (Re : Candragomin).

WZKM, XIII, pp. 308-15 (about Candragomin).

CATALOGUES

Sāstri's Cat. of MSS. in Durbar Lib. of Nepal (about Rāmacandra's Prakriyākaumudī).

New Catalogus Catalogorum, Madras, different vols. for information about authors and works.

Oxford Catalogue (Aufrecht), p. 162 — List of works utilised by Buaṭṭoji.

PURĀṆAS

TEXTS

All the Mahāpurāṇas have been edited in *Aṣṭādaśa Mahāpurāṇa*, Bombay, loose-leaves. The Purāṇa Text Series, Varanasi, has undertaken to publish the texts of all Mahāpurāṇas. Some have already been published. All-India Kashiraj Trust, Varanasi, is publishing critical editions of Purāṇas and studies relating to them. An Eng. tr. of all the Mahā- and Upa-purāṇas is being published, in 50 vols., under the caption *Ancient Indian Tradition and Mythology*, by Motilal Banarsidass, Delhi, Vols. 1-4 *Śiva Purāṇa*, Vols. 5-6, *Liṅga Purāṇa*, Vols. 7-11 *Brāgavata Purāṇa*, Vols. 12-14 *Garuḍa Purāṇa*, 15-19 *Nārada*, 20-21 *Kūrma*, 22-26 *Brahmāṇḍa*, 27-30 *Agni*, 31-32 *Varāha* and 33-36 *Brahma* have been published.

STUDIES

Agrawala, V.S., *Matsya Purāṇa — A Study*, Vārāṇasī, 1963.

———, *Vāmana Purāṇa — A study*, Vārāṇasī , 1964.

Aiyar, N., *The Purāṇas in the Light of Modern Sciences.*

Ali, S.M., *The Geography of the Purāṇas*, New Delhi, 1966.

Awasthi, A.B.L., *Purāṇic Index*, New Delhi, 1992.

Banerji, J.N., *Purāṇic and Tāntric Religion —Early Phase*, Calcutta, 1966.

Banerji, S.C., *Studies in the Mahāpurāṇas*, Calcutta, 1991.

———, *New Perspectives in the Study of the Purāṇas*, Delhi.

Bhattacharya, R.S., *Subject Index of the Agni Purāṇa with Important Proper Names*, Vārāṇasī.

Chatterjee, A., *Padma Purāṇa — A Study*, Calcutta, 1967.

Coburn, T., *Devi-māhātmya*, Delhi, 1984.

Dange, S.S., *The Bhāgavata Purāṇa — A Mytho-social Study*, 1984.

Dange, S.A., *Encyclopaedia of Purānic Beliefs and Practices*, New Delhi, 1986.

Devi, A.K., *A Bibliographical Dictionary of Puranic Personages*.

Diksitar, V.R.R., *The Matsya Purāṇa — A Study*, Madras, 1935.

———, *Purāṇa Index*, 3 vols., Madras, 1951, 1955.

Gangadharan, N., *Garuḍa Purāṇa, A Study*, Vārāṇasī, 1972.

———, *Liṅga Purāṇa* — A *Study*, Delhi, 1980.

Gyani, S.D., *Agni Purāṇa, A Study*, Vārāṇasī.

Hazra, R.C., *Studies in the Purānic Records on Hindu Rites and Customs*, Dacca, 1940.

———, *Studies in the Upapurāṇas*, Vols. I-III, Calcutta.

Iyer, K.N., *The Purāṇas in the Light of Modern Science*, Adyar.

Kantawala, S.G., *Cultural History from the Matsya Purāṇa*, Baroda, 1964.

Mani, V., *Purānic Encyclopaedia*, Delhi.

Mishra, B.B., *Polity in the Agni Purāṇa*, Calcutta, 1966.

Pargiter, F.E., *Purāṇa Text of the Dynasties of Kali Age* (ed. with Eng. tr.), Banaras, 1962.

———, *Ancient Indian Historical Tradition*, London, 1922.

Patil, D.R., *Cultural History from the Vāyu Purāṇa*.

Rawal, A.J., *Indian Society, Religion and Mythology — A Study of Brahmavaivarta Purāṇa*, Delhi, 1982.

Rukmani, T.S., *A Critical Study of the Bhāgavata Purāṇa.*

Sen Sarma, P., *Military Wisdom in the Purāṇas*, Calcutta, 1979.

———, *Plants in the Indian Purāṇas*, Calcutta, 1989.

Solis, B.P., *The Kṛṣna Cycle in the Purāṇas*, 1984.

Tandon, Y., *Purāṇa-viṣaya-samanu-kramaṇikā*, Hoshiarpur, 1952.

Wilson, H.H., Eng. trs. of *Viṣṇu Purāṇa* (Intro.).

Winternitz, M., *History of Indian Literature*, Vol. I.

TANTRA

(Works on Tantra)

These are divided into the following classes: Published and Unpublished.

PUBLISHED WORKS

A. Texts, Lexicons, Translations.

B. Works in Western Languages

C. Works in Hindi

D. Works in Bengali

E. Miscellaneous Works

F. Periodicals, Proceedings, Reports, etc.

In this bibliography, we have taken into account only the published Tāntric works. Due to various reasons, it has not been possible to note the place and/ or the year of publication in every case.

UNPUBLISHED WORKS

The unpublished texts far outnumber the published ones. The titles of a good many unpublished texts of some importance have been collected, with the respective places of deposit, in the present author's work, entitled *New Light on Tantra*, Calcutta, 1992.

Published Works

[In Engligh alphabetical order]

A. TEXTS, LEXICONS, TRANSLATIONS

Besides Tāntric texts, some other works, influenced by Tantra, are also included; the works of the latter class are important in the history of Tantra literature.

Advaya-vajra-saṁgraha, GOS.

Adyadi-mahālakṣmi-hṛdaya-stotra, in Bṛhat-stotra-multahara, pt. 2, Bṛhat-stotra-ratnākara, pt. 1.

Āgama-tattva-vilāsa, ed. by P. Sastri, Calcutta, 1985.

Ahirbudhnya-saṁhitā, with Eng. tr. by Nityasvarupananda, Calcutta, 1964.

Ajitagama, I, II, Pondicherry, 1963, 1967.

Ākāśa-bhairava-kalpa, N.C. Sharma.

Anandakanda, Tanjore Sarasvati Mahal Series, 15, 1952.

Ānandalaharī, ed. and tr. by Avalon, Madras, 1961 (5th edn.).

Aniruddha-saṁhitā, ed. by A.S. Iyenger, Mysore, 1956.

Ārya-mañjuśrī-mūlakalpa, TSS, Trivandrum, 1920-5.

Aṣṭāvakra-saṁhitā, with Eng. tr. by Nityasvarupananda, Calcutta, 1964.

Aṣṭottara-śatopaniṣatsu Śākta Upaniṣad, Adyar (Madras), 1950.

Bhāradvāja-saṁhitā (Telugu), ed. by P. Aiyyangar, Mysore.

Bhāradvāja-saṁhitā (from Nārada-pañcarātra), Venkatesvara Press, Bombay, 1905.

Bhargavatantra, ed. by R.P. Chowdhury.

Bhāvopahāra (Cakrapāṇi), with *vivaraṇa* by Ramyadeva, KSS, No. 14, 1918.

Bījanighaṇṭu, ed. by A. Avalon, Tantrik Texts, I.

Bṛhad-brahma-saṁhitā (from Nārada-pañcarātra), ed., H.N. Apte, Anandasrama Series No. 68 (Telugu), Tirupati, 1909.

Bṛhannila-tantra, ed. by M. Kaul, 1984.

Bṛhat-tantra-sāra (Kṛṣṇānanda), Calcutta, 1341 BS.

Cakra-saṁvara (sambhara)-tantra, Tantric texts, 7, Calcutta, 1919. (First Section).

Cid-gagana-candrika, with comm. of R. Misra, *Divyacakorikā* comm. ed. by K.A. Sastri, Letukura, East Godavari District, 1943, 2 pts.

Dakṣiṇāmūrti-saṁhitā, Varanasi, 1937.

Dakṣiṇāmūrti-stotra (Śaṅkarācārya) with comm. of Svayamprakasa and *Vārttika* of Sureśvarācārya, Bombay, 1902.

Dattātreya-tantra, with Hindi comm., Bombay, 1983.

Devībhāgavata, ed. by R. Pandeya, Varanasi, Saṁvat, 1984; Venkatesvar Press, with Nīlakaṇṭha's *Tilaka* comm., Saṁvat 1984; Vangavasi, Calcutta, Śaka 1932 (2nd edn.).

Devī Purāṇa, ed. with Bengali tr. by P. Tarkaratna, Calcutta, 1334 BS (2nd edn.); with Hindi comm., Bombay, 1983.

Durgā-dakārādi-sahasra-nāma (from *Kulārṇava-tantra*), Calcutta, 1921 (in a collection).

Durgāsaptaśatī, with seven Skt. comms., ed. by K.K. Sharma, 1984.

Ekākṣarakośa (Puruṣottama), A. Avalon, Tāntrik Texts, I.

Gaṇapati-tattva, old Javanese text, ed., with notes and Eng. tr. by S. Singhal, New Delhi, 1958.

Gandharva-tantra, ed. by Kak and Sastri, Srinagar, 1934.

Gandhottama-nirṇaya (by son of Viśveśvara), Haridwar, 1900.

Gāyatrīkavaca (from *Vasiṣṭha-saṁhitā of Pañcarātra*), Amritsar, 1902.

Gāyatrīkavaca (from *Rudrayāmala*)—*Bṛhat-stotra-muktāvalī*, Pt. I, *Stotra* No. 245), 1st & 2nd edn., 1912, 1923; with *Suryokavaca*, pp. 29-31, 1918, in Telugu script.

Gāyatrī-rahasya, ed. by Sarma Gaud.

Gāyatrī-tantra (from *Agastya-saṁhitā*) (ed.) *Sulabha-tantra-prakāśa*, 1886; also with Hindi comm., ed. by M. Pal, Calcutta, Saṁvat 1948; with Hindi tr., 1916; in Kṛṣṇānanda's *Tantrasāra*.

Gopāla-mantra-kramadīpikā — Same as *Kramadīpikā* (q.v.).

Gorakṣa-siddhānta-saṁgraha, Sarasvati-bhavana texts, No. XVIII, 1925.

Guhyasamāja-tantra, GOS, liii, 1931; HOS.

Gupta-sādhana-tantra, Calcutta.

Gurutantra, ed. and tr. into Bengali by J. Tarakalamkara, Calcutta, 1335 BS.

Haṭhayoga-pradīpikā, Bombay, 1952.

Hayasīrsa-saṁhitā, Ādikāṇḍa, Rajshahi (now in Bangladesh), 2 vols. 1952, 1957.

Hevajra-tantra, ed. by D.L. Snellgrove.

Īśāna-śiva-gurudeva-paddhati, TSS.

Īśvara-pratyabhijña-kārikā of Utpala, with his own com. up to 3/20, pub. with *Siddhitrayī*, KSS. 34; ed. by M.S. Kaul, 1921.

Īśvara-pratyabhijña-vimarśini of Abhinavagupta, 3 pts.; KSS, Nos. LX (1938), LXII (1941), LXV (1943), ed. by M.S. Kaul.

Īśvara-saṁhitā, Conjeevaram, 1923; Mysore, 1890 (Telugu Script).

Jñānasaṁkalini (or *-saṁkuli*)*-tantra*, with Bengali tr., in *Aruṇodaya*, Calcutta, 1891 ff.

Kakṣapuṭa (or, -*ṭi*), pub. in *Arunodaya* (Part); pub. under title *Siddha-nāgārjuna-kakṣapuṭa* in *Indrajālādi-saṁgraha*, Vasumati, Calcutta (31 ch.), ptd. at Belgaum; with Telugu trs. by Venkatachalapati (Rani), Vijayawada, 1958; in 196 verses (perhaps only an extract). Extracts in P.C. Ray, *History of Hindu Chemistry*, II, App. Skt. Texts, pp. 1-17.

Kālacakra-tantrarāja, ed. by B. Banerjee, Asiatic Society, Calcutta, 1985.

Kālīkākalpa or *Kālīkalpa* in *Bṛhat-stotra-ratnākara*, II.

Kalikā Purāṇa, Bombay, Śaka 1829 (= AD1907). Also ed. by P. Tarkaratna, with Bengali tr., Calcutta, 1316 BS.

Kālikārcā-mukura, by K. Nyayaratna in *Ṣaṭ-cakra-nirūpaṇa*, 1850.

Kālīrahasya, with Hindi comm., ed. by S. Mishra.

Kālī-tantra, with Skt. *ṭippaṇī* and Bengali tr., Calcutta, 1922; in *Śāktapramoda*, Bombay, 1933. A different text of same title pub. by K. Vidyaratna, Calcutta, 1892. A *Kālī-tantra*, with Hindi tr., Moradabad, 1902.

Kālīvilāsa, London, 1917.

Kālīvilāsa-tantra, Tāntrik Texts, VI, Calcutta, 1917.

Kalpacintāmaṇi, ed. and tr. by J. Hopkins, London, 1985.

Kālyarcana-candrikā of N. Lahidi, Mursidabad, 1877-79 (in Bengali script).

Kāmadhenu-tantra in *Vividha-tantra-saṁgraha* and *Sulabhamantra-prakāśa*, Calcutta, (ed. by R. Shukla).

Kāmakalāvilāsa of Puṇyānandanātha.

Kāmākhya-tantra, in *Tantra-sāra*, 1877-84; *Sulabha-tantra-prakāśa*, 1886; *Vividha-tantra-saṁgraha*, Calcutta, 1877-81

Kāmaratna-tantra.

Kāmarūpa-tantra-mantra, with Bengali tr., Calcutta, 1912. Compiled by C. Vasak, with Bengali tr., Calcutta, 1929.

Kapiñjala-saṁhitā, Cuddapet, 1896 (Telugu script).

Karaṅkiṇī-mahātantra, included in Rasaratnākara (Rasagranthamālā, Gondal, 1926), title *Kiṅkiṇī-meru-tantra*.

Karpūra-stavarāja of Mahākāla, ed. by S. Dikshit, Delhi.

Kaśyapa-jñānakāṇḍa, ed. by R. Parthasarathi Bhattachar, Tirupati, 1948.

Kaulajñāna-nirṇaya, ed. by P.C. Bagchi, Calcutta, 1934.

Kaulamārga-rahasya, Tāntrik Texts, XIV.

Kaulāvalī-nirṇaya, Tāntrik Texts, XIV.

Kaulāvalī-tantra, ed. by R.M. Chattopadhyay.

Kauśikasūtra, ed. by M. Bloomfield, New Haven, 1890. Important Sections, referring to magic, tr. into German by W. Caland in *Altindisches Zauberritual*, Amsterdam, 1900.

Kauśikasūtra-dārilabhāṣya, ed. by R.N. Dandekar, Poona, 1972.

Kramadīpikā, with comm., ed. by D.P. Sukla, Varanasi, 1917.

Kramastotra of Abhinavagupta, pub. as Appendix C. to *Abhinavagupta*, etc., by K.C. Pandey, Varanasi, 1963 (2nd edn.).

Kubjikā-mata-tantra, ed. by J. Schoterman.

Kulacūḍāmaṇi-tantra, in Tāntrik Texts, IV, London, Calcutta, 1915; 2nd edn., Madras, 1956.

Kulārṇava-tantra, Tāntrik Texts, V, 1971; ed. and tr. by R.K. Rai, Varanasi, 1983. Also ptd. in *Tantrasāra*, Compiled by R.M. Chattopadhyay, 1877-84; Sulabha-tantra-prakāśa, 1886. Aslo ptd. in Calcutta, 1897.

Kumāratantra, ed. and tr. into French by J. Filliozat, Paris, 1937.

Kumārī-tantra, in Śāktapramoda, compiled by Devananda, 1890, ed. by Krishnamacharya, with Hindi comm.; ed. by A.K. Kalia.

Lakṣmī-tantra, with Hindi comm. of C.L. Gautam, Varanasi; Eng. tr. with notes by S. Gupta, Leiden, 1972.

Lalitā-sahasranāma, ed. by V. Krishnamacharya, Adyar, 1959.

Lalitā-sahasranāma, with Bhāskararāya's comm. and Eng. tr. by R.A. Sastri, Madras, 1951 (3rd edn.).

Luptāgama-saṁgraha, ed. by G. Kaviraj, Pt. 1, Varanasi, Śaka 1892 (= AD 1970).

Mahābhāgavata Purāṇa, crit. edn. with intro. and index, by P. Kumar, Delhi, 1933; ed. by P. Tarkaratna, with Bengali tr., Calcutta, 1321 BS.

Mahākāla-saṁhitā, pub. by G.N. Jha, Allahabad, 1971.

Mahānirvāṇa-tantra, ed. by Ādi Brāhmasamāj, Calcutta, 1876; W. Alex. Delhi. Eng. tr. by A. Avalon, London, 1913. Prose Eng. tr. by M.N. Dutt, Calcutta, 1900.

Mahārtha-mañjarī of Maheśvarānanda, with Parimala comm., ed. by Ganapati Sastri, *TSS*., No. 66, 1919.

Mahāvairocana-tantra, M.N. Dutt, A. Wayman.

Maheśvarīya-tantra, ed. by L. Tikakar, with Hindi comm., Bombay 1983; ed. by R. Sharma (with Hindi comm.), Varanasi.

Mahimnaḥ-stotra of Puṣpadanta, with comm. of M. Sarasvati, Varanasi, 1964. Eng. tr. with comm., by A. Avalon, Madras, 1963.

Mālinī-vijayottara-tantra, ed. by M.S. Kaul, Delhi, 1984.

Mālinīvijayottara-vārttika—Abhinavagupta's comm. on *Mālinī-vijayottara-tantra*, ed. by M.S. Kaul, 1911, KSS. No. XXI.

Mantrābhidhāna (part of *Rudrayāmala*), ed. by A. Avalon, Tāntrik Texts, I.

Mantramahārṇava, with Hindi tr. by R.K. Rai, Devīkhaṇḍa, Devatākhaṇḍa, Miśrakhaṇḍa.

Mantra-mahāvijñāna, pts. 1-4.

Mantramahodadhi of Mahīdhara, with Skt. comm., Bombay, 1983, with *Naukāṭīkā* and Eng. intro., ed. by J.W. Dejong, Canberra (3 vols. in one). Eng. tr. by T.V.P. Iyer; ed. with *Naukā* comm., Hindi tr. and Hindi comm. by S. Chaturvedi, Varanasi, 1981. Text and comm. with Eng. tr. by a Board of Scholars, 1988.

Mantrayoga-saṁhitā, text and Eng. tr. by R.K. Rai.

Mātaṅgaparameśvarāgama, I. Vidyāpāda, with comm. of Rāmakaṇṭha, ed. by N.R. Bhatta, Pondicherry, 1977.

Mātṛkābheda-tantra, ed. by C. Bhattacharya, Calcutta, 1933; ed. by R.K. Rai, Varanasi, 1983.

Mātṛkā-cakra-viveka of Svatantrānandanātha, Varanasi, 1934.

Mātṛkānighaṇṭu, ed. by A. Avalon, Tāntrik Texts, I.

Māyā-tantra, Calcutta.

Meru-tantra, Venkatesvara Press, Bombay, 1908.

Mṛgendrāgama (*Kriyāpāda*, *Caryāpada*), with comm. of Bhatta Narayana-kantha, ed. by N.R. Bhatt, Pondicherry, 1962.

Mṛgendrāgama (section of *Yoga*), with comm. of Bhatta Narayana Kantha.

Mṛgendra-tantra (Vidyāpāda, Yogapāda), with comm. of Bhatta Narayana kantha, ed. by D.M.S. Kaul, 1930.

Mudrānighaṇṭu (from *Vāmakeśvara Tantra*), ed. by A. Avalon, Tāntrik Texts, I.

Muṇḍamālā Tantra, Calcutta, 1387 B.S. Also ed. by R.N. Chattopadhyay.

Nārada-pañcarātra, ed. by K.M. Banerji, Calcutta, 1965. Eng. tr. in *SBH*, 23, 1921. Also ed., with Hindi comm., by R.K. Rai.

Nāradīya Saṁhitā, ed. by R.P. Choudhari.

Netratantra, ed. by V. Dvivedi, with comm. of Kṣemarājācārya, Delhi, 1985; ed. by J. Das, with Bengali tr., Calcutta, 1388 BS.; ed. by M.S. Kaul, Bombay, I, 1926; II. 1939.

Nīlatantra, ptd. in *Tantrasāra* by Kṛṣṇa Bhattacharya, Calcutta, 1877-84.

Niruttara-tantra, ed. by R. Chattopadhyay; ed. by B. Sharma; ed. by D. Tripathi, with Bengali tr., Calcutta, 1385 BS.

Nirvāṇa-tantra, ed. by R.M. Chatterji, B. Sharma; ed. by N. Smrtitirtha, with Bengali tr., Calcutta, 1385 BS.

Niṣpannayogāvali by Abhayākaragupta, ed. by B. Bhattacharya, Baroda, 1944.

Nityaṣoḍaśīkārṇava (Part of *Vāmakeśvara Tantra*), ed. with *Setubandha* comm. of Bhāskara Rāya; with comms. of Śivānanda and Vidyānanda, ed. by V.V. Dvivedi, included in *Yoga-tantra-saṁgraha*, Varanasi, 1968.

Nityotsava of Umānanda (*Paraśurāma-kalpasūtra*, II), GOS, XXIII, 1984.

Pādmatantra, Bangalore, 1927 (2 Vols.), Telugu script; Mysore, 1891.

Pādukāpañcaka, Tāntrik Texts, II, 1913.

Pañcarātrāgama, I, II.

Paramānanda-tantra, with comm. of Maheśvarānandanātha, ed. by R. Mishra.

Paraśurāma-kalpasūtra, ed. by M. Sastri, with Rāmeśvara's comm.; by S.Y. Sastri Dave, GOS, 1950; ed. by B. Sharma.

Parama-puruṣa-saṁhitā, ed. by P. Sitaramacarya, Bhadrachalam.

Paramārtha-sāra, Abhinavagupta, with comm. of Yogarāja; ed. by J.C. Chatterji, KSS.: VII, 1916; with Eng. tr. and notes by L.D. Barnett, London, 1910.

Parameśvara-saṁhitā, Srirangam, 1953.

Parāpraveśikā of Kṣemarāja, with notes by M.R. Sastri, 1918.

Parāśara-saṁhitā (Telugu), ed. by Raghavacharya, I, Bangalore, 1898.

Parātriṁśikā, Kashmir Series, No. 18, 1918.

Parātriṁśikā-vivaraṇa, Abhinavagupta, ed., with notes, by M.R. Shastri, KSS. No. XVIII, 1918.

Pauṣkara-saṁhitā, A.S. Iyengar and M.C. Thirumalachariar.

Pracaṇḍacaṇḍikā, Same as *Chinnamastā*.

Parātriṁśikā-laghuvṛtti of Abhinavagupta, ed. by J.D. Jadoo, 1947.

Prajñopāya-viniścayasiddhi of Anaṅgavajra GOS ed., XLIV, Baroda, 1929.

Prāṇatoṣiṇi, ed. by J. Vidyasagar, Calcutta, 1898.

Prāṇatoṣiṇi, with Hindi trs., by R.D. Shukla.

Prapañcasāra, ed., with *Vivaraṇa* comm. of Padmapāda, *Prayogakramadīpikā* comm. on *Vivaraṇa*, Intro. by A. Sarasvati, Delhi, 1981.

Pratyabhijñā-hṛdaya of Kṣemarāja, with Eng. tr. and notes, by Thakur J. Singh, Delhi, 1963. With Eng. tr. and comm. (under title *The Secret of Self-realistion*): 1. K, - Taimni, Adyar, Madras, 1974.

Puraścaraṇa-dīpikā of Kāśīnātha or Śivānandanātha, Varanasi, 1973.

Puraścaryārṇava, ed. by P. Varma, 3 Pts., Calcutta, 1901, 1902, 1904.

Puraścaryārṇava, by Pratap Sinha; ed. by M. Jha.

Puruṣottama-saṁhitā, ed. by P. Sitaramacarya, Bhadrachalam, 1932 (Telugu script).

Rādhātantra, ed. by K. Mukhopadhyay, Calcutta, 1383 BS.

Rasārṇava-tantra, ed. by P.C. Ray and H.C. Kaviratna, Calcutta, 1910.

Rasārṇava-tantra, ed. by T. Panta, Varanasi, 1939. Reptd. : I. 1985.

Rasārṇavaṁ nāma Rasa-tantram, with gloss., called Bhāgīrathī and Hindi exposition, called *Rasacandrikā*, by I. Tripathi.

Rasārṇavakalpa, Eng. tr. by M. Ray; B.B. Subharayappa.

Rauravajāmala, I, II, Pondicherry, 1961, 1972, ed. by N.R. Bhatt.

Ṛgvidhāṇa, ed. by R. Meyer, Berolini, 1878.

Rudrayāmala-tantra, with Hindi comm., Bombay, 1983; *Uttaratantra*, ed. by J. Vidyasagara, Calcutta, 1937 and by R.K. Rai, Varanasi, 1986.

Sādhanamālā, ed. by B. Bhattacharya, Baroda, 1968, GOS, I, II.

Sādhanarahasya, I, Compiled by A. Kavibhusana, Śaka 1852 (AD 1930).

Sādhanarahasya-prariśiṣṭa, compiled by A. Kavibhusana.

Śāktānanda-taraṅgiṇī, ed. by P. Sastri (with Beng. tr.), Calcutta, 1349 BS., ed. by R. Chattopadhyay, *Vividhatantra-saṁgraha*, Calcutta, 1881-86; R.N. Tripathi, Varanasi. Append. (Yogatantra Granthamālā, Vol. II).

Śāktapramoda, ed. by R. Singh, 1951.

Śākta Upaniṣads, ed. by A.K. Warrier, Adyar, Madras.

Śāktavijñāna of Somānandanātha, ed. by J.D. Jadoo, 1947.

Śaktibhāṣya (On *Brahmasūtra*) by P. Tarkaratna, ch. I, Śaka 1959; ch. II, 1861.

Śaktisaṁgama-tantra, ed. by B. Bhattacharya, Vols. I. III, Baroda, 1932-47. *Sundarī-khaṇḍa* and *Chinnamastākhaṇḍa*, published separately. Hindi summary by R.D. Shukla.

Śaktisūtra, Sarasvatī-bhavana Series, X, Varanasi.

Samurtārcanādhikaraṇa, ed. by P. Raghunatha Cakravarti Bhattacharya, M.R. Kavi, Tirupati.

Sanatkumāra-tantra pub. GOS, Baroda, 2 vols.

Sannyāsatantra, Swami Saraswati.

Śāradātilaka of Lakṣmaṇa Deśika, ed. by A. Avalon, Delhi, 1982 (with comm. of Rāghava Bhaṭṭa); ed. with Hindi exposition, C. Gautam.

Eng. tr. by a Board of Scholars, 1988.

Sarasvatītantra, Calcutta.

Sarva-durgati-pariśodhana-tantra, ed. by T. Skorupski, Delhi, 1983.

Ṣaṭcakranirūpaṇa, *Ṣaṭcakravivṛtti* (Part of *Śrītattvacintāmaṇi* of Pūrṇānanda), ed. by T.N. Vidyaratna, Calcutta/London, 1913. Eng. tr. by Avalon in *The Serpent Power*, Madras, 1972.

Ṣaṭcakravivṛti, ed. by T.N. Vidyaratna, Tāntrik Texts, II, Calcutta, 1913.

Sāttvata-saṁhitā, ed., with Skt. Comm., by Trivedi, Varanasi; ed. by P.B. Anathachariar, Conjeevaram, 1902.

Saubhāgya-bhāskara, comm. on *Latitāsahasranāma*, by Bhāskara Roy, Bombay, 1935.

Saubhāgyalakṣmī-tantra, Calcutta.

Saundaryalaharī of Śaṅkarācārya, ed., with comm. and Eng. tr. by Woodroffe, Adyar, 1937; ed. by N. Brown, with Eng. tr., Cambridge Mass, 1958; ed., with nine expositions, Eng. tr., notes, Hindi tr. etc., by Kuppusvami, Delhi, 1976; ed. with three comms., Eng. tr. and notes, by R.A. Sastri and R.K. Guru, Madras, 1957.

Siddhalaharītantra, Same as *Kālīvilāsa* (q.v.).

Siddha-nāgārjuna-kakṣapuṭa, See *Kakṣapuṭa*.

Siddhasiddhānta-saṁgraha, G.N. Kaviraj.

Siddha-siddhānta-paddhati and other works of Nātha Cult., by Mullick, Poona, 1954.

Siddhāntasāra, Collected by B.L. Sarkar, Pub. by S.L. Sarkar, Calcutta.

Śiva-dṛṣṭi, Somānanda, with Utpaladeva's comm., ed. by M.S. Kaul, KSS. LIV, 1934, ch. I, tr. and comm. by R. Gnoli, pub. in *East and West*, New Series, VIII, 1957.

Śivasūtra, Vasugupta, with five commentaries, ed. by K. Sagar, with Kṣemarāja's comm. and Eng. tr.

Śivasūtravārttika, comm. by Bhāskara, ed. by J.C. Chatterji, 1916.

Śivasūtravārttika, comm. by Varadarāja, ed. by M.S. Kaul, KSS. No. XLIII, 1925.

Śivasūtra-vimarśinī, Kṣemarāja, ed. by J.C. Chatterji, KSS. I. Do, Eng. tr. by P.T.S. Iyengar, 1911, Allahabad, 1912.

Spanda-kārikā, with Kallaṭa's *Vṛtti* and *Śiva-sūtra-vārttika* of Bhāskara, ed. by J.C. Chatterji, 1916.

Spanda-kārikā-vivṛtti, Rāmakaṇṭha, ed. by J.C. Chatterji, KSS. VII, 1913.

Spanda-nirṇaya, comm. of Kṣemarāja on *Spanda-Kārikā*, ed. with Eng. tr. by M.S. Kaul, KSS No. XLII, 1925.

Spanda-pradīpikā, comm. of Bhaṭṭa Utpala or Utpala Vaiṣṇava, ed. by V. Islampurkar, 1898.

Spanda-sandoha, Kṣemarāja's comm. on the first verse of *Spandakārikā*, ed. by M.R. Shastri, KSS. XVI, 1917.

Śrīcakrasaṁbhāra, Tibetan text and Eng. tr. by K.D. Sandeep ed. in Tāntrik Texts, VII, 1919.

Śrīdevi-rahasya, ed. by R.C. Kak (with *Jvālāmukha-sahasra-nāmādi-bṛhat-pariśiṣṭa*).

Śrīgurutantra, with Hindi tr., Hardwar, 1967.

Śrīpraśna-saṁhitā (Kumbhakonam, 1904) (Grantha script) ed. by J.R. Bhattacharya, with Hindi tr., Hardwar, 1967.

Śrītantranidhi Śaktinidhi, with Eng. trns., by B.R. Srivastava.

Śrītattva-cintāmaṇi, Calcutta Skt. Series. No. 19; with comm. by Bhuvana on chs. I-XVIII and by Cintāmaṇi on ch. XIX-XXVI, Delhi, 1994.

Śrīvidyāratnasūtra, ed. by G.N. Kavirāj, Varanasi, 1919.

Sulabha-tantraprakāśa, Calcutta, 1887.

Svacchanda-tantra, ed. with Kṣemarāja's comm., by V.V. Dvivedi, Pts. I, II.

Śyāmārahasya, with Bengali tr., ed. by S. Tirthanath, Calcutta, 1389 BS.

Tantra of Svayambhu Vidyāpāda, with comm. of Sadyojyoti, Delhi.

Tantrābhidhāna, with Eng. tr. by R.K. Rai.

Tantrakaumudī of Devanātha, ed. by R. Jha, Darbhanga, 1969.

Tantrāloka of Abhinavagupta, ed., with Jayaratha's *Viveka* comm. by K. Sagar; ed., with Skt. comm., Eng. intro. and indices, by R.C. Dwivedi and N. Rastogi, in 8 vols., Delhi.

Āhnika IV, with *Viveka* comm. of Jayaratha, ed. by M.S. Kaul, KSS. No XXX, 1921.

It is learnt that the *Tantrāloka* has been translated into Italian by R. Gnoli.

Ed. by L. Shastri, Intro. by Avalon, Delhi, 1981 (with comm.).

Tantra-saṁgraha of Nīlakaṇṭha Somayājī, with *Yuktidīpikā* and *Laghuvivṛti* of Śaṅkara, ed. by K.V. Sarma, Ed. R.P. Tripathi, Pt. III, Varanasi, 1979; V.V. Dvivedi, Pt. IV.

Tantrasāra-saṁgraha of Nārāyaṇa, Madras, 1950.

Tantrasamuccaya (Nārāyaṇa), with comm. of Śaṅkara and *Vivaraṇa*. TSS Nos. 67, 71, 151, 169.

Partial text in N.V. Mallya's *Studies in Sanskrit Texts on Temple Architecture, with special reference to Tantra-sammuccaya,* Chidambaram, Annamalai University, 1949.

Tantrasāra of Kṛṣṇānanda.

Same as *Bṛhat-tantrasāra* (q.v.), ed. by P.K. Sastri, 3rd. edn. by R.M. Chatterji, Calcutta, 1929.

Tantrasāra of Abhinavagupta.

ed. with notes, M.R. Sastri, 1918. Under the title *Essenza dei Tantra*.

Tantrasāra tr. into Italian by P. Boringhieri, with exhaustive introduction by R. Gnoli, Torin, 1960.

Tantra-śuddha-prakaraṇa, ed. by T. Ganapati Sastri, Trivandrum, 1915.

Tantra-vaṭa-dhānikā, Abhinavagupta, ed. by M.R. Shastri, KSS. XXIV, 1918.

Tāntrika Abhidhāna, Svami, S.N., Calcutta, 1910.

Tārābhaktisudhārṇava, Tāntrik Texts, Vol. XXI, Calcutta, 1940. Ed. by P. Bhattacharya, Delhi, 1983 (Reprint).

Tārārahasya of Brahmānanda, ed. by P.C. Pal and others, Calcutta, 1948 VS; ed. by J. Vidyasagara, Calcutta, 1896; ed. by T. Giritirtha, with Bengali tr., Calcutta, 1384 BS.; ed. by P. Sastri, Calcutta, 1313 BS.; with Hindi tr. by H. Shankar, S. Sankar, 1926.

Tārārahasya-vṛttikā, Varendra Research Society, Rajshahi (Bangladesh), 1961.

Tārātantra, ed. by A.K. Maitra, Delhi, 1983. Pub. by Varendra Res. Soc., Rajshahi (Bangladesh); ed. with Hindi Notes.

Tripurā-rahasya, ed. by G. Kaviraj (Jñānakhaṇḍa), with *Tātparya-dīpikā* comm. of Śrīnivāsa, Varanasi, 1965.

Tripurā-rahasya, (Jñānakhaṇḍa), with Hindi comm., by S.D. Maharaj.

Tripurā-rahasya, Eng. tr. and comparative study of the process of individuation by A.U. Vasavada, Varanasi, 1965.

Tripurā-rahasya, (Māhātmya Khaṇḍa), Varanasi, 1932.

Tripurāsāra-samuccaya of Nāgabhaṭṭa, with Skt. Commentary of Govindācārya, Varanasi.

Tripurasundarīdaśaka, Ptd. in Stotrārṇava, p. 654, Madras.

Ucchiṣṭa-gaṇeśa-sahasra-nāma-stava (from *Huramakhalatantra*), Ed. V. Raghavan Madras, 1959. Ptd. in a collection of *Ucchiṣṭa-gaṇapati*

Texts, Venkatesvar Press, Bombay, 1931.

Uḍḍāmara-tantra, Varanasi, 1897.

Uddhārakośa (A dictionary of the Secret Code of Tāntric Syllabic Code), Raghuvir and Shodo Taki, 1978.

Uddīśa Tantra, I. 20 ch., ptd. in *Indrajālādi-saṁgraha*, Calcutta, 1579. *Sulabha-tantra-prakāśa*, Calcutta, 1887; Lucknow 1822, with Hindi tr., Moradabad, 1898; with Hindi comm. of S. Mishra, Varanasi.

Ugratārā-sahasra-nāma, Pub. by Varendra Res. Society, Rajshahi, Bangladesh.

Vāmakeśvara-tantra, Anandasrama, (ed.), Series No. 56, 1908.

Vāmakeśvarī-mata, with *Vivaraṇa* by Jayaratha; ed. by M.K. Shastri, 1945.

Varivasyā-rahasya of Bhāskara, ed. S.C. Sastri, with author's own comm., Eng. trs. and notes, Adyar, Madras, 1948.

Vāsanā-tattva-bodhikā, Same as *Tārā-rahasya-vṛttikā* (q.v.).

Vātulanātha-sūtra, with comm. by Ananta Śaktipada, ed. and tr. into French by L. Silburn, Paris, 1959.

Vidyā-kalpasūtra, Same as *Paraśurāma-kalpasūtra* (q.v.).

Vijñānabhairava, with Beng. tr. and exposition, by R.C. Adhikari, Burdwan, West Bengal, 1980; with Eng. tr. by J. Singh; with comm. by Kṣemarāja up to verse 23 and by Śivopādhyāya onwards, ed. with notes, by M.R. Shastri, 1918. with comm. of Ānanda Bhaṭṭa, ed. with notes, by M.R. Shastri KSS No. IX, 1918; text and comm., tr. with notes into French by L. Silburn, Paris, 1961, with subtitle *Samagra Bhāratīya Yogaśāstra* and with Skt. and Hindi comm., ed. by V.V. Dvivedi, Delhi, 1978.

Vinaśikha-tantra (Śaiva Tantra of left current), ed. by T. Goudriaan, Delhi, 1985, with Intro., Romanised text, Eng. tr., Notes, Index of half-Ślokas (odd *pādas*) and index of Sanskrit words.

Viṣṇu-saṁhitā, Trivandrum, 1925.

Viṣṇutilaka (Telugu), Bangalore, 1896.

Yantra-cintāmaṇi, with Hindi comm., Varanasi.

Yogaratnamālā of Nāgārjuna, P. Kumar.

Yogatantra-granthamālā, ed. by B. Shukla, Varanasi, 1970.

Yoginī-hṛdaya (Being ch. VI-VIII of *Nityāṣoḍaśikārṇava*), with *Dīpikā* of Amṛtānanda and *Setubandha* of Bhāskara Rāya, ed. by G. Kaviraj, Varanasi (1963), ed. by K. Chattopadhyay, 2nd edn., Varanasi, 1963.

Yoginī-tantra, ed., with Hindi tr. by K. Misra, Bomaby, 1983; B.N. Sastri,

1982; ed. by B. Sastri (with intro. in Eng.), ed. by R.M. Chatterji.

Yonitantra, ed. by J.A. Schoterman, New Delhi, 1980.

B. BOOKS IN WESTERN LANGUAGES

Aiyer, K.N., *Thirty-two Vidyās*.

Allan., *Catalogue of Gupta Coins,* LXXXIII.

Allen, M.R., *The Cult of Kumārī*.

Alpar, H.P., *Understanding Mantras*, Delhi.

Anand, M.R., *Kāmakalā*, New York, 1958; *Tāntric Magic* (with A. Mookherjee), New Delhi, 1977.

Angiras, R.S., *Trilogy of Tantra*, Haryana, 1989.

Arguelles & Arguelles, *Maṇḍala*, etc.

Arundale, G.S., *Kuṇḍalinī*.

Avalon, A., (John Woodroffe), *Principles of Tantra*, Madras, 1960 (2 vols.); (Eng. trs. of *Tantra-tattva* of Śiva Candra Vidyāraṇava); Intro. to *Kaulajñānanirṇaya*, Calcutta, 1934; *Śakti* and *Śākta*, Madras; *The Great Liberation*, Madras, 1956; *Mahāmāyā*; *Intro. to Tantra-śāstra*; *The World as Power*, Madras, 1957; *Serpent Power*, Madras, 1957; *Wave of Bliss* (Eng. tr. of *Ānandalaharī* and comm.), Madras, 1957; *Chakras*.

Ayyar, C.V.H., *Origin and Early History of Śaivism in South India*, Madras, 1974.

Bagchi, P.C., *Studies in the Tantras*, Pt. I, Calcutta, 1939, (Reprint 1975).

Bagchi, S., *Eminent Indian Śākta Pīṭhas*, etc., in the background of the *Pīṭhas* of Kalighat, Vakreswar and Kamakhya, Calcutta, 1980.

Bajpai, Ira, *The Philosophy of Tantrāloka* (Āhnikas 1-3 with Eng. tr.), Ph.D. thesis, 1971, Lucknow University.

Bandyopadhyay, P., *The Goddess of Tantra* (2nd edn.).

Banerji, J.N., *Purāṇic and Tāntric Religion, Early Phase*, Calcutta.

———, *Development of Hindu Iconography,* Calcutta, 1956.

Banerji, S.C., *Tantra in Bengal,* New Delhi, 1992, (2nd edn.)

———, *Fundamentals of Ancient Indian Music and Dance*, Ahmedabad, 1976.

———, *A Brief History of Tantra Literature*, Calcutta, 1988.

———, *New Light on Tantra*, Calcutta, 1992.

Barnard, T., *Haṭhayoga*, London, 1950.

Barth, A., *The Religions of India*, London, 1989.

Basu, M., *Tantras, a General Study*, Calcutta, 1976.

———, *Fundamentals of the Philosophy of Tantra*, Calcutta, 1986.

Bedekar, V.M., See Hinze O.M.

Bernard, T., *Haṭhayoga*, London, 1950.

Benard, E.A., *Chinnamastā*, the awful Buddhist and Hindu Tāntric goddess, 1994.

Beyer, G., *The Cult of Tārā*, London, 1973 (Magic and Ritual in Tibet).

Beyer, S., *The Cult of Tantra; Magic and Ritual in Tibet.*

Bhandarkar, *Collected Works*, IV.

Bhandarkar, R.G., *Vaiṣṇavism, Śaivism and Minor Religious Systems*, Strasburg, 1913, Varanasi, 1965.

Bharati, A., *The Tāntric Tradition*, London, 1965.

———, *The Ochre Robe*, London, 1961.

Bhat, M.S., *Vedic Tāntrism, a study of Ṛgvidhāna of Śaunaka* (with Text, tr.) Delhi.

Bhattacharya, B., *Indian Buddhist Iconography, Mainly Based on Sādhanamālā and Cognate Tāntric Texts of Rituals*, 2nd edn., Calcutta, 1958.

———, *Introduction to Buddhist Esoterism*, Oxford, 1932.

———, *World of Tantra.*

———, *Sādhanamālā*, Baroda, 1968.

Bhattacharya, D., *Mythological and Ritual Symbolism: A study with ref. to the Vedic and Tāntric Agni.*

Bhattacharya, D.C., *Tāntric Buddhist Iconographic Sources*, New Delhi, 1974.

Bhattacharya, N.N., *History of Śākta Religion*, New Delhi, 1974.

———, *The Indian Mother Goddess*, 2nd edn., New Delhi, 1977.

———, The *History of Tāntric Religion*, New Delhi, 1987.

———, *History of Indian Cosmogonical Ideas*, New Delhi, 1971.

———, *History of Indian Erotic Literature*, New Delhi, 1975.

———, *Rituals and their Social Contents*, New Delhi, 1975.

———, *A Glossary of Indian Religious Terms and Concepts*, New Delhi, 1990.

Bhattasali, N.K., *Iconography of Buddhist and Brahmaṇical Sculptures in Dacca Museum*, 1972.

Blofeld, J., *The Way of Power — A Practical Guide to Tāntric Mysticism of Tibet*, London, 1970.

———, *Mantras, Sacred Words of Power*, New Delhi, 1981.

Bloomfield, J., *Mantras* (Sacred words of power).

Bose, N.K., *Canons of Orissan Architecture*, pp. 92, 154.

Bose, M.M., *Caitanya Sahajiyā Cults of Bengal*, Calcutta, 1930.

Bose and Halder, *Tantras — Their Philosophy and Occult Secrets*, Calcutta, 1956.

Brahma, N.K., *Philosophy of Hindu Sādhanā*, Calcutta, 1932.

Briggs, G.W., *Gorakhnāth and the Kānphaṭa Yogīs*, Calcutta, 1938.

Capra, F., *The Tao of Physics*, 1979.

Caristedt, G., *Studies in Kulārṇava-tantra*, Upsala, 1974.

Chakrabarti, C., *The Tantras, Studies on their Religion and Literature*, Calcutta, 1946.

Chakrabarti, P.C., *Doctrine of Śakti in Indian Literature*, Calcutta, 1940.

Chakraborti, H. (ed.), *Pāśupata-sūtra*, Calcutta, 1970.

Chakravarti, C., *Tantras*, etc., Calcutta, 1963.

Chandra, L., *Maṇḍalas of the Tantrasamuccaya*.

Chatterji, J.C., *Kashmir Śaivism*, KSS. II, 1944. Delhi, 1959.

Chatterji, K.K., *The History of Dakṣiṇeśvara Kālī Temple*.

Chattopadhyay, A., *Atīśa and Tibet*, Calcutta, 1967.

Chattopadhyay, S., *Reflections on the Tantras*.

Chaudhuri, L.R., *Practicals of Mantras and Tantras*.

Chen, C.M., *Discrimination between Buddhist and Hindu Tantras*.

Chimmoy, *Kuṇḍalīnī, the Mother Power*, 1974.

Coburn, T.B., *Devī-māhātmya*, Crystallisation of the Goddess Tradition, 1984.

Colaabovala, F.D., *Tantra, the Erotic Cult*.

Cunningham, *Archaeological Survey Report*, IX.

Dacca University, *History of Bengal*, I (P.C. Bagchi — Religion of Bengal).

Dasgupta, S.N., *A History of Indian Philosophy*, Vol. III.

———, *A History of Indian Philosophy*, III, Indian edn. New Delhi, 1988.

Dasgupta, S.B., *Introduction to Tāntric Buddhism*, Calcutta, 1958.

———, *Aspects of Indian Religious Thought*, Calcutta, 1957.

———, *Obscure Religious Cults*, Calcutta, 1946.

Desai, D., *Erotic Sculptures of India*, New Delhi, 1975.

De, S.K., *Bengali Literature in the Nineteenth Century*, Calcutta, 1962.

Devasenapati, V.A., *Śaiva Siddhānta*, Madras, 1958.

Diksitar, V.R.R., *The Lalitā Cult*, Madras, 1942.

Douglas, N., *Tantrayoga*, New Delhi, 1971.

Dutta, M.N. (tr.), *Mahānirvāṇa Tantra*.

Dvivedi, V.V., *Tantra-yātrī* (Essays on Tantra), Varanasi, 1982.

Dvivedi and Shashni, *Bauddha Tantra-kośa*, Pt. I; Varanasi, 1990.

Dyczkowski, M.S.G. : *The Doctrine of Vibration*, State University of New York Press.

———, *The Canon of the Śaivāgama and the Kubjikā Tantras of the Western Kaula Tradition*.

Desika, N.R., *Śrīvidyā-upāsanā* (*Lalitāsahasra-nāma stotra*), Bangalore, 1992.

Ehrenfels, O.R., *Mother-right in India*, Hyderabad, 1941.

Eliade, M., *Yoga-Immortality and Freedom*, 2nd edn., New York, 1958.

Eliot, *Hinduism and Buddhism*, 3 vols, Vol. II, London, 1957.

Encyclopaedia Britannica, Vols. dealing with Tantra and its different aspects.

Evans Wentz, W.Y., *Tibetan Yoga and Secret Doctrines*, London, 1958.

Farquhar, J.N., *Outline of the Religious Literature of India*, London, 1920, 1968.

Farrow, G.W., and Menon, I., *The Concealed Essence of the Hevajra Tantra*, Delhi.

Filliozat, J., *Classical Doctrine of Indian Medicine*, Delhi, 1964.

Foucher, A., *Etude sur l' Iconographie Bouddhiquede L'Inde*, 2 Pts.

Frazer J.G., *Adonis Attis Osiris*, London, 1907.

Freud, S., *Kuṇḍalinī, energie, etc*.

Garrison, O.V., *Tantra, the Yoga of sex*, New York, 1964.

Gavin and Frost, *Tāntric Yoga*, the royal path to raising Kuṇḍalinī Power, Delhi, 1994.

Geden, A.S., *Tantras* (Entry in *Ency. of Rel. and Ethics*, T. Hastings, Vol. XII, 1951).

Getty, A., *Gods of Northern Buddhism*, New York, 1964.

Ghosh, Aurobindo, *The Life Divine*, 1939.

———, *The Mother.*

Goel, B.S., *Third Eye and Kuṇḍalinī*, Kuruksetra, 1985.

Gopi Krishna, *Kuṇḍalinī.*

Goudriaan, T., *The Sanskrit Tradition and Tāntrism*, Leiden, 1990.

———, (ed.), *Ritual and Speculation in Early Tāntrism*, 1993.

Goudriaan, T. and Gupta, S., *Hindu Tāntric and Śākta Literature*, Pub. in the Series *History of Indian Literature*, Wiesbaden, 1981.

———, Vol. II, Fasce. 2, Hoshiarpur, Punjab (India).

Guenther, H.V. and C. Trungpa, *Dawn of Tantra*, ed. by M. Kohn, 1975.

———, *Yuganaddha, the Tāntric View of Life,* Benares, 1964.

———, *The Tāntric View of Life*, Berkeley and London, 1972.

Gupta, Goudriaan and Moens, *Hindu Tāntrism*, Leiden, 1979.

Hastings, *Encyclopaedia of Religion and Ethics.*

Hazra, R.C., *Studies in Purāṇic Records*, etc., Dacca, 1940.

Hinze, O.M., *Tantra-vidyā* (tr. by V.M. Bedekar).

Hopkins, J., *The Tāntric Distinction*, an intro. to Tibetan Buddhism, ed. by A.C. Klain, London, 1984.

Jacobs, H., *Western Psychotherapy and Hindu Sādhanā*, London, 1961.

James, E.O., *The Cult of the Mother-Goddess*, London, 1959 (pp. 99-124 deal with India).

Jash, P., *History of Śaivism*, Calcutta, 1974.

———, *Pratyabhijñā System — Its Religious and Philosophic Background*, 1960.

———, *Pratyabhijña System* — Some Controversial View-points, 1959, 1960.

Jha, S.K., *A Critical and Comparative Study of Pratyabhijñā Philosophy* (Ph.D. Thesis, 1972, Darbhanga).

Joshi, L.M., *Lalitā-Sahasranāma — A Comprhensive Study of One Thousand Names of Lalitā Mahā-Tripurasundarī.* With original text in Sanskrit, Roman Transliteration and Critical Explanation of each name, 1998.

Jung, C.G., *Maṇḍala Symbolism, to Śrī Bhairava-Padmāvatī-kalpa.* Tr. by R.F.C. Hull, Princeton, 1972.

Kakati, B.K., *The Mother-Goddess Kāmākhyā*, 1914.

Kane, P.V., *History of Dharmaśāstra.*

Kapur, T.B., *Dhyānamaṇḍala.*

Kaviraj, G.N., *Śākta Philosophy.*

———, *History of Philosophy, Eastern and Western*, ed. by Radhakrishnan, London, 1952-53.

———, *Philosophy of Tripurā-tantra*, Varanasi, 1931.

———, *Some Aspects of the Philosophy of Śākta Tantra*, Varanasi, 1967.

Kavory, M.B., *Comparative and Critical Study of Mantraśāstra*, 1944.

Kaw, R.K., *The Doctrine of Recognition*, Hoshiarpur, 1967.

Khanna, M., *Yantra*, London, 1979.

Kramrisch, S., *Unknown in India.*

———, *Ritual art in Tribe and Village*, Philadelphia, 1968.

Krishna, G., *Kuṇḍalinī, in Time and Space*, New Delhi.

———, *Secrets of Kuṇḍalinī in Pañcastavī.*

———, *Kuṇḍalinī, the Biological Basis of Religion and Genus.*

Kumar, P., *Tāntric Goddess Tārā*

———, *Shakti Cult in Ancient India.*

———, *Śāktism — a Study.*

———, *Śakti and Her Episodes*, 1981.

Kundu, N.L., *Non-dualism in Śaiva and Śākta Philosophy*, Calcutta.

Lal, K., *The Cult of Desire*, Delhi, 1966 (2nd edn.).

Lal, P., *Hindu Religion and Iconology.*

Lansdowne, Z.F., *The Chakras and Esoteric Healing*, Maine, 1988.

Leedbeater, C.W., *Cakras*, Adyar, 1927.

Lele, W.K., *Doctrine of the Tantrayukti.*

Lennoy, R., *The Eye of Love*, London, 1977.

Lessing and Wayman, *Introduction to Buddhist Tāntric Systems,* Delhi, 1983.

Lhalungpa, L.P. (tr.), *The Life of Milarepa*, Boudder, Colorado, 1982.

Lorenzen, D.N., *The Kāpālikas and Kālāmukhas*, New Delhi, 1991.

Mahadevan, T.M.P., *Kashmir Śaivism*, 1952.

Mahajan, S.N., *The Science of Yoga and Consciousness.*

Majithia, S.S., *The Great Yogic Sermon*, 1969.

Malik, A.D., *Kuṇḍalinī and Meditation*, Delhi, 1991.

Marr, G.S., *Sex in Religion*, London, 1936.

Mehta, R.J., *Konārk Sun-Temple of Love*, Bombay, 1969.

Mehta, Rohit, *The Secret of Self-transformation: A Synthesis of Tantra and Yoga*, Delhi, 1987.

Mishra, K., *Significance of Tāntric Tradition*, Varanasi, 1981.

*Mookherji, A., *Tantra Art*, Delhi, 1966.

———, *Tantra Āsana*, Basel, New York, 1971.

———, *The Tāntric Way* (with M. Khamara).

———, *Kuṇḍalinī*, Delhi, 1982.

———, *Kālī, the Feminine Force*, London, 1988.

Mookherji, Khanna, *Tāntric Way — Art, Science, Ritual*, London, 1989.

Muller Ortega, P.E., *The Triardic Heart of Śiva, Kaula Tāntricism of Abhinavagupta in the non-dual Śaivism of Kashmir*, Albany, 1989.

Mullin, G.H. and Richards, M. (eds.), *Meditations on Lower Tantras*, Dharamsala, 1983.

Mullin, G.H. (comp. and tr.), *Bridging the Sūtras and Tantras*, a collection of Ten Minor Works by the First Dalai Lama (1319-1474), Dharamsala, 1981.

Muses, C.A., *Esoteric Teachings of the Tibetan Tantra*, tr. by C.C. Chi, York Beach, 1982.

Nagaswamy, R., *Tāntric Cult of South India*, Delhi, 1980.

Nandimath, S.C., *Hand-Book of Vīra Śaivism*, Dharwar, 1942.

Nath, R.G., *The Yogīs of Bengal*, Calcutta, 1909.

Nawels, S.M., *Jaina Paintings*, Vol. I, Ahmedabad, 1980.

Needham, J., *Science and Civilisation in China*, 2 vols. Cambridge, 1954-56.

Neumann, E., *The Great Mother*, New York, 1961.

Padoux, A., *Vāc, the concept of the word in selected Hindu Tantras* (tr. from French original by J. Gontier), Albany.

Pandey, K.C., *An Outline of History of Śaiva Philosophy*.

Pandit, M.P., *More on Tantras*, New Delhi, 1985.

———, *Kuṇḍalini-yoga*, Madras,

———, *Gems from the Tantra*, Pts. I, II, Madras, 1967.

———, *Thoughts of a Shākta*.

———, *Lights on the Tantra*, Madras, 1968.

———, *Tāntric Sādhanā*, 1964.

———, *Studies in the Tantras and the Veda*, Madras, 1967.

———, *Aurobindo on the Tantra*, Madras.

---

* Mishra, T.N., *Impact of Tantra on Religion and Art*, 1997.

Pandit, B.N., *Aspects of Kashmir Śaivism*, Srinagar, Kashmir, 1947.

———, *Comparative Study of Kashmir Śaivism* (Thesis for Ph.D. 1964, Panjab University).

Paranjyoti, V., *Śaiva Siddhānta*, London, 1954.

Pathak, V.S., *Śaiva Cult in Northern India*, Varanasi, 1960.

Pott, P., *Yoga and Tantra*, Leiden, 1961.

Prabhavananda, Swami, *The Spiritual Heritage of India*, London, 1962.

Prajñananda, Swami, *Historical Study of Indian Music*, Calcutta, 1975.

Pyne, E., *The Śāktas — an Introduction and Comparative Study*, Calcutta, 1938.

Radha, Swami, S., *Kuṇḍalinī Yoga*, Delhi.

———, *Mantras, Words of Power*, Delhi.

Radhakrishnan, S., *History of Indian Philosophy — Eastern and Western*, I (exposition of Śākta belief by G. Kaviraj), London, 1952.

Rajneesh, *The Book of Secret Discourses on Vishāna Bhairava-Tantra*, 5 Vols., Poona, 1974, ed. by A. Prem, A. Teerth.

Rao, T.A.G., *Elements of Hindu Iconography*, I, pt. II, Madras, 1914 (For Kālī image).

Rao, S.K.R., *Tantra, Mantra, Yantra.*

———, *Tāntric Tradition*

———, *Elements of Hindu Iconography,* Madras, 1916.

———, *Yantras, Text and Plates*, 1988.

———, *Śrī Chakras*, Text and Plates, 1989.

———, *Meditation on Lalitā-sahasra-nāma*, Bangalore, 1990.

———, *The Tāntric Practices in Śrīvidyā* (with *Śrī Sāradā-catuśtī*), Bangalore, 1990.

Rastogi, N., *Tāntric Thought of Kashmir, a Framework of the Monistic Culture.*

———, *Krama Tāntricism of Kashmir*, Vol. I, Delhi, 1979, Vol. II, shortly.

———, *Introduction to the Tantrāloka*, Delhi, 1987.

———, *Kālī as a Metaphysical Concept in the Krama System of Kashmir*, 1986.

Rawson, P., *Tantra*, London, 1973.

———, *Erotic Art of the East*, New York, 1968.

Ray, N.R., *Sanskrit Buddhism in Burma.*

Ray, P., *History of Chemistry in Ancient and Medieval India*, Calcutta, 1956.

Rele, V.G., *Mysterious Kuṇḍalinī*, Bombay, 1927.

Rend C.I.P., *Introduction to the Cakras*, 1974.

Rendel, P., *Introduction to the Cakras*, Northamptonshire, 1974.

Rolland, R., *Ramkrishna*.

Rudrappa, J.C., *Kashmir Śaivism*, Bangalore.

Samuel, G. *et al*, *Tantra and Popular Religion in Tibet*, New Delhi, 1994.

Sankaranarayanan, S., *Śrīcakra*, 1970.

———, *Glory of the Divine Mother*, Delhi.

Saran, P., *Tantra, Hedonism in Indian Culture*, New Delhi, 1994.

Sarasvati, Swami, S., *Meditation from the Tantras*.

———, *Āsana, Prāṇāyāma, Mudrābandha*, Monghyr, (Bihar), 1983.

———, *Kuṇḍalinī Tantra*, Munger (Bihar), 1984.

———, *Light on Guru-Disciple Relationship*, 1984.

———, *Yogic Management of Asthma and Diabetes*, Munger (Bihar), 1984.

Sarasvati, P. and Woodroffe, *Sādhanā for Self-realisation* (*Mantras, Yantras* and *Tantras*), Madras, 1963.

Sarasvati, S.K., *Tantrayāna Art Album*, Calcutta, 1979.

Sastri, H., *Origin and Cult of Tārā*, Calcutta, 1925.

Sastri, H.C., *Tantra Darshan*.

Sastri, K., *The Veda and the Tantra*, Madras, 1951.

Sastri, K.T.V., *Further Lights: The Veda and the Tantra*, 1951.

Sastri, M.R., *Tantrasāra of Abhinavagupta*, Bombay, 1918.

Saunders, E.D., *Mudrā*, London, 1966.

Scharpes, E., *Tāntrik Doctrine of Immaculate Conception*, 1933.

Schrader, F.O., *Introduction to the Nārada Pañcarātra and the Ahirbudhnya-saṁhitā*, Madras, 1916.

Sengupta, A., *Parampuruṣ Rāmkṛṣṇa*, Calcutta, 1358 BS.

Sen Sharma, D.B., *Studies in Tantrayoga*, 1985.

Shah, P.R., *Tantra: Its Therapeutic Aspect*, Calcutta, 1987.

Sharma, L.N., *Kashmir Śaivism*, Varanasi, 1972.

Sharma, P.K., *Śakti and Her Episodes*, etc., Delhi, 1981.

Sharma, S.R., *Tāntric Mahāvijñāna*, Bareilly, 1970.

Shastri, V.D., *Mālinīvijayottara-tantra—a source-book*, etc. (Ph.D. Thesis,

1956, Punjab University).

Shende, J.N., *Religion and Philosophy of the Atharvaveda*, Poona, 1952.

Shivananda, *Tantra-yoga, Nāda-yoga and Scientific basis*.

Shubhakaran, K.T., *Mystical Formulae*, Pt. II, *Yantras*, New Delhi, 1992.

Siddhantasastri, R.K., *Śaivism Through the Ages*, Delhi, 1975.

Silburn, L., *Kuṇḍalinī, the Power of the Depths*.

Singh, L.P., *Tantra: Its Mystic and Scientific Basis*, Delhi, 1976.

Sinha, A.K., *Science and Tantrayoga*, Kuruksetra, 1981.

Sinha, J., *Śākta Monism; Cult of Śakti; Schools of Śaivism*, Calcutta, 1970.

Sircar, D.C., *The Śākta Pīṭhas*, Calcutta, 1960.

———, *Shakti Cult and Tārā*, Calcutta, 1960.

Sivapriyananda, Svami., *Secret Power of Tāntric Breathing*, 1983.

Snellgrove, D.L., *A Critical Study of the Hevajra Tantra*, London, 2 vols., 1980, Vol. I, Bibliography, Diagrams, Glossary, Index (Intro. & Eng. tr.). Vol. II. Romanised text.

Srivastav, B., *Iconography of Śakti*.

———, *Tantra, the Supreme Understanding* (Discourses of *Tilopā's Song of Mahāmudrā*).

———, *Tāntric Mysticism of Tibet*, New York, 1974.

———, *Tāntrism, its Secret Principles and Practice*, Northamptonshire, 1982.

Svami, S.N., *Tāntrik Abhidhān*, Calcutta, 1910 BS.

Tagore, R.N., *The Religion of Man*, 1930.

Taimini, T.K., *Śiva-sūtra* with Eng. tr. and comm. (Ultimate Reality and Realisation).

Taranatha, *History of Buddhism in India*, tr. into German by A. Schiefner, St. Petersburg.

Tattvananda (Swami), *The Vaiṣṇava Sects*, 1989.

———, *The Śaiva Sects, Mother-worship*.

———, *The Tantra Vision* (*Discourse on the Royal Song of Saraha*).

Thomas, P., *Kāmakalpa*, 1963.

———, *Kāmakalā*, Bombay, 1960.

———, *Incredible India*, Bombay, 1966.

Thomas, E.J., *History of Buddhist Thought*, Reprint, 1953.

Thompson and Spencer: *Bengali Religious Lyrics — Sākta* (Heritage of India Series).

Trungpa, C., *Journey without Goal, Tāntric Wisdom of the Buddha,* Boston, 1985.

Tsong Ka-pa, *Tantra in Tibet — The Great Exposition of Secret Mantra*, tr. into Eng. under the title *Tantra in Tibet*, by J. Hopkins, London, 1977.

Tucci, G., *Theory and Practice of Maṇḍala*, London, 1961.

———, *Ratilīlā*, an interpretation of the Tāntric images of the temples of Nepal, Geneva, 1969.

Tulkes, D. and Mullin, G.H., *Atīśa and Buddhism in Tibet.*

Turstig, Hans-Georg, *Yantracintāmaṇi of Dāmodara on magic (related to Tāntrism)*, Stuttgart, 1988.

Upadhyay, R.K., *Concept of God in the Śaiva Tantra.*

Vajapeya, K., *Science of Mantras.*

Vandyopadhyay, J.N., *Pañcopāsanā*, Calcutta, 1960.

Vasavada, A.U., *Tripurā-rahasya* (*Jñānakhaṇḍa* — Eng. tr., and a comparative study of the process of individuation).

Vasu, S.C., *Gheraṇḍa-saṁhitā* (tr.), 1979.

Vatsyayana, K., (Gen. ed), *Prakṛti*, Vol. 3 (The Āgamic tradition and the Arts), New Delhi, 1995.

Vira, R.V., Taki, S., *A Dictionary of Secret Tāntric Syllabic Code,* Lahore, 1938.

Visnutirtha, Swami, *Devātma Śakti*, 1949.

Waddel, L.A., *Lamaism*, London, 1985.

Walker, B., *Tāntricism: its Secret Principles and Practices.*

Wall, O.A., *Sex and Sex-worship*, London, 1919.

Warrier, A.G.K. (tr.), *Śākta Upaniṣads*, Adyar, 1967.

Wayman, A., *Yoga of Guhyasamāja-tantra*, ed. by K.V. Sarma, Hoshiarpur, 1979; Text in Roman script with Eng. tr. *Buddhist Tantras* (Light on Indo-Tibetan esotericism, New York, 1973).

White, J., (ed.), *Kuṇḍalinī, Evolution and Enlightenment*, New York, 1979.

Wilson, H.H., *Works*, II.

Winternitz, M., *History of Indian Literature*, Vols. I, II, Calcutta, 1927, 1933.

Woodroffe, J., See Avalon, *The World as Power.*

Woodroffe and Mukhopadhyay, *Mahāmāyā*, Madras, 1954.

Yeshe, Lama T., *Introduction to Tantra.*

Zannas, E. and Auboyer, J., *Khajuraho*. The Hague, 1960.

Zimmer, H., *Myths and Symbols in Indian Art and Civilization*, ed. by J. Campbell.

C. HINDI WORKS

Avasthi, S.S., *Mantra aur Mātṛkāon Kā Rahasya*.

Dvivedi, H.P., *Nātha Sampradāya*, 1966.

Kamalesh, S., *Śaktibhāṣya Kā Adhyayan*.

Kaviraj, G.N., *Tantrik Vāṅgmay men Śāstra-dṛṣṭi*, Patna, 1963.

———, *Tantra aur Āgam Śāstron Kā Digdarśan*, tr. by H.K. Tiwari, Varanasi.

———, *Tāntrik Sādhanā aur Siddhānta*, tr. by H.K. Tiwari, Varanasi.

———, *Tāntrik Sāhitya*, Varanasi.

———, *Bhāratīya Saṁskṛti aur Sādhanā*, Varanasi.

Sastri, G., *Tantradarśan*.

Sastri, D., *Tantrasiddhānta aur Sādhanā*.

Vasavada, A., (Hindi rendering by B.S. Upadhyay) *Tripurārahasya Kā Tantra-viśleṣaṇa*, Varanasi.

D. BENGALI WORKS

Bandyopadhyay, J.N., *Pañcopasanā*, Calcutta, 1960.

Bandyopadhyay, S.C., *Śaktiraṅga-vaṅgabhūmi*, Calcutta, 1991.

Basu, Manoranjan, *Rāmakṛṣṇa-sādhanā-parikramā*, Calcutta, 1978.

Basu, S.P., *Niveditā Lokamātā*, Vol. I, Calcutta, 1971.

Bhattacharya, Mahendranath, *Bhāratiya Dharmer Itihās*, Calcutta, 1977.

Bhattacharya, H., *Hinduder Devdevī*, Calcutta, I, 2nd edn., 1982; II, 1978; III. 1980.

Bhattacharya, S., *Tantra-paricaya*, Santiniketan, 1359 BS.

Bhattacharya, A., *Bāṁglā Maṅgal Kāvyer Itihās*, Calcutta, 1964.

Bhaumik, H., *Kālīkṣetra-dīpikā*, Calcutta.

Brahmachari, T.P., *Tāntrik Sādhanā O Tantrakāhinī*, Calcutta, 1381 BS.

Chakraborti, C., *Tantrakathā*, Calcutta, 1362 BS.

Chakraborti, J.K., *Śākta Padāvalī O Śakti-sādhanā*, Calcutta, 1382 BS (5th edn.).

———, *Prācīn Bhāratīya Sāhitya O Bāṅgālīr Uttarādhikār*, 1382 BS (2nd edn.).

Chakravarti, N., *Ūnaviṁśa Śātābdīr Kavioyālā O Bāṁlā Sāhitya*, Calcutta, 1884.

Chakravarti, D., (ed.), *Ādyāpīṭher Ṭhākur Śrī Annadār Kathā O Gān*.

Chakravarti, S., *Mehārer Sarvānanda*, Calcutta.

Chatterjee, J.N., *Vāmākhyāpā*.

Chatterjee, R.M., *Vividha-tantra-saṁgraha*, Calcutta, 1981-86.

Chattopadhyay, P., *Tantrābhilāṣīr Sādhusaṅga*, Calcutta, 1983.

Das, U.K., *Śāstramūlak Bhāratiya-śakti-sādhanā*, 2 vols., Birbhum, 1373 BS.

Das Gupta, Nalini, *Bāṁlāy Bauddha-Dharma*.

Dasgupta, S.B., *Bhārater Śakti-sādhanā O Śākta Sāhitya*, Calcutta, 1365 BS.

Gangopadhyay, B., *Mahāpīṭh Tārāpīṭh*, Calcutta.

Ghosh, B., *Paścim Baṅger Saṁskṛti*, Calcutta, 1957.

Ghosh, N., *Daśa Mahāvidyā*, Calcutta.

Ghosh, Satyadev, *Sādhanā Samar*.

Gupta, M. (Śrīma), *Śrī Śrī Rāmkṛṣṇa-kathāmṛta*, 5 vols., Calcutta, 1904-32.

Kaviraj, G.N., *Tāntrik Sādhanā O Siddhānta*, I, 2nd edn., Burdwan, 1983; II. 2nd edn., 1983.

———, *Tantra O Āgama-śāstrer Digdarśan*, Calcutta, 1963.

Lahidi, D., (ed.), *Bāṅgālīr Gān*, Calcutta, 1312 BS.

Majumdar, R.C., *Bāṁlā Deśer Itihās, Madhya-yuga* (Chs., 12, 13), Calcutta, 1373 BS.

Malik, K., *Nāth Samprodāyer Itihās*, etc., Calcutta, 1950.

Mitra, S., *Aviśvāsya Satya*, Calcutta.

———, *Daśamātṛkā*, Calcutta.

Mukherji, A.C., *Ardhakālī*.

Mukhopadhyay, B.N., *Śakti rūp Bhārate O Madhya Eśiyāy*, Calcutta, 1990.

Mukhopadhyay, Sitanath, *Prācīn Kavīoyālār Gān*, Calcutta

Nandi, Sunil, *Kāli-rahasya*, Calcutta.

Nigudhananda, *Khunje Phiri Kuṇḍalinī*, Calcutta.

———, *Mahātīrtha Ekānna Pīṭher Sandhāne*, Calcutta.

———, *Ekānna Pīṭher Sādhak*, Calcutta.

——, *Śaktikṣetra Cavviś Upapīṭher Sandhāne*, Calcutta.

Nivedita (Sister), *Svāmījīke Ye rūp Dekhiyāchi* (trs. by Svami Madhavananda), Calcutta, 1983.

Omkarnath, Sītaramdas, *Mātṛgāthā*, 1372 BS.

Prajnananda (Svāmī), *Bhāratīya Saṁgīt Itihās*, I, Calcutta, 1961 (2nd edn.), II (1st half), Calcutta 1978 (3rd edn.); II (2nd half), Calcutta, 1879 (3rd edn.).

Raghuvir and Shodotaki, *Uddhārakośa of Dakṣiṇāmūrti*, 1978.

Ramprasāder Granthāvolī — Vasumati ed., Calcutta.

Ray, A., *Śāktapadavālī*, Calcutta.

Ray, Diptimay, *Paścim Baṅger Kālī O Kālīkṣetra*, Calcutta.

——, *Tantra-tattva, praveśīkā*, Calcutta, 1398 BS.

——, *Tantra-tattva O Sādhāna*, Calcutta.

Sanyal, N., *Bhāratīya Bhāskarye Mithun*, Calcutta.

Saradananda (Svāmī), *Gītātattva O Bhārate Śaktipūjā*, Calcutta, 1983.

Sarasvati, S., *Pāl Yuger Citrakalā*, Calcutta, 1378 BS.

Sarasvati, Padmanath, *Prabandhāṣṭaka*.

Sarkar, M., *Tantrer Ālo*, Calcutta, 1354 BS.

Sastri, H.P., *Bauddha Gān O Dohā*, Calcutta, 1916.

Sastri, S., *Tantraparicay*, Santiniketan, 1359 BS.

——, *Saṁskṛtānuśīlane Rabīndranāth*, Calcutta, 1984.

Sen, K.M., *Bāṁglār Sādhanā*, Calcutta, 1352 BS.

Sen, Sukumar, *Baṅgabhūmikā*, Calcutta, 1974.

——, *Bāṁglār Bāūl*.

Siddhantabhusana S.C., *Kaula-mārga-rahasya*, Calcutta, 1335 BS.

Svami, S.N., *Tāntrik Abhidhān*, Caclutta, 1910.

Vidyabhusan, A.C., *Sarasvatī*, I, 1340 BS.

Vidyarnava, S.C., *Tantratattva*, I, 1317 BS.

Bengali Journals and Papers

Ānandabājār Patrikā (Calcutta daily) — 13.9.81

Ārati, Vaiśākh, 1314 BS.

Bābā Tāraknāth (Monthly journal), from Tarakesvar Math, Hughly, West Bengal, V. II, 1392 BS; K.K. Sen Gupta's paper — 'Śaktivād O Durgāpūjā'.

Desh, (Calcutta Weekly), dated 27.2.82 (p. 9), 24.4.82 (p. 3), 8.5.82 (p. 3), 15.3.82 (p. 3), 10.7.82 (p. 6), 17.10.87, p.15, B.N. Mukherji's paper on 'Kālidevīr Mūrti-tattva'.

Devayāna (monthly journal), Vol. VII, No. 41 (article by Dinesh Bhattacharya)

Baṅgīya Sāhitya Pariṣat Patrikā, Calcutta, Vols. 58, 59 (Article by C. Chakravarti), Vol. 62, No. 3 (articles by R. Tarkatirtha); Vol. 45 (pp. 222-31); Vol. 46 (p. 80).

Viśvabhāratī Patrikā, Māgha-Caitra, 1362 BS. (article by S.B. Dasgupta).

E. MISCELLANEOUS WORKS

Volume of Studies Presented to F. Thomas (article by B. Bhattacharya).

Āchārya Rāy Commemoration Volume (V. Bhattacharya's article captioned 'Sanskrit Treatises on alchemy as translated into Tibetan'; K.C. Viraraghava's article, entitled 'The Study of Alchemy').

Memoirs of Archaeological Survey of India, No. 66 *Encyclopaedia of Indo-Aryan Research*, Vol. III, 6 (R.G. Bhandarkar's article on The Pañcarātra or *Bhāgavata* system), 1913.

Aruṇa Bhāratī — A.N. Jani Fel. Vol.

(i) Paper on *Pañcarātra* by K.D. Bharadwaj.

(ii) Dhal's paper — *Virajākṣetra — a Śākta Pīṭha.*

(iii) Joshi's paper — *Śākta Tāntrism in Gupta Age.*

(iv) Desai's paper — *Mother-Goddess and Her Partner.*

Vatsyayana, K. (Gen. ed.), *Prakṛti*, vol. 3, The Āgamic Tradition and the Arts, New Delhi, 1995.

Cultural Heritage of India, R.K. Mission, Calcutta; vol. III, pt. 3 (*Philosophy of Tantras*, 1953, vol. IV, pt. 1 (*Evolution of Tantras, etc.*), 1956.

F. JOURNALS, PROCEEDINGS REPORTS, ETC.

English

Journals

Ancient Tantra, dealing exclusively with Tāntric matters, is published from Ancient Tantra, Jalandhar.

Kuṇḍalinī, on *Tantra-yoga*, Kuṇḍalinī Research and Publication Trust, New Delhi.

ABORI, XV, IX, XVI (articles by R.C. Hazra).

ABORI, X, 1930 (Article by B. Bhattacharya).

ABORI Dimond Jubilee Vol., 1978 (article by S.A. Dange).

ABORI, XIX, 1938. A.K. Coomaraswamy, The Tāntric Doctrine.)

Adyar Library Bulletin, XXI (article by C. Chakravorty).

Annual Reports of Faculty of Arts and Letters, Tohuk University, 1958. (H. Hadamo, Human existence in Tāntric Buddhism).

Archaeological Survey of India.

Report, IX (Temple of 64 *Yoginīs* in Bherāghāṭ)

Bhāratkaumudī, II, Allahabad, 1947 (U.P. Shah, A. Peep into the Early History of Tantra in Jaina Literature).

Cunningham, *Archaeological Survey Report*, IX.

Bulletin of R.K. Mission, Calcutta, D. Sen's paper on Advaitism in Tantra.

Bulletin of School of Oriental and African Studies, London, LIV, Pt. 2, 1991 (G. Bühnemann, Selecting and Perfecting *Mantras* in Hindu Tāntrism).

Eranos Jahrbuch, I, Zurich, 1933. (H. Zimmer, *Zue Bedentong des Indischen Tantra Yoga*).

Glory of India, Motilal Banarsidass, Delhi, Vol. VI, 1-4. (Article—Laksesvara Rath, a lesser known Tāntric by P. Mishra).

Harvard Journal of Asiatic Studies, VII, 1945, (Chou-yi-liang, Tāntrism in China).

IHQ, V, VI (P.C. Bagchi, On some Tāntric texts studied in Ancient Kambuja).

VII, 1931 (D.R. Sastri, The Lokāyatas and Kāpālikas).

IX, 1933 (R.C. Hazra, Influence of Tantra on *Tattvas* of Raghunandana).

XII, 1936 (S. Levi, On a Tāntric fragment from Kucha).

VI, X, XXVII (articles by C. Chakraborty).

Sept. 1951 (*Śākta* festivals of Bengal).

XXXI, 1935 (*Matsyendranātha* and his *Yoginī* Cult by Karambelkar).

XXXII, 1956 (article by B. Bhattacharya).

Indian Antiquary, IV, 101 ff. (Eng. tr. of portions of Tāranātha's *History of Buddhism*).

Indian Culture, II, 1934 (Przylusky, J., *Mudrā*).

Indian Culture, VIII (article by S.B. Dasgupta).

JAOS, VI, 23, 1902 (A.H. Ewing, The *Śāradātilaka Tantra*).

JASB, Letters, XVII (article by B. Banerji).

JASB, New Series, XXIX (article by C. Chakravarti).

JASB, New Series, XVIII.

Jha Comm. Vol. (articles by C. Chakravarti).

JOR, Madras, XIX, Pt. 4, 1950 (Tāntric Cult in Epigraphs by B.P. Desai).

Journal of Asiatic Soc. of Bangladesh, XVIII, No. 1 (Pāül Poets on Chāri Chandra by H.C. Pal).

JRAS, 1984 (L.A. Waddell, The Indian Buddhist Cult of Avalokita and His Consort Tārā).

JRAS, 1910 (On Tantras in Malabar).

JRAS, 1911 (A.G. Svamin's paper — The *Pañcarātras* or *Bhagavat-Śāstra*

Journal of Music Academy, Madras, XI, 1-4, 1940.

K.B., Pathak Comm. Vol. (article by C. Chakravarti).

Lalitakalā 1-2, 1955 (P. Chandra, *The Kaula-Kapotika* Cult at Khajuraho).

Marg, Bombay, March, 1965 (Plastic Situation by M. Anand; Sculptures of Nagarjuna Konda, A. Roy).

June, 1963. (The Lesser Vehicle, etc., by M. Anand).

MASI, No. 20 (H. Sastri, Origin and Cult of Tārā).

Melanges Chinois et Bouddhiques III, Brussels, 1934-35. (Tucci, G., Some Glosses upon the *Guhyasamāja*).

New Indian Antiquary, I, 1938, (S.K. De, The Buddhist Tāntric Sanskrit Literature of Bengal).

Ostasiatesche Zeolgchrift, XII, N.S. Berlin, 1936, (H.V. Glasenapp, Tantrismus and Saktismus).

Poona Orientalist, XXI, pp. 47-49 on *Śaktisaṁgama-tantra*.

Proc. of Indian Hist. Cong. VIII (Panigrahi, K.C., Obscene Sculptures of Orissan Temples).

Quest, XXV, 1962 (A. Bharati, Metaphysics of Tāntrism).

Rupam, 1920 (*Mithuna in Indian Art* by O.C. Gangoli) *Summaries of Papers*, 5th World Skt. Conf., 1981. (Tāntrism, *Śakti* Cult, Śākambharī Classification of Śaiva Tantras).

Studies in Honour of Andre Padover, Albany, New York. (G. Bühnemann — On Puraścaraṇa: *Kulārṇava Tantra*, ch. 15, in Goudriaan's edn.).

Tāntric and Taoist Studies in Honour of R. Stein, Vol. I, ed. by M. Strickmann, 1981. (A Padoux — Un Japa tantrique, *Yoginīhṛdaya* 3, 172-90).

ZDMG, Supplement, III, 2 (1977), paper by J.A. Schoterman.

BENGALI

CATALOGUES OF MANUSCRIPTS

Bodleian Catalogue, I, — T. Aufrecht.

Catalogue of Palm-leaf and Selected

Paper Mss. in Durbar Library, Nepal, — H.P. Sastri, Calcutta, 1905.

Catalogue of Skt. MSS in Asiatic Society, Calcutta, vol. VIII.

Des. Cat. of Skt. MSS. in Govt. Oriental Mss. Library, Madras — M. Rangacharya, Vols. XII, XIII.

India Office Catalogue, IV — Eggeling.

New Catalogorus Catalogorum, Madras

PHILOSOPHY

(General *Nÿaya-Vaiśeṣika*, Mīmāṁsa, Vedānta, Sāṁkhya, Yoga, Buddhist and Jaina Philosophies, Cārvāka system under separate heads.)

There are many editions and translations of original philosophical texts. We have selected the prominent among them, preferring later editions and translations to the earlier ones. The editions and translations have been noted under the respective entries in the work.

There is a number of modern works dealing with the individual systems separately. Numerous are the works of a general nature. So, we have mentioned only those works of a general nature which are prominent or well-known. Then, we have mentioned the works under the different systems separately.

It should be stated that this bibliography is not exhaustive. We have mentioned only the very important works which will facilitate the study of Indian philosophy in a general way, and not in a specialised manner.

In some cases, the places and years of publication could not be ascertained.

General

Agarwal, N.M., *Some Aspects of Indian Philosophy*.

Aleaj, K.P., *The Role of Pramāṇas in Hindu and Christian Epistemology*, Calcutta, 1991.

Aung and Rhys Davids, *Compendium of Philosophy*.

Banerji, S.C., *A Companion to Indian Philosophy*, Delhi, 1996.

——, *A Companion to Middle Indo-Āryan Literature*, Calcutta, 1977.

Barua, B.M., *Pre-Buddhistic Indian Philosophy*.

Bhartiya, M.G., *Causation in Indian Philosophy*.

Bhatt, G.P., *The Basic Ways of Knowing*, Delhi, 1989.

Bhattacharya, G.M., *Essays in Analytical Philosophy*.

Bhattacharya, K.C., *Studies in Philosophy*, Vols. I, II, Calcutta, 1958.

Brunton, P., *Indian Philosophy and Modern Culture*, Delhi, 1981.

Chattopadhyay, D.P., *et al* (eds.), *Phenomenology and Indian Philosophy*, Delhi, 1991.

Chennukesavan, S., *Concept of Mind in Indian Philosophy*, Delhi, 1991.

Choubey, O.P.S., *Traces of Indian Philosophy in Persian Poetry*.

Coward, H.G., *Derrida and Indian Philosophy*, 1991.

Das Gupta, S.N., *History of Indian Philosophy*, 5 vols.

Das Gupta, Surama, *Development of Moral Philosophy in India*, Calcutta, 1961.

Edgerton, F., *The Beginnings of Indian Philosophy*, London, 1965.

Encyclopaedia of Indian Philosophies (by a team of scholars). For details, see *Reference Books* (*infra*).

Frauwallner, E., *History of Indian Philosophy*, 2 vols., Eng. tr. by V.M. Bedekar.

Garbe, *Philosophy of Ancient India*.

Harris, R.B. (ed.), *Neo-Platonism and Indian Thought*, 1992.

——, *Śabda-pramāṇa — an epistemological analysis*, 1968.

Hindrey, R., *Comparative Ethics in Hindu and Buddhist Traditions*, Delhi.

Ingalalli, R.I., *Meaning and Knowledge — an Interpretation of Indian and Contemporary Epistemological Concepts*, 1989.

Jha, V.N., *Relations in Indian Philosophy*, 1992.

Jwala Prasad, *History of Indian Epistemology*.

Kaviraj, G.N., *Aspects of Indian Thought*, University of Burdwan, West Bengal, 1966.

Krishna, Daya, *Indian Philosophy, a Counterperspective*.

Lad, A.K., *A Comparative Study of the Concept of Liberation in Indian Philosophy,* Berhampur, M.P.

Layek, S., *An Analysis of Dream in Indian Philosophy*, 1990.

Maitra, S.K., *Fundamental Questions of Indian Metaphysics.*

Mishra, G.N., *Problems of Nescience in Indian Philosophy.*

Mishra, R.K., *Theory of Creation in Main Orthodox Schools of Indian Philosophy,* Allababad, 1992.

Misra, U., *History of Indian Philosophy*; vols. I, II.

Modi, P.M., *Akshara, the Forgotten Chapter in the History of Indian Philosophy*, 1985.

Mukherji, A., *A Critique of Verbal Testimony,* Calcutta.

Müller, M., *Six Systems of Philosophy,* 1903.

Nakamura, H., *Ways of Thinking of Eastern Peoples.*

Organ, T.W., *Self in Indian Philosophy.*

Pandey, R.C., *Problem of Meaning in Indian Philosophy*, Delhi 1963.

Pandey, R.R., *Man and the Universe in the Orthodox Systems of Hindu Philosophy*, Delhi, 1978.

Potter, K.H., *Presuppositions of Indian Philosophies*, Delhi, 1991.

Prasad, H.S., *Time in Indian Philosophy,* 1992.

Radhakrishnan, S., *Indian Philosophy,* Vols. I, II, London (Rev.), 1929, 1931.

———, *History of Philosophy, Eastern and Western,* 2 Vols., London, 1952-53.

Radhakrishnan and Moore (eds.), *A Source-book of Indian Philosophy*, Princeton 1957.

Raja, C.K., *Some Fundamental Problems of Indian Philosophy.*

Raja, K.K., *Indian Theories of Meaning*, 1969.

Raju, P.T., *The Philosophical Tradition of India,* Delhi.

Rao, V.R., *Selected Doctrines from Indian Philosophy.*

Sastri, M.N., *Hindu Metaphysics*, New Delhi, 1978.

Schultz, M., *Hindu Philosophy*, New Delhi, 1978.

Sharma, P.N., *Reign of Realism in Indian Philosophy.*

Sharma, R.K., *Researches in Indian and Buddhist Philosophy,* Vol. in honour of A. Wayman, Delhi.

Shastri, H., *Philosophical Conception of Word in Sanskrit Literature.*

Sinari, *The Structure of Indian Thought,* Delhi, 1990.

———, *Concept of Man in Philosophy,* Shimla, Delhi, 1991.

Sinha, K.P., *The Absolute in Indian Philosophy,* Varanasi, 1991.

———, *The Self in Indian Philosophy*, Calcutta, 1991.

Tarkalamkar, C.K., *Hindudarśana*, Śrīgopāl Basu Mallik Lecture, Calcutta University, 5 Vols. in Bengali.

Zimmer, H., *Philosophies of India*, ed. by J. Campbell, New York, 1951.

Nyāya-Vāiśeṣika

Bahadur, K.B., *Wisdom of Nyāya,* New Delhi, 1978.

Bandyopadhyay, N., *Concept of Logical Fallacies* (*Hetvābhāsa* according to Gaṅgeśa and Raghunātha).

Bhaduri, S., *Nyāya-Vaiśeṣika Metaphysics*, Calcutta.

Bhattacharya, G.M., *Navyanyāya — Some Logical Problems in Historical Perspective*, Calcutta.

———, *Studies in Nyāya-Vaiśeṣika Theism*, Calcutta.

Bhattacharya, A.T.S., *Nature of Vyāpti according to Navyanyāya*, Calcutta.

Bhattacharya, B.K., *Inference in Indian and Western Logic.*

Bhattacharya, D.C., *History of Navyanyāya in Mithilā*, Darbhanga.

Bülcke, C. , *Theism of Nyāya-Vaiśeṣika*, Delhi.

Chakrabarti, K.K., *Logic of Gotama,* 1978.

Chatterji, J.C., *Hindu Realism* (*Nyāya-Vaiśeṣika*), Calcutta, 1975.

Chatterji, S.C., *Nyāya Theory of Knowledge.*

Das, S.K., *The Nyāya Theory of Supernormal Perception.*

Gajendragadkar, V.S., *Kaṇāda Doctrine of the Padārthas*, 1988.

Gokhale, P.P., *Inference and Fallacies in Ancient Indian Logic*, 1992.

Junnarkar, N.S., *Gautama, The Nyāya Philosophy*, Delhi, 1975.

Kaviraj, G.N., *History and Bibliography of the Nyāya-Vaiśeṣika Literature.*

———, *Gleanings from the History of Bibliography of the Nyāya-Vaiśeṣika Literature.*

Motilal, B.K., *Nyāya-Vaiśeṣika,* Wiesbaden, 1977.

Narain Harsh, *Evolution of Nyāya-Vaīśeṣika Categoriology.*

Potter, K.H., *Bibliography of Encyclopaedia of Indian Philosophies*, Vol. II, (Pt. I, *Nyāyavaiśeṣika*, Pt. II, Do from Gaṅgeśa onward).

Sen, S., *A Study of Mathurānātha's Tattva-cintāmaṇirahasya*, 1924.

Suguira, *Hindu Logic as Preserved in China and Japan.*

Vidyabhusan, S.C., *Medieval Systems of Indian Logic.*

———, *History of Indian Logic.*

Wada, T., *Invariable Concomitance in Navyanyāya,* 1990.

Mīmāṁsā, Vedānta

Adams, G.C., *The Structure and Meaning of Bādarāyaṇa's Brahmasūtras* (tr. and analysis of Adhyāya I).

Aiyar, C.N.K., *Life and Times of Śaṅkara*, Madras.

Aiyyar, A.S.N., *Mīmāṁsā Jurisprudence.*

Belvalkar, Multiple Authorship of the Vedāntasūtras, *Indian Philosophical Review,* October, 1918.

Betty, L.S., *Vādirāja's Refutation of Śaṅkara's Non-dualism,* etc., 1978.

Bhatkhande, S.M., *Chāndogya Upaniṣad and Brahmasūtras — A Comparative Study*, Bombay, 1982.

Bhatt, G.P., *Epistemology of the Bhāṭṭa School of Pūrvamīmāṁsā.*

Bhattacharya, A., *Studies in Post-Śaṅkara Dialectics*, 1986.

Bhattacharya, H.B., *Status of the World in Advaita Vedānta,* Varanasi.

Bhattacharya, Kālidāsa , *A Modern Understanding of Advaita Vedānta*, Ahmedabad, 1975.

Chakravarti, N., *Advaita Concept of Falsity*, Calcutta.

Chaudhuri, Roma, *Ten Schools of Vedānta*, (3 vols.) Calcutta.

———, *Sufism and Vedānta.*

Clooney, F.X., *Thinking Ritually, Rediscovering the Pūrvamīmāṁsā of Jaimini,* Vienna, 1990.

Comans, M., *Advaitāmoda — A study of Advaita and Viśiṣṭādvaita*, 1988.

Date, V., *Vedānta Explained,* 2 Vols.

Deussen, *System of the Vedānta.*

Devaraja, N.K., *An Introduction to Śaṅkara's Theory of Knowledge,* ed. with comm. of Advaitānanda, by S.R. Krishnamurthi Sastri, Vol. I, Pts. 1, 2, Madras, 1976.

Devasthali, G.V., *Mīmāṁsā* (The ancient Indian science of sentence interpretation, ed. by V.N. Jha), Delhi, 1991.

Dvivedi, R.C., *Studies in Mīmāṁsā.*

Frauwallner, E., *Materialiner Zur Karmamīmāṁsā,* Wien, 1968.

Ghate, V.S., *The Vedānta — A Study of the Brahmasūtras with comms. of* Śaṅkara, Rāmānuja, Nimbārka, Madhva and Vallabha, 2nd edn., Poona, 1960.

Guha, A.K., *Jīvātman in the Brahmasūtras,* Calcutta.

Isherwood, C., *Vedānta for Modern Man,* London, 1952.

———, *Vedānta for Western World.*

Iyer, N.N.V., *Advaita Vedānta,* Bombay, 1964.

Iyer, B.R.R., *Rambles in Vedānta,* Delhi, 1991.

Jha, G.N., *Prabhākara School of Pūrvamīmāṁsā,* 1911.

———, *Pūrvamīmāṁsā in its Sources.*

Joshi, S.N., *A Critique of Indian Dualism.*

Kirtikar, V.J., *Studies in Vedānta.*

Kulasrestha, S., *The Concept of Salvation in Vedānta.*

Lal, B.K., Vedānta and the contemporary problem of man's estrangement, *Bulletin of R.K. Mission Inst. of Culture,* Calcutta, 42(8), Aug. 1991.

Mazumdar, P.K., *The Philosophy of Language,* an Indian approach in the light of Pāṇinian and the Mīmāṁsā Schools of Indian Philosophy, Calcutta.

Mehta, J.L. *et al.*, *Vedānta and Buddhism.*

Mehta, N.D., *Vedānta-siddhānta-bheda* or an account of various followers of Śaṅkarācārya School, Delhi, 1985.

Modi, P., *Critique of Brahmasūtra,* 2 Vols.

Moghe, S.G., *Studies in the Pūrvamīmāṁsā.*

Nag, A., *Six Systems of Vedānta Philosophy,* Calcutta.

Nakamura, H., *History of Early Vedānta Philosophy.*

Pandey, *Śrī Aurobindo and Vedānta.*

Pandey, S.L., *Pre-Śaṅkara Advaita Philosophy.*

Panse, U., *A Reconstruction of the Third School of Pūrvamīmāṁsā,* 1989.

Raghavan, V.K.S.N., *History of Viśiṣṭādvaita Literature,* Delhi, 1979.

Rao, P.N., *Epistemology of Dvaita Vedānta,* Madras, 1976.

Raphael, *Tat Tvam Asi,* Delhi.

Raphael (tr. Mccarthy), *The Pathway of non-duality—Advaitavāda,* Delhi.

Sahasrabuddha, M.T., *Survey of Pre-Śaṅkara Advaita.*

Santina, P.D., *Mādhyamaka Schools in India,* Delhi.

Sarasvati, K. (ed.), *Mīmāṁsā-kośa* (Jaimini Mīmāṁasāsūtra concordance) Pts. 1-2, 1952-53.

Sarma, R.N., *Mīmāṁsā Theory of Meaning,* 1988.

———, *Verbal Knowledge in Prabhākara Mīmāṁsā,* 1989.

Sastri, A.M., *The Vedānta Doctrine of Śrī Śaṅkarācārya*, 1984.

Sastri, M.G., *An Examination of Śaṅkara's Refutation of the Sāṁkhya Theory*, Ahmedabad, 1926.

Satpathy, D.R., *Doctrine of Māyā in Advaita Vedānta*, Calcutta, 1922.

Sharma, A., *The Experiential Dimension of Advaita Vedānta*.

Sharma, R.M., *Encyclopaedia of Vedānta*, Delhi, 1993.

Sinha, D., *The Metaphysics of Experience in Advaita Vedānta*.

Sinha, J.N., *Problems of Post-Śaṅkara Advaita*

Sircar, M.N., *The System of Vedāntic Thought and Culture*.

Sitananda, *Yoga-Vedānta Dictionary*, Delhi.

———, *Vedānta and Modern Science*, 1968.

Srinivasachari, P.N., *A Synthetic View of Vedānta*, 1952.

Srivastava, L.K., *Advaitic Concept of Jīvanmukti*, Delhi, 1990.

Staal, J.F., *Advaita and Neoplatonism*.

Tiwari, K.N., *Dimensions of Renunciation in Advaita Vedānta*.

Tripathi, R.S., *Brahmasūtra-pramukha-bhāṣya-pañcaka-samīkṣaṇam*.

Upadhyay, V.N., *Lights on Vedānta*.

Vajapeyi, G., *Advaitika darśana-saṁgraha*.

Victor, P.G., *Social Philosophy of Vedānta — A Study of the Gītā, Brahmasūtra and Śaṅkara's Commentaries on Them*, Calcutta, 1991.

Warrier, A.G.K., *God in Advaita*, Simla, 1977.

Warrier, E.I., *Aurobindo's Integral Yoga and Śaṅkara's Advaita: A Comparative Study*.

X.D'sa., *Śabdapramāṇam in Śabara and Kumārila*, Vienna, 1983.

Sāṁkhya, Yoga

Abhedananda, *Yoga Psychology*, Calcutta, 1960.

Acharya, T., *Relevance of Indian Philosophy to Modern Society*, 1960.

Ananda (Śrī), *The Complete Book of Yoga-harmony of Body and Mind*, Delhi, 1981.

Arya, U., *Philosophy of Haṭhayoga*, Pennsylvania, 1985.

Atreya, B.L., *The Philosophy of Yogavāśiṣtha*, Adyar, Madras.

Aurobindo (Śrī), *Bases of Yoga*, Calcutta.

———, *Yoga and its Object*, 1972.

———, *The Synthesis of Yoga,* Pondicherry, 1973.

———, *Letters on Yoga,* Pts. 1-3.

Bahadur, K.B., *Wisdom of Sāṁkhya,* New Delhi.

Bedekar, V.M., Studies in Sāmkhya, Pañcaśikha and Caraka, *ABORI*, Vol. 38.

———, Studies in Sāṁkhya, the teaching of Pañcaśikha in the *Mahābhārata, Ibid., BEFEO,* 1904.

Behanan, K.T., *Yoga — A Scientific Evaluation*, New York, 1937.

Bhattacharya, B.N., *Sāṁkhyadarśana,* Calcutta.

Bhattacharya, G.N., *An Analytical Study of Yoga Philosophy*, Calcutta University 1985.

Catalina, F.V., *The Study of the Self-concept of Sāṁkhya-Yoga Philosophy,* 1968.

Chakravarty, P.B., *Origin and Development of the Sāṁkhya System of Thought,* Calcutta, 1951.

Chang, G.C.C., *Teaching of Tibetan Yoga,* New York.

———, *The Six Yoga Systems of Nāropā and Teachings on Mahāmudrā.*

Chappel, C., *The Yogasūtra of Patañjali*, 1990.

Chattopadhyay, N.K., *Indian Philosophy — An Exposition in the Light of Vijñānabhikṣu's Bhāṣya and Yogavārttika,* Calcutta, 1979.

Chattopadhyay, E., and Mohanty, *Phenomenology and Indian Philosophy*, Delhi.

———, *Bhāratīya Darśane Sāṁkhya-Yogadarśana-pramāṇa-tattva* (in Bengali), Calcutta, 1988.

Cheng, H., *Empty Logic — Mādhyamika Buddhism from Chinese Sources*, Delhi, 1991.

Clark, W.E., *Indian Conceptions of Immortality*, Cambridge, 1934.

Coster, G., *Yoga and Western Psychology*, Delhi, 1968.

Devi, M., *Yoga for Expectant Mothers and Fathers,* Pondicherry, 1974.

Davies, J., *Hindu Philosophy — An Exposition of Sāṁkhya.*

Dasgupta, S.N., *A Study of Patañjali,* Calcutta, 1989 (2nd edn.).

———, *Yoga Philosophy in Relation to other Systems of Indian Thought,* Calcutta, Delhi, 1975.

Douglas, N., *Tantrayoga,* New Delhi, 1971.

Evans Wentz, W.Y., *Tibet's Great Yogī, Milarepa*, New York, 1928.

Feuerstein, G., *The Philosophy of Classical Yoga,* Manchester, 1980.

——, *Text-book of Yoga,* London, 1975.

Fromm, E. and Suzuki, *Zen Buddhism and Psycho-analysis,* New York, 1960

Ganguly, H.K., *Philosophy of Logical Construction,* Calcutta, 1963.

Garbe, R., *Die Sāṁkhya Philosophie,* 1894.

Gavin and Frost, *Tāntric Yoga, etc.,* Maine, 1989.

Ghosh, J., *Sāṁkhya and Modern Thought,* Calcutta, 1930.

Giles, L., *Taoist Teachings,* London, 1925.

Gosvami, S.S., *Haṭhayoga.*

Garde, R.K., *Yoga Therapy* (principles and practice), Bombay, 1975.

Guyot, F., *Yoga, the Science of Health* (in French, tr. into Eng. by J. Carling), London, 1937, (3rd edn.).

Hall, F.E., *Intro. to Sāṁkhya-pravacana-bhāṣya,* B-1. Series, Calcutta, 1856.

Harrison, M.H., *Hindu Monism and Pluralism,* Bombay, 1932.

Heimann, B., *Indian and Western Philosophy,* Unwin Bros., Great Britain, 1937.

Hittleman, R.E., *Be Young with Yoga,* 4th edn., London, 1967.

Hulin, M., *Sāṁkhya Literature,* Wiesbaden, 1978.

Jaggi, O.P., *Yogic and Tāntric Medicine,* Delhi, 1973.

Jackson, R.J., *Indian's Quest for Reality,* London, 1947.

Jarmil and Vicenik, *Effect of Haṭhayoga on Heart-activity in Exercising Women,* Bratislava, Activ. Nerv. Sup, Praha, No. 2.

Jarrell, H.R., *International Yoga Bibliography, 1950-80,* London.

Javalgekar, R.R., *The Yoga Science* (for everyone), Varanasi, 1990.

Johnston, E.H., *Early Sāṁkhya,* Royal Asiatic Society of Great Britain, 1937.

Kenghe, C.T., *Yoga as Depth Psychology and Para-psychology,* Vols. I, II, Varanasi, 1975.

Krishnamacharya Yoga Mandiram, *Teaching Yogāsana to mentally retarded.* Vijaya Human Services. A Report on the Training Programme, Madras.

Krishna Prem, *Initiation into Yoga,* London, 1976.

Krishna, G., *Yoga — A Vision of its Future.*

——, *The Purpose of Yoga,* New Delhi, 1993.

Kumar, S., *Sāṁkhya Thought in the Brāhmaṇical Systems of Indian*

Philosophy.

Larson, G.J., *Classical Sāṁkhya*, Delhi, 1969.

Legget, T., *Śaṅkara on the Yogasūtras*, Delhi.

Malik, A.D., *Kuṇḍalinī and Meditation,* Delhi, 1991.

Mishra, S., *Yoga and Āyurveda,* 1989.

Motoyama, H., *A Psycho-physiological Study of Yoga,* Tokyo, 1975.

Mumford, J., *Psychosomatic Yoga.*

Nair, T.J., *Yogic Exercises*, Bombay, 1987.

Pandit, S.C., *Yoga Against Spinal Pain,* London, 1975.

Pelletier, K.R., *Mind as Healer, Mind as Slayer — A Holistic Approach to Preventing Stress and Disorder*, New York, 1977.

Pranavananda (Yogī), ed. by T. Rodriguez and K. Ram, *Pure Yoga,* Delhi.

Rai, P.K., *Encyclopaedia of Yoga.*

Rajlaksmi, *Yoga Therapy in Diabetes, Bronchial Asthma and Hypertension,* Indian Institute of Yoga and Allied Sciences.

Raju, P.T., *The Philosophical Traditions of India,* Delhi.

Raman, R., *Haṭhayoga for All,* Delhi, 1991.

Rao, K.B.R., *Theism of Pre-classical Sāṁkhya*, Mysore, 1966.

Rele, V.G., *Yogic Āsanas for Health and Vigour,* 10th edn., Bombay, 1972.

Rodriguez, T. (ed.), *Pure Yoga by Yogī Praṇavānanda.*

Ruben, W., Beginnings of Epic Sāṁkhya, *ABORI*, Vol. 37, 1958.

Saksena, S.K., *Nature of Consciousness in Hindu Philosophy,* Benares, 1944.

Sarasvati, *Effects of Yoga on Hypertension,* Monghyr, 1978.

Sarasvati, Y., *Blood-pressure: Management through Yoga*, 2nd edn., 1951.

Sen Gupta, A., *Classical Sāṁkhya: A Critical Study,* 1969.

Sen Gupta A., *Sāṁkhya and Advaita Vedānta, A Comparative Study*, 1973.

Sinha, A.K., *Perspective in Yoga*, Varanasi, 1974.

Sovani, V.V., *A Critical Study of the Sāṁkhya System*, Poona, 1935.

Surath, *Scientific Yoga.*

Suzuki, D.T., *An Introduction to Zen Buddhism* (ed. by C. Humphreys), London, 1988.

——, *Living by Zen*, London, 1950.

Udupa, K.N., *Stress and its Management by Yoga*, Delhi, 1985 (2nd edn.), Rep. 1989.

Udupa K.N. and Singh, *Yoga in Relation to Brain Pituitary-Adrenocortical axis.* In a special vol. on brain-pituitary-adrenocortical axis, London, 1979.

Varenne, J., *Yoga and Hindu Tradition,* tr. from French, by D. Coltman, London, 1976.

Vidyabhusan, S.C. , Sāṁkhya Philosophy in the Land of the Lāmās, *JRASB,* III, 1907.

Vivekananda, *Rājayoga*, Calcutta.

———, *Bhaktiyoga*, Calcutta.

———, *Karmayoga,* Calcutta.

Walls, A.W., *Psychotherapy: East and West,* London, 1971.

Warrier, E.I., *Aurobindo's Integral Yoga and Śaṅkara's Advaita — A Comparative Study.*

Wayman, A., *Buddhist Dependent Origination and the Sāṁkhya Guṇas,* Ethnos, 1962.

Yesudian, S. and Haich, E., *Yoga and Health,* London, 1953.

Vaiṣṇava Philosophy

Bhandarkar, R.G., *Vaiṣṇavism*, etc., Poona, 1928.

Chakrabarti, Ramakanta, *Vaiṣṇavism in Bengal: A historical study, 1486-1900*, Calcutta.

Chari, S.M.S., *Viṣṇavism — A Philosophy, Theology and Religious Description.*

Chatterji, C., *The Philosophy of Caitanya and His School,* Delhi, 1993.

De, S.K., *Early History of the Vaiṣṇava Faith and Movement in Bengal,* Calcutta, 1942.

Roy Chaudhuri, H.C., *Materials for the Study of the Early History of the Vaiṣṇava Sect*, Calcutta, 1962.

Śaiva Philosophy

Barnett, L.D., *The Heart of India.*

Chatterji, J.C., *Kashmir Śaivism,* Srinagar, 1914.

Pandey, K.C., *Abhinavagupta,* Benares, 1935.

Rastogi, N., *Introduction to Tantrāloka*

———, *Krama Tantricism of Kashmir*, Vol I, Delhi, 1979, Vol. II.

Sen Sharma, D.B., *The Philosophy of Sādhanā*, with special reference to the Trika Philosophy of Kashmir, Albany, 1990.

Buddhist and Jaina Philosophies

Bagchi, P.C., *Le Canon Bouddhique en Chine,* tome 1, Paris, 1927.

Barua, B.M., *A History of Pre-Buddhistic Indian Philosophy*, Calcutta University.

Bülert, V.A. Van, *Epistemology and Spiritual Authority* (development of epistemology and logic in old Nyāya and Buddhist School of Epistemology).

Bothra, P., *Jaina Theory of Perception*, Delhi.

Chang, C.C., *A Treasury of Mahāyāna Sūtra*, Delhi.

Das, S.C., *Indian Puṇḍits in the Land of Snow.*

Davids, R., *Dialogues of the Buddha* (Eng. tr. in 2 parts), Sacred Books of the Buddhist Series.

Davids, R. (Mrs.), *Buddhism* (Home University Library).

Eckel, M.D., *Jñānagarbha's commentary on the Distinction between the Two Truths,* an eighth century handbook of Mādhyamika Philosophy, Albany, 1987.

Fatone, V., *The Philosophy of Nāgārjuna*, Delhi, 1991.

Ganguly, S., Treatise in Thirty Verses on Mere Consciousness (*Vijñaptimātratā-daśaśāstra-kārikā*), Delhi.

Glasenapp, H., *Vedānta and Buddhism*, 1958.

———, *Brahma and Buddha,* 1926.

Govinda, Lama A., *The Psychological Attitude of Early Buddhist Philosophy*, Delhi, 1991.

Hindrey, R., *Comparative Ethics in Hindu and Buddhist Traditions*, Delhi.

Huntington, C.W. with G.M. Wengchen, *The Emptiness of Emptiness: An Introduction to Early Indian Mādhyamika*, Honolulu, 1989.

Jaini, *Outlines of Jainism.*

Jenning, J.G., *Vedāntic Buddhism of the Buddha,* Delhi.

Keith, A.B., *Buddhist Philosophy of India and Ceylon,* Oxford, 1923.

Kloetzli, R., *Buddhist Cosmology,* Delhi, 1980.

Kuppuram, G. and Kumudamani, K. (eds.), *Buddhist Heritage in India and Abroad*, Delhi, 1991.

Law, B.C., *Heaven and Hell in the Buddhist Perspective.*

Lindtner, Chr., *Nāgārjuniana, Studies in the Writings and Philosophy of Nāgārjuna*, Delhi, 1990.

McGovern, *Introduction to Mahāyāna Buddhism.*

Mitra, R.L., *Nepalese Buddhist Literature.*

Mookerji, S., *Jaina Philosophy of Non-absolution,* Delhi.

Nagao, G.M. (tr. by J.P. Keenam), *The Fundamental Standpoint of Mādhyamaka Philosophy*, 1990.

———, (trs. by L.S. Kawamura), *Mādhyamika and Yogācāra*, 1992.

Nakamura, H., *Indian Buddhism*: A *Survey with Bibliographical Notes,* Delhi, 1987.

Nanjio, B., *Catalogue of the Chinese Translation of the Buddhist Tripiṭaka*, Oxford, 1883.

Nariman, *Literary History of Sanskrit Buddhist Literature.*

Padmarajiah, Y.J., *A Comparative Study of the Jaina Theories of Reality*, Delhi.

Prasad, H.S., *The Buddhist Philosophy of Time*, 1992.

Radhakrishnan, S., The teaching of Buddha by speech and silence, *Hibbert Journal*, April, 1931.

Ruegg, D. Sr. and S. Lambert (eds.), *Earliest Buddhism and Mādhyamaka,* Leipzig, 1990.

Sacred Books of the Jainas In this series, several philosophical works of the Jainas are translated into English.

Sharma, R.K. (ed.), *Researches in Indian and Buddhist Philosophy* (Vol. in honour of A. Wayman).

Sikdar, J.C., *Theory of Reality in Jaina Philosophy,* Varanasi, 1991.

Sogen, Y., *Systems of Buddhistic Thought*, Calcutta University.

Stcherbatsky, *Buddhist Logic,* 2 vols, New York, 1962.

Stevenson, S., *The Heart of Jainism*, Oxford Uni. Press, Oxford.

Suzuki. D.T., *Outlines of Mahāyāna Buddhism*, Luzac & Co.

Tsong-Ka-Pa, *The Yoga of Tibet,* Delhi.

Tucci, G., *Pre-Diṅnāga Buddhist Texts on Logic from Chinese Sources*, 1981.

Tuck, A.P., *Comparative Philosophy and the Philosophy of Scholarship: On Western Interpretation of Nāgārjuna*, New York, 1990.

Upadhyaya, B., *Bauddha-darśana-mīmāṁsā*, Varanasi, 1978.

Upadhyaya, K.N., *Early Buddhism and the Bhagavad Gītā*, Delhi 1971.

Vijayadharmasuri, *Jaina-tattvajñāna* in *Festschrift Winternitz.*

Vijaya Bhuvanabhanusuri, *Ganadharavada* (essentials of Mahāvīra's Philosophy), Delhi.

Warner, H.C., *Buddhism in Translations*, Harvard University Press.

Watanbe, F., *Philosophy and its Development in the Nikāyas and Abhidhamma.*

Wayman, A., *Yoga of the Guhyasamāja-tantra*, Delhi.

Williams, R., *Jaina Yoga* (a survey of the medieval Śrāvakācāras), Delhi.

Williams, P., *Mahāyāna Buddhism: The Doctrinal Foundations*, London and New York, 1989.

Cārvāka System

Chattopadhyay, D.P., *Lokāyata*, New Delhi, 1951.

Dasgupta, S.N., *A History of Indian Philosophy*, IV, Cambridge, 1955.

Ruben, W., *Studies in Ancient Indian Thought,* Calcutta, 1966.

Shastri, D.R., *A Short History of Indian Materialism*, Calcutta, 1957 (2nd edn.)

Shastri, H.P., *Lokāyata*, Dacca 1925.

Reference Books

Bhāratīya Darśana-koṣa, published from Govt. Sanskrit College, 3 vols., Calcutta,

Bhimacarya, *Nyāyakośa*.

Encyclopaedia of Indian Philosophies, 7 vols., Delhi.

Addendum: The *Tattvopaplava-siṁha*, attributed to Jayarāśi of uncertain date, is the only surviving Sanskrit work of the Cārvāka-Lokāyata school. In it, full-fledged scepticism has been propounded. Different sections of the work are devoted to the different definitions of the means of knowledge in general and perception in particular.

The schools criticised are Nyāya (Ācārya and Vyākhyātṛ schools), Mīmāṁsā (Bhāṭṭa and Prābhākara as also older commentaries), epistemological school of Buddhism (Diṅnāga and Dharmakīrti), Sāṁkhya (Vārṣa-gaṇya and Vindhyasrāmin).

The work ed. and tr. (first half of the text into English) by E. Franco, Delhi, 1994, with Introduction, detailed analysis, exhaustive notes on which, *inter alia*, the opponents behind the different arguments are identified, their positions reconstructed and put into a historical perspective. Besides parallel passages from the work and later works have been collected and translated.

Originally published, Stuttgart, 1987 ed., with English and Hindi Introduction by S. Sanqkavi and R.C. Parikh, Varanasi, 1987.

ARTHAŚĀSTRA

TEXT AND TRANSLATION

Ed. by T. Ganapati Sastri, with *Śrīmūlā* comm., *TSS*, 3 Vols., 1921, 1924, 1925.

Ed. and tr. by L.N. Rangarajan, New Delhi, 1992.

Eng. tr. by R.P. Kangle, Bombay, 1963.

Kangle, R.P., *The Kauṭilīya Arthaśāstra*, Pt. III — A Study, Bombay, 1965.

Chaudhary, R.K., *Kauṭilya's Political ideas and Institutions,* Banaras.

Sen Sarma, P., *Ethno-biological information in Kauṭilīya Arthaśāstra*, Calcutta, 1998.

Sternbach, L., *Bibliography of Kauṭilīya Arthaśāstra*, Hoshiarpur, 1973.

SMṚTI-ŚĀSTRA

For references to the *Mahābhārata*, the *Smṛti Material in the Mahābhārata* by the author of this work, has been used.

Prācīna Smṛti

DHARMASŪTRA

Āpastamba-dharmasūtra, ed. with *Ujjvalā* comm. by M. Sastri, Mysore.

Baudhāyana-dharmasūtra, ed. with *Vivaraṇa* comm., by A.C. Sastri, Benares, 1931.

Gautama-dharmasūtra, (ed.), Ānandāśrama, with *Mitākṣarā*-comm., Poona, 1931.

Vaikhānasa-Smārta-sūtra, ed. by K. Rangachari, Madras, 1930.

Vaśiṣṭha-dharmaśāstra, ed. with *Vidvannodinī* comm., by K. Dharmadhikari, Benares, Śaka 1781; ed. by A. Führer, Poona, 1930.

Viṣṇu- Smṛti, ed. with extracts from *Vaijayantī* comm. by J. Jolly, Calcutta, 1881.

DHARMAŚĀSTRA

Kātyāyana-smṛti-sāroddhara, ed. by P.V. Kane, Bombay, 1993.

Manu-smṛti, with Kullūkabhaṭṭa's comm., Delhi, 1983. With comms. of Medhātithi and Kullūka (in Bangali scripts) and Bengali translation, Calcutta, Eng. tr. by Bühler, *SBE*, Vol. XXV.

Nārada-smṛti, ed. by J. Jolly, with extracts from Asahāya's comm., as revised by Kalyāṇabhaṭṭa, up to verse 21 of the fifth title (Abhyupetyā-śuśūṣā), B. 1 Series, Calcutta, 1885.

Parāśara-smṛti, with gloss of Mādhavan, Bombay Skt. Series.

Yājñavalkya-smṛti, N.S. Press (edn.), Bombay, 1926.

Navya Smṛti

BENGAL SCHOOL

Aniruddha Bhaṭṭa, *Hāralatā*, B.1. Series, Calcutta, 1909.

———, *Pitṛdayitā*, (ed.), Skt. Sāhitya Pariṣat, Calcutta.

Ballālasena, *Dānasāgara*, B.1. (ed.), Calcutta, 1953.

———, *Adbhutasāgara*, ed. by M. Jha, Varanasi, 1905.

Bhavadeva Bhaṭṭa, *Prāyaścitta-prakaraṇa*, pub. by Varendra Res. Soc., Rajshahi, Bangladesh, 1927.

———, *Karmānuṣṭhāna-paddhati*, ed., S. Kaviratna, Calcutta, 1348 BS.

———, *Śavasūtakā-śauca-prakaraṇa*, ed. by R.C. Hazra, Calcutta, 1959.

Govindānanda, *Dānakriyā-kaumudī*, B.1. (ed.), Calcutta, 1903.

———, *Śuddhi-kaumudī*, B.l. (ed.), Calcutta, 1905.

———, *Śrāddha-kriyā-kaumudī*, B.l. (ed.), Calcuṭta, 1904.

———, *Varṣakriyā-kaumudī*, B.l. (ed.), Calcutta, 1902.

Halāyudha, *Brāhmaṇa-sarvasva* (ed.) by D.M. Bhattacharya, Calcutta, 1960.

Jīmūtavāhana, *Kālaviveka*, B.1. (ed.), Calcutta, 1905.

———, *Dāyabhāga*, ed., by J. Vidyasagara, Calcutta, 1893.

———, *Vyavahara-mātṛka*, ed. A.T. Mukherji, Calcutta.

Raghunandana, *Smṛti-tattva*, Vols. I. II, ed. by J. Vidyasagara, Calcutta.

Śrīnātha Ācāryacūḍāmaṇi — *Vivāha-tattvārṇava*, ed. by S.C. Banerji, *ABORI*, Poona, 1951.

Śūlapāṇi, *Śrāddha-viveka*, ed. by C. Smṛtībhūṣaṇa, Calcutta, 1299 BS.

———, *Prāyaścitto-viveka*, ed. by J. Vidyasagara, Calcutta, 1893.

———, *Sambandha-viveka*, ed. by J.B. Chaudhuri, Calcutta, 1942.

——, *Durgotsava-viveka*, ed. by Sanskrit Sahitya Parisad, Calcutta.

——, *Dīpakalikā*, ed. by J.R. Gharpure, Bombay.

MITHILĀ SCHOOL

Caṇḍeśvara, *Gṛhastha-ratnākara*, B.1. Series, Calcutta, 1928.

——, *Kṛtya-ratnākara*, B.1. Series, Calcutta, 1925.

——, *Rājanīti-ratnākara*, ed. by K.P. Jayaswal, *JBORS,* XXII, 1936, Appendix.

——, *Vivāda-ratnākara*, B.1. Series, Calcutta, 1931.

Mishra, Rudradhara, *Varṣakṛtya*, Old Benares, ed. (?).

——, *Śuddhi-viveka* (ed.) Venkatesvara Press, Bombay, Saṁvat, 1951.

——, *Śrāddha-viveka*, Chowkhamba Skt. Series, Benareṣ, 1935.

Śrīdattopādhyāya, *Ācārādarśa* Benares edn., Saṁvat, 1939.

Vācaspatimiśra, *Dvaita-nirṇaya*, ed. by S. Shukla, Benares, 1995 V.S.

——, *Kṛtya-cintāmaṇi*, ed. by M. Smṛtitirtha, Benares, 1814 SE.

——, *Sambandha-cintāmaṇi*, ed. by S. Tarkasarasvati, Silchar, (Assam), 1850.

——, *Śrāddha-cīntāmaṇi*, ed. by M. Smrtitirtha, Benares, 1814 SE.

——, *Śuddhi-cintāmaṇi*, ed. by M. Smrtitirtha, Benares, 1813 SE.

——, *Tīrtha-cintāmaṇi*, B.L. Series, Calcutta, 1912.

——, *Vivāda-cintāmaṇi*, ed. by R.C. Vidyavagish, Calcutta, 1837.

——, *Vyavahāra-cintāmaṇi*, ed. by L. Rocher, Gent, 1956.

Vardhamāna, *Daṇḍaviveka*, GOS, Baroda, 1931.

Vidyāpati, *Durgā-bhakti-taraṅgiṇi*, ed. by 1.C. Vidyavinod, Srihatta (Assam), 1856, SE.

——, *Gaṅgā-vākyāvalī*, ed. by J.B. Chaudhuri, Calcutta, 1940.

VĀRĀṆASĪ SCHOOL

Kamalākarabhaṭṭa, *Nirṇayasindhu*, N.S. Prass edn., Bombay, 1905.

——, *Śūdra-kamalākara, ibid.*, 1895.

Nandapaṇḍita, *Dattaka-mīmāṁsā*, ed. by B. Śiromani, with comm., Calcutta, 1885.

Nārāyaṇa Bhaṭṭa, *Antyeṣṭi-paddhati*, N.S. Press edn.

——, *Prayoga-ratna*, N.S. Press edn., Bombay AD 1915.

——, *Tristhali-setu*, Anandāśrma Press edn., Poona.

SOUTH INDIAN SCHOOL

Devaṇṇa Bhaṭṭa, *Smṛticandrikā*, ed. by J.R. Gharpure (up to *Śrāddha*), Bombay. Pub. in Mysore Govt. Oriental Series (up to *Aśauca*).

Hemādri, *Caturvarga-cintāmaṇi*. Sections on *Vrata*, *Dāna*, *Śrāddha* and *Kāla* have been published. The last two are parts of the *Pariśesa-khaṇḍa*.

Kāśīnātha Upādhyāya, *Dharmasindhu*, N.S. Press edn., Bombay, 1926.

Nīlakaṇṭhabhaṭṭa, *Bhagavanta-bhāskara*, Benares, 1879-80.

Mādhavācārya, *Parāśara-mādhavīya*, pub. in B.1. Series, Calcutta, and in Bombay Skt. Series.

———, *Kālanirṇaya*, pub. in B.1. Series, Calcutta.

ORISSA SCHOOL

Gadādhara, *Gadādhara-paddhati* (including 18 sections called *sāras* which have been printed).

———, *Ācārasāra*, B.1. edn., Calcutta.

———, *Kālasāra*, B.1. edn., Calcutta.

———, *Dānasāra*, B.1. edn., Calcutta.

Narasiṁha Vājapeyin-*Nityācāra-pradīpa*, B.1. edn., Calcutta.

Pratāparudradeva, *Sarasvatī-vilāsa*, *Dāyabhāga* portion. Published, with Eng. tr. by T. Foulkes, 1881.

———, Entire *Vyavahāra* section pub. in Mysore Govt. Publication Series.

OTHER WRITERS

Anantadeva, *Smṛti-kaustubha*, N.S. Press edn., Bombay, 1909.

———, *Saṁskāra* section, *ibid.*, 1913; also printed at Baroda, 1914.

Mitramiśra, *Vīramittrodaya*, Vyvahāra section pub. by. J. Vidyasagara, Calcutta, 1875.

———, Sections on *Paribhāṣā*, *Saṁskāra*, *Rājanīti*, *Āhnika*, *Pūjā*, *Tīrtha* and *Lakṣaṇa* pub. in Benares (Chowkhamba). *Dāyabhāga* portion of *Vyavahāra* pub. with Eng. tr. by G. Sarkar Sastri.

COLLECTIONS OF DHARMAŚĀSTRAS

Dharmaśāstra-saṁgraha, ed. by J. Vidyasagara, Calcutta, 1876.

Dharmaśāstra-saṁgraha, ed. by V. Upadhyaya, 2 vols.

Smṛtīnāṁ Samuccaya, Anandāśrama Skt. Series, 1905.

Smṛti-sandarbha, Calcutta, 1952-53.

Smṛti-sandarbha, (a Collection of Dharmaśāstras), 6 vols., ed. by H. Smith, Delhi, 1988.

Ūnaviṁśati-saṁhitā, ed. by P. Tarkaratna, with Bengali tr., Calcutta, 1909.

MISCELLANEOUS WORKS

Agrawala, V.S., *India as Described by Manu*, Varanasi, 1970.

Ambedkar, B.R., *Who were the Śūdras*, Bombay, 1946.

———, *Riddles in Hinduism*.

Apte, V.M., *Sacrament of Marriage* etc, Delhi, 1978.

Banerji, N.N., *Manu and Modern Times*, New Delhi.

Banerji, G.D., *Marriage and Strīdhana*, Calcutta.

Banerji, S.C., *Dharmasūtras: A Study, etc*., Calcutta, 1962.

———, *The Costaway of Indian Society*, Calcutta, 1939.

———, *Smṛtiśāstre Bāṅgāli* (in Bengali), Calcutta, 1368 BS.

———, *Crime and Sex in Ancient India*, Calcutta.

———, *A Glossary of Smṛti Literature*, Calcutta.

———, *Society in Ancient India*, New Delhi, 1993.

———, *Principles of Hindu Jurisprudence*, 2 Vols. Delhi.

Bharadwaj, S.K., *Linguistic Study of Dharmasūtras*, Rohtak, 1982.

Bhattacharya, Bhavatosh, *Raghunandana's indebtedness to his predecessors*, Calcutta, 1955.

———, *Studies in Dharmaśastra*, Calcutta, 1964.

Brough, J., *Early Brahmanical system of Gotra and Pravara*, Cambridge, 1953.

Bühler, G., *The Laws of Manu*, SBE, XXV, Oxford, 1886.

Bühneman, G., *Pūjā: A study in Smārta Ritual*.

Chakrabarti, Bani, *Samāja-saṁskāraka Raghunandana*, (in Bengali), Calcutta, 1970 (2nd, ed.)

Chatterji, H., *Studies in Some Aspects of Hindu Saṁskāras in Ancient India*, Calcutta, 1967.

———, *The Law of Debt in Ancient India*, Calcutta, 1971.

———, *Studies in the Social background of the forms of Marriage in Ancient India*, vols. I, II, Calcutta.

Crawford, S.G., *Evolution of Hindu Ethical Ideals*, Calcutta, 1974.

C.S., *Śrīnivāsāchari Volume*, Madras, 1950 (Paper, entitled 'The Modernity of Manu', by R. Sathianathier).

Das, B., *The Seience of Social Organisation or the Law of Manu*, Madras, 1932.

Das, R.M., *Women in Manu and His Seven commentators.*

Derrett, J.D.M., *Hindu Law, Past and Present*, Calcutta, 1957.

Ganguly, J., *Darmaśāstra in Mithilā*, Calcutta, 1972.

Gharpure, J.R., *Sāpiṇḍya.*

———, *Teachings of Dharmaśāstra.*

Ghosh, B.K., *Hindu Law and Custom.*

Hazra, R.C., *Studies in the Purāṇic Records,* etc., Dacca.

Jayaswal. K.P., *Manu and Yājñavalkya.*

Kane, P.V., *History of Dharmaśāstra*, Vols. I-V (Vol. I rev. in two parts).

Lariviere, R.W., *Studies in Dharmaśāstra*, Calcutta, 1984.

Lingat, R., *Les Sources du Droit class le systeme traditional du L. Inde*, The Hague, 1969.

Mitra, V., *India of Dharmasūstras.*

Motwani, K., *Manu Dharmaśāstra* (for influence of Manu outside India), Madras, 1958.

Patwardhan, M.V., *Manusmṛti* — the Ideal Democratic Republic of Manu, Delhi, 1968.

Raghavan, V., *New Catalogus Catalogorum.*

Ramgopal, *India of Vedic Kalpasūtras.*

Sharma, N.R., *The Kāmarūpa School of Dharmaśāstra*, 1993.

Sing, B., *Social Life in Ancient India.*

Sternbach, L., *Bibliography of Dharma and Artha in Ancient and Medieval India.*

Supakar, S., *The Law of Evidence in Ancient India*, Calcutta, 1940.

Thakur, U., *History of Mithilā*, ch. VIII.

Tiwari, C., *Śūdras in Manu*, Delhi, 1963.

Ved-Mitra, *India of Dharmasūtra.*

Papers

Annals of Bhandarkar Oriental Research Institute, Poona, 1935, 1951.

Indian Historical Quarterly, Vols. VIII, IX.

Journal of Oriental Institute, Baroda, Vol. VI, Nos. 2-3.

Journal of Bihar and Orissa Research Society, Vol. XXIII.

Journal of Asiatic Society (of Bengal), Calcutta, 1912, 1915, 1938, 1953. (*New Series, Letters* — Hora on *Fish in Smṛti Literature*).

Journal of Oriental Research, 1953 — 3rd series (S.L. Hora on Fish in Smṛti Literature) Madras, Vol. XVIII.

New Indian Antiquary, Vols. V-VII.

Our Heritage (Journal of Calcutta Sanskrit College), Vols. I, II, XII, XVI (Articles by R.C. Hazra on Source of Dharma, Judicial Pramāṇas)

KĀMAŚĀSTRA

Texts and Translations

Anaṅgaraṅga of Kalyānamalla, ed. by R.S. Kusala, Lahore, 1890; with Eng. tr. by S.N. Prasad.

Kāmasūtra of Vātsyāyana, ed. with Skt. comm. *Jayamaṅgalā* and a Hindī comm., Vārāṇasī, 1964; ed. and illustrated by L. Dane, Eng. tr. by R.W. Burton, New York, 1962 (New edn.); S.C. Upādhyāya with line-drawings and illustrations. German tr. by R. Schmidt, W. Friedrich, Leipzig, 2nd edn., L. Varlay, Berlin, 1706. French tr. by F. Lemairesse, G. Garre, Paris, 1891.

Kandarpa-cūḍāmaṇi of King Vīrabhadra of Vaghela dynasty, ed. by R.S. Kusala, Lahore, 1926.

Kucimāratantra, Lahore, 1922.

(2) *Dhanvantari-granthāvalī* 17, Aligarh, Vijayagarh, 1925.

Nāgarasarvasva of Padmaśrī, with Jagajjyotirmallā's comm. ed. by T. Sarma, Bombay, 1921.

Pañcasāyaka of Maithila Jyotirīśvara Kaviśekhara, ed. by S.S. Ghiladia, Lahore, 1921.

Ratiramaṇa of Siddha Nāgārjuna, Calcutta, 1909.

Ratirahasya of Kukkoka, ed. with Kāñcināthā's comm. by D. Parajuli, Lahore. Eng. tr. by R. Schmidt, Lotus Verlag, Berlin, 1903.

Ratimañjarī of Jayadeva, ed. by P.E. Pavolini, Giornale della societa Asiatica Italiana, xvii, 1904. Text available also in *Kāvya-saṁgraha*, compiled by J. Vidyāsāgara, vol. III, Calcutta, 1888.

Ratiratna-pradīpikā of Mahārāja Devarāja, with Eng. tr., ed. by R. Iyengar, Mysore, 1923.

Studies

N.B.:- About the 64 subsidiary *Śilpa-kalās*, mentioned in the *Kāmasūtra*, see A. Veṅkaṭasubbiāh and E. Müller in *Journal of Royal Asiatic Society*, 1914.

Agrawala, P.K., *The Unknown Kāmasūtras*, Vārāṇasī, 1988.

Burton and Arbuthnot, *Kāmasūtra*.

Chakladar, H.C., *Studies in Vātsyāyanā's Kāmasūtra: Social Life in Ancient India*, Calcutta, 1929.

De, S.K., *Ancient Indian Erotics and Erotic Literature*, Calcutta, 1959.

———, *Treatment of Love in Sanskrit Literature*, 1929.

Ghosh, M., *Glimpses of Sexual Life in Ancient India*, Calcutta.

Hampiholis, V.K., *Kāmaśāstra in Classical Sanskrit Literature*.

Kapadia, B.H., Paper on flora and fauna in *Kāmasūtra*, *Journal of Oriental Institute*, XI, 1961.

Meyer, J.J., *Sexual Life in Ancient India*, 2 vols., London, 1930 (Deals mainly with the Epics, and has very little direct bearing on Erotics).

Peterson, P., Vātsyāyana on the Duties of a Hindu Wife, *Journal of Anthropological Society of Bombay*, 1892.

———, Courtship in Ancient India (as given in *Kāmasūtra*), *Journal of Bombay Branch of Royal Asiatic Society*, 1892.

Raghavan, V., *Journal of G. Jhā Res. Institute*, I. IV. 1944, pp. 472-3.

Rai, R.K., *Encyclopaedia of Indian Erotics*, Vārāṇasī, 1983.

Schmidt, R., Beitrage zur indischen Erotik, Berlin (Extracts from all texts arranged in encyclopaedic tr.), Leipzig, 1902, 2 te. Aufl. XI, 691, Berlin, 1911. 3 te. Aufl. . . 1922. Winer. Zeitschrift fur die Kunde des Morgenlandes, XVIII, 1904 and XXIII, 1909.

———, Vātsyāyana's Kāmasūtra, *Indische Erotik*.

———, *Liebe und Ehe im alten Indien*, Berlin, 1904. (mostly tr. of selected texts).

———, *Wiener Zeitschrift für die Kunde des Morganlandes*, XVII, 1904 (For specimen text with tr. of another work, named *Ratiśāstra* of Nāgārjuna with *Smara-tattva-prakāśikā* comm. of Rāvaṇārādhya).

Veṅkaṭasubbiah, A. and Müller, E., *Paper in Journal of Royal Asiatic Soc.*, 1914.

Wilhelm, F., The quotations in Kāmasūtra of Vātsyāyana, *Indologica Taurinensia* 6, 1978/80.

POETICS

Texts and Translations

Dhvanyāloka, ed. with *Locana* comm., Hindī tr. of both text and comm. and a *vyākhyā*, Delhi. Ed. by K. Sastri and others, with *Locana*, *Kaumudī* and *Upalocana*, Uddyota I, Madras, 1944; K. Krishnamoorthy, with Intro., Eng. tr. and notes Mysore, 1974. German tr. by H. Jacobi, Leipzig, 1903; Russian tr. by Y. Ali-khanova, with comments, Bengali tr. by S.S. Sengupta and K.P. Bhattacharya, Calcutta.

Kāvyālaṁkāra of Bhāmaha; ed. with Eng. tr. and notes, by P.V.N. Sastry, Tanjore, 1970 (Rev. edn.).

See R. Gnoli, *Udbhaṭa's comm. on K.L. of Bhāmaha*, ed. with critical notes.

Kāvyālaṁkāra of Rudraṭa, ed. by Durgaprasad and Parab, NSP, 1909, with Namisādhū's comm.

Kāvyādarśa of Daṇḍin, ed. with Eng. tr., by S.K. Belvalkar, Poona, 1924; with an original comm. by R. Raddi Sastri, Poona, 1938 (2nd edn.) Russian tr., Leningrad.

Kāvyālaṁkāra-sūtra-vṛtti of Vāmana, ed. with N.N. Kulkarni, with extracts from *Kāmadhenu* comm., Poona 1927. Eng. tr. by G. Jha, Allahabad.

Kāvyaprakāśa of Mammaṭa, ed. with *Dīpikā* comm. by S.P. Bhattacharya, Banaras, 1933. Eng. tr. by G. Jha, Allahabad, 1925.

Rasagaṅgādhara of Jagannātha, ed. by Durgaprasad and Parab, with Nāgoji's comm., Bombay, 1947 (6th edn.); R. Ojha, with *Rasacandrikā* comm., Varanasi, 1977; vol. I. ed. with Eng. and Bengali tr., by C. Chatterji, Calcutta.

Sāhitya-darpaṇa of Viśvanātha, ed. by K.M. Sastri, with comm. *Lakṣmī*, Varanasi, 1955; H.D. Siddhāntavāgīśa, with Skt. comm., subject-index, verse-index, index of authors and works cited, Calcutta, Śaka 1867; P.V. Kane (chs. I, II, X, with notes and History of Sanskrit Poetics, Bombay, 1951. Eng. tr. by J.R. Ballantyne and P.D. Mitra, Asiatic Soc., Calcutta.

Vakrokti-jīvita of Kuntaka ed. by S.K. De, Calcutta, 1961 (3rd edn.), Chs. I part of III with a resume of the unedited portion. Crit. edn. with fresh MS. material, with Eng. tr. by K. Krishnamoorthy, Karnataka University, Dharwar, 1977.

Studies

Amaladass, A., *Philosophical Implications of Dhvani*, Vienna, 1984.

——, *Dhvanyāloka Concordance*, Delhi.

Bhatt, G., *Splendour of Sanskrit Poetics*.

Bhattacharya, S.P., *Studies in Indian Poetics*, Calcutta.

De, S.K., *History of Sanskrit Poetics*, 2 Vols., Calcutta, 1960, 2nd edn.

——, *Sanskrit Poetics as a Study of Aesthetics*, Bombay, 1963.

——, *Early History of Vaiṣṇava Faith and Movement in Bengal*, Calcutta, 1961 (2nd edn.).

——, *Some Problems of Sanskrit Poetics*, 1981 (Reprint).

Gangopadhyay, A.L., *Paṇḍitarāja Jagannātha on Esthetic Problem*, Calcutta.

Gerow, E., *A Glossary of Indian Figures of Speech*.

Gnoli, R., *The Aesthetic Experience According to Abhinavagupta*.

Goswami, B., *A Critique of Alaṁkāras in Rasagaṅgādhara*, Calcutta.

Jha, B., *Concept of Poetic Blemishes in Sanskrit Literature*, Benares.

Krishnamoorthy, K., *Dhvanyāloka and its Critics*, Mysore, 1968.

Kulkarni, V.M. (ed.), *Prākrit Verses in Sanskrit Works on Poetics*, Vols. I, II, Delhi, 1994.

Lahiri, P.C., *Concepts of Rīti and Guṇa in Sanskrit Poetics*.

Mainkar, T.G., *Ṛgvedic Foundations of Classical Poetics : Some Thoughts on Indian Aesthetics sand Literary Criticism*, Mysore, 1969.

Mukherji, R., *Jagannātha's Literary Theories*.

Nagendra, *Dictionary of Sanskrit Poetics*, Delhi, 1987.

Raghavan, V., *Some Concepts of Alaṁkāra-śāstra*, Madras, 1973.

——, *The Number of Rasas*, Adyar, 1940.

Rajendra, C., *A Transcultural Approach to Sanskrit Poetics*, Calicut, 1994.

Shukla, C.P., *Treatment of Alaṁkāras in Rasagaṅgādhara*, 1977.

Swaroop, S., *The Role of Dhvani in Sanskrit Poetics*, Moradabad.

DRAMATURGY

Nāṭya-śāstra of Bharata, ed. with *Abhinavabhāratī* comm. by M.R. Kale, 4 vols., GOS, 1926 onwards. Eng. tr. by M.M. Ghosh, *Bib. Ind.*, Vols. I, II, 1951, 1961. Rev. 2nd edn., of Vol. I, Calcutta, 1967.

Daśarūpaka of Dhanañjaya, ed. with Dhanika's comm., notes, Eng. tr, etc. by J.K. Shastri.

Sāhityadarpaṇa of Viśvanātha, (Ch. VI deals with dramaturgy) Ed. by H.D. Sidhantavagisa, with comm., Calcutta, Śaka 1867. Eng. tr. by J.R. Ballantyne and P.D Mitra, *Bib. Ind.*, Calcutta. See also A.B. Keith, *Sanskrit Drama.*

METRICS

Chandomañjarī of Gaṅgādāsa, ed. with notes in English, by D.K. Kanjilal, Calcutta, 1970; by A. Sastri Vetala with Skt. and Hindi comm., Benares, 1959.

Piṅgala-chandaḥsūtra, ed. with Halāyudha's comm., *Kāvyamālā* Series 81, 1908; Ed. with Yādavapradkāśa's comm. by H. Sinha Roy, *Bib. Indica*, Calcutta, 1977. See also Arnold, *Vedic Metre*. A.D. Mukherji, *Sanskrit Prosody in its Evolution*, Calcutta.

MUSIC AND DANCE (VOCAL MUSIC, INSTRUMENTAL MUSIC AND DANCE)

Original Works in Sanskrit

Ahobala, *Saṁgītapārijāta*, ed. by K. Vedāntavāgīśa, Calcutta, 1936; Hathras (U.P.) 1941; Calcutta, 1959 (with Beng. tr.).

Aśokamalla, *Nṛtyādhyāya*, GOS, 1963.

Bharata, *Nāṭyaśāstra*, ed. by M. Ghosh, Calcutta, Vol. I, 1967, Vol. II, 1961. Eng. tr. by the same scholar, Calcutta. I, II, 1951, 1961.

Dāmodara, *Saṁgītadarpaṇa*, Hathras (U.P.), 1950.

Dattilam, ed. by S. Śāstrī, Trivandrum, 1930.

Dhanañjaya, *Daśarūpaka*, ed. by G.C.O. Haas, 1912.

Ghanaśyāmadāsa, *Saṁgītasāra-Saṁgraha*, ed. by Prajñānānanda, Calcutta, 1956.

Govindācārya, U., *Nāṭyaśāstra-saṁgraha*, ed. by A.K.M. Row Sahib & others, Vol. I, 1953, Vol. II, 1961.

Jagadekamalla, *See Kavicakravartī.*

Jāyasenāpati, *Nṛttaratnāvalī*, ed. by Rāghavan, Madras, 1965.

Kāśīnātha Apātulasī, *Saṁgītasudhākara*, 1917.

Kavicakravartī Jagadekamalla, *Saṁgīta-cūḍāmaṇi*, GOS, 1958.

Kumbha or Kumbhakarṇa, *Saṁgītarāja*, ed. by P. Śarmā, Vol. I, Varanasi, 1963.

Kumbha, Maharana, *Nṛtyaratnakośa*, ed. by R.C. Parikh, P. Shah, Vol. I, 1957.

Mātaṅga, *Bṛhaddeśī*, ed. by S. Sastri, Trivandrum.

Nandikeśvara, *Abhinayadarpaṇa*, ed. by M. Ghosh, Calcutta, 1943.

Nānya Bhūmipāla, *Bharatabhāṣyam*.

Nārada, *Saṁgītamakaranda*, GOS, 1920.

Nāradī Śikṣā — Kasi (Benares), 1893; ed. by S. Sāmaśrami, Calcutta edn. of tr. into Eng. by S.C. Banerji, Calcutta, 1983.

Narahari Cakravarti, Alias Ghanaśyāmadāsa (q.v.).

Nṛttasaṁgraha, ed. by P. Ghosh, 1956.

Pārśvadeva, *Saṁgīta samayasāra*, TSS, 1925.

Rāmacandra and Guṇacandra, *Nāṭyadarpaṇa*, GOS, 1959.

Rāmāmātya, *Svaramela-Kalānidhi*, ed. by M.S.R. Aiyar, Annamalainagar, 1932.

Rūpagosvāmin, *Nāṭakacandrikā*, ed. by B.L. Sukla, Varanasi, 1964.

Sāgaranandin, *Nāṭaka-lakṣaṇa-ratnakośa* ed. by Sukla, Benares, 1972 Also see *Nāṭaka-lakṣaṇa-ratnakośa* by S. Chattopadhayay.

Śāradātanya, *Bhāva-prakāśa*, GOS, Baroda, 1968.

Śārṅgadeva, *Saṁgītaratnākara*, Vol. I (chap. I), Madras, 1943. Vol. II (chapters II-IV), Madras, 1959; Vol. III (chaps. V-VI), Madras, 1951. and Vol. IV (chap. VII), Madras, 1953; ed. and tr. Shringy and Sharmā, Vols. I, II (up to ch. IV), Varanasi, 1978, New Delhi, 1989.

Śiṅgabhūpāla, *Raṣārṇavasudhākara*, TSS, 1916.

Someśvara, *Mānasollāsa*, Vol. III, GOS, 1961.

Somanātha, *Rāgavibodha*, ed. by S. Śāstri, Madras, 1945.

Śrīnivāsa, *Rāgatattva-vibodha*.

Śubhaṁkara, *Saṁgītadāmodara*, ed. by G. Śāstri and G. Mukhopādhyaya, Calcutta, 1960.

Sudhākalaśa, *Saṁgītopaniṣat-śāroddhāra*, GOS, 1961.

Viṣṇuśarmā (V. Bhātkhaṇḍe), *Abhinayarāgamañjarī*, 1921.

The following Purāṇas are noteworthy:

Agni

Mārkaṇḍeya, I.34-5, XXII, *Vāyu,* chs. 86-87, *Viṣṇudharmottara* section II.

Modern Works

ENGLISH

Agrawala, V.K., *Traditions and Trends in Indian Music.*

Ambrose, K., *Classical Dances and Costumes of India*, 1950.

Augustus, W.N., *Music of India*.

Bandyopadhyay, S., *The Music of India*, Bombay, 1970.

———, *The Origin of Rāga*, New Delhi, 1979.

Banerji, S.C., *Fundamentals of Ancient Indian Music and Dance*, Ahmedabad.

Banerji, P., *Basic Concept of Indian Dance*.

Beduri, G.N., *Saṅgīta-Nāṭaka Rama Kumbhe*, Jodhpur, 1968.

Bhandarkar, P.R., *Contributions to the Study of Ancient Hindū Music*, Bombay, 1912.

Bhate, D.D., *The Śruti Theory of Indian Music*, Satara, 1931.

Bhātkhande, V.N., *A Short Historical Survey of the Music of Upper India*, Bombay, 1934.

Bhatt, G.K., *Bharata Nātya-mañjarī*, Poona, 1975.

Bhattacharya, A., *A Treatise on Ancient Music*, Calcutta, 1978.

Boatwright, H., *Indian Classical Music and the Western Listener,* Bombay, 1960.

Bose, M., *Classical Indian Dancing*, Calcutta, 1970.

Burnell, A.C., *The Ārṣeya Brāhmaṇa of the Sāmaveda and Their Music*, Mangalore, 1876.

Clements, E., *Introduction to the Study of Indian Music*, London, 1913.

Coomaraswamy, A.K., & Duggirala, *The Mirror of Gesture* (Eng. tr. of *Abhinayadarpaṇa*), 1970.

Danielou, A., *Purāṇas and Music*, Pondicherry 1951.

De, S.K., *Sanskrit Poetics*, Calcutta.

Deva, C.B., *Classical Musical Instruments of India*, Calcutta, 1979.

Deval, K.B., *The Hindu Musical Scale and the Twenty-two Śrutis*, Poona, 1910.

Devi, R., *Dance of India*.

Engle, C., *The Music of the Ancient Nations*, London, 1915.

Felber, E., *The Indian Music of the Vedic and the Classical Period*, Vienna, 1912.

Fox-Strangways, A.H., *The Music of Hindusthān*, Mittal Publications, New Delhi, 1995 (Rpt.).

———, A.H., *The Hindu Scale*, Leipzig, 1907-08.

Framji, F., *Bhāratīya Śruti, Svara and Rāga Theory*, Poona, 1935.

French, P.T., *Catalogue of Indian Musical Instruments.*

Ganguli, O.C., *Rāgas and Rāgiṇīs*, Baroda, 1948.

Garratt, G.T., *The Legacy of India*, Oxford, 1938.

Gautam, M.R., *Evolution of Rāga and Tāla in Indian Music.*

Chosh, N., *Fundamentals of Rāga and Tāla with a New System of Notation*, Bombay, 1968.

Gupta, B., *Studies in Nāyaka-Nāyikā-bheda.*

Gupta, P.S., *A Fresh Light . . . Śṛṅgāra-rasa in Nāṭyaśāstra.*

Hariharan, M., *Jayadeva and Gīṭagovinda — A Study*, Trivandrum, 1980.

Holroyde, P., *Indian Music*, London.

Jairazbhoy, N.A., *The Rāgas of North Indian Music*, Oxford, 1998.

Jones, W., *On the Musical Modes of the Hindus.*

Kavi, M.R., *Bharatakośa*, Tirupati, 1951, Rev. ed. of V. Rāghavan's *Bharatakośa.*

Keith, A.B., *Sanskrit Drama*, Oxford, 1924.

———, *Indian Mythology*, Mittal Publications, Delhi.

Keskar, B.V., *Indian Music, Problems and Prospects*, Bombay, 1967.

Kuppuswamy, G. and Hariharan, M., *Indian Dance and Music Literature, A Select Bibliography*, New Delhi, 1981.

———, *Jayadeva and Gītagovinda — a Study*, Trivanndrum, 1980.

Lath, M., *A Study of Dattilam*, Delhi, 1978.

Mankad, D., *Types of Sanskrit Drama*, 1936.

Mainkar, T.G., *Studies in Sanskrit Dramatic Criticism.*

Massey, R., *Indian Dances, Their History and Growth*, London, 1967.

Mehta, M., *22 Śrutis and Grāmas of Music*, Bombay, 1938.

Menon, B.K., *Indian Classical Dances*, Calcutta, 1967.

Naidu, B.V.N. *et al.*, *Tāṇḍavalakṣaṇam or the Fundamentals of Ancient Hindu Dancing*, 1971.

Nayak, J., Religious Sects in the *Nāṭyaśāstra*, *Summaries of Papers*, AIOC, 1974.

Peterson, J.D., *On the Grāmas or Musical Scales of the Hindus.*

Pingle, B.A., *Indian Music*, 1938.

Popley, H.A., *The Music of India*, New Delhi, 1966.

Prajñānānanda, S., *The Developmental History of Indian Music*, Calcutta, 1965.

Raja, C.K., *Saṁgītaratnākara*, Eng. trs. (Ch. I), Madras, 1945.

Raja, C.K. and Burnier, R., *Saṁgītaratnākara*, Eng. tr. (ch. VII), *Adyar Library Bulletin*, Vol. XXIII. Pts. 3-4, Madras, 1959.

Ram, V.B., *Glimpses of Indian Music.*

Raṅgāchārya, A., *Introduction to Bharata's Nāṭyaśāstra*, Bombay, 1966.

Rao, G.P., *Alaṁkāraratnākara of Śobhākaramitra*, Mittal Publications, New Delhi. 1992.

Rao and Śāstrī , *A Monograph on Bharata's Nāṭyaśāstra.*

Rao, T.V.S., *Studies in Indian Music.*

Rawson, P., *Music and Dance in Indian Art*, Edinburg, 1963.

Rosenthal, E., *The Story of Indian Music and Its Instruments*, London, 1928 (Reprint, 1971).

Roy Choudhuri, H.K., *The Musicians of India.*

Sāmbamoorthy, P., *History of Indian Music.*

Sānyāl, A.N., *Rāgas and Rāgiṇīs*, Bombay, 1969.

Shastry, S.N., *Laws and Practice of Sanskrit Drama.*

Simon, R., *The Musical Compositions of Somanatha*, Madras, 1904.

Sinha, P., *An Approach to the Study of Indian Music*, Calcutta, 1970.

Subbarao, B., *Rāganidhi*, Vol. I.

Swarup, B., *Theory of Indian Music*, Mittal Publications, New Delhi, (Rpt.)

Tagore, S.N., *Six Principal Rāgas of the Hindus*, Calcutta, 1877.

Tagore, Sourindro Mohan, *Universal History of Music*: Compiled from Diverse Sources. Together with various original notes on Hindu Music, Mittal Publications, New Delhi, 1989.

———, *Indian Music by Various Authors*, Vols. I, II (2nd, 1982).

———, *Short Notice of Hindu Musical Instruments*, Calcutta, 1912.

———, *Seven Principal Musical Notes of the Hindus*, etc., Calcutta, 1892.

———, *Hindu Music*, Calcutta, 1875.

———, *The Musical Scales of the Hindus*, Calcutta, 1884.

Tarlekar, G.S., *Studies in the Nāṭyaśāstra*, Delhi, 1975.

———, *Musical Instruments in Indian Sculpture*, Pune, 1972.

Vātsyāyana, K., *Classical Indian Dance in Literature and the Arts*, 1969.

Vermā, K.M., *Seven Words in Bharata.*

———, *Nāṭya, Nṛtta* and *Nṛtya*, 1957

White, E., *Appreciating Indian Music.*

Williard, N.A., *A Treatise on the Music of Hindostan*, Calcutta, 1834.

Wilson, A.C., *A Short Account of the Hindu System of Music*, London, 1904.

Wood, A., *The Physics of Music*, 1945.

FRENCH

Sur la musique Edition critique traduction *Francaise et introduction Par Daniclou et* N.R. Bhatt, Pondicherry, 1959.

HINDI

Miśra, R., *Pālaprakāśa*.

BENGALI

Bandyopādhyāy, Suresh Chandra, *Saṁgita-ratnākara* of Śārṅgadeva, Bengali tr., Calcutta.

Chaudhurī, P. and I. Chaudhurāṇi, *Hindu Saṁgīta*, Viśvavidyāsaṁgraha.

Gosvami, K., *Saṁgītsāra*, 2nd edn., 1879.

Gupta, M., *Saṁgītaprakāśikā*.

Mukhopādhyāya, H.N., *Saṁgīte Parivartan*, 1931.

Mukhopādhyāy, D.P., *Sur O Saṁgati*.

Prajñānānada, *Saṁgīta O Saṁskṛti*, Vol. I, Calcutta, 1953; Vol. II, Calcutta, 1956.

———, *Rāg O Rūp*, Darjeeling.

———, *Bhāratīyasaṁgīter Itihās*, Vols. 1-3, Calcutta.

Roy Choudhury, B.K., *Bhāratīya Saṁgītakoṣa*, Calcutta, 1372 BS.

———, *Hindusthānī Saṁgīte Tānsener Sthān*, Calcutta, 1346 BS.

Sānyāl, A., *Prācīn Bhārater Saṁgita-cintā*, Viśvavidyāsaṁgraha

Sen, R.M., *Saṅgīta-taraṅga*, Calcutta.

Thakur, S.M., *Yantrakoṣa*, 1875.

MĀRĀṬHĪ

Bhātkhaṇḍe, V.N., *Hindusthānī Saṁgītapaddhati*, Vol. I, 1910; Vol, II, III, 1914; Vol. IV, 1932.

Articles

ENGLISH

Agrawala, V.S., Some Early Refs. to Musical Rāgas and Instruments, *Journal of Music Academy*, Madras, XXIII, 1952.

———, Dance-terminology from Kālidāsa, *USIC Centre News*, Almora, 1942.

Aiyangar, C.R.S., 'The Cultural aspect of Indian Music and Dancing', *Cultural Heritage of India,* R.K. Mission, Vol. III.

Āiyar, M.S.R., 'The question of *Grāmas*', *Journal of Royal Asiatic Society of Great Britain and Ireland*, 1936.

———, 'Sāmagāna', *Journal of Music Academy,* Madras V, 1934.

Bāgchi P.C., 'The Diffusion of Indian Music in Ancient Times', *Uttaramandrā* (a journal), Vol. I, 1940.

Coomaraswamy, A.K., 'Dīpaka-rāga', *Year Book of Oriental Art*, London, 1925.

———, 'Somanāntha', *Sanskrit Research*, 1916.

Dharma, P.C., 'Musical Culture in the *Rāmāyaṇa*', *Indian Culture*, Vol. IV, 1939.

Felber, E., 'The Indian Music of the Vedic and Classical Period', (text, tr.), *Journal of Music Academy*, Madras.

Fox-Strangways, A.H., 'The *Gāndhāra grāma*', *Journal of Royal Asiatic Society of Great Britain and Ireland,* 1935.

Gānguli, O.C., 'Non-Āryan Contribution to Āryan Music', *Annals of ABORI,* Poona, XV, 1934.

———, 'Dhruvā type of Old Indian Stage-songs', *Journal of Music Academy*, Madras, XIV.

———, 'The Meaning of Music', *The Hindoostan*, 1940.

———, 'A New Document of Indian Dancing', *USIC Centre News*, Almora, Vol. V. 1943.

Halugur, C. 'Introduction to study of Bharatiya Saṁgīta Śāstra', *Journal of Music Academy*, Madras, 1930.

———, 'Why is the *mṛdaṅga* so called', *Journal of Music,* Madras, XXIV.

———, 'Some Names in Early Saṁgīta Literature', *Ibid.*, II, IV.

———, 'Some Early References to Musical *Rāgas* and Musical Instruments', *Ibid.*, XXIII.

———, 'The Indian Origin of the Violin', *Ibid.*, XIX.

Rao, T.V.S. 'A Plea for a Rational Interpretation of *Saṁgītaśāstra*,' *Journal of Music Academy*, Madras, IX, 1938.

Sankaran, C.R. and B. Chaitanya Deva, 'Postulational Methods and Indian Musicology', *Journal of University of Bombay*, XVIII, 1949.

Note: Also see H.D. Krishna Rao in *The Indian Music Journal*, Vols.

I, II (1912-13).

The Bengali *magnum opus* of Prajñānānanda, entitled *Saṅgīta O Saṁskṛti* has been mentioned already. So, the articles, published by him prior to the publication of the above book, are not mentioned here.

JOURNALS

The noteworthy journals, dealing with Indian music, are mentioned below:

(1) *Journal of Indian Musicological Society*, Baroda.

(2) *Saṁgīta* — monthly published from Saṁgīta Kāryālaya, Hathras (U.P.).

(3) *Saṁgīta-kalāvihāra* — monthly published from Gāndharva Mahāvidyālaya, Poona.

(4) *Surachandā* — monthly pub. from Calcutta.

(5) *The Indian Music Journal.*

(6) *Viśvavīṇā* — quarterly pub. from Calcutta.

A noteworthy journal is also published from Saṁgīta-Nāṭaka Academy, Delhi.

TEXTS AND TRANSLATIONS

ARCHITECTURE

Mānasāra, ed. and tr. into Eng. by P.K. Acharya in 5 Vols., 1927 onward.

Mayamata, ed. with Eng. tr. by B. Dagens — *An Indian Treatise on Architecture and Iconography*, New Delhi, 1985.

Samarāṅgana-sūtradhāra, ed. T. Ganapati Sastri, in 2 vols., revised by V.S. Agrawala, *GOS*, 1966; with Hindī tr. by D. Sukla, Delhi, 1965.

Śilparatna, attributed to Śrīkumāra, ed. T. Ganapati Sastri, TSS, 1922-29.

Vāstusūtra-upaniṣad, attributed to Pippalāda, ed. with Eng. tr. and notes, by A. Boner *et al*, Delhi, 1982.

Studies

Acharya, P.K., *Hindu Architecture in India and Abroad* Mānsāra Series, Vol. VI, Rep., Delhi, 1996.

———, *A Dictionary of Hindu Architecture,* London, 1927.

———, *Encyclopaedia of Hindu Architecture*, Bhopal, 1978.

———, *India Architecture according to Mānasāra Śilparatna*, Patna, 1979.

———, *Mānasāra on Architecture and Scrulpture*, Mānasāra Series, Vol. III, 1995.

Bakshi and Sareen, *Temples of India*.

Begde, P.V., *Ancient and Medieval Town Planning in India*, New Delhi.

Bhattacharya, T.P., *The Canons of Indian Art*.

———, *A Study on Vāstuvidyā*, Calcutta, 1963, 2nd ed.

Brown, P., *Indian Architecture*, 2 vols., Bombay, 1959.

Courens, J.H., *Principles of Indian Śilpaśāstram with text of Mayaśāstra*.

Das, P.K., *The Secrets of Vāstu*, Secunderabad, 1989.

Dutt, B.B., *Town Planning in Ancient India*, Calcutta, 1925.

Havell, E.B., *Ancient and Medieval Architecture of India*, London, 1915.

Kramrisch, S., *Hindu Temples*, 2 vols, Delhi, 1976.

Rao, S.K.R., and Vikhanasacharyulu, D., *Devālaya-vāstu*, Bangalore, 1997.

Sen, N.N., On some remarkable words from the *Silparatna, Indian Linguistics, Taraporewala Mem. Vol.*, 1957; *Turner Jubilee Vol.*, 1958.

Sukla, L., *A Study of Hindu Art and Architecture with special ref. to Terminology*.

Sukla, D.N., *Vāstu-śāstra* (with special ref. to Bhoja's *Samarāṅgana-sūtra-dhāra*), Lucknow, Vols. I, II, Lucknow.

HORSELORE AND ELEPHANTLORE

Nīlakaṇṭha: *Mātaṅgalīlā*, ed. G. Sastri, Trivandrum, 1910. Eng. trs. by Edgerton, Yale, 1931. German tr. by Zimmer, Berlin, 1929. On authorship, see A.B., Keith, *History of Skt. Lit.*, 1930, p. 465.

Pālakāpya, *Hastyāyurveda*, Poona, 1894.

N.B. See M.S. No 12295 of an unknown author, preserved in Sarasvatī Mahal Library, Tanjore, dealing with the subject.

Jayadatta, *Aśvavaidyaka*, *Bib. Ind.* ed., Calcutta, 1887.

Nakula, *Aśvaśāstra*, ed. Gopalan, Tanjore, 1952.

AGRICULTURE

A Collection of Agricultural Sayings in Orissa — through the courtesy of Dr. Parija, Cuttack.

For an up-to-date bibliography, see G. Wojtilla, *History of Kṛṣiśāstra*, Acta Antiqua et Archaeologica, Supplement IX, SZEGED, Hungaria, 1999.

A Collection of Kanarese Sayings and Proverbs bearing on Agriculture — Bulletin No. 35. Department of Agriculture, Govt. of Madras, 1934.

Agriculture and Allied Arts in Vedic India, A.K.Y.N. Aiyer, Bangalore City, 1949.

Agricultural Practices in Ancient India, S.P. Ray Chauduri, ICAR, New Delhi, Review Series, No. 4.

Agriculture in Ancient India, S.P. Ray Chaudhuri, Dacca University Studies.

Amarakośa — (see *Nāmaliṅgānuśāsana*).

Ancient Indian Life by J.C. Ray, Calcutta, 1948.

Arthaśātra of Kauṭilya, Ch. 42 (sec. 41), Sītādhyakṣa.

Asamiya Sāhityer Chanaki, Vol. I, Calcutta University, 1929.

A Short Account of the Agricultural Methods Practised in Ancient India, S.P. Ray Chaudhuri, *Science and Culture*, VII, 1941.

Bhāratīya-kṛṣi-śāstra-vāṅmaya-sūcī — Reprint from Shilpa-Sansar, Poona. (30th, April, 1955, and 19th Feb., 1955). In this *sūcī* some references to works, published and unpublished, on Agriculture are given under *kṛṣi-śāstra* — *vṛkṣavidyā*, pp. 283-4).

Bṛhat-saṁhitā of Varāhamihira, ed. by S. Dvivedi. Vizianagram Sanskrit Series.

Buddhist Records of the Western World, Vol. II, Beal, London, 1884.

Epigraphia Indica, Vol. XXI.

Ghāg aur Bhandarī, Ramnaresh Tripathi, Hindusthan Academy, Allahabad, 1949.

Grām-Sāhitya, Part II, Ramnaresh Tripathi, Atmaram & Sons, Delhi, 1952.

History of Botany and Allied Sciences in India (*c*. 2000 BC to AD 100) III. Science of Agriculture, Arcives Internationales'd' Histoire des Sciences, UNESCO, Paris, 1951 — G.P. Majumdar.

India Through Chinese Eyes, Surendranath Sen, University of Madras.

Inscriptions of Bengal, Vol. III, N.G. Majumdar.

Jyotistattva of Raghunandana. (In the *Smṛti-tattva*, Vol. I, ed. by J. Vidyasagar, Calcutta).

Kāśyapīya kṛṣi-sūkti, a Skt. work on Agriculture by G. Wojtilla. *Acta orientalia*, Hungery, XXXIII fasc. 2, 1979, pp. 209-52.

Kāśyapiy Kṛṣi-sūkti, Eng. tr. in *Acta Orientalia*, Hungary, Vol. XXXIX (1), pp. 85-136, 1985.

Khanār Vacan, pub. Visvadeva Mukhopadhyaya, Calcutta.

Kṛṣi-parāśara (in Oriya) Dutt Press, Cuttack, 1930.

Kṛṣi-parāśara (in Skt.) ed. and tr. into English by G.P. Majumdar and S.C. Banerji. Asiatic Society, Calcutta, 1960.

Kṛṣi-saṁgraha, tr. into English by S.P. Ray Chaudhuri, Imperial Bureau of Soil Science, England, *Monthly Bulletin No. 59*, 1936.

Mahābhārata.

Manu-smṛti, N.S.P. edn., Bombay.

Mohenjo-Dāro and its Civilization of Ancient India with Reference to Agriculture by N.C. Choudhary.

Nāmaliṅgānuśāsana, ed. by Śivadatta Śāstrī, Bombay, 1929.

Origin and Development of the Science of Agriculture in Ancient India, G.P. Majumdar, *Proc. All India Oriental Conf.*, Section Technical Sciences, pp. 113-16, Nagpur, 1946.

Raghuvaṁśa of Kālidāsa, ed. by Kale, Vol. I, Bombay, 1900.

Rāmapāla-carita of Sandhyākaranandin, ed. by R.C. Majumdar *et al.*, Rajshahi, 1939.

Ṛgveda.

Some Materials for the Study of Agriculture and Agriculturists in Ancient India, R.C. Ganguli, Serampore (West Bengal), 1932.

The Antiquity of Some Field and Forest Flora of India, A.K.Y.N. Aiyer, Sankarapuram, Bangalore, 1953.

Vanaspati, Book III — Botany and Science of Agriculture, pp. 186-219, G.P. Majumdar, Calcutta University, Calcutta, 1927.

Vedic Index, Vols. I and II — Macdonell and Keith

MATHEMATICS

Agrawala, V.S., *Vedic Mathematics*.

Bag, A.K., *Mathematics of Ancient and Medieval India*, Banares, 1980.

Bose, D.M. *et al*, *A Concise History of Science in India*, New Delhi, 1971.

ĀYURVEDA

TEXTS AND TRANSLATIONS

Caraka Saṁhitā.

Ed. with Eng., Hindī and Gujarāṭī tr., 6 vols., by Āyurvedic Soc., Jamnagar, 1949.

See A.C. Kaviratna and P. Sharma, *The Caraka Saṁhitā*, vols. 1-4.

Text with Eng. tr. (4 vols.) by P.V. Sharma, Delhi, 1994.

Suśruta Saṁhitā

Ed. with Ḍalhaṇa's comm by J. Trikamji, Bombay, 1931.

Eng. tr. by K. Bhiṣagratna, Calcutta, 1907.16.

Studies

Filliozat, J., *The Classical Doctrine of Indian Medicine*, Delhi, 1964.

Mukherjee, G.N., *Surgical Instruments of the Hindus* (with a comparative study of surgical instruments of Greek, Roman, Arab and Modern European Surgeons), Calcutta, 1913-14.

Roy, P., Gupta, H., and Roy, M., *A Scientific Synopsis of Suśruta Saṁhitā*), New Delhi, 1980.

Roy, P., and Gupta, H.N., *Caraka Saṁhitā: A Scientific Approach.*

Sankaran, P.S., *Suśruta's Contribution to Surgery.*

BOTANY

Banerji, S.C. and Majumdar, G.P., *Kṛṣi-parāśara.*

———, *Flora and Fauna*, Calcutta, 1980.

Bose, D.M. *et. al* (eds.), *A Concise History of Science in India*, New Delhi, 1971.

Hooker, *Flora of British India.*

Majumdar, G.P., *Aspects of Indian Civilisation*, etc., Calcutta.

———, *Upavana-vinoda* Calcutta, 1935.

———, *Vanaspati*, Calcutta, 1927.

Seal, B.N., *The Positive Sciences of the Ancient Hindus*, Varanasi, 1958.

Papers

B.C. Law Volume, I, Calcutta (*Vedic Plants* by G.P. Majumdar).

Cultural Heritage of India, III, R.K. Mission, Calcutta (*Botany — Past and*

Present by G.P. Majumdar).

WORKS CONTAINING ARTICLES BY P.K. GODE

Acharya Dhruva Smāraka Grantha (*The Role of Yava and Caṇaka*, etc).

B.C. Law Volume, I, 1944 (*Studies in the History of Indian Plants antiquity of Jawar or Jondhlā from 2200 B.C. to AD 1850*).

D.K. Potdar Commemoration Volume, Poona, 1950 (*The History of Maize in India between AD 1500 and 1900*).

Sārdha-śatābdī Comm. Vol., Asiatic Society, Bombay, 1957.

Sarūpa Bhāratī (L. Sarup Mem. Vol.) Hoshiarpur, 1954.

New Indian Antiquary, VI, 1944 — *The Mahāśāli Variety of Rice in Mgadha* (between AD 600 and 1100)

———, VIII, 1946, — *Some Notes on the History of Candana*, etc.

Poona Orientalist, XIV, 1949.

Prācyavāṇī, Calcutta, III, Nos. 1, 2; 1946 — *The Use of Caṇaka, etc.*

PAPERS BY P.K. GODE

(Titles of Journals are in Alphabetical Order)

Annals of Bhandankar Oriental Research Institute, Poona, Vols.:

XIX — Kaiyadeva and Medical or Botanical Glossary ascribed to him — before AD 1450.

XXVI, 1946 — History of Caṇaka, etc. between AD 1800 and 1870.

XXVIII — History of Mendi between 2000 BC and AD 1850.

XXIX, 1949 — Some notes on the history of almond in India between *c.* AD 100 and 1900.

XXXI, 1959 — On history of Tāmbūla.

XXXIII, 1953 — History of Fenugreek and Alfalfa, etc. between *c.* 700 BC and AD 1800.

Aryan Path, 1947 — Plant-lore in Ancient India.

Bhāratīya Vidyā, VII, 1946 — *Aśvabalā*, etc.

Journal of Oriental Institute, Baroda, I, No. 1, 1951 — Some references to *Aśvabalā* (and No. 3, 1952).

Journal of Kalinga History Res. Soc., II. No. 3, 1947 — References to Candana, etc.; II, No. 4; III, Nos. 1-3, 1950. Some references to Sugar-cane, etc.

Journal of Travancore University MSS. Library, Trivandrum, VI, Nos. 1, 2. History of Tāmbūla II.

Indian Culture, XIII, No. 1, 1946 — History of the art of grafting plants between *c.* 500 BC and AD 1800.

WORKS IN BENGALI

Biswas, K. and Ghosh, E., *Bhāratīya Vanauṣadhi*, I, II.

Majumdar, R.C., *Prācīn Bhārate Vijñān-carcā*, Calcutta.

Sen Gupta, V., *Vanauṣadhi-darpaṇa*, I, II, Calcutta, 1908.

POPULAR BELIEFS AND PRACTICES

Adbhutasāgara of Ballālasena, ed. by M. Jha, Banares, 1905.

Vasantarāja-śakuna, Veṅkaṭeśvara Press, Bombay, 1906 with Skt. comm. and Hindī tr.

Chakraborty C., *Common Life in Ṛgveda and Atharvaveda*, Calcutta.

Sharma, K.L., *Vaidik Sāhitya men śakun evaṁ adbhut ghaṭanāye* (Hindi), Saharanpur (U.P.), 1970.

Stutley, M., *Ancient Indian Magic and Folklore*, Delhi.

WAR

Chakravarti, P.C., *Art of War in Ancient India*, 1941.

Dikshitar, V.R.R., *War in Ancient India*, Madras, 1944.

Majumdar, B.K., *The Military System in Ancient India*, Calcutta, 1955.

Sen Sarma, P., *Military Wisdom in the Purāṇas*, Calcutta, 1979.

Index